Sixth Edition

MULTICULTURAL LAW ENFORCEMENT

STRATEGIES FOR PEACEKEEPING IN A DIVERSE SOCIETY

Robert M. Shusta

Deena R. Levine

Herbert Z. Wong

Aaron T. Olson

Philip R. Harris

PEARSON

Boston   Columbus   Indianapolis   New York   San Francisco   Upper Saddle River
Amsterdam   Cape Town   Dubai   London   Madrid   Milan   Munich   Paris   Montreal   Toronto
Delhi   Mexico City   Sao Paulo   Sydney   Hong Kong   Seoul   Singapore   Taipei   Tokyo

Editorial Director: Andrew Gilfillan
Acquisitions Editor: Gary Bauer
Editorial Assistant: Lynda Cramer
Director of Marketing: David Gesell
Senior Marketing Manager: Mary Salzman
Senior Marketing Coordinator: Alicia Wozniak
Project Management Team Lead: JoEllen Gohr
Project Manager: Jessica H. Sykes
Procurement Specialist: Deidra Skahill
Senior Art Director: Diane Ernsberger
Cover Designer: Wanda Espana Wee Design Group
Media Project Manager: Leslie Brado
Full-Service Project Management: Jogender Taneja
Composition: Aptara®, Inc.
Printer/Binder: RR Donnelley/Willard
Cover Printer: Phoenix Color/Hagerstown
Text Font: Minion Pro

Many of the designations by manufacturers and sellers to distinguish their products are claimed as trademarks. Where those designations appear in this book, and the publisher was aware of a trademark claim, the designations have been printed in initial caps or all caps.

Library of Congress Cataloging-in-Publication Data

Shusta, Robert M.
    Multicultural law enforcement: strategies for peacekeeping in a diverse
society / Robert M. Shusta, Deena R. Levine, Aaron T. Olson, Herbert Z. Wong,
Philip R. Harris. – Sixth edition.
      pages cm
    ISBN 978-0-13-348330-7
    ISBN 0-13-348330-4
    1. Police-community relations—United States.   2. Discrimination in law
enforcement—United States.   3. Multiculturalism—United States.
4. Intercultural communication—United States.   I. Title.
HV7936.P8M85 2015
363.2'3—dc23   2014022545

3   16

PEARSON

ISBN 13: 978-0-13-348330-7
ISBN 10:   0-13-348330-4

Dedication

To our inspirational co-author, Dr. Philip R. Harris, whose vision for Multicultural Law Enforcement more than 20 years ago continues to shape criminal justice programs throughout the United States

CONTENTS

FOREWORD

One of the most profound social changes to impact American law enforcement is the changing nature of diversity. While police agencies across America have struggled for many years with the issues of race and ethnicity, the nature of that struggle has been essentially binary. Black/White, male/female, similar/other; whatever the local issue, it has generally been narrowly defined.

However, over the last 50 years, these struggles have become even more complex and challenging as large numbers of non-English-speaking immigrants, documented and unauthorized, have come to America seeking economic, religious, or political freedom. The barriers of language, culture and social expectations have added significantly to the challenges of policing a heterogeneous society. Law enforcement professionals frequently encounter cultural and racial tensions, as well as strongly held suspicion, if not outright fear, of the police that the immigrants bring with them. Such suspicion and fear are often a result of personal experience in their countries of origin. Clearly, effective policing of multicultural communities remains an enormous challenge. However, there is good reason for optimism as police agencies become more diverse, enhance their training, and seek to build strong relationships with specific communities.

By embracing the philosophy of community partnerships and community policing strategies, law enforcement agencies, together with citizens, have created some safer towns and cities. To be effective, police officers cannot operate alone; they require the active support and assistance of citizens in their jurisdictions. Central to maintaining that support is the recognition that law enforcement agencies must reflect the diversity of the communities they serve. Every day, officers come into contact with individuals from different cultural backgrounds, socioeconomic classes, religions, sexual orientations, as well as differing physical and mental abilities. Each of these groups brings a different perspective to police community relations and, as a result, our officers must be prepared to respond appropriately to each group. Failure to recognize and adjust to community diversity can foster confusion and resentment among citizens, quickly leading to a breakdown in the critical bond of trust between a law enforcement agency and its community.

Policing has changed dramatically since the publication of the first edition of this book. There has been a generational shift within the law enforcement community, both in terms of age and diversity. Nevertheless, the challenge of policing an increasingly complex society remains. The need to find ways to address this challenge helps explain the continued interest in this work.

The publication of this sixth edition of *Multicultural Law Enforcement: Strategies for Peacekeeping in a Diverse Society* is significant, considering that over 95 percent of published books never enter into their second edition. Clearly, the authors have filled a gap in the law enforcement literature, and the global sales of this volume confirm that its authors have produced a highly relevant text, one that is rich with instruction. Thus, readers are fortunate now to have access to this sixth edition. Since its first publication in 1995, this work has established itself as a classic in the criminal justice field. The fact that the text has been adopted by and used in police and corrections academies, advanced officer courses, and criminal justice courses is testimony to its far-reaching acceptance.

Multicultural Law Enforcement's major sections effectively address the key cultural needs of law enforcement as practitioners, in increasing numbers have discovered for themselves. The practical contents of the book provide critical information and insight that will improve police performance and professionalism. The subject matter herein, especially the cultural-specific information, continues to be on the leading edge. Instructors and trainers will welcome this current edition of *Multicultural Law Enforcement* as a complete learning system that offers the following supplements to the main text: an Instructor's Manual, chapter quizzes, and PowerPoint presentations for each chapter.

Finally, this edition of *Multicultural Law Enforcement* enables agencies and departments to prepare officers to form partnerships for successful community policing practices within our multicultural communities. It touches on other related topics too, such as gangs, the homeless, the mentally ill, global terrorism, and international politics and their impact on policing in America.

The authors' diversity and collective competence are quite impressive. The five coauthors have a combined total of 58 years of active state and local law enforcement experience. They also have spent years conducting training, teaching criminal justice college classes, and consulting. Each author has sought additional cultural information and input from criminal justice professionals from the diverse backgrounds about which they write. I feel confident in recommending this text, and I encourage all who use it to put into action the strategies and tools of this exceptional work for the betterment of your agencies, communities, and the larger society.

Chief Bernard Melekian (Ret.), DPPD
Former Chief of Police, Pasadena Police Department
Former Director, U.S. Department of Justice's Community Oriented Policing Services

PREFACE

This sixth edition of *Multicultural Law Enforcement: Strategies for Peacekeeping in a Diverse Society* is a continuing tribute to all our readers who enthusiastically received the first five editions. It is a textbook designed for use in police departments and academies as well as college and university criminal justice programs; it is used in a wide range of agencies for in-service training programs and advanced officer courses. While the text's focus has primarily been on police officers, in addition to law enforcement, the content applies to other criminal justice professionals, emergency service personnel, correctional officers, border patrol agents, marshals, federal agents, and campus and military police.

Multicultural Law Enforcement, with accompanying instructional tools, is a complete learning package designed to assist users in understanding the pervasive influences of culture, race, ethnicity, gender, and sexual orientation in the workplace and in multicultural communities.

NEW TO THIS EDITION

The sixth edition contains updated and expanded information for leaders, officers, managers, supervisors, new recruits, and instructors. It is based on research of current issues facing law enforcement professionals and the communities they serve. For some new sections, authors have conducted interviews with criminal justice professionals from diverse backgrounds. The content revision includes:

- Updated demographics throughout the chapters from the latest census figures and U.S. Department of Justice statistics
- Additional in-depth background on refugees and immigrants
- Updated information and examples of law enforcement workforce diversity and workplace inclusion
- Expanded sections on hate crimes and on violence against immigrant and Native American women
- Additional cultural-specific information on such varied topics as Muslim cultural identity and Indian country crime
- New and updated coverage of federal laws pertaining to crimes motivated by hate/bias and information on racial profiling
- Expanded information on homeland security, counterterrorism and citizen programs to benefit multicultural communities in disaster preparedness
- Additional information on law enforcement contact with gangs, homeless and mentally ill populations

Throughout the text we stress the need for awareness and understanding of cultural differences and respect toward those of different backgrounds. We encourage readers to examine preconceived notions they might hold of particular groups. We outline why agency executives and managers should build awareness and promote cultural understanding and tolerance within their agencies.

An increasing number of leaders in law enforcement and criminal justice agencies and their employees have accepted the premise that greater cross-cultural competency and improved cross-racial and interethnic relations must be a key objective of all management and professional development. Demographic changes have had a tremendous impact not only on the types of crimes committed, but also on the composition of the workforce and the people with whom officers make contact. To be effective, executives must understand and be responsive to the diversity in their workforces and in their changing communities. Professionalism today includes the need for greater consideration across cultures and improved communication with members of diverse groups.

In an era when news is accessed instantaneously, the public can witness cross-cultural and interracial contact between law enforcement agents and citizens, seconds after interactions occur. Community members have become increasingly sophisticated and critical with regard to how members of diverse cultural and racial groups are treated by public servants. Police departments, criminal justice and emergency services agencies are now serving communities whose members carefully observe them and hold them accountable for their actions.

With cross-cultural knowledge and sensitivity, those who are charged with the responsibility of peacekeeping and public safety will improve their image while demonstrating greater professionalism within the changing multicultural workforce and community.

We offer instructors and trainers using *Multicultural Law Enforcement: Strategies for Peacekeeping in a Diverse Society* a complete learning package, including an Instructor's Manual, PowerPoint slides, and chapter quizzes. We hope our readers will find our revised and updated text an enhancement to their law enforcement and criminal justice programs.

Robert M. Shusta, MPA
Deena R. Levine, MA
Herbert Z. Wong, PhD
Aaron T. Olson, MEd
Philip R. Harris, PhD

INSTRUCTOR SUPPLEMENTS

Instructor's Manual with Test Bank Includes content outlines for classroom discussion, teaching suggestions, and answers to selected end-of-chapter questions from the text. This also contains a Word document version of the test bank.

MyTest This computerized test generation system gives you maximum flexibility in preparing tests. It can create custom tests and print scrambled versions of a test at one time, as well as build tests randomly by chapter, level of difficulty, or question type. The software also allows online testing and record-keeping and the ability to add problems to the database. This test bank can also be delivered formatted for use in popular learning management platforms, such as Black-Board, WebCT, Moodle, Angel, D2L, and Sakai. Visit www.PearsonMyTest.com to begin building your tests.

PowerPoint Presentations Our presentations offer clear, straightforward outlines and notes to use for class lectures or study materials. Photos, illustrations, charts, and tables from the book are included in the presentations when applicable.

To access supplementary materials online, instructors need to request an instructor access code. Go to **www.pearsonhighered.com/irc**, where you can register for an instructor access code. Within 48 hours after registering, you will receive a confirming email, including an instructor access code. Once you have received your code, go to the site and log on for full instructions on downloading the materials you wish to use.

ALTERNATE VERSIONS

eBooks This text is also available in multiple eBook formats including Adobe Reader and Cours-eSmart. *CourseSmart* is an exciting new choice for students looking to save money. As an alternative to purchasing the printed textbook, students can purchase an electronic version of the same content. With a *CourseSmart* eTextbook, students can search the text, make notes online, print out reading assignments that incorporate lecture notes, and bookmark important passages for later review. For more information, or to purchase access to the *CourseSmart* eTextbook, visit **www.coursesmart.com.**

ACKNOWLEDGMENTS

This sixth edition has benefited from expert contributions by numerous people. Cultural resources and experts read and checked our chapters for accuracy and interpretations of cultural behavior. Other contributors gave us written, up-to-date material that we incorporated in our revision. Still others provided invaluable editorial and research assistance, enhancing the overall quality of this edition.

In particular, for this sixth edition, we would like to express our thanks to the following individuals, some of whom have also contributed to previous editions: Judi Lipsett, editorial assistant; Kay Jones, intercultural specialist and research assistant; Humera Khan, Executive Director at Muflehun, Washington, D.C.; Christopher Martinez, Program Director—Refugee and Immigrant Services of the Catholic Charities of San Francisco; Mitchell Grobeson, Sergeant (retired), Los Angeles Police Department; Lubna Ismail, President, Connecting Cultures, Washington, D.C.; Anthony Pan, Asia Cross-Cultural Consultant; Ilana Lipsett, Researcher; James Johnson, PhD, Social Science Analyst, Administrative Office of the U.S. Courts; Thomas Kochman, Founder and COO of KMA Associates, internationally known diversity specialist; Lieutenant Matt Nemeth, Executive Director of PAL in Jacksonville, Florida; Larry Becker, Deputy Chief of S'Klallam Tribes in Kingston, Sequim, and Port Angeles, Washington; Betsy Brantner-Smith, Sergeant (retired), Naperville Police Department, Illinois; Kathy Bierstedt, Sergeant (retired), Metro Dade, Florida Police Department; and Steven P. Wallace, PhD, UCLA Chair and professor, Department of Community Health Sciences, Los Angeles, California.

We would like to thank additional contributors for valuable input that helped to shape previous editions and upon which we have developed further material. We owe appreciation to the following people for their helpful cross-cultural wisdom and its application to law enforcement and criminal justice: Kim Ah-Low, Georgia; Chung H. Chuong, California; Ondra Berry, retired Assistant Police Chief, Reno, Nevada Police Department; Jim Cox, retired Police Chief, Midwest City Police Department, Oklahoma; Ronald Haddad, Police Chief, Dearborn, Michigan; Captain S. Rob Hardman, USCG (retired), Virginia; Wilbur Herrington, Massachusetts; Jim Kahue, Hawaii; Chief Susan Jones (retired), Healdsburg, California Police Department; Charles Marquez, Colorado; Mohammed Berro, (retired) Corporal, Dearborn Police Department, Michigan; Sarah Miyahira, PhD, Hawaii; Margaret Moore, Washington, D.C.; Jason O'Neal, Police Chief Chickasaw Nation Lighthorse Police, Ada, Oklahoma; Jim Parks, J.D., Criminal Justice Department Chair, Portland Community College, Portland, Oregon; JoAnne Pina, PhD, Washington, D.C.; Eduardo Rodela, PhD, Washington, D.C.; Darryl McAllister, Captain, Hayward Police Department, Hayward, California; (late) George Thompson, Founder of Verbal Judo Institute, Inc.

The following additional individuals provided important input to past editions: David Barlow, PhD, Professor and Interim Dean, Fayetteville State University, North Carolina; Danilo Begonia, JD, Professor, Asian American Studies, San Francisco State University, San Francisco, California; Peggy Bowen, PhD, Assistant Professor of Criminal Justice, Alvernia College, Reading, Pennsylvania; John Brothers, Executive Director, Quincy Asian Resources, Inc., Quincy, Massachusetts; Patricia DeRosa, President, ChangeWorks Consulting, Randolph, Massachusetts; Ronald Griffin, Pastor and Community Leader, Detroit, Michigan; Sari Karet, Executive Director, Cambodian American Foundation, San Francisco, California; Marilyn Loden, Organizational Diversity Consultant with Loden Associates, Inc., Tiburon, California; A.L. "Skipper" Osborne, CEO of TAJFA (Truth and Justice for All), Portland, Oregon; Paula Parnagian, World View Services, Revere, Massachusetts; Oscar Ramirez, PhD, Police and Court Expert Consultant, San Antonio, Texas; Jose Rivera, retired Peace Officer, Education Director—Native American Museum, Sausalito, California; Greg Patton, Criminal Justice Cultural Diversity Instructor at Portland Community College; Lourdes Rodriguez-Nogues, EdD, President, Rasi Associates, Boston, Massachusetts; Helen Samhan, Executive Director, Arab American Institute Foundation,

Washington, D.C.; Margaret D. Shorter, Sgt., Royal Canadian Mounted Police and officer of the International Association of Women and Policing; Victoria Santos, President, Santos & Associates, Newark, California; Michael Stoops, Executive Director of the National Coalition for the Homeless, Washington D.C.; Reverend Onasai Veevau, Pastor and Pacific Islander Community Leader, San Mateo, California; Norita Jones Vlach, PhD, Professor, School of Social Work, San Jose State University, San Jose, California; James Zogby, PhD, Director, Arab American Institute Foundation, Washington, D.C.; John Zogby, PhD, President, Zogby International, New York, New York; Brian Withrow, Professor, School of Community Affairs, Wichita, Kansas.

We would also like to thank the following reviewers: Vincent Benincasa, Hesser College; Cindy Brown, Rose State College; Douglas Evans, Sullivan Community College; Kelly Gould, Sacramento City College; Patrick Ibe, Albany State University; Charles Kocher, Cumberland County College; Richard Michelson, Grossmont College; Kimberly Tenerelli, Marian University; and Jun Xing, Oregon State University.

ABOUT THE AUTHORS

Robert M. Shusta, Captain (retired), MPA, served over 27 years in law enforcement, and retired as a Captain at the Concord, California Police Department. He has been a part-time instructor at numerous colleges and universities in northern California and at police academies. He is a graduate of the 158th FBI National Academy and the fourth California Command College conducted by POST. He has served on state commissions responsible for developing POST guidelines and state policy recommendations. (Retired) Captain Shusta has conducted extensive training on cultural awareness and hate crimes as well as Train the Trainer programs on combatting domestic violence.

Deena R. Levine, MA, has been providing consulting and training to organizations in both the public and the private sectors since 1983. She is the principal of Deena Levine & Associates LLC, a firm specializing in multicultural workplace training as well as global cross-cultural business consulting. She and her associates, together with representatives from community organizations, have provided programs to law enforcement agencies, focusing on cross-cultural and human relations. She began her career in cross-cultural training at the Intercultural Relations Institute, formerly at Stanford University, developing multicultural workforce understanding for managers and supervisors. She has written an additional widely used text on the cultural aspects of communication, entitled *Beyond Language: Cross-Cultural Communication* (Regents/Prentice Hall).

Herbert Z. Wong, PhD, a clinical and organizational psychologist, provides cultural awareness and diversity training to law enforcement officers on local, state, and federal levels nationwide. He is a professor of psychology and research director at the Graduate School of Professional Psychology, John F. Kennedy University. He is the president of Herbert Z. Wong & Associates, a management consulting firm to over 350 businesses, universities, government agencies, and corporations, specializing in multicultural management and workforce diversity. In 1990, Dr. Wong cofounded and was president of the National Diversity Conference, which became the Society for Human Resource Management's Workplace Diversity Conference. He developed and provided the national Training-of-Trainers programs for the seven-part "Valuing Diversity" videotape series used in over 4,000 organizations worldwide. Dr. Wong specializes in diversity assessments and open systems analysis for cultural competency in human services programs.

Aaron T. Olson, MEd, is an adjunct professor at Portland Community College (PCC), Portland, Oregon, and Eastern Oregon University (EOU), La Grande, Oregon, where he teaches cultural diversity courses. He designed the first cultural diversity courses and curricula for PCC's criminal justice program in 2001, fire protection program in 2009, and EOU's fire service administration program in 2011. Outside of academia, he is an organization and training consultant, specializing in staff development for businesses and government agencies, and conducts multicultural training workshops for public safety and nonpublic safety personnel. He is a retired Oregon State Police patrol sergeant and shift supervisor with 26 years of police experience in communications, recruiting, and patrol assignments. He taught a variety of topics at Oregon's Department of Public Safety Standards and Training to students at the recruit, supervisory, mid-management, and executive management levels. In 2002, he established public safety workshops for immigrants and refugees at the Immigrant Refugee Community Organization (IRCO), Portland, Oregon, and continues to provide instruction for IRCO.

Philip R. Harris, PhD, is a retired management psychologist with extensive experience in human resource development, including law enforcement and criminal justice systems. As President of Harris International, La Jolla, California, he also served as a POST Command College research consultant. In his global consulting practice, he conducted leadership training for such institutions as the U.S. Marine Corps, the U.S. Customs Service, the District of Columbia and Philadelphia Police Departments. Dr. Harris has written or edited myriad texts, articles, and books, including *Managing Cultural Differences*, *Toward Human Emergence*, *Managing the Knowledge Culture*, and *Developing High Performance Leaders* (2013). In 2013, at 88 years of age, having authored or coauthored 53 books, Dr. Harris retired as a global consultant on diversity.

PART ONE

Impact of Cultural Diversity on Law Enforcement

Part One of *Multicultural Law Enforcement: Strategies for Peacekeeping in a Diverse Society* introduces readers to the implications of a multicultural society for law enforcement, both within and outside the police agency. Chapter 1 discusses aspects of the changing population and presents views on diversity. The case studies in Chapter 1 exemplify how the presence of different cultures can affect the very nature and perception of crime itself. We present the subject of prejudice and its effect on police work, providing specific examples of its consequences in law enforcement. The chapter ends with suggestions for improving law enforcement in multicultural communities.

Chapter 2 discusses demographic changes taking place within law enforcement agencies, as well as reactions to diversity in the law enforcement workplace and responses to it. In addition to data on ethnic and racial groups, this chapter provides information on women and on gay men and lesbians in law enforcement across the country. We include a discussion of how law enforcement agencies and the community must be proactive about the elimination of discrimination and racism. In addition, we illustrate the realities of the new workforce and the corresponding need for flexibility in leadership styles.

Chapter 3 discusses challenges in the recruitment, retention, and promotion of police personnel from multiple perspectives, including those associated with race, ethnicity, and sexual orientation. We emphasize that the pool of qualified applicants for law enforcement jobs has significantly reduced not only because of the economy, but also because of societal changes and trends. We present strategies for recruitment, emphasizing the commitment required by law enforcement chief executives and the need to look inward—that is, to assess the level of comfort and inclusion that all employees experience in a given agency. If the levels are not high, hiring, retention, and promotion will be difficult. Chapter 3 describes the pressing need facing all agencies to build a workforce of highly qualified individuals of diverse backgrounds and in which all people have equal access to the hiring, retention, and promotion processes. It also presents a creative model for recruitment using community policing.

Chapter 4 provides practical information highlighting the dynamics of cross-cultural communication in law enforcement. The chapter includes a discussion of the specific problems involved when officers communicate with speakers of other languages. We present typical styles of communication that people may display when they are uncomfortable with cross-cultural contact. The chapter includes a section on the need for communication sensitivity after the tragedy of September 11, 2011 (referred to in this text as "9/11"). In addition, it covers differences in nonverbal communication across cultures and addresses some of the communication issues that arise between men and women in law enforcement agencies. Finally, we present skills and techniques for officers to apply in situations of cross-cultural contact.

Each chapter ends with discussion questions and a list of references. The following appendices correspond to the chapter content in Part One:

A. Multicultural Community and Workforce: Attitude Assessment
B. Cultural Diversity Survey: Needs Assessment
C. Cross-Cultural Communication Skills Assessment for Law Enforcement Professionals

1

Multicultural Communities
Challenges for Law Enforcement

LEARNING OBJECTIVES

After reading this chapter, you should be able to:

- Discuss the impact of diversity on law enforcement.
- Understand the references "melting pot" and "mosaic" society as well as the historical context in which these terms have evolved.
- Summarize key demographic trends in the United States related to the growth of minority populations.
- Provide an overview of key issues associated with immigration directly affecting law enforcement.
- Define "culture" and "ethnocentrism" and discuss the contexts in which they are relevant to law enforcement.
- List the primary and secondary dimensions of diversity.
- Apply the concepts of prejudice and stereotyping to everyday police work.

OUTLINE

- Introduction
- The Interface of Diversity and Law Enforcement
- Typology of Immigrants and Refugees
- Culture and Its Relevance to Law Enforcement
- Dimensions of Diversity
- Prejudice in Law Enforcement
- Summary
- Discussion Questions and Issues

INTRODUCTION

Multiculturalism in the United States has a long silent history. The United States has, from its founding, taken in immigrants from different cultural backgrounds, many of whom were, at the time, controversial. First, it was the Germans about whom questions were raised as to whether they could or would become "real Americans." Then questions were raised about the Chinese and after them Irish and the Eastern European immigrants. Now it is Hispanic-Americans and Muslim-Americans of whom we ask those questions.

—*Stanley Renshon, Professor of Political Science, CUNY Graduate Center, 2011*

The American experience has always been a story of color. In the 20th century it was a story of the black-white line. In the 21st century we are moving into a new off-white moment.

—*Suárez-Orozco (Global Expert on Immigration), 2013*

Multiculturalism and diversity are at the very heart of America and accurately describe the demographics of our nation. The word *multiculturalism* does not refer to a movement or political force, nor is it an anti-American term. The United States is an amalgam of races, cultures, and ethnic groups, evolving from successive waves of immigration. The United States, compared to virtually all other nations, has experienced unparalleled growth in its multicultural population. Reactions to these changes range from appreciation and even celebration of diversity to an absolute intolerance of differences. In its extreme form, intolerance resulting in crimes of hate is a major law enforcement and criminal justice concern.

THE INTERFACE OF DIVERSITY AND LAW ENFORCEMENT

Those whose professional ideal is to protect and serve people equally from all backgrounds must face the challenges and complexities of a diverse society. A lack of communication effectiveness, coupled with minimal understanding of individuals' backgrounds, can result in inadvertent violation of individuals' rights as well as officer safety and risk issues. Officers, even more than others, must ensure that their prejudices remain in check and that they refrain from acting on any biased thought.

In an interview, Ondra Berry, Retired Deputy Police Chief, Reno, Nevada, states:

Law enforcement is under a powerful microscope in terms of how citizens are treated. Minority and ethnic communities have become increasingly competent in understanding the role of law enforcement, and expectations of law enforcement for professionalism have been elevated from previous years. In an age when information about what happens in a police department on the East Coast speeds across to the West Coast in seconds, law enforcement officials must be aware. They must be vigilant. They must do the right thing. (Berry, 2013)

Although our nation has been enriched by diversity, many police procedures and interactions with citizens are, consequently, more complex. Racial tensions and communication challenges with immigrants, for example, are bound to complicate some police encounters. It would be naive to preach to law enforcement officers, agents, and managers about the value of diversity when day-to-day activities can be more complicated because of it. At a minimum, a basic acceptance of our multicultural society on the part of all criminal justice representatives is required as a precursor to improving interpersonal relations and contact across cultural, ethnic, and racial lines.

The United States has always been a magnet for people from nearly every corner of the earth, and, consequently, U.S. demographics continue to undergo constant change. In their efforts to be both proactive and responsive to diverse communities, police officers and groups from many backgrounds around the country are working to become more closely connected in direct relationships promoted in community-based policing models. Leaders from both law enforcement agencies and the community have realized that both groups benefit when each group seeks mutual assistance and understanding. The job of law enforcement requires a certain level of comfort and professionalism in interacting with people from all backgrounds whether one is working with community members to build trust or dealing with suspects, victims, and coworkers.

Through increased awareness, cultural knowledge, and skills, law enforcement as a profession can increase its cultural competence. Acquiring cultural competence is not an instantaneous process; it is multilayered and complex, and includes:

- Exploration of officers' belief systems and biases
- Awareness of an officer's perspectives and perceptions, especially as they may differ from those associated with minority viewpoints
- Acquisition of cultural information relevant to the concerns of law enforcement, and the capacity to apply that knowledge in ethnic, racial, and other diverse communities
- Increased communication skills leading to effective rapport building and communication with all community members
- Development of a set of principles, attitudes, and policies that will enable all individuals in an organization to work effectively and equitably across all cultures and ethnicities

The strategies an individual uses to approach and build rapport with his or her own cultural group may result in unexpected difficulties with another group. The acts of approaching, communicating, questioning, assisting, and establishing trust with members of culturally diverse groups require special knowledge and skills that have nothing to do with the fact that "the law is the law" and must be enforced equally. Acquiring knowledge and skills that lead to sensitivity does not imply preferential treatment of any one group; rather it contributes to improved communication with members of all groups.

Individuals must seek a balance between downplaying and even denying the differences of others, and, on the other hand, distorting the role of culture, race, and ethnicity. In an effort to simply "respect all humans equally," we may inadvertently diminish the influence of culture or ethnicity, including the role it has played historically in our society.

The Melting Pot Myth and the Mosaic

Multiculturalism, also called cultural pluralism, violates what some consider the "American way of life." However, from the time the United States was founded, Americans were never a homogeneous people. The indigenous peoples of America, the ancestors of the American Indians, were here long before Christopher Columbus "discovered" them. There is even strong evidence that the first Africans who set foot in this country came as free people, 200 years before the slave trade from Africa began (Rawlins, 1992). Furthermore, the majority of people in America can claim to be the children, grandchildren, or great-grandchildren of people who have migrated here. Americans did not originate from a common stock. Until fairly recently, America has been referred to as a melting pot, a term depicting an image of people coming together and forming a unified culture. One of the earliest uses of the term was in the early 1900s, when a famous American playwright, Israel Zangwill, referring to the mass migration from Europe said, "America is God's crucible, the great Melting-Pot where all the races of Europe are melting and re-forming. . . . Germans and Frenchmen, Irishmen and Englishmen, Jews and Russians—into the Crucible with you all! God is making the American!" (Zangwill, 1908).

This first use of the term *melting pot* was not designed to incorporate anyone except Europeans. Did the melting pot ever exist, then, in the United States? No, it never did. Yet people still refer to the belief, which is not much more than a romantic myth about the "good old days." African Americans, brought forcibly to this country between 1619 and 1850, were never part of the early descriptions of the melting pot. Likewise, Native American peoples were not considered for the melting pot. It is not coincidental that these groups were nonwhite and were therefore not "meltable." Furthermore, throughout our past, great efforts have been made to prevent any additional diversity. Most notable in this regard was the Chinese Exclusion Act in 1882, which denied Chinese laborers the right to enter America. Early in the twentieth century, organized labor formed the Japanese and Korean Exclusion League "to protest the influx of 'Coolie' labor and in fear of threat to the living standards of American workingmen"

(Kennedy, 1986,). Immigration was discouraged or prevented if it did not add strength to what already existed as the European-descended majority of the population (Handlin, 1975).

Even at the peak of immigration in the late 1800s, New York City exemplified how different immigrant groups stayed separate from each other, with little of the "blending" that people often imagine taking place (Miller, 2013). Three-fourths of New York City's population consisted of first- or second-generation immigrants, including Europeans and Asians. Eighty percent did not speak English, and there were 100 foreign-language newspapers in circulation. The new arrivals were not accepted by those who had already settled, and newcomers found comfort in an alien society by choosing to remain in ethnic enclaves with people who shared their culture and life experiences.

The first generation of every immigrant and refugee group, who saw the United States as the land of hope and opportunity, had always experienced obstacles in acculturation and integration into the new society. In many cases, people resisted Americanization and kept to themselves. Italians, Irish, Eastern European Jews, Portuguese, Germans, and virtually all other groups tended to remain apart when they first came. Most previously settled immigrants were distrustful and disdainful of each newcomer group. "Mainstreaming" began to occur only with children of the immigrants, although some people within certain immigrant groups tried to assimilate quickly. For the most part, however, society did not permit a quick shedding of previous cultural identity. History has never supported the metaphor of the melting pot, especially with regard to the first and second generations of most groups of newcomers. Despite the reality of past multicultural disharmony and tension in the United States, however, the notion of the melting pot prevailed.

The terms *mosaic* and *tapestry* more accurately portray diversity in America. They describe a society in which all colors and backgrounds contribute their parts to form society as a whole, but one in which groups are not required to lose their characteristics in order to "melt" together. The idea of a mosaic portrays a society in which all races and ethnic groups are seen as separate and distinct in contributing their own color, shape, and design to the whole, resulting in an enriched society.

Reactions to Multiculturalism: Past and Present

Accepting multiculturalism and diversity has always been a difficult proposition for many Americans (Miller, 2013). Typical criticisms of immigrants, now and historically, include "They hold on to their cultures," "They don't learn our language," "Their customs and behavior are strange," "They form cliques," and "They take our jobs." Many newcomers, in fact, have historically resisted Americanization, keeping themselves to ethnic enclaves. They were not usually accepted by mainstream society.

Are the reactions to newcomers today so different from people's reactions to earlier waves of immigrants? Let us look at the reactions to the Irish, who, by the middle of the nineteenth century, constituted the largest group of immigrants in the United States, making up almost 45 percent of the foreign-born population. Approximately 4.25 million people left Ireland, mainly because of the potato famine. Many of these immigrants had come from rural areas, but ended up in cities on the East Coast. Most were illiterate; some spoke only Gaelic (Kennedy, 1986). Their reception in America was anything but welcoming, exemplified by the plethora of signs saying, "Jobs available, no Irish need apply."

> The Irish . . . endure[d] the scorn and discrimination later to be inflicted, to some degree at least, on each successive wave of immigrants by already settled "Americans." In speech and in dress, they seemed foreign; they were poor and unskilled and they were arriving in overwhelming numbers. . . . The Irish found many doors closed to them, both socially and economically. When their earnings were not enough . . . their wives and daughters obtained employment as servants. (Kennedy, 1986)

If this account were written without specific references to time and cultural group, it would be reasonable to assume that it describes contemporary reactions to newcomers. We could have taken this passage and substituted Jew, Italian, or Polish at various points in history. Today, it could be used in reference to Afghans, Mexicans, Haitians, Chinese, Koreans, or Indians. If we compare immigration today with that during earlier periods in U.S. history, we find similarities as well as significant differences. In the past few decades, we have received people from cultures more dramatically different than those from Western Europe. For example, many of our "new Americans" from parts of Asia or Africa bring values and languages not commonly associated with or related to mainstream American values and language. Middle Easterners bring customs unknown to many U.S.-born Americans. (For cultural specifics, refer to Chapters 5–9.) Many refugees bring scars of political persecution or war trauma, the nature of which the majority of Americans cannot even fathom. The relatively mild experiences of those who came as voluntary migrants do not compare with the tragedies of many of the more recent refugees. Desperate economic conditions compelled many early European immigrants to leave their countries and thus their leaving was not entirely voluntary. However, their experiences do not parallel those, for example, of war-torn Eastern European refugees who came to the United States in the 1990s or Afghan and Iraqi refugees who came after 2000 or Central and South Americans fleeing gang violence or Africans escaping state violence in the past decade.

Disparaging comments were once made toward the very people whose descendants would, in later years, constitute much of mainstream America. Many fourth- and fifth-generation immigrants have forgotten their history (Miller, 2013) and are intolerant of the "foreign ways" of emerging immigrant groups. Every new group seems to be met with some suspicion and, in many cases, hostility. Adjustment to a new society is and has always been a long and painful process, and the first-generation immigrant group suffers, whether Irish, Polish, Afghani, Filipino, Central American or African. It must also be remembered that many groups did not come to the United States of their own free will but rather were victims of a political or an economic system or circumstance such as war that forced them to abruptly cut their roots and escape their homelands. Although grateful for their welcome to this country, such newcomers did not want to be uprooted. Many new Americans did not have any part in the creation of events that led to their flight from their countries.

Changing Population

Demographic estimates and projections in the twenty-first century are likely to fall short of counting the true mix of people in the United States. In the culture-specific chapters of this book, we discuss Asian and Pacific Americans, African Americans, Latino and Hispanic Americans, Arab Americans and other Middle Eastern groups, and Native Americans. These categorizations are merely for the sake of convenience; an individual may belong to two or more groups. For example, black Latinos, such as people from the Dominican Republic or Brazil, may identify themselves as both black and Latino. Race and ethnic background (e.g., in the case of a black Latino) are not necessarily mutually exclusive. Hispanic is considered an ethnicity, not a race. Therefore, people of Latino descent can count themselves as part of any race. Selecting a clear-cut category is not as simple as it may appear. In fact, in the 2010 census, the Hispanic population predominantly identified themselves as either White or "some other race" (Census Bureau Reports, 2011).

Beginning with the 2000 census, biracial individuals could report being a multiple-race combination. The U.S. Census information released in 2008 projected that, by 2050, the number of people who identify themselves as being of two or more races will more than triple, from 5.2 million to 16.2 million (U.S. Census Bureau, 2012) In fact, data from the 2010 census showed a population well on its way to surpassing that estimate, with 9 million people, or 3 percent of the population, reporting more than one race. Of those 9 million, 92 percent reported being of exactly two races, with 8 percent reporting three races (Census Bureau Reports, 2012).

Law enforcement officials need to be aware of the overlap between race and ethnicity and that many individuals consider themselves to be multiracial. According to historian Edward Ball, "We are not separate tribes of Latinos and whites and blacks in America. We've all mingled, and we have done so for generations." (Swarns & Kantor, 2009)

Heterogeneous   Dissimilar, or composed of unrelated or unlike elements. A **heterogeneous society** is one that is diverse, and frequently refers to racial and ethnic composition.

The face of America has been changing for some time. In 1860, there were only three census categories: black, white, and "quadroon" (i.e., a person who has one black grandparent, or the child of a mulatto and a white). Beginning with the 2000 census, there were 63 possible options for marking racial identity, or twice that if people responded in the affirmative to whether or not they were of Hispanic ethnicity. Furthermore, as of 2012, the US Census Bureau even established a National Advisory Committee on Racial, Ethnic, and Other Populations to "help us meet emerging challenges the Census Bureau faces in producing statistics about our diverse nation," according to Census Bureau acting director Thomas L. Mesenbourg (Census Bureau Reports, 2012).

Minority Populations

Documented changes in population characteristics between 2000 and 2010 have been dramatic, and this trend is projected to continue this through the next decade and beyond. The 2010 census projections show that, "The next half century marks key points in continuing trends—the U.S. will become a plurality nation, where the non-Hispanic white population remains the largest single group, but no group is in the majority," according to Mesenbourg. Minorities, defined as all but the single-race, non-Hispanic white population, currently comprise 37 percent of the U.S. population, or 116.2 million people. This number is expected to rise to 241.3 million, or 57 percent of the population, by 2060 (Census Bureau Reports, 2012).

Consider the following data released in 2012 (Census Bureau Reports, 2012):

- The U.S. is projected to become a majority-minority nation for the first time in 2043.
- The Hispanic population is projected to increase from 53.3 million in 2012 to 128.8 million in 2060, meaning nearly one in three U.S. residents would be Hispanic, up from about one in six today.
- The non-Hispanic white population is projected to peak in 2024, at 199.6 million, but unique from any other race or ethnic group, is expected to slowly decrease, falling by nearly 20.6 million from 2024 to 2060.
- The black population is expected to increase from 41.2 million to 61.8 million from 2024 to 2060, increasing its share of the total population from 13.1 percent in 2012 to 14.7 percent in 2060.
- The Asian population is projected to more than double, from 15.9 million in 2012 to 34.4 million in 2060, with its share of nation's total population climbing from 5.1 percent to 8.2 percent in the same period.
- The number of people who identify themselves as being of two or more races is projected to more than triple, from 7.5 million in 2024 to 26.7 million in 2060.

Minority group   A group that is the smaller in number of two groups that constitute a whole; part of the population that, because of certain characteristics, differs from the majority population and may be subjected to differential treatment.

Exhibit 1.1 shows projected rates of growth of nonwhite groups through 2050 and the corresponding decline in the white (non-Hispanic ethnicity) population.

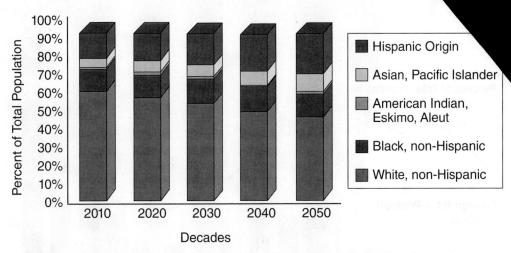

EXHIBIT 1.1 Resident population by race and Hispanic origin status—Projections: 2010 to 2050
Source: U.S. Census Bureau, Statistical Abstract of the United States, 2002.

Some of these population shifts give rise to nuances and controversies associated with the word "minority." U.S. Census information released in 2013 indicated that approximately 11 percent of counties (353 of over 3,000 counties) across the United States are a "majority-minority" county (see Exhibit 1.2). Four states—California (60.6% minority), Hawaii (77.2%), New Mexico (60.2%), and Texas (55.5%)—and the District of Columbia (64.5%) are majority-minority states; this means that the percentage of minority residents in these counties and states has exceeded 50 percent (Census Bureau Reports, 2013). Majority-minority counties are growing in rural and urban areas alike. This change has had a huge impact on many institutions in society, including the law enforcement workforce.

EXHIBIT 1.2 Largest Majority-Minority Counties
Source: Badger, "6 More U.S. Counties are now Majority-Minority," The Atlantic Cities, 2013.

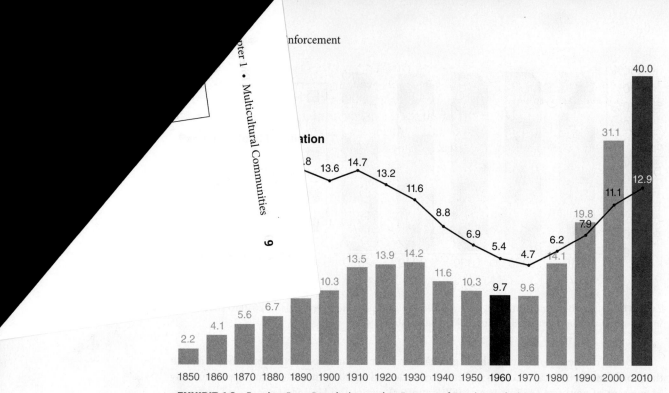

EXHIBIT 1.3 Foreign-Born Population and as Percent of Total Population.
Source: U.S. Census Bureau, 1850-2000 Decennial Census; 2010 American Community Survey. Reprinted with permission.

Immigrants and Refugees

Immigration is not a new phenomenon in the United States. Virtually every citizen, except for indigenous peoples of America, can claim to be a descendent of someone who migrated, whether voluntarily or not, from another country. Immigration levels per decade reached their highest absolute numbers ever at the end of the last century, when the number of immigrants surpassed 9 million from 1991 to 2000 (see Exhibit 1.3), not including the estimated 11 million undocumented immigrants living in the United States. The U.S. Census Bureau American Community Survey (ACS) reported that in 2010 there were 39.9 million foreign-born living in the United States, comprising 13 percent of the total population. This represents an increase of 11.5 million people more than a decade earlier, according to the March 2000 Current Population Survey.

Immigrant or **"Permanent Resident Alien"**   "An [individual] admitted to the United States as a lawful permanent resident. Permanent residents are also commonly referred to as immigrants; however, the Immigration and Nationality Act (INA) broadly defines an immigrant as any alien in the United States, except one legally admitted under specific nonimmigrant categories [e.g., temporary workers] . . . Lawful permanent residents are legally accorded the privilege of residing permanently in the United States. They may be issued immigrant visas by the Department of State overseas or adjusted to permanent resident status by the Department of Homeland Security (DHS) in the United States." (Department of Homeland Security, 2013)

Unauthorized Immigrants and Related Terminology

The terms *illegal immigrant, illegal alien, undocumented immigrant* and *unauthorized immigrant* are sometimes used interchangeably, but there is controversy around the use of each of these labels, in part, related to people's views on immigration. (Discussion of this controversy is beyond the scope of this chapter.) In this text, we use two common terms—*undocumented immigrant* and *unauthorized immigrant*. The latter term is increasingly in use (e.g., Pew Research and ICE references), however, as of the writing of this sixth edition, it has not entirely replaced the former term. There are two major groups of undocumented or unauthorized immigrants: those who cross the U.S. borders without having been "inspected" and those who enter the country with legal documents as temporary residents, but have violated their legal admission status by extending their stay.

> **Refugee** "Any person who is outside his or her country of nationality who is unable or unwilling to return to that country because of persecution or a well-founded fear of persecution. Persecution or the fear thereof must be based on . . . race, religion, nationality, membership in a particular social group, or political opinion. People with no nationality must generally be outside their country of last habitual residence to qualify as a refugee." (Department of Homeland Security, 2013)

In addition, immigrants from 1980 to the present have come from many more parts of the world than from where they arrived at the turn of the twentieth century. In the middle of the twentieth century, 75 percent of the immigrants were from European countries. As shown in Exhibit 1.4, by 2009, over 80 percent of immigrants were from countries in Latin America and Asia (Census Bureau Reports, 2010). From the U.S. Census 2009 American Community Survey data, the top seven countries of birth for foreign-born populations were, in descending order, Mexico, China, the Philippines, India, El Salvador and Vietnam, and Korea (see Exhibits 1.5 and 1.6). Exhibit 1.7 shows foreign-born population by state; 56 percent of the total foreign-born population lived in California, New York, Texas and Florida, with at least 3.5 million immigrants in each state (U.S. Census Bureau, 2010). Despite this historical high immigrant population, the proportion of the total population is lower than during the late 1800s and early 1900s, when it fluctuated between 13 percent and 15 percent (U.S. Census Bureau, 2010).

Seven states experienced over 23 percent of their foreign-born population entering between 2005 and 2009 (U.S. Census Bureau, 2010). The states with the highest percentage of recent immigrants were North Dakota (34 percent), Kentucky (28 percent) and South Dakota (26 percent), followed by South Carolina, Alabama, Indiana and West Virginia (U.S. Census Bureau, 2010).

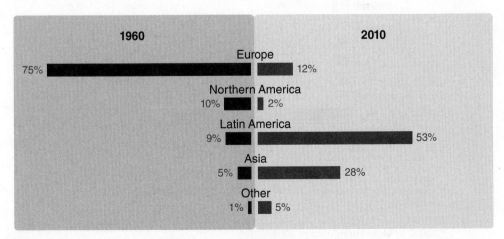

EXHIBIT 1.4 Change in Foreign-Born Population by Region of Birth.
Source: U.S. Census Bureau 1960 Decennial Census; U.S. Census Bureau, 2010 American Community Survey.

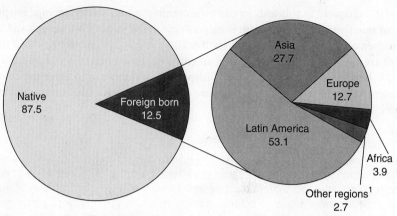

¹Other regions include Oceania and Northern America.

EXHIBIT 1.5   Total Population by Nativity and Foreign-Born Population by Region of Birth: 2009.

Source: U.S. Census Bureau, American Community Survey, 2009. Reprinted with permission.

A 2012 report showed Asian immigrants for the first time outpacing Hispanic immigration, making Asians the fastest growing racial group in the United States (Pew Research Social & Demographic Trends, 2012). According to Pew Research demographers, the Hispanic immigrant population has almost tripled the rate of undocumented immigrants compared to the Asian immigrant population. Therefore, tougher border enforcement has had a larger impact on Hispanic immigrants; Hispanic immigration dropped 31 percent from 2007 to 2010, while Asian immigration grew 10 percent in that same time period.

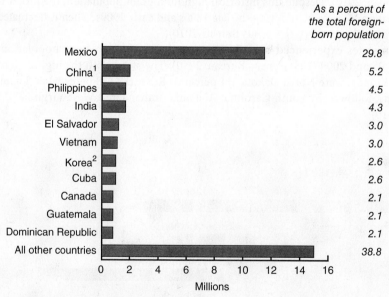

¹Includes respondents who reported their country of birth as China, Hong Kong, Macau, Paracel Islands, or Taiwan.
²Includes respondents who reported their country of birth as Korea, North Korea, or South Korea.

EXHIBIT 1.6   Foreign-Born Population by Country of Birth for Countries with 750,000 or More Foreign-Born: 2009.

Source: U.S. Census Bureau, American Community Survey, 2009. Reprinted with permission.

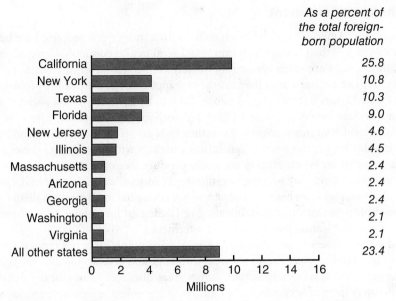

As a percent of the total foreign-born population

State	Percent
California	25.8
New York	10.8
Texas	10.3
Florida	9.0
New Jersey	4.6
Illinois	4.5
Massachusetts	2.4
Arizona	2.4
Georgia	2.4
Washington	2.1
Virginia	2.1
All other states	23.4

EXHIBIT 1.7 Foreign-Born Population by State for States with 750,000 or More Foreign-Born: 2009

Source: U.S. Census Bureau, American Community Survey, 2009. Reprinted with permission.

> The **foreign-born** population includes naturalized U.S. citizens, legal permanent residents, temporary migrants (e.g., foreign students), humanitarian migrants (refugees), and unauthorized migrants. (U.S. Census Bureau, State and Country Quick Facts: Foreign-Born Persons, 2010)

Further Distinctions between Immigrants and Refugees

Because a large proportion of minorities with whom law enforcement officers encounter are born outside the United States, it is important to understand some of the key differences that relate to immigration status as people enter the country.

Refugees are sponsored into the United States under the authority of the U.S. government. Although many ethnic groups have come in under the sponsorship of the federal government with refugee or émigré status, the largest numbers came from Southeast Asia as a result of the upheaval brought on by the Vietnam War. Refugees, sponsored into the United States by the government, are expected to receive fully public support services such as welfare, tuition reimbursement, job training programs, and "English as a second language" programs. Case managers are often assigned to refugee families to ensure that family members utilize all of the services provided. Some believe that such participation in public programs may create dependency and learned helplessness; others feel that refugees have escaped terror, torture or war and require support for being uprooted, that is, a choice to leave their country that was not their own.

Immigrants, on the other hand, enter into the United States under the direct sponsorship of their families. The federal government mandates that immigrants be allowed to enter the United States only if their families can support or provide work for them. In fact, one criterion for being able to attain permanent residence status (a "green card") is that the immigrant will not become a burden to the government; this means that participation in any public-funded program may jeopardize that individual's chances for attaining permanent residence status.

Anti-Immigrant Sentiment

Even though most Americans, with the exception of the indigenous peoples, have been immigrants at some time in their lineage, anti-immigrant sentiment is common. Especially in times of recession, immigrants are often blamed for society's woes. However, the issues surrounding immigration are not as clear-cut as they may at first appear to be. Despite the problems that are inevitably created when large groups of people have to be absorbed into a society, immigrant groups can stimulate the economy, revitalize neighborhoods, and eventually become fully participatory and loyal American citizens. Nevertheless, if an officer has an anti-immigrant bias, negative attitudes may surface when that officer interacts with immigrants, especially under stressful circumstances. When officers are under pressure, negative attitudes become apparent and their communication may become unprofessional. Indeed, some citizens have claimed that officers with whom they have been in contact had not attempted to understand them or that they demonstrated little patience in communicating or finding an interpreter. (See Chapter 4 for a discussion of communication issues and law enforcement.)

In addition, officers must be aware of "racial flash points" that are created when immigrants move into economically depressed areas with large and diverse populations. Some people feel that immigrants' moving into certain urban areas displaces economically disadvantaged groups or deprives them of access to work. Thus law enforcement representatives may see hostility between, for example, blacks and Korean or Arab immigrants in such cities as Los Angeles, New York, and Detroit. Although officers cannot be expected to solve these deep-seated problems, they may find themselves in situations in which they can serve as cultural mediators, helping each group to increase understanding and toleration of the other. For example, police can point out that the absence of a Korean grocer's smile or greeting of a customer is not necessarily a sign of hostility or an expression of distrust, but possibly a cultural trait. When a person complains that an Arab liquor store owner does not hire outside his or her community, officers can explain that it is usually because the business is a small, family-run operation in which employees are family members. It would be too simplistic to attribute all or even the majority of problems as cultural, but with an understanding of immigrants' backgrounds, officers can help explain points of tension to members of other ethnic groups.

Community Policing Outreach to Immigrants and Refugees

As part of his community policing outreach, Aaron T. Olson (coauthor of this textbook), established through IRCO (Immigrant Refugee Community Organization) ongoing police outreach to Portland area immigrants and refugees beginning in 2002. The educational sessions, focusing around police and emergency services, continue through the present (Olson, 2013). New immigrants and refugees, for example, are oriented on interaction with American police and on how to use 911. What instructors learn from the immigrant community is also shared with police officers in various police departments. People in law enforcement have learned that there are some predictable social and cultural differences for which education should be provided to help newcomers with acculturation to the U.S. law enforcement expectations. For example, consider the following:

- In the United States, most police departments do not allow the driver or the passengers to exit their car and walk back to the police car.
- In other countries like Cuba, Japan, Mexico, Russia, and some countries in the Arab world it is expected that motorists exit their car and walk back to the police officer. Getting out of the car is even a sign of courtesy toward officers in some countries.
- The police in such regions as Eastern Europe and South America expect bribes when they stop a motorist.
- Interpreters (especially those who work for the court), and new immigrants are excellent sources of information on customs of their country.

To better serve new immigrants and refugees coming to the United States from all countries in the world, organizations such as the Immigrant Refugee Community Organization (IRCO) in Portland, Oregon have offered public-safety and basic-law workshops. The sessions provide an orientation on America's police, laws, and emergency services.

Immigrants and refugees attending these workshops typically have been in the United States for one month, and have had no previous orientation on the American police, laws, or emergency services. Sessions, with interpreters, include such basic topics as:

- FBI and ICE
- State Police
- Sheriff's departments and city police departments
- Traffic and criminal laws
- Domestic violence
- What to do if stopped by a police officer
- How to use 911 for emergencies and other alternatives for nonemergencies

EXHIBIT 1.8 Workshops for Immigrants and Refugees on U.S. Police, Laws, and Emergency Services
Source: Olson, Aaron T., 2013. Used with permission.

- Men from Eastern Europe and South America find it difficult to believe that a man can be arrested for touching a woman and find it silly that the U.S. police do prostitution sting decoy operations.
- Domestic violence laws are basically nonexistent in Eastern European countries as those governments view family matters as personal and private.
- There are cultures where children are allowed to play outside and where neighbors feel some responsibility for children other than their own (i.e., in some group-oriented cultures). Immigrants and refugees from such cultures need to be educated about the vigilance required to supervise children in U.S. neighborhoods.
- Domestic violence laws in the United States are very specific; some immigrants and refugees do not understand that they do not have to endure abuse by their domestic partners.

The more cultural knowledge that officers gain on ethnic and immigrant communities, the more they will be able to anticipate and deal with reactions and behavior (see Exhibit 1.8 on workshops provided to immigrants and refugees).

TYPOLOGY OF IMMIGRANTS AND REFUGEES

We have developed a seven-part typology that is useful in understanding and summarizing some of the differences among individuals within immigrant, refugee, and minority groups. Our typology suggests that as law enforcement and public safety organizations prepare and train their personnel to work with minority communities, a focus on key differences and motivational components within each of the typological groups would be beneficial. Following the typology shown in Exhibit 1.9 is a detailed explanation of each "type" of immigrant, refugee, or minority group.

Typology of Immigrant, Refugee, and Minority Individuals

The key to understanding the behavior of the most recent immigrant and refugee group (Type I) is to realize that members are in survival mode. Many people from this category remember that law enforcement and police officers in their country of origin were corrupt, aligned with a repressive government and the military, and/or swayed by bribes from those who were more affluent. All their activities tend to be guided by this framework, which is to survive; to get through. This perspective also makes sense in terms of the traumatic ordeals faced by refugees in their journeys to the United States. Encounters of these people with law enforcement personnel usually involve

Type	Description	Key Motivating Perspective
Type I	Recently arrived adult immigrant or refugee (fewer than [approximately] five years in the United States with major life experiences in the country of origin)	Survival
Type II	Adult immigrant or refugee with five or more years in the United States (with major life exprinces in the country of origin)	Preservation
Type III	Immigrant or refugee as youth (major life experiences in the United States)	Adjustment
Type IV	Second-generation minority individual (offspring of immigrant or refugee)	Change
Type V	Third generation or more minority individual	Choice
Type VI	Foreign-country national (anticipates return to home country; includes visitors and tourists)	Maintenance
Type VII	Foreign-country national (global workplace and residency)	Expansion

EXHIBIT 1.9   Immigrant/Ethnic Group Typology

saying and doing anything to discontinue the contact because of possible fears of personal harm (e.g., not speaking English; not producing identification; blindly saying "Yes, I will cooperate!").

With regard to Type II immigrants, understanding their behavior relates to their need to preserve their home cultures as the motivating perspective. Given that the majority of their life experiences occurred outside the U.S., members are trying to preserve much of the values and traditions of their home cultures. Intergenerational conflict between grandparents or parents and youths tends to occur within this group. Members are inclined to keep to their ethnic communities (e.g., Chinatowns) and have as little to do with law enforcement as possible.

Type III immigrants whose major life experience is in the United States, focus much energy on changes (through assimilation or acculturation)—that must be made in order to succeed—although these individuals tend to continue to value the cultural and ethnic elements of their former homelands as well. Members of this group reflect the socioeconomic standings of the different waves upon which each entered the United States. For members of this group, reactions to law enforcement officials vary depending on their time of immigration and socioeconomic experiences.

People who are second-generation U.S.-born or later (Type IV) work very hard at being assimilated into society, adjusting and changing to be part of mainstream America. Often, the expectations of their parents are high, sacrificing so that their offspring will "make it" in their lifetimes. Type IV minority members may interact primarily with mainstream Americans and take on many of the values and norms of U.S. culture. Despite these individuals' efforts to become like the mainstream (i.e., "become white"), they may still be considered "marginal" by some and may be viewed as outsiders. People from this group try to minimize their contact with law enforcement personnel and agencies primarily because of the immigration and other experiences relayed to them by their parents' generation.

The Type V category includes individuals who are more able to choose which aspects of their old cultures to keep and which of the new culture to accept. The focus is on selecting activities, values, norms, and lifestyles that blend the best of their families' traditions and American cultures. Being bicultural is a unique and important aspect of this group. Many may no longer have as much skill with their native languages as they have with English, and may rely on English as their primary or only language (thus an individual can be bicultural and not bilingual). Contact by members of this group with law enforcement personnel might not be any different than contact with other Americans.

For the last two categories, foreign country nationals, we make a key distinction between those who plan to return to their own countries following work assignments in the United States (Type VI) and those whose work is truly global, in that individuals may have several residences in different parts of the world (Type VII). Those who are on temporary work assignments in the United States maintain their home-base cultural orientation and experiences knowing that when the work assignment is over, they will go back to their home countries again. Because they want to maintain their native cultures, some individuals of this group may be inadequately prepared to understand many of the laws and practices of the United States.

For the second group of foreign nationals (Type VII), the key focus is on their ability to "expand" their actions and behavior effectively in differing global environments. These individuals see themselves as being able to adapt to life in a variety of circumstances; many speak three or more languages (including English). Individuals within this group pride themselves in knowing about the different laws, norms, values, and practices of the countries they encounter. Law enforcement personnel should find this group able to understand and follow the laws and practices of a given community.

European Americans

In learning about multiculturalism in U.S. society, focus is often centered on the diversity among immigrants and foreign-born from cultures very different from "mainstream" U.S. culture. However, there is also a great deal of diversity among European Americans. One of the myths about European Americans is that they are all alike. The majority of people in the United States are of European descent, although as of July 2011, for the first time in history, children born to minority parents outnumbered those born to whites of European ancestry. From July 2010 to July 2011, 50.4 percent of children born belonged to a minority group, up from 48.6 percent in the same period ending in 2009 (Dougherty & Jordan, 2012). According to the 2010 American Community Survey, approximately 12 percent of all foreign-born people living in the United States were from Europe, with roughly two-thirds of those born in Southern and Eastern Europe (American Community Survey, 2011).

Most Europeans are not of the same ethnicity or nationality, nor do they even have the same physical characteristics. Europe is a continent that is divided into four regions—east, west, north, and south—and has a population of 740 million people (Population Reference Bureau, 2013). Europe has 46 different countries, each with a unique national character, government, and, for the most part, language. To illustrate Europe's diversity and heterogeneity, the European Union has 23 different official languages for its European Parliament compared to the United Nations (which has six official languages). The European Union holds the world's largest translation operation and has 60 interpreters in use when its 28-member state Parliament is in session (European Parliament, 2007). The countries listed in Exhibit 1.10 represent the continent of Europe.

According to the 2010 U.S. Census, 12 percent of the foreign-born population living in the United States was from Europe, a sharp decline from previous decades. In 1960, Europeans comprised nearly 75 percent of the U.S. foreign-born population (Census Bureau Reports, 2010). Under the "Iron Curtain" communist regimes in Eastern European countries, there was little immigration from that region. However, since the democratization of many of these countries in the late 1980s and early 1990s, the U.S. has seen an uptick in immigration numbers from Eastern Europe.

An estimated 44 percent of European immigrants, or 2.1 million people, were born in Eastern Europe, with the highest numbers coming from Poland, Russia, Ukraine, Romania, and Bosnia and Herzegovina, respectively (Russell & Batalova, 2012). Many Eastern European immigrants to the

1. Albania	17. Holy City (Vatican City)	32. Norway
2. Andorra	18. Hungary	33. Poland
3. Austria	19. Iceland	34. Portugal
4. Belarus	20. Ireland	35. Romania
5. Belgium	21. Italy	36. Russia
6. Bosnia and Herzegovina	22. Kosovo	37. San Marino
7. Bulgaria	23. Latvia	38. Serbia and Montenegro
8. Croatia	24. Liechtenstein	39. Slovakia
9. Cyprus	25. Lithuania	40. Slovenia
10. Czech Republic	26. Luxembourg	41. Spain
11. Denmark	27. Macedonia, the former	42. Sweden
12. Estonia	Yugoslav Republic	43. Switzerland
13. Finland	28. Malta	44. Turkey
14. France	29. Moldova	45. Ukraine
15. Germany	30. Monaco	46. United Kingdom
16. Greece	31. Netherlands	

EXHIBIT 1.10   The Countries of Europe

United States came to reunite with family or escape ethnic violence and wars that followed the dissolution of the Soviet Union. The State Department assists refugees—distinct from immigrants who came to the United States for other reasons—with their resettlement, looking for locations with housing, jobs, available services and a "welcoming attitude" (Gilsinan, 2013). The State Department contracts with local agencies to place refugees in cities that immigrants might otherwise not choose. The result is large populations of Eastern European refugee communities found in cities with small nonrefugee immigrant populations. St. Louis, Missouri, for example, is home to the largest Bosnian community outside of Bosnia, many of whom were "settled" prior to 2001 but now make up a thriving Bosnian community (Gilsinan, 2013).

Unauthorized Immigrants: Demographic Information

The census bureau does not ask about legal migrant status of respondents as there is no legislative mandate to do so. (U.S. Citizenship and Immigration Services [USCIS], 2013). In its 2003 report on undocumented immigrants, the former Immigration and Naturalization Services (INS), now the USCIS, placed the growth of this population at 350,000 annually. This figure was 75,000 per year higher than was estimated before the 2000 census, primarily because of improved means of counting a hard-to-track population. Exact figures are difficult to obtain, but estimates put the number of undocumented immigrants in the United States at 11.1 million in 2011, a decrease from a peak of 12 million in 2007 (Census Bureau Reports, 2012). (See Exhibit 1.11)

Unauthorized Immigrants: Background Information

As noted previously, undocumented or unauthorized immigrants can be broadly divided into two major groups: those who enter the U.S. illegally and those who enter legally, but have stayed beyond their permitted time. Initially, Mexicans and other Latin Americans come to most people's minds when they hear the terms *illegal alien* and *undocumented worker*. In addition, however, there are people from the Dominican Republic who enter through Puerto Rico; since Puerto Ricans are U.S. citizens, they are considered legal. Therefore, officers may come in contact with "Puerto Ricans" who are actually from the Dominican Republic and have come to the United States under an illegal pretext. Asians are also smuggled into the United States, including women brought in for sex trade. People from other parts of the world may come to the United States on a tourist visa and then decide to remain permanently (e.g., Canadians).

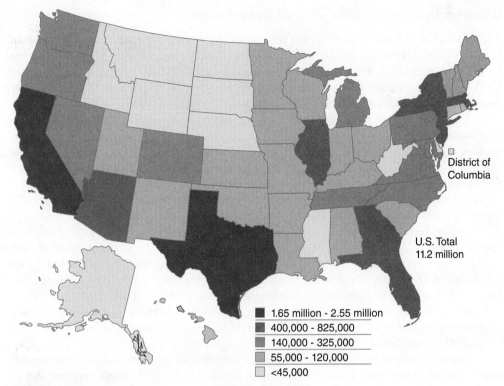

EXHIBIT 1.11   Unauthorized Immigrant Population by State
Source: Passel and Cohn, Pew Research Center, 2011. Used with permission.

Asylee   A foreign-born individual in the United States or at a port of entry who is found to be unable or unwilling to return to his or her country of nationality, or to seek the protection of that country, because of persecution or a well-founded fear of persecution. Persecution or the fear thereof must be based on the individual's race, religion, nationality, membership in a particular social group, or political opinion (U.S. Citizenship and Immigration Services, 2013).

Some come to the United States with the hope that they can remain legally by proving that they had escaped from the political repression in their homeland. Those who seek asylum would face persecution or death if they were to return to their native countries.

People who are often deported as undocumented arrivals are those who come as "economic refugees" (i.e., their economic status in their home country may be desperate). They generally have few occupational skills and are willing to take menial jobs that many American citizens will not accept. They fill economic gaps in various regions where low-wage labor is needed.

Outer appearances are not an accurate guide to who has legal status and who does not. Both the illegal and the legal immigrants may live in the same neighborhoods. In addition, the U.S. government has occasionally legalized significant numbers of some populations of formerly illegal immigrants, usually in recognition of special circumstances in those persons' home countries, such as large-scale natural disasters or serious political instability.

Undocumented immigrants lack the papers necessary to obtain legal residence in the United States. The societal consequences are far-reaching. Law enforcement officials, politicians, and social service providers, among others, have had to deal with many concerns related to housing, education, safety, employment, spousal violence, and health care. The undocumented segment of the immigrant population poses some difficult challenges for law enforcement officials.

Unauthorized Immigrants: Fear of Deportation

The principal barrier to establishing trust with undocumented immigrants revolves around fears of being reported to the U.S. Immigration and Customs Enforcement (USICE), the largest investigative arm of the DHS. Entire communities may resist reporting crimes because of the fear of deportation. These immigrants are often already located in high-crime areas, and become even more vulnerable because of their fears of deportation.

An argument exists that supports leaving undocumented immigrants alone, unless they have committed a criminal act or are creating a disturbance. It is based on the perspective that tracking down and deporting immigrants has technically been the job of the USICE and not that of the state or local police. Sometimes the trust of the entire community, including both the illegal and the legal immigrants, is at stake. If immigrant communities know that police officers will not turn over illegal immigrants to the USICE, then there is less fear of the police when it comes to reporting crimes.

Although law enforcement agencies in Prince William and Frederick counties [Virginia] have agreed to help federal authorities enforce immigration laws, officials in many other parts of the country remain reluctant to do so, saying they fear losing the trust of the immigrant communities and worry about being accused of racial profiling. Raleigh, NC, Police Chief Harry Dolan agrees that undocumented immigrants are hesitant to report crimes, particularly those of which they are the victim. "The challenge today that we're finding is that the trust is diminishing because they're concerned what would happen to a family member if they called the police" (Pardo, 2010).

Law enforcement's involvement with undocumented immigrants had been the focus of controversy for years prior to the publication of this text. "The ICE 287(g) Program: A Law Enforcement Partnership" actively began in 2006 with 29 participating law enforcement agencies. This partnership gave the authority to the secretary of Homeland Security to enter into agreements with state and local law enforcement agencies, allowing officers to perform immigration law enforcement functions. Under 287(g), ICE provides state and local law enforcement with the training and delegated authority to enforce immigration law within their jurisdictions (U.S. Immigration and Customs Enforcement, 2013).

Under the new administration in 2009, the ICE 287(g) program began to undergo tremendous scrutiny. Many immigrant groups claimed that 287(g) had become a vehicle for the racial profiling of Hispanic immigrants, and that deportation by police officers for minor crimes had begun to occur with alarming frequency. Congressional hearings in early 2009 called for the monitoring, improved assessment, and closer supervision of the 287(g) program, and many local law enforcement agencies recognized 287(g) as a problem. From February to July 2009, and the Office of the Inspector General (OIG) conducted a review of 287(g) and published its findings in March of 2010, and has since made fundamental reforms to address findings of the review. The 287(g) program now partners with the DHS Office of Civil Rights and Civil Liberties to create courses and policies, including "supervisory responsibilities, victim-witness assistance, constitutional protections, and civil rights." DHS OIG released a follow-up report in 2012, "The Performance of 287(g) Agreements FY 2012 Follow-Up," in which OIG indicated the following results of the review:

- *"Since our initial 287(g) report in March 2010, ICE has made significant progress in implementing our recommendations. To close a recommendation, we must agree with the actions ICE has taken to resolve our concerns. Of the 62 total recommendations included in our prior reports, 60 have been closed based on corrective action plans and supporting documentation provided by ICE"* (USICE, 2013).

Budget cuts are reducing the number of communities with active 287 (g) task forces. As of August 2013, there were 36 participating agencies in 19 states (USICE, 2013), down from 67 participating agencies in 23 states in May 2009, partly due to budget cuts and partly due to a shift in focus toward Secure Communities (see below). The 2013 budget report for the Department of Homeland Security (DHS) announced a $17 million cut for the 287(g) program, citing Secure Communities as "more consistent, efficient and cost effective in identifying and removing criminal and other priority aliens . . . ICE will begin by discontinuing the least productive 287(g) task force agreements in jurisdictions where Secure Communities is already in place" (Department of Homeland Security, 2013).

Secure Communities has led to fears of deportation as well. Under this program, local law enforcement agents send fingerprints collected during the booking process to the FBI, which then checks them against the DHS immigration database. While local law enforcement is involved in the collection process, federal ICE agents determine a course of action to take to enforce applicable laws. As of July 2012, Secure Communities was activated in 94 percent of U.S. jurisdictions (USICE, 2013). However, some jurisdictions, including San Francisco, Cook County, IL, and Los Angeles have declined to participate in the program, arguing that it undermines trust that has been built between law enforcement agencies and immigrant communities. Los Angeles Police Chief Charlie Beck, in announcing withdrawal from this program, said that it had reduced trust between the Police Department and the communities in Los Angeles.

"Community trust is extremely important to effective policing," he said. "So it's my intent, by issuing this change in procedures, that we gain this trust back" (Lovett, 2012).

Unauthorized Immigrants: The "U" Visa and the Safe Reporting of Crimes

With the passage of the Victims of Trafficking and Violence Protection Act of 2000 (including VAWA, Violence Against Women Act), Congress also created the "U" visa, a relatively unknown piece of legislation that can affect communities and law enforcement. When undocumented immigrants call the police, chances are that they are victims of or witnesses to a crime. If they actively cooperate with law enforcement in providing information about the crime, they are entitled to a U visa or a nonimmigrant visa, which can eventually be used in the application for a legal work permit and a social security number. The U visa is distinct from the T visa, another protective measure designed for victims of trafficking in persons, which includes sex trafficking or labor trafficking. While there are many hurdles associated with obtaining the U visa, undocumented immigrants who are granted it may eventually apply for residency. Application for the U visa is an extremely challenging process, and needs to include a "certification of helplessness" from a certifying agency. This means that the individual petitioning for the U visa must "provide a Nonimmigrant Status Certification from a federal, state or local law enforcement official that demonstrates the petitioner 'has been helpful, is being helpful or is likely to be helpful' in the investigation or prosecution of the criminal activity." As of 2007, the United States Citizenship and Immigration Services has been able to grant up to 10,000 U nonimmigrant visas in any one fiscal year (USICE, 2013).

According to Christopher Martinez, Program Director for refugee and immigrant services of the Catholic charities CYO in San Francisco, between 2007 (when regulations for the "U" visa were issued) and 2009 only approximately 13,000 people across the country had applied for the U visa. Of these, only 65 had received the visa. Since 2009, when filing and approval processes were streamlined, over 65,000 cases have been filed (up to 10,000 per year), and about 77 percent of them have been approved (Martinez, 2013) Nonprofits such as the Catholic Charities have forged relationships with police departments to maximize cooperation, and have been in a position to educate officers about this provision in the Act. In Martinez's experience in San Francisco, the city has had the support of the police department and the District Attorney's Office for these nonimmigrant visa applications.

If more of the community knew about this law, more undocumented immigrants would likely come forward and out of the shadows to cooperate with law enforcement. In doing so, they could work with the police to create safer communities. It is not an easy road to obtain this kind of visa, but it can be an incentive to speak out and to help avoid becoming victimized again. About 10 years ago, a woman and her child living on the East Coast witnessed a heinous crime involving the husband. While at the time of the crime the law did not exist, this woman came forward cooperating fully with the authorities. Ultimately, the perpetrator was caught and convicted. The woman became eligible for a U visa, and had the full backing of the District Attorney's office in the city in which she and her child live (Martinez, 2013).

Immigrant Women: Victims of Domestic Violence

In a 2003 report to a congressional subcommittee on immigration, Leslye E. Orloff, director of the Immigrant Women's Program (National Organization of Women's Legal Defense and Education Fund), presented a full account of problems that continue to beset battered immigrant women. Even though the frequency of domestic violence is consistent across socioeconomic classes, racial groups, and geographic areas, according to Orloff, immigrant women still face additional challenges in seeking help from their communities.

> [The] Violence Against Women Act (VAWA), passed by Congress in 1994 and improved in 2000 [then reauthorized in 2005 and 2013], set out to reform the manner in which officers responded to domestic violence calls for help. Although significant improvement following the passage of VAWA has been noted, the response continues to be lacking. Some police officers' personal attitudes regarding domestic violence (i.e., it is a private problem) and how it should be handled (through mediation rather than arrest or formal charges), in essence, marginalizes victims of domestic violence. In extreme cases, victims' requests for help are disregarded. The lack of appropriate response to domestic violence from the police is further compounded when the battered woman is an immigrant. The police often do not have the capacity to communicate effectively with the immigrant victim in her own language. The police may use her abuser or her children to translate for her, and/or police may credit the statements of her citizen spouse or boyfriend over her statements to the police due to gender, race or cultural bias. (Orloff, 2003)

VAWA was reauthorized by the Congress first in 2000, after its passage in 1994, and then in December 2005. On January 5, 2006, the bill was signed into law by President George W. Bush, and was reauthorized by President Barack Obama in March 2013. The most recent reauthorization includes expansions of protections for immigrants, including the addition of stalking to the list of serious crimes covered by the U visa. It also added an "age-out" providision to protect children of immigrants who filed for the U visa. Previously, children who turned 21 before a U visa application was approved were not protected, but the 2013 VAWA reauthorization extended the reach of the protections to include children who were younger than 21 at the time of the U Visa filing.

Domestic violence is a phenomenon that exists among people from all socioeconomic classes, races, and backgrounds. Nevertheless, there are particular factors contributing to the high rate of domestic violence that some immigrant women experienced in their native countries and that Native American women face in the United States. One in three Native American women is raped over her lifetime (Erdrich, 2013), and in many cases, have little recourse due to jurisdictional challenges with tribal and federal courts. In 2010, President Obama signed into law the Tribal Law and Order Act, which "address crime in tribal communities and places a strong emphasis on decreasing violence against American Indian and Alaska Native women" (Department of Justice, 2013). Further information on violence against Native Americans can be found in Chapter 9.

Women subjected to domestic violence in their home countries confront societal, familial, and legal systems that refuse to acknowledge the seriousness of the problem or to protect the victim. In many countries, the voices of the victims go unheard, drowned out by age-old traditions that perpetuate the idea that women should serve their husbands no matter how they are treated. Often victims' own families do nothing to help the victim of spousal abuse and force her to "endure"—as generations of women have done. Outside the family network, women find little assistance in the legal system. Many countries do not codify domestic violence as a separate crime, and some countries regard domestic violence as strictly a family issue to be dealt with in a private manner. In many countries, the law fails to recognize rape by a spouse . . . Few countries have enacted protections for domestic violence victims. And, measures that have been enacted all too often fall short due to little or no enforcement. While a growing number of countries have laws on domestic violence, 102 countries have no such specific legal provisions, and marital rape is not considered a prosecutable offence over 53 nations (UNIFEM, 2013)

When women who have been battered come to the United States, they carry with them the traumas they experienced earlier owing to their culture and traditions. There are multiple problems facing battered immigrant women in the United States. The following summarizes some of these, and should help law enforcement representatives understand the larger context in which an immigrant may fail to report a crime (Tiede, 2001):

- Some battered immigrant women are completely isolated in the United States. They may live secret lives, never having established a legal identity in the United States.
- Batterers frequently add to victims' fears by threatening to call ICE about deportation.
- Women fear losing their families and being deported to a hostile society upon their return. (In certain places in Latin America, for example, a woman returning to her own village without her husband and children is often ostracized.)
- Victims are often not aware that protection is available, nor do they know how to find it.
- Many victims do not speak English and have no understanding of U.S. criminal and immigration laws and systems.

In addition, a battered immigrant woman may not understand that she can personally tell her story in court, or that a judge will believe her. Based on her experience in her native country, she may believe that only those who are wealthy or have ties to the government will prevail in court. Batterers often manipulate these beliefs by convincing the victim that he will prevail in court because he is a male, is a citizen, or has more money (Orloff, 2003).

A 2013 report in Public Radio International (PRI) details additional hardships undocumented immigrant women face when it comes to domestic violence. The following quote is from Sister Rosemary Welsh, Executive Director of Casa de Misericordia, or House of Mercy, a shelter for battered women in Laredo, Texas.

"One of the ways men would keep [undocumented immigrant women] in a domestic violence situation [is] saying that 'I am a U.S. citizen,' or 'I am a legal permanent resident, and you call the police, and they will deport you and I will stay with the kids. It was a way of terrorizing the women and also keeping them in bondage and keeping them in a violent situation." (PRI, 2013).

Police can assist by being ready with resources to provide to victims. In the case of immigrant women, both documented and undocumented, officers need to be aware of community assistance programs specifically created to address their needs. In some jurisdictions, management may even encourage or mandate that officers make an initial call for help, while still with the victim, to a community organization, for example. The Women's Justice Center in Santa Rosa, California, is one such example of a community resource. Exhibit 1.12 lists advice from the Center and lets immigrant women know that their issues and fears are shared.

Immigrant Barriers to Positive Relationships with Police

Immigrants must learn a great deal about U.S. laws, the law enforcement system in general, and the role of police officers. Many fear the police deeply because police in their native countries engaged in arbitrary acts of brutality in support of repressive governments (e.g., in Central America). A Central American refugee who was granted asylum in the United States recalled a police act of "handcuffing" that took place in the 1980s. He explained that such actions, and

---

Women's Justice Center
HELP
Special for Immigrant Women

1. You deserve help, and as a crime victim, you have a right to all the same crime victim services as any crime victim born in the United States.
   —Do not be shy about calling police, using women's shelters, calling rape crisis centers . . . or going to restraining order clinics.
2. What if the person abusing you says that he will call ICE and get you deported if you call the police or try to get help?
   —It is very, very common for violent men to make this threat to immigrant women who are their victims. But it is virtually impossible for these men to carry out the threat.
3. If you are still afraid to seek help, ask someone to make the phone calls for you, and to be with you when you deal with police and other crisis workers.
   —It's a very good idea when you get help for domestic violence and rape to have someone at your side.
4. What if you can't find anyone who can go with you?
   It's very common for abusers and men who rape to isolate you from human contact, especially if you have just arrived to the U.S. You can ask others for help even if you don't tell them everything. For example, you can say, *"Will you call this number for me and ask if they have someone who speaks Spanish?"* Or, you can say, "I have been a victim of a crime and I need to go to court. Will you watch my children for the afternoon?" Or, you can say, *"My husband is abusive and I need a ride to the police."*
5. Insist on good translations.
   —The U.S. Constitution says that all persons must be given equal protection of the laws. The courts have repeatedly ruled that this means everyone from native born citizens to newly arrived immigrants, whether or not they have the proper documentation. Every human being has a right to equal protection under the laws.

EXHIBIT 1.12   Advice to Immigrant Women from the Women's Justice Center
Source: De Santis, Women's Justice Center, 2013, www.justicewomen.com. Used with permission.

worse, were common practice for police. (Would it compromise his safety if you mentioned the state and agency?)

> I was about 14 years old. My father and I were in the car driving home late in the afternoon. It was very common to have to go through checkpoints, and we were unfortunately pulled aside at one of them. My father was asked to produce paperwork, including a license. Unfortunately, he had forgotten his wallet that day. Even though my father had also worked for the government, the police did not believe him. They took my father out of the car, put his arms behind his back, and with a string tightly tied his thumbs together as they had no handcuffs. Right away, I could see his thumbs start becoming purple. The police demanded that I go home and get his wallet. It took me about one hour to run home and back. Thankfully, I got the wallet. But, when I returned to see my father, his thumbs had turned completely black from the tight string around them. There was no way we could complain about this—things would have gotten much worse for us if we had. There was too much fear at that time in our history. We could not even look an officer in the eye without getting into some kind of trouble. . . . (Central American asylee, personal. communication., 2013)

To illustrate this fear even further, the Central American interviewee added, after he shared the above story: "Please do not ever identify me by name or associate me with this anecdote. There could still be consequences for my family back home if they knew that I was speaking about the authorities like this" (Central American asylee, personal communication, 2013).

In some other countries, citizens disrespect police because the officers are poorly educated, inefficient, corrupt, and have a very low occupational status (e.g., in Iran). The barriers immigrants bring to the relationship with police suggest that American officers have to double their efforts to communicate and to educate. A further challenge for law enforcement is that, for the reasons mentioned above, new immigrants often become victims of violent crimes. In part, the acculturation and success of immigrants in this society depend on how they are treated while they are still ignorant of the social norms and laws. Law enforcement officials who have contact with new Americans will need extraordinary patience at times. Adaptation to a new country can be a long and arduous process. Without the knowledge of citizens' cultural and national backgrounds, law enforcement officers may observe citizens' reactions that they do not fully understand.

CULTURE AND ITS RELEVANCE TO LAW ENFORCEMENT

An understanding of accepted social practices and cultural traditions in citizens' countries of origin can provide officers with insight into predicting some of the reactions and difficulties new immigrants will have in America. However, some customs are simply unacceptable in the United States, and arrests must be made in spite of the cultural background. Regardless of the circumstances, immigrant suspects need to be treated with respect; officers and all others in the criminal justice system must understand the innocent state of mind the citizen was in when committing the "crime." For example, female circumcision is illegal under all circumstances in the United States but is still practiced in certain African countries. The Hmong, mountain people of Southeast Asia, and particularly Laos, have a tradition considered to be an acceptable form of eloping. This Hmong tradition allows a male to capture and take away a female for marriage; even if she resists, he is allowed to take her to his home, and it is mandated that he consummate the union. However, "Marriage by capture" translates into kidnap and rape in the United States. Perpetrators of such crimes in the United States must be arrested.

In interviews with a deputy public defender and a deputy district attorney, a legal journal posed the following question: Should our legal system recognize a "cultural" defense when it comes to crimes? The deputy district attorney's response was, "No. You're treading on shaky ground when you decide something based on culture, because our society is made up of so many different cultures. It is very hard to draw the line somewhere, but [diverse cultural groups] are living in our country, and people have to abide by [one set of] laws or else you have anarchy." The deputy public defender's response to the question was: "Yes. I'm not asking that the [various cultural groups] be judged differently, just that their actions be understood according to their own history and culture" (Sherman, 1986). This counsel, dispensed in the late 1980s, continues to reflect on current legal decisions about culturally influenced "criminal" actions today.

If law enforcement's function is to protect and serve citizens from all cultural backgrounds, it becomes vital to understand the cultural dimensions of crimes. Obviously, behaviors or actions that may be excused in another culture must not go unpunished if they are considered crimes in this country (e.g., spouse abuse). Nevertheless, there are circumstances in which law enforcement officials at all levels of the criminal justice system would benefit by understanding the cultural context in which a crime or other incident occurred. Law enforcement professionals must use standard operating procedures in response to specific situations, and the majority of these procedures cannot be altered for different groups based on ethnicity.

In a multicultural society, however, an officer can modify the way he or she treats a suspect, witness, or victim, given the knowledge of what is considered "normal" in that person's culture. When officers suspect that an aspect of cultural background is a factor in a particular incident, they may earn the respect of—and therefore cooperation from—ethnic communities if they are willing to evaluate their arrests in lesser crimes. For example, certain aspects of what is considered "normal" in the Sikh culture and religion can cause confusion for officers who have not been exposed to Sikh traditions and practices (Sikhism is a religion followed by a minority of people who are mainly from Northern India). Sikh men wear turbans as they are required to cover their hair in public. Removing a turban in public can be likened to a strip search and would need to be done in a culturally sensitive manner. Sikh men carry a *kirpan* (sheathed knife); a *kirpan* is not a concealed weapon.

Many officers say that their job is to uphold the law, but it is not up to them to make judgments. Yet discretion when deciding whether to take a citizen into custody for a lesser crime may be appropriate. When officers understand the cultural context for a crime, the crime will and should be perceived somewhat differently. The Sikh religious requirements are one example. Consider Pacific Islanders having barbecues in their garages, where they roast whole pigs. Or a Tongan driving under the influence of "Kava," a relaxing elixir; the Kava ritual is considered to be an integral part of life popular with Pacific Islanders. What about a Vietnamese family that eats dog meat? When officers understand the cultural context within which a "crime" takes place, then it is much easier to understand a citizen's intent. Understanding the cultural dimensions of a crime may result, for example, in not taking a citizen into custody. With lesser crimes, this may be the appropriate course of action and can result in the preservation of good police–community relations. Before looking at specific case studies of incidents and crimes involving cultural components, we present the concept of culture and its tremendous impact on the individual.

All people, except for very young children, adhere to cultural dos and don'ts, and both consciously and unconsciously identify with their group; individuals have varying degrees of attachment to their cultural group's traditional values. A persona's identity is sanctioned and reinforced by the society in which he or she has been raised. According to some experts, culture has a far greater influence on people's behavior than does any other variable such as age, gender, race, and socioeconomic status (Hall, 1959) and often this influence is unconscious. It is virtually impossible to lose one's culture completely when interacting in a new environment, yet change will inevitably take place.

The Definition of Culture

Although there are many definitions of culture, we are using the term to mean beliefs, habits, attitudes, values, patterns of thinking, behavior, and everyday customs that have been passed on from generation to generation. Culture is learned rather than inherited and is manifested largely in unconscious and subtle behavior. With this definition in mind, consider that most children have acquired a general cultural orientation by the time they are five or six years old. For this reason, it is difficult to change behavior immediately to accommodate a new culture. Many layers of cultural behavior and beliefs are subconscious. In addition, many people assume that what they take for granted is taken for granted by all people ("all human beings are the same"), and they do not even recognize their own culturally influenced behavior. Anthropologist Edward T. Hall (1959) said, "Culture hides much more than it reveals and, strangely enough, what it hides, it hides most effectively from its own participants." In other words, people are blind to their own deeply embedded cultural behavior.

Ethnocentrism   An attitude of seeing and judging other cultures from the perspective of one's own culture; using the culture of one's own group as a standard for the judgment of others, or thinking of it as superior to other cultures that are merely different; an ethnocentric person would say there is only one way of being "normal" and that is the way of his or her own culture.

Ethnocentrism is a barrier to accepting that there is another way, another belief, another communication style, another custom, or another value that can lead to culturally different behavior. Ethnocentrism often causes a person to assign a potentially incorrect meaning or attribute an incorrect motivation to a given act. Consider how the outcome could have differed if only one person in the chain of authorities had viewed the bruises as something other than abuse.

To further understand the hidden nature of culture, picture an iceberg. The only visible part of the iceberg is the tip, which typically constitutes about 10 percent of the mass. Like most of culture's influences, the remainder of the iceberg is submerged beneath the surface. What this means for law enforcement is that there is a natural tendency to interpret behavior, motivations, and criminal activity from the officer's cultural point of view. This tendency is due largely to an inability to understand behavior from alternative perspectives and because of the inclination toward ethnocentrism.

When it comes to law enforcement, there is only one set of laws to which all citizens, whether native-born or not, must adhere. However, the following case studies illustrate that culture does affect interpretations, meaning, and intention.

Mini Case Studies and Cultural Practices: Does Culture Matter?

The following descriptions of cultural practices or mini case studies involve "crimes" or "offenses" with a cultural component. If the crime is a murder or something similarly heinous, most people will not be particularly sympathetic, even with an understanding of the cultural factors involved. However, consider that understanding other cultural patterns gives one the ability to see and react in a different way. The ability to withhold judgment and to interpret a person's intention from a different cultural perspective is a skill that will ultimately enable a person to identify his or her own cultural blinders.

The examples describe "crimes" of varying severity. The corresponding questions at the end of the chapter (page 38) will allow you the opportunity to discuss the degree to which culture matters, or does not matter, in each of the following cases:

1. Culture Matters? The Sword in a Public Park

A City University of New York (CUNY) study entitled, "Police Narratives about Racial and Ethnic Identity" illustrates culture and "crime" involving a cultural practice in parts of Asia and associated with the martial art of Tai Chi. It is customary for some followers of Tai Chi to carry a sword with them to parks, and then proceed with the movements, using the sword. For the immigrant who does this, there is clearly no criminal intent since the practice is accepted as "normal" in the person's country of origin. Yet, in the United States, this would potentially be considered a crime.

2. Culture Matters? The Turban and the *Kirpan*

In a previous section entitled, "Culture and its Relevance to Law Enforcement," you learned that removing a Sikh's turban in public is tantamount to doing a strip search. Sikh men must keep a *kirpan* (sheathed knife) at all times, and for some, this extends to when they sleep. A police officer arrives at the home of a Sikh couple after a neighbor calls the police to say that she heard specific verbal threats (with intimations of violence) toward the wife and that she also heard. The officer arrests the husband, pats him down and searches him, and finds, incidental to the arrest, the husband's *kirpan*. The Sikh is now additionally charged with "possession of a concealed weapon."

3. Culture Matters? A Tragic Case of Cross-Cultural Misinterpretation

In parts of Asia, there are medical practices unfamiliar to many law enforcement officials (as well as medical practitioners) in the West. A number of these practices result in marks on the skin that can easily be misinterpreted as abuse by people who have no knowledge of these culturally based medical treatments. The practices include rubbing the skin with a coin ("coining," "coin rubbing," or "wind rubbing"), pinching the skin, touching the skin with burning incense, or applying a heated cup to the skin ("cupping"). Each practice leaves highly visible marks, such as bruises and even burns. The following is an account of a serious misreading of some very common Southeast Asian methods of traditional folk healing on the part of U.S. school authorities and law enforcement officials.

A young Vietnamese boy had been absent from school for a few days with a serious respiratory infection. His father, believing that coining would help cure him, rubbed heated coins on specific sections of his back and neck. The boy's condition seemed to improve and he was able to return to school. Upon noticing heavy bruising on the boy's neck, the teacher immediately informed the school principal, who promptly reported the "abuse" to the police (who then notified Child Protective Services). When the police were notified, they went to the child's home to investigate. The father was very cooperative when questioned by the police and admitted, in broken English, that he had caused the bruising on his son's

(continued)

neck. The man was arrested and incarcerated. While the father was in jail, his son, who was under someone else's custody, apparently relapsed and died of his original illness. On hearing the news, the father committed suicide in his jail cell. Of course, it is not known whether the father would have committed suicide as a response to his son's death alone. The tragic misinterpretation on the part of the authorities involved, including the teacher, the principal, and the arresting police officers, provides an extreme case of what can happen when people attribute meaning from their own cultural perspective.

Cultural understanding would not have cured the young boy, but informed interaction with the father could have prevented the second tragedy. All of the authorities were interpreting what they saw with "cultural filters" based on their own belief systems. Ironically, the interpretation of the bruises (i.e., child abuse) was almost the opposite of the intended meaning of the act (i.e., healing). Even after some of the parties involved learned about this very common Southeast Asian practice, they still did not accept that it existed as an established practice, and they could not fathom how others could believe that coining might actually cure illness. Their own conception of medical healing did not encompass what they perceived as such "primitive treatment."

4. Culture Matters? Latino Values as a Factor in Sentencing

In a court of law, a cultural explanation or rationalization (i.e., a cultural defense) rarely affects a guilty or not-guilty verdict. Nevertheless, culture may affect sentencing. Consider the following case, in which, according to retired Judge Lawrence Katz, cultural considerations lessened the severity of the sentence:

A Mexican woman living in the United States became involved in an extramarital affair. Her husband became outraged when the wife bragged about her extramarital activities at a picnic at which many extended family members were present. At the same time, the wife also made comments about her husband's lack of ability to satisfy her and how, in comparison, her lover was far superior. On hearing his wife gloat about her affair, the husband left the picnic and drove five miles to purchase a gun. Two hours later, he shot and killed his wife. In a case such as this, the minimum charge required in California would be second-degree murder. However, because the jury took into consideration the cultural background of this couple, the husband received a mitigated sentence and was found guilty of manslaughter. It was argued that his wife's boasting about her lover and her explicit comments made specifically to emasculate him created a passion and emotion that completely undermined his machismo, masculine pride and honor. To understand the severity of the wife's offense, the law enforcement officer and the prosecutor had to understand what it means to be humiliated in such a manner in front of one's family, in the context of Latino culture. (Katz, 2013)

The purpose of these "Culture Matters" descriptions or mini case studies is not to discuss the "rightness" or "wrongness" of any group's values, customs, or beliefs but to illustrate that the point of contact between law enforcement and citizens' backgrounds must not be ignored. Officers must be encouraged to consider culture when investigating and presenting evidence regarding an alleged crime or incident involving people from diverse backgrounds. This consideration does not mean that standard operating procedures should be changed nor does it imply that heinous crimes such as murder or rape should be excused on cultural grounds. However, as a matter of course, officers need to include cultural competence as a variable in understanding, assessing, and reporting certain kinds of incidents and crimes.

Law enforcement representatives have the ultimate authority to arrest or admonish someone suspected of a crime. According to retired Judge Katz, "Discretion based on cultural competence at the police level is much more significant than what happens at the next level in the criminal justice system (i.e., the courts)." Individual police officers have the opportunity to create positive public relations if they demonstrate cultural sensitivity and respect toward members of an ethnic community. Katz cited the example of police contact with the San Francisco Bay Area Samoan community, in which barbecues and parties can include a fair amount of drinking, resulting in fights. In Katz's opinion, the police, responding to neighbors' complaints, could come in with a show of force and the fighting would cool down quickly. However, word would spread that the police officers had no cultural understanding or respect for the people involved. This would widen the gap that already exists between police and many Pacific Islander and other Asian groups and would not be a way to foster trust in the Samoan community. Alternatively, the police could locate the leader, or the "chief," of this group and let that person deal with the problem in the way that he would have handled the conflict in Samoa. There is no question about the chief's ability to handle the problem. He has a prominent role to play and can serve as a bridge between the police and the community. The *matai* is also a resource; he is an elder who has earned the respect of the community.

The heads of Samoan communities are traditionally in full control of members' behavior, although this is changing somewhat in the United States. Furthermore, according to traditional Samoan values, if a family member assaults a member of another family, the head of the family is required to ensure punishment. Given the power entrusted to the chiefs, it is reasonable to encourage officers first to go through the community and elicit assistance in solving enforcement problems. This recommendation does not imply, in any way, that groups should be left to police themselves; instead, understanding and working with the leadership of a community represents a spirit of partnership.

The awareness of and sensitivity to such issues can have a significant impact on the criminal justice system, in which police have the power to either inflame or calm the people involved in a particular incident. According to Katz, "Many cases, especially those involving lesser offenses, can stay out of court." He asks, "Do you always need a show of force? Or can you counsel and admonish instead?" In certain situations, such as the one described earlier, officers can rethink traditional police methods in order to be as effective as possible. Doing so involves knowledge of ethnic communities and a desire to establish a positive and trustworthy image in those communities (Katz, 2013).

DIMENSIONS OF DIVERSITY

To make sense of the different groups in our workplace and society, we need to have functional categories and terms. Marilyn Loden, organizational diversity consultant, describes and outlines the primary and secondary dimensions of diversity (Loden, 2013). The specific categories within the dimensions of diversity are not new but rather provide a functional construction of individual and group characteristics for understanding the people in the workforce and our society. This awareness and the ability to view differences as sources of strength often results in improved interpersonal relationships and improved citizen contacts.

Primary Dimensions of Diversity

A primary dimension is a core characteristic with which a person is born that remains with the individual in all stages of his or her life. According to Loden, people have a minimum of six primary dimensions (Loden, 2013):

1. Age
2. Ethnicity
3. Gender
4. Mental/physical abilities and characteristics
5. Race
6. Sexual orientation

Most people are aware of the meaning of these categories. For the sake of clarity, the following terms are included in the category "sexual orientation": heterosexual, homosexual, lesbian, gay, bisexual, transgender, transsexual, asexual, and queer. All of the six primary dimensions are characteristics that contribute to being advantaged or disadvantaged in the workforce and in society. Victims of hate bias crimes have been targeted because of these six dimensions of diversity—age, ethnicity, gender, disability status, race, and sexual orientation. The primary dimension associated with age also includes generational differences. In the law enforcement agency workforce, values may collide among the generations; leaders and managers need to be cognizant of this dimension of diversity. Recruiting someone from "Generation Y," for example, could involve an understanding of some of the unique characteristics associated with this age group. Generation Y members (born between 1977 and 1994, and compromising 20 percent of the population) have been characterized by one global human resource and recruitment firm as a tolerant group (NAS Insights, 2006). "With the ever growing diverse population, the word 'minority' may no longer have meaning to this and future generations . . . Working and interacting with people outside of their own ethnic group is the norm, and acceptable" (NAS Insights, 2006). A 2008 survey of students at California State University, Fullerton, showed that members of the younger generation are more tolerant of immigrants (Fiber-Ostrow & Hill, 2011).

Secondary Dimensions of Diversity

A secondary dimension is a characteristic a person acquires as the result of a choice he or she made or a choice someone else made for him or her (Loden, 2013). Nearly all of the secondary dimensions' characteristics contribute to the micro level demographic data. The secondary dimensions of diversity include, but are not limited to,

1. Communication style
2. Education
3. Family status
4. Military experience
5. Organizational role and level
6. Religion
7. First language
8. Geographic location
9. Income
10. Work experience
11. Work style
12. Others

Both primary and secondary dimensions of diversity influence the personal and professional lives of law enforcement personnel. Police officers need to be cognizant of these dimensions with their coworkers, and leaders with their subordinates. Tensions between supervisors and coworkers are often caused by the differences in secondary dimensions. Similarly, a police officer's ability to establish rapport with citizens can also be related to either the actual or the perceived degree to which dimensions are shared.

Exhibit 1.13 shows how the primary and secondary dimensions of diversity influence people in the workforce and society. "While each dimension adds a layer of complexity, it is the dynamic interaction among all the dimensions of diversity that influences one's self-image, values, opportunities, and expectations. Together, the primary and secondary dimensions give definition and meaning to our lives by contributing to a synergistic, integrated whole—the diverse person" (Loden, 2013).

Further Diversity within and among Ethnic Groups in the United States

As much as we may try to categorize people into distinct ethnic categories, it must be recognized that there are some unique factors that should be taken into account that can increase understanding and improve communications between law enforcement and the members of minority communities. Take, for example, "age" as a primary dimension of diversity. Some people, especially those who are Asian American, for a variety of reasons might self-report a different age than what is shown on official identification. In some cultures, children are considered to be one year old when they are born; in yet other cultures, birthdays are based on the lunar calendar and thus at certain times of the year, reported ages don't match "official" ages. Among immigrants, entry papers are sometimes falsified leading to discrepancies. So as we can see, there are nuances even with this primary dimension of culture.

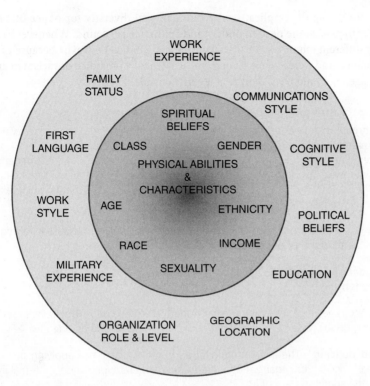

EXHIBIT 1.13 Dimensions of Diversity

Models such as the diversity wheel, designed by Loden Associates, facilitate understanding of a broad range of primary and secondary dimensions of diversity.

Source: Loden Associates Inc. 2013. Reprinted with Permission of Marilyn Loden. http://www.loden.com

Other diversity factors to be considered are as follows:

- people's comfort with and competence in English;
- generational status in the United States (refer to the section on typology presented earlier in the chapter; first-generation refugees or immigrants are likely to deviate from cultural norms more than their second- or third-generation offspring);
- their degree of identification with the home country and/or region of self or parents' origin;
- their family composition and the extent of family dispersion in the United States and globally;
- their participation in and degree to which they are embedded in their ethnic community network;
- their cultural values; and
- the extent to which they relate to issues, concerns, and problems shared by other ethnic/racial groups.

PREJUDICE IN LAW ENFORCEMENT[*]

The following questions were asked of police officers participating in a cultural diversity program:

"Raise your hand if you are a racist." Not a single officer raised a hand.

"Raise your hand if you think that prejudice and racism exist outside this agency." Most officers raised their hands.

The instructor then asked with humor: "From where were you recruited?" (Berry, 2013).

---

[*]Racial profiling is discussed in Chapter 13 as well as in the culture-specific chapters (5–9).

When discussing the implications of multicultural diversity for police officers, it is not enough simply to present the need to understand cultural background. Whenever two groups are from entirely different ethnic or racial backgrounds, prejudice may exist because of fear, lack of contact, ignorance, and stereotypes. To deny the existence of prejudice or racism in any given law enforcement agency would be to deny that it exists outside the agency.

To stereotype   To believe or feel that people conform to a pattern or manner with all other individual members of that group, lacking any individuality. People who are prone to stereotyping often categorize the behavior of an entire group based on limited experience with a very small number of people in that group. Negative stereotyping classifies many people in a group by the use of slurs, innuendoes, names, or slang expressions that depreciate the group as a whole as well as individuals in it.

Prejudice   A judgment or opinion formed before facts are known, usually involving negative or unfavorable thoughts about groups of people.

To scapegoat   To blame one's failures and shortcomings on innocent people or those only partly responsible.

Bias   A preformed negative opinion or attitude toward a group of persons based on their race, religion, disability, sexual orientation, ethnicity, gender, or gender identity.

Bias-based policing   The act—intentional and unintentional—of applying or incorporating personal, societal, or organizational biases and/or stereotypes in decision-making, police actions, or the administration of justice.

Prejudice and Bias

Prejudice is a judgment or opinion formed before facts are known, usually involving negative or unfavorable thoughts about groups of people. Bias, which can be conscious or unconscious, influences behavior, decision-making or action and reflects an inclination to make certain choices based on the inclination. Discrimination is action based on prejudiced thought and biases. Increasingly, researchers in the social science field contend that all people have biases, and that they are largely out of our awareness.

How Prejudice Influences People

Prejudice is encouraged by stereotyping which is a shorthand way of thinking about people who are different. The stereotypes that form the basis of a person's prejudice can be so fixed that he or she easily justifies his or her racism, sexism, or other bias and even makes such claims as "I'm not prejudiced, but let me tell you about those—I had to deal with today." Coffey, Eldefonson, and Hartinger (1982) discuss the relationship between selective memory and prejudice:

> A prejudiced person will almost certainly claim to have sufficient cause for his or her views, telling of bitter experiences with refugees, Koreans, Catholics, Jews, Blacks, Mexicans and Puerto Ricans, or Indians. But in most cases, it is evident that these "facts" are both scanty and strained. Such a person typically resorts to a selective sorting of his or her own memories, mixes them up with hearsay, and then overgeneralizes. No one can possibly know all refugees, Koreans, Catholics, and so on. (Coffey et al., 1982)

Indeed, individuals may be so convinced of the truths of their stereotypes that they claim to be experts on "those people." One of the most dangerous types of prejudice can be subconscious. Subconscious prejudice (sometimes called "character-conditioned prejudice") usually runs deep; the person with this character deficiency may hold hostile attitudes toward many ethnic groups, not just one or two. People who tend to mistreat or oppress others because of their prejudices often were mistreated themselves, and this experience can leave them extremely distrustful of all others. In addition, people who have strong prejudices can be insecure and frustrated because of their own failures. Consequently, they blame or scapegoat others. They have a great deal of stored-up anger that often began to build in childhood because of dysfunctional relationships with their parents. Quite often, members of racial supremacist organizations fit the description of the extremely prejudiced person for whom mistrust and hate of all others is a way of life.

Another type of prejudice is acquired during "normal" socialization. This type of prejudice results when a person belongs to a group that holds negative views of other specific groups (e.g., southern whites and blacks, Arabs and Jews, Chinese and Japanese, Puerto Ricans and Mexicans). When there is a pattern of prejudice within a particular group, the "normal" person is the one who conforms to the prejudice. From childhood, parents pass on stereotypes of the out-group into the child's mind because of their "normal" prejudices. By adulthood, the person who has learned prejudice against a particular group can justify the prejudice with rationalizations (Coffey et al., 1982).

If you are normal, you have cultural blind spots that will give you an unbalanced view of people who are different from you. Officers must look at themselves and understand their own biases first before getting into situations in which they may act upon them (Berry, 2013).

Furthermore, biases are powerful, and often largely hidden. "Project Implicit" has resulted from the collaboration of scientists from three universities, including Harvard; researchers have devised assessments, tools, and laboratory methods to assess individuals' biases (Project Implicit, 2011).

Captain Tracey Gove of the West Hartford, Connecticut Police Department summarizes key findings and methods from Project Implicit in an article entitled, "Implicit Bias and Law Enforcement," published in the journal *The Police Chief* (Gove, 2011).

Project Implicit key findings include:

Implicit biases are pervasive.

People are often unaware of their implicit biases.

Implicit biases predict behavior.

People differ in levels of implicit bias.

In Gove's summary of key findings related to implicit bias and law enforcement, she cites Criminal Justice Professor Dr. Lorie Fridell who has made recommendations that "help agencies to address the ill-intentioned officers who engaged in biased policing and the overwhelming majority of well-intentioned officers who aspire to police fairly and impartially, but who are human" (Gove, 2011).

In law enforcement, the expression of prejudice as bias, discrimination, and racism is illegal and can have tragic consequences. It is not possible to force people to abandon their own prejudices and biases in the law enforcement workplace or when working in the community. Because prejudice and biases are thoughts or preferences, they are private and do not violate a law. According to Gove, "While individual police leaders and personnel may have their own thoughts or beliefs on the topic [of implicit bias], its pervasiveness requires implications for the law enforcement field (Gove, 2011).

Although police chiefs cannot mandate that their officers banish prejudicial thoughts, police management can help officers understand the nature of prejudice and unconscious bias, and how decision-making can, in a split second, reflect a bias. While some police officers say they have every right to believe what they want, the chiefs of all departments must be able to guarantee, with as much certainty as possible, that officers will not act on their prejudices or be so unaware of unconscious biases that officers do not see the connection between their actions and their biases. All officers must understand where the line is between prejudice and discrimination, whether in the law enforcement agency with coworkers or with citizens. It becomes eminently clear that prejudice and biased in the law enforcement agency must be addressed before it turns into racism and discrimination. Indeed, an agency cannot be expected to treat its multicultural population fairly if people within the agency are likely to act on their prejudiced thoughts.

Police prejudice has received a great deal of attention since the late 1990s when it was addressed as a topic of concern in the President's Initiative on Race ("One America" 1998).

> Racial disparities and prejudices affect the way in which minorities are treated by the criminal system. Examples of this phenomenon can be found in the use of racial profiling in law enforcement and in the differences in the rates of arrest, conviction, and sentencing between whites and minorities and people of color. Law enforcement professionals have recognized, especially as they enter the twenty-first century, that prejudices unchecked and not acted on can result in not only citizen humiliation, lawsuits, loss of jobs, and long-term damage to police–community relations but in personal tragedy as well.

Sometimes, training can be successful in changing behavior and possibly attitudes. Consider the example of firing warning shots. Most officers have retrained themselves to refrain from this action because they have been mandated to do so. They have gone through a process of "unfreezing" normative behavior (i.e., what is customary) and have incorporated desired behavior. Thus explicit instruction and clear directives from the top can result in profound changes of police actions. Clear policies that, in no uncertain terms, condemn racist acts or forms of speech will prevent most outward demonstrations of prejudice. It is not acceptable to ask a citizen, "What are you doing here?" just because he or she is of a different background than those of a particular neighborhood. Officers pay attention to these specific and unambivalent directives coming from the top. It may be difficult to impossible to rid an officer of stereotypes, but eliminating acts of prejudice becomes the mandate of the department.

Peer Relationships and Prejudice

Expressions of prejudice in police departments may go unchallenged because of the need to conform or to fit into the group. Police officers do not make themselves popular by questioning peers or challenging their attitudes. It takes a leader to voice an objection or to avoid going along with group norms. Some studies have shown that peer behavior in groups reinforces acts of racial bias. For example, when someone in a group makes ethnic slurs, others in the group may begin to express the same hostile attitudes more freely. This behavior is particularly relevant in law enforcement agencies given the nature of the police subculture and the strong influence of peer pressure. Thus law enforcement leaders must not be ambiguous when directing their subordinates to control their expressions of prejudice, even among peers. Furthermore, according to some social scientists, the strong condemnation of any manifestations of prejudice can at times affect a person's feelings. Authorities or peers who keep prejudiced people from acting on their biases can, in the long run, weaken the prejudice itself, especially if the prejudice is not virulent. People conform and can behave differently, even if they hold the same prejudicial thoughts. Even if they are still prejudiced, they will be reticent to show it. National authorities have become much more vocal about dealing directly with racism and prejudice in law enforcement as an institution, especially in light of the quantity of allegations of racial profiling in police departments across the country.

A process of socialization takes place when top management has mandated change and a person is forced to adopt a new standard of behavior. When a mistake is made and the expression of prejudice occurs, a police department will pay the price in adverse media attention, lawsuits, citizen complaints, human relations commission's involvement, or dismissal of the chief or other management. What may have been acceptable at one time is now definitely not and may result in discipline and monetary sanctions.

When police officers are not in control of their prejudices, either in speech or in behavior, the associated negative publicity affects the reputation of all police officers. It reinforces the popular stereotype that police are racists or bigots. Yet, because of publicized instances of discrimination, officers become increasingly aware of correct and incorrect behavior toward ethnic minorities. One example of this was a police department that was besieged by the press and outraged citizens for over two years. Several police officers had exchanged racist messages on their patrol car computers, using the word *nigger* and making references to the Ku Klux Klan. The citizens of the town in which the incident took place ended up conducting an investigation of the department to assess the degree of racism in the institution. In their report, the committee members wrote that the disclosure of the racial slurs was "an embarrassment and a crushing blow" to the image and credibility of the city and the police department. In addition, citizens demanded the chief's resignation. In a cultural diversity workshop, some of the officers said they believed that the entire incident was overblown and that there was no "victim." These officers failed to understand that the use of derogatory terms alone is offensive to citizens. Officers who do not grasp the seriousness of the matter may not realize that citizens feel unprotected knowing that those entrusted with their safety and protection are capable of using such hateful language. While the language is offensive, the problem is more with the attitudes it conveys. Such incidents are extremely costly from all points of view; it may take years for a department to recover from one incident connected to an officer's prejudice or racism.

Officers need to be aware that anything they say or do with citizens of different backgrounds that even hints at prejudice automatically creates the potential for an explosive reaction. Here the experience of the minority and the nonminority do not even begin to approach each other. An officer can make an unguarded casual remark and not realize it is offensive. For example, an officer can offend a group member by saying "You people" (accentuating a we–they division) or by implying that if a member of a minority group does not fit a stereotype, he or she is exceptional (e.g., "She's Hispanic, but she works hard" or "He's African American, but very responsible").

Members of culturally diverse groups are up against the weight of history and tradition in law enforcement. Ethnic groups have not traditionally been represented in police work (especially in top management), nor have citizens of some ethnic groups had reasons to trust the police. The prejudice that might linger among officers must be battled constantly if they are to increase trust with ethnic communities. The perception of many ethnic group members is that police will treat them more roughly, question them unnecessarily, and arrest them more often than they arrest whites. Awareness of this perception is not enough, though. The next step is to try harder with ethnic groups to overcome these barriers. Officers should go out of their way to show extra respect to those citizens who least expect it. It is important to create nondefensiveness in citizens who have traditionally been the object of police prejudice and who expect rude or uncivil behavior from the officers.

Beyond eliminating the prejudice manifested in speech, police management can teach officers how to reduce or eliminate acts of bias and discrimination. A large metropolitan police department hired several human relations consultants to help assess community–police problems. The chief insisted that they ride in a police car for four weekends so that they would "appreciate the problems of law officers working in the black ghetto." Every Friday through Sunday night, the consultants rode along with the highway patrol, a unit other officers designated as the "Gestapo police." When the month ended and the chief asked what the consultants had learned, they replied, "If we were black, we would hate the police." The chief, somewhat bewildered, asked why. "Because we have personally witnessed black citizens experiencing a series of unjust, unwarranted intimidations, searches, and series of harassments by unprofessional police." Fortunately, that chief, to his credit, accepted the feedback and introduced a successful course in human relations skills. After this training, the officers demonstrated greater professionalism in their interactions with members of the black community.

When it comes to expressions of prejudice, people are not powerless. No one has to accept sweeping stereotypes (e.g., "You can't trust an Indian," "All whites are racists," "Chinese are shifty," and so on). To eliminate manifestations of prejudice, people have to begin to interrupt biased and discriminatory behavior at all levels. Officers have to be willing to remind their peers that ethnic slurs and offensive language, as well as differential treatment of certain groups of people, is neither ethical nor professional. Officers need to change the aspect of police culture that discourages speaking out against acts or speech motivated by prejudice. An officer or a civilian employee who does nothing in the presence of racist or other discriminatory behavior by his or her peers becomes a silent accomplice.

Eight Tips for Improving Law Enforcement in Multicultural Communities*

- Make positive contact with community group members from diverse backgrounds. Don't let them see you only when something negative has happened. Allow the public to see you as much as possible in a non-enforcement role.
- Make a conscious effort in your mind, en route to every situation, to treat all people objectively and fairly.
- Remember that all groups have some bad, some average, and some good people within them.
- Go out of your way to be personable and friendly with minority group members. Remember, many don't expect it.
- Don't appear uncomfortable with or avoid discussing racial and ethnic issues with other officers and citizens.

- Take responsibility for patiently educating citizens and the public about the role of the officer and about standard operating procedures in law enforcement. Remember that citizens often do not understand "police culture."
- Don't be afraid to be a change agent in your organization when it comes to improving cross-cultural and interracial relations within your department and between police and community. It may not be a popular thing to do, but it is the right thing to do.
- Remember the history of law enforcement with all groups and ask yourself the question, "Am I part of the past, or a part of the future?"

*Tips and quotes are from Ondra Berry, retired Deputy Chief of Reno Police Department, 2013.

Summary

- A diverse society contributes to the challenges of a law enforcement officer's job. Although our nation has been enriched by diversity, many police procedures and interactions with citizens can become more complex because of it. Racial tensions and communication challenges with immigrants are bound to complicate some police encounters. Officers have to work harder at building trust with certain communities. As individuals, officers need to increase their own cultural competence; as a profession, law enforcement needs to ensure that agencies promote the ideal of officer effectiveness across all backgrounds and equitable principals, policies, and structure throughout police organizations.
- Multiculturalism has been a way of life in this country since its founding; U.S. society has never been homogeneous. Until fairly recently, America has been referred to as a melting pot, a term depicting an image of people coming together and forming a unified culture. However, the melting pot did not really ever exist. The first generation of every immigrant and refugee group in the United States has always experienced obstacles to acculturation into the new society. History does not support the metaphor of the melting pot, especially with regard to the first and second generations of most groups of newcomers. The terms *mosaic* and *tapestry* more accurately portray diversity in America. They describe a society in which people of all colors and backgrounds contribute to form society as a whole—and one in which groups are not required to lose their characteristics in order to "melt" together. The idea of a mosaic portrays a society in which each group is seen as separate and distinct in contributing its own color, shape, and design to the whole, resulting in an enriched society.
- The face of America has been changing for some time. Minorities constitute one-third of the U.S. population, and are expected to become the majority by 2043. By 2050, minorities are expected to reach 54 percent of the

population. U.S. Census information released in 2013 showed that 11 percent of counties across the United States was already a "majority-minority" county; this meant that the percentage of minority residents in these counties had exceeded 50 percent.

- New immigrants can present challenges for law enforcement officers. Immigrants must learn a great deal about U.S. laws, the law enforcement system in general, and the role of police officers. Many immigrants fear law enforcement because police in their native countries engaged in arbitrary acts of brutality in support of repressive governments. In some other countries, citizens disrespect police officers because officers are poorly educated, inefficient, and corrupt, and have a very low occupational status. The barriers immigrants bring to the relationship with police suggest that American officers have to double their efforts to communicate with and to educate new immigrants. A further challenge for law enforcement is that, for a variety of reasons, new immigrants often become victims of violent crimes. Law enforcement faces additional challenges with respect to undocumented immigrants and its own enforcement role. With the debate on immigration in the United States and transitional relationships between ICE and some law enforcement agencies going on, issues await resolution regarding the enforcement role of the police officer.

- "Culture" is defined as beliefs, values, patterns of thinking, behavior, and everyday customs that have been passed on from generation to generation. Culture is learned rather than inherited and is manifested largely in unconscious and subtle behavior. If law enforcement's function is to protect and serve citizens from all cultural backgrounds, it becomes vital to understand the cultural dimensions of crimes. Obviously, behaviors or actions that may be excused in another culture must not go unpunished if they are considered crimes in this country. Nevertheless, there are circumstances in which law enforcement officials at all levels of the criminal justice system would benefit by understanding the cultural context in which a crime or other incident occurred. Law enforcement professionals must use standard operating procedures in response to specific situations; the majority of these procedures cannot be altered for different groups based on ethnicity. In a multicultural society, however, an officer can modify the way he or she treats a suspect, witness, or victim given the knowledge of what is considered "normal" in that person's culture. It is important for an officer to understand where "ethnocentrism" comes into play. "Ethnocentrism" is defined as an attitude of seeing and judging other cultures from the perspective of one's own culture. An ethnocentric person would say there is only one way of being "normal" and that is the way of his or her own culture. When officers suspect that an aspect of cultural background is a factor in a particular incident, they may earn the respect of—and therefore cooperation from—ethnic communities if they are willing to evaluate their arrests in lesser crimes.

- A "primary dimension of diversity" is a core characteristic with which a person is born and which remains with the individual in all stages of his or her life. People have a minimum of six primary dimensions: age, ethnicity, gender, mental/physical abilities and characteristics, race, and sexual orientation. A "secondary dimension of diversity" is a characteristic that a person acquires as the result of a choice he or she made or a choice someone else made for him or her. The secondary dimensions of diversity include, but are not limited to, communication style, education, family status, military experience, organizational role and level, religion, income, first language, geographic location, income, work experience, and work style. Among various ethnic groups, there are nuanced diversity factors that should be further considered, including how age is seen in different cultures, comfort with and competence in English, generational status, family composition and extent of family dispersion, among others.

- When discussing the implications of multicultural diversity for police officers, it is not enough simply to present the need to understand cultural background. Whenever two groups are from entirely different ethnic or racial backgrounds, there is the possibility that prejudice exists because of fear, lack of contact, ignorance, and stereotypes. To deny the existence of prejudice or racism in any given law enforcement agency would be to deny that it exists outside the agency. Members of the law enforcement profession have to examine their words, behaviors, and actions to evaluate whether they are conveying professionalism and respect to all people within the workplace and on the streets, regardless of their race, culture, religion, or ethnic background. All officers and civilian employees must be free of all expressions of prejudice and must recognize when stereotypes are contributing to biased judgments and potentially differential treatment of citizens.

Discussion Questions and Issues

1. *Views on the Multicultural Society.* The following viewpoints regarding our increasingly multicultural population reflect varying levels of tolerance, understanding, and acceptance. Discuss the following points of view and their implications for law enforcement:
   - Diversity is acceptable if there is not too much of it, but the way things are going today, it is hard to absorb and it just may result in our destruction.
   - They are here now, and they need to do things our way.
   - To advance in our diverse society, we need to accept and respect our differences rather than maintain the myth of the melting pot.

2. *Police Work and Multiculturalism.* Describe three reasons why police officers need to show multicultural respect to their coworkers and citizens in their community. Also list three ways to demonstrate this respect and the benefits that will result.

3. *Dealing with Illegal Immigrants.* Does the police department in which you work (or in the city in which you reside) have a policy regarding undocumented immigrants? Are officers instructed not to inquire into their status unless a crime has been committed? How do you think police officers should deal with undocumented immigrants?

4. *Mini Case Studies and Cultural Practices: Does Culture Matter? – Discussion Questions*

   4. A. *Culture Matters?* Reread, then discuss.

   ### The Sword in a Public Park
   - What are the laws pertaining to knives or swords in the jurisdiction where you live or work?
   - What would you do if you were a police officer encountering an individual practicing Tai Chi with a sword in a public park?
   - What would you say and what would your approach be?

   4. B. *Culture Matters?* Reread, then discuss.

   ### The Turban and the *Kirpan*
   - What are the general laws that pertain to the *kirpan* (sheathed knife) in your city, county or state?
   - How are Sikh *kirpans* handled within the school district in which you live or work? How about within public buildings in which you live or work?

   - Regardless of the guilt or innocence of the Sikh individual who is arrested in any police-related incident, the surrounding close-knit Sikh community will likely make judgments about the manner in which a Sikh community member is treated. If you were a police officer in a situation such as the one described above, what would you want the community to say specifically about the way you confiscated the *kirpan* and removed the turban (i.e., assuming you also had reason to do the latter)?

   4. C. *Culture Matters?* Reread, then discuss.

   ### A Tragic Case of Cross-Cultural Misinterpretation
   - Do you think this case would have proceeded differently if all the authorities involved understood the cultural tradition of the medical practice ("coin rubbing") that caused the bruising? Explain your answer.
   - Discuss whether you think Southeast Asian refugees should give up this medical practice because it can be misinterpreted.

   4. D. *Culture Matters?* Reread, then discuss.

   ### Latino Values as a Factor in Sentencing
   - Discuss whether culture should play any part in influencing the sentencing of a criminal convicted of violent crimes such as murder and rape. Was the lighter verdict in this case justified? Explain your answer.
   - According to retired Superior Court Judge Katz, culture influenced the sentencing in this case. In your opinion, if the husband involved were not Latino, would the sentence have been the same?

5. *Prejudice and Discrimination in Police Work.* In your own words, define prejudice and discrimination. Give examples of (a) discrimination in society in general, (b) discrimination against police officers, and (c) discrimination toward minorities by police officers. Discuss two strategies for each one to help eradicate the discrimination and the benefits that will result.

References

American Community Survey Briefs. (2011). Place of Birth of the Foreign-Born Population: 2009. Retrieved July 2, 2013, from www.census.gov/prod/2010pubs/acsbr09-15.pdf

Badger, Emily. (2013, June 13). "6 More U.S. Counties are now Majority-Minority," *The Atlantic Cities*. Retrieved May 24, 2013, from www.theatlanticcities.com/neighborhoods/2013/06/6-more-us-counties-are-now-majority-minority/5901/

Berry, Ondra. (2013, March). Retired Deputy Police Chief, Reno, Nevada, Police Department, personal communication.

Coffey, Alan, Edward Eldefonson, and Walter Hartinger. (1982). *Human Relations: Law Enforcement in a Changing Community*, 3rd ed. Englewood Cliffs, N.J.: Prentice-Hall.

Department of Homeland Security. (2013). FY 2013 Budget in Brief. Retrieved June 5, 2013, from www.dhs.gov/xlibrary/assets/mgmt/dhs-budget-in-brief-fy2013.pdf

Department of Homeland Security. (2013). Definition of Terms. Retrieved May 18, 2013, from www.dhs.gov/definition-terms

Department of Justice. (2013). Tribal Law and Order Act. Retrieved July 5, 2013, from www.justice.gov/tribal/tloa.html

De Santis, Marie. (2013). "Help: Special for Immigrant Women." Women's Justice Center. Retrieved April 15, 2013, from www.justicewomen.com

Dougherty, Conor and Miriam Jordan. (2012, May 17). "Minority Births are the New Majority." *Wall Street Journal.* Retrieved July 5, 2013, from http://online.wsj.com/article/SB100014240 52702303879604577408363003351818.html

Erdrich, Louise. (2013, February 27). "Rape on the Reservation," *New York Times,* p. A25..

European Parliament. (2007). The European Parliament's Interpreters. Retrieved August 27, 2013, from www.europarl.europa.eu/sides/getDoc.do?type=IM-PRESS&reference=2006 0403FCS06935&language=EN

Fiber-Ostrow, Pamela and Sarah Hill. (2011, February). "Immigration Opinion and Generation Y: A Study of Tolerance," *California State University, Fullerton.* Retrieved June 17, 2013, from www.researchgate.net/publication/228198190_Immigration_Opinion_and_Generation_Y_A_Study_of_Tolerance

Gilsinan, Kathy. (2013, February 15). "Why Are There So Many Bosnians in St. Louis?" *The Atlantic Cities.* Retrieved August 4, 2013, from www.theatlanticcities.com/politics/2013/02/why-are-there-so-many-bosnians-st-louis/4668/

Gove, Tracey G. (2011, October). "Implicit Bias and Law Enforcement," *The Police Chief.* Retrieved May 14, 2013, from www.policechiefmagazine.org/magazine/index.cfm?fuseaction=display_arch&article_id=2499&issue_id=102011

Hall, Edward T. (1959). *The Silent Language.* Greenwich, Conn.: Fawcett.

Handlin, Oscar. (1975). *Out of Many: A Study Guide to Cultural Pluralism in the United States.* Anti-Defamation League of B'nai B'rith. Louisville, KY: Brown & Williamson Tobacco Corporation.

Katz, Lawrence. (2013, January). Retired Presiding Judge, Juvenile Court of Contra Costa (California) County, personal communication.

Kennedy, John F. (1986). *A Nation of Immigrants.* New York, NY: Harper & Row, p. 14.

Loden Associates Inc. (2013). Primary and Secondary Dimensions of Diversity. Retrieved July 24, 2013, from www.loden.com/Web_Stuff/Dimensions.html

Loden, Marilyn. (2013, June). Organizational Diversity Consultant, Loden Associates Inc., personal communication.

Lovett, Ian. (2012, October 5). "Los Angeles to Cease Transferring Some Immigrants," *New York Times,* p. A14.

Martinez, Christopher. (2013, March). Program Director for Refugee & Immigrant Services, Catholic Charities CYO, San Francisco, Calif., personal communication.

Miller, Char. (2013, February). (Former) Professor of history, Trinity College, San Antonio, Tex, personal communication.

NAS Insights. (2006). "Generation Y: The Millenials. Ready or Not, Here They Come." NAS Recruitment Communications. Retrieved February 14, 2009, from www.nasrecruitment.com/talenttips/NASinsights/GenerationY.pdf

Olson, Aaron T. (2013). Helping Immigrants and Refugees: Police and Emergency Training. Retrieved July 24 2013, (IRCO sponsored sessions). Retrieved June 1, 2013, from http://atolson.com/helpingimmigrantsandrefugees.html

"One America in the 21st Century: Forging a New Future," Executive Summary, Advisory Board to the President's Initiative on Race, September 1998.

Orloff, Leslye. (2003, February 27). Testifying as the director of the Immigrant Women Program, NOW Legal Defense and Education Fund, before the Subcommittee on Immigration, Border Security, and Claims House Judiciary Committee.

Pardo, Charles C. Duncan. (2010, January 14). "Crimes go unreported by undocumented immigrants, RPD chief says," *Raleigh Public Record.* Retrieved July 29, 2013, from http://raleighpublicrecord.org/news/2010/01/14/crimes-go-unreported-by-undocumented-immigrants-rpd-chief-says/

Passel, Jeffrey and D'Vera Cohn. (2011, February 1). "Unauthorized Immigrant Population: National and State Trends, 2010," Pew Research Hispanic Trends Project. Retrieved August 25, 2013, from www.pewhispanic.org/2011/02/01/appendix-c-maps/

Pew Research Hispanic Trends Project. (2013, January 29). A Nation of Immigrants. Retrieved May 24, 2013, from www.pewhispanic.org/2013/01/29/a-nation-of-immigrants/

Pew Research Social & Demographic Trends. (2012, June 19). The Rise of Asian Americans. Retrieved May 24, 2013, from www.pewsocialtrends.org/2012/06/19/the-rise-of-asian-americans/

Population Reference Bureau. (2013). 2012 World Population Data Sheet. Retrieved May 19, 2013, from www.prb.org/Publications/Datasheets/2012/2012-world-population-data-sheet.aspx

Project Implicit. (2011). Project Implicit. Retrieved June 29, 2013, from https://implicit.harvard.edu/implicit/

Rawlins, Gary H. (1992, October 8). "Africans Came 200 Years Earlier." *USA Today,* p. 2a.

"The Changing Face of Race in America." (2000, September 18). *Newsweek,* p. 38.

Renshon, Stanley. (2011, February 8). "Multiculturalism in the U.S.: Cultural Narcissism and the Politics of Recognition," *Center for Immigration Studies.* Retrieved August 6, 2013, from www.cis.org/renshon/politics-of-recognition

Russell, Joseph and Jeanne Batalova. (2012, July). "European Immigrants in the United States,"

Migration Information Source. Retrieved July 24, 2013, from www.migrationinformation.org/usfocus/display.cfm?ID=901

Sherman, Spencer. (1986). "When Cultures Collide." *California Lawyer,* 6(1), 33.

"Some immigrant women, victims of domestic violence, afraid to seek help." (2013, March 23). *Public Radio International.* Retrieved May 19, 2013, from www.pri.org/stories/politics-society/social-justice/some-immigrant-women-victims-of-domestic-violence-afraid-to-seek-help-13299.html

Suárez-Orozco cited in Yen, Hope. (2013, March 17). "Rise of Latino population blurs US racial lines," *Associated Press.* Retrieved June 18, 2013, from www.kjonline.com/news/Rise-of-Latino-population-blurs-US-racial-lines.html?pageType=mobile&id=1

Swarns, Rachel L. and Jodi Kantor. (2009, October 8). "In First Lady's Roots, A Complex Path from Slavery," *The New York Times*. P. A1.

Tiede, Lydia Brashear. (2001). "Battered Immigrant Women and Immigration Remedies: Are the Standards too high?" *Human Rights Magazine*. Section Individual Rights and Responsibilities, American Bar Association, Winter 2001; Vol. 28, No. 1. (Excerpted with permission June, 2009)

UNIFEM. (2013). UN Women: Violence Against Women. Retrieved May 24, 2013, from www.unifem.org/gender_issues/violence_against_women/

U.S. Census Bureau. (2013, June 13). "Asians Fastest-Growing Race or Ethnic Group in 2012, Census Bureau Reports." Retrieved June 27, 2013, from www.census.gov/newsroom/releases/archives/population/cb13-112.html

U.S. Census Bureau. (2012, October 12). "Census Bureau Establishes National Advisory Committee on Race, Ethnic and Other Populations." Retrieved June 27, 2013, from www.census.gov/newsroom/releases/archives/miscellaneous/cb12-195.html

U.S. Census Bureau. (2013). How Do We Know? Retrieved June 27, 2013, from www.census.gov/how/infographics/foreign_born.html

U.S. Census Bureau. (2011). Overview of Race and Hispanic Origin: 2010. Retrieved June 26, 2013, from www.census.gov/prod/cen2010/briefs/c2010br-02.pdf

U.S. Census Bureau. (2010, October). Place of Birth of the Foreign-Born Population: 2009. Retrieved May 27, 2013, from www.census.gov/prod/2010pubs/acsbr09-15.pdf

U.S. Census Bureau. (2010). State and Country Quick Facts: Foreign-Born Persons. Retrieved May 27, 2013, from http://quickfacts.census.gov/qfd/

U.S. Census Bureau. (2012). The Two or More Races Population: 2010. Retrieved May 27, 2013, from www.census.gov/prod/cen2010/briefs/c2010br-13.pdf

U.S. Census Bureau. (2012, December 12). "U.S. Census Bureau Projections Show a Slower Growing, Older, More Diverse Nation a Half Century from Now." Retrieved June 14, 2013, from www.census.gov/newsroom/releases/archives/population/cb12-243.html

U.S. Citizenship and Immigration Services. (2013). Information Resources and Immigration Services, Data Integration Division, U.S. Census Bureau. Retrieved June 29, 2013, from www.uscis.gov/portal/site/uscis

U.S. Immigration and Customs Enforcement. (2013). Fact Sheet: Delegation of Immigration Authority Section 287(g) Immigration and Nationality Act. Retrieved August 4, 2013, from www.ice.gov/news/library/factsheets/287g.htm

Zangwill, Israel. (1908). *The Melting Pot: Drama in Four Acts*. New York, NY: Macmillan.

2

The Changing Law Enforcement Agency
A Microcosm of Society

LEARNING OBJECTIVES

After reading this chapter, you should be able to:

- Identify how the ethnic, racial, and gender composition of law enforcement agencies is changing in the United States.
- Define racism and understand the steps organizational managers and supervisors can take to identify and control prejudicial conduct by employees.
- Describe methods for defusing conflicts within the organization and community related to issues of gender, sexual orientation, race, and ethnicity.
- Explain the history of women in law enforcement, the issues confronting them, and how support and mentoring programs help them make transitions into the workplace.
- Define the terms lesbian, gay, bisexual, transgender and LGBT.
- Explain what law enforcement chief executives need to do in order to convey zero tolerance for and disciplinary action in response to discrimination based on sexual orientation.
- Explain the role of supervisors, managers, and the chief executive in providing a workplace environment that is comfortable for all employees, especially for women and individuals from diverse backgrounds.

OUTLINE

- Introduction
- Changing Workforce
- Racism within the Law Enforcement Workforce
- Women in Law Enforcement
- Sexual Orientation in Law Enforcement
- Police Leadership, Professionalism, and Synergy
- Supervisors, Managers, and the Chief Executive
- Summary
- Discussion Questions and Issues

INTRODUCTION

In Chapter 1, we reviewed the evolution of multicultural communities and the demographic changes that the United States has experienced in recent decades. The most notable demographic changes mentioned involve the increases in racial, ethnic, and immigrant populations in our country. Diversity is becoming so commonplace in communities that terms such as *majority group* and *minority group* have been questioned for some time. There is often a negative reaction to the term *minority*, which critics find not just outmoded but offensive. The word carries overtones of inferiority and inequity. The word, technically, is used to describe numerical designations, but over the years it has come to have much larger implications. While in this book we continue to use the term in some contexts, we also want to remind the reader of the controversy around the term.

The range of reactions to these changes in society as a whole is no different from the reactions within law enforcement agencies. Members of police communities across the country have demonstrated both tolerance of and resistance to the changing society and workforce. Some officers dislike the multicultural workforce and the involvement of women in policing, although the latter is becoming a nonissue. They may resent diversity because of their own prejudices or biases. This resentment is due in part to perceived or actual advantages others receive when competing for law enforcement positions, either entry level or promotional. In addition, because of inept affirmative action hiring in the past (in which management rushed to fill quotas but did not focus on competence), some officers perceive that affirmative action (where still being used) means lowering standards. Indeed, where standards have been lowered, everyone suffers, especially the less-qualified employees hired because of affirmative action. (This issue is discussed further in Chapter 3.)

Leading positively and valuing the diversity within an agency are the keys to meeting the challenge of policing multicultural communities. As discussed in Chapter 1, racial and ethnic tensions still exist in the law enforcement community. Agency personnel must address the conflicts in their own organizations before dealing with racial, ethnic, or sexual orientation issues in the community. For example, if there are allegations of harassment, a hostile work environment, or differential treatment within the agency, these allegations must be addressed on a timely basis, or they fester and result in lawsuits, court injunctions, and unhappy employees who do not remain with the organization.

Law enforcement agencies themselves determine, by their action or inaction, whether social problems that manifest within the agencies are resolved. Across the United States, the national press has reported numerous cases in which law enforcement agencies did nothing or took the wrong action. Whether they like it or not, police officers are primary role models for citizens and are judged by a higher standard of behavior than are others. While supervision of police officers is important to ensure that this higher standard of behavior is maintained, no amount of supervision of officers working with the public, no matter how thorough and conscientious, will prevent some officers from violating policies; there simply are too many police officers and too few supervisors. Thus, it is important that police officers demonstrate integrity and a stable set of core virtues. These virtues must include the ability to remain professional in protecting and serving a diverse public.

As stated in Chapter 1, those concerned with peacekeeping and enforcement must accept the realities of a diverse society as well as the heterogeneity within their workforce. The irony is that the peacekeepers sworn to uphold laws pertaining to acts of bias sometimes themselves become perpetrators, even against their peers. If police departments are to be representative of the populations served, police executives must effect changes. These changes have to do with the treatment of peers as well as recruitment, selection, and promotion of employees who have traditionally been underrepresented in law enforcement. The argument (Chapter 1) that the United States has never really been a melting pot applies also to the law enforcement community. In some cases, relationships within the law enforcement workplace, especially as diversity increases, are characterized by disrespect and tension. Although many in the police subculture would argue that membership implies brotherhood or familial relationship (and therefore belonging), this membership has traditionally excluded certain groups in both subtle and obvious ways.

CHANGING WORKFORCE

As microcosms of their communities, law enforcement agencies increasingly include among their personnel more women, members of ethnic and racial minorities, and gay males and lesbians. Although such groups are far from achieving parity in most law enforcement agencies in the United States, advances have been made. The U.S. Bureau of Labor Statistics prepares reports quarterly which analyze the labor workforce participation. Labor workforce refers to the number of people ages 16 or older who are either working or looking for work. The Winter 2013-14 workforce report shows the overall percentage of men and women in the workforce (Exhibit 2.1), percentage by race (Exhibit 2.2), and by ethnic origin (Exhibit 2.3) projecting those numbers to 2022. Quarterly reports have shown that the rates for men and women in the workforce have been converging over the last several decades.

This profound shift in demographics has resulted in notable changes in law enforcement. In many regions of the country, today's law enforcement workforce differs greatly from the workforce of the past. For one example, the Hispanic population is growing at such a rate that it is difficult for public sector agencies, especially law enforcement, to achieve parity. It is also difficult to keep up

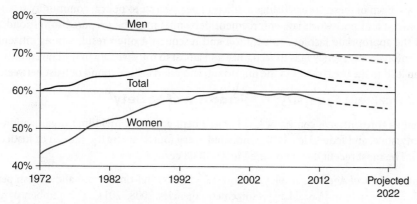

EXHIBIT 2.1 Labor force participation rates for men and women, 1972–2012 and projected 2022, in percent
Source: Occupational Outlook Quarterly. (Winter 2013-2014). U.S. Bureau of Labor Statistics.

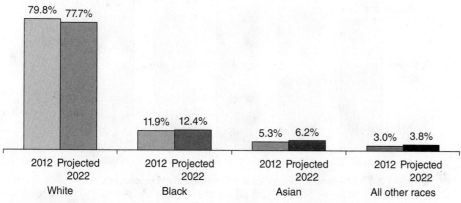

EXHIBIT 2.2 Percent distribution of labor force by race, 2012 and projected 2022
Source: Occupational Outlook Quarterly. (Winter 2013-2014). U.S. Bureau of Labor Statistics.

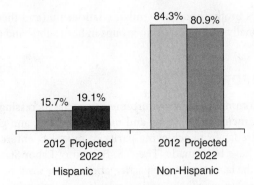

EXHIBIT 2.3 Percent distribution of labor
force by ethnic origin, 2012 and projected 2022
Source: Occupational Outlook Quarterly. (Winter
2013-2014). U.S. Bureau of Labor Statistics.

with the organizational change required not only to provide police services, but also to recruit and retain personnel from this subset of the population. For a law enforcement agency to maintain the support and trust of any community, it is essential that the organization reflect the diversity of the area it serves. In communities across the nation, officers come into contact with persons from different cultural or ethnic backgrounds, socioeconomic classes, religions, and sexual orientations on a daily basis. Each of these groups brings a different perspective to police–community relations. As a result, sworn and nonsworn law enforcement personnel must be prepared to respond to each group in the appropriate fashion. Frustration and resentment often result among citizens when their law enforcement agency fails to recognize and adjust to the diversity in the community. Such a failure can lead to the breakdown of the important, and often critical, bond of trust between them.

Law Enforcement Diversity: A Microcosm of Society

A nationally representative census of law enforcement agencies, including organizations at the city, county, state, and federal levels, is conducted every four years by the Bureau of Justice Statistics (BJS). The most recent data contained in the 2008 census shows:

> ***State and Local Agencies*** employed about 1.13 million full-time sworn and civilian personnel ("Census of State and Local Law Enforcement Agencies, 2008," 2011). The numbers of full-time state and local law enforcement employees between 1992 and 2008 are shown in Exhibit 2.4.

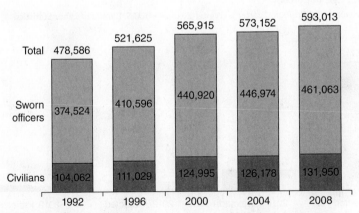

EXHIBIT 2.4 Full-time state and local law enforcement employees, 1992–2008
Source: "Census of State and Local Law Enforcement Agencies, 2008." (2011, July). Bureau of Justice Statistics. NCJ 233982. Retrieved from www.bjs.gov/content/pub/pdf/csllea08.pdf

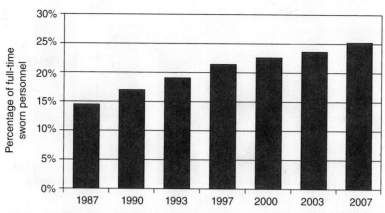

EXHIBIT 2.5 Minority representation among local police officers, 1987-2007

Source: "Local Police Departments, 2007," (2010, December). U.S. Department of Justice, Office of Justice Programs, Bureau of Statistics. NCJ231174. Retrieved from www.bjs.gov/content/pub/pdf/lpd07.pdf.

The breakdown by gender, race, and/or ethnic group for sworn, full-time personnel in 2007 was:

- Approximately 1 in 4 sworn personnel (about 117,113 individuals) were members of a racial or ethnic minority group. This was an increase of about 10,500 (10%) over 2003. From 2003 to 2007, minority representation among local police officers increased from 23.6 percent to 25.3 percent. In 1987, minorities comprised 14.6 percent of officers (Exhibit 2.5). Of these officers, there were:

  1. An estimated 55,267 black or African American officers, which was about 2,400 (5%) more than in 2003. In 2007, however, because the total number of officers also rose since 2003, the percentage of black officers remained the same. In 1987, blacks comprised 9.3 percent officers.
  2. An estimated 47,678 Hispanic or Latino officers, which was about 6,600 (16%) more than in 2003. From 2003 to 2007, the percentage of officers who were Hispanic rose from 9.1 percent to 10.3 percent. In 1987, 4.5 percent of officers were Hispanic.
  3. An estimated 12,564 officers (2.7%) were members of other minority groups including Asians, Pacific Islanders, and American Indians/Alaska Native—about the same number (2.8%) as in 2003 but more than in 1987 (0.8%).

- Approximately 1 in 8 sworn personnel were women (about 55,305 individuals), representing an increase of about 4,300 (8%) from 2003. Female representation increased from 11.3 percent to 11.9 percent between 2003 and 2007. The survey does not have a breakdown by race or ethnicity for female officers.

Sheriffs' Offices employed about 353,461 full-time sworn and civilian personnel. Sheriffs' offices can be found in almost every county and independent city throughout the United States, with a total of 3,085 nationwide as of 2008. Of the approximately 172,241 full-time sworn personnel, the equivalent of 59 percent were assigned to law enforcement, 23 percent to jails, 12 percent to courts, and 6 percent to other operations or duties ("Census of State and Local Law Enforcement Agencies, 2008," 2011). Exhibit 2.6 reflects the number of full-time employees in sheriffs' offices in the period from 1992 to 2008. The breakdown by women, race, and/or ethnic group for sworn, full-time personnel in 2007 was:

- 18.9 percent, or 1 in 5, were members of a racial or ethnic minority group, estimated to be 32,554 individuals. Of these,

  1. An estimated 15,500 (9%) were black or African American, slightly less than in 2003 (10%), but equal to the proportion employed in 1987.

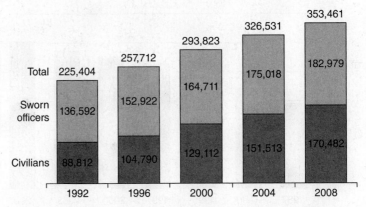

EXHIBIT 2.6   Full-time employees in sheriffs' offices, 1992-2008
Source: "Census of State and Local Law Enforcement Agencies, 2008." Reaves,
Brian A. BJS NCJ 233982. Retrieved from www.bjs.gov/content/pub/pdf/csllea08.pdf

2. An estimated 13,900 (8%) were Hispanic or Latino. From 2003 to 2007, the number of Hispanic or Latino deputies increased by 16 percent.
3. An estimated 3,154 were Asian or Pacific Islander (1.1%) or American Indian or Alaska Native (0.4%).
• Women were estimated to be 20,800 (12%). There is no breakdown available as to the race or ethnicity of the sworn women deputies.

Federal Agencies employed approximately 120,000 full-time law enforcement officers who were authorized to make arrests and carry firearms in the United States. The largest number of these, about 45,000 (37%), performed criminal investigations and enforcement duties. The next largest job function was police response and patrol, with about 28,000 officers (23%). Approximately 18,000 (15%) performed immigration or customs inspections, and around 17,000 (14%) performed corrections and detention duties. See Exhibit 2.7 for the percentages in each category. There are 24 federal agencies, excluding

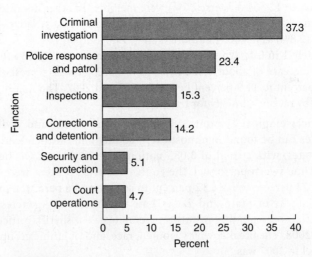

EXHIBIT 2.7   Percent of full-time federal officers . . . by primary function, 2008
Source: "Federal Law Enforcement Officers, 2008." (June 2012). U.S. Department of Justice, Office of Justice Programs, Bureau of Statistics. NCJ 238250. Retrieved from www.bjs.gov/content/pub/pdf/fleo08.pdf

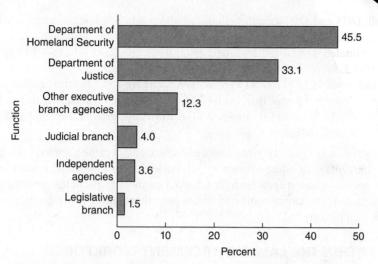

EXHIBIT 2.8 Percent of federal officers by department or branch, 2008.

Source: "Federal Law Enforcement Officers, 2008." (June 2012). U.S. Department of Justice, Office of Justice Programs, Bureau of Statistics. NCJ 238250. Retrieved from www.bjs.gov/content/pub/pdf/fleo08.pdf

inspectors general's offices, which in 2008 employed more than 250 full-time officers with arrest and firearms authority in the United States. These agencies employed 96 percent of all federal officers. The four largest (see Exhibit 2.8) included two in the Department of Homeland Security (DHS) and two in the Department of Justice (DOJ).

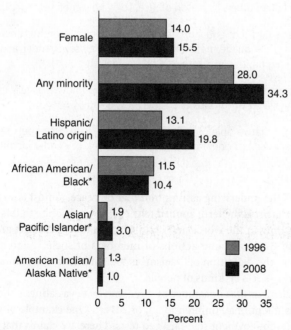

*Excludes persons of Hispanic/Latino origin.

EXHIBIT 2.9 Percent of female and minority federal officers, 1996 and 2008

Source: "Federal Law Enforcement Officers, 2008." (June 2012). U.S. Department of Justice, Office of Justice Programs, Bureau of Statistics. NCJ 238250. Retrieved from www.bjs.gov/content/pub/pdf/fleo08.pdf

...d DOJ agencies employed about 4 in 5 federal officers. The breakdown ...group, and women in 2008 was:

...d 41,160 (34.3%), or 1 in 3, were members of a racial or ethnic group ...9).

...ted 18,600 (15.5%) were women with arrest and firearm authority. This was a ...ower percentage than in 2004 (16.1%) but higher when compared to 1996 (14%). ...s no breakdown for women as to race or ethnic group ("Federal Law Enforcement ...rs, 2008," 2012).

...icreases in minority percentages in these agencies came a corresponding reduction ...percentage of white officers and deputies in law enforcement workforces. Some ...r law enforcement agencies have achieved parity in terms of the percentage of diverse ...ups in their workforce compared to the percentage in the community; most have not, ...t the numbers are improving.

RACISM WITHIN THE LAW ENFORCEMENT WORKFORCE

There are three major types of racism: personally mediated, institutional, and internalized. Personally mediated racism is what most people think of when they hear the word *racism* (Feagin, 2006). It includes specific attitudes, beliefs, practices, and behaviors involved in acts of prejudice, discrimination, bias, and stereotyping by individuals directed toward others. Institutional racism is the failure of an organization (public or private) to provide goods, services, or opportunities to people because of their color, culture, or ethnic origin. It is beyond the scope of this text to delve into the third type, internalized racism.

Racism   Total rejection of others by reason of race, color, or, sometimes more broadly, culture.

Discrimination   The denial of equal treatment to individuals or groups because of their age, disability, employment, language, nationality, race, ethnicity, sex, gender and gender identity, sexual orientation, religion, or other form of cultural identity.

Prejudice   A judgment or opinion formed before facts are known, usually involving negative or unfavorable thoughts about groups of people.

Bias   A preformed negative opinion or attitude toward a group of persons based on their race, religion, disability, sexual orientation, ethnicity, gender, or gender identity.

Racism involves the underlying assumption that one race, almost always the white race, is superior to all others. *Racist* is the term applied to those who subscribe to this belief. Examples of racism are found not only in the words and actions of white supremacist groups, however, but also, unfortunately, in the words and actions of members of society who are not part of hate groups. However, often the definition of "racism" is too simplistic. Racism takes many forms, is often unconscious, and affects all kinds of people.

Institutional racism, or the appearance of same, can be devastating to those impacted by the practice, whether it is intentional, unintentional, or covert. One example of institutional racism could be the use of pre-employment standardized tests. There are claims that this kind of assessment can be significantly biased toward people of a certain cultural and social background, so that in much of the Western world, racial minorities tend to score lower. Unpaved roads in predominantly black neighborhoods could be seen as another example of institutionalized racism, as could the presence of older-edition, used textbooks in schools that are predominantly black.

Racism within law enforcement agencies, which can be personally mediated or institutional, has been documented for decades. An African American history display at the New York

Police Academy contains the following written account of the experiences of one of the first black officers in the New York Police Department:

> Seven years before the adoption of the charter creating New York City, Brooklyn, then an independent city, hired the first black policeman. Wiley G. Overton was sworn in on March 6, 1891.... His first tour of duty was spent in civilian clothing because fellow officers breaking with tradition refused to furnish him with a temporary uniform.... Officers in his section refused to sleep in the same room with him.... The officers in the precinct ignored him and spoke only if it was necessary in the line of duty.

The New York Police Department is not alone. Racism can occur in police departments regardless of size or region. Unfortunately, racism has been an issue for decades.

The authors, over the years of producing this textbook, have spoken with officers from different states about racism in their departments. Those interviewed requested that their names not be included, because they felt they might face repercussions. One African American officer recalled almost coming to blows with a white officer who used a racial slur against him; the use of such slurs was commonplace for the white officer and his friends. A Cuban American officer recounted the story of a nonresistant Latino suspect who was caught in the commission of a minor crime and beaten by the white arresting officers, who used racial epithets. One major city in Massachusetts suspended a deputy superintendent of police for using the word "nigger" directed toward one of his own officers. An African American officer in a large city in Florida was fired after using racial epithets against other blacks in violation of a strict citywide policy. In this particular case, the African American officer's conduct was reported by another officer at the scene. In yet another city, an African American officer was overheard telling a white prisoner, "Wait until you get to central booking and the niggers get hold of you."

Institutional or personally mediated racism and discrimination is combated by using federal law. Under Title VII of the Civil Rights Act of 1964, the Americans with Disabilities Act, and the Age Discrimination in Employment Act, it is illegal to discriminate in any aspect of the hiring process or in employment. The three Acts applied to state and local governments the provisions of federal laws concerning discriminatory practices. A U.S. government agency, the Equal Employment Opportunity Commission (EEOC), investigates, litigates, and resolves complaints and allegations of discrimination in both the public and the private sector. EEO laws were passed to correct a history of unfavorable treatment of women and minority group members. All workers in the United States are protected from harassment, discrimination, and employment decisions based on certain criteria. To be protected, individuals must be part of a "protected class" as described by federal or state law, policy, or similar authority; however, they must still exhibit necessary qualifications for the job, follow all company guidelines, and conduct themselves in a manner expected and required of all employees. The "protected class" designation means that workers are protected from employment discrimination on the basis of sex, race, religion, color, national origin, age (over 40), and physical or mental disability. In addition, Title II of the Genetic Information Nondiscrimination Act of 2008 (GINA) prohibits genetic information discrimination in employment. The Pregnancy Discrimination Act (PDA) forbids discrimination based on pregnancy when it comes to any aspect of employment, layoff, training, fringe benefits, such as leave and health insurance, and any other term or condition of employment (U.S. Equal Employment Opportunity Commission, n.d.). Nor is it legal for employers to retaliate against any employee or applicant who has filed a complaint about discrimination; the U.S. Supreme Court in 2009 ruled that workers who cooperate with their employers' internal investigations of discrimination may not be fired in retaliation for implicating colleagues or superiors ("Court rules on worker retaliation," 2009). For the fiscal year 2012, the EEOC investigated 37,836 charges of retaliation, which was higher than all other categories of discrimination (38.1% of the total) ("Enforcement and Litigation Statistics," 2012).

Title VII of the Civil Rights Act of 1964 also prohibits employment decisions based on stereotypes and assumptions about the abilities, traits, or performance of individuals of certain racial and ethnic groups. Also prohibited are both intentional discrimination and neutral job policies that disproportionately exclude minorities and that are not job-related. For fiscal year 2012, the EEOC received 99,142 charges of employment discrimination and obtained $365.4 million in relief through its administration program and litigation. The number of charges, of those pertinent to this section of the chapter, by category and percent of the total, were:

- *Race discrimination:* 33,512 charges (33.7%)
- *Religion-based discrimination:* 3,811 charges (3.8%)
- *National origin–based discrimination:* 10,883 charges (10.9%)
- *Color discrimination:* 2,662 charges (2.7%)

The numbers in almost all categories represent an increase over previous years ("Enforcement and Litigation Statistics," 2012). Chief executives, managers, supervisors, and employees should recognize from these figures the importance of defusing and controlling institutional or personally mediated racism and discrimination in the workplace.

Defusing Racially and Culturally Rooted Conflicts

To defuse racist attitudes, behaviors, and/or practices in any organization (public or private) or school, the organization must be upfront and proactive about racism. It is essential that employers and parents (or elders) get involved in any concerted effort to defeat this problem. A good place to start is to recognize that all cultures, races, ethnic groupings, and nations are susceptible to racist (or exclusionary) attitudes, practices, and behaviors. It should be understood that white people are no more—or less—inclined toward racism than are people of other races or ethnicities. This must be established before any useful dialogue, experience, or insight can take place.

One of the greatest challenges for police officers is dealing with their own conscious or unconscious negative bias, stereotypes, and prejudices. No one can be forced to simply abandon long-held prejudices. However, police must recognize that in law enforcement, acting in discriminatory or racist ways is not only unprofessional, but also can lead to tragic consequences.

The first step in addressing the problem is for police department personnel, on all levels, to admit, rather than deny, that racism exists. Police researcher David Shipler, after two years of interviews across the country, maintained that he encountered very few black officers who had not been "hassled by white cops." He was quick to point out, however, that not every white police officer is a bigot and not every police force a bastion of racism; in fact, some agencies have made great strides in improving race relations within their organization and the community they serve ("Report Recommends Using Military Model," 1992). Shipler recommends that law enforcement should combat and defuse racism by using the U.S. Army model developed during a time of extreme racial tension in the military in the early 1970s ("Report Recommends Using Military Model," 1992). Obviously, no model of training will bring guaranteed success and alleviate all acts of prejudice and racism. However, professional groups can build on each other's attempts, especially when these efforts have been proven to be fairly successful. Shipler recognizes that police officers are not identical to soldiers, because the former have constant contact with the public (where they see the worst) and must use personal judgment in dangerous and ambiguous situations. Nevertheless, he suggests that some military approaches are adaptable to law enforcement. According to Shipler, the basic framework for combating and defusing racism in the military has been:

- *Command commitment:* The person at the top sets the tone all the way down to the bottom. Performance reports document any bigoted or discriminatory behavior.
- *Training of advisers:* Military personnel are trained at the Defense Equal Opportunity Management Institute in Florida as equal opportunity advisers. The advisers are assigned to military units with direct access to commanders. They conduct courses locally to train all members of the unit on race relations.

- *Complaints and monitoring:* The advisers provide one channel for specific complaints of racial and gender discrimination, but they also drop in on units unannounced and sound out the troops on their attitudes. Surveys are conducted and informal discussions are held to lessen racial tensions. ("Report Recommends Using Military Model," 1992)

Shipler, still a consultant and author regarding race issues, confirms that his recommendations for defusing tensions are still valid today (Shipler, 2013).

Sondra Thiederman (1991) is an author of five books and principal of Cross-Cultural Communications, a business specializing in bias reduction and skills for diffusing conflict in a diverse workplace. In one of her books, *Bridging Cultural Barriers for Corporate Success,* published in 1991, she provides nine tips that will help organizational managers or leaders identify and resolve conflicts that arise because of cultural (not only racial) differences in the workplace, tips that are still useful and applicable no matter what cultures, races, religions, or lifestyles are involved:

1. Give each party the opportunity to voice his or her concerns without interruption.
2. Attempt to obtain agreement on what the problem is by asking questions of each party to find out specifically what is upsetting each person.
3. During this process, stay in control and keep employees on the subject of the central issue.
4. Establish whether the issue is indeed rooted in cultural differences by determining:
   a. If the parties are from different cultures or subcultures.
   b. If the key issue represents an important value in each person's culture.
   c. How each person is expected to behave in his or her culture as it pertains to this issue.
   d. If the issue is emotionally charged for one or both of the parties.
   e. If similar conflicts arise repeatedly and in different contexts.
5. Summarize the cultural (racial, religious, or lifestyle) differences that you uncover.
6. State the negative outcomes that will result if the situation is not resolved (be specific).
7. State the positive outcomes that will result if the situation is resolved (be specific).
8. Negotiate terms by allowing those involved to come up with the solutions.
9. Provide positive reinforcement as soon as the situation improves.

Conflict resolution, a key component of any community policing program or partnership, is defined as a process whereby the parties involved may achieve some measure of success without leaving either party devoid of respect. Thiederman's approach is based on conflict resolution and crisis intervention techniques that many law enforcement and correctional officers learn in either their academy or in-service training. Civilians working in the criminal justice system should receive similar training. Police department command must encourage the use of conflict resolution techniques by officers of all backgrounds as a way of handling issues prior to their becoming flash points. With professionalism and patience, the use of conflict resolution techniques to reduce racial and ethnic problems will work within both the workforce and the neighborhoods.

Conflict Resolution Tips

The National Crime Prevention Council has developed the following list of things to remember when managing conflict ("Conflict Resolution Tips"):

1. Note that anger is a normal feeling.
2. How we handle our anger and how we deal with other people who are angry can make the difference between managing conflict effectively and having conflict end in violence.
3. Be aware of triggers, which are any verbal or nonverbal behaviors that result in anger or other negative emotional reactions that can get in the way of resolving conflicts.
4. Triggers are like lightning bolts. When they strike, they can interfere with communication.
5. To avoid pulling others' triggers, pay particular attention to your own behavior, even your body language.

6. Note that people already use strategies to control their anger (for example, walking away from a dangerous situation), and that all they need to do is build on that foundation.

7. Point out that, even though we sometimes think of ourselves as being "out of control," we often choose to blow up at some times and stay calm at other times. For example, there's a difference between how we handle anger with our friends and anger with a parent or grandparent. To resolve the conflict, you must stay calm to communicate.

8. The less "hot" the anger, the more you can control it.

9. Even though your anger may be legitimate, it usually doesn't help to show your anger to the other person. Sometimes the other person will take you more seriously if you remain calm and courteous.

10. Remember that your goal is to be able to get angry without becoming abusive or violent, and to communicate your wants and needs effectively without threatening others.

Departmental General Order for Control of Prejudicial Conduct

As a result of allegations of racism against it, the Alameda (California) Police Department developed a series of general orders as one approach to remedy the problem. Violation of the department general orders (DGOs) carries progressive disciplinary ramifications up to and including termination. The general orders deal with control of prejudicial conduct based on race, religion, ethnicity, disability, sex, age, or sexual orientation and are as follows:

1. *Code of ethics:* [Officers] commit to personal suppression of prejudice, animosities, malice, and ill will, as well as respect for the constitutional rights of all persons.

2. *Discrimination:* Discrimination or racism in any form shall never be tolerated.

3. *Impartiality:* DGO 80-2 requires impartiality toward all persons and guarantees equal protection under the law and prohibits exhibition of partiality due to race, creed, or influence.

4. *Harassment:* DGO 90-3 deals with harassment in the workplace based on race, religion, color, national origin, ancestry, disability, marital status, sex, age, or sexual preference.

The Alameda Police Department also produced an in-service training guide listing "mortal sins," or actions not condoned, which include:

1. Racism, racial slurs, racial discrimination
2. Sexism, offensive sexual remarks, sexual harassment, sexual discrimination
3. Discrimination or harassment for sexual orientation
4. Religious discrimination

This department sent a clear message to its employees that its leaders will not tolerate discriminatory behavior. The same department adapted a San Diego Police Department attitude assessment survey instrument on perceptions regarding contact with the multicultural community and workforce. The survey instrument is reproduced in Appendix A.

Police Fraternal Organizations

Police fraternal religious and ethnic organizations offer their members social activities, fellowship, counseling, career development, resources, and networking opportunities with persons of common heritage, background, or experience. The New York Police Department, for example, has many clubs, societies, and associations to address the needs of its pluralistic organization. The Irish are represented by the Emerald Society, African Americans by the Guardians Association, Christian officers by Police Officers for Christ, those of Asian or Pacific Islander heritage (which includes Chinese, Japanese, Korean, Filipino, and Asian Indian officers) by the Asian Jade Society, Italian officers by the Columbia Association, and so on. The police subculture can be a stressful environment, so it is only natural that persons different from the majority workforce members seek emotional comfort zones with those of similar background. Membership in these groups provides emotional sanctuary from the stereotyping, hostility, indifference that members encounter within their organizations and communities.

Occasionally we hear of criticism within a department or by the public that such organizations actually highlight the differences between groups of people. At a National Organization of Black Law Enforcement Executives (NOBLE) conference, a white female (nonparticipating attendee) asked the meaning of the acronym NOBLE. When given the answer, she asked: "Is it ethical for blacks to have their own organization? Could whites have an organization called the 'National Organization of White Law Enforcement Executives' without being referred to as racists? Why can't the multicultural, social, and professional organizations that already exist satisfy the needs of everyone?"

The woman's concern was brought up directly with one of the conference participants, Sergeant Thomas Hall, an African American who at the time was a Virginia state trooper. He explained:

> In America, we need independent black institutions . . . to foster cultural pride, and have a place where we can go and feel comfortable. We cannot express ourselves in society. We cannot assimilate in society. We cannot even assimilate like some Hispanic groups can because of their complexions. I can't assimilate on a bus. As soon as I step on the bus, you are going to realize there is a black guy on the bus. I can't assimilate in a police organization . . . so without these black institutions, I cannot survive. We all have survival mechanisms. I have cultural needs and I have to be around people that share my needs and frustrations. I cannot do that in organizations that are predominantly white. The whites don't suffer from the racial pressures and tensions that I suffer from. So how can they [mostly white organizations] meet my interests and needs? It is impossible. (Hall, 1992)

Hall stressed that African American law enforcement organizations provide him with a network of persons with similar interests, concerns, and backgrounds.

Another nonprofit organization is the Hispanic National Law Enforcement Association (HNLEA), which was formed in 1988. According to its Web site, HNLEA is involved in the administration of justice and dedicated to the advancement of Hispanic (Latino) and minority interests within the law enforcement profession. The organization is trying to increase the representation of Hispanics and other minorities in the law enforcement field, and acts as a liaison to various communities, minority officers, and law enforcement agencies.

The racial, ethnic, religious, and sexual orientation organizations within law enforcement are not meant to divide but rather to give support to groups that traditionally were not accepted in law enforcement fully and had no power within the organization. Yet the sentiment expressed by the white female who inquired into the meaning of NOBLE is not uncommon among police officers. Police command officers and supervisors must not ignore this debate (whether expressed or not). They must address the issues underlying the need for the support groups within the department. They must also foster dialogue and shared activities between all formalized groups within the organization. All officers must hear an explanation of the benefit they receive from membership in the groups of different ethnic, racial, and sexual orientation perspectives. Officers must be willing to discuss ways to guard against divisiveness, either real or perceived, within their agencies.

Assignments Based on Diversity

There has been limited research on the assumption that an increase in the proportion of any underrepresented group in a police agency would have a positive effect in the community. Some believe that an increase in Hispanic, African American, or Asian officers in a neighborhood of the same race or ethnicity would improve police–community relations. The same argument could be made regarding gay and lesbian officers. We might speculate that there would be a more sensitive response of "like folks," who are aware of needs and issues of "their kind." In fact, historically, immigrants (Irish, Italians, and Germans) were hired by police departments because they could communicate and operate more effectively than could nonimmigrant officers in neighborhoods with large concentrations of immigrants.

aving officers of their own color or national origin work
result in unfairness because it can result in a career path
nt from that of white officers. Furthermore, officers of the
nt ethnicity or race in the neighborhood do not necessarily
oblem solvers there. Not all racially or ethnically diverse offi-
ork with their own cultural or racial group. Assignments based
e generally unfair and may be a disservice to both the officer and
hould not be restricted to working in specific areas based on the
nity relations will improve automatically. In addition, it cannot be
the same background as the citizens will always show sensitivity to

n, a retired Washington, D.C., Metropolitan police officer and past execu-
ational Black Police Officers Association, illustrated this point at a NOBLE
e discussed the reasons why a new African American recruit wanted to work
Washington, D.C. The recruit said that he could tell people of his own race
could not always do so in predominantly white neighborhoods. Hampton noted,
the young recruit "called people from his neighborhood 'maggots.'" Hampton
nt that supervisors must hold subordinates accountable for their conduct, and the
ch   tive must make it known that inappropriate behavior will be disciplined no matter
what the neighborhood (Hampton, 2009). We present this example to illustrate that some officers may have internalized the hatred society has directed toward them and consequently are
not automatically the most effective officers in certain neighborhoods.

When Chief Robert Burgreen was the top executive of the San Diego Police Department,
he, like many other law enforcement managers, did not deploy officers according to color, sexual
orientation, or ethnicity. Deployment was based on the best fit for the neighborhood and was
related to an officer's competence and capabilities. However, Chief Burgreen had four community
relations sergeants, each acting as a liaison for one major group in the city: Hispanic, African
American, Asian, and gays and lesbians. He described these sergeants as his "eyes and ears" for
what was going on in the various communities. Some cities use cultural affairs committees to
perform a similar function, made up of people from diverse groups in the community and the
officers who provide them service.

WOMEN IN LAW ENFORCEMENT

Women in the Workforce

Women have long been part of the general workforce in American society, although for many
years in primarily traditional female employment roles, such as nurses, secretaries, schoolteach-
ers, waitresses, and flight attendants. The first major movement of women into the general workforce occurred during World War II, although there is an argument that this also took place as
early as the Civil War. With men off to war, women entered the workforce in large numbers and
successfully occupied many nontraditional employment roles. A nontraditional occupation for
women is defined as one in which women comprise 25 percent or less of total employment. After
World War II, 30 percent of all women continued working outside the home ("History of Women
in the Workforce," 1991).

According to a United States Department of Labor report completed in 2012, the number of women in the labor force increased at an extremely rapid pace between 1950 (18 million,
or 34%) and 1999 (66 million, or 60%), which was an annual growth rate of 2.6 percent. In
2011, this percentage had dropped slightly to 58.1 percent. The study anticipated that the participation of women in the labor force would slow markedly in the next 50 years, projecting
that it would reach 92 million by 2050 on the basis of an annual growth rate of 0.7 percent
("Women in the Labor Force: A Databook," 2012). The report indicates that women continued

to be concentrated in traditionally female occupations. In 2011, they accounted for nearly 51 percent of all persons employed in management, professional, and related occupations and 20.6 percent of those employed in service occupations, which includes criminal justice jobs. In 2011, employed Asian and white women were more likely (44 and 42% respectively) to work in higher-paying management, professional, and related occupations than were employed which comprised black (34%) and Hispanic (25%) women. Meanwhile, Hispanic women (31%) and black women (28%) were more likely than white (20%) and Asian women (22%) to work in service occupations.

Women hired as police officers during the early years were given duties that did not allow or require them to work street patrol. Assignments and roles were limited to positions such as juvenile delinquency and truancy prevention, child abuse, crimes against women, and custodial functions (Bell, 1982). In 1845, New York City hired its first police "matron," and in 1888, Massachusetts and New York passed legislation requiring communities with a population over 20,000 to hire police matrons to care for female prisoners. According to More (1992), during the first half of the nineteenth century, a number of police practices were challenged, thus allowing for the initial entry of women into the police field. In 1905, the Portland (Oregon) Police Department boasted of its first woman sworn to uphold duties of a police officer; however, she did not work patrol. In 1922, the International Association of Chiefs of Police passed a resolution supporting the use of policewomen; no women worked patrol or as detectives at the time. Historically, it has been a predominant belief that women were not capable of performing the law enforcement functions of exercising authority and using force.

It was not until 1968 that the Indianapolis Police Department made history by assigning the first two female officers to patrol on an equal basis with their male colleagues (Schulz, 1995), finally overcoming this perception. Other landmarks for women in law enforcement occurred in 1985, with the appointment of the first woman chief of police in a major city (Portland, Oregon), and in 1994, with the appointment of the first African American woman chief of police in Atlanta.

Title VII of the Civil Rights Act of 1964 was discussed earlier in this chapter. This law played an important role in opening up police departments to women. Adoption of affirmative action policies, now illegal in many states, along with court orders and injunctions, also played a role in bringing more women into law enforcement. Although more women were entering law enforcement, they still encountered blatant and open skepticism, resentment, and hostility from male officers.

Historically, law enforcement agencies' requirements or standards pertaining to minimum height and weight, strength, and agility posed one of the many barriers to female entry into the police field (Polisar & Milgram, 1998). Most civil service tests modified these requirements in order to comply with court-ordered legal mandates and injunctions by the early 1980s (Balkin, 1988). However, a study published by the National Center for Women and Policing (NCWP) in 2003 concluded that there is still an adverse impact on women due to entry-level physical agility testing that eliminates a large number of women. NCWP suggests that there are other options that will yield the benefits of qualified women entering the profession and eliminate this obstacle to their being hired (Lonsway, 2003). This study is discussed more fully in Chapter 3.

Number of Women in Law Enforcement

The number of women in law enforcement remains small and is increasing only very slowly. As noted earlier, as of 2007, the latest year for which statistics are available, sworn women officers represented about 12 percent of local police departments, 6.5 percent of state agencies, and 11.2 percent of sheriffs' offices (Langton, 2010). All of these percentages showed a decline from previous years (see Exhibit 2.10). Among federal law enforcement agencies employing more than 500 full-time sworn officers, women accounted for approximately 16 percent. Over the 12-year

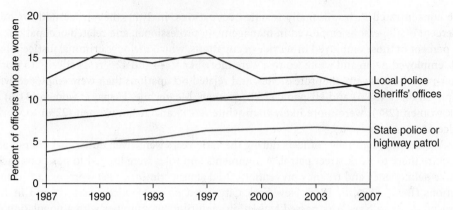

EXHIBIT 2.10   Percent of full-time sworn law enforcement officers who are women 1987-2007

Source: BJS June 2010 NCJ 230521. Retrieved from www.bjs.gov/content/pub/pdf/wle8708.pdf

period from 1996 to 2008, the percentage of women officers over all federal agencies increased slightly, from 14 percent to 15.5 percent (see Exhibit 2.11). Researchers in the late 1980s had made various predictions of the numbers of women expected to be in law enforcement professions by the turn of the twenty-first century, ranging from 47 to 55 percent of the workforce, but those predictions never materialized.

Women in local police agencies were gaining in numbers at approximately half a percentage point per year from 1987 to 2007. Women in sheriffs' offices gained in numbers between 1987 and 1990, then dropped the next three years, then increased until 1997. The trend halted or even reversed in 2003 and has continued to decline since then. Researchers studying this phenomenon believe that the decline of women in law enforcement can be attributed to the decrease in the number of consent decrees still in effect among the agencies surveyed: eight consent decrees mandating the hiring or promotion of women or minorities had expired. Also, because of the recession that began in 2007, most departments across the nation laid off the most recently hired and were not filling vacancies for budgetary reasons. This impacted the numbers of not only women, but also of minority officers within agencies.

A review of the statistics makes it clear that women are underrepresented in law enforcement. However, law enforcement was not the only field that saw a reduced number of women, as the following statement from an article based on a study by the Federal Reserve of Dallas,

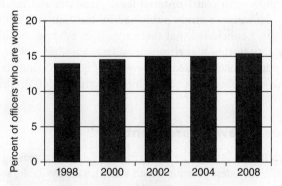

EXHIBIT 2.11   Percent of women federal law enforcement officers

Source: Women in law Enforcement, 1987-2008 June 2010, NCJ 230521. Retrieved from www.bjs.gov/content/pub/pdf/wle8708.pdf

Texas, indicates: "[S]ince the start of this decade, the workforce participation of women in prime working years—between 25 and 54—has experienced its largest sustained decline since World War II" ("More Women Leaving the Labor Market," 2005). This research found that most of the women dropping out of the workforce were educated, married, with children, and with higher incomes, and that many others were leaving to go back to school or to have families. The study did not focus on women in law enforcement, so further research is needed to verify if retention problems are occurring in this occupation for the same reasons.

Workplace Issues

The integration of women into policing and the problems with their retention have led many law enforcement chief executives, managers, and supervisors to grapple with workplace issues within their departments. Women still face some unique challenges, including overcoming the attitudes of society and of some of their male coworkers and bosses. Workplace issues confronting law enforcement agencies, and especially women in law enforcement, involve sexual harassment, gender discrimination, role barriers, the "brotherhood," a double standard, differential treatment, and career-versus-family issues.

SEXUAL HARASSMENT   The following are considered sexual harassment in the workplace:

- *Hostile environment,* which consists of unwelcome sexual behavior, such as "jokes," cartoons, posters, banter, repeated requests for dates, requests for sexual favors, references to body parts, or physical touching, that has the purpose or effect of unreasonably interfering with an individual's work performance or creating an intimidating, hostile, or offensive working environment.
- *Quid pro quo sexual harassment,* which means one is asked to perform sexual acts in return for a job benefit. For example, you are told you will pass probation, get a promotion, get a good performance evaluation, or not be written up for doing something wrong if you will engage in some type of sexual behavior.
- *Gender harassment,* which is behavior that is not based on sexual behavior but is based on gender. It is also known as sex-based harassment. Examples include comments such as "women are not brave enough to be police officers," and "women should stay home and have babies and leave policing to real men." ("Workplace Issues," 2005)

Sexual harassment can occur in a variety of circumstances including, but not limited to, the following:

1. The victim, as well as the harasser, may be a woman or a man. The victim need not be of the opposite sex.
2. The harasser can be the victim's supervisor, an agent of the employer, a supervisor in another area, a coworker, or a nonemployee.
3. The victim need not be the person harassed, but could be anyone affected by the offensive conduct.
4. Unlawful sexual harassment may occur without economic injury to or discharge of the victim.
5. The harasser's conduct must be unwelcome.

Employers are encouraged to take steps necessary to prevent sexual harassment from occurring, because prevention is the best tool to eliminate sexual harassment in the workplace. They should clearly communicate to employees that sexual harassment will not be tolerated. They can do so only by establishing an effective complaint or grievance process and taking immediate and appropriate action when an employee complains ("Facts about Sexual Harassment," 2008). Although sexual harassment exists in both private and public sectors, we believe it is particularly problematic in law enforcement—an occupation that is still mostly male-dominated.

The majority of women officers interviewed for each edition of this book (who requested that their names not be used) said they had been sexually harassed in the workplace. Most of the women indicated that when male officers exhibited offensive behavior, they remained quiet for fear of negative backlash from the men. This lack of reporting can also be directly attributed to the code of silence in law enforcement agencies and the severe retaliation that occurs when women report misconduct. Even outside of law enforcement, however, women are reluctant to report harassment; "it has been estimated that only 5 to 15 percent of harassed women formally report problems of harassment to their employers or employment agencies such as the EEOC" ("Sexual Harassment in the Workplace," 2010). Those interviewed revealed that sexual harassment occurs at all levels of an organization and is not limited to male harassment of women.

Department executives must institute a zero-tolerance sexual harassment policy and send that message throughout the department. Policy-specific training must also be provided on sexual harassment and its prevention. Some departments have revised their promotional exam to include questions on the department's sexual harassment policies and procedures. The Albuquerque (New Mexico) Police Department went so far as to move the investigation of sexual harassment complaints from within the department to an external city agency with expert Equal Employment Opportunity investigators on staff. According to the Albuquerque PD, this approach tends to speed up the process, ensure impartiality, and increase confidence in the procedures. Officers who make a complaint do not have to go through the chain of command. An eight-hour police-specific training course for sworn supervisors on preventing sexual harassment, developed by the Institute for Women in Trades, Technology and Science (IWITTS), is also of value. It is presented in a case-study format that analyzes police legal cases, and it has been highly rated by those who have attended. The IWITTS course provides those who attend with a "Law Enforcement Assessment Tools" kit, which enables law enforcement agencies to conduct a self-assessment and develop a strategic plan to recruit women, prevent sexual harassment, and ensure fair promotion.

When harassment takes place, the results can be devastating in terms of the involved employees' careers, the internal environment of the organization, and the department's public image. The importance of training all law enforcement employees (sworn and nonsworn) on the issues of sexual harassment cannot be stressed enough. The once male-dominated occupation of law enforcement is in a process of transition to a multicultural work environment, with increased representation of both men and women with differing cultural identities in race, ethnicity, and sexual orientation. As judicious policies and directives are put in place in this new environment, and training and procedures are developed and presented, sexual harassment can be expected to decrease. Training on discrimination and sexual harassment should deal not only with legal and liability issues but also with deep-seated attitudes about differences.

GENDER DISCRIMINATION Gender discrimination occurs when a person is subjected to unequal treatment in the workplace on the basis of sex. A few examples of what might constitute workplace gender discrimination are:

- Assigning women to jobs or programs that are considered "traditionally women's" instead of the nontraditional positions such as SWAT teams, K9, gang units, and narcotics
- Using tests for promotions or other job opportunities that are not job-related or represent a small part of the job duties, which result in women not getting promoted at the same rate that men are promoted
- Holding women to a higher or different level on performance evaluations
- Not giving women equal consideration for specialized training, conferences, specialty job assignments, and the like
- Not giving pregnant women light duty, but giving such assignments to men who are injured off-duty ("Workplace Issues," 2005).

The federal Pregnancy Discrimination Act (PDA) requires employers to treat "women affected by pregnancy, childbirth or related conditions" the same "as other persons not so affected but similar in their ability or inability to work" ("Pregnancy Discrimination & Temporary Disability," n.d.). One of the biggest complaints from pregnant sworn officers is that when they notify their department that they are pregnant, they are removed from their position and there is little or no effort to find a light-duty position. Discrimination on the basis of pregnancy, childbirth, or a related medical condition is discrimination on the basis of gender. Nor may a law enforcement agency refuse to preserve a job for an employee on maternity leave when it protects the jobs of others temporarily disabled; deny seniority status upon return from maternity leave; or refuse to grant pension service time for the period of leave unless other disabled employees are similarly disadvantaged. City, county, state, and federal employers must know the laws pertaining to such workplace issues and train their employees accordingly to avoid costly lawsuits. For example, the National Center for Women and Policing (NCWP) has produced a document titled "Model Pregnancy Policy Guidelines," which should be referred to for more information.

ROLE BARRIERS   Barriers and hostility toward women in the workplace based on gender have diminished, both in the general population and within law enforcement. For example, ideas about protection differ by gender—who protects whom? In American society, women may protect children, but it has more socially acceptable and traditional for men to protect women. In the act of protecting, the protectors become dominant and the protected become subordinate. Although this gender-role perception has not completely broken down, especially in the law enforcement and corrections workforce, it is subsiding because of the number of women and young male officers in those professions today. There are now fewer veteran male officers who have never worked with women. Many veteran police and correctional officers initially had difficulty with the transition as women came into the dangerous, male-dominated, nontraditional occupations that men felt required "male" strength and abilities. The result has been described as a clash between cultures— the once male-dominated workforce versus the new one in which women are integral parts of the organizational environment. The veteran male police or correctional officers, socially conditioned to protect women, often feel that in addition to working with inmates or violent persons on the streets, they have the added responsibility of protecting the women officers with whom they work.

These feelings, attitudes, and perceptions can make men and women in law enforcement positions uncomfortable with each other. Women sometimes feel patronized, overprotected, or merely tolerated rather than appreciated and respected for their work. Again, these attitudes and perceptions are diminishing as many in the new generation of male officers are more willing to accept women in law enforcement. In our numerous interviews with veteran officers, we found that, with few exceptions, women were generally accepted by men, but the acceptance was related to how well a specific woman performed her duties.

According to Retired Sergeant Betsy Brantner Smith (personal communication), there are fewer role barriers to women in law enforcement than in the past. Although still not a perfect world, there are more opportunities for women in special assignments and promotions if they prepare themselves to meet the standards and requirements. She says that women must make an effort to be "marketable" for the position they want, whether it be a promotion or special assignment, and that they need to raise their competency level and acquire the skill sets, knowledge, and abilities required for the position. Smith further added that when we strive to treat everyone equally, we, in fact, run the risk of ignoring gender differences and this may end up being the wrong thing to do. Smith believes that we should admit that we are not all equal, pointing out that the word, diversity does not mean equality, but rather the state of being different. (Smith, personal communication, 2013).

> Many leaders and managers attempt to treat everyone equally by ignoring gender differences or by going to the opposite extreme and overcompensating. An example of overcompensation would be retaining and promoting women on the basis of gender and not their competence. Most women cops would much rather work for a male boss who knows how to lead and treats people fairly rather than for an incompetent female boss. Just making a department look more diverse should not be the objective. (Smith, personal communication, 2013)

THE BROTHERHOOD   Women who are accepted into the "brotherhood" of police or correctional officers have generally had to become "one of the guys." (Refer to Chapter 4 for more information on how language used in the brotherhood excludes women.) According to Susan Jones, former Chief of Police of the Healdsburg (California) Police Department and now mayor of that city, the term *brotherhood* still exists today, along with the associated behaviors. Jones hopes that one day there will be just the "family of law enforcement" (Jones, 2013). The term *brotherhood* is outdated in today's coed law enforcement environment, and those who still use it demonstrate a lack of cultural competency. Sergeant Betsy Brantner Smith (2013) said that while she agrees that "the family of law enforcement" is also valid, she doesn't see *brotherhood* as a negative term, as it describes what it is.

Often a woman who tries to act like one of the guys (be part of the brotherhood) on the street or in a jail or prison is considered too hard, too coldhearted, or too unemotional and may be criticized by peers and supervisors. Although perhaps this is a little exaggerated, some women have been described as "Jane Waynes" because they swagger, swear, spit, and are highly aggressive. Yet if a female officer is too feminine or not sufficiently aggressive, men will not take her seriously and she will not do well either in police or in correctional work. So women are confronted with a dilemma: They must be aggressive enough to do the job but feminine enough to be acceptable to male peers, and they must also be able to take different approaches to problems.

When women feel compelled to behave like men in the workplace, the results can be counterproductive and can even result in disciplinary action. Women may feel that to succeed they have to stay within the narrow bands of acceptable behavior and exhibit only certain traditionally masculine or feminine qualities. Walking this fine line is difficult. This phenomenon is not unique to law enforcement, as women in construction trades, historically male-dominated turf, have asserted.

Studies have found that most women police officers have a different style of policing, a "service-oriented style," and they see their roles as peace restorers (Skolnick & Bayley, 1988), while male officers typically view their roles as crime fighters and use physical force more often than their women counterparts. According to a 2010 study by the National Center for Women and Policing, which involved seven major U.S. police agencies,

> Women officers are substantially less likely than their male counterparts to be involved in problems of excessive force. . . . Given that women currently comprise 12.7% of sworn personnel in big city police agencies, we would expect that female officers in these agencies should be involved in approximately 12.7% of the citizen complaints, sustained allegations, or payouts for excessive force. Yet the data indicate that only 5% of the citizen complaints for excessive force and 2% of the sustained allegations of excessive force in large agencies involve female officers. The average male officer is two to three times more likely than the average female officer to have a citizen name him in a complaint of excessive force. ("Men, Women, and Police Excessive Force: A Tale of Two Genders," 2010)

Captain Keith Foster, a veteran of the Fresno (California) Police Department, suggests that the differences in officers' willingness to use force to resolve conflict may be explained by men being, in most cases, inherently stronger than women:

> Some might suggest that male officers are more concerned with improving their physical characteristics [i.e., strength training and tactical skills] rather than their intellectual capacities [i.e., persuasion and negotiation skills]. This notion may be due to the belief that strength counts when persuasion and negotiation fail. Generally speaking, female police officers often rely on negotiation, persuasion, and effective communication to resolve conflict. (Foster, 2006)

Foster's study suggests that most women who come into law enforcement with limited upper body strength or knowledge of arrest and control techniques develop physical strength and become proficient in the tactics of arrest over time. He asserts, however, that "female police officers never forget how to use their most valuable tool in law enforcement—their ability to prevent and/or defuse conflict rather than provoking it and/or responding to it" (Foster, 2006).

Sergeant Kathy Bierstedt, who recently retired from a large police department in Florida, said that "usually men are physically stronger than women. But even so, women can use this to their advantage when arresting a male subject. Because it's a given that a male is stronger, he usually does not feel the need to prove his masculinity by fighting with a female officer. However, in a confrontation with a male officer, the male subject might feel the need to prove 'he's a man,' and fight back with the male officer" (Bierstedt, 2013). Sgt. Kathy Bierstedt related that on many occasions she had told an aggressive male that he was stronger and would probably win if he resisted arrest, but that he could let her handcuff him and go quietly with dignity. If not, she could have other officers respond to subdue him, at which time, he would likely receive injuries as well as additional charges for resisting arrest and the battery of the officers. That seldom failed to ensure compliance. Verbal skills are a must not only for the female officers, but for all officers.

The sergeant, mentioned earlier, explained that "gender intelligence is important to understand. Most women officers instinctively will utilize verbal skills to handle situations wherein a male officer may resort to force more quickly." However, she questioned whether men and women law enforcement and corrections trainers are trained to teach these verbal skills to both genders. If not, she suggested, they should be (Smith, 2013). Another woman police officer said her approach was to work every job in the department, including gangs, narcotics, sex crimes, and street patrol. She was one of the first women hired by a West Coast Police Department in 1980, and, she said, "I got tough. I didn't want a reputation for being a softy." She summarized the different approach to law enforcement this way: "Women can do (police work), we just don't get in as many fights" (wished to remain anonymous). Additionally, women officers, and especially those who are members of minority groups, often feel that they have to go out of their way to prove themselves, including putting on a brave face.

A DOUBLE STANDARD   Interviews with women officers for each edition of this book showed clearly that the majority felt they had to perform better than male officers just to be considered equal—a double standard. These women spoke of how they imposed pressures on themselves to perform up to or exceed the expectations of their male peers. (Note that minority, gay, and lesbian employees often express the same sentiment.) One female officer explained that many women were using a community policing philosophy long before it became the practice of their agency. She mentioned that when she tried to do problem solving, she was criticized in her evaluations. Her supervisor rated her negatively for "trying too hard to find solutions to complainants' problems" and said she "spends too much time on calls explaining procedures" and "gets too involved" (Jones, 2013). Today, however, women police officers report that the double standard is less common because of the emphasis that law enforcement places on community policing. Now this approach is seen as the norm and is expected of all officers (Jones, 2013).

DIFFERENTIAL TREATMENT   Many women in law enforcement, when interviewed for prior editions of this text, indicated that they were treated differently from men by staff members. They said that they were frequently held back from promotions or special assignments in areas like special weapons and tactics, homicide investigations, and motorcycle units because of the perception that these are "male" jobs. They reported feeling that they were also held back from training for these assignments and were not promoted at the same rate as men. Over the years, some change has occurred: More women officers are now serving in special assignment and showing no special problems with performance. However, a study regarding women participating on special weapons and tactical (SWAT) teams concluded that "Although the research is exploratory and the findings are difficult to generalize, the results suggest that law enforcement's militaristic nature and role specialization continue to impede integrating female officers into

SWAT subcultures." The study indicated that although male SWAT members surveyed were somewhat receptive to women on the team, they generally felt that women lacked the needed strength and skills ("Women on SWAT Teams: Separate but Equal?" 2011).

Police executives must determine if their female officers are receiving equal opportunities for assignments and training that will provide the groundwork and preparation for their eventual promotion. They need to determine if female officers are applying for promotions in numbers proportionate to their representation in the department. If not, perhaps women officers need encouragement from their supervisors, mentors, and informal network associates. It is also possible that the promotion process disproportionately screens out female officers. Research shows that the more subjective the process is, the less likely women are to be promoted. The use of assessment center and "hands-on" testing is said to offer some safeguards against the potential for the perception of bias against women. Utilizing structured interviews and selecting interview board members who represent different races and both sexes can also minimize this risk. Many departments are now training interview board members on interviewing techniques. The IWITTS has developed a well-received half-day training session for supervisors, "Creating a Supportive Work Environment," to address issues of integration and retention of women.

CAREER VERSUS FAMILY Women in law enforcement are faced with another dilemma—trying to raise a family and have a successful career, two goals that are often difficult to combine. Women, especially single parents, who had children when they entered law enforcement frequently find that they have difficulty balancing their commitments to family and work. If they had children after entering the occupation, they may be confronted with inadequate pregnancy policies and maternity-leave policies (see earlier discussion). In both cases, women often feel a sense of guilt, stress, and frustration in trying to both do well in a job and maintain a family. Progressive criminal law enforcement organizations offer innovative work schedules, modified duty assignments during pregnancy, child care programs, mentoring and support groups, and a positive work atmosphere for women. Such programs benefit all employees within the organization. Today, men are taking a more active role in parenting and family; therefore, child care, creative work schedules, and even maternity or parental leave should be of importance to them as well.

Sergeant Kathy Bierstedt, mentioned earlier, said that during the hiring process, officers sign a document that informs them they are required to work various shifts and sites, including graveyard. The form also notifies them that assignments are based upon seniority. However, based upon extenuating circumstances, such as a severely ill family member, they can submit a "hardship" request. If granted, it is a one-time exception and only for a period of one shift change, approximately four months. This is to allow time to make arrangements as necessary. This "hardship" is usually requested for officers in Uniform Patrol, as specialized units make adjustments as their staffing needs allow. Also, having children does not constitute a "hardship." She also said that women with children in a two-parent home are reminded that their spouse should also care for their child or children in the event this was needed (Bierstedt, 2013).

Mentor and Informal Networking Programs for Women

Women's performance and attitudes can be enhanced if they have access to a **mentor** and to **informal network** programs. The mentor provides information, advice, support, and encouragement to someone who is less experienced. Mentoring involves leading, developing, and guiding by example to facilitate the protégé's personal development, for the benefit of both the individual and the organization. There is a great deal of research on the topic of mentoring and networking for women as well as for minorities. Law enforcement management is well advised to consult these studies, the information from which will contribute to the successful creation of such programs.

Mentor   A trusted counselor or guide.

Informal networks   A system of influential colleagues who can, because of their position or power within an organization, connect the employee with information, resources, or other contacts helpful to the employee's promotion or special-assignment prospects.

Usually mentoring occurs in a one-on-one coaching context over a period of time through suggestions, advice, and support on the job. There are many reasons for law enforcement agencies to provide for or encourage the use of mentor and support programs. Studies over the years have found that women who had one or more mentors reported greater job success and job satisfaction than women who did not have a mentor. Lack of access to such networks can be a key barrier to promotions and special assignments. Sgt. Smith firmly believes in mentoring as a tool to improve and build the person mentored, either male or female, to make them more successful (Smith, personal communications, 2013). In an article she wrote for *PoliceOne*, she said, "Find a mentor, preferably several, but choose wisely. Look for not only supervisors and FTOs, but informal leaders in the organization as well as other personnel from other agencies. Make sure they have good reputations and good attitudes, and that you adhere to the chain of command. Surround yourself with positive people in general; it makes life easier" (Smith, 2013).

The *Catalyst* Barriers series focuses on women's perception that lack of access to networks of influential colleagues is a key barrier to promotions and special assignments to women in the workforce. The report states:

> This issue is particularly pronounced for women of color who face "double exclusion" in the workplace, based on both their gender and race/ethnicity. In fact, lack of access to networks of influential colleagues underlies all major barriers identified by women of color, including lack of influential mentors or sponsors (as one needs connections with others to obtain mentors and sponsors); lack of company role models of the same racial/ethnic group (reflecting a shortage of similar others who might form part of an influential network); and lack of high-visibility assignments (which are often facilitated by personal relationships with those wielding influence). ("Connections that Count," 2006)

Several associations provide an organized voice for the interests of women in policing: the International Association of Women Police (IAWP), the National Association of Women Law Enforcement Executives (NAWLEE), and the National Center for Women and Policing (NCWP). The NAWLEE focuses on helping women to strengthen their leadership roles in policing, while the NCWP focuses on growth and leadership. However, while these organizations provide excellent resources, they cannot take the place of departmental, in-house mentoring programs or informal networks for women.

In both *Catalyst* Barriers surveys, Latinas and Asian American women said they encounter stereotypes in the workplace. Asian women said they often feel overlooked by their organizations' diversity programs, in part, because they are labeled "overachievers" who don't require specific diversity efforts. Both reports suggest that managers should encourage more experienced Asian American women and Latinas to serve as mentors for younger women, as well as make more of an attempt to understand the cultural background of their diverse workforce. It is stressed, however, that those in need of a mentor should be able to "choose from a wide range of networking opportunities. Women of color should not be limited to networking only with people of their own race or ethnicity, nor should they feel compelled to network exclusively with others in the work environment who do not share their cultural background" ("Connections that Count," 2006).

The Transition of Women into Law Enforcement

Although women are still a minority in numbers, they now see themselves as at least equal to and perhaps even more capable than their male peers. They perceive that their working conditions have improved and that there is less harassment than in the past. Now a woman's ability to perform the job is increasingly less likely to be measured by traditional standards. For example, verbal communication skills are equally and potentially more important than physical strength (after all, an officer's nondefensive communication can help to defuse many situations where aggressive behavior may otherwise occur). The progress of women in law enforcement can also be seen in leadership. There have been many women who have worked their way up the ranks and serve as Chiefs of Police or Sheriffs in small and large agencies across the country. And in March 2013, the president "named 30-year veteran Secret Service agent Julia Pierson as the agency's first female director, signaling his desire to change the culture at the male dominated service" ("Obama picks first female Secret Service chief," 2013).

SEXUAL ORIENTATION IN LAW ENFORCEMENT

The terms *homosexual, lesbian, gay, bisexual, transgender*, and *LGBT* are used in our discussion of sexual orientation.

Homosexual   Of or relating to people who are physically, romantically, and/or emotionally attracted to people of the same gender.

Gay   A male homosexual. (See Glossary for additional information)

Lesbian   A homosexual woman. (See Glossary for additional information)

LGBT   Common initialism for "lesbian, gay, bisexual, and transgender."

Bisexual   Of or relating to people who are physically, romantically, sexually, and/or emotionally attracted to both men and women.

Transgender   Of or relating to a person who identifies as a different gender from their gender as assigned at birth. Covers a range of people, including heterosexual cross-dressers, homosexual drag queens, and transsexuals who believe they were born in the wrong body, and may take hormones or undergo a sex change operation to alter their gender.

Most authors and police administrators group "gay" and "lesbian" together as if the experiences of the two groups are identical. However, nowhere is the dichotomy more visible than within law enforcement. Many officers still assume that "macho" women are lesbians and that stereotypically "feminine" women are heterosexual, although such mapping of gender roles onto sexual orientation is frequently erroneous. This topic is discussed later in this chapter.

Policy versus Practice

According to Mitchell Grobeson (2013), a retired Los Angeles Police Department sergeant who is gay, the past two decades have seen the removal of the explicit ban on employing gay men and lesbians by most law enforcement agencies. Some agencies did so out of fear of litigation and negative publicity, and some because research indicated gay men and lesbians should not be excluded from law enforcement professions. The rejection of homosexuals in law enforcement by some agencies continues, although surreptitiously, despite studies that have shown that the presence of openly LGBT personnel enhanced service and did not negatively impact morale or unit cohesion in integrated police departments. A deputy chief of a large department, one of the highest-ranking openly gay officers, told *Frontiers* magazine that in terms of how gay and lesbian officers are treated currently, "The discrimination is much more sophisticated than discrimination in the past . . ." (Brooke, 2005).

Recruitment

Law enforcement administrators seeking to have a workforce on parity with their community need to be cognizant of artificial barriers. To ensure equal opportunity, it is important to conduct applicant tracking, in which applicant information is taken at an event and contact with the applicant is maintained to determine if the applicant is hired or at which point in the process he or she is disqualified. If a disproportionate number of these applicants are failing during a specific part of the hiring process, such as oral interviews, background investigations, or polygraph exams, then administrators must be able to capture this information starting from the original point of contact. Further, this approach can help determine if committing resources for LGBT events or advertisements is an effective use of public funds. Another area to monitor to determine if a department provides equal opportunity is the number of openly gay and lesbian officers who voluntarily participate in events within the LGBT communities and the number of those who are willing to be named when interviewed by the mainstream media.

The Controversy

Some police officers view openly gay and lesbian individuals as extremist militant types who publicly display their sexuality in offensive or socially unacceptable ways. This is a stereotype; most LGBT officers do not draw attention to their sexual orientation any more than do heterosexual officers who display framed photographs of their significant other on their desks or in their lockers. Concerns about homosexuals in the military or in law enforcement used to include beliefs that gay soldiers or police officers will walk hand in hand, dance together at clubs, make passes at non-gay colleagues, or display other socially unacceptable aspects of their private lives. These arguments for bans are not based in reality, however, since most gays in the military and the criminal justice system are as work-oriented as their heterosexual colleagues. They do not wish to provoke anyone in the system; rather, like most other officers, homosexual officers want to accomplish their missions, work special assignments, be promoted, and avoid confrontation. In fact, gay and lesbian officers and military personnel are much less likely than their heterosexual counterparts to engage in behaviors that draw attention away from their occupational performance (Grobeson, 2013). Gay and lesbian officers are no different from others in wanting to support the disciplinary processes, and they believe that any inappropriate conduct should be handled with proper discipline.

Research at the beginning of the twenty-first century on the subject of homosexuals in the military and in law enforcement concluded that the presence of gays and lesbians has not caused morale to drop in either setting. The research also determined that there were no negative consequences within urban police departments that adopt nondiscrimination statutes and actively recruit and hire homosexual officers.

Differences in Treatment of Gay versus Lesbian Officers

Many law enforcement professionals have voiced opinions that because of the "macho" requirements of police work, a double standard exists with respect to the way gay and lesbian officers are viewed. The traditional male dominance of the profession has made it difficult for many male officers to accept that women or gay men are equally able to perform the same tasks they do. They view their work as an occupation for only the "strongest and the toughest." Male officers' self-esteem can be threatened by the ability of women and gay men to do "their" job. (This issue has already been discussed under the section "Women in Law Enforcement.")

According to Grobeson, there has been a trend of acceptance of "macho" lesbians into law enforcement. Many male officers are more accepting of lesbian officers, particularly those who are not openly homosexual, than they are of heterosexual women. It appears that male officers are more fearful that "feminine" women will not provide them with sufficient backup where physicality is required. They are more willing to rely on lesbian officers, whom they stereotype as being macho and athletic. Grobeson believes that there is still a degree of discrimination directed toward women who break the cultural mores and choose to be open or apparent about their sexual orientation.

In addition, the pervasive stereotype of gay men as effeminate remains a factor in most officers' bias against the hiring of and working with gay men. Allowing openly gay men to serve as officers is perceived by many as threatening to the macho image of police work: If a gay man can successfully complete the necessary tasks, then their job is less macho. Further, those officers whose self-image is based on their job, perceiving themselves as "John Wayne," are generally the most uncomfortable with the concept of working with gay officers.

Grobeson asserts that gay men are relegated to the least desirable status of any minority group in terms of acceptance in police culture. Homophobic jokes and nicknames, for example, are still prevalent locker room banter, whereas racial epithets have mostly been eliminated. One stereotype characterizes effeminate men as unworthy of trust as partners, despite the fact that many gay officers are military combat veterans with awards and accolades for bravery, heroism, and service under fire.

Gay male officers also assert that management in some law enforcement agencies serving large LGBT populations gives preferential treatment to lesbian officers. These assignments have included recruitment, background investigation, internal affairs/management control, community relations, and liaisons from the chief's office. There have been two reasons cited for this reverse discrimination: first, managers get a "3-for" in which their selection is approved by personnel departments and policymakers because it fulfills affirmative action obligations in as many as three protected categories: gender, sexual orientation, and, often, ethnicity or race. Second, law enforcement managers believe that by involving lesbian officers in both the disqualification of gay male applicants and in disciplinary actions against gay officers, they have decreased their liability with regard to claims of bias based upon sexual orientation. In short, lesbian officers are used against gay men, as well as against their fellow lesbian officers, to avoid claims of sexual orientation discrimination or harassment (Grobeson, 2013).

The Transition of LGBT Individuals into Law Enforcement

Problems sometimes surface within law enforcement agencies as gay and lesbian officers "come out of the closet." Many organizations and employees have been hesitant to welcome such a major change and have resisted it unless measures were taken to allay their fears. In many agencies, officers thought to be or who are openly gay or lesbian have encountered discriminatory treatment and/or hostility because of other employees' negative stereotypes and attitudes. In addition, people without proper education on acquired immune deficiency syndrome (AIDS) have expressed fear of transmission solely due to a male officer's perceived sexual orientation. This and other fears may mean that gay men will have an even more difficult time assimilating into departments than ethnic or racial minorities, heterosexual women, or lesbians.

As more officers who are openly gay or lesbian are recruited and hired or "come out of the closet," the law enforcement organizational atmosphere will undoubtedly become more tolerant. Individual and group prejudices and assumptions about LGBT employees, for example, will be challenged. Because of the small number of openly gay and lesbian officers in law enforcement today, especially within small agencies, there are currently few policies dealing specifically with inappropriate displays of sexuality; obviously, discipline would have to be applied equally to both the homosexual and the heterosexual officers who behave unprofessionally. Among gay and lesbian law enforcement officers, however, there is a strong desire to conform to the norms of the organization and to prove their worth as members of that organization. Law enforcement agencies should have written policies to assist gay and lesbian officers' transition into the department as well as operational plans to promote employee acceptance of these officers.

With notable exceptions such as the San Francisco Sheriff's Department and the police departments of San Francisco, San Diego, and New York, the presence of openly gay and

lesbian officers within law enforcement agencies is relatively
important that agency officials establish openly gay and lesb
munity. This assignment provides role models to qualified L(
career in law enforcement. Critically, with the increasing pre
gives an agency the ability to provide victims with the exper
officers, which will likely elicit both cooperation and informati
come of an investigation. Police officials realized years ago tha
provide women rape victims the comfort of being interviewed
is duplicated when it comes to LGBT hate crime victims (see (
the reticence of LGBT crime victims to come forward due to the
enforcement personnel, the availability of an LGBT officer help
victimization." In the end, the community as a whole, as well as t
benefit from the presence of such forthright and honest personne

Part 1 • Impact of Cultural Diversity on Law E

However,
governments
punish ins
ing the
priv

68

Policies against Discrimination and Harassment

Even though there have been gains in the reduction of discriminatio
employees after decades of complaints and lawsuits, the practice still   ome of these
high-profile cases have resulted in millions of dollars of jury awards and settlements by city,
county, and state employers nationwide. A few of those include:

- California: The Los Angeles City Council approved a $1.5 million settlement in a case
  involving a gay police officer who alleged he was the victim of harassment and retaliation
  by a supervisor. ("Sgt. Ronald Crump, Gay LAPD Officer, To Receive $1.5 Million Settle-
  ment in Harassment Lawsuit," 2013).
- New Jersey: The town of Dover settled an employment discrimination suit brought by a
  lesbian police sergeant in 2008 for $750,000. She claimed she was harassed and discrimi-
  nated against because of her gender and sexual orientation. (Kwoh, 2008)
- New York: The city of New York, based on a jury verdict in 2007, paid an NYPD sergeant
  $500,000 for employment discrimination based on the perception that he was gay. A lieu-
  tenant and captain sued for retaliation for speaking out against it. Each recovered approximately $500,000 in a jury verdict. ("N.Y. Jury Charges $1.5M to City," 2007)

Statutes and Company Policy Pertaining to Discrimination Based on Sexual Orientation

Discrimination based on an individual's sexual orientation occurs in both private and government workplaces. An employee of the federal government is protected from sexual orientation
discrimination in the workplace. However, unlike race, gender, and other types of discrimination
covered by EEOC laws, no single law applies to ban such misconduct across the nation uniformly.
On November 7, 2013, Senate Bill 815 (S.815), Employment Non-Discrimination Act of 2013,
was passed by the Senate and sent to the House of Representatives. The legislation was referred by
the House of Representatives on January 8, 2014, to the Subcommittee on the Constitution and
Civil Justice.

S.815 prohibits covered entities (employers, employment agencies, labor organizations, or
joint labor-management committees) from engaging in employment discrimination on the basis
of an individual's actual or perceived sexual orientation or gender identity. The legislation provides
an exception from this protection to religious organizations and to non-profit membership-only
clubs. Under S.815, employers would be prohibited from making decisions about hiring, firing,
promoting or compensating an employee based on sexual orientation or gender identity. S.815
would also prohibit preferential treatment of gay, lesbian, bisexual, and transgendered employees
as well as using quotas requiring an employer to hire a certain number of such employees. Similar
legislation has been introduced in previous Congresses since 1974 without being passed.

ue to a growing awareness of the issue within some cities, counties, and state
and private companies, more and more employers have taken steps to prevent and
ances of sexual orientation discrimination. The following states (almost half, includ-
District of Columbia) have laws that prohibit sexual orientation discrimination in both
ate and public workplaces. As of 2013, these states include:

California	Colorado	Connecticut	Hawaii	Illinois
Iowa	Maine	Maryland	Massachusetts	Minnesota
Nevada	New Hampshire	New Jersey	New Mexico	New York
Oregon	Rhode Island	Vermont	Washington	Wisconsin

If a state does not have such a law, the city, county, or law enforcement agency should adopt an antidiscrimination policy with regard to sexual orientation or gender identity in the workplace. There are a few states that prohibit sexual orientation discrimination only in public workplaces, such as for state employees: Delaware, Indiana, Michigan, Montana, and Pennsylvania. In some states, city and county governments have established policies against sexual orientation workplace discrimination in the form of city ordinances. There are also some companies that have enacted policies that prohibit sexual orientation discrimination and impose disciplinary actions against those who do discriminate.

The EEOC court decisions have ruled that sexual orientation and transgender discrimination by federal employees is unlawful. The Commission has also found that claims by lesbian, gay, and bisexual individuals alleging sex stereotyping are entitled to a sex discrimination claim under Title VII of the Civil Rights Act of 1964. (See *Veretto v. U.S. Postal Service*, EEOC Appeal No. 0120110873, July 1, 2011; *Castello v. U.S. Postal Service*, EEOC Request No. 0520110649, Dec. 20, 2011.) The EEOC recently held that discrimination by federal agencies and employees against an individual because that person is transgender (also known as gender identity discrimination) is discrimination because of sex and therefore is covered under Title VII. (See *Macy v. Department of Justice*, EEOC Appeal No. 0120120821, April 20, 2012.)

Some court cases that seek to protect LGBT personnel are filed as class action lawsuits because state and local ordinances prohibiting harassment and discrimination are seldom used. Even where there are policies in place, often there is neither enforcement nor means of forcing compliance by the law enforcement agency. Municipalities often choose to settle lawsuits rather than risk a court trial. The elimination of discrimination and harassment of LGBT employees should remain an area of concern to agency leadership, whose success in preventing the development of a hostile workplace environment will have the added benefit of fewer lawsuits.

> The chief executive must establish departmental policies and regulations regarding LGBT officers. These policies must clearly state that discrimination, harassment, and failure to assist fellow LGBT officers are unacceptable and will result in severe disciplinary action. The chief executive must obtain the support of his or her supervisors and managers to ensure that the intent of these rules, policies, and procedures is clear and that all employees adhere to these regulations. All employees must be held accountable, and those who do not support these antidiscrimination policies should not be promoted or awarded special assignments. Department executives must be aware that gay and lesbian officers might not report victimization by other employees.

City or county officials must support and possibly even champion legislation. Any proposed or enacted policy should establish that:

- Sexual orientation is not a hindrance in hiring, retention, or promotion.
- Hiring is based solely on merit and all individuals meet objective standards of employment.
- Hiring is done on the basis of identical job-related standards and criteria for all individuals.

Law enforcement managers and supervisors must routinely check to ensure that the policy is being carried out as intended.

Training on Gay, Lesbian, and Transgender Issues

Cultural awareness programs that train department personnel on diversity within communities and in the workforce must also educate employees on LGBT issues. The training should address and demonstrate the falsehood of stereotypes and myths. It must also cover legal rights, including a discussion of statutes and departmental policies on nondiscrimination and the penalties for violating them. These penalties include liability for acts of harassment and discrimination. Often, involving openly gay or lesbian officers (from other agencies, if necessary) in these training programs provides the best outcome. Ideally, this training will enable employees to know the gay or lesbian officers they work with as human beings, reduce personal prejudices, and dispel false assumptions, and thus change behavior. This type of training furthers the ideal of respect for all people. A secondary benefit of this training is the decreased likelihood of personnel complaints and lawsuits by gay or lesbian employees or community members against a city, county, or individual officer.

For a nondiscrimination policy to be implemented effectively, managers must provide regular and ongoing training at all levels of their department (see curricula in the Instructor's Manual associated with this textbook). The RAND National Defense Research Institute conducted a study on the compatibility of homosexuality within the U.S. military, which was published in 1993 and remains one of the best resources on the topic of diversity training today. The RAND study addressed the efficacy of types of training on LGBT issues relative to both military and paramilitary (law enforcement) organizations. The finding was one that had been supported by many law enforcement trainers, including those in the San Francisco Police Department, and was contrary to the positions maintained by a number of LGBT community and professional groups. The report stated that because homophobic attitudes are present among the rank and file, and because sensitivity training and similar programs usually provoke resentment rather than tolerance, the emphasis on training is most successful when it focuses on strict standards of professional conduct and behavior. According to Grobeson (2013), this is the strategic difference between "diversity" training (which is marked by role playing and command officer disciplinary statements) versus "sensitivity" training (which is what is usually presented by LGBT groups within the business and professional community). Grobeson also points out that localized surveys have shown that due to the media, acceptance of gay men and lesbians is increasing among younger generations. The increasing tolerance may improve the ability to host effective recruit academy training on many LGBT issues, especially as young gay or lesbian recruit officers are gradually becoming more willing to be open about their sexual orientation. Grobeson is quick to point out that such may still not be the case for in-service training for officers, with tenured veterans tending to be the most vocal opinion leaders. Grobeson states that this tendency has proven true among current military veterans, who often comprise a primary hiring pool for law enforcement agencies.

Cultural diversity training, which is much more confrontational than sensitivity training but is not abrasive, challenges officers' current attitudes without being condescending. In measuring officers' attitudes, beliefs, feelings, and knowledge, this type of training has been shown to have a positive impact. The training uses simulated situations in which officers deal with partners who are gay. Managers and supervisors are required to handle situations in which a fellow officer is being harassed for perceived homosexuality. Such presentations are most successful when conducted by gay or lesbian officers who are experienced diversity trainers, but this is not to suggest that trainers will be qualified or successful merely because of their sexual orientation.

It is recommended that the training include discussion panels made up of local LGBT community members, business owners, service providers, and community groups, as well as representatives of gay youth services. For supervisors and managers, additional panels comprising attorneys, including municipal attorneys who prosecute hate crimes and those who specialize in defense work dealing with homosexual arrestees, HIV issues, and sexual orientation employment discrimination, should be provided.

DOMESTIC VIOLENCE IN LGBT RELATIONSHIPS   Another new critical area for law enforcement training pertaining to the LGBT community involves the issue of domestic violence. Just as in heterosexual relationships, domestic violence occurs among gay and lesbian couples, and in all cases, it is very problematic. In fact, "the percentage of domestic violence among homosexual couples is the same as straight couples—up to 33 percent, studies show" ("Manslaughter case spotlights gay domestic abuse," 2010). For police officers, domestic violence calls are often the most difficult and the most dangerous part of their job. The added problem for police officers in communities today is how to recognize and handle cases involving violence between gay domestic partners or those in a same-gender marriage. One reason that domestic violence between LGBT persons might be especially challenging for officers is the lack of training by their agencies and appropriate resources and referrals within the immediate community. According to Grobeson, for some law enforcement officers, it may be difficult to recognize such incidents, determine who the victim is, and respond effectively with appropriate action and referrals. The problem can be particularly difficult for police officers to recognize within the lesbian community because of a perception that women don't hurt each other. The fact that batterers are often skilled at presenting themselves as victims presents another problem. "Additionally, domestic partner violence can be difficult for LGBT communities to publicly acknowledge and address at a time when there is a struggle for legal recognition of LGBT relationships. Traditional domestic violence programs do not always offer services specific to LGBT victims of domestic violence, which may prevent some LGBT victims from seeking services" (Grobeson, 2013).

Another issue is that few officers are aware of "domestic partnership" laws within their jurisdiction when they are responding to incidents of LGBT domestic violence. The same problem exists in states that recently established same-gender marriage laws. As of July 2013, 13 states and the District of Columbia have legalized same-gender marriage: California, Connecticut, Delaware, Iowa, Maine, Maryland, Massachusetts, Minnesota, New Hampshire, New York, Rhode Island, Vermont, and Washington. In June 2013, the United States Supreme Court struck down the federal Defense of Marriage Act (DOMA), which had allowed states to refuse to recognize same-sex marriage laws of other states; on the same day, the court also ruled against California's Proposition 8, which had made same-gender marriage illegal in that state. New laws on same-gender marriage will require law enforcement and correctional agencies to create policies and procedures and provide training to their officers. For example, some correctional facilities allow for conjugal visits by spouses, but do not allow for same-gender privileges, which would be grounds for legal action. For those officers and deputies working in the field, when both occupants of a residence have equal standing under the law, it is no easy decision in determining who shall be forced to leave the house when responding to domestic disputes between same-gender married couples.

The rapidly changing social and legal picture also means that most officers as well as court personnel are unlikely to be knowledgeable about issues of custody, adoptions (16 states allow "joint" gay adoptions), and visitation within LGBT relationships. They also may hesitate to assist because the cases are seen as being too complicated, or there are no policies or procedures in place on how to handle these issues and situations.

The recommendations for the criminal justice system regarding LGBT domestic violence are to:

1. prepare policies, procedures, and protocol regarding victims and abusers;
2. determine what resources and referrals are available in the community for the victims and abusers;
3. develop appropriate referral and resources forms.

GENDER-NEUTRAL TERMINOLOGY   Although the total number of LGBT marriages and adoptions is low, the statistics make it clear that not only have the numbers increased, but also that they are continuing to increase substantially both small and large cities throughout the

United States. Police and sheriff academies and in-service training courses will have to rewrite their curricula to train instructors to use gender-neutral terminology. No longer should a responding law enforcement officer ask simple questions such as, "Is your mother or father home?" Instead, in both written materials and in verbal commands, instructors will need to provide training that uses terms such as, "Is your parent or guardian at home?" This makes the parties—especially juveniles—feel more comfortable and law enforcement agencies more professional and progressive. It is also more courteous by allowing for inclusion of gay or lesbian parents, whether single or legally recognized couples consisting of two fathers or two mothers.

TRANSGENDER POLICIES, PROTOCOL, AND TRAINING Most law enforcement personnel are unlikely to have had any significant contact with members of the transgender community prior to or even during their careers, depending upon where they work. Most problems for police officers in their encounters with transgender individuals involve a lack of experience, education, training, department policy and procedure, or protocol. According to Grobeson (2013) and a study by Galvan and Bazargan (2012) for the UCLA Williams Institute, in communities where there are transgender persons, the relationship between law enforcement and those members continues to be one that demands attention. According to the National Coalition of Anti-Violence (NCAV) Projects, police harassment and brutality against transgender individuals continues to be one of the largest areas of complaints of misconduct against law enforcement and corrections personnel. According to the NCAV, of the 6,450 transgender and gender-nonconforming respondents contacted in the 2011 National Transgender Discrimination Survey who had interacted with police, 22 percent reported being subjected to harassment or abuse—with the rate being much higher for transgender people of color. Almost 50 percent of transgender individuals surveyed stated that if they were the victim of a hate crime, they would not be comfortable reporting it to the police. ("Ask Lambda Legal: Transgender Community and Police," 2013).

Police officers are the protectors of individuals in a diverse society that includes LGBT people. Although we recognize that these officers are human and entitled to their personal beliefs, they cannot display biased behavior or engage in discriminatory actions. Police officers who are prejudiced against LGBT people must still uphold their rights. When prejudice or bias by an officer results in an overt discriminatory act, he or she must be appropriately punished. Officers also cannot remain silent if they witness a harassing or discriminatory act or crime of any kind committed by fellow employees. These same officers must maintain a good working relationship with peers who may be different from themselves. Police officers represent the entire community. Any discriminatory act they commit while on (or off) duty can bring dishonor not only to them but also to their agency, the community they serve, and the entire profession of law enforcement.[1]

Most departments, especially smaller agencies, have no specific policy ("Transgender Protocol") regarding interaction with transgender people, so guidelines must be developed to assist sworn and nonsworn employees on the arrest and search of transgender individuals. A recommended protocol for law enforcement or corrections should include the following:

1. Officers should refer to the transgender person either by the name on the identification, the person's adopted name, or in the gender pronoun for which he or she is dressed or seeking to be perceived (i.e., address a transgender man in woman's attire as "miss" or "ma'am").
2. In investigative circumstances, an officer may respectfully ask gender- and name-related questions. Once those questions have been answered, an officer should refer to that person by the name the individual regularly uses.
3. If a frisk or search is necessary, under governing legal standards and barring exigent circumstances, two officers of the gender requested by the transgender individual should

---

[1]For more information on conducting diversity training, refer to the Instructor's Manual for this textbook, which offers suggestions for a cultural diversity training program that includes LGBT awareness.

search the person. The frisk or search should be consistent with maintenance of not only physical integrity and human dignity of the person, but also officer safety. If a transgender individual does not specify a preference, then officers of the same gender presentation should conduct the search (i.e., a transgender female who expresses no preference should be searched by female officers).

4. Officers should avoid any behavior that harasses transgender persons.

5. If incarcerated, transgender persons should be housed in the appropriate location according to his or her gender identification.

6. A narrative report, in its first paragraph, should indicate the gender the individual is living as and should state that he or she is transgender. The person should thereafter be referred to throughout the report by the adopted name or appropriate pronoun based upon gender presentation.

7. Statistical or booking pages are based upon the legal name and gender (genitalia) of the individual. ("Chief Charlie Beck instructs officers to treat transgender people with respect," 2012)

Departments should also have programs or designated liaison officers to work with transgender organizations or transgender individuals in the community. Departments that have policies, liaison, and employee training improve rapport and relations with the transgender community, which also reduces exposure to complaints and lawsuits.

Mini Case Study: How Should This Situation Have Been Handled by the Police Department?

Officers respond to a call at a motel and are met by a nude, intoxicated individual who has breasts but also male genitalia. The individual is arrested for public intoxication. All indications are that the individual is living as a woman, but because of the male genitalia, the individual is placed in the all-male jail. Officers learn that she is a "pre-op" transsexual, a person who is undergoing sex reassignment procedures.

Support Groups for Lesbian, Gay, Bisexual, and Transgender Officers

It is important that agency executives and managers provide opportunities for LGBT individuals to not only enter into law enforcement careers, but also assimilate comfortably into the organization. LGBT officers benefit from support groups and peer counselors in their own or neighboring police agencies.

POLICE LEADERSHIP, PROFESSIONALISM, AND SYNERGY

Within diverse communities facing the myriad challenges of transition and integration, economic constraints, and the complexity of crimes, representatives of the justice system need to act proactively, sensitively, and knowledgeably. If social order is not to be replaced by chaos, law enforcement representatives of all types not only need to be culturally sensitive but also must actively avoid racist, sexist, and homophobic behavior that may trigger violent social protest. Clearly, the diverse images of law enforcement as held by the multicultural communities rest upon the professionalism that today's peace officers display with regard to cultural competence, technical knowledge, and communication skills. The image of law enforcement projected to the public by police officers, their organizations, and the media is especially important within multicultural venues.

Lack of professionalism and inadequate personnel development can be very costly to any organization. But when it occurs within the public sector, it can prove damaging to both individuals and their careers, as well as to agencies and society. The following subsections cover three key concepts, which will be defined especially because of their implications for law enforcement and peacekeeping within a multicultural society (Barlow, 2000; Dantzker, 2000; Hunter, Barker, and Mayhall, 2008; White, 2007).

Leadership

Leadership   Exercised when one takes initiative, guides, or influences others in a particular direction.

Leaders are said both to possess a good balance of conceptual, technical, and professional competence and to demonstrate judgment and people skills. Leaders are not only creative change agents but also practical futurists, exercising foresight and the capacity for the "big picture" and the "long view" (White, 2007). Today as we transition into an information age and multicultural work environment, leaders need to be both transformational and transcultural. That is, strong leaders are those who advance innovations in the following initiatives:

- Transforming workplaces from the status quo to appropriate environments
- Renewing organizations and becoming role models by transmitting intellectual excitement and vision about their work
- Helping personnel to manage change by restructuring their mind-sets and values
- Helping to improve their organizations by preparing the next generation of supervisors and professionals, primarily through human resource development programs that they initiate and/or supervise. At a more personal level, they become mentors and coaches to high-performing personnel with organizational potential. (Kennedy, 2008)

In terms of multicultural diversity and inclusion, such leaders deal with all persons fairly, regardless of gender, race, color, religion, or cultural differences. A leader seeks to empower a more diverse workforce in law enforcement to be reflective of the communities they serve. Furthermore, culturally sensitive leaders cut across cultural barriers while combating prejudice, bigotry, or racism wherever found in the organization and community (Kennedy, 2008). Police supervisors, for example, exercise this leadership through anticipatory thinking, strategic planning, creative decision-making, and effective communications (White, 2007). Similarly, chiefs of police provide leadership when they annually present their departmental goals, both orally and in writing, for the benefit of the city council and their agency workforce, ensuring over the year that these goals are systematically achieved.

Professionalism

Professionalism   Approach to one's occupation or career, with a sense of dedication and expertise.

In contrast to an amateur, a professional is a committed high performer. A professional possesses integrity and demonstrates competence—regardless of the role, career activity, or sport in which he or she is engaged. Following is a description of some of the characteristics of professionalism, particularly as relevant to law enforcement. A professional in criminal justice systems is concerned about:

- Doing an effective job or rendering an effective service
- Developing and maintaining his or her career skill or competency level
- Exhibiting ethical and sensitive behavior and ensuring that other departmental members do the same

- Capitalizing on diversity in people and organizations and seeking to develop human potential with regard to diversity
- Being aware of the latest developments in the criminal justice field

In law enforcement, professionals make it a point to understand the law and legal system in which they work, as well as key issues in criminal justice. To increase their competence, these professionals are familiar with aspects of criminal and deviant behavior. Whether writing a report, conducting an investigation or an interview, or commanding a police action, professional peace officers do the work consistently well (White, 2007). They are high performers who meet their own goals and targets, not just for self-advancement or to please command officers, but because of the important nature of their duties. Their performance observes the code of ethics expected of public employees. With growing multiculturalism both in the community and in the workforce, law enforcement professionals support policies and programs that promote collaboration among people of diverse backgrounds. (Kennedy, 2008). Furthermore, they work with colleagues or the community to rectify any divisiveness, intolerance, discrimination, and even violence in the workplace. As is noted later in this chapter, competence in emerging computer technology, digital communication, and research tools are also a necessary part of law enforcement today.

Synergy

Synergy   The benefit produced by the collaboration of two or more systems in excess of their individual contributions.

Synergy occurs through working together in combined action, attaining a greater total effect than the sum of the individual parts. Cultural synergy builds on the differences in people to promote mutual growth and accomplishment. Through such collaboration, similarities, strengths, and diverse talents are shared to enhance human activities and systems. For team management and teamwork, synergistic relations are essential (Harris & Moran 2000; Gehl 2004; Kennedy 2008). In law enforcement, synergistic leaders:

- Facilitate interagency and inter-precinct cooperation
- Create consensus, which enables disparate people and groups to work together by sharing perceptions, insights, and knowledge
- Promote participation, empowerment, and negotiation within an organization or community, so that members work for mutual advantage and are committed to teamwork and the common good over personal ambition or need
- Demonstrate skills of facilitating, networking, conflict resolution, and coordination
- Are open-minded, effective cross-cultural communicators

Synergistic leaders give priority to the professional development of subordinates, especially through training and team building (Justice & Jamieson 1999).

Thus leadership, professionalism, and synergy are three powerful, interrelated concepts. When applied to the criminal justice system in general, or law enforcement and peacekeeping in particular, they may alter one's role, image, and performance. Leadership, professionalism, and synergy are illustrated at both the organizational and the individual levels in the context of the new work culture (Gido, 2009).

SUPERVISORS, MANAGERS, AND THE CHIEF EXECUTIVE

Supervisors, managers, and chief law enforcement executives should follow specific guidelines to meet the challenge of policing a diverse community. As emphasized previously, these leaders must first effectively manage the diversity within their own organizations. Progressive law enforcement executives are aware that before employees can be asked to value diversity in the community, it must be made clear that diversity is valued within the organization. Managing differences in the law enforcement workplace is therefore of high priority.

> Perhaps the biggest challenge facing police executives of the 21st century will be to develop police organizations that can effectively recognize, relate and assimilate the global shifts in culture, technology and information. Changing community expectations, workforce values, technological power, governmental arrangements, policing philosophies, and ethical standards are but a sample of the forces that must be understood and constructively managed by the current and incoming generation of chief executives. (Moody, 1999)

Leadership and team building are crucial to managing a diverse workforce and establishing good minority–community relations. The supervisory and management team must take the lead in this endeavor by:

- Demonstrating commitment
- Developing strategic, implementation, and transition management plans
- Managing organizational change
- Developing police–community partnerships (community-based policing)
- Providing new leadership models

Demonstrating Commitment

The organization must adopt and implement policies that demonstrate a commitment to policing a diverse society. These policies must be developed with input from all levels of the organization and community. The chief executive must reflect the imperative to value diversity and treat all persons with respect. His or her personal leadership and commitment are the keystones to implementing policies and awareness training within the organization and to successfully building bridges to the community. One of the first steps is the development of a "macro" mission statement for the organization; it should elaborate the philosophy, values, vision, and goals of the department to foster good relationships within a diverse workforce and community. All existing and new policies and practices of the department must be evaluated to determine how they may affect women, members of diverse ethnic and racial groups, gay men, lesbians, bisexuals, and transgender employees on the force. Recruitment, hiring, and promotional practices must be reviewed to ensure that there are no institutional barriers to particular groups in an agency. The chief executive must stress, via mission and values statements, that the agency will not tolerate discrimination, abuse, or crimes motivated by hate against protected classes within the community or within the agency itself. The policy statements should also include references to discrimination or bias based on physical disability or age. It is also an opportunity to be proactive by training and informing employees about federal EEOC regulations and any state, local, or agency laws and regulations pertaining to discrimination, and the consequences for violating them. The information should include statutes and consequences for retaliation against individuals for their involvement in discrimination actions.

The executive must use every opportunity to speak out publicly on the value of diversity and to make certain that people both inside and outside the organization know that upholding those ideals is a high priority. He or she must actively promote policies and programs designed to improve community relations and use marketing techniques to sell these programs, both internally and externally. Internal marketing is accomplished by involving senior management and the police association in the development of the policies and action plans. The chief or sheriff can use this opportunity to gain support for these policies by demonstrating the value of community support to increasing both the department's and the officers' effectiveness. External marketing is accomplished by involving representatives of community-based organizations in the process.

Police leaders must institute policies that develop positive attitudes toward a pluralistic workplace and community even as early as the selection process (see discussion in Chapter 3).

Using background interviews, polygraphs, and psychological exams, candidates for law enforcement employment must be carefully screened. The questions and processes can help determine candidates' attitudes and beliefs and, at the same time, make them aware of the agency's strong commitment to a diverse workforce.

Developing Strategic, Implementation, and Transition Management Plans

Textbooks and courses that teach strategic, implementation, and transition management planning are available to law enforcement leaders. The techniques, although not difficult, are quite involved and are not the focus of this book. Such techniques and methodologies are planning tools, providing the road map that the organization uses to implement programs and to guide the agency through change. Action plans that identify specific goals and objectives form an essential component. These plans include budgets and timetables and establish accountability—who is to accomplish what by when. Multiple action plans involving the improvement of police–community relations in a diverse society would be necessary to cover such varied components as policy and procedural changes; affirmative action recruitment, hiring, and promotions (where legal); cultural awareness training; and community involvement (i.e., community policing).

Managing Organizational Change

The department leadership is responsible for managing change processes and action plans. This is an integral part of implementation and transition management, as discussed previously. The chief executive must ensure that any new policies, procedures, and training result in increased employee responsiveness and awareness of the diversity in the community and within the organization's workforce. He or she must require that management staff continually monitor progress on all programs and strategies to improve police–community relations. In addition, the chief must ensure that all employees are committed to those ideals. Managers and supervisors need to ensure application of these established philosophies and policies of the department, and they must lead by example. When intentional deviation from the system is discovered, retraining and discipline should be quick and effective. Employees (especially patrol officers) must be rewarded and recognized for their ability to work with and within a pluralistic community. The reward systems for employees, especially first- and second-line supervisors, would recognize those who foster positive relations with individuals of different gender, ethnicity, race, or sexual orientation both within and outside the organization. As we have illustrated, the chief executive, management staff, and supervisors are role models and must set the tone for the sort of behavior and actions they expect of employees.

Developing Police–Community Partnerships

Progressive police organizations have adopted community policing as one response strategy to meet the needs and challenges of a pluralistic workforce and society. The establishment of community partnerships is a very important aspect of meeting today's challenges. For example, a cultural awareness training component will not be as effective if police–community partnerships are not developed, utilized, and maintained. The chief executive must establish and maintain ongoing communication with all segments of the community. These lines of communication are best established by community policing (discussed in detail in Chapter 14).

Providing New Leadership Models

In the past, all methods or models of management and organizational behavior were based on implicit assumptions of a homogeneous, white male workforce. Even bestsellers such as *The One-Minute Manager* (Blanchard & Johnson, 1983) and *In Search of Excellence* (Waterman & Peters, 1984) that continue to be useful management tools are based on that assumption.

Managers in today's society must learn to value diversity and overcome personal and organizational barriers to effective leadership, such as stereotypes, myths, and unwritten rules and codes (one of those being that the organizational role model is a white male). New models of leadership must be incorporated into law enforcement organizations to manage the diverse workforce.

Good leaders not only acknowledge their own ethnocentrism, but also understand the cultural values and biases of the people with whom they work. Consequently, such leaders can empower, value, and communicate more effectively with all employees. Developing others involves acquiring mentoring and coaching skills, important tools for modern managers. To communicate responsibly, leaders must understand the diverse workforce from a social and cultural context and be able to use a variety of verbal and nonverbal communication strategies with employees. Modern leaders are also familiar with conflict mediation in cross-cultural disputes.

To be leaders in the new workforce, most managers will have to unlearn practices rooted in old mind-sets, change the way their organization operates, shift organizational culture, revamp policies, create new structures, and redesign human resource systems. The vocabulary of the future managers involves leading employees rather than simply managing them. People want to be led, not managed, and the more diverse the working population becomes, the more this type of leadership is needed. This approach to leadership was echoed in the introduction to *Transcultural Leadership—Empowering the Diverse Workforce*:

> Today productivity must come from the collaboration of culturally diverse women and men. It insists that leaders change organizational culture to empower and develop people. This demands that employees be selected, evaluated, and promoted on the basis of *performance and competency*, regardless of sex, race, religion, or place of origin. Beyond that, leaders must learn the skills to enable men and women of all backgrounds to work together effectively. (Simons, Vazquez, & Harris, 2011).

Management, to build positive relationships and show respect for a pluralistic workforce, must be aware of differences, treat all employees fairly (but not necessarily in identical ways), and lead. The differing needs and values of a diverse workforce require flexibility by organizations and their leaders. Modern leaders of organizations recognize not only that different employees have different needs, but also that these needs change over time. Bridging cultural and racial gaps within their organizations must be a goal of law enforcement leaders.

Professional law enforcement leaders must also take the initiative to guide their departments to cultural competence. They must capitalize on the diversity of people within the organization and community, establish synergy, and seek to develop human potential for the betterment of both. The challenges for law enforcement in particular are to recognize and appreciate diversity within both the community and the workforce, while using such insights advantageously. Human diversity must become a source of renewal rather than tolerable legislated requirements within our agencies, communities, and society. To accomplish this goal within criminal justice systems, multicultural awareness and skills training must become an integral part of the human resource development of peacekeepers.

Summary

- In the United States, there has been a profound shift in demographics, which has resulted in notable changes in the composition of the workforce in law enforcement agencies. Every agency has more women, ethnic and racial minorities, and gay and lesbian members.
- Racism exists within our law enforcement organizations; police are not immune to social ills. The basic

framework for combating and defusing racism in law enforcement agencies is to use the military model involving command commitment, training of advisers, and the investigation of complaints and monitoring of results. Officers must have knowledge of conflict resolution techniques to reduce racial and ethnic problems within the community they serve.

- In 1972, the passage of the Equal Employment Opportunity (EEO) Act applied to state and local governments the provisions of Title VII of the Civil Rights Act of 1964. EEO laws were passed to correct a history of unfavorable treatment of women and minority group members. All workers in the United States are protected from harassment, discrimination, and employment decisions based on certain criteria. To be protected, individuals must be part of a "protected class" as described by federal or state law, policy, or similar authority; however, they must still exhibit necessary qualifications for the job, follow all company guidelines, and conduct themselves in a manner expected and required of all employees. The "protected class" groups protected from employment discrimination include men and women on the basis of sex; any group which shares a common race, religion, color, or national origin; people over 40; and people with physical or mental handicaps. The U.S. Supreme Court in 2009 ruled that workers who cooperate with their employers' internal investigations of discrimination may not be fired in retaliation for implicating colleagues or superiors. The EEO Act played an important role in opening up police departments to women.

- The past two decades have seen the removal of the explicit ban against employing gay men and lesbians by most law enforcement agencies. The rejection of homosexuals in law enforcement by some agencies continues despite studies that have shown that the presence of openly LGBT personnel enhanced service and did not negatively impact morale or unit cohesion in integrated police departments. The chief executive must establish departmental policies and regulations regarding LGBT officers. These policies must clearly state that discrimination, harassment, and failure to assist fellow LGBT officers are unacceptable and will result in corrective, including disciplinary, action.

- Law enforcement leaders must be committed to setting an organizational tone that does not permit racism or discriminatory acts and must act swiftly against those who violate these policies. They must monitor and quickly deal with complaints both from within their workforce and from the public they serve.

- Professional law enforcement leaders must take the initiative to guide their departments to cultural competence and must capitalize on the diversity of people within the organization and community, establish synergy, and seek to develop human potential for the betterment of both.

Discussion Questions and Issues

1. *Measuring Responsiveness to Diversity.* Using the check-off and scoring sheet (Exhibit 2.12), determine how responsive your police department has been to the diversity of the jurisdiction it serves. If you are not affiliated with an agency, choose a city or county police department and interview a command officer to determine the answers and arrive at a score. Discuss with the command officer what initiatives his or her department intends to undertake to address the issues of community diversity.

2. *Defusing Racially and Culturally Rooted Conflicts.* What training does the police academy in your region provide on defusing racially and culturally rooted conflicts? What training of this type does your local city or county law enforcement agency provide to officers? What community (public and private) agencies are available as referrals or for mediation of such conflicts? Discuss what training should be provided to police officers to defuse, mediate, and resolve racially and culturally rooted conflicts. Discuss what approaches a law enforcement agency should utilize.

3. *Women in Law Enforcement.* How many women officers are there in your local city or county law enforcement agency? How many of those women are in supervisory or management positions? Are any of the women assigned to nontraditional roles such as special weapons and tactics teams, motorcycle enforcement, bomb units, hostage negotiations, or community relations? Have there been incidents of sexual harassment or gender discrimination against women employees? If so, how were the cases resolved? Has the agency you are examining implemented any programs to increase the employment of women, such as flextime, child care, mentoring, awareness training, or career development? Has the agency been innovative in the recruitment efforts for women applicants? Discuss your findings in a group setting.

4. *Diversity in Law Enforcement.* Comment on the diversity in your local city or county law enforcement agency. What is the breakdown in your agency's hierarchy? For example, who holds supervisory or management positions? Have there been reported acts of discrimination against people of diverse backgrounds? Has the agency you are examining implemented any programs to increase the employment of minorities? Discuss your findings in a group setting.

Use the following simple assessment to analyze your organization's diversity and multicultural profile. If the majority of the responses are below 3, your management and leadership should consider taking actions to alter both the organizational practices as well as its image.

1......2......3......4......5
(1 = minimally; 5 = to a great extent)

A. To what extent does your organization integrate policies related to various workforce/community demographics, including religion, race, ethnicity, sexual orientation and multicultural relations into its overall mission and vision statements?

B. To what extent does your organization integrate policies related to religion, race, ethnicity, sexual orientation and multicultural relations into its strategic plan (i.e., to what extent do leaders prepare officers to "walk the talk")?

C. To what extent does your organization's hiring practices, assignments and promotions consider officers' knowledge related to community policing within diverse communities?

D. To what extent does your organization recruit culturally diverse and minority candidates in an attempt to achieve parity?

E. To what extent do ethnically and culturally diverse community groups provide input into your organization's educational programs focusing on crime prevention and/or cultural awareness?

F. To what extent has your organization provided cross-cultural awareness training focusing on specific immigrant and refugee populations in your city?

G. To what extent has your organization provided diversity education, focusing on workforce issues such as respect for differences (including sexual orientation, religious background, etc.)?

H. To what extent does your organization use interpreters to assist with non-English or English as a Second Language speakers?

I. To what extent is your organization's Web site or other publicity bilingual or multilingual (i.e., in multicultural communities)?

J. To what extent does your organization's Web site and other publicity portray a multicultural and/or multiracial community?

EXHIBIT 2.12   Analyzing Your Organization'S Diversity and Multicultural Awareness Profile

References

"Ask Lambda Legal: Transgender Community and Police." (2013, January 31). *Lambda Legal Blog*, M. Dru Levasseur. Retrieved July 24, 2013, from www.lambdalegal.org/blog/201301_ask-lambda-legal

Balkin, J. (1988). "Why Policemen Don't Like Policewomen." *Journal of Police Science and Administration, 16*(1), 29–38.

Barlow, Hugh D. (2000). *Criminal Justice in America*. Upper Saddle River, NJ: Prentice-Hall.

Bell, Daniel. (1982). "Policewomen: Myths and Reality." *Journal of Police Science and Administration, 10*(1), 112.

Bierstedt, Kathy. (2013, March). Sergeant retired, Florida police department, personal communication.

Blanchard, Kenneth H., and Spencer Johnson. (1983). *The One-Minute Manager*. New York, NY: Berkley.

Brooke, Aslan. (2005, October 19). "David vs. Goliath," *Frontiers* magazine, p. 18.

"Census of State and Local Law Enforcement Agencies, 2008." (2011, July 26). Bureau of Justice Statistics. NCJ 233982. Retrieved July 1, 2013, from www.bjs.gov/content/pub/pdf/csllea08.pdf

"Chief Charlie Beck instructs officers to treat transgender people with respect." (2012, April 19). *Los Angeles Times*, p. 1.

"Conflict Resolution Tips." National Crime Prevention Council. Retrieved July 7, 2013, from www.ncpc.org/topics/conflict-resolution/conflict-resolution-tips

"Connections That Count: The Informal Networks of Women of Color in the United States." (2006). Catalyst.org. Retrieved August 19, 2013, from www.catalyst.org/knowledge/connections-count-informal-networks-women-color-united-states

"Court Rules on Worker Retaliation." (2009, January 27). *Contra Costa* (Calif.) *Times*, p. A13.

Dantzker, M. L. (2000). *Understanding Today's Police*. Upper Saddle River, NJ: Prentice-Hall.

Equal Employment Opportunity Commission. "Enforcement and Litigation Statistics FY 2012." Retrieved August 4, 2013, from eeoc.gov/eeoc/statistics/enforcement/

"Facts about Sexual Harassment." (2008). U.S. Equal Opportunity Commission. Retrieved July 1, 2013, from www.eeoc.gov/eeoc/publications/fs-sex.cfm

Feagin, Joe R. (2006). *Systemic Racism: A Theory of Oppression*. New York, NY: Routledge.

"Federal Law Enforcement Officers, 2008." (2012, June 26). Bureau of Justice Statistics. NCJ 238250. Retrieved July 1, 2013, from www.bjs.gov/content/pub/ascii/fleo08.txt

Foster, Keith. (2006, August). "Gender and Excessive Force Complaints." *Law and Order*, 54(8), pp. 95–99.

Galvan, Frank H. and Mohsen Bazargan. (2012, April). "Interactions of Latina Transgender Women in Law Enforcement." *The Williams Institute–UCLA School of Law*. Retrieved July 8, 2013, from www.williamsinstitute.law.ucla.edu

Gehl, A. R. (2004). "Multiagency Teams: A Leadership Challenge." *The Police Chief*, 70(10). Retrieved July 1, 2013, from policechiefmagazine.org/magazine/index.cfm?fuseaction=display_arch&article_id=1395&issue_id=102004

Gido, R. L. (2009). The world is flat: Globalization and criminal justice organizations and workplaces in the twenty-first century. In R. Muraskin and A. R. Roberts, *Visions for Change: Crime and Justice in the Twenty-First Century*, 5th ed. Upper Saddle River, NJ: Prentice Hall.

Grobeson, Mitchell. (2013). Sergeant retired, Los Angeles (Calif.) Police Department, personal communication.

Hall, Thomas. (1992, October). Sergeant, Virginia State Troopers retired, personal communication.

Hampton, Ron. (2009). "Unfinished Business: Racial and Ethnic Issues Facing Law Enforcement II." Paper presented at a conference sponsored by the National Organization of Black Law Enforcement Executives and the Police Executive Research Forum, Reno, Nevada.

Harris, P. R., and R. T. Moran. (2000). *Managing Cultural Differences Instructor's Guide*. Boston, Mass.: Gulf Publications Series/Butterworth-Heinemann.

"History of Women in the Workforce." (1991, September 19). *Business Week*, p. 112.

Hunter, R. D., T. D. Barker, and P. D. Mayhall. (2008). *Police Community Relations and the Administration of Justice*, 7th ed. Upper Saddle River, NJ: Prentice-Hall.

Jones, Susan. (2013). Former Chief of Police, Healdsburg (Calif.) Police Department, personal communication.

Justice, T., and D. Jamieson. (1999). *The Complete Guide to Facilitation: Enabling Groups to Succeed*. Amherst, Mass.: Human Resource Development Press.

Kennedy, Debbe. (2008). *Putting Our Differences to Work: The Fastest Way to Innovation, Leadership, and High Performance*. San Francisco, Calif.: Berrett-Koehler.

Kwoh, Leslie. (2008, August 1). "Dover to Pay Ex-Sergeant $750,000 to Settle Suit." *The Star-Ledger* (Newark, NJ), p. 1.

Langton, Lynn. "Women in Law Enforcement, 1987–2008." (2010, June). NCJ 230521. U.S. Department of Justice, Office of Justice Programs, Bureau of Justice Statistics. Retrieved July 8, 2013, from www.bjs.gov/content/pub/pdf/wle8708.pdf

"Local Police Departments and Sheriffs' Offices 2007." Bureau of Justice Statistics. Retrieved January 5, 2013, from www.bjs.gov/content/pub/pdf/lpd07.pdf

Lonsway, Kimberly A. "Tearing Down the Wall: Problems with Consistency, Validity, and Adverse Impact of Physical Agility Testing in Police Selection." (2003, September). *Police Quarterly*, 6(3), 237–277.

"Manslaughter case spotlights gay domestic abuse." (2010, January 11). *Contra Costa* (Calif.) *Times*, p. A7.

"Men, Women, and Police Excessive Force: A Tale of Two Genders." (2010). *National Center for Women and Policing*. Retrieved July 8, 2013, from www.womenandpolicing.com/PDF/2002_Excessive_Force.pdf

Moody, Bobby D. (1999, May). "Police Leadership in the 21st Century: Achieving and Sustaining Executive Success." International Association of Chiefs of Police. Retrieved August 19, 2013, from www.theiacp.org/Portals/0/pdfs/Publications/policeleadership.pdf

More, Harry. (1992). *Male-Dominated Police Culture: Reducing the Gender Gap*. Cincinnati, OH: Anderson Publishing, pp. 113–137.

"More Women Leaving the Labor Market." (2005, December 21). *Dallas Morning News*, p. C5.

"N.Y. Jury Charges $1.5M to City." (2007, February 1). LRP Publications. Employment Practice Liability Verdicts and Settlement Publications No.126981-2002 (N.Y. Sup. Ct.), Vol. 8, No.11.

"Obama picks first female Secret Service chief." (2013, March 27). *Contra Costa* (Calif.) *Times*, p. A5.

"Occupational Outlook Quarterly." (Winter 2013-14). U.S. Bureau of Labor Statistics. Retrieved March 25, 2014 from www.bls.gov/ooq/ooqindex.htm.

Polisar, J., and D. Milgram. (1998, October). "Recruiting, Integrating and Retaining Women Police Officers: Strategies That Work." *Police Chief*, pp. 46–60.

"Pregnancy Discrimination & Temporary Disability." U.S. Equal Employment Opportunity Commission. (n.d.). Retrieved August 4, 2013, from www.eeoc.gov/laws/types/pregnancy.cfm

"Report recommends using military model to defuse racism in police departments." (1992, May 26). *The New York Times*, p. A17.

Schulz, Dorothy M. (1995). *From Social Worker to Crime Fighter: Women in United States Municipal Policing*. Westport, CT: Praeger, p. 5.

"Sexual Harassment in the Workplace." (2010). Sexual Harassment Practice Group of Outten & Golden LLP. Retrieved July 8, 2013, from www.workharassment.net/index.php/sexual-harassment-in-the-workplace.html

"Sgt. Ronald Crump, Gay LAPD Officer, To Receive $1.5 Million Settlement in Harassment Lawsuit." (2013, January 16). *Los Angeles Daily News*.

Shipler, David. (March 2013). Personal communication.

"Sheriffs' Offices, 2007 - Statistical Tables." (2012, December). Bureau of Justice Statistics. NCJ 238558. Retrieved July 1, 2013, from www.bjs.gov/content/pub/pdf/so07st.pdf

Simons, George, Carmen Vazquez, and Philip Harris. (2011). *Transcultural Leadership—Empowering the Diverse Workforce.* New York, NY: Routledge.

Skolnick, Jerome H., and David Bayley. (1988). *The New Blue Line: Police Innovation in Six American Cities.* New York, NY: Free Press.

Smith, Betsy Brantner. (2013). Sergeant, retired, Naperville (Illinois) Police Department, owner of The Winning Mind LLC Tucson, AZ, personal communication.

Smith, Betsy Brantner. (2007, September). "What Advice Would You Give a Female Rookie?" *PoliceOne.com.* Web posted at www.policeone.com/women-officers/articles/1354260-What-advice-would-you-give-a-female-rookie/ (accessed July 8, 2013).

Thiederman, Sondra. (1991). *Bridging Cultural Barriers for Corporate Success.* San Francisco, CA: Jossey-Bass.

Thiederman, Sondra. (2013, March). Personal communication.

Waterman, Robert H., and Tom Peters. (1984). *In Search of Excellence.* New York, NY: Harper & Row Publishers, Inc.

White, M. D. (2007). *Current Issues and Controversies in Policing.* Boston, Mass.: Allyn and Bacon.

"Women in the Labor Force: A Databook (2012 Edition)." United States Department of Labor, Bureau of Labor Statistics. Report 1040. Retrieved July 8, 2013, from www.bls.gov/cps/slf-intro-2012.htm

"Women on SWAT Teams: Separate but Equal?" (2011). *Policing: An International Journal of Police Strategies and Management,* *34*(4), Emerald Group Publishing Limited, 699–712.

"Workplace Issues." (2005). National Center for Women and Policing. Retrieved May 5, 2009, from www.womenandpolicing.org

3 Multicultural Representation in Law Enforcement
Recruitment, Retention, and Promotion

LEARNING OBJECTIVES

After reading this chapter, you should be able to:

- Recognize the historical perspectives of women and minorities in law enforcement.
- Discuss the ongoing challenges of recruitment trends with respect to women and minorities in law enforcement agencies.
- Explain recruitment difficulties and strategies for success.
- Describe the importance of retention and promotion of minorities and women in law enforcement careers.
- Identify promotional policies and practices in law enforcement agencies that would demonstrate the valuing of differences in our workplaces and communities.

OUTLINE

- Introduction
- Recruitment of a Diverse Workforce
- Attracting and Retaining Women and Minorities
- Selection Processes
- Retention and Promotion of a Diverse Workforce
- Summary
- Discussion Questions and Issues

INTRODUCTION

Our increasingly diverse society has created a demand for law enforcement officers and agents who can work effectively with many different types of people. For this reason, hiring and retaining qualified employees, especially women, blacks, Asians, Hispanics, and members of other nontraditional groups, continues to be a concern and a priority of law enforcement agencies nationwide. Many agencies have had difficulty finding qualified applicants, however, which has led to a recruitment crisis. This crisis, although influenced by economic circumstances, appears to be primarily the result of changing societal and demographic trends.

Chapter 3

RECRUITMENT OF A DIVERSE WORKFORCE

The recruitment of women and members of **diverse groups** is not a
U.S. law enforcement. In 1967, for example, a President's Crime C
mended that more minorities be hired, and that they receive oppor
Soon after the Watts riots in Los Angeles, the 1968 Kerner Commis
underrepresentation of blacks in law enforcement as a serious problem.
improved hiring and promotion policies and procedures for minorities
Commission report on the Los Angeles Police Department, released soo
lowing the first Rodney King trial, cited problems of racism and bias wit
mission recommended, among other things, improved hiring and p
would benefit all groups.

> **Diverse Groups** Diverse groups, in this textbook, will refer to person
> or ethnicity than the majority population. The term also includes those
> lesbian, bisexual, or transgender.

Recruitment Crisis and Trends

The past two decades have seen major shifts in employment trends in law enforcement agencies
nationwide. Among these changes is the difficulty in recruiting qualified candidates for law
enforcement positions. This reduction in the pool of qualified applicants can be attributed not
only to the economy, but also to significant societal changes during this period.

GOOD ECONOMY In the late 1990s and into 2000, the United States experienced the lowest
unemployment rate in 30 years (approximately 4%) because of a robust economy. Although there
were plenty of jobs in law enforcement, the number of applicants was substantially lower than in
the past. Due to the employees' market, those seeking jobs could be very selective. Many jobs in
private industry, especially high-tech jobs, came with high salaries, stock options, signing and
year-end bonuses, company cars, and broader opportunities for advancement. Public sector
employers had difficulty competing with such incentives and opportunities; thus, public safety
occupations seemed less attractive. Court decisions (and pretrial settlements) against such companies as Coke, Texaco, and Wall Street's Smith Barney in race bias lawsuits also factored into
recruitment difficulties during this time. Many large companies, aware that the populations
within their recruitment areas were diversifying, knew that their employee demographics had to
match those of the world outside or they, too, would be subject to lawsuits and/or criticism. As a
result, they scrambled to recruit and promote talented women and minorities. This was particularly true for companies that sell products or services to the public. The wide-open market also
made for transitory employees, especially those with experience, causing retention problems for
employers. During this period, smaller law enforcement agencies lost staff as larger agencies
lured experienced officers away with promises of better benefits. The recruitment effort, in which
everyone was competing for the same pool of qualified candidates, has been compared to the
National Football League draft.

At the same time, police departments experienced a reduction in staff because many
officers who had been hired in the police expansion wave of the 1960s and 1970s (known as the
Baby Boomers) began to retire. Most law enforcement officers retire before age 55, earlier than
is typical in civilian occupations. As the baby-boom-era officers began retiring at an acceler-
ated rate, due in part to improved retirement benefits that became an industry standard during
the early 2000s, the result was a shortage of employees. A further strain on law enforcement
agencies and their ability to recruit occurred as a result of the September 11, 2001, terrorist
attacks on our country. Police departments were now asked to assume new homeland security

nce duties in addition to their normal, ongoing public safety responsibilities. As
for police services expanded, agencies, with limited resources, still tried to recruit
ed personnel.

Another consequence of the 9/11 attacks was that law enforcement agencies began to face
competition for recruits from an expanding number of federal and private security jobs created
by the two-front war in Afghanistan and Iraq. In addition, the national military response to
terrorism also affected the ability of existing police officers to meet traditional and new police
missions, particularly in small and rural police departments where the call-up of even one or two
officers who serve in the National Guard or Reserves can have a noticeable impact.

BAD ECONOMY   Beginning in late 2007, the United States experienced what some economists
describe as the worst economic downturn since the Great Depression, seriously impacting local,
state, and federal governments. By June 2009, unemployment was at 9.5 percent, according to the
Bureau of Labor Statistics (Bureau of Labor Statistics, 2009). In April 2013, the unemployment
rate had declined to 7.6 percent, but may have actually been higher because many discouraged
job seekers had stopped looking for work (Bureau of Labor Statistics, 2013). During this period,
cities and counties were forced to reduce personnel through layoffs and attrition, as well as by
freezing department size and limiting the number of trainees in academies. Unfortunately, layoffs
disproportionately affect employees who were the most recently hired, so that women and people
of diverse ethnic and racial groups are often the first to lose their jobs, canceling any gains made
in achieving a multicultural and multiracial workforce.

One of the causes of the economic woes of city and county agencies was that tax revenues
were shrinking while costs for police and firefighters' wages and benefits were escalating. Some
municipalities had been saddled with labor contracts they could no longer afford to maintain.
For example, some government agencies entered into contracts with their law enforcement and
firefighters' unions that called for enhanced retirement benefits known as "3-at-50." This benefit
allows employees to retire at age 50 with retirement pay of 3 percent of their highest annual salary
multiplied by the number of years they served. If any agency in a given region offers this benefit,
others must follow suit in order to stay competitive and retain personnel. As more and more
eligible employees reached the age of 50, a major exodus of workers took place, severely impacting the budgets of many public agencies and creating vacancies that could not be filled because of
the poor economy.

In short, there were conflicting trends. Cost cutting throughout local, state, and federal
government forced layoffs, cutbacks in service, and unfillable vacancies. At the same time, there
was public pressure for more effective services and protection from terrorist threats.

TURNING THE CORNER   In 2013, law enforcement agencies across the country, after about five
years of cutbacks, layoffs, and the inability to hire new and replacement employees, began to see
a turnaround. Most agencies began to hire to restore their numbers after the cuts they had been
required to make. Because so many people had been laid off from downsizing industries, there
was an abundance of applicants, diverse and better educated, trying to get into law enforcement.
There were more "free agents" putting themselves through police academies. Agencies could
once again hire the very best of those who applied.

Recruitment Difficulties

These shifting economic forces, combined with social and demographic changes, have led to
challenges for agencies in recruiting qualified workers. These challenges are intensified by
recruitment standards set by local, state, and federal law enforcement agencies, which have
historically eliminated many candidates. For example, in California, according to Peace Officer
Standards and Training (POST) spokesman Bob Stresak, "out of every 1,500 new law enforcement applicants, only 100 make it through the intensive hiring process that includes a thorough

background and credit check, physical, psychological, and polygraph test. Of those 100 who make the initial cut, 10 percent drop out of the training academy and another 10 percent that graduate leave before completing field training" ("Law Enforcement Agencies Statewide Compete to Find Enough Qualified Candidates to Serve Their Communities," 2007).

A study by Mission: Readiness, a nonpartisan organization of senior retired military leaders, found "an alarming 75 percent of Americans ages 17-24 would not qualify for military service today because they are physically unfit, failed to finish high school or have criminal records" ("Ready, Willing, and Unable to Serve," 2009). According to the report, those findings are particularly true in low-income areas. The study cites three important reasons that young Americans cannot join the military: poor education (approximately one out of four lack a high school diploma); involvement in crime (approximately one in 10 have at least one prior conviction for a felony or serious misdemeanor); and poor health (nearly 32% have health problems, including asthma, vision or hearing problems, mental health issues, or recent treatment for Attention Deficit Hyperactivity Disorder). In addition to the health issues, weight problems disqualify 27 percent of young persons from joining the military. Because law enforcement organizations recruit from the same demographic groups, the ramifications for hiring are clear.

Like the military, law enforcement agencies screen job applicants using standards that address age, height, weight, education, drug use, criminal history, credit rating (departments don't want recruits who may be hounded by creditors or lawsuits), and physical and mental fitness. Because many of those interested in a career in law enforcement cannot meet these rigorous standards, some standards have had to change in response to social forces. In the past, for example, a previous misdemeanor conviction may have been an automatic disqualifier; however, that is no longer the case for most agencies today.

AGE, HEIGHT, AND WEIGHT   As the population has aged, some agencies have raised their upper age limit for new hires, including Boston (from 32 to 40), the Indiana State Police (from 35 to 40), and Houston (from 36 to 44). There are even agencies that have no upper age limit, usually out of fear of age-discrimination lawsuits. However, older job candidates are still required to meet the same physical fitness requirements during the testing processes and in the academy as their younger colleagues. Most agencies have also eliminated height requirements, requiring only that the candidate's weight be proportional to height and that they pass the training academy. In the past decade, the national obesity epidemic has also had an impact on law enforcement and military recruitment.

DRUG USE AND CRIMINAL HISTORY   For many years, most law enforcement organizations would not consider job candidates who had any history of drug use. However, agencies have found it increasingly difficult to locate suitable applicants unaffected by the drug culture, and have therefore eased their standards. The trend is that agencies no longer disqualify candidates for minor drug use or even drug convictions that occurred well prior to their application. Numerous studies have found that teenage girls are just as likely to use illegal drugs as their male counterparts, thus women too have difficulty passing background investigations. More women than in the past are being incarcerated for offenses that make them ineligible for law enforcement careers. These trends pose a challenge to law enforcement agencies desiring to increase the number of women in their departments. For all these reasons, many criminal justice agencies no longer require that candidates for jobs have a perfectly clean criminal record.

EDUCATION   Despite years of research by academics and practitioners into the relationship between higher education and policing skills, there has been little agreement concerning the optimal extent of education recommended for an entry-level officer. A high school education is usually required of applicants for most police departments and, historically, these officers have performed well. An increasing number of departments require 1 or 2 years of college coursework or more, and a few expect a 4-year college degree. This trend is based on the argument that

> The movement from traditional policing to community-oriented problem solving requires skill sets, such as critical and analytical reasoning, enhanced understanding of socioeconomic causes of crime, and advanced interpersonal and intercultural communications, that are best developed in higher education programs. (Hilal & Erickson, 2010)

The 2009 "Ready, Willing and Unable to Serve" study found that approximately one out of four young Americans lacks a high school diploma. However, by 2013, according to a study by the U.S. Department of Education, "the high school graduation rate is the highest since 1976, but more than a fifth of students are still failing to get their diploma in four years" ("High school graduation at 36-year high-Officials: Increase reflects weak job market, economy," 2013). The study indicates that the steady rise of students completing their high school education is a reflection of a poor job market and thus the increased competition for jobs. The report found that "nationally, white and Asian and Pacific Islander students were among the least likely to leave school without a degree, with only 2 percent dropout rates. Hispanic students posted a 5 percent dropout rate, followed by blacks at 6 percent and American Indians and Alaska Natives at 7 percent" ("High school graduation at 36-year high-Officials: Increase reflects weak job market, economy," 2013). A Pew Research report found that 69 percent of Hispanic high school graduates in the class of 2012 enrolled in college the following fall. This was two percentage points higher than the rate for white students. (Fry & Taylor, 2013).

Although the graduation trend appears to be improving, there are still concerns about the eligibility of minority officers, especially in diverse, urban areas from which an agency may be trying to recruit. For this reason, only a small fraction of agencies now require that candidates hold a 4-year college degree. Typically, those recruits who do possess such a degree can expect a higher salary than their peers with fewer years of education. Most potential applicants do not have a college degree, however, and those who do are attracted to careers other than law enforcement for many reasons, including salary and benefits.

To increase their applicant pools, agencies such as St. Petersburg and Tampa, Florida, have eliminated the requirement of 2 years of college if the candidate has military or law enforcement experience. The relaxation of standards has been prompted in large part by a dire need to fill vacancies. At the same time, agencies are attempting to recruit candidates who are wiser, more worldly, and cooler-headed in a crisis.

ADDITIONAL FACTORS   There are other reasons why many individuals have been deterred from or are reluctant to seek a career in law enforcement. Highly publicized scandals involving police departments in some major cities have had a negative effect on recruitment. In addition, because of a history of acrimonious relationships between members of minority communities and the police, members of those communities—the very people law enforcement seeks to attract—may shy away, fearing disapproval from their peers for joining with the perceived enemy.

Many immigrants and first-generation people from South and Central America, Puerto Rico, Cuba, and Mexico "have perceptions about the police [that] were heavily shaped by their experiences in their country of origin" (Menjivar & Bejarano, 2004). In essence, these communities may not call upon or cooperate with the police in the United States because of distrust or a lack of understanding of the role of law enforcement here. These perceptions are passed on to their children who are born in the United States so that, in many cases, they too are reluctant to apply for criminal justice jobs. Thus although Hispanics are the nation's largest minority group, the criminal justice system is not attracting a large pool of applicants. Hispanics make up 16 percent of the U.S. population now, and by some projections, that number will rise to nearly 30 percent by mid-century. Among Latinos, ages 18 and older, some 52 percent are immigrants and 48 percent were born in the United States (Taylor, Lopez, Martinez & Velasco., 2012).

Criminal justice educators and authors David and Melissa Barlow, in an unpublished article, "Hiring Latino/a Officers: What Police Administrators Need to Know," concluded that "strategies for hiring Latino/a police officers to represent a subset of the United States population may be more complex than for other minority groups." Their research refers to a Pew Research Hispanic Center report which determined that a majority of Hispanic/Latino respondents reject the notion that there is a common Hispanic culture. They are connected by a common language, but their experiences vary widely based upon their country of origin and where they live in the United States. The report indicated that many prefer to be identified not as Hispanic or Latino, but by their family's country of origin, such as Mexican, Puerto Rican, Cuban, Salvadorian, and the like. These factors need to be taken into consideration when planning recruitment strategies that will appeal to the Latino/a population. The Barlows suggest that "[at] a minimum, police leaders should make it a point to know the demographic make-up of their community and seek the appropriate cultural representation" (Barlow & Barlow, 2013). Departments with employees who match in ratio the demographics of their community secure legitimacy for the agency and promote the democratic principle of representation. Although Latino and Latina officers should not be required to work only in Hispanic communities, when they do they may be more likely to receive cooperation and support from the community than non-Hispanic officers.

Finally, another reason for the reluctance of young people to apply for careers in law enforcement is that the hierarchical paramilitary structure of most agencies may be unappealing to today's youth. In addition, most young people do not like to be micromanaged. For these reasons, policing has become a less attractive profession.

ATTRACTING AND RETAINING WOMEN AND MINORITIES

A study by the National Center for Women and Policing (NCWP) produced a self-assessment guide to assist agencies seeking to recruit and retain more women in sworn law enforcement positions. The resulting publication, *Recruiting and Retaining Women: A Self-Assessment Guide for Law Enforcement*, provides assistance to federal, state, and local law enforcement agencies in examining their policies and procedures to identify and remove obstacles to hiring and retaining women at all levels of the organization. The guide also provides a list of resources for agencies to use when they plan or implement changes to their current policies and procedures. The guide recommends increasing the number of women at all ranks of law enforcement as a strategy to strengthen community policing, reduce the use of force, enhance police response to domestic violence, and provide balance to the workforce.

To assist law enforcement agencies that wish to increase the number of women employees in their workforce, the NCWP offers the following services:

- A regional training seminar on recruiting and retaining women. This 2-day seminar helps law enforcement agencies develop effective recruiting programs to increase the number of female employees.
- Online updates to the self-assessment guide. New programs in law enforcement agencies across the country are described on the Web site, where readers can access the latest research about women in policing and other critical issues.
- On-site consulting by a team of professional law enforcement experts to help agencies identify and remove obstacles to recruiting and retaining women.

For additional information on these services, contact the NCWP.

RECRUITMENT OF NONSWORN PERSONNEL   The same factors impeding the recruitment of sworn personnel apply to nonsworn law enforcement staff as well. For example, most agencies today have a shortage of civilian dispatchers. This is a highly stressful job for which sound judgment and coolness under pressure are crucial. Candidates for dispatcher typically must pass a written and an oral test, a criminal background check, a polygraph, and a psychological exam. The job is so stressful that retention of good dispatchers is difficult. The long hours and night, weekend, and holiday shifts contribute to the high turnover rate for this position. Competition among agencies for seasoned dispatchers is fierce, and openings are frequent.

Recruitment Strategies

Recruitment strategies to attract diverse candidates for both law enforcement and civilian jobs within the department involve:

1. *Commitment:* The chief executive and the department must demonstrate a genuine commitment.
2. *Marketing plan:* A strategic marketing plan must be developed that includes action steps, objectives, goals, budget, accountability, and timetables.
3. *Resources:* Adequate resources, including money, personnel, and equipment, must be made available to the recruitment effort.
4. *Social media platforms:* Recruiters must make use of new and emerging social media technology to seek and prescreen applicants for department jobs.
5. *Selection and training of recruiters:* Recruiters are ambassadors for the department and must be selected carefully, be trained to reflect the diversity within the community, and include women.
6. *Recruiting incentives:* Police executives should consider using financial and other incentives to recruit women and minorities.
7. *Community involvement:* The community should be involved in recruiting and hiring women and minorities for sworn and nonsworn positions.
8. *Military involvement:* Efforts should be made to network with the various military branches to recruit discharged veterans.
9. *Internship, cadet, reserve, explorer scout, and high school police academy programs:* High school and college students are potential future recruits, so programs should be available that address these groups.

To build a diverse workforce, recruitment strategies used in the past are no longer sufficient and will not provide agencies with high-quality applicants. Agencies with maximum success in recruiting women and minorities have had specific goals, objectives, and timetables in place; these policies must be established at the top level of the organization.

COMMITMENT   Recruiting minority and women applicants, especially in highly competitive labor markets, requires commitment and effort. Police executives must communicate that commitment to their recruiting staff and devote the resources necessary to achieve recruitment goals. This genuine commitment must be demonstrated both inside and outside the organization. Internally, chief executives should develop policies and procedures that emphasize the importance of a diverse workforce. Affirmative action and/or programs that target certain applicants (where legal) will not work in a vacuum. Chief executives must integrate the values that promote diversity and affirmative action into every aspect of the agency, from its mission statement to its roll-call training. Externally, police executives should publicly delineate the specific hiring and promotion goals of the department to the community through both formal (e.g., media) and informal (e.g., community-based policing, networking with organizations representing the diverse groups) methods. While chief executives promote the philosophy, policies, and procedures, committed staff members, who are sensitive to the need for affirmative hiring and promotions, carry them out. Executives should also build partnerships with personnel officials so that decisions clearly reflect the hiring goals of the department. It is recommended that police executives audit the personnel selection process to ensure that neither the sequencing of the testing stages nor the length of the selection process is hindering the objective of hiring women and minorities.

Although chiefs may be genuine in their efforts to champion diversi
action hiring, care must be taken that their policies and procedures do not
the Civil Rights Act of 1964. Also, agencies in states that have enacted
affirmative action hiring programs and the targeting of "protected classes"
Proposition 209, passed in 1996, which is discussed later in this chapter) mu
regulations. A knowledgeable personnel department or legal staff should re
procedures prior to implementation.

MARKETING PLAN A strategic marketing plan should be developed that inc
steps that commit the objectives, goals, budget, accountability, and timetables for
campaign to paper. Demographic data should form one of the foundations for
must also take into account the current political, social, and economic condition
ment and the community. Deputy Chief Chris Skinner of the Hillsboro, Oregon
ment researched what attracts candidates for law enforcement to a particular agency. His
recommendation for recruiting effectively in a competitive market is that agencies separate themselves from others by creating market position:

> One way agencies can differentiate themselves is to achieve law enforcement "brand" as related to
> their position in the marketplace, to become the brand name when people discuss law enforcement
> services in the area. More important, each department should strive to have prospective officers con-
> sider it the brand name to work for. (Skinner, 2010)

Deputy Chief Skinner indicates that "creating the brand name or look is easy; the real challenge is creating a unique brand experience" with the candidate for employment. In essence,
this involves establishing a positive emotional connection between a potential applicant and
the agency; "otherwise, applicants will evaluate the agency based solely on the rational factual
information that applies to every law enforcement organization" (Skinner, 2010). The agency
must create a special allure that presents it as a great place to work and thus the better choice
among others. Some examples of how to achieve this include ride-along programs; introduc-
tions to good role models within the department, especially those of the same gender and/or
background of the candidate; an informative and attractive Web site; and positive press
releases about the department.

To avoid losing qualified applicants to other agencies or private industry, the marketing
plan should provide for fast-tracking the best candidates through the testing and screening processes. Fast-tracking is an aggressive recruitment strategy wherein a preliminary, qualifying check
quickly takes place concerning the driving, credit, and criminal history of the applicant before
any other screening occurs. Applicants who do not meet established standards are immediately
notified. The remaining applicants are then interviewed by a trained, ranking officer or civilian
holding the position for which the candidate is applying. Applicants earning a passing score on
the personal interview immediately receive a letter advising them that they passed, thereby giving
them tangible evidence that the agency is seriously considering hiring them. The letter also
informs them that they must pass additional qualifying steps, including a background investigation, which must commence immediately. The applicant must complete the final testing within
10 days, or the agency may withdraw the offer.

To streamline the process, background investigators have established blocks of time for
other testing such as polygraphs and psychological and medical evaluations. Streamlining is
important because in today's labor market, the best-qualified applicants will not wait for months
while testing proceeds at a slow pace; they will get hired and take positions elsewhere.

Additionally, the strategic recruitment plan should include an advertising campaign
that targets:

- Colleges and universities, including ROTC and sports departments
- Military bases and reserve units
- Churches, temples, mosques, synagogues, and other places of worship

- Community centers in minority neighborhoods; associations for Hispanics, Native Americans, Asians, and African Americans
- Gymnasiums, fitness and martial arts studios, athletic clubs, and the like

Participation of women and minority officers within the department is crucial in recruitment efforts (see "Recruiting Incentives"), as is the involvement of groups and organizations that represent the target groups. If within the community there are high-profile minorities and women, such as athletes and business executives, they should be enlisted to promote police work as a career through media releases and endorsements on flyers and brochures. Application packages should be made available at police stations 24 hours a day, 7 days a week so that they are available to potential candidates even when the personnel office is closed.

RESOURCES   Adequate resources, including money, personnel, and equipment, must be made available to the recruitment effort. Financial constraints challenge almost every organization's recruitment campaign. The size or financial circumstances of an agency may necessitate less expensive—and perhaps more innovative—approaches. For example, many small law enforcement jurisdictions can combine to implement regional testing. One large county on the West Coast successfully formed a consortium of agencies and implemented regional testing three times per month for law enforcement candidates. To participate, each agency pays into an account based on the population of its jurisdiction. Alternatively, each agency can pay according to how many applicants it hired from the list. The pooled money is then used for recruitment advertising (for example, billboards, radio, television, newspapers) and the initial testing processes (reading, writing, and agility tests, including proctors). The eligibility list is then provided to each of the participating agencies, which continue the screening process for applicants in whom they have an interest. By combining their efforts, they may be able to:

- Save money
- Develop a larger pool of applicants
- Become more competitive with private industry and other public agencies
- Test more often
- Reduce the time it takes from application to hire

In terms of recruiting a diverse workforce, the second benefit listed above—developing a larger pool of applicants—is central to reaching beyond the traditional applicant pool. Law enforcement agencies, taking advantage of the Internet's global coverage, can post position openings on their Web sites in an effort to recruit individuals with a wide variety of backgrounds and skills. Agencies now commonly maintain their own Web sites describing their departments and offering information on jobs available, testing dates, and how to obtain applications. Department Web sites have been found to be valuable recruiting tools when used to highlight the work of women and minorities within an agency, and can be used to attract returning military veterans.

Law enforcement career fairs, usually lasting no more than 2 or 3 hours, should be held on a weekend or an evening, so that people who are already employed have the opportunity to attend. A media and publicity campaign should be used to attract women and minorities to the event. At the career fair, a role-model panel of women and minority officers from a variety of assignments within the agency can describe their jobs and answer questions. The sort of information that might be provided by the panel could include:

- the history of the agency,
- what the testing processes are and how they can prepare,
- programs available to assist them in preparation for tests,
- information about agency volunteer programs, civilian positions, cadets, explorers, internships, and reserves,
- academy requirements, dates, expectations, location and contact information,

- information about the Field Training Program for new hires and expectations,
- examples of work schedules and career ladders,
- availability of, if possible, ride-along programs with the agency,
- the importance of problem solving and communications skills—community policing,
- what the department is looking for in a candidate for employment.

A high-ranking minority or female officer should also address those in attendance to persuade them to consider becoming employees. Information about the application and selection process, the physical agility test, and the academy should also be available.

SOCIAL MEDIA PLATFORMS   As mentioned, progressive agencies advertise openings and career fairs on their own Web sites and on free Web sites such as YouTube, Facebook, and Craigslist, as well as continuing to utilize more traditional venues. This technology is an inexpensive way to reach thousands of potential candidates in many demographic groups for both sworn and nonsworn positions. It provides an opportunity for the agency to give job-hunters in-depth information about the department, and also about the recruitment and selection process. Social media platforms provide a way to announce testing dates and locations for picking up and returning applications, and can also refer users to the department Web site and promote careers in law enforcement.

One agency on the West Coast discovered that in the year they created a women's section on their recruitment Web site, the percentage of females in the academy jumped from 8 percent to 50 percent. The Web site featured biographies and photos of the department's diverse workforce. The Internet has become the number-one way that candidates for law enforcement careers learn about job openings and agencies across the country.

New technology offers other benefits, as well. Video conferencing can be used by agencies to prescreen applicants for law enforcement jobs to determine if they are eligible and meet all the requirements, so that neither the department nor the candidate's time is wasted. The same applies for background investigators, who can perform interviews long-distance, saving the agency time and money for travel.

SELECTION AND TRAINING OF RECRUITERS   A recruiter is an ambassador for the department and must be selected carefully. Police recruiters should reflect the diversity within the community and include women. Full-time recruiters are a luxury most often found only in large agencies. The benefit of a full-time recruiter program is that frequently the employees in this assignment have received some training in marketing techniques. They have no other responsibilities or assignments and can therefore focus on what they do, and do it well. They develop the contacts, resources, and skills to be effective. Whether recruiters are full-time, part-time, or assigned on an as-needed basis, however, the following criteria should be considered when selecting them:

- Commitment to the goal of recruiting
- Belief in a philosophy that values diversity
- Ability to work well in a community policing environment
- Belief in and ability to market a product: law enforcement as a career
- Comfort with people of all backgrounds and ability to communicate this comfort
- Ability to discuss the importance of entire community representation in police work and its advantages to the department without sounding patronizing

Recruiters must be given resources (such as a budget and equipment) and must have established guidelines. They must be highly trained with respect to their role, market research methods, public relations, and cultural awareness. They must also understand, appreciate, and be dedicated to organizational values and ethics. They must be aware and in control of any biases they might have toward individuals, or groups of people, who might be different from themselves.

Almost every state's Commission on Peace Officer Standards and Training (POST) has developed a course on the techniques and methods of recruitment. Large, progressive agencies (or a consortium of agencies) could develop an in-house program patterned after these model courses. The Institute for Women in Trades, Technology and Science (IWITTS) can provide resources and training programs on recruiting and retaining women. The organization conducts national workshops, and also provides technical assistance to departments via personal contact or the Internet. Their materials include a law enforcement environmental assessment tool (LEEAT) involving institutional checklists and data collection methods to help determine the best recruiting strategies for a particular law enforcement agency.

RECRUITING INCENTIVES Employee referral systems (ERS) are a very effective recruitment technique that sometimes involves incentives. ERS success requires that officers informally assess an applicant to determine if he or she can perform well within the organization, and if so, make a recommendation to the agency. Research has suggested that officers who are recruited through employee referral systems are more likely to succeed in the selection process, be hired, and stay with the agency.

To implement ERS, it is recommended that police executives consider using financial and other incentives, after first determining that such programs are lawful in their jurisdiction (monetary incentive programs may be adversely affected by Fair Labor Standards Act considerations). The percent of state and local law enforcement officers employed by agencies offering selected incentives to recruit applicants for sworn positions in 2008 is shown in Exhibit 3.1. Financial and other incentive programs are especially useful to agencies that cannot afford full-time recruiters. They are used to encourage officers to recruit bilingual whites, women, and ethnically and racially diverse candidates, informally, while on or off duty. One possible program would give officers overtime credit for each person they recruit in those categories who makes the eligibility list, additional credit if the same applicant is hired, and

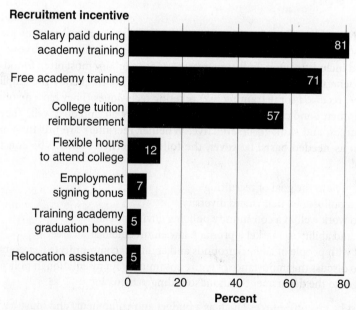

Recruitment incentive

EXHIBIT 3.1 Agencies incentives to recruit applicants for sworn positions, 2008

Source: "Hiring and Retention of State and Local Law Enforcement Officers, 2008." (2012, October). Brian A. Reaves, Ph.D. NCJ 238251. Retrieved from www.bjs.gov/index.cfm?ty=pbdetail&iid=4514

further credit for each stage the new officer passes until the probation period ends. Some departments offer officers who are not specifically assigned to recruiting up to 20 hours compensatory time for recruiting a lateral police officer. Department members can also receive an additional 40 hours of compensatory time for recruiting a lateral who is bilingual or from a protected class.

One East Coast agency awards $250 to employees who recruit applicants (of any racial or ethnic group) who complete all phases of the background process, are hired, and start the academy. The same department awards $250 to employees who recruit lateral police officer candidates once they complete all phases of the background process, are hired, and report for duty. When these recruits make it through probation, the employee who recruited them receives $250 as an additional incentive. Encouraging all department members to be involved in the recruitment effort, including the promotion of law enforcement as a career, is usually effective.

To be competitive in recruiting employees, especially minorities and women, agencies must offer incentives just as corporations do. Some cities and counties offer signing bonuses to experienced officers from other agencies. For example, in 2008, the city of Oakland, California, offered experienced officers from the city of Vallejo a $25,000 signing bonus to join their department ("Vallejo Police Recruiting a Tough Go," 2008, p. A32). Some departments offer academy-trained applicants a $3,000 signing bonus. The amounts vary, but the practice of offering these bonuses has been used in other cities and counties across the nation by agencies that can afford it. Some jurisdictions also offer law enforcement officers help with down payments and interest-free loans on their first home. Such offers are used not only to encourage current police officers to stay with the department, but also to recruit new hires who might not be able to live in a high-cost community ("San Francisco Housing Aid for Teachers, Police," 2007, p. A36). Watching personnel leave for greener pastures can be frustrating for the department that invested time and money in the employee. It takes about a year to hire a new officer, at a cost of approximately $4,000 for the screening processes, and thousands more for academy training. Thus the use of incentives to attract and retain personnel with experience ultimately saves the agency money.

COMMUNITY INVOLVEMENT   Successful law enforcement agencies involve the community in recruiting and hiring women and minorities. Representatives from protected classes should be involved in initial meetings to plan a recruitment campaign. They can assist in determining the best marketing methods for the groups they represent, and can help by personally contacting potential candidates. They should be provided with recruitment information (such as brochures and posters) that they can disseminate at religious institutions, civic and social organizations, schools, and cultural events. Community-based policing also offers the best opportunity for officers to put the message out regarding agency recruiting.

Community leaders representing the diversity of the community should also be involved in the selection process, including sitting on oral boards for applicants. The San Francisco Police Department utilizes community leaders in all the processes mentioned. Many progressive agencies have encouraged their officers to join community-based organizations, in which they interact with community members and are able to involve the group in recruitment efforts for the department.

MILITARY VETERANS   Some law enforcement agencies commit time and resources to recruiting veterans who discharge, separate, or retire from military service. Veterans often make excellent law enforcement employees because of their experience within a military organizational structure.

As the wars in Iraq and then Afghanistan came to a close, more and more military veterans looked for criminal justice jobs. In 2012, the military also started downsizing by reducing recruitment and asking fewer members to re-enlist after they serve their commitment. Unlike prior wars, these troops have been formally trained in techniques used in inner-city combat. Referred to as "peacekeeping," these techniques are much like policing, such as the searching and "clearing" of houses and other structures. Today's military veterans have also received training on one of the largest tasks of sheriff's departments and correctional personnel—detention. The International Association of Chiefs of Police published a study in 2011, "Employing Returning Combat Veterans as Law Enforcement Officers-Recruitment Strategies," which provides useful approaches to recruiting combat veterans.

An emerging trend is the increase in the number of lesbian, gay, bisexual, and transgender (LGBT) military veterans (see Chapter 2) who apply for law enforcement or corrections occupations. Given the traditional recruiting strategies employed by many law enforcement agencies, the effect of the repeal of preventing openly gay and lesbian individuals from serving in the armed forces will necessitate that managers and supervisors, as well as those working in backgrounds and recruitment, evaluate their agencies' written and unwritten policies. In traditional law enforcement, homosexuality has been both a real and an artificial barrier.

The availability of LGBT military veterans for employment is an issue of major importance to executives and managers within the criminal justice system. Prior to the end in 2013 of "Don't Ask, Don't Tell," there had been an increasing number of *dishonorable* discharges based solely upon discovered or believed homosexuality. This becomes an employment issue when the person applies for a criminal justice position. In the past, the armed forces had agreed to release homosexual personnel under the category of general discharge ("The Military Discharged about 12,340 People between 1994 and 2007 under 'Don't Ask, Don't Tell,'" 2008). Virtually all law enforcement and correctional agencies, however, mandate disqualification of persons who have been discharged from military service with anything less than "honorable."

In order for criminal justice executives to make informed decisions, they must know the difference between *discharge* and *separation* from military service, and whether the discharge/ separation was voluntary or involuntary. The vast majority of those leaving the service after completing an initial enlistment obligation are *separated* (voluntary) rather than discharged. This may mean there is an additional military service obligation to be carried out in the Individual Ready Reserve. The key difference is that a *discharge* completely relieves the veteran of any unfulfilled service obligation. A separation may also be involuntary when the service member is released for punitive reasons based upon specifically identified conduct. It is important to know the type or *basis* of the discharge or separation and the *characterization of service. Basis* is the reason for which the person is being administratively separated (for example, a pattern of misconduct, convenience of the government for parenthood, weight control failure). *Characterization of service* refers to the quality of the individual's military service: honorable, general (under honorable conditions), other than honorable, bad conduct, or dishonorable (Uniform Code of Military Justice [UCMJ], 1950).

There have, however, been some LGBT veterans discharged under the characterization "general." The "general" characterization means:

> If a member's service has been honest and faithful, it is appropriate to characterize that service under honorable conditions. Characterization of service as general (under honorable conditions) is warranted when significant negative aspects of the member's conduct or performance of duty outweigh positive aspects of the member's military conduct or performance of duty. ("Military Justice 101— Part 3, Enlisted Administrative Separations," 1998)

Thus, a general discharge is given to a service member whose performance is satisfactory but is marked by a departure from duty performance and conduct expected of military members. The reasons for such a characterization of service vary, but general discharge is always preceded by some form of nonjudicial punishment (i.e., no court-martial). The nonjudicial punishment is typically utilized by the service member's unit commander to correct unacceptable behavior prior to initiating discharge action.

Punitive discharges are punishments authorized by a court-martial and result in either a dishonorable discharge or bad conduct discharge. A court-martial is generally held for the most serious violations of the Uniform Code of Military Justice.

Major cities, particularly those with large LGBT communities now accept applicants who have a general discharge, when the sole issue was sexual orientation with no "related misconduct." Within the past decade, those agencies progressive enough to hire an LGBT military veteran who has been discharged solely for being "homosexual" (where there was no misconduct) have found that these individuals have been some of the most outstanding and well-respected members of their organizations. This has been especially noted within the San Diego Police Department, which employed a large number of active and former military personnel.

INTERNSHIP, CADET, RESERVE, EXPLORER SCOUT, AND HIGH SCHOOL POLICE ACADEMY PROGRAMS   Law enforcement agencies should have various programs available to high school students, as they are potential future recruits. These are often referred to as "grow your own cops" programs. One such innovative recruitment tool was launched in San Jose, California, in 1988, called the "Santa Teresa High School Police and Fire Academy." It was a year-long academy program that helped students prepare for careers in fire services or law enforcement. The Academy provided recruiters with a pool of candidates. The program was offered to about 60 students at a time from six school districts in Santa Clara County, California. The students spent half of each day at the academy and the other half at their own schools. Students, who wore uniforms, learned police and fire job skills, which helped prepare them for those vocations. Another purpose of the Academy was to instill a sense of community service and spirit in the youth who attend, and to provide positive mentor/role-model guidance from professional law officers, firefighters, graduate students, and community members. Cadets collectively performed 6,000 to 8,000 hours a year of community service.

As a part of a high school police academy, or of other programs geared toward this age group, role model and mentoring components should be incorporated. Mentoring would involve police officers associating with youth in positive ways before the young people have made the decision to use drugs, commit crimes, or drop out of school. Such programs would include an emphasis on the importance of developing good speaking and writing skills; weaknesses in these areas disqualify many candidates from careers in law enforcement. Police Athletic Leagues, which have operated in many agencies across the nation for decades, have also traditionally filled this mentorship role.

Young people are clearly a very important part of any recruitment effort, so law enforcement agencies should develop and use surveys of the demographics and attitudes of this age group. Such surveys could help gauge the level of interest in law enforcement careers, and help determine what changes police might need to make to attract the best candidates. The survey can also provide an opportunity to promote such programs as police intern, cadet, explorer, and high school academy.

SELECTION PROCESSES

Prior to initiating any selection process, law enforcement agencies must assess the satisfaction level of current employees and the workplace environment of the department.

Satisfaction Level of Employees

The first step before outreach recruitment can take place is for the department to look inward. Are any members, sworn or nonsworn, experiencing emotional pain or suffering because of their race, ethnicity, nationality, gender, or sexual orientation? A department seeking to hire applicants from these groups cannot have internal problems, either real or perceived, related to racism, discrimination, or hostility toward female, gay male, or lesbian officers. A department with a high turnover rate or a reputation for not promoting women, minorities, or gays and lesbians will also deter good people from applying. The department must resolve any internal problems before meaningful recruitment can occur. To determine the nature and extent of any such problems, law enforcement agencies can perform an assessment of all their employees through anonymous surveys about their work environment. There should be a review of policies and procedures (especially those related to sexual harassment and gender discrimination) and an examination of statistical information such as the number of officers leaving the department and their reasons for doing so, as well as which employees are promoted. The goal is not only to evaluate the workplace environment for women and minorities, but also to determine what steps need to be taken to dissolve barriers confronting them. See Appendix A for a sample survey that can be used for this purpose.

Supervisors and managers must talk with all members of their workforce on a regular basis to find out if any issues are disturbing them. They must then demonstrate that they are taking steps to alleviate the sources of discomfort, whether this involves modifying practices or simply discussing behavior with other employees.

The field training program for new recruits should also be reviewed and evaluated to ensure that new officers are not being arbitrarily eliminated or subjected to prejudice or discrimination. By the time a recruit has reached this stage of training, much has been invested in the new officer; every effort should be made to see that he or she completes the program successfully. Negligent retention, however, is a liability to an organization. When it is well documented that a trainee is not suitable for retention, release from employment is usually the best recourse regardless of race, ethnicity, sexual orientation, or gender.

Role models and networking and mentoring programs should be established to give recruits and junior officers the opportunity to receive support and important information from senior officers of the same race, ethnicity, gender, or sexual orientation. Many successful programs, however, include role models of different backgrounds than the recruits.

Applicant Screening (Employment Standards)

Historically, law enforcement agencies hired men for sworn positions and it was considered a male occupation. Traditionally, applicant screening involved tests with an emphasis upon physical strength and little upon communications skills or problem solving. Now most agencies have removed obstacles that prevented most women and some men from becoming law enforcement officers. Testing and pre-employment screening now involve assessing skills, abilities, and fitness required of today's law enforcement officers in their use of community policing. Departments across the country are seeking employees who can communicate and cooperate with citizens and use problem-solving skills.

A bad hire, in any occupation, can be very costly to an organization. Law enforcement agencies, therefore, must create a complete plan to recruit, screen, and hire solid candidates to fill openings. The hiring agency must have an accurate, up-to-date job description and an understanding of current standards for the position(s) for which they are hiring. An applicant should know exactly what the standards for employment are and what the job requires so there are no surprises. Those agencies needing assistance in establishing effective and defensible standards for the employment and training of peace officers should contact the International Association of Directors of Law Enforcement Standards and Training (IADLEST).

Law enforcement agencies must assess applicants along a range of dimensions (employment standards) that include, but are not limited to:

- Basic qualifications such as education, requisite licenses, and citizenship
- Intelligence and problem-solving capacity
- Psychological fitness
- Physical fitness and agility
- Current and past illegal drug use

- Character as revealed by criminal record, driving record, work history, military record, credit history, reputation, and polygraph examination
- Aptitude and ability to serve others (see "Innovations in Police Recruitment and Hiring: Hiring in the Spirit of Service," 2001)
- Racial, ethnic, gender, sexual orientation, and cultural biases

The last dimension, testing for biases, deserves particular attention. An agency whose hiring procedures screen for unacceptable biases demonstrates to the community that it seeks police officers who will carry out their duties with fairness, integrity, diligence, and impartiality—officers who will respect the civil rights and dignity of the people they serve and with whom they work. Such screening should include not only the use of psychometric testing instruments developed to measure attitudes and bias, but also careful background investigation of the candidate by personnel staff. The investigation should consider the applicant's own statements about racial issues, as well as interviews with personal and employer references that provide clues about how the applicant feels about and treats members of other racial, ethnic, gender, and sexual-orientation groups. These interviews would include questions on:

- How the applicant has interacted with other groups
- What people of diverse groups say about the applicant
- Whether the applicant has ever experienced conflict or tension with members of diverse groups or individuals, and how he or she handled the experience

Because of the emphasis on community policing, law enforcement recruiters must also seek applicants who demonstrate the mentality and ability to serve others (not just fight crime). Recruiters therefore are looking for candidates who are adaptable, analytical, communicative, compassionate, courageous (both physically and morally), courteous, culturally sensitive, decisive, disciplined, ethical, goal-oriented, incorruptible, mature, responsible, respectful, and self-motivated. Agencies also expect officers to have good interpersonal and communication skills, as well as sales and marketing abilities, so applicants should be screened for these attributes, and for their desire for continued learning and ability to work in a rapidly evolving environment. Officers more and more are encountering the challenges of different languages, cultural and generational differences, and the diverse opinions of members of the communities they serve. Agencies must develop means of generating trust among the diverse groups. The importance of bilingual officers and officers with cultural understanding is paramount in today's communities.

Today, effective law enforcement officers work closely with neighborhood groups, social welfare agencies, housing code officials, and a host of others in partnerships to control crime and improve quality of life. Law enforcement agents must be eager to understand a task, draw up a plan, and follow it through to completion in concert with others. Without an agreeable nature, officers and deputies faced with today's changing attitude toward crime fighting would not have a chance. Thus, the search for recruits should focus on those who demonstrate an ability to take ownership of problems and work with others toward solutions. These potential officers must remain open to people who disagree with them or have opinions that differ from their own. Law enforcement agencies should make their goals and expectations clear to candidates for employment, recognizing that some candidates will not match the department's vision, mission, and values, and therefore should be screened out at the beginning of the process. Screening should include determining the applicants': (1) emotional stability, (2) extroversion versus introversion, (3) openness to experience, (4) agreeableness versus toughness, and (5) conscientiousness.

It is in the best interest of law enforcement agencies to complete a job analysis before implementing tests. Although it is a time-consuming process, the final result is a clear description of the job for which applicants are applying and being screened. Utilizing the job analysis data, tests and job performance criteria can be developed and made part of the screening process. Applicants when provided with a copy of the job analysis can decide in advance if they fit the criteria.

Aptitude for a law enforcement career can also be determined from structured oral interviews. The oral interview panel should be gender- and racially diverse, and include members of the local community to reduce the possibility of bias. The panel should also include both sworn and civilian law enforcement employees. It is important that all raters are supportive of women and protected classes in policing, and thoroughly trained in the rules of the interview process. Questions should be developed in advance for the oral interview, and should test for the skills and abilities needed for community policing, including the ability to work with all types of people, to de-escalate violence, to mediate disputes, and to solve problems. The same questions should be asked of each candidate, regardless of whether the candidate is male or female.

The authors believe that one of the most useful new tools for law enforcement recruitment, one that represents a paradigm shift in recruitment philosophy, comes from the findings of the federally funded project Hiring in the Spirit of Service (HSS). The project's recommendations represent a major change in recruitment strategy, as agencies using HSS are seeking and hiring service-oriented law enforcement personnel.

HIRING IN THE SPIRIT OF SERVICE   The HSS program, developed in the late 1990s, suggests ways of recruiting applicants who are not drawn to a law enforcement career because of the spirit of adventure ("crime fighter") associated with the profession, but are attracted because they are service-minded. Recruitment should not just be for those who are educated, but for those who will work well within community-oriented policing (COP) and problem-oriented policing (POP) philosophies. These philosophies require intelligent individuals who can solve problems. The individuals' size (a move away from recruiting "big tough cops") should not matter if they have interpersonal and service-oriented skills. Those recruited must be able to accept diversity not only within the community they work, but also within their own workforce.

The HSS program targets persons whose qualifications are consistent with other service-oriented professions, like teaching, nursing, and counseling, as long as they are able to meet strict physical training and fitness demands. Historically, candidates who did not fit the "crime fighter" mentality were discouraged from applying or disqualified at some point in the testing process. Those departments using the HSS selection process reach out to service-minded candidates, attracting them to law enforcement professions they might not have considered. The HSS project involved a cooperative agreement awarded to the Community Policing Consortium (CPC) by the U.S. Department of Justice Office of Community-Oriented Police Services (the COPS Office). The CPC examined the components of traditional screening procedures in order to find creative ways to revise traditional practices to make them consistent with the principles of community (service-oriented) policing:

> The CPC was particularly interested in a strong emphasis on community engagement—the core of community policing—which enables the building of trust, the development of collaborative problem-solving partnerships, and greater accountability to the community. These emphases set community policing apart from the professional model of policing and have been instrumental in introducing change to the police culture. ("Innovations in Police Recruitment," 2001, p. 1)

Through a competitive process, five law enforcement agencies were selected to serve as demonstration sites for the study. The five agencies were selected because they represent the gamut of law enforcement challenges in the United States. The sites were Burlington, Vermont, a small department with a growing multicultural community; Sacramento, California; Detroit, Michigan; Hillsborough County, Florida; and King County, Washington (both of the latter are full-service sheriffs' offices).

The HSS project report noted the great lengths to which the agencies went to involve citizens in substantive ways in the processes, and how the communities influenced strategies and outcomes. The report also stressed that the processes of HSS are neither easy nor quick, especially the involvement of community members. All the agencies encountered many challenges during the study. The study findings and recommendations resulted in revisions to each agency's recruitment and hiring practices, which are now based on the identified personal characteristics and required competencies necessary to perform the community policing function.

Other useful resources include *Recruitment and Retention of Qualified Police Personnel—A Best Practices Guide*, published by the International Association of Chiefs of Police; *Hiring and Keeping Police Officers*, the findings of a study that examined experiences of police agencies nationwide in hiring and retaining sworn officers, published by The National Institute of Justice (NIJ); and *Tearing down the Wall*, by the NCWP, which also provides insights on physical agility testing.

Examples of Successful Recruiting Programs

Successful recruitment programs vary by community. If recruitment efforts result in a large enough pool of qualified applicants, the pool will contain individuals of all backgrounds. The following agencies have had success in recruiting female and minority applicants, and might be contacted to determine the strategies they used: Portland, Oregon; Madison, Wisconsin; Pittsburgh, Pennsylvania; Albuquerque, New Mexico; Tucson, Arizona; Burlington, Vermont; Sacramento, California; Detroit, Michigan; Hillsborough County, Florida; and King County, Washington.

A program, "Vermont Works for Women's Step Up to Law Enforcement," has been successful in preparing women (of all races and ethnicities) for criminal justice jobs. The three key components of the program are physical conditioning geared to the physical exam administered by the police academy and taught by licensed trainers at a local gym; a focus on the soft skills of career planning in law enforcement professions; and training in technical topics specific to law enforcement, taught by policing and corrections partners (Tuomey & Jolly, 2009). The percent of state and local law enforcement officers employed by agencies using selected methods to recruit applicants for sworn positions in 2008 is shown in Exhibit 3.2.

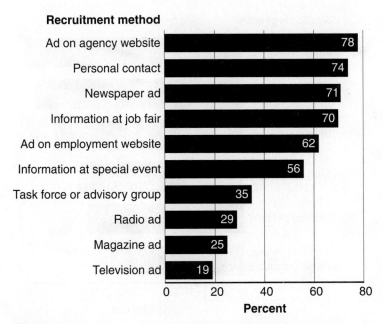

EXHIBIT 3.2 Agencies methods to recruit applicants for sworn positions, 2008

Source: "Hiring and Retention of State and Local Law Enforcement Officers, 2008." (2012, October). Brian A. Reaves, Ph.D. NCJ 238251. Retrieved from www.bjs.gov/index.cfm?ty=pbdetail&iid=4514

Legal Issues and Affirmative Action

In some states or jurisdictions, there may be some controversial and even legal aspects of recruitment efforts that target women and protected class candidates for law enforcement jobs. Generally, it is not permissible to recruit only members of a particular race, ethnicity, or gender. Federal law prohibits programs that require meeting specific *hiring* goals for any particular group except when necessary to remedy discrimination. However, outreach programs and recruiting efforts seeking to broaden the pool of potential candidates by reaching a greater number of qualified individuals that includes women and members of diverse groups would be lawful. Such programs and efforts should be designed to make employment opportunities known to all potential applicants regardless of their race, ethnicity, national origin, sexual orientation, or gender.

In California, Proposition 209, which outlawed governmental discrimination and preferences based on race, sex, color, ethnicity, or national origin, was passed in 1996. The law provides that any government agency that offers preferential treatment in hiring or promoting employees could be penalized by having the state cut off its tax dollars. In September 2000, justices of the California Supreme Court affirmed that the proposition was legal. The justices, in their decision, placed strict limits on employers regarding the types of outreach programs they can legally use to recruit employees; any outreach program that gives minorities and women a competitive advantage is a violation of Proposition 209. Many other states followed California's example by enacting similar legislation, but not all. In 2008, Colorado voters became the first in the nation to reject a ballot proposition that would have banned affirmative action programs allowing the consideration of race or gender in state hiring, contracting, and college admissions. Agencies need to research what strategies are legal and appropriate within their state and jurisdiction. The percent of state and local law enforcement officers employed by agencies targeting specific applicant groups with special recruitment efforts in 2008 can be seen in Exhibit 3.3.

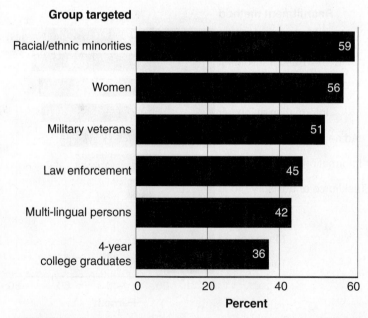

EXHIBIT 3.3   Agencies' targeting specific applicant groups with special recruitment efforts, 2008

Source: "Hiring and Retention of State and Local Law Enforcement Officers, 2008" October 2012. Brian A. Reaves, Ph.D. October 29, 2012. NCJ 238251 Retrieved from www.bjs.gov/index.cfm?ty=pbdetail&iid=4514

Affirmative action and consent decrees have enjoyed only moderate success in attempts toward achieving parity in the hiring of women and individuals from ethnically and racially diverse backgrounds. There has been even less success with promotions of members of these groups to command ranks. An unfortunate problem that can be associated with the promotion of women and nonwhites is that doubts are raised about their qualifications: Are they qualified for the job, or are they products of affirmative action? Peers may subtly or even explicitly express to each other that the promotion was not the result of competence, and the promoted candidate may feel that his or her success is not based entirely on qualifications. Consequently, employees may experience strained relationships and lowered morale. There is no denying the potential for a strong negative internal reaction in an organization when court orders have mandated promotions. Some white and/or male employees feel anger or frustration with consent decrees or affirmative action–based promotions. Clearly, preventive work must be done to avoid such problems.

The National Organization of Black Law Enforcement Executives (NOBLE) has consistently endorsed affirmative action to increase the numbers of minorities in the profession. NOBLE has met with recruiters and other representatives of law enforcement across the nation to discuss potentially successful minority recruitment strategies. One such strategy involves the creation of a pilot project with 10 historically black colleges to increase the number of graduates pursuing law enforcement careers. The project includes workshops, lectures, and miniconferences, as well as internships in law enforcement. NOBLE has also sponsored job fairs that attract prospective candidates for employment, who then meet with representatives from participating agencies.

Mini Case Study: What Would You Do?

You are the new personnel sergeant responsible for a department with 50 sworn officers. The department has one African American man, two Hispanic men, and two women officers. There has never been a large number of minority or women candidates applying for sworn positions in the department, and your agency does not reflect the demographics of the city. Your city has an affirmative action program, but to date, no outreach programs have been initiated to recruit women and minorities. Your chief has asked that you provide a proposal on what strategies you would suggest to recruit women and minorities. Develop a list of what you would propose. Make a list of what other departmental processes should take place prior to applicant testing.

RETENTION AND PROMOTION OF A DIVERSE WORKFORCE

Recruiting officers who reflect the gender, racial, ethnic, and sexual orientation demographics of the community is one important challenge for law enforcement agencies. Retention and promotion of these officers are equally important. Employees leave their agencies for a variety of causes. As Mark J. Terra explains:

> Exit surveys have identified several reasons why individuals choose to leave employment. The most common was a perceived limited potential for professional growth, characterized as a lack of hope in the present position. Others included a lack of respect or support from supervisors; compensation-related issues pertaining to the individual's value or worth; the perception that supervisors lack leadership skills; and issues related to the employee's work hours (for example., inflexible schedule, not enough overtime, or an undesirable shift). (Terra, 2009, pp. 11–12)

Exit interviews should be utilized to determine why an employee is leaving. Even if the stated purpose is a higher salary, "leaders should personally meet with them and ask questions to clarify whether that is the real reason" (Gladis & Pomerantz, 2008).

Retention

Retention of any employee is usually the result of good work on the part of the employee and a positive environment wherein all employees are treated with dignity and respect. In fact, once an agency earns a reputation for fairness, talented men and women of all ethnicities, races, and sexual orientations will seek out that agency and will remain longer. Job satisfaction, thus retention of employees, including women and protected classes, can often be attributed not only to fair compensation and benefits, but also to the following:

- Leadership
- Mentoring
- Training and Development
- Addressing bias, discrimination, and harassment
- Communication
- Performance Evaluations
- Job Descriptions

LEADERSHIP   Job satisfaction and employee commitment are often attributed to good leadership. Patrick Lencioni proposes that there are three leadership functions that significantly impact employee satisfaction and engagement. These entail creating an atmosphere in which the employee:

1. can see the value in his or her work,
2. sees and has access to the leader (supervisor or manager) and feels valued and appreciated,
3. is provided the skills and abilities to measure the success of his or her contribution to the mission of the organization and particularly of his or her assigned unit (Lencioni, 2007).

Employees who don't see or understand the value of their work sometimes think, therefore, that it is irrelevant. If they don't have communication with their leader, they feel invisible. If they don't know how to measure their contribution to the unit in which they work, they are frustrated. Such employees are usually miserable. Leaders that look for these signs and make necessary changes can transform an unhappy employee into one that is satisfied and less likely to leave the organization.

MENTORING   The importance of mentoring, supporting, and informal networking programs for women and members of diverse groups is covered in Chapter 2. Mentoring, which is not a new concept or practice, can be both formal and informal. Formal mentoring involves establishing policy and procedures, defining roles and responsibilities, and training senior members who will become mentors on the processes and goals of the organization. Mentoring involves providing a system wherein less experienced employees receive information, advice, support, and encouragement from more senior colleagues. Mentoring involves leading, developing, and guiding by example to facilitate the protégé's personal development, for the benefit of both the individual and the organization. Because mentoring and providing networking opportunities contribute to employee satisfaction, there is a greater likelihood of retention.

It should be noted that the role of a mentor and that of a field training officer (FTO) are not the same. The FTO is responsible for the training and development of an effective new officer and evaluates his or her effectiveness continually during the process. The role of a mentor for the same officer is supportive, relational, and does not involve a performance evaluation. The mentor maintains contact with the officer not only during his or her field training, but also upon completion to provide continuing support, guidance and encouragement.

Mentoring and support programs are intended not only for new officers, but also for veterans. Even seasoned officers exposed to or involved in violence or distressing cases (child pornography, pedophiles, rape, deaths, major traffic accidents) need support. Support programs are particularly important when a death involves a fellow officer. Officers typically learn to compartmentalize or hold in their feelings. They need a way to vent and share, but typically do not turn to spouses, intimate others, friends, or family members. Some departments have peer counseling programs that provide support for those members, both sworn and civilian, who need help. Such programs are another means of providing a working environment that is more conducive to retaining employees.

More information about mentoring is available in publications from the International Association of Chiefs of Police, such as *Best Practices Guide for Institutionalizing Mentoring into Police Departments*, *Developing a Mentoring Process*, and *Mentoring for Law Enforcement*. Another source is "Optimizing Mentoring Programs for Women of Color," available from *Catalyst*.

TRAINING AND DEVELOPMENT Development of employees through in-service training, educational opportunities, and access to special assignments within an organization are three factors leading to job knowledge, experience, and satisfaction—and therefore to retention. Departments with programs that help their employees obtain advanced degrees find that such a practice often results in happy and productive members who stay with that agency.

"To be successful in a constantly changing occupation, employees must increase their skills," notes Mark J. Terra in *The FBI Law Enforcement Bulletin*. "If they work for an organization that does not provide such benefits, they will go elsewhere to find them" (Terra, 2009, p.12). Community policing and advances in technology, the emergence of domestic security threats, and the growth of cybercrime and identity theft mean that the skills of officers must be constantly updated.

Training for officers of all ranks should continue throughout their careers. Such training should not only address the necessary, practical skills involving search and seizure, firearms, defensive tactics, arrest procedures, and so on, but also "include current issues, especially pertaining to interaction in a diverse community and communications skills" (Terra, 2009, p. 12). Also, development of employees is important for meeting the requirements for special assignments that increase the chances of promotion within the organization. Special assignments include such highly sought-after positions as those in SWAT, gang, narcotics, canine, or motorcycles units; horse patrol; and field training.

Some law enforcement agencies have formed partnerships with higher education institutions. One example is the Phoenix, Arizona Police Department that partnered with a university where officers can earn a master's degree in leadership in two years. Participants can receive almost $4,000 per year in tuition reimbursement as part of their compensation package (Terra, 2009). Other agencies increase job satisfaction by offering incentives for those pursuing a degree.

Departments that provide incentives and encouragement for college education will find that the opportunities correlate with improved performance and that "degreed officers often have a career advantage over their colleagues who do not have degrees" (Friedman, 2006). Conversely, if an agency does not provide these opportunities, officers will look for agencies that do. Online courses are now making it even easier to acquire knowledge and degrees.

ADDRESSING BIAS, DISCRIMINATION AND HARASSMENT A department seeking to retain employees cannot have internal problems, either real or perceived, related to racism, harassment, discrimination, or hostility toward women, gay male, or lesbian officers. Ethnic slurs, racial or gender jokes, offensive or derogatory comments or other verbal or physical conduct is unlawful and interferes with the individual's work performance.

Departments should analyze statistical information pertaining to the number of officers leaving and their reasons for doing so. Exit interviews should be conducted especially if there is a high turnover rate for women, minorities, or gays and lesbians to ascertain whether there has been discrimination or harassment of any sort that caused the employee to leave and to evaluate how the problem can be corrected.

COMMUNICATIONS   Retention is also higher within agencies where supervisors and managers talk with all members of their workforce on a regular basis. Supervisors and managers are then able to take action to alleviate the sources of discomfort, whether this involves modifying practices or simply discussing behavior with other employees.

Communication between supervisors and employees should be both formal and informal. Formal feedback most often takes the form of a performance evaluation, but it might also take the form of a commendation or even a thank-you note commending the good work of the employee. Positive reinforcement is often achieved by recognizing good performance, and when this is not done, the employee may become unhappy and his or her performance may suffer.

It is important not only that an agency has effective top-down communications, but also communication that flows freely in both directions. Employees who cannot communicate upward become frustrated and angry, which negatively affects their performance level, and may lead to their disengagement from the organization, figuratively or literally.

PERFORMANCE EVALUATION   A good employee performance evaluation system is an important factor in personnel satisfaction and retention. Evaluation systems should be used that involve factors that are job-related and objective rather than subjective. To be objective, the evaluation must focus on traits and behaviors that are measurable and related to the position's job description. It must also be related to the goals of the department or unit to which the officer is assigned. A performance evaluation requires giving accurate feedback to the employee that helps him or her determine personal strengths and weaknesses. It should be a vehicle to encourage improvement and provide guidelines to do so. The evaluation should also focus on the employee's short- and long-term goals so that the officer receives help not only in his or her own professional development, but also in becoming the kind of officer that meets the organization's needs. Performance evaluations should take place annually; if they do not, everyone is slighted, especially women and members of diverse groups.

JOB DESCRIPTIONS   Every sworn and nonsworn employee should have a job description that identifies the position title and describes the essential functions, duties, and tasks the position performs for the employer. The job description lists the knowledge, skills, and abilities required of the position. Further, it delineates the qualifications, such as education and/or experience, license/certificates, and working conditions. The job description is a living document and should be updated when there are changes in the position that impact the employee. It should be reviewed by the employee and his or her supervisor each year at the time of the employee's annual performance evaluation to insure the document provides adequate directions to achieve success in the job. The job description is an excellent tool in eliminating bias and discrimination in the workforce.

Promotion

The limited number of promotions of protected classes and women to supervisor and command ranks has been cited as a severe problem in policing for over three decades by scholars and police researchers alike. Faced with this lack of opportunity, some officers leave the organization for other employment or relocate to law enforcement agencies where they can get promoted. Some agencies do not provide leadership training opportunities or only provide them to those who are on a promotion list or have just been promoted. Agencies that have a succession plan in place and offer opportunities and training to all employees who choose or aspire to be leaders create an environment that encourages participation in promotion processes and career progression. Given the right motivation and tools for self-improvement, even some poor test-takers can make good leaders.

Authors and advocates for the promotion of women have used the term *glass ceiling* to describe an unacknowledged barrier that inhibits women from reaching ranks above entry level. Whether there is a glass ceiling or not, women still constitute only a small proportion of police supervisors and managers. Within organizations, women and others of diverse backgrounds are frustrated when promotional opportunities seem more readily available to white males than to them. The disenchantment that often accompanies frustration frequently leads to low productivity and morale, early burnout, and resignation; to those individuals, opportunities appear better elsewhere. Lack of attention to equal opportunity and lack of transparent promotion policies and practices at some law enforcement agencies have resulted in court-ordered promotions. These have a negative impact on a department's operations and relationships, both internally and externally, and often lead to distrust and dissatisfaction. The dearth of mentors and role models for women and members of diverse groups has also been cited as a reason these employees fail to learn what it takes to get promoted within an organization.

Chief executives need to measure results of efforts to promote women and minorities by determining if these groups are applying for promotions in numbers that are proportional to their numbers in the department. If not, perhaps female and minority officers need encouragement from their supervisors, mentors, or informal network associates. It is also possible that the promotion process disproportionately screens out female and minority officers. Some safeguards against bias include weighting the process toward "hands-on" tasks (for example, assessment center testing), conducting structured interviews, selecting board members who represent different races and both sexes, and training the board members on interviewing techniques.

Failure to promote qualified candidates representative of the diverse populations agencies serve, including women, can result in continued distrust of the police by the communities. Underrepresentation within police departments also aggravates tensions between the police and the community. Some scholars and criminal justice experts argue that underrepresentation at all levels within law enforcement agencies hurts the image of the department in the eyes of the community.

Police executives and city or county managers cannot afford to minimize the consequences of poor retention and inadequate promotional opportunities for women and diverse members of their organizations. Some departments have done very well in recruiting and hiring women, but, for reasons that are yet to be established, women have left departments more quickly than men. The reasons vary, but family pressures are the most frequently cited cause.

GENERATION Y   In Chapter 1, the authors introduced the subject of "Generation Y" or Millennials referring to those persons born between 1977 and 1994. Employers, managers, and supervisors wishing to recruit and retain members of this generation will benefit from understanding their characteristics, learning styles, and work attitudes (NAS Insights, 2006). One particular characteristic that sets members of this generation apart is their technological proficiency, especially when compared to preceding generations. Other characteristics include a generally higher level of education than previous generations (especially women); an expectation of equality and a strong social conscience; an assumption of promotion in less than two years; and the expectation that they will move on from their job within five years (Eisner & Harvey, 2009). These generational differences impact not only how recruiters will attract new law enforcement personnel, but also how supervisors and managers will interact and direct their work and provide an environment in which they will stay and be promoted. Good leaders are aware of these differences and develop and use leadership strategies that work best with these employees.

Mini Case Study: How Would You Handle It?

You are a male lieutenant in charge of the special weapons and tactics unit. The first female officer will soon be assigned to your unit. The special weapons and tactics team members are voicing negative opinions about having a female officer in the unit. They are complaining that standards will be lowered because women are not as physically fit as men. When you have overheard these conversations, or when they have been addressed to you directly, you have refuted them by pointing to the women in the department who are in outstanding physical shape. This strategy has not been effective, as the squad members continue to complain that women officers can't do the job and that their personal safety might be in jeopardy. What would you do?

Summary

- Population changes, particularly those that result in greater diversity, create a demand for law enforcement personnel who have the ability to work with different types of people. The nature of policing has also broadened, requiring officers to master a complex set of skills. The adoption of the community-policing model requires departments to be more representative of and responsive to the communities served.

- Recruiting, hiring, retaining, and promoting a diverse workforce will remain a challenge in law enforcement for a long time. The number of people available and qualified for entry-level jobs will continue to decrease; more employers, both public and private, will be vying for the best candidates. Hiring and promoting women and minorities for law enforcement careers are achievable goals.

- Successful recruiting involves *commitment* by the chief executive; *planning*, including an assessment of current recruitment practices; adequate *resources*; properly selected and trained *recruiters*; the use of *incentives*; and *community involvement*. Law enforcement will have to use innovative and sophisticated marketing techniques and advertising campaigns to reach the desired population of potential applicants, and it must develop fast-track hiring processes.

- The Hiring in the Spirit of Service (HSS) program suggests that to recruit applicants who historically would not be targeted by law enforcement agencies, departments must seek service-minded individuals having qualifications consistent with professions such as teaching, nursing, and counseling. In the past, candidates who did not fit the "crime fighter" image were discouraged from applying or disqualified during the testing process.

- Law enforcement is still in transition away from the aggressive, male-dominated (and predominantly white) culture of the past, so must now overcome the common perception that policing is a profession that requires only physical strength. With the shift to community policing, women can thrive. Departments are looking for people with good interpersonal skills who are community and service-oriented, and they are finding that women meet these qualifications. Law enforcement executives should seek minority employees for the same reasons.

- Prior to initiating any recruitment effort, every agency must assess the satisfaction level of the current employees and evaluate the workplace environment. A department seeking to hire applicants from women and minority groups must first resolve internal problems, either real or perceived, related to racism, discrimination, or hostility toward female, gay male, or lesbian officers. A high turnover rate or a reputation for not promoting women, minorities, or gays and lesbians will also deter potential applicants.

- Retention of employees is crucial and requires a positive environment wherein all employees are treated with dignity and respect. Retention also requires good supervisors and managers and an agency in which there is two-way communication and job-related performance evaluations. A high rate of retention is most likely to occur in organizations that meet the basic needs of employees, offer reasonable opportunities for ongoing professional career development, and have mentoring and networking programs. It is important that the agency addresses any claims of bias, discrimination and harassment within the organization. Once an agency earns a reputation for fairness, talented men and women of all ethnicities and races will seek out that agency and will remain longer.

- Opportunities for promotions of protected classes and women to supervisor and command ranks must be available within the organization. This is accomplished through providing leadership training and mentoring to those who seek advancement. Promotional processes that disproportionately screen out females and minorities should be identified and

removed. Failure to promote qualified candidates representative of the diverse populations agencies serve, including women, can result in continued distrust of the police by the community and hurt the image of the department.

- Employers, managers, and supervisors wishing to recruit and retain members of the Gen Y or Millennial generation will need to understand their unique characteristics, learning styles, and work attitudes.

Discussion Questions and Issues

1. *Institutional Racism in Law Enforcement.* Law enforcement agencies typically operate under the pretense that all their members are one color, and that the uniform or job makes everyone brothers or sisters. Many members of diverse ethnic and racial groups, particularly African Americans, do not agree that they are consistently treated with respect, and believe that there is institutional racism in law enforcement. Caucasians clearly dominate the command ranks of law enforcement agencies. Discuss with other students in your class whether you believe this disparity is the result of subtle forms of institutional racism, or actual conscious efforts on the part of the persons empowered to make decisions. Consider whether tests and promotional processes give unfair advantage to white applicants, and whether they discriminate against department employees of other races and ethnicities. Do officers from diverse groups discriminate against members of other, different cultures?

2. *Employment of a Diverse Workforce and Police Practices.* How has the employment of a diverse workforce affected police practices in your city or county? Is there evidence that significant changes in the ethnic or racial composition of the department alter official police policy? Can the same be said of gay male and lesbian employment? Does employment of protected classes have any significant effect on the informal police subculture and, in turn, on police performance? Provide examples to support your conclusions.

References

Barlow, David E. and Barlow, Melissa H. (2013). "Hiring Latino/a Police Officers: What Police Administrators Need to Know." Paper presented to Academy of Criminal Justice Science conference, April 2013.

Bureau of Labor Statistics, U.S. Department of Labor Retrieved April 5, 2013, from www.bls.gov/ooh/protective-service/police-and-detectives.htm

Eisner, Susan P. and Mary Ellen O'Grady Harvey. "C-change? Generation Y and the glass ceiling." *SAM Advanced Management Journal*, Winter 2009, 74(1).

Friedmann, Robert R., (2006, August). "University Perspective: The Policing Profession in 2050." *The Police Chief,* 73(8).

Fry, Richard and Paul Taylor, "Hispanic High School Graduates Pass Whites in Rate of College Enrollment." (2013, May 9). Pew Research Center. Retrieved June 3, 2013, from www.pewresearch.org

Gladis, Steve and Suzi Pomerantz, "Executive Coaching for Law Enforcement." (2008, February). *FBI Law Enforcement Bulletin,* 77(2), 18–23.

"High school graduation at 36-year high-Officials: Increase reflects weak job market, economy." (2013, January 22). *Contra Costa (Calif.) Times,* p. A4.

"Hiring and Retention of State and Local Law Enforcement Officers, 2008." (2012, October). Brian A. Reaves. NCJ 238251. Retrieved March 24, 2014, from www.bjs.gov/content/pub/pdf/hrslleo08st.pdf

Hilal, Susan M. and Timothy E. Erickson, "The Minnesota Police Education Requirement-A Recent Analysis." (June 2010). *FBI Law Enforcement Bulletin,* 79(6).

"Innovations in Police Recruitment and Hiring: Hiring in the Spirit of Service." (2001). U.S. Department of Justice, Office of Community Oriented Policing Service. Project #2001-CK-WX-K094, p. 1.

International Association of Chiefs of Police (IACP), *Best Practices Guide: Recruitment, Retention, and Turnover in Law Enforcement,* International Association of Chiefs of Police. *Employing Returning Combat Veterans as Law Enforcement Officers-Recruitment Strategies.* (2011, March). Bureau of Justice Assistance Grant No. 2009-D2-BX-K008.

"Law Enforcement Agencies Statewide Compete to Find Enough Qualified Candidates to Serve Their Communities." (2007, February 6). *Contra Costa (Calif.) Times,* pp. 1, 19.

Lencioni, Patrick. (2007). *The Three Signs of a Miserable Job.* Jossey-Bass, San Francisco, CA, p. 217.

Menjivar, Cecilia and Cynthia L. Bejarano. (2004). "Latino immigrants' perceptions of crime and police authorities in the United States: A case study from the Phoenix metropolitan area." *Ethnic and Racial Studies* 27(1), 120–148.

"The Military Discharged about 12,340 People between 1994 and 2007 under 'Don't Ask, Don't Tell.'" (2008, November 18). *Servicemembers Legal Defense Network*. Retrieved March 4, 2009, from www.sldn.org

"Military Justice 101—Part 3, Enlisted Administrative Separations." (1998). Retrieved March 1, 2009, from www.usmilitary.about.com/od/justicelawlegislation/a/miljustice.htm

NAS Insights. (2006). "Generation Y: The Millenials. Ready or Not, Here They Come." NAS Recruitment Communications. Retrieved February 14, 2009, from www.nasrecruitment.com/talenttips/NASinsights/GenerationY.pdf

"Percent of state and local law enforcement officers employed by agencies offering selected incentives to recruit applicants for sworn positions, 2008." (2012, October). Bureau of Justice Statistics, Census of State and Local Law Enforcement Agencies. NCJ 238251. Retrieved April 20, 2013, from www.bjs.gov/index.cfm?ty=pbdetail&iid=4514

"Ready, Willing, and Unable to Serve." (2009). Mission: Readiness- Military Leaders for Kids, Washington D.C., p. 1. Retrieved April 5, 2013, from www.cdn.MissionReadiness.org

"San Francisco Housing Aid for Teachers, Police." (2007, October 21). *Contra Costa (Calif.) Times*, p. A36.

Skinner, Chris, "Recruiting with Emotion and Market Positioning." (2010, July 1). *FBI Law Enforcement Bulletin*, 79(7), 20–27.

Taylor, Paul, Mark Hugo Lopez, Jessica Martinez, and Gabriel Velasco, "When Labels Don't Fit: Hispanics and Their Views of Identity." (2012, April 4). Pew Hispanic Center. Washington, DC: Pew Research Center.

Terra, Mark J., "Increasing Officer Retention through Educational Incentives." (2009, February). *FBI Law Enforcement Bulletin*, 78(2), 11–15.

Tuomey, Lianne and Rachel Jolly, "Step Up to Law Enforcement: A Successful Strategy for Recruiting Women into the Law Enforcement Profession." (2009, June). *The Police Chief*. International Association of Chiefs of Police, Alexandria, VA. Retrieved from www.policechiefmagazine.org

Uniform Code of Military Justice. (**UCMJ**, 64 Stat. 109, 10 U.S.C. ch. 47, 1950). Retrieved May 5, 2009, from www.ucmj.us

"Vallejo Police Recruiting a Tough Go." (2008, March 30). *Contra Costa (Calif.) Times*, p. A 32.

4 Cross-Cultural Communication for Law Enforcement

LEARNING OBJECTIVES

After reading this chapter, you should be able to:

- Identify the impact of language barriers in everyday law enforcement situations.
- Develop skills that are effective with speakers of English as a second language.
- Describe cultural frameworks, including hierarchy and "context," that influence communication.
- Explain typical communication dynamics in cross-cultural, cross-racial, and cross-ethnic encounters.
- List key interviewing and data-gathering skills that contribute to an officer's effectiveness.
- Accommodate verbal and nonverbal communication style differences across cultures.
- Demonstrate understanding of appropriate male-female communication in law enforcement settings.

OUTLINE

- Introduction
- Language Barriers and Law Enforcement
- Attitudes toward Limited-English Speakers
- Cross-Cultural Communication in the Law Enforcement Context
- Cross-Cultural Communication Dynamics
- Interviewing and Data-Gathering Skills
- Nonverbal Communication
- Male-Female Communication in Law Enforcement
- Summary
- Discussion Questions and Issues

INTRODUCTION

In multicultural training sessions for officers, we sometimes hear that there are too many groups about which to learn, and that it is impossible to modify behavior accordingly. Indeed, officers do not have to remember every minute detail about culturally influenced communication, and this is especially true when officers are responding

Understanding cultural differences and how they impact communication is critical. But there's a huge caveat. Let's also understand how we are similar, and what kinds of communication works with people of all backgrounds:

1. Remember that everyone, in all cultures, wants to be respected.
2. For all cultural, racial, or ethnic groups, it is better to provide options than to make threats.
3. All people would like a second chance. Ask: "Is there anything I (we) can say or do to get your cooperation? I (we) would like to think there is."

EXHIBIT 4.1   Effective Communication Across All Backgrounds
Source: Adapted with permission of George Thompson, Founder of Verbal Judo, Personal Communication, 2009.

to emergencies. Officers *are* correct when they point out that the key to effective communication with citizens is respect. They are also correct when they say that, no matter what the background of the citizen is, they have to enforce the law and be consistent with everyone. That said, there are generalities related to cross-cultural communication (including language issues), and recognition of these will enhance overall understanding of certain communication components that officers experience or observe.[*] In other words, there are not hundreds of details to learn despite the myriad cultural, national, and racial groups that officers might encounter.

After years of working with citizens from nearly every background, the late Dr. George Thompson, former police officer and founder of the Verbal Judo Institute, expressed a belief that there are certain communication essentials that contribute to effectiveness regardless of background. Exhibit 4.1 introduces and outlines these items.

To paraphrase Thompson, the default is always respectful communication. Thompson took the key concept of respect one step further: "Talking about respecting people [from all cultural backgrounds] is vague. But treating people with respect is an act that is highly specific" (Thompson, 2009). That said, displays of respect can vary from culture to culture especially in cultures where a hierarchy is strongly emphasized.

In some cultures, for example, respect is offered through indirect eye contact; in many parts of Asia, Africa, and the Middle East, people often show respect by making intermittent eye contact or by looking off into space ("sustained indirect" eye contact). Some officers interpret this behavior as defiant or as a sign of dishonesty, but first-generation refugees or immigrants from these parts of the world are, in fact, communicating respect in the default way that they have learned. Former FBI agent, Joe Navarro, says, "Little or no eye contact is erroneously perceived by some as a classic sign of deception, especially during questioning, while the truthful should 'lock eyes.' This is not supported by research or experience and is completely false" (Navarro, 2009). In addition, when citizens speak in a certain tone of voice or are talking loudly, an officer may assume that they are exhibiting aggression or going out of control. Because of learned ethnocentrism, any officer can easily fall into the trap of making judgments about citizens just by the way they talk or use body language.

Not knowing how to cope with communication style differences can add stress to situations that are already tense. Human beings are programmed and signaled to be "on alert" when something strange or unexpected occurs. It is as if there is a bell or alarm that sounds loudly when people are faced with diversity such as a group of people to which they are not accustomed. This mechanism for alertness and alarm results in stress. Thus, for law enforcement officials whose work by nature can be tense and stressful, it is all the more crucial to build solid skills for leveraging differences in communication styles.

---

[*] *Appendix C on pages 425 is a 15-question assessment, entitled: Cross-Cultural Communication Skills Assessment for Law Enforcement Professionals. It is a tool to help readers identify in what areas they can make improvements in their communication across cultures.*

In dealing with an individual who is not a native speaker of English, it is of key importance to keep three points in mind:

- A listener can easily misinterpret speech patterns—intonation, in particular, can be perceived to carry emotion and intentionality. What one hears is not always what is intended.
- A listener can easily misunderstand spoken words when a speaker is not fluent in English.
- A listener should use multiple indicators for interpreting correctly what a citizen is attempting to say.

LANGUAGE BARRIERS AND LAW ENFORCEMENT

With the increasing emphasis on community policing and staff diversity in law enforcement, cross-cultural communication skills have become more and more essential not only in establishing good relationships with citizens, but also with professional colleagues. In developing cross-cultural communication and competency skills, police officers who were not born in this country or who spoke another language at home can be a valuable resource, offering insights that can alleviate frustration in encounters with those who are not fluent in English. The following is a personal account of a Vietnamese police officer and his struggles with English when he first came to the United States:

> For the first few months of being here, I was always tired from speaking the language. I had to strain my ears all day long and all my nerves were bothered. It was hard work to make people understand my broken English and to listen to them. Sometimes, I just could not communicate any more and I just stopped speaking English. Sometimes I had to pretend I understood what others said and why they were laughing. But inside I felt very depressed. I am an adult and my language sounded worse than a child's. Sometimes it was better not to say anything at all.

Nationwide, changing demographics have resulted in the need for law enforcement to deal increasingly with a multicultural population that includes speakers of other languages who do not have equivalent skills in English. From citizens who report crimes using limited English to crime witnesses, suspects, and victims, there is no absolute assurance that officers will understand them. Officers are justifiably frustrated by language barriers and find it difficult to do their jobs in the way they have been trained. On a "good day" some officers make it a point to modify their English so that they will be better understood; on a stressful day, many officers are frustrated at having to slow down their speech and listen more patiently. Some law enforcement officers are noticeably impatient when they deal with nonnative English speakers. Even citizens who do not speak English well may sense when police are not listening to their side of the story. As a result, citizens who face language barriers are often not successful at communicating even the minimum amount of necessary information. Perhaps most difficult is the situation in which a person with limited English skills is traumatized, further affecting the victim's ability to speak English. Officers need to be aware of the potential for inadvertent discrimination based on a citizen's language background, which could fall under "language and national origin discrimination" (Ho, 2013).

In one case in Oregon, the friends of an Asian man named Hung Minh Tran were accused of involvement in a barroom assault. One miscommunication led to another; eventually Tran was hauled outside and knocked into some chairs by a female police officer. "Tran said [the officer] was giving him confusing commands, such as go against the wall, back up against the wall, and back away from the wall. He didn't understand what she wanted so he did what he's seen on TV: got down on his knees, with his hands locked behind his head, facing away from her, 'so I'm not a threat.'"(Do I see three characters or do I need a better prescription on my bifocals? Please excuse my attempt at humor). At that point, the officer used a Taser on Tran. In the end, over \$80,000 was paid out in a federal civil rights suit for police conduct that was "unnecessary, unreasonable and an excessive use of force" (Bernstein, 2011). Had the officer used good cross-cultural communication skills from the start, this situation might have been avoided.

Clearly, the higher the number of bilingual officers a department has, the more efficient and effective the contact is with non-English-speaking citizens. Many agencies subsidize foreign-language training for their personnel or seek recruits with multiple language skills. When the resources are not available for such programs, however, there can be serious and sometimes tragic consequences. Non-English-speaking citizens may not understand why they are being arrested or searched. They may not know their rights if they are unfamiliar with the legal system, as is the case with many recently arrived immigrants and refugees. Using the wrong interpreter can mislead officers, so much so that a victim and his or her interpreter might give two completely different versions of a story—for example, using the friend of a suspected child abuser to translate the allegations of the child who has been abused. As further illustrated in a Department of Justice notice, . . . when police officers respond to a domestic violence call . . . use of family members or neighbors to interpret for the alleged victim, perpetrator, or witnesses may raise serious issues of competency, confidentiality, and conflict of interest and is thus inappropriate (DOJ, 2002).

Language barriers can lead to serious problems for those who cannot speak English. In some cases there is no sensitivity when it comes to language obstacles. For example, in a largely Spanish-speaking area of Los Angeles, a deputy, according to witnesses, asked a Hispanic male to get out of his car. The man answered in Spanish, "I'm handicapped," and reached down to pull his left leg out of the car. The deputy apparently believed that the man was reaching for a weapon and consequently "struck him on the head with the butt of his gun" (Kolts, 1992). This incident, while dated, is a lesson for all existing and future generations of police officers not to overreact on a motorist traffic stop.

Another Spanish language example has to do with the word *molestar*, which means "to bother" or "to annoy." In the extreme, a Spanish-speaking individual could answer "yes" to an officer's question "Did you molest your niece?" The answer could be "yes" if the non-English-speaking individual thought there was something about his behavior that irritated or annoyed his niece. Certainly, the greater the number of bilingual officers there are, the better. However, even without learning another language, officers can learn about features of other languages that may confuse an interaction when a limited-English speaker communicates with a police officer. For example, some languages do not have verb tenses (e.g., most dialects of Chinese and certain languages of India), and thus you might hear, "I eat tomorrow," or "I eat yesterday." When recounting a crime observed, individuals not fluent in English might make verb-tense errors, potentially leading officers to think that they are not reliable witnesses or that they are not telling the truth. Similarly, in some Asian languages such as Tagalog (one of the main languages spoken in the Philippines), there are no terms to distinguish gender in the he/she form. Thus, when speaking English, some Filipinos mix up gender, again potentially giving the impression that they are dishonest or confused about the facts.

Intolerance of language differences and difficulties is sometimes voiced by police officers in cultural diversity in-service training workshops; similarly, recruit police officers attending cultural diversity classes in police academies echo this sentiment. It is not uncommon to hear, "Why do I have to learn about their language and their customs?" In response to such questions, students need to be challenged and asked, "Who benefits in citizen/police contacts when police officers have effective communication skills?" The response clearly would be that the community, police officers, and the non- or limited-English speaking individual all benefit.

Communication across cultures and with people for whom English is a second language can be frustrating and exacts a great deal of patience from officers. Exhibit 4.2 lists basic guidelines for communicating with others for whom English is a second language. Sensitivity to the

1. Speak slowly and enunciate clearly.
2. Face the person and speak directly even when using an interpreter.
3. Avoid concentrated eye contact if the other speaker is not making direct eye contact.
4. Do not use jargon, slang, idioms, or reduced forms (e.g., "gonna," "gotta," "wanna," "couldja").
5. Avoid complex verb tenses (e.g., "If I would have known, I might have been able to provide assistance").
6. Repeat key issues and questions in different ways.
7. Avoid asking questions that can be answered by yes or no; rather, ask open-ended questions (e.g., instead of "Will you do this?" ask "How will you meet this requirement?").
8. Use short, simple sentences; pause between sentences.
9. Use visual cues such as gestures, demonstrations, and brief written phrases.
10. Use active rather than passive verbs (e.g., "I expect your attention" [active] rather than "Your attention is expected" [passive]).
11. Have written materials duplicated in bilingual format.
12. Pause frequently and give breaks. Monitor speed when talking.
13. Limit to only one idea per sentence.
14. Respect the silence that nonnative English speakers need to formulate their sentences and translate them in their minds.
15. Check comprehension by having the listener repeat material or instructions, and summarize frequently.
16. Provide encouragement and positive feedback on the person's ability to communicate.
17. Listen even more attentively than when communicating with a native speaker of English.
18. Be patient. Every first-generation immigrant struggles with the acquisition of English.
19. Do not speak more loudly than usual. It will not help.

EXHIBIT 4.2 Basic Guidelines for Communicating with People for Whom English Is a Second Language

difficulties of those who do not speak English is in order, but that is only a partial solution to the problem. In attempting to cope with the problem of dealing with non-English-speaking citizens, suspects, and criminals, many departments not only have increased the number of bilingual officers in their forces but have also begun to utilize telephone interpreting services, several of which operate in multiple languages around the clock. Some 911 emergency centers have interpreters available 24 hours a day for many languages.

Government agencies that serve the public are required by Executive Order 13166 (see Exhibit 4.3) to provide "meaningful access" to all of their services. Commercial language services have made it possible to support 911 call centers, extend victim support, issue Miranda rights, and even assist officers with routine traffic stops. Having access to multilingual interpretation services as well as community referrals is a first step in addressing the challenge of communication with those who speak no or limited English, but it is not a long-term solution. Having bilingual officers or bilingual nonsworn personnel constitutes a more direct method of addressing the problem. Many departments across the country encourage on-the-job

Executive Order 13166
Improving Access to Services for Persons with Limited English Proficiency (LEP)

On August 11, 2000, President Bill Clinton signed Executive Order 13166. "Each Federal agency shall examine the services it provides and develop and implement a system by which LEP persons can meaningfully access those services . . ."

EXHIBIT 4.3 Executive Order Mandating Access to Services for LEP
Source: U.S. Department of Justice, Civil Rights Division, 2000.

language training with tuition reimbursement for classes, and offer extra pay for second-language proficiency. Police department personnel are encouraged to look for classes specially designed for law enforcement. If they do not exist, a few select officers and language educators should form a partnership so that officers can guide language teachers in the development of police-specific second-language curricula (i.e., to meet the specialized needs of officers on the street).

A certain amount of distrust among cross-cultural and racial groups undoubtedly originates with language and communication problems. There is a strong and positive message to the community when departments provide officers with some type of language training as well as matching appropriate language skills to a community's particular demographics.

Increasing bilingual hires is one of the most practical directions in which to go; as an additional advantage, bilingual officers often have a better understanding of the communities they serve. Some community policing programs use trained citizen volunteers to assist in situations in which English is not the primary language spoken. When interpretation services are not available, officers have no choice but to rely on English. In such situations, the tips listed in Exhibit 4.2 on modifying one's language will be helpful.

ATTITUDES TOWARD LIMITED-ENGLISH SPEAKERS

It is important not to stereotype those who speak with accents or have little knowledge of English. An individual might have immigrated to the United States after the age at which people lose their accents (usually in the early teens). Many immigrants speak broken English, and may give all appearances of being "foreign" because their English is not perfect—yet they may be intelligent and highly educated. People who speak English poorly might be diplomatic personnel from another country, or tourists. Treating any of these people with less than the utmost patience and respect can have serious consequences for the community; not to mention the reputation of the local police force. The key is to avoid making inferences about individuals based on their accents or levels of fluency; this includes avoiding assumptions as to whether they are documented or undocumented immigrants.

Citizens' use of a second language and the accompanying frustrations for officers can be overwhelming. In some cases, whether the society at large (or police as a microcosm of society) is concerned about a particular group's use of their native language seems to be directly related to the population size of that group. For example, when large groups of Cubans or Puerto Ricans speak Spanish there is often a higher level of anxiety among the dominant white population than when a few Armenians speak their native language. In other cases, U.S. citizens who do not speak any languages other than English sometimes take it personally when people speak other languages around them, expressing concern that people are talking about them "behind their backs" or—particularly in the case of law enforcement situations—strategizing about criminal activity. While this might be true, it is always more likely *not* to be the case.

Virtually every immigrant group is said to resist learning English, yet the pattern of language acquisition among the generations of immigrants follows a predictable course. Members of the second and third generations of an immigrant family almost always become fluent in English, while many first-generation immigrants (the grandparents and the parents) struggle, sometimes partly learning English and sometimes not learning it at all. This is because most first-generation immigrants arrive in the United States as adults, and thus face the same problem learning English that many Americans face in foreign-language classrooms—that is, they begin their studies as teens or adults, when it is more difficult to learn a new language, rather than as children. Because of this, adults often believe that they are "no good" at the new language and give up trying to learn it.

Many immigrants, however, are extremely motivated to learn English and become productive members of society. In urban areas, access to English classes is often limited (e.g., there have been known to be four- and five-year waiting lists for English programs at Los Angeles community colleges). Newcomers are fully aware that without English they will not be able to integrate into society.

Nevertheless, some people, including established immigrants, have a tendency to over-generalize their observations about newcomers. It is true that some people do not want to learn English and that even some middle-class U.S.-born Americans do not make efforts to improve their language abilities. How often do we hear that high school graduates who are native English speakers have not learned to write or speak well? In such cases, laziness or lack of high-quality education or both may have contributed to this aspect of illiteracy. In fairness, all groups have a percentage of lazy people, but people tend to stereotype others. Although not all first-generation immigrants learn English, there is a great deal of mythology around the "masses" of immigrants who hold on to their native languages. Interestingly, in the reverse, many people born in the United States find it completely normal for an American business executive who is sent to work in Japan, for example, to learn little or no Japanese during his entire stay in the country. In other words, many Americans are tolerant of other Americans who struggle to learn a foreign language but are intolerant of immigrants who struggle with English. Other languages seem "difficult," while one's own language seems "easy." *Any* language can be challenging to master.

The native language of an immigrant family is the language of communication for that family, and speaking it is essential if children in the family are to communicate with relatives who might still be living in the family's country of origin. It is not uncommon to hear comments from U.S.-born citizens such as, "They'll never learn English if they insist on speaking their native tongue at home." But most individuals are severely challenged to express affection, resolve conflicts, show anger, and even to simply relax in a second language. In addition, language is an integral part of a person's identity. During the initial months, and even years, of communicating in a second language, a person does not truly feel like himself or herself. Initially, an individual often has a feeling of play acting or taking on another identity when communicating in a second language.

From a physiological perspective, communicating in a foreign language and adjusting to life in a new culture can be exhausting. Everyday tasks require tremendous mental energy to accomplish. Listening to a foreign language for extended periods of time is absolutely draining, as shown in the case of the Vietnamese police officer presented earlier in this chapter. And in speaking any given language, a person uses a set of muscles to articulate the sounds of that language. Changing to another language, particularly as an adult, requires the use of an entirely new set of muscles. Doing so causes mental strain and facial tension. All of these things combined can lead to a person's "shutting down"—the result of which is an inability to communicate in the new language. It is no wonder that in the multicultural workforce, clusters of people from different ethnic groups can be seen having lunch and taking breaks together. Simply put, it conserves mental and physical energy to be able to speak one's own language.

Sometimes police officers say, "I know they speak English because they speak it among themselves" (i.e., when the group is culturally mixed). "The minute I'm on the scene, it's 'No speak English.' Why do they have to play dumb? What do they think I am—stupid?" It would be naïve to say that this situation does not occur. There will always be some people who try to deceive others and use or not use English to their own advantage. However, there may be other reasons that people "feign" not knowing English. Several factors affect an immigrant's ability to use English at any given moment. A few of these are of particular significance to law enforcement officers. Generally speaking, an immigrant's ability to express himself or herself in English is at its best when that person is comfortable with the officer. So, the more intimidating an officer is, the higher the likelihood that anxiety will affect the speaker's ability in English. Language breakdown is one of the first signs that a person is ill at ease and stressed to the point of not being able to cooperate and communicate. It is in the officer's best interest to increase the comfort level of the citizen, whether a victim, a suspect, or simply a person requiring help. However, language breakdown in a person who is otherwise conversationally competent in English can also occur as a result of illness, intoxication, fatigue, and trauma.

Yet another reason why people might be hesitant to speak English with a police officer is instinctive self-preservation, particularly when they have experienced corrupt or brutal treatment by law enforcement officers in their own countries, or if they are unfamiliar with the U.S. legal system. (See Chapter 1 for examples of this.)

Finally, officers' attitudes toward immigrants and nonnative English speakers, whether positive or negative, are likely to affect their interactions with them. This is especially true when an officer is under pressure and negative attitudes are more likely to surface in communication. A calm demeanor and sincere efforts to listen and understand will pay high returns.

CROSS-CULTURAL COMMUNICATION IN THE LAW ENFORCEMENT CONTEXT

To understand the need for skillful communication with members of culturally and ethnically diverse groups, as well as with women from one's own cultural group, officers should recognize some of the special characteristics of cross-cultural communication in the law enforcement context (Exhibit 4.4). To best protect and serve communities made up of individuals from many different racial and cultural backgrounds, officers as peacekeepers, crime fighters, and law enforcement representatives need to look beyond the "mechanics" of policing and examine what takes place in the process of cross-cultural communication. Communication, in general, is a challenge because "although the words are the same the meaning can be completely different. The same expression can easily have a different connotation or emotional emphasis. Misinterpretation is so common and consistent that eventually we develop limiting perspectives of each other" (Gray, 2002). Most people think that talking to others, making one's points, and giving explanations should not be so difficult. Effective communication, however, results in *mutual* understanding; it is not a one-way process.

Every communication act involves a message, a sender, and a receiver. Given that any two human beings are fundamentally different, there will always be a psychological distance between the two involved (even if they have the same cultural background). Professional police officers are usually trained in various methods of bridging the gap, or psychological distance,

---

- Officers have traditionally used styles of communication and language that at one time were considered acceptable. Now, because of diverse groups within the police agency and within our cities, the unspoken rules about appropriate and inappropriate communication are changing.
- Communication can be tense in crises and in culturally unfamiliar environments.
- Officers' perceptions of a cultural group may be skewed by the populations they encounter.
- Communication will be enhanced when officers are aware of
  1. Perceptions
  2. Cultural filters
  3. High- and low-context communication styles (see explanation in text)
  4. Possible biases and stereotypes
- Through communication, officers have tremendous power to influence the behavior and responses of the citizens they contact. A lack of knowledge of the dynamics of cross-cultural communication will diminish this power.
- Improved communication with all citizens will result in safer interactions for officers.

EXHIBIT 4.4   Key Cross-Cultural Areas in Communication for Officers to Consider

between the two very different worlds of sender and receiver. In instances of cross-cultural communication, including cross-racial and cross-ethnic interactions, in which the sender and receiver are from different cultures, officers have an even greater gap to try to bridge. Exhibit 4.4 summarizes key factors that can potentially contribute to cross-cultural and cross-racial communication challenges. Psychological distance exists between any two human beings because every individual is "wired" differently from the next. Styles of communication that differ across cultures can contribute to perceptions or misperceptions and incorrect filtering of communication "data."

The Influence of Hierarchy and Formality on Communication

Hierarchy A deeply embedded system of societal structure whereby people are organized according to how much status and power they have. Hierarchical societies have specific and defined ways in which people must behave toward those lower and higher on the hierarchy. Communication is restricted in hierarchical societies, and people are always aware of where they stand in terms of status and power vis-à-vis other individuals.

Most Americans, to some extent, believe in equality and reject notions of hierarchy; interpreting hierarchy as the idea that one person is better than another. (Hence the saying, "Everyone puts on their pants one leg at a time.") Related to this belief is an emphasis in American culture on informality. But differences in communication style due to cultural beliefs about hierarchy and formality are not truly foreign to Americans. For example, they tend to communicate differently with their bosses as compared to their siblings or best friends—especially when the topic under discussion is emotionally charged. Communication in *every* culture is influenced by hierarchy and formality to one degree or another.

For people who come from cultures in which differences in hierarchy and formality are emphasized rather than downplayed, communication styles vary widely depending on the status of the person to whom they are speaking. Law enforcement officials who randomly encounter people from cultures in which hierarchy and formality are emphasized must realize that an officer's status is that of a stranger (requiring formality) and of an authority figure (requiring deference based on hierarchy). Relationship building, at least in the initial stages, may be challenging. Law enforcement should recognize that "opening up" can take longer, and that the need to gain trust, a critical step with all citizens, may take more effort. (The reader can review the section on undocumented immigrants in Chapter 1 to understand other elements of the fear factor and communication with law enforcement.)

There is a strong link among the elements of hierarchy, formality, and communication. This has implications for law enforcement workforce interaction not only because agencies are hierarchical, but also because of workforce cultural diversity within an agency and attitudes that may be brought to work by first-generation immigrants and refugees. In terms of understanding the influence of hierarchy and formality on communications under stressful conditions, one of the most studied areas is the airplane cockpit.

A 1999 plane crash in London involving Korean Airlines was "partly blamed on rigid relations between senior and junior pilots . . . The plane's captain, who had a malfunctioning cockpit indicator, censured his first officer who was communicating correct information to the control tower, according to British investigators" (Park, 2013). In a study published the year after that crash, pilot respondents (First Officers) who indicated that their aviation companies had a relatively autocratic or directive leadership style reported that "subordinates [more frequently] are afraid to express disagreement . . . with the Captains" (Merritt, 2000). While accounting for other factors contributing to plane crashes, the researchers of the study concluded that "effects of national culture can be seen over and above the professional pilot culture . . ." (Merritt, 2000).

Interestingly, one writer has pointed out that, "In fact, cultural characteristics generally associated with 'western' culture have also been implicated in fatal air accidents . . . In one of the worst air accidents . . . the [American] crew had been chatting informally with one another on their descent and had not been paying adequate attention to their surroundings . . . These incidents—and others like them—clearly illustrate that while excessive rigidity in an airplane cockpit is a liability, excessive informality is equally dangerous" (Freeland, 2012). Eventually, rules were put in place by U.S. aviation authorities to restrict cockpit conversations "to matters related to the operation of the aircraft during critical phases of the flight" (Freeland, 2012). What this demonstrates is that cultural influences can have serious consequences, and have implications for the communication that takes place among different levels of hierarchy in culturally diverse law enforcement settings.

High- and Low-Context Communication

Edward Hall is the author of three dated but still seminal books in the field of cross-cultural communication: *The Silent Language, Beyond Culture*, and *The Hidden Dimension* (Hall, 1959, 1966, 1976). He coined the terms *high-context* and *low-context* to describe very different frameworks of communication across cultures and individual styles. (Exhibit 4.5 depicts a view of the high- to low-context communication spectrum across regions.) An understanding of this spectrum of high- to low-context communication—which can be related to hierarchy—will contribute to officers' understanding of direct/indirect or explicit/implicit communication.

In low-context (or direct/explicit) communication, people depend on words to create meaning, and rely little on other factors such as the setting, people's body language, the levels of hierarchy involved in the discussion, and so on. High-context (or indirect/implicit) communicators, in contrast, take many of their cues from the context rather than from words. In communication,

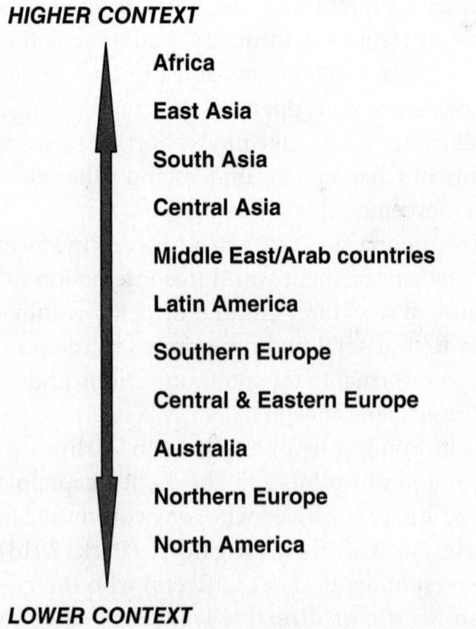

HIGHER CONTEXT

↑

Africa

East Asia

South Asia

Central Asia

Middle East/Arab countries

Latin America

Southern Europe

Central & Eastern Europe

Australia

Northern Europe

North America

↓

LOWER CONTEXT

EXHIBIT 4.5   High- and Low-Context Spectrum across Regions
Source: Adapted from Edward Hall, *Beyond Culture* (1976) and Geert Hofstede (2010).

people or cultural groups who tend toward the high-context end of this communication spectrum exhibit the following characteristics, to varying degrees:

- "Yes" means "I'm listening"; tendency to avoid saying no directly
- Desire to maintain harmony and avoid disagreement/conflict
- Difficulty answering yes/no and either/or type questions; awareness of shades of gray and broad context or scope
- Concern about maintaining face (theirs and others)
- Preference for getting to the point slowly and/or indirectly
- Appearance of "beating around the bush" (i.e., this is a low-context communicator's perception and filter of the higher-context style); in high-context communication, beating around the bush is seen as a polite style of communication and the "right" way to communicate

Lower-context communication tendencies include the following:

- "Yes" equals "yes" and "no" equals "no"
- Ease with direct communication and responding directly to conflict
- Belief that "the truth" is more important than issues of "face"
- Preference for getting right to the point; "beating around the bush" seen as negative

Exhibit 4.6 expands on these tendencies and provides a list of other cultural behavior associated with them.

High-Context Cultures	Low-Context Cultures
Relationships among people and the situation (or "context") determine, in large part, how communication should take place.	Styles of communication are similar among people regardless of their relationships or the setting. People do not generally speak more formally to an authority figure.
• There is deference to authority. • There is formality between people in authority and others. • This formality often manifests itself in restrained and polite communication.	• There is an emphasis on equality. • It is acceptable for casual and informal communication to take place between people at differing levels of a hierarchy.
Individuals who are subordinate tend to offer respectful silence and/or statements of agreement in the presence of an authority figure.	Open and transparent communication is characteristic of low-context cultures, in general. (Organizations, however, can still be hierarchical, even in low-context cultures.)
• In a high-context culture, people tend to tell authority figures what they think the authority figures want to hear.	• There is less emphasis on pleasing authority than on speaking one's mind.
There is a greater focus on the importance of relationships rather than on completion of tasks.	There is greater focus on completing tasks than on nurturing relationships.
• Accordingly, timing allows for interruptions and attention to people (vs. tasks).	• Accordingly, there is a high value placed on task achievement and getting things done. • To a high-context individual, task orientation may appear cold and rude, and can interfere with rapport building.
To a low-context, task-oriented person, constant interruptions may appear unfocused, and the communication style may seem digressive.	

EXHIBIT 4.6 Characteristics of High- and Low-Context Cultures
Source: Adapted from Edward Hall, *Beyond Culture* (1976). Garden City, NY: Doubleday.

As officers know, rapport-building with all citizens is essential for building trust, and this is often preliminary to people's willingness to communicate freely with the officers. This is especially true when communicating with people who have higher-context communication styles. Typically, these styles are more characteristic of Asian and Latin American cultures. Within any given culture, there are gender differences as well (i.e., women tend to have a higher-context style than do men). The style of communication in law enforcement is essentially a lower-context communication style, but police officers should at least be able to identify when individuals are using a higher-context communication style. Chapter 5 provides several examples of high-context communication in the law enforcement context and makes recommendations for responding effectively to this style. (See section entitled, "Communication Styles of Asian/Pacific Americans" in Chapter 5).

One of the key tools for building rapport in law enforcement is neurolinguistic programming (NLP), a communication model and a set of techniques for establishing rapport. Officers have successfully used this communication tool to build rapport in interviews with witnesses and victims of crimes. The techniques involved have to do with a fundamental principle in interpersonal relationships, which is the need to create harmony with others in order to establish rapport. As such, one type of communication used with NLP is that of "modeling," or matching nonverbal and verbal behavior with a witness, victim, or interviewee. Doing so may prove to be especially challenging with people from different cultural backgrounds, but it is useful as a way to minimize the cultural gap between the officer's style and that of the citizen with whom he or she is interacting. It is beyond the scope of this chapter to detail the theory behind and steps involved in NLP. For additional information, see the FBI Law Enforcement Bulletin article entitled, "Subtle Skills for Building Rapport" (Sandoval & Adams, 2001).

CROSS-CULTURAL COMMUNICATION DYNAMICS

It is naturally less challenging to interact with people from one's own background than with those from a different group. Communication can be strained and unnatural when there is no apparent common ground. The "people are people everywhere" argument and "just treat everyone with respect" advice both fall short when we understand that there can be basic differences in the areas of behavior and communication across cultures. Some police officers feel that understanding of cross-cultural communication is unnecessary if respect is shown to every person. Yet, if officers have had limited contact with people from diverse backgrounds, they may inadvertently communicate their lack of cross-cultural competence. In the next few sections, we exemplify typical ways people attempt to accommodate or react to cultural or racial differences and how they may cover up their discomfort in communication across cultures.

Using Language or Language Style to Become Just Like One of "Them"

Black officer to a white officer: "Hey, what kind of arrest did you have?"
White officer: "Brotha-man was trying to front me . . ."

Captain Darryl McAllister from the Hayward, California, Police Department uses the preceding example to illustrate how obviously uncomfortable some white people are when communicating cross-racially. One of his pet peeves is hearing other officers trying to imitate him in speech and trying to act like a "brother." He explains that this type of imitative language is insincere and phony. The artificiality makes him feel as if people are going overboard to show just how comfortable they are when, in fact, they may not be. He explained that he does not feel that this style of imitation is necessarily racist but that it conveys others' discomfort with his "blackness" (McAllister, 2013).

Similarly, officers attempting to establish rapport with citizens should not pretend to have familiarity with the language and culture or use words selectively to demonstrate how "cool" they are (e.g., using *señor* with Spanish-speaking people, calling an African American "my man," or referring to a Native American as "chief"). People of one cultural background may find themselves in situations in which an entire crowd or family is using a particular dialect or slang. If officers lapse into the manner of speaking of the group, they will likely appear to be mocking that style. Ultimately, police officers should be sincere and natural. "Faking" another style of communication can have extremely negative results.

Walking on Eggshells

When in the presence of people from different cultural backgrounds, some people have a tendency to work hard not to offend. Consequently, they are not able to be themselves or do what they would normally do. In a cultural diversity session for city government employees, one white participant explained that he normally has no problem being direct when solicitors come to the door trying to sell something or ask for a donation to a cause. His normal response would be to say, "I'm not interested," and then he would promptly shut the door. He explained, however, that when a black solicitor comes to the door, he engages the person in conversation, and most of the time ends up making a donation to whatever cause is being promoted. His inability to be himself and communicate directly stems from his concern about appearing to be racist. It is not within the scope of this subsection to analyze this behavior in depth, but simply to bring into awareness some typical patterns of reactions in cross-cultural and cross-racial encounters. A person must internally recognize the tendency to overcompensate in order to eventually reach the goal of communicating in a sincere and authentic manner with people of all backgrounds (Exhibit 4.7).

"Some of My Best Friends Are . . ."

In an attempt to show how tolerant and experienced they are with members of minority groups, some people feel the need to demonstrate this strongly by saying things such as, "I'm not prejudiced," or "I have friends who are members of your group," or "I know . . . people," or, worse, "I once knew someone who was also [for example, Jewish/Asian/African American]." Although the intention may be to break down barriers and establish rapport, these types of statements often sound patronizing. To a member of a culturally or racially different group, this type of comment comes across as extremely naïve. In fact, many people would understand such a comment as signifying that the speaker actually does have prejudices toward a particular group. Minority-group members would question a nonmember's need to make a reference to others of the same background when there is no context for doing so. These types of remarks indicate that the speaker is probably isolated from members of the particular group. Yet the person making a statement such as "I know someone who is Asian" is trying to establish something in common with the other person and may even go into detail about the other person he or she

- Self-awareness about one's early life experiences that helped to shape perceptions, filters, and assumptions about people
- Self-awareness about how one feels toward someone who is "different"
- Management of assumptions and discomfort in dealing with people who are different (e.g., do I try to deny that differences exist and laugh differences away, or imitate "them" in order to appear comfortable?)
- Ability to be authentic in communication with others by modifying communication style when necessary

EXHIBIT 4.7   Key Areas for Officers to Consider: Self-Awareness

knows. As one Jewish woman reported in a cross-cultural awareness session, "Just because a person I meet is uncomfortable meeting Jews or has very little experience with Jews doesn't mean that I want to hear about the one Jewish person he met ten years ago while traveling on a plane to New York!"

"You People" or the We/They Distinction

Some may say, "I'd like to get to know you people better," or "You people have made some amazing contributions." The use of "you people" may be another signal of prejudice or divisiveness in a person's mind. When someone decides that a particular group is unlike his or her own group (i.e., not part of "my people"), that person makes a simplistic division of all people into two groups: "we" and "they." Often accompanying this division is the attribution of positive traits to "us" and negative traits to "them." Members of the "other group" (the out-group) are described in negative and stereotypical terms (e.g., "They are lazy," "They are criminals," "They are aggressive") rather than neutral terms that describe cultural or ethnic generalities (e.g., "They have a tradition of valuing education," or "Their communication style is more formal than that of most Americans"). The phenomenon of stereotyping makes it very difficult for people to communicate with each other effectively because they do not perceive others accurately. By attributing negative qualities to another group, a person creates myths about the superiority of his or her own group. Cultural and racial put-downs are often attempts to make people feel better about themselves.

"You Stopped Me Because I'm . . ." or Accusations of Racial Profiling

There are three recurring situations in which an officer may hear the accusation: "You stopped me because I'm [black, Arab, etc.]." The first situation is when citizens from a neighborhood with residents predominantly from one race or culture are suspicious of any person who shows up in their neighborhood who is obviously from a different cultural or racial background. Thus they may call 911 reporting a "suspicious character" and may even add such statements as, "I think he has a gun," when there is no basis for such an accusation. In this situation, the police officer must understand the extreme humiliation and anger the "suspicious characters" feel when they are the object of such racist perceptions. Once the officer determines that there is no reason to arrest the citizen, it is most appropriate for the officer to apologize for having made the stop and to explain that department policy requires that officers are obliged to investigate all calls.

Indeed, incidents occur all over the country in which citizens call a police department to report a "suspicious character" just because he or she does not happen to fit the description of the majority of the residents in that area. Given that there is a history of stopping minorities for reasons that are less than legitimate, the officer must go out of his or her way to show respect to the innocent citizen who does not know why he or she has been stopped and is caught totally off guard. Many people reported to be "suspicious" for merely being of a different race would appreciate an officer's making a final comment such as "I hope this kind of racism ends soon within our community" or "It's too bad there are still people in our community who are so ignorant." Comments such as these, said with sincerity, may very well get back to the community and contribute to improved future interactions with members of the police department. Of course, some people who are stopped will not appreciate any attempt that the officer makes to explain why the stop was made. Nevertheless, many citizens will react favorably to an officer's understanding of their feelings.

A second situation in which an officer may hear, "You stopped me because I'm . . ." may occur not because of any perceived racist intentions of the officer but rather as a "reflex response" of the citizen (in other words, it has no bearing on reality). Many people have been stopped without reason in the past or know people who have; they carry this baggage into each encounter with an officer. One police officer explained: "I don't consider myself prejudiced. I consider myself a fair person, but let me tell you what happens almost every time I stop a black in city X. The first words I hear from them are 'You stopped me because I'm black.' That's bugging the hell out of me because that's not why I stopped them. I stopped them because they violated the traffic code. It's really bothering me and I'm about to explode."

Officers accused of racially or ethnically motivated stops truly need to remain professional and not escalate a potential conflict or create a confrontation. Law enforcement officials should not only try to communicate their professionalism, both verbally and nonverbally, but also try to strengthen their self-control. The best way to deal with these types of remarks from citizens is to work on one's own reactions and stress level. One could potentially receive such remarks on a daily basis. People react to officers as symbols and are using the officer to vent their frustration.

Let's assume that an officer did not stop a person because of his or her ethnicity or race and that the officer is therefore not abusing his or her power. The late George Thompson, founder and president of the Verbal Judo Institute, believed that in these situations, people bring up race and ethnicity to throw the officer off guard. According to Thompson (who was white and a police officer), the more professional an officer is, the less likely he or she is to let this type of statement become a problem. Newer officers, especially, can be thrown off guard by such allegations of racism when, in fact, they are simply upholding the law and keeping the peace as they have been trained to do. Thompson advocated using "verbal deflectors" when citizens make such remarks as "You stopped me because I'm. . . ." He recommended responses such as "I appreciate that, but you were going 55 miles an hour in a 25-mile-per-hour zone," or "I hear what you're saying, but you just broke the law." Verbal deflectors: (1) are readily available to the lips, (2) are nonjudgmental, and (3) can be said quickly. Thompson believed that statements from citizens should not be ignored. Silence or no response can make people even more furious than they already were because they were stopped (Thompson, 2009).

> Pay attention to what citizens say, but deflect their anger. You are not paid to argue with citizens. You are paid to keep the peace. If you use tactical language and focus every word you say so that it relates to your purpose, then you will sound more professional. The minute you start using words as defensive weapons, you lose power and endanger your safety. If you "springboard" over their arguments and remain calm, controlled, and nonjudgmental, you will gain voluntary compliance most of the time. The results of this professional communication are that: (1) you feel good, (2) you disarm the citizen, and (3) you control them in the streets (and in courts and in the media). Never take anything personally. Always treat people with respect and explain the "why" in your communication with them. (Thompson, 2009)

The third and final situation in which an officer may hear "You stopped me because I'm . . ." is when the citizen is correct and, indeed, racial profiling is taking place. Police department personnel are not immune from the racism that still exists in our society. Reflecting biased attitudes outside the law enforcement agency, some officers use their positions of power to assert authority in ways that cannot be tolerated. We are referring not only to the white officer who subjugates citizens from different backgrounds, but also, for example, to an African American officer who has internalized the racism of the dominant society and may actually treat fellow group members unjustly. Alternatively, this abuse of power could take place between, for example, a black or Latino officer and a white citizen. (See Chapter 13 for a detailed description of racial profiling.)

Officers must consider the reasons a citizen may say, "You stopped me because I'm . . ." and respond accordingly. The situations described above (i.e., citizens call in because of racist perceptions and the "suspicious character" is innocent; the citizen stopped is simply "hassling" the officer, and may or may not have been unjustly stopped in the past; and the citizen making the accusation toward the officer is correct) call for different responses on the part of the officer. The officer would do well, in all three situations, to remember the quote included in the final section of Chapter 1: "Remember the history of law enforcement with all groups and ask yourself the question, 'Am I part of the past, or a part of the future?'" (Berry, 2013).

Communication Considerations Post-9/11

Many Arab Americans, in particular, feel that they are automatic suspects when approached by law enforcement representatives. Since 9/11, there has been what Lobna Ismail, an Arab American cross-cultural specialist, characterizes as collateral damage to the entire Arab American community. They may hesitate to call the police when they are victims of crimes, and they fear being treated as suspects rather than victims of a crime (Ismail, 2013). While there has been progress in some jurisdictions in bridging the cultural gap with police in the years following 9/11, mutual distrust between some Arab American communities and law enforcement lingers. Some of this has come about because of 9/11, but, in addition, some immigrants bring with them a fear of law enforcement from their native countries where widespread police corruption as well as police brutality were and are facts of life (NIJ, 2008). It is therefore imperative to consider the importance of building trust, rapport, and relationships with Arab Americans and people from the Middle East. According to Dr. James Zogby, president of the Arab American Institute Foundation in Washington, D.C., the more a community-policing mindset has developed in a particular locale, the more easily do communication barriers come down between law enforcement and Arab Americans. "We have found that when FBI and police department leadership, for example, are willing to sit down and dialogue with community leaders, then it is much more likely that citizens will be willing to share information and provide tips because officers have gone out of their way to build trust" (Zogby, 2013).

Regarding communication with Arab Americans (and this applies to communication with other cultural groups as well), officers should not try too hard, in an unnatural way, to demonstrate cultural understanding. An officer should accommodate differences in communication style where they exist, but should not act stiff or uncomfortable in an attempt to "get it right." With cultural groups that may appear very different from one's own, or when sensitivities may be high, as with members of the Arab American community, law enforcement representatives should think about approaching others in a way that will increase the comfort level of all concerned. This means being natural; not beginning with the assumption that others are foreign and strange; and avoiding such thoughts as "I can't communicate with them unless I know their ways" (Zogby, 2013). In the end, the spirit of respect toward fellow human beings, with some knowledge of cultural detail, will lead to effective communication. See Chapter 8 for in-depth coverage of law enforcement contact with Arab Americans and other groups from the Middle East.

INTERVIEWING AND DATA-GATHERING SKILLS

Interviewing and data-gathering skills form the basic techniques for communication and intervention work with multicultural populations. For the officer, the key issues in any interviewing and data-gathering situation are as follows:

- Establishing interpersonal relationships to gain trust and rapport for ongoing work
- Bringing structure and control to the immediate situation
- Gaining information about the problems that require the presence of the law enforcement officer
- Giving information about law enforcement guidelines, resources, and assistance available
- Providing action and intervention as needed
- Bolstering and supporting the different parties' abilities and skills to solve current and future problems on their own

Listed in Exhibit 4.8 are helpful guidelines for providing and receiving information in appropriate ways in a multicultural context.

In the area of data gathering and interviewing, the officer in a multicultural law enforcement and peacekeeping situation cannot assume that his or her key motivators and

1. Be knowledgeable about who is likely to have information. Ask questions to identify the head of a family or respected community leaders.
2. Consider that some cultural groups have need extra efforts at rapport and trust building before they are willing to share information. Do not consider the interval that it takes to establish rapport a waste of time.
3. Provide background and context for questions, information, and requests. Cultural minorities differ in their need for contextual (i.e., background) information before getting down to the issues or business at hand. Remain patient with those who want to go into more detail than you think is necessary.
4. Expect answers to be formulated and expressed in culturally different ways. Some people tend to be linear in their answers (i.e., giving one point of information at a time in a sequential or chronological order); some present information in a zigzag fashion (i.e., they digress frequently); and others tend to present information in a spiral or circular style (i.e., they may appear to be avoiding the point). And, of course, in addition to cultural differences, there are individual differences in ways of presenting information.
5. It is important to speak simply, but do not make the mistake of using simple or "pidgin" English. Remember, people's comprehension skills are usually better than their speaking skills.
6. "Yes" does not always mean "yes"; do not mistake a courteous answer for the facts or the truth or even for understanding.
7. Remember that maintaining good rapport is just as important as coming to the point and getting work done quickly. Slow down!
8. Silence is a form of speech; do not interrupt it. Give people time to express themselves by respecting their silence.

EXHIBIT 4.8   Interviewing and Data Gathering in a Multicultural Context

values are the same as those of the other parties involved. Recognizing such differences in motivation and values will result in greater effectiveness. For example, the values of maintaining face and/or preserving one's own honor as well as the honor of one's family are extremely strong motivators for many people from Asian, Latin American, and Mediterranean cultures. An Asian gang expert from the Oakland, California, Police Department illustrated this value system with the case of a niece who had been chosen by the police to translate for her aunt, who had been raped. The values of honor and face prevented the aunt from telling the police all the details of the crime of which she was the victim. Her initial story, told to the police through her niece's translation, contained very few of the facts or details of the crime. Later, through a second translator who was not a family member, the rape victim gave all the necessary information. Precious time had been lost, but the victim explained that she could not have revealed the true story in front of her niece because she would have shamed her family.

Exhibit 4.9 lists key values or motivators for police officers. In any given situation, these values may be at odds with what motivates the victim, suspect, or ordinary citizen of any background. However, when the officer and the citizen are from totally different backgrounds, additional cultural or racial variables may also be in conflict.

1. Survival or injury avoidance
2. Control and structure
3. Respect and authority
4. Use of professional skills
5. Upholding laws and principles
6. Avoiding conflict and tension
7. Harmony and peacekeeping
8. Conflict resolution and problem solving
9. Self-respect and self-esteem

EXHIBIT 4.9   Key Values or Motivators in Law Enforcement

Finally, when interviewing and gathering data on hate incidents and crimes (including threats conveyed by telephone call or letter) targeted at individuals of particular backgrounds, the officer's need for control and structure may have to encompass hysterical or at least highly emotional reactions from other people of that same background. In the officer's attempt to control the situation, he or she must consider that there is also a community needing reassurance. For example, an officer must be willing to respond sensitively to heightened anxiety on the part of group members and not downplay their fears. Interviewing and data gathering may therefore last much longer when the officer is required to deal with multiple community members and widespread fears.

NONVERBAL COMMUNICATION

Up to this point in the chapter, we have primarily discussed verbal communication across cultures and its relevance to the law enforcement context. Nonverbal communication, including tone of voice, plays a key role in the dynamics between any two people. Dr. Albert Mehrabian of the University of California, Los Angeles, described in the classic and highly quoted book *Silent Messages* (1971) the general impact on the interaction between two or three people when a person's verbal and nonverbal messages contradict each other. In this scenario, it is almost always tone of voice and body language, including facial expressions that convey an individual's true feelings. Obviously, low-context (direct/explicit) people pay attention to other aspects of communication in addition to words; it is simply a matter of degree of emphasis. Of course officers have to attend to citizens' words; however, tone of voice and body language can reveal much more. In addition, across cultures, there are other considerations that relate directly to the interpretation of meaning.

Consider the following examples of reactions to differences in nonverbal communication across cultures and their implications for day-to-day police work:

> *He didn't look at me once. I know he's guilty. Never trust a person who doesn't look you in the eye.*
>
> AMERICAN POLICE OFFICER

> *Americans seem cold. They seem to get upset when you stand close to them.*
>
> JORDANIAN TEACHER

As in the first example, if an officer uses norms of eye contact as understood by most Americans, he or she could make an incorrect judgment about someone who avoids eye contact; or, as in the second example, an officer's comfortable distance for safety might be violated because of a cultural standard defining acceptable conversational distance. The comments demonstrate how people can misinterpret nonverbal communication when it is culturally different from their own. Misinterpretation can happen even with two people from the same background, but it is more likely when there are cultural differences. Universal emotions such as happiness, fear, and sadness are expressed in similar nonverbal ways throughout the world; however, nonverbal variations across cultures can cause confusion.

Take the example of the way people express sadness and grief. In many cultures, such as Arab and Iranian cultures, people express grief openly and out loud. In contrast, in other parts of the world (e.g., in China and Japan), people are generally more subdued or even silent in their expressions of grief. In Asian cultures, the general belief is that it is best to contain one's emotions (whether sadness or happiness) if it is not an appropriate time or place to express them, and so that others will feel comfortable in one's presence. Without this cultural knowledge, in observing a person who did not openly express grief, for example, one might conclude that he or she is not in emotional distress. This would be an incorrect and ethnocentric interpretation based on one's own culture.

The expression of friendship is another example of how cultural groups differ in their nonverbal behavior. Feelings of friendship exist everywhere, but their expression varies. In some cultures, it is acceptable for men to embrace and kiss each other (in Saudi Arabia and Russia, for example) and for women to hold hands (in China, Korea, Egypt, and other countries). Russian gymnasts of the same sex have been seen on television kissing each other on the lips; this is an acceptable gesture in their culture and does not imply that they are gay or lesbian. What is considered "normal" behavior in one culture may be viewed as "abnormal" or unusual in another.

The following areas of nonverbal communication have variations across cultures; the degree to which a person displays nonverbal differences depends, in part, on the age of the person and the degree of his or her acculturation to the United States.

1. *Gestures:* A few American gestures are offensive in other cultures. For example, the OK gesture is obscene in Germany and Latin America—and in France, it means "zero"; the crossed-fingers-for-good-luck gesture is offensive in Vietnam; and the "come here" gesture (beckoning with a curled index finger and with the palm up) is very insulting in most of Asia and Latin America.

2. *Position of Feet:* A police sergeant relaxing at his desk with his feet up, baring the soles of his shoes, would most likely offend a Thai or Saudi Arabian (and other groups as well) coming into the office. To show one's foot is insulting in many cultures because the foot is considered the dirtiest part of the body. (Another example of this was the intended insult toward Saddam Hussein when Iraqis hit a statue of him with their shoes.) Officers need to be mindful of this taboo with respect to the feet, and should refrain, whenever possible, from making physical contact with their feet when, for example, someone is lying on the ground.

3. *Facial expressions:* Not all facial expressions mean the same thing across cultures. The smile is a great source of confusion for many people in law enforcement when they encounter people from Asian cultures. A smile or giggle can cover up pain, humiliation, and embarrassment. Some women (e.g., Japanese, Vietnamese) cover their mouths with their hands when they smile or giggle. Upon hearing something sad, a Vietnamese person may smile. Similarly, an officer may need to communicate something that causes a loss of face to a person, resulting in the person smiling. This smile does not mean that the person is trying to be a "smart aleck"; it is simply a culturally conditioned response.

4. *Facial expressiveness:* People in law enforcement have to be able to "read faces" in certain situations in order to assess situations correctly. The degree to which people show emotions on their faces depends, in large part, on their cultural background. Whereas Latin Americans, African Americans and people from Mediterranean regions tend to show emotions facially, other groups, such as many of the Asian cultural groups, tend to be less facially expressive and less emotive. An officer may thus incorrectly assume that a person is not being cooperative or would not make a good witness.

5. *Eye contact:* In many parts of the world, eye contact is avoided with authority figures. In parts of India, for example, a father would discipline his child by saying, "How dare you look me in the eye when I'm speaking to you"; whereas an American parent would say, "Look me in the eye when I'm talking to you." Direct eye contact with some citizens can be perceived as threatening to that citizen; for a citizen to maintain direct eye contact with a police officer would be disrespectful in some cultures. A security officer in a large store in San Jose, California, offered the example of officers looking directly at Latino/Hispanic young people suspected of stealing items from the store. On a number of occasions, the officers' direct eye contact was met with a physical reaction (i.e., the young person attempting to punch the officer). He explained that the Latino/Hispanic individual mistook the eye contact as confrontation and a challenge for a fight.

6. *Physical or conversational distance:* All people subconsciously keep a comfortable distance around them when communicating with others, resulting in invisible walls that keep people far enough away. (This subcategory of nonverbal communication is called *proxemics.*) Police officers are perhaps more aware than others of the distance they keep from people in order to remain safe. When someone violates this space, a person often feels threatened and backs away or, in the case of an officer, begins to think about protective measures. Although personality and context also determine interpersonal distance, cultural background comes into play. In general, Latin Americans and Middle Easterners are more comfortable at close distances than are northern Europeans, Asians, and the majority of Americans. In some cultures, the amount of acceptable space depends on whether the other person is of the same sex or the opposite sex. A male police officer should not necessarily feel threatened, for example, if approached by an Iranian or Greek male in a manner that feels uncomfortably close. While maintaining a safe distance, the officer should also consider cultural background. Consider the example of a Middle Eastern suspect who ignores an officers' command to "step back." The social distance for interacting in the Middle East (as in many other areas of the world) is much closer than it is in the United States. For officers, for whom safety is paramount, this could easily lead to misinterpretation. Generally, Americans are comfortable at a little more than an arm's distance from each other.

For the law enforcement professional, nonverbal communication constitutes a major part in all aspects of peacekeeping and enforcement—but as an FBI article on interviewing skills cautions, "Investigators must remember that no 'silver bullet' for identifying deception exists" (Matsumoto, Hwang, Skinner, & Frank, 2011). A combination of two skills: (1) the detection of microexpressions (fleeting expressions of emotions observed in the face) and (2) "statement analysis" (examination of word choice and grammar) are said to be reliable indicators of truthfulness, but training and practice are necessary in order for officers to employ these skills reliably (Matsumoto et al., 2011). In addition, while some microexpressions are believed to be fairly consistent across cultures, they must be interpreted within the context of a situation, and statement analysis is most likely to be reliable only when applied to native speakers. Thus, when working with multicultural populations, it is crucial for officers to be aware of the variety of nuances and differences that may exist from one group to another. (Exhibits 4.10 and 4.11).

---

1. Body language and nonverbal messages can override an officer's verbal content in high-stress and crisis situations. For example, the officer's statement that he or she is there to help may be contradicted by a body posture of discomfort and uncertainty in culturally unfamiliar households.
2. For people of different ethnic backgrounds, stress, confusion, and uncertainty can communicate unintended messages. For example, an Asian may remain silent and look nervous and anxious at the scene of a crime. He or she may appear to be "uncooperative" when in fact this person may have every intention of helping the officer.
3. For people with limited English skills, the nonverbal aspects of communication become even more important. Appropriate gestures and nonverbal cues help the nonnative English speaker understand verbal messages.
4. It is important for officers to learn about and avoid offensive gestures and cultural taboos. However, immigrants and international visitors are quick to forgive and overlook gestures and actions made out of forgetfulness and ignorance. Officers should realize, too, that, in time, newcomers usually learn many of the nonverbal mannerisms with which officers are more familiar. Nevertheless, learning about offensive gestures can help officers avoid interpersonal offenses.

Note: Each of the culture-specific chapters (Chapters 5–9) contains information about nonverbal characteristics of particular groups.

EXHIBIT 4.10 Nonverbal Communication: Key Points for Law Enforcement

- When is touch appropriate and inappropriate?
- What is the comfortable physical distance between people in interactions?
- What is considered proper eye contact? What do eye contact and lack of eye contact mean to the people involved?
- What cultural variety is there in facial expressions? For example, does nodding and smiling mean the same in all cultures? If someone appears to be expressionless, does that mean he or she is uncooperative?
- What are appropriate and inappropriate gestures for a particular cultural group?
- Is the person in transition from one culture to another and, therefore, lacking knowledge of American-style communication?

EXHIBIT 4.11 Key Questions Concerning Nonverbal Communication across Cultures

Officers must be authentic in their communication with people from various backgrounds. When learning about both verbal and nonverbal characteristics across cultures, officers do not need to feel that they must communicate differently each time they are in contact with someone of a different background. However, understanding that there are variations in communication style will help the officer interpret people's motives and attitudes more accurately and, overall, assess situations without a cultural bias.

MALE-FEMALE COMMUNICATION IN LAW ENFORCEMENT

You have to go along with the kind of kidding and ribbing that the guys participate in; otherwise, you are not one of them. If you say that you are offended by their crass jokes and vulgar speech, then you are ostracized from the group. I have often felt that in the squad room men have purposely controlled themselves because of my presence, because I have spoken up. But what I've done to them is make them act one way because of my presence as a woman. Then they call me a prude or spread the word that I'm keeping track of all their remarks for the basis of a sexual harassment suit down the road. I have no interest in doing that. I simply want to be a competent police officer in a professional working environment. (Comments by a woman police officer, wishing to remain anonymous, at a Women Peace Officers' Association [WPOA] Conference)

With the changing workforce, including increasing numbers of women in traditionally male professions, many new challenges in the area of male-female communication are presenting themselves. Within law enforcement, in particular, a strong camaraderie characterizes the relationships mainly among the male members of a police force, although, in some cases, women are part of this camaraderie. Women allowed into what has been termed the "brotherhood" have generally had to "become one of the guys" to gain acceptance into a historically male-dominated profession. Many of these women have learned to communicate in a more male style—more directly and assertively. "It is frequently observed that male speakers are more likely to be confrontational by arguing, issuing commands, and taking opposing stands for the sake of argument, whereas females are more likely to avoid confrontation by agreeing, supporting, and making suggestions rather than commands . . . fighting with each other and banding together to fight others can create strong connections among males . . ." (Tannen, 2001).

Camaraderie results when a group is united because of a common goal or purpose; the glue cementing the camaraderie is the easy communication among its members. The extracurricular interests of the members of the group, the topics selected for conversation, and the jokes that people tell all contribute to the cohesiveness or tightness of police department members. In some departments, women find that they or other women are the objects of jokes about sexual topics or that there are simply numerous references to sex. Because certain departments within cities have consisted mostly of men, they have not had to consider the inclusion of women on an equal basis and have not had to examine their own communication with each other.

Young women who are new to a department feel that they must tolerate certain behaviors in order to be accepted. A female sheriff participating in a WPOA conference said that on a daily basis she confronts vulgar language and sexual references in the jail where she works. Her list was long: "I am extremely bothered about the communication of the men where I work. Without mincing words, I'll tell you—at the county jail, officers are very degrading to women. They sometimes make fun of rape victims, they are rude and lewd to female inmates, and they are constantly trying to get me to join into the 'fun.' A woman is referred to as a 'dyke,' a 'cunt,' a 'douche bag,' a 'whore,' a 'hooker,' a 'bitch,' and I'm sure I could come up with more. The guys don't call me those names, but they use them all the time referring to other women." This sheriff also noted that she did not experience the disrespectful verbal behavior in one-on-one situations with male deputies, but only when they were in a group. She wondered out loud, "What happens to men when they group with each other? Why is there the change?"

It is not only the male grouping phenomenon that produces this type of rough, vulgar, and sexist language. One study of a large urban police department conducted for California Law Enforcement Command College documented inappropriate communications from patrol cars' two-way radios and computers. The language on the official system was often unprofessional—rough, vulgar, offensive, racist, and sexist. Obviously, both discipline and training were needed in this agency.

Certainly, not all men behave and talk in offensive ways, but the phenomenon is frequent enough that women in traditionally male work environments mention this issue repeatedly. Some women join in conversations that make them uneasy, but they do not let on that their working environment is uncomfortable and actually affecting their morale and productivity. Some women seem to be comfortable with the sexual comments of their male counterparts and may not object to the use of certain terms that other women find patronizing (e.g., "honey," "doll," "chick"). Through sexual harassment policies, both women and men have learned that, for some, sexual innuendoes and patronizing terms can contribute to a hostile working environment.

In male-dominated institutions, vocations, and professions, women find that speaking out against this type of talk and joking creates discomfort for them and puts them in a double bind. A female police officer at a cross-cultural training workshop on discrimination in the workplace said she felt that women's choices regarding communication with fellow male officers were limited. She explained that when a woman objects or speaks up, she risks earning a reputation or label that is hard to shed. If she remains quiet, she must tolerate a lot of verbal abuse and compromise her professionalism. This particular police officer decided to speak up in her own department, and, indeed, she earned a reputation as a troublemaker. In fact, she had no interest in going any further than complaining to her supervisor but nevertheless was accused of preparing for a lawsuit. She explained that a lawsuit was the farthest thing from her mind and that all she wanted was professional respect.

Some women who have objected to certain mannerisms of their male counterparts' communication say that when they come into a room or office, the men stop talking. The result is that the communication that normally functions to hold a group together is strained and tense. The ultimate result is that the workplace becomes segregated by gender. When shut out from a conversation, many women feel excluded and unempowered; in turn, many men feel resentful about having to modify their style of communication.

Women in traditionally male work environments such as police and fire departments find that they are sometimes put in a position of having to trade their professional identity for their personal one. A woman officer who proudly tells her sergeant about the arrest she made may be stunned when he, totally out of context, compliments the way she has been keeping in shape and tells her how good she looks in her uniform. This is not to say that compliments are never acceptable. But in this context, the woman is relating as a professional and desires reciprocal professional treatment. Men and women often ask, "Where do I draw the line? When does a comment

- Use terms that are inclusive rather than exclusive. Examples: "police officer," "chairperson," "commendations" (instead of the informal "atta boys").
- Avoid using terms or words that many women feel diminish their professional status. Examples: "chick," "babe"
- Avoid using terms or words that devalue groups of women or stereotype them. Example: Referring to women officers as "dykes"
- Avoid sexist jokes, even if you think they are not offensive. (Someone is bound to be offended; the same applies to racist jokes.)
- Avoid using terms that negatively spotlight or set women apart from men. Examples: "For a woman cop, she did a good job" (implying that this is the exception rather than the rule); this also applies to references about other cultural groups: "He's Latino, but he works hard"; "He's black, but he's really skilled."

EXHIBIT 4.12   Inclusive Workplace Communication

become harassment?" In terms of the legal definition of sexual harassment, when the perpetrators are made aware that their comments are uninvited and unwelcome, then they must be reasonable enough to stop making them. It is not within the scope of this chapter to detail sexual harassment and all its legal implications (see Chapter 2). However, it should be noted that everyone has his or her own limits. What is considered harassment to one individual may be appreciated by another. When communicating across genders, each party must be sensitive to what the other party considers acceptable or insulting (see Exhibit 4.12). It is also the responsibility of the individual who has been offended, whether male or female, to make it clear that certain types of remarks are offensive.

In addition, it is wise to remember that male-female communication difficulties do not all fall within the realm of sexual harassment. Differences in directness and other subtleties also play a part. Women tend to apologize more then men—for interrupting, for not being clear, or simply as a soothing phrase to make others feel comfortable. Statements from female witnesses or victims that include apologies, for example, should not necessarily be interpreted by police officers as being any less reliable than statements from males that do not include such apologies. The way women and men present themselves in professional settings also differs. "Ask a man to explain his success and he will typically credit his own innate qualities and skills. Ask a woman the same question and she will attribute her success to external factors, insisting she did well because she 'worked really hard,' or 'got lucky,' or 'had help from others'" (Sandberg, 2013).

The bottom line is that effective communication skills are necessary for police officers interacting with colleagues and citizens alike, but can be extremely difficult to achieve. Constant effort, vigilance, empathy, and compassion are required for long-term success.

Summary

- Communication with people for whom English is a second language can exact a great deal of patience from officers. The language barriers can lead to serious problems for non–English speakers and law enforcement. Using inappropriate interpreters can mislead officers, so much so that a victim and his or her interpreter may give two completely different versions of a story. In some cases, extra sensitivity on the part of law enforcement is needed when it comes to language obstacles. Increasing bilingual hires is one of the most practical solutions if budget allows; as an additional advantage, bilingual officers often have a better understanding of the communities they serve. At a minimum, officers should know what the basic guidelines are for communicating with speakers of other languages. In addition, officers can become sensitive to features of other languages that frequently cause confusion when limited- or non-English speakers attempt to communicate in English.

- Officers' attitudes about immigrants and nonnative English speakers, whether positive or negative, are likely to affect their interaction with them. One important guideline is to refrain from making inferences about individuals based on their accent or level of fluency. From a physiological perspective, communicating in a foreign language can be exhausting and cause mental strain, potentially resulting in a person's "shutting down" or not being able to communicate in the new language. In general, limited-English-speaking individuals' ability to express themselves in the second language is at its best when they are comfortable with officers. Language breakdown is one of the first signs that a person is ill at ease and stressed to the point of not being able to cooperate and communicate. It is in the officers' best interest to increase the comfort level of the people with whom they interact, whether victims, suspects, or simply people requiring help.

- Rapport-building with all citizens is essential for building trust, and this is often preliminary to people's willingness to communicate freely with officers. This is especially true when communicating with people who have relatively "high context" (indirect/implicit) communication styles. Typically, these styles are characteristic of cultural groups coming from Asian, African, and Latin American cultures. There are gender differences within cultures as well (i.e., women tend to have a higher-context style than do men). The style of communication in law enforcement is a relatively low context (direct/explicit) communication style; police officers must understand the framework of "context" when interacting with individuals who exhibit different styles than their own.

- Officers' own filters and perceptions influence the responses they choose to exhibit in cross-cultural and cross-racial encounters. As with all people, officers have blind spots and emotional "hot buttons" that may negatively affect communication with individuals from races, ethnicities, and backgrounds different from their own.

Officers may unknowingly communicate biases or a lack of comfort with members of certain groups.

- Interviewing and data-gathering skills form the basic techniques for communication and intervention work with multicultural populations. For the officer, key issues include establishing interpersonal relationships to gain trust and rapport; bringing structure and control to the immediate situation; gaining information about the problems that require the presence of a law enforcement officer; giving information about law enforcement guidelines, resources, and assistance available; providing action and interventions as needed; and supporting the different parties' abilities and skills to solve current and future problems on their own.

- Nonverbal communication across cultures can have a direct impact on police/citizen interaction and police perception of behavior. Body language can include gestures, eye contact, physical or conversational distance, and the degree to which an individual is facially expressive. For law enforcement professionals working within multicultural populations, it is important to be aware of a variety of nuances and differences that may exist from one group to another.

- Officers have used styles of communication and language in the past that were considered acceptable not only within the police agency but with citizens as well. Because of cultural diversity in the population and the accompanying need to respect all individuals, the unspoken rules about what is appropriate have changed dramatically. This includes the need to use inclusive communication with women within the law enforcement profession. Through communication, officers have tremendous power to influence the behavior and responses of the citizens with whom they have contact. This is true of all citizens, regardless of background. A lack of knowledge of the cross-cultural aspects of communication will diminish that power with people whose backgrounds differ from that of the officer.

Discussion Questions and Issues

1. **Communicate with Respect.** The introduction to this chapter presents a view of what all people would like in communication, and that is respect. "Remember that everyone in all cultures wants to be respected . . . talking about respecting people [from all cultural backgrounds] is vague. But treating people with respect is an act that is highly specific" (Thompson, 2009). Describe in detail the behavior that defines, for you, "respectful communication." In your experience, does this behavior work with all cultural groups? Explain your answer.

2. **The Origins of Stereotypes.** In this chapter, we argue that officers need to recognize how their early experiences in life and later adult experiences shape their perceptions and "filters" about people from groups different from their own. What do you remember learning about various ethnic and racial groups when you were young? Did you grow up in an environment of tolerance, or did you hear statements such as "That's the way they are," or "You've got to be careful with those people" or "They are lazy [or dishonest, etc.]"? Also, discuss your experiences as an adult interacting with people

from different ethnic or cultural groups and how those experiences may be affecting your perceptions.

3. ***Police Officer Interaction with Speakers of Other Languages.*** The following dialogue illustrates a typical interaction between a police officer and a nonnative speaker of English, in this case a Vietnamese man. Judging from the English that the Vietnamese person is speaking, how would you rate the officer's use of English?

  The following dialog takes place when an officer pulls a car over, gets out of his car, and approaches the driver. The driver, who is Vietnamese, says, in poor English, "Why you stop me?"

  OFFICER: I pulled you over because you ran a red light.

  CITIZEN: (Blinking; no response)

  OFFICER: This is a traffic violation. (Receives no feedback). Do you understand?

  CITIZEN: (Nodding) Yes.

  OFFICER: I'm going to have to issue you a traffic citation.

  CITIZEN: (Looking through the front windshield of the car; no response)

  OFFICER: Let me see your registration and driver's license.

  CITIZEN: License? Just a minute. (Leans over to open glove compartment, but finds nothing; gets out of car and goes to trunk)

  OFFICER (IRRITATED AND SLIGHTLY NERVOUS):   *Hey!* (In a loud voice) What's going on here? I asked to see your driver's license. Are you the registered owner of this car?

  CITIZEN: Yes. I get my license.

  OFFICER (SPEAKING MUCH LOUDER):   Wait a minute. Don't you understand? Are you not the owner of this car? Do you even have a license?

  CITIZEN: Wait. (Finds license in trunk and produces it for officer)

  OFFICER: Okay. Would you mind getting back into the car now?

  CITIZEN: (Does nothing) Yes.

  OFFICER (POINTING TO THE FRONT SEAT):   Back into the car!

  CITIZEN: (Gets back into the car)

  The officer could make improvements in at least four areas: (1) choice of words, (2) manner of asking questions, (3) use of idioms (there are at least two or three that could be changed to simple English), and (4) tone and attitude. Analyze this interaction by being specific as to how the officer could improve.

4. ***Police Officers' "Hot Buttons."*** Discuss how citizens (e.g., suspects, victims, complainants) affect your reactions in communication. Specifically, what words and attitudes do they use that break down your attempts to be professional? What emotionally laden language "sets you off?"

5. ***Professional Communication with Citizens.*** After you have discussed Question 4, conduct role-plays with fellow officers that involve situations in which you must respond professionally to abusive language. (Refer back to the section on accusations of racial profiling if you need suggestions.)

6. ***Cultural Observations.*** Make a list of your observations for each of the cultural groups with which you have had a substantial amount of contact. Then try to find someone from that culture with whom you can discuss your observations.
  a. Display of emotions and expression of feelings
  b. Communication style: loud, soft, direct, indirect
  c. Expressions of appreciation; conventions of courtesy (i.e., forms of politeness)
  d. Need (or lack thereof) for privacy
  e. Gestures, facial expressions, and body movements
  f. Eye contact
  g. Touching
  h. Interpersonal space (conversational distance)
  i. Taboo topics in conversation
  j. Response to authority

7. ***Discomfort with Unfamiliar Groups.*** Try to recall a situation in which you found yourself in a culturally unfamiliar environment (e.g., responding to a call in an ethnically different household or being the only person of your background among a group of people from another cultural or ethnic group). How much discomfort, if any, did you experience? If the situation was uncomfortable, did it affect your communication effectiveness or professionalism?

8. ***Accusations of Racially or Ethnically Motivated Stops.*** Have you encountered, "You stopped me because I'm [any ethnic group]?" If so, how did you handle the situation? How effectively do you think you responded?

References

Bernstein, Maxine. (2011, February 27). "Portland officers use Tasers on 2 men who had surrendered, costing city almost $140,000 to settle lawsuits." *The Oregonian.*

Berry, Ondra. (2013, March). Retired Assistant Police Chief, Reno, Nevada, Police Department, personal communication.

DOJ: Department of Justice. (2002, June 18). "Guidance to Federal Financial Assistance Recipients Regarding Title VI Prohibition Against National Origin Discrimination Affecting Limited English Proficient Persons." *Federal Register, Vol. 67, No. 117.*

Freeland, Ben. (2012, August 6). "When Bad Communication Kills—The Korean Air Saga." *Brush Talk.*

Gray, John. (2002). *Mars and Venus in the Workplace.* New York: Harper Collins, p. 23.

Hall, Edward. (1959). *The Silent Language.* Garden City, NY: Doubleday.

Hall, Edward. (1966). *The Hidden Dimension.* Garden City, NY: Doubleday.

Hall, Edward. (1976). *Beyond Culture.* Garden City, NY: Doubleday.

Ho, Christopher. (2013, August). Senior Staff Attorney for the Language Rights Project, Employment Law Center/Legal Aid Society, San Francisco, CA, personal communication.

Hofstede, Geert, Gert Jan Hofstede, and Michael Minkov. (2010). *Cultures and Organizations: Software of the Mind.* New York: McGraw-Hill.

Ismail, Lobna. (2013). President of Connecting Cultures, a training and consulting organization specializing in Arab American culture, personal communication.

Kolts, James G. and Staff. (1992, July). *The Los Angeles County Sheriff's Department*, p. 199.

Matsumoto, David, Hyi Sung Hwang, Lisa Skinner, and Mark Frank. (2011, June). "Evaluating Truthfulness and Detecting Deception." *FBI Law Enforcement Bulletin.*

McAllister, Daryl. (2013, March). Captain Hayward Police Department, (California) personal communication.

Mehrabian, Albert. (1971). *Silent Messages.* Belmont, CA: Wadsworth Publishing.

Merritt, Ashleigh. (2000, May). "Culture in the Cockpit: Do Hofstede's Dimensions Replicate?" *Journal of Cross-Cultural Psychology*, 31(3), 283–301.

Navarro, Joe. (2009, December 11). "The Body Language of the Eyes." *Psychology Today.*

NIJ: National Institute of Justice. (2008, July). *Policing in Arab-American Communities after September 11.* U.S. Department of Justice, Office of Justice Programs.

Park, Chan-Kyong. (2013, July 12). "S. Koreans dismiss cockpit culture as cause of crash." *Fox News.*

Sandberg, Sheryl. (2013). *Lean In: Women, Work, and the Will to Lead.* New York: Alfred A. Knopf, p. 30.

Sandoval, Vincent A., and Susan H. Adams. (2001, August). "Subtle Skills for Building Rapport." *FBI Law Enforcement Bulletin*, pp. 1–5.

Tannen, Deborah. (2001). *Talking from 9 to 5: How Women's and Men's Conversational Styles Affect Who Gets Heard, Who Gets Credit, and What Gets Done at Work.* New York: Harper Collins Publishers, p. 236.

Thompson, George. (2009, March). Founder of Verbal Judo (www.verbaljudoglobal.com), personal communication.

U.S. Department of Justice. (2000). Executive Order 13166. Web posted at www.usdoj.gov/crt/cor/Pubs/eolep.php (accessed August 20, 2013).

Zogby, James. (2013). Director of the Arab American Institute Foundation, personal communication.

PART TWO

Cultural Specifics for Law Enforcement

Part Two presents information on Asian/Pacific, African American, Latino/Hispanic, Middle Eastern, and Native American cultures with regard to the needs of law enforcement and criminal justice representatives. These cultural groups were selected, as opposed to others for one or more of the following reasons: (1) the group is a relatively large ethnic or racial group in the United States; (2) the traditional culture of the group differs widely from that of mainstream American culture; and/or (3) typically or historically there have been problems between the particular group and law enforcement officials.

In these chapters, general information is presented on demographics, historical background, and diversity within each cultural group. Also included are specific details relevant to law enforcement and criminal justice as to stereotypes, communication styles, group identification terms, offensive labels, and family structures.

Important note: Although specific cultural and racial groups are presented in this part of the book, we wish to remind our readers that individuals in the U.S. multicultural population do not always easily fall into neat categories of only one race or culture. There can be an overlap of race and ethnicity, as in the case of a black Latino. Our categorization of different groups is simply a convenient way of presenting information.

5 Law Enforcement Contact with Asian/Pacific Americans

LEARNING OBJECTIVES

After reading this chapter, you should be able to:

- Describe the historical background of the Asian/Pacific American community in the United States.
- Highlight the demographic features and diversity of this population.
- Discuss the implications of group identification terms for Asian/Pacific Americans.
- Identify myths and stereotypes applied to this group.
- Understand select characteristics of traditional Asian/Pacific American extended family structures as they relate to law enforcement contact.
- Recognize the communication styles used by Asian/Pacific Americans.
- Utilize key skills, resources, and practices for addressing law enforcement concerns relating to this group.

OUTLINE

- Introduction
- Asian/Pacific American Defined
- Historical Information
- Demographics: Diversity among Asian/Pacific Americans
- Labels and Terms
- Myths and Stereotypes
- The Asian/Pacific American Family
- Communication Styles of Asian/Pacific Americans
- Key Issues in Law Enforcement
- Summary
- Discussion Questions and Issues

INTRODUCTION

For the past five decades, the Asian/Pacific American (sometimes referred to as Asian American/Pacific Islander) population has experienced the largest proportional increases of any ethnic minority population in the United States (over 100% growth for the decades from 1960 to 1990, 76% growth for the decade from 1990 to 2000, and 46% growth from 2000 to 2010). This growth can be attributed to: (1) high immigration from Pacific Rim countries; (2) relative longevity; (3) high birth rates; and (4) admission of immigrants with special skills and expertise for work in high-technology industries in the United States. The numbers of Asian/Pacific Americans now living in major urban areas is particularly striking, with the highest concentrations found in New York City, Los Angeles, San Jose (CA), San Francisco, Honolulu, San Diego, Chicago, Houston, Seattle, Philadelphia, Fremont (CA), and Sacramento (CA). Increasing numbers of Asian/Pacific Americans are engaged in politics, business, education, community leadership, and public service areas. Law enforcement contact with people from the Asia/Pacific region has likewise increased because of their greater presence in communities. Asian/Pacific Americans have one of the highest naturalized citizenship rates among all foreign-born groups: in 2011, 58 percent of the immigrants from Asian/Pacific countries were naturalized citizens (Gryn & Gambino, 2012).

ASIAN/PACIFIC AMERICAN DEFINED

The term *Asian/Pacific Americans* is a contraction of two terms: *Asian Americans* and *Pacific Islander* peoples. Although used throughout this chapter as referring to a single ethnic/cultural group, *Asian/Pacific Americans* is, in fact, a convenient summary label for a very heterogeneous group—an ever-emerging, ethnic mosaic of people from diverse backgrounds. Groups are added and removed based on self-definition and needs for self-choice. In our definition, we have not included immigrants or refugees from the South Central Asian nations of Kazakhstan, Kyrgyzstan, Tajikistan, Turkmenistan, or Uzbekistan (i.e., countries that were part of the former Soviet Union). We also do not include certain countries that are physically located on the Asian continent even though they are listed as such in the "World Population Data Sheet" (Population Reference Bureau, 2012) because of the self-choice issue. (People from Jordan or Israel, for example, might not identify with the term "Asian.") Clearly, the pooling of separate Asian and Pacific Islander groups under the label of Asian/Pacific Americans emerged, in part, out of the necessity to have a collective whole when a large numerical count might make a difference (especially in political and community issues).

At least 40 distinct ethnic and cultural groups can be included under the Asian/Pacific American designation.

1. Bangladeshi
2. Belauan (formerly Palauan)
3. Bhutanese
4. Bruneian
5. Cambodian
6. Guamanian/Chamorro
7. Chinese
8. Fijian
9. Hawaiian (or Native Hawaiian)
10. Hmong
11. Indian (Asian)
12. Indonesian
13. Japanese
14. Kiribati
15. Korean
16. Laotian
17. Malaysian
18. Maldivian
19. Marshallese (of the Marshall Islands, to include Majuro, Ebeye, and Kwajalein)
20. Micronesian (to include Kosrae, Pohnpei, Chuuk, and Yap)
21. Mongolian
22. Myanmarese/Burmese
23. Nauruan
24. Nepalese
25. Ni-Vanuatu
26. Okinawan
27. Pakistani
28. Filipino
29. Saipan Carolinian (or Carolinian, from the Commonwealth of the Northern Marianas)
30. Samoan
31. Singaporean
32. Solomon Islander
33. Sri Lankan (formerly Ceylonese)
34. Tahitian
35. Taiwanese
36. Tibetan
37. Tongan
38. Thai
39. Tuvaluan
40. Vietnamese

While there are marked differences among the groups listed, individuals *within* any of these groups may also differ in a vast number of ways. From the viewpoint of law enforcement, it is important to recognize some of the factors that may either diverge or be common to all Asian/Pacific ethnic groups. Certain aspects of culture might be similar, for example, while English-language abilities might vary widely.

One research study (Pew Research, 2013) found that "62% [of Asians] say they most often describe themselves by their country of origin" (e.g., "Korean" for those whose ancestry is from Korea, "Vietnamese" for those whose ancestry is from Vietnam); however, there may be other demographic variables of greater importance than that of nationality. For example, whether a person of Chinese descent is from the Central Asian nation of Uzbekistan, the Southeast Asian nation of Vietnam, or the Pacific Island nation of Micronesia, the demographic variable of ethnicity (being Chinese) may be a more important identifier than national origin. As another example, religion might be a more important group identifier than either ethnicity and/or nationality, as seen with some Muslims (i.e., people who practice Islam). Given that the four countries with the largest Muslim populations—Indonesia, India, Pakistan, and Bangladesh (Pew Research, 2012)—are in southern Asia, Asian/Pacific American people who practice Islam might see religion as a more important identifier than ethnicity or nationality.

HISTORICAL INFORMATION

The first Asians to arrive in the United States in sizable numbers were the Chinese in the 1850s, who immigrated to work in the gold mines in California and later on the transcontinental railroad. In the late 1800s and early 1900s, the Chinese were followed by the Japanese and Filipinos (and in smaller numbers by Koreans and South Asian Indians). Large numbers of Asian Indians eventually entered the United States as a result of Congressional action in 1946 for "persons of races indigenous to India," as well as Filipinos, to have the right of naturalization—although both Indians and Filipinos were limited to 100 persons per year becoming naturalized citizens (Hayes, 2012). Most immigrants in those early years were men, and most worked as laborers and at other domestic and menial jobs. Until the change of the immigration laws in 1965, the number of Asian and Pacific Islander peoples coming into the United States was severely restricted, and families often had to wait a decade or longer before members could be reunited. With the change in the immigration laws, large numbers of immigrants came to the United States from Hong Kong, Taiwan, China, Japan, Korea, South Asia (e.g., India, Sri Lanka, Bangladesh), the Philippines, and other parts of Southeast Asia (e.g., Vietnam, Thailand, Singapore, Cambodia, Malaysia). After the Vietnam War, large numbers of Southeast Asian refugees were admitted in the late 1970s and early 1980s. The need for engineering and scientific expertise and skills in "high-tech" and Internet companies resulted in many Asian/Pacific nationals (under special work visas) immigrating to the United States in the late 1990s and early 2000s. Skilled workers entering with "high-tech visas" (i.e., H-1B visas) continue to contribute to the growth of the Asian/Pacific American population in the United States. (See Exhibit 5.1.)

Law Enforcement Interactions with Asian/Pacific Americans

Early experiences of Asians and Pacific Islanders were characterized by the majority population's wanting to keep them out of the United States and putting tremendous barriers in the way of those who were already here. Many Asian/Pacific Americans found the passage and enforcement of "anti-Asian" federal, state, and local laws to be more hostile and discriminatory than racially motivated community incidents. It was the role of law enforcement and criminal justice agencies and officers to be the vehicle to carry out these laws. Thus, from the beginning, the interactions

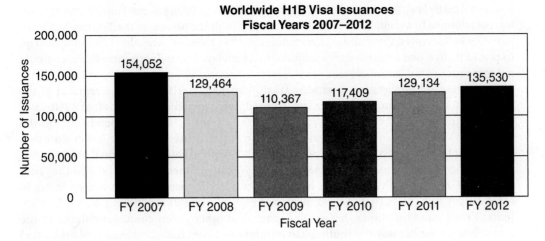

Worldwide H1B Visa Issuances
Fiscal Years 2007–2012

EXHIBIT 5.1 Worldwide H-1B Visa Issuances

of Asian/Pacific Americans with law enforcement officials were fraught with conflicts, difficulties, and mixed messages.

ANTI-ASIAN FEDERAL, STATE, AND LOCAL LAWS Almost all early U.S. federal immigration laws were written such that their enforcement made Asian newcomers feel neither welcomed nor wanted. Following the large influx of Chinese in the 1850s to work in the gold mines and on the railroad, many Americans were resentful of the Chinese for their willingness to work long hours for low wages. With mounting public pressure, the Chinese Exclusion Act of 1882 banned the immigration of Chinese laborers for 10 years, and subsequent amendments extended this ban indefinitely. Because of this ban and because the Chinese population in the United States was predominantly male, the Chinese population in the United States dropped from 105,465 in 1880 to 61,639 in 1920 (Takaki, 1998). But the Chinese Exclusion Act applied only to the Chinese; Japanese immigration started in large numbers in the 1890s to work as laborers and in domestic jobs on farms on the West Coast. Similar to the case of the Chinese, public pressure to restrict Japanese immigration ensued. In the case of the Japanese, however, the Japanese government did not want a "loss of face" or loss of international prestige through having its people "banned" from immigrating to the United States. Rather, a "Gentleman's Agreement" was negotiated with President Theodore Roosevelt in 1907, which resulted in the Japanese Government voluntarily restricting the immigration of Japanese laborers to the United States. Family members of Japanese already in the United States, however, were allowed to enter. Under the Gentleman's Agreement, large numbers of "picture brides" began entering the United States, resulting in a substantial increase in Japanese American population—25,000 in 1900 to 127,000 in 1940 (Daniels, 1988). Subsequent laws banned or prevented immigration from Asian countries. The Immigration Act of 1917 banned immigration from all countries in the Pacific Rim except for the Philippines (a U.S. territory at the time). The Immigration Act of 1924 restricted migration from all countries to 2 percent of the countries' national origin population living in the United States in 1890; this went unchanged until 1965. Moreover, it was not until 1952 that most Asian immigrants were eligible to become naturalized citizens of the United States and therefore have the right to vote. (African and Native Americans were able to become citizens long before Asian/Pacific Americans were given the same rights.)

While Filipinos had been immigrating to the United States since the early 1900s, large numbers of Filipino laborers began entering in the 1920s because of the need for unskilled laborers (and due in part to the unavailability of Chinese and Japanese immigrants whose entry was restricted by law). Similar to the immigration of previous Asian groups, Filipino immigration was soon limited to a quota of 50 immigrants per year with the passage of the Tydings-McDuffie Act of 1934. Moreover, Congressional resolutions in 1935 reflected clear anti-Filipino sentiment by providing free, one-way passage for Filipinos to return home on the agreement that they would not come back to the United States.

Anti-Asian immigration laws were finally repealed starting with the removal of the Chinese Exclusion Act in 1943. Other laws were repealed to allow immigration of Asians and Pacific Islanders, but the process was slow. It was not until 1965 that amendments to the McCarran-Walter Act opened the way for Asian immigrants to enter in larger numbers (a fixed quota of 20,000 per country, as opposed to 2% of the country's national origin population living in the United States in 1890). The 1965 amendment also established the "fifth preference" category, which allowed highly skilled workers needed by the United States to enter. Under this category, a second major wave of immigrants from Hong Kong, Taiwan, India, Korea, the Philippines, Japan, Singapore, and other Asian countries entered in the mid-1960s. An earlier wave of South Asian immigrants (from India, Pakistan, and Sri Lanka) with expertise to help in America's space race against the Soviets led to large numbers of professional and highly educated South Asians immigrating into the United States under the "fifth preference" category after 1965. For example, 83 percent of the Asian Indians (about 60,000) who immigrated under the category of professional and technical workers between 1966 and 1977 were engineers (about 40,000) and scientists with PhDs (about 20,000) (Prashad, 2001).

The third major wave of close to 1 million refugees and immigrants arrived in the United States from Vietnam and other Southeast Asian countries starting in the mid-1970s and lasting through the mid-1980s. The Refugee Act of 1980: (1) established the definition for "refugee"; (2) reduced limits on the numbers of refugees entering the United States; (3) created the Office of Refugee Resettlement; and (4) permitted refugees to adjust their statuses after one year to become permanent residents and after four more years, to become U.S. citizens (Povell, 2005). From the mid-1990s to the early 2000s, the need for personnel with high-tech, engineering, and Internet skills led to an additional influx of immigrants from India, Pakistan, Singapore, Korea, China (including Hong Kong), Taiwan, and other Asian locales.

Although many immigrant groups (e.g., Italians, Jews, Poles) have been targets of discrimination, bigotry, and prejudice, Asian/Pacific Americans, like African Americans, have experienced extensive legal discrimination, hindering their ability to participate fully as Americans. This discrimination has gravely affected their well-being and quality of life. Some states had laws that prohibited intermarriage between Asians and whites. State and local laws imposed restrictive conditions and taxes specifically on Asian businesses and individuals. State courts were equally biased; for example, in the case of *People v. Hall*, heard in the California Supreme Court in 1854, Hall, a white defendant, had been convicted of murdering a Chinese man on the basis of testimony provided by one white and three Chinese witnesses. The California Supreme Court threw out Hall's conviction on the basis that state law prohibited blacks, mulattos, or Indians from testifying in favor of or against whites in court. The court's decision read:

> Indian as commonly used refers only to the North American Indian, yet in the days of Columbus all shores washed by Chinese waters were called the Indies. In the second place the word "white" necessarily excludes all other races than Caucasian; and in the third place, even if this were not so, I would decide against the testimony of Chinese on the grounds of public policy. (*People v. George W. Hall*, 4 Cal. 399 [October 1854])

This section on anti-Asian/Pacific American laws and sentiments cannot close without noting that Japanese Americans are the only immigrants in the history of the United States who have been routed out of their homes and interned without due process. President Roosevelt's Executive

Order 9066 resulted in the evacuation and incarceration of 100,000 Japanese Americans in 1942. For Asian/Pacific Americans, the internment of Japanese Americans represents how quickly anti-Asian sentiments can result in victimization of innocent people.

DEMOGRAPHICS: DIVERSITY AMONG ASIAN/PACIFIC AMERICANS

As noted in the section defining Asian/Pacific Americans, this is an extremely heterogeneous population comprising many different ethnic and cultural groups with educational and socioeconomic diversity as well as other background, generational, and life experience differences. See the "Typology" in Chapter 1 on page 15 for a review of motivational and behavioral differences among minority populations related to immigration and generational status.

Asian/Pacific Americans currently number about 17.3 million and represent just over 5 percent of the U.S. population (Hoeffel, Rastogi, Kim, & Shahid, 2012). While longevity and birth rates have contributed to population increases, the major contributor to the growth of the Asian/Pacific American population is immigration from Pacific Rim countries. Currently, as evident in Exhibit 5.2, Chinese are the largest group comprising 23.4 percent of the total Asian/Pacific American population, followed by Asian Indians (19.4%) and then Filipinos (16.9%), Vietnamese (11.1%), Koreans (9.7%), Japanese (5.0%) and 14.5 percent for "all other Asian/Pacific groups." In the "all other" category, there was an increase of 5.2 percent from 2007 to 2011 per census calculations, with the four largest groups, in order of their numbers, being: Pakistani, Cambodian, Hmong, Thai, Laotian, and Bangladeshi.

For law enforcement officers, the key Asian/Pacific American groups to understand are the six largest groups: Chinese, Filipino, Asian Indian, Vietnamese, Korean, and Japanese (considering, in addition, local community trends and unique qualities of the community's populations). Knowledge of growing trends among these Asian/Pacific American populations is also important for officer recruitment and other human resource considerations. Currently, the Asian/Pacific Americans involved in criminal justice careers are largely Japanese, Chinese, and Korean Americans. To accommodate the changing Asian/Pacific American population base, it is critical to recruit and develop officers from the Filipino, Vietnamese, and Asian Indian communities. Moreover, given the anticipated growth of the world population in the coming decades, it would be wise to recruit and develop officers with cultural knowledge, languages, and skills pertaining to China, India, Indonesia, and Pakistan—Asian nations with the largest populations (Population Reference Bureau, 2012).

Asian/Pacific American Groups*	Percentage of Total Asian/Pacific American Population
Chinese (including people from Taiwan)	23.4
Asian Indian	19.4
Filipino	16.9
Vietnamese	11.1
Korean	9.7
Japanese	5.0
All other Asian/Pacific groups	14.5
All Asian/Pacific Americans	100.00

EXHIBIT 5.2 Asian/Pacific American Population by Groups
Source: Calculated from 2011 American Community Survey data (U.S. Census Bureau).

Country of Birth	Number of Foreign-Born
China, Hong Kong, Macau, Taiwan	2,231,000
India	1,857,000
Philippines	1,814,000
Vietnam	1,259,000
Korea	1,083,000

EXHIBIT 5.3   Distribution of Foreign-Born Asian/Pacific Americans by Country of Birth
Source: Gryn & Gambino, (2012). The Foreign-Born from Asia: 2012, U.S. Census Bureau.

More than half of all Asian/Pacific Americans are foreign-born (11.6 million) and comprise over 25 percent of the foreign-born population in the United States (Gryn & Gambino, 2012). Five countries contributed the largest numbers of foreign-born Asian/Pacific Americans, as seen in Exhibit 5.3.

As noted earlier, foreign-born Asian/Pacific Americans constitute the second highest percentage of immigrants becoming naturalized citizens at 58 percent; only those born in Europe had a higher rate (Gryn & Gambino, 2012). Most of the Japanese, Filipinos, Cambodians, and Indonesians reside in the western states. Chinese, Koreans, Vietnamese, Laotians, and Thais are fairly widely distributed in the large urban areas of the United States. Most of the Asian Indians and Pakistanis live in the eastern states. The state of Minnesota and the city of Fresno, California, have the largest Hmong populations in the country. Proficiency in English language varies within groups: groups that have immigrated most recently (Southeast Asians) have the largest percentage of those unable to speak English well.

Law enforcement officers, depending on their jurisdictions, need to determine what additional languages and skills training might be appropriate in their work with Asian/Pacific American communities.

For many Asian/Pacific American groups, especially those who have recently immigrated into the United States, the law enforcement system is somewhat of a mystery. Thus, some Asian/Pacific Americans newcomers may initially hesitate to communicate openly or cooperate with police.

> In Vietnam, if you are arrested, then the work of the attorney is to prove that you are innocent. You remain locked up in jail until your innocence is proven. In the United States, a suspect who is arrested is released either upon posting bail or on their own recognizance, usually within 24 hours. To the Vietnamese immigrant, it would seem that if you have the money, you can buy your way out of jail! (Vietnamese community advocate's comments at a community meeting about a local merchant's reluctance to cooperate with police)

LABELS AND TERMS

As noted earlier, the term *Asian/Pacific Americans* is a convenient summarizing label used to refer to a heterogeneous group of people. There is no universal acceptance of this labeling convention, but for practical purposes it has been adopted frequently, with occasional variations (e.g., Asian and Pacific Americans, Asian Americans/Pacific Islanders, Asians and Pacific Islanders). As of 1997, the U.S. government divided this group into two categories: "Asian" and "Native Hawaiian and Other Pacific Islander." Which particular terms are used is based on the principle of self-designation and self-preference. Asian and Pacific Islander people are sensitive about the issue because up until the 1960 census, the population was relegated to the "Other" category. With the ethnic pride movement and ethnic minority studies movement in the late 1960s, people of

Asian and Pacific Islands descent began to designate self-preferred terms for group reference. The terms were chosen over the previous term *Oriental*, which many Asian/Pacific Americans consider to be offensive. *Oriental* symbolizes to many the past references, injustices, and stereotypes of Asian and Pacific people. It was also a term designated by those in the West (i.e., the Occident/ Western Hemisphere) for Asian people, and reminds many Asian/Pacific Americans of the colonial mentality and its effects on Pacific Rim countries (not to mention that is most often used to refer to carpets!).

By individuals within any of the groups, as previously mentioned, often the more specific names for the groups are preferred (e.g., Chinese, Japanese, Vietnamese, Pakistani, Hawaiian). Some individuals may prefer that the term *American* be part of their designation (e.g., Korean American, Filipino American). For law enforcement officers, it is best to ask individuals which ethnic or cultural group(s) they identify with and what they prefer to be called.

The use of slurs such as "Jap," "Chink," "Gook," "Chinaman," "Flip," and other derogatory ethnic slang terms is never acceptable in crime fighting and peacekeeping, no matter how provoked an officer may be. The use of other stereotype depictions, including "Chinese fire drill," "DWO (Driving While Oriental)," "Fu Man Chu mustache," "Kamikaze kid," "yellow cur," "yellow peril," "Bruce Lee Kung Fu type," "slant-eyed," "towel head," "Vietnamese bar girl," and "dragon lady," does not convey the professionalism and respect for community diversity important to law enforcement and must be avoided. Officers hearing these words used in their own departments (or with peers or citizens) should provide immediate helpful feedback about such terms to those who use them. Officers who, out of habit, routinely use these words may find themselves or their superiors in the embarrassing situation (in other words, on the evening news) of having to explain to offended citizens and communities why these terms were used.

MYTHS AND STEREOTYPES

Knowledge of and sensitivity to Asian/Pacific Americans' concerns, diversity, historical background, and life experiences will facilitate the crime-fighting and peacekeeping missions of law enforcement officers. It is important to have an understanding about some of the myths, environmental messages, and stereotypes of Asian/Pacific Americans that contribute to the prejudice, discrimination, and bias they encounter. Many Americans do not have much experience with the diversity of Asian/Pacific American groups and learn about these groups only through stereotypes, often perpetuated by movies and the media. The effect of myths and stereotypes is to reduce Asian/Pacific Americans to simplistic, one-dimensional characters whom people then lump into one stereotypic group. Often, the complexities of the diverse Asian/Pacific American groups in terms of language, history, customs, cultures, religions, and life experiences become confusing and threatening, and it is easier to deal with stereotypes. Nonetheless, it is important for law enforcement officers to be aware of the different stereotypes of Asian/ Pacific Americans. The key to effectiveness with any ethnic or racial group is not the complete elimination of myths and stereotypes about the group, but rather the awareness of these stereotypes and management of one's behavior when the stereotypes are not true of the person with whom one is dealing.

Some of the stereotypes that have affected Asian/Pacific Americans in the law enforcement setting include the following:

1. *Viewing Asian/Pacific Americans as "all alike."* That is, because there are many similarities in names, behavior, and physical features, many law enforcement officers make comments about their inability to tell people apart, or may deal with Asians in group fashion (e.g., they are all "inscrutable"; involved in gangs).
2. *Viewing Asian/Pacific Americans as successful "model minorities" or as a "super minority."* Some hold the stereotype that Asian/Pacific Americans are all successful, which is further reinforced by the media (Kawai, 2005). This has resulted in intergroup hostilities

and hate crimes directed toward Asian/Pacific Americans and has served to mask true differences and diversity among the various Asian and Pacific Islander groups. Some Asian/Pacific American groups have had to highlight the inaccurate perceptions of the "model minority" stereotype. The language barriers and adjustment issues associated with new immigrant groups affect the cohesiveness of some Asian families, contributing to delinquency among youth and high crime rates (e.g., Southeast Asian youth in the San Francisco Bay Area). Thus the model minority stereotype does not apply across the board, yet is a common stereotype when people do not recognize distinctions among and within groups.

Clearly, no group of people can be "all successful" or "all criminals." Nonetheless, the "success" and the "model minority" stereotypes have affected Asian/Pacific Americans negatively. For example, because of their implied success, law enforcement organizations may not spend the time to recruit Asian/Pacific American individuals for law enforcement careers (assuming that they are more interested in other areas such as education and business pursuits). This stereotype also hides the existence of real discrimination for those who are successful, as seen in glass (or "bamboo") ceilings in promotional and developmental opportunities, for example. The success stereotype has resulted in violence and crimes against Asian/Pacific persons. Two examples, one older but etched in the memories of many Asian/Pacific Americans, and the other more recent, are representative of issues very salient to Asian/Pacific Americans today.

> The murder of Vincent Chin, and the subsequent inability of the court system to bring the murderers to justice, is now a well-known case among Asian/Pacific American communities. The perpetrators in this case, Ronald Ebens and Michael Nitz, were two white automobile factory workers who blamed Vincent Chin (a Chinese American) for the success of the Japanese automobile industry that was, in turn, blamed for taking away American jobs in the automobile factory. (Takaki, 1989)

> A year after more than two dozen Asian American students were attacked at a high school in South Philadelphia, the Justice Department has reached an agreement with school officials there, resolving a high-profile investigation into school bullying. The Philadelphia incident, which involved a day-long assault on the students and sent 13 to the hospital, was one of several glaring cases of school harassment across the country last year. The attack made international news when it triggered an eight-day boycott by Asian American students, many of them recent immigrants, who said they would not return to school until they felt safe. (Thompson, 2010)

3. *Viewing some Asian/Pacific Americans as possible "foreign" terrorists because of their skin color, religious affiliation, and/or native dress.* Many Asian/Pacific Americans immigrate from countries with large populations that practice Islam (e.g., Indonesia, Pakistan, Bangladesh, and India) and stay close to their cultural traditions and native dress. It is unfortunate that people sometimes come to inappropriate conclusions about who might be a "foreign" terrorist based solely on such outward appearances. In addition, Sikhs—who wear turbans and grow beards—originate in India and Pakistan and are often mistaken for Muslims. These type of examples followed the 9/11 tragedy—one of the first suspects detained for questioning was a Sikh who was wearing a turban and was misidentified as an Afghani Taliban member (who also wear turbans, but different kinds); additionally, South Asians (e.g., Bengalis) with dark skin tones were misidentified as Arabs and detained for questioning on homeland security issues.

   From a law enforcement perspective, many hate crimes against Asian/Pacific Americans are related to the stereotyping of the group as foreigners and not Americans.

4. *Misunderstanding Asian/Pacific cultural differences and practices and viewing differences as a threat to other Americans.* The more than 40 Asian/Pacific American groups encompass great differences in languages, backgrounds, cultures, and life experiences. When we lack specific information about any group, it is natural to draw conclusions based on our own stereotypes, assumptions, and filtering systems. Most of the time, inappropriate assumptions and stereotypes are modified by favorable contact and actual interpersonal

relationships with Asian/Pacific American people. From a law enforcement perspective, the thrust of community policing, as well as cultural competency training, is to provide opportunities to modify stereotypes and learn about ethnic communities. Law enforcement agencies, however, have to intervene in situations in which individuals and/or groups view Asian/Pacific American cultural differences as perceived threats. Stereotypical and racially biased views of Asian/Pacific Americans as threats require the ongoing attention of law enforcement agencies.

THE ASIAN/PACIFIC AMERICAN FAMILY

Obviously, with so many different cultural groups falling under the label of Asian/Pacific Americans, great differences exist in how families operate within the various subgroups. There are, however, certain common characteristics of Asian/Pacific American families that might be of value in crime fighting and community peacekeeping. Asian/Pacific American families generally exhibit very strong ties among family members. It is not unusual for three to four generations of the same family to live under one roof. Moreover, the extended family can have an ongoing relationship network that spans great geographic distances. For example, family members (all of whom consider themselves as one unit) can be engaged in extensive communications and activities with members of the same family in the United States, Canada, Hong Kong, and Vietnam, all simultaneously. It is not uncommon for an officer to come into contact with members of the extended Asian/Pacific American family in the course of servicing these communities.

Culture Shock and the Asian/Pacific American Family

Because the traditional cultures of Asia and the Pacific Islands are so very different from that of the United States, many Asian/Pacific American families (whether refugees, immigrants, businesspersons, students, or tourists) experience some degree of culture shock when they enter and reside in the United States. Culture shock results not only from differences in values and traditions but also from differences in urbanization, industrialization, and modernization owing to technology that may be different from that in their homeland. Peace officers need to be aware that Asian/Pacific Americans may cope with their culture shock by becoming "clannish" (e.g., Chinatowns, Koreatowns). Other survival mechanisms include avoiding contact and interaction with those who are different (including police officers). One key to the success of law enforcement officers in working with Asian/Pacific Americans is the knowledge of how best to communicate with families residing in these "clannish" communities, and which family members to speak to for information, help, and referral.

The Roles of Family Members

In most Asian/Pacific American families, relationship and communication patterns tend to be hierarchical, with an elder (parent or grandparent) as the head of the household. Although many decisions and activities may appear to be determined by the elder, other individuals may be influential. Generally, if there are grandparents in the household, the parent might act as the spokesperson for the family, but would consult the grandparents and others regarding any major decision. It is important in any kind of law enforcement contact that requires a decision and/or choice to allow the family time to discuss issues in, as much as feasible, a "private" manner. This might involve giving the family members an extensive amount of time to speak among themselves in their native language, which some Americans find excruciatingly uncomfortable. In addition, self-control and keeping things within the family are key values for Asian/Pacific Americans. An officer thus may find that there is more leverage in a situation by allowing an Asian/Pacific American to come to the same conclusion as the officer with respect to a situation. For example, the officer can explain an arrest situation to an elder family member, and instead of saying directly to the individual to be arrested that he or she has to leave with the officer, the officer can allow the elder to suggest to the family member that he or she leave with the officer. What may appear to be a minor consideration in this case can result in a great degree of persuasion, control, and cooperation by all parties concerned.

Although there are no clear-cut rules as to whether one goes to a male head of the household or to a female head to make a law enforcement inquiry, it should be noted that for most Asian/Pacific American families, the role of the mother in discipline and decision making is very important. In other words, even when a household appears to be "ruled" by a father or grandfather, the women's roles could be major.

Children, Adolescents, and Youths

Most Asian/Pacific American families comprise at least two or more individuals within the same household working outside of the home. Thus, if young children are present, there is a high reliance on either family members or others to help care for them while the parents are at work. It is not uncommon for older children to care for younger children within a household.

In recent immigrant and refugee families, Asian/Pacific American children have a special role in being the intermediaries between parents and the external community because of the ability of the younger individuals to learn English and American ways of doing things. Children often serve as interpreters for peace officers in their communication and relations with Asian/Pacific American families comprising recent immigrants and refugees, which can put the children in extremely awkward situations. It is suggested that officers review the role expected of a youthful family member and determine how sensitive any translated content might be to the different family members and the consequences if messages are interpreted incorrectly. For example, asking a juvenile to interpret for his or her parents who speak no English when the juvenile has been involved in a sexual abuse situation at school may result in significant omissions and/or changed content because of shame. Likewise, due to the emphasis on hierarchy in most Asian families, children will dutifully tell police officers whatever an elder family member says at the time, even if the child knows the information to be false. Thus it is extremely wise to procure the services of an interpreter when interviewing Asian families. And in all cases, even when a child is acting as an interpreter, officers should direct communication to elder family members lest they view the officers' lack of attention to them as an insult.

Asian/Pacific American Family Violence

Keeping sensitive issues within the family and using self-help and personal effort strategies are part of Asian/Pacific cultural values and norms. Research studies on family violence (e.g., spousal physical abuse; child abuse; sexual abuse) by Asian/Pacific Americans show an increasing trend. It is only during recent decades that researchers and community advocates have begun collecting such data. The few reported studies that exist seem to indicate significant and emerging problems with family violence within the Asian/Pacific American community. Tjaden and Thoennes (2000) conducted a telephone survey of a nationally representative sample of 8,000 men and 8,000 women of all ethnic backgrounds. Results showed that 12.8 percent of the Asian/Pacific American women reported having been physically assaulted by an intimate partner at least once during their lifetimes, and 3.8 percent reported having been raped. A study released in 2010 (Dabby, Patel, & Poore) showed that 78 percent of homicides involving Asian/Pacific Americans were perpetrated by intimate partners of their victims. (Only 10% of perpetrators were female; 90% were male.) And unfortunately, as researchers Cho and Kim (2012) point out, "Asian victims of IPV [intimate partner violence] are less likely to use mental health services than any other racial groups. The odds of other racial groups seeking mental health services [are] more than four times those for Asians." The availability of bilingual outreach services is of key importance to the Asian/Pacific American community.

The role of peace officers in detecting, assessing, and intervening in family violence situations within Asian/Pacific American communities is a critical one given this area of emerging needs and problems. The sensitivity of the peace officer to cultural influences and patterns of communication (as noted in the next section) will be significant in the effective gathering of initial information and subsequent referral and interventions with Asian/Pacific American families involved in domestic violence and other issues of abuse.

COMMUNICATION STYLES OF ASIAN/PACIFIC AMERICANS

There are key generalizations that can be made concerning Asian/Pacific American verbal and nonverbal communication styles. Misunderstandings resulting from style differences can lead to conflicts and perceptions of poor service from police agencies, as well as safety and control issues for peace officers.

1. It is important that officers take the time to get information from witnesses, victims, and suspects even if individuals speak limited English. The assistance of interpreters, language bank resources, and officers who speak Asian/Pacific dialects or languages can greatly enhance this process. Often Asian/Pacific Americans have not been helped in crime-fighting and peacekeeping situations because officers could not or did not take information from individuals who could not speak English well.

2. Asian/Pacific Americans tend to hold a greater "family" and/or "group" orientation. As such, the lack of the use of "I" statements and/or self-reference should not be evaluated as being evasive. Officers may be concerned because an Asian/Pacific American may use the pronoun "we" when the situation may call for a personal observation involving an "I" statement. For example, concerning a traffic accident, the Asian/Pacific American may describe what he or she saw by saying, "We saw. . . ." Using such group statements to convey what the individual saw is consistent with the family and group orientation of Asian/Pacific Americans. Another area of some concern to law enforcement is the tendency of certain Asian language speakers to confuse pronouns, switching back and forth between "he" and "she" to refer to an individual. One reason for this is that in some languages, such as various spoken dialects of Chinese, there is no difference in the pronunciation of "he" and "she." Be patient when taking witness statements or during interrogations; Asian Americans are not trying to be deceptive, and any nervousness on their part—or any sense that an officer is becoming impatient—will only make matters worse.

3. Officers should be aware that for many Asian/Pacific Americans, it is considered rude, impolite, and to involve a "loss of face" (for the officers; not for the speaker) to directly say "no" to an authority figure. Peace officers must understand the following possibilities when an answer of "yes" is heard from an Asian/Pacific American. It can mean (1) "Yes, I heard what you said (but I may or may not agree with you)"; (2) "Yes, I understand what you said (but I might not do it)"; (3) "Yes, I can see this is important for you (but I do not share your sense of urgency)"; or (4) "Yes, I agree (and will do what you said)." Because both the context of the communication and nonverbal aspects of the message are equally meaningful, it is vital for law enforcement officers to be sure of the "yes" answers received, as well as of other language nuances from Asian/Pacific Americans. Two examples might be illustrative: (1) If an Asian/Pacific American says that he or she will "try his or her best to attend," this generally means that he or she will not be there, especially for voluntary events and situations such as community neighborhood safety meetings. (2) If an Asian/Pacific national says in response to a question "It is possible," this generally means, "Do not wait for it to happen." Such communications, as noted previously, may be more applicable to some Asian/Pacific Americans than others, but sensitivity on the part of law enforcement officers to these language nuances will

facilitate understanding. In a communication situation in which the response of "yes" may be ambiguous, it is suggested that law enforcement officers rephrase the question so that the requested outcome in action and understanding are demonstrated in the verbal response. For example:

Asking a yes/no question that prompts an ambiguous response:

OFFICER: "I need you to show up in court on Tuesday. Do you understand?"

ASIAN WITNESS: "Yes!"

Providing context and rephrasing the question to elicit a response that shows understanding and outcome:

OFFICER: "It is important to tell this information to a judge. How will you come to court on Tuesday?"

ASIAN WITNESS: "Yes. My brother has a car. He will take me to court on Tuesday."

4. Asian/Pacific Americans tend to be "high context" (indirect; implicit) in communication style. This means that officers must provide both interpersonal and situational context for effective communication. Context for Asian/Pacific Americans means that members of the community know the officers in the community. Community members may have had previous working relationships with the officers (e.g., crime prevention meetings, police athletic league). Moreover, other members of the community may help to provide information and context for police cooperation based on past relationships. Context also means providing explanations and education to Asian/Pacific American individuals or groups about procedures and laws before asking them questions and/or requesting their participation in an activity. By providing background information and establishing prior community relationships, Asian/Pacific American individuals have context for cooperating with law enforcement agencies and officers.

5. Be aware of nonverbal and other cultural nuances that may detract from effective communication between officers and members of the Asian/Pacific American community. Many Asian/Pacific Americans find it uncomfortable and inappropriate to maintain eye contact with those of higher status, or with authority figures like police officers. As such, many Asian/Pacific Americans look down on the ground and/or avert their eyes while talking. Police officers should not automatically read this nonverbal behavior as indicating a lack of trust or respect, or as dishonesty. Likewise, police officers should be aware of possible nonverbal gestures and actions that may detract from their professional roles. For example, in many Asian cultures, gesturing with a curled index finger for a person to come forward is used primarily for servants, children, and/or dogs.

6. Asian/Pacific Americans may not display emotions in ways that officers expect. The central thesis guiding some Asian/Pacific Americans is the Confucian notion of "walking the middle road." This means that extremes—too much or too little of anything—are not good. As such, Asian/Pacific Americans tend to moderate displays of positive and/or negative emotion. Often, in crisis situations, nonverbal displays of emotions are controlled to the point that the affect of the Asian/Pacific American appears "flat." Under such circumstances, the officer needs to correctly understand and interpret such unemotional displays appropriately. For example, just because the parent of a murder victim does not appear shaken by an officer's report does not mean that the person is not experiencing a severe emotional crisis.

KEY ISSUES IN LAW ENFORCEMENT

Underreporting of Crimes

Asian/Pacific Americans, because of their past experiences with certain law enforcement agencies (e.g., anti-Asian immigration laws; health and sanitation code violations in restaurants; perceived unresponsiveness by police), are reluctant to report crimes and may not seek police assistance and help. Many Asian/Pacific Americans remember how police in their home countries brutalized and violated them and others (e.g., in Southeast Asian and other Asian countries). Crimes that occur within a family's home (e.g., home invasion; family violence) or within the confines of a small family business (e.g., robbery of a Chinese restaurant) often go unreported unless these crimes are connected to larger criminal activities.

Many immigrants and refugees are simply not knowledgeable about the legal system of the United States and therefore avoid any contact with law enforcement personnel. Outreach and community-policing efforts will enhance the contact and relationship with Asian/Pacific American communities, helping to correct the underreporting of crimes.

Asian/Pacific American Community and Law Enforcement Interaction

Increasingly, when there are collaborative and cooperative efforts among law enforcement, criminal justice, and community advocacy systems, Asian and Pacific American communities begin to gain greater trust and confidence resulting from effective multicultural and multidisciplinary law enforcement actions. Numerous "Citizen Police Academies" exemplify how police, community advocates, and citizens join together to collaborate on police services in the Asian community. The programs are intended to open lines of communication between citizens and the police and to help citizens understand the complexities of its policies and regulations. Monterey Park, California has a Citizen Police Academy in which classes are presented in Spanish, English and Chinese. In 2003, this Police Citizen Academy presented the entire program in Mandarin and Cantonese. (City of Monterey Park, 2014)

The Los Angeles Police Department Airport Police Bureau was one of the first units to establish storefront outreach efforts that resulted in improved police/community relationships and better service benefits to the Asian/Pacific American neighborhood in the Korean area of Los Angeles (Chin, 1985). Storefront outreach efforts are now utilized in most urban centers with large Asian/Pacific American communities such as San Francisco, New York, Oakland, Chicago, Boston, and Seattle. (See Chapter 14 for further information on community policing.) Another outreach approach is the use of Asian/Pacific American bilingual community service officers (CSOs)—nonsworn officers with badges and uniforms—who provide police department supportive services to Southeast Asian communities in San Diego, California.

Increasing Asian/Pacific American Peace Officers

There is a noticeable underrepresentation of Asian/Pacific Americans in federal, state, and local law enforcement and criminal justice positions. According to a survey conducted by the Bureau of Justice Statistics in 2008, of the 120,000 full-time federal personnel authorized to make arrests and carry firearms in the 50 states and the District of Columbia, only 3 percent were Asian/Pacific Islanders. The federal agencies that employed the largest number of Asian/Pacific Islanders were: (1) the Internal Revenue Service; (2) the U.S. Postal Inspection Service; (3) the Bureau of Diplomatic Security; and (4) the Federal Bureau of Investigation (Reaves, 2012).

The small numbers of Asian/Pacific American officers has hampered many departments in neighborhoods with large Asian/Pacific American populations in effectively serving those communities with appropriate role models and bicultural expertise. A variety of reasons exist for such underrepresentation, including: (1) the history of law enforcement relationships with Asian/Pacific American communities; (2) interest (or more specifically, the lack thereof) of Asian/Pacific Americans in law enforcement careers, to some extent due to the perception of a "bamboo ceiling" of limited career advancement possibilities; (3) the image of law enforcement personnel in Asian/Pacific American communities; (4) a lack of knowledge about the different careers and pathways in law enforcement (again, exacerbated by the "bamboo ceiling" perception); (5) concern with and fear of background checks, physical requirements, and the application process; and (6) a limited number of role models and advocates for law enforcement careers within Asian/Pacific American communities. With growing Asian/Pacific American populations in areas throughout the United States, law enforcement has begun to emphasize the importance of diversity in its recruitment efforts.

Hate Crimes against Asian/Pacific Americans

By far, the greatest number of hate crimes motivated by racial bias are targeted toward black Americans (see Chapter 6). However, such crimes extend beyond racism associated with skin color. Immigrant Americans and those who are *perceived* to be immigrants are often scapegoated as responsible for the poor state of the economy, a lack of jobs, and the failure of some to get ahead. Asian/Pacific immigrants, whether first-, second-, third- or fourth-generation Americans, are often lumped into one category—"immigrant."

> In examining the underlying and historical context for these hate crimes, it is important to note that the persistent stereotype of Asian Americans as "perpetual foreigners" has fueled discrimination, hostility, and even violence against Asian American and NHPI [Native Hawaiian and Pacific Islander] individuals. Political or economic tensions between the U.S. and Asian countries during rough economic times have also led to increased violence against Asian Americans and NHPIs in the past. More recently, inflammatory rhetoric targeting immigrants has instigated an increase in hate-based violence against those perceived to be immigrants—including Asian Americans and NHPIs. (APALC, 2012)

In 2011, there were just under 3,500 hate crime offenses motivated by racial bias (i.e., single-bias), based on data collected as part of mandatory law enforcement agency reporting. Nearly 5 percent of those offenses were targeted toward Asian/Pacific Americans (i.e., there were other hate crimes reported vis-à-vis individuals reporting to be more than one race). (FBI, 2012a)

In August 2013, the Department of Justice announced that a number of additional groups would be included in the national program that tracks hate crime, that is, the Uniform Crime Reporting Program (discussed in Chapters 11 and 12). These groups include individuals from South Asia such as Sikhs and Hindus (as well as Buddhists who are from many different parts of Asia). Speaking as a member of the Congressional Asian Pacific American Caucus (CAPAC), California Congressman Ami Bera stated:

> I am pleased that Director Mueller has approved the FBI Advisory Policy Board's recommendation to add several categories in its tracking of hate crimes, including offenses committed against Sikh, [and] Hindu . . . Americans. As we near the one-year anniversary of the tragic Oak Creek shootings where six Sikh Americans were killed in a horrific hate crime, I am confident this change will protect domestic civil rights and aid law enforcement in securing our communities. By ensuring that all Americans—regardless of religion, race, gender or creed—feel safe in their communities, we can heal our families and honor the memories of those killed in Oak Creek. (CAPAC, 2013)

Thus the 2011 hate crime figures reported above do not reflect offenses against individuals from these newly accepted Asian categories. Taking into account South Asians mistaken as Arabs and Muslims, the number of hate crimes against all Asian/Pacific Americans has increased.

Crimes within Asian/Pacific American Communities

Many crimes committed in Asian/Pacific American communities, particularly among Asian/Pacific refugee and Asian/Pacific immigrant groups, are perpetrated by members from within the same community. Law enforcement officials have often found it difficult to get cooperation from refugee and immigrant victims of human trafficking, extortion, home robbery, burglary, theft, and other crimes. In part, the lack of cooperation stems from a fear of retaliation by the criminals, who are often known to the victims. Other concerns of Asian/Pacific American victims include: (1) a perceived level of responsiveness of peacekeeping officers and agencies; (2) a lack of familiarity with and trust in police services; (3) the perceived level of effectiveness of law enforcement agencies; and (4) prior stereotypes and images of law enforcement agencies as discriminatory (e.g., immigration laws) and unresponsive to crimes against Asian/Pacific Americans. Recent Asian/Pacific American refugees and immigrants are often prime targets, in part because of their distrust of most institutions (e.g., banks; police departments; hospitals). As a result, they are more inclined to hide and store cash and other valuables in their homes. A key challenge for police agencies is to educate this group and to work cooperatively with Asian/Pacific Americans to reduce crime within these communities.

Human trafficking has been highlighted as one of the crimes perpetuated by Asian/Pacific Americans on others within their own communities. The International Labour Organization estimates that more than 20.9 million people worldwide (including 11.7 million from the Asia-Pacific region) are victims of forced labor (ILO, 2012).

> **Human trafficking** The transportation of persons for sexual exploitation, forced labor, or other illegal or criminal activities.

Human trafficking has become a global business, with many victims coming from Asian countries; such illegal activities generate billions of dollars in profits for traffickers and organized criminal groups (United Nations, 2012). Because of its secretive and hidden nature, human trafficking is likely to remain an increasingly underreported crime. As noted by the Asian Anti-Trafficking Collaborative (AATC), "Preying on the desperation and dreams of vulnerable immigrants around the world, human traffickers lure their victims to the U.S. with false promises and tales of living the American dream. Most victims are pulled to the U.S. by the hope of opportunity and pushed from their home country by the lack of the same chances of making a better life for themselves and their loved ones. But once in the U.S., the experiences of these individuals are strikingly similar: abuse, threats of violence and retaliation, elimination of personal liberty and free agency, and dehumanizing treatment that crushes the dignity, self-esteem, and self-worth of the victim" (API Legal Outreach, 2013). Law enforcement officers' involvement with Asian/Pacific American communities on human trafficking has emerged as one of the major areas of work. There are approximately 100,000 to 300,000 American-born children, annually, who are sold into the sex trade. The FBI and other law enforcement agencies have initiated numerous national programs to help combat this phenomenon. FBI initiatives center around combating the exploitation of individuals who end up in agricultural and domestic service as slave laborers, as well as on protecting those who are forced into prostitution. As of 2012, the FBI participated in over 80 human trafficking task forces and various other groups across the U.S. in collaboration with local, state and federal law enforcement agencies as well as advocacy groups (FBI, 2012b).

Many of the victims are young immigrants or the children of immigrants whose parents face extreme poverty in the U.S. and continue to be traumatized by memories of war or genocide. In Northern California, there is a particular demand for Cambodian American girls (Brown, 2011). These girls and young women are from families whose parents and grandparents experienced or escaped from one of the worst tragedies in modern history. (The Cambodian genocide resulted in the killing of 1.7 million people or 21% of the population. [CGP, 2013]). Within a Cambodian family, the emotional scars from genocide are likely to be passed on from generation to generation, and the fallout affecting family dynamics is considerable. Human trafficking abusers can be family members (e.g., brothers as pimps). Many domestic minors forced into the sex trade still live with parents, and end up working in massage parlors or strip clubs, with escort services, or even as acupuncturists (Professor Richard J. Estes, University of Pennsylvania, as quoted in Brown, 2011).

> Veronica, 26, [is] a Cambodian-Filipina community college freshman whose purse bulges with college papers. It also holds the red velvet heels she wears on weekends to make "out calls" in San Francisco for men who find her on the Internet. When Veronica was 12, her stepfather, a custodian, would take her into empty buildings and touch her. On April 29, 2000, a date she remembers

exactly, a man who flattered her persuaded her to become "occupied," as she put it. He beat her repeatedly for seven years. "He would beat me for simple things, like not making enough money or worse, getting pulled over by a cop," she said. (Professor Richard J. Estes, University of Pennsylvania, as quoted in Brown, 2011)

Families whose members have been victims of violence and genocide often fear law enforcement and do not ask for help. Law enforcement professionals have to work hard at building relationships and encouraging such victims to open up.

Perhaps most important in these cases is earning the trust of the victims of commercial sexual exploitation. These cases often require the victims' willingness to cooperate in the investigation and, ultimately, testify against these defendants. Where trust is established with the victim, these victims will often notify detectives with new cell phone numbers, addresses and changes in work status. Even simple changes in outreach can make a difference. For example, recognizing that most of these individuals are awake at night and have cell phone contact that is viable at night means regular contact is more likely. Limiting victim outreach to the 8 a.m. to 5 p.m. workday, on the other hand, precludes most reasonable chances of staying in touch with the victims in these cases. (Tiapula & Turkel, 2008)

Worldwide efforts to end this situation are being led by the United Nations with the "Protocol to Prevent, Suppress and Punish Trafficking in Persons, Especially Women and Children." As of August 2012, 152 countries had ratified the Protocol (United Nations, 2012).

Summary

- As a result of early immigration laws and other discriminatory treatment received by Asian/Pacific Americans in the United States, the experiences of Asian/Pacific Americans with law enforcement officials have been fraught with conflicts, difficulties, and mixed messages. Some Asian/Pacific Americans remember this history and carry with them images of police services as something to be feared and avoided. Law enforcement officials may need to go out of their way to establish trust and to win cooperation in order to accomplish their goals effectively when serving and protecting Asian/Pacific Americans.

- The label Asian Americans/Pacific Islanders encompasses over 40 very diverse ethnic and cultural groups. Significant differences exist among these groups (e.g., different cultures and languages) in addition to differences *within* the groups as a result of individual life and generational experiences. While it is difficult to understand individual subtleties within these communities, officers can learn about the various motivational determinants of individuals within different generational and immigrant groups.

- The preferred term for referring to Asian/Pacific Americans varies with context, groups, and individual preferences. Law enforcement officials need to be aware of terms that are unacceptable and derogatory as well as terms that are preferred. When in doubt, officers should ask Asian/Pacific Americans which terms they prefer. Officers are advised to provide helpful feedback to peers when offensive terms, labels, and/or actions are used concerning Asian/Pacific Americans. This will reduce the risk of misunderstanding and improve the working relationships between officers and Asian/Pacific American communities. Moreover, it will help enhance the professional image of the department within those communities.

- The complexities of the diverse Asian/Pacific American groups in terms of language, history, customs, cultures, religions, and life experiences can be confusing and threatening. Accordingly, it can be easy to fall back on stereotypes of these groups. A key stereotype of great concern to Asian/Pacific Americans is that they are regarded by mainstream Americans as very much alike. It is important that peace officers show awareness of diversity among Asian/Pacific Americans. Some hold the stereotype that Asian/Pacific Americans are all successful; this stereotype is further reinforced by the media. Such stereotypes have resulted in intergroup hostilities and hate crimes directed toward Asian/Pacific Americans.

- With so many cultural groups falling under the label of Asian/Pacific Americans, we find great differences in how families operate within the various subgroups. Asian/Pacific American families generally exhibit very strong ties among extended family members. It is not unusual for three to four generations of the same family to live under one roof. One key to the success of law enforcement officers in working with Asian/Pacific American families is knowledge of how best to address family members for information, help, and referral. Peace officers need to be aware that Asian/Pacific Americans may cope with culture shock by seeking solace within the family or community; in other words, becoming "clannish" (e.g., Chinatowns, Koreatowns).

• Many Asian/Pacific Americans are concerned with their inability to communicate clearly, and this is of particular concern among Asian/Pacific Americans who are immigrants and refugees. Peace officers must recognize that bilingual individuals and nonnative English speakers want to communicate effectively with officers, and officers must take the time to allow them to do so. Maintaining contact, providing extra time, using interpreters, and being patient with speakers will allow Asian/Pacific Americans to communicate their concerns. Officers should be aware of nonverbal aspects in the communication styles of Asian/Pacific Americans, including eye contact, touch, gestures, and affect (show of emotions). Accents, limited vocabulary, and incorrect grammar may give officers the impression that Asian/Pacific Americans do not understand what is communicated. It is important to remember that the English listening and comprehension skills of Asian/Pacific American immigrants and refugees are usually better than their speaking skills.

• In most Asian/Pacific American families, relationship and communication patterns tend to be hierarchical, with a parent or grandparent as the head of the household. Elder family members are typically consulted regarding any major decision. In recent immigrant and refugee families, Asian/Pacific American children have a special role in being interpreters or intermediaries between parents and the external community because of their English-language abilities and awareness of the American ways of doing things.

• Asian/Pacific Americans, because of their past experiences with law enforcement agencies along with concerns about privacy and other factors, are reluctant to report crimes and may not seek police assistance and help. Law enforcement departments and officials need to build relationships and working partnerships with representative groups from Asian/Pacific American communities. Relationship building is often helped by outreach efforts such as community storefront offices, bilingual officers, and participation of officers in community activities.

Discussion Questions and Issues

1. *Law Enforcement Interactions.* Many anti-Asian/Pacific American laws and events leave Asian/Pacific Americans with the view that law enforcement agencies are not user-friendly. What are the implications of this view for law enforcement? Suggest ways to counteract negative points of view.

2. *Diversity among Asian/Pacific Americans.* The Asian/Pacific American category comprises over 40 diverse ethnic and cultural groups. Which groups are you most likely to encounter in crime fighting and peacekeeping? Based on trends within your community, which groups do you anticipate encountering in your future work?

3. *How Asian/Pacific American Groups Differ.* In Chapter 1, we presented a typology for understanding motives for the behavior of immigrants and refugees in terms of their generational and immigration status in the United States (see Chapter 1, page 10). How might you apply this typology to better understand (a) an Asian/Pacific American refugee involved in a traffic moving violation? (b) an Asian/Pacific American immigrant involved as a victim of a house robbery? (c) an Asian/Pacific national involved as a victim of a burglary? (d) Southeast Asian youths involved in possible gang activities?

4. *Choice of Terms.* The term *Asian Americans and Pacific Islanders* is used in many publications and by many people to refer to members of the diverse groups included in this category. How might you find out which is the best term to use in reference to an individual if ethnic and cultural information of this kind is necessary?

5. *Offensive Terms and Labels.* We strongly urge that offensive terms such as Chinks, Gooks, and Flips not be used in law enforcement work at any time. Give three practical reasons for this perspective.

6. *Effects of Myths and Stereotypes.* Myths and stereotypes about Asian/Pacific Americans have greatly affected this group. What are some of the Asian/Pacific American stereotypes that you have heard of or encountered? What effects would these stereotypes have on Asian/Pacific Americans? Suggest ways to manage these stereotypes in law enforcement. How might awareness of Asian/Pacific American stereotypes be helpful in an interview with an Asian/Pacific American about homeland security issues?

7. *Communication Style Variations among Cultures.* How do you think that the information in this chapter about verbal and nonverbal communication styles can help officers in their approach to Asian/Pacific American citizens? Does understanding the cultural components of the styles and behavior help you to become more sensitive and objective about your reactions? Provide some examples of rephrasing questions to elicit responses that show understanding and intended actions on the part of Asian/Pacific Americans.

8. ***Self-Monitoring and Avoidance of Law Enforcement.*** Why do you think many Asian/Pacific Americans keep to their own communities and express the desire for self-monitoring and community resolution of their problems? When are such efforts desirable? When are they ineffective? How can police agencies be of greater service to Asian/Pacific American communities in this regard?

9. ***Human Trafficking and Other Populations.*** This chapter highlights human trafficking within the context of Asian

Americans or Asians brought to the U.S. for trafficking purposes. It is well known that criminals use the massage industry as a means for sex trafficking in the United States, and that many owners and workers in such "massage" parlors are of Asian origin. However, human trafficking in the United States is not limited to Asians. Do some research about the jurisdiction in which you live or work (or choose the nearest metropolitan area), and list demographic characteristics of other trafficking victims (e.g., age, gender, ethnic and national origin).

References

APALC: Asian Pacific American Legal Center. (2012, September 17). Statement of APALC. Hearing on Hate Crimes and the Threat of Domestic Extremism.

API: Asian Pacific Islander Legal Outreach. (2013). "Asian Anti-Trafficking Collaborative (AATC)." Retrieved July 24, 2013, from www.apilegaloutreach.org/trafficking.html

Brown, Patricia Leigh. (2011, May 23). "In Oakland, Redefining Sex Trade Workers as Abuse Victims." *The New York Times.*

CGP: Cambodian Genocide Program, a Program of the Genocide Studies Program of Yale University. (2013). Retrieved July 25, 2013, from www.yale.edu/cgp

CAPAC: Congressional Asian Pacific American Caucus. (2013, August 2). "CAPAC Applauds New FBI Hate Crime Tracking Data." Press release.

Chin, James. (1985). "Crime and the Asian American Community: The Los Angeles Response to Koreatown." *Journal of California Law Enforcement*, 19, 52–60.

Cho, Hyunkag and Woo Jong Kim. (2012, April 22). *Intimate Partner Violence Among Asian Americans and Their Use of Mental Health Services: Comparisons with White, Black, and Latino Victims.* Springer Science and Business Media, LLC.

City of Monterey Park. (2014) Retrieved December 18, 2013, from www.ci.monterey-park.ca.us/

Dabby, C., Hetana Patel, and Grace Poore. (2010, February). *Shattered Lives: Homicides, Domestic Violence and Asian Families.* San Francisco: Asian & Pacific Islander Institute on Domestic Violence, APIA Health Forum.

Daniels, Roger. (1988). *Asian America: Chinese and Japanese in the United States since 1850.* Seattle, WA: University of Washington Press.

FBI: Federal Bureau of Investigation, (2012a). "Hate Crime Statistics, 2011." *Uniform Crime Report.* U.S. Department of Justice.

FBI: Federal Bureau of Investigation. (2012b). "Human Trafficking—FBI Initiatives." Retrieved July 31, 2013, from www.fbi.gov/about-us/investigate/civilrights/human_trafficking/initiatives

Gryn, Thomas and Christine Gambino. (2012, October). "The Foreign Born From Asia: 2011." U.S. Census Bureau, *American Community Survey Briefs.*

Hayes, Patrick. (Ed.). (2012). *The Making of Modern Immigration: An Encyclopedia of People and Ideas.* Santa Barbara, CA: ABC-CLIO, LLC.

Hoeffel, Elizabeth M., Sonya Rastogi, Myoung Ouk Kim, and Hasan Shahid. (2012, March). "The Asian Population: 2010."

U.S. Census Bureau, *2010 Census Briefs.* Washington, D.C.: U.S. Government Printing Office.

ILO: International Labour Organization. (2012). *ILO 2012 Global estimate of forced labour, Executive Summary.* Geneva, Switzerland: ILO Special Action Programme to combat Forced Labour.

Kawai, Yuko. (2005). "Stereotyping Asian Americans: The Dialectic of the Model Minority and the Yellow Peril." *The Howard Journal of Communications.* 16, 109–130.

Pew Research Center. (2012, December 18). *The Global Religious Landscape: A Report on the Size and Distribution of the World's Major Religious Groups as of 2010.* Forum on Religion & Public Life. Washington, D.C.

Pew Research Center. (2013, April 4). *The Rise of Asian Americans.* Washington, D.C.

PRB: Population Reference Bureau. (2012). *World Population Data Sheet.* Washington, D.C.

Povell, Marc. (2005). *The History of Vietnamese Immigration.* Washington, D.C.: The American Immigration Law Foundation. Retrieved August 28, 2013, from www.ailf.org/awards/benefit2005/vietnamese_essay.shtml

Prashad, V. (2001). *The Karma of Brown Folk.* Minneapolis, MN: University of Minnesota Press.

Reaves, Brian A. (2012, June). "Federal Law Enforcement Officers, 2008." U.S. Department of Justice, Office of Justice Programs. Bureau of Justice Statistics Bulletin NCJ 238250.

Takaki, R. (1998). *Strangers from a Different Shore: A History of Asian Americans.* Boston, MA: Little, Brown and Company.

Takaki, R. (1989). "Who Killed Vincent Chin?" In G. Yun (Ed.), *A Look Beyond the Model Minority Image: Critical Issues in Asian America.* New York: Minority Rights Group, Inc., p. 23–29.

Thompson, Krissah. (2010, December 15). "Justice Reaches pact with Philadelphia schools in '09 attacks on Asian American students." *Washington Post.* Retrieved from www.ndaa.org/pdf/prosecut092008_feat_identvic.pdf

Tiapula, Suzanna, and Allison Turkel. (2008, April/May/June). "Identifying the Victims of Human Trafficking." *The Prosecutor.*

Tjaden, Patricia, and Nancy Thoennes. (2000). *Extent, Nature, and Consequences of Intimate Partner Violence.* Washington, D.C.: National Institute of Justice and the Centers for Disease Control and Prevention.

United Nations. (2012). *Global Report on Trafficking in Persons 2012.* Vienna: United Nations Office on Drugs and Crime.

6 Law Enforcement Contact with African Americans

LEARNING OBJECTIVES

After reading this chapter, you should be able to:

- Describe the historical background of African Americans, especially as it relates to the dynamics between citizens and police.
- Recognize key aspects of diversity within African American communities, including those of class, culture, and religion.
- Explain the evolution of African American identity movements and self-identification terms.
- Understand the impact of African American stereotypes on law enforcement and cross-racial perceptions.
- Identify select characteristics of African American youth, extended families, gender roles, and single mothers as they relate to contact with law enforcement.
- Illustrate the potential for misunderstanding by describing characteristics of African American verbal and nonverbal communication styles as distinguished from mainstream styles.
- List and discuss key issues associated with law enforcement contact in African American communities.

OUTLINE

- Introduction
- Historical Information
- Demographics: Diversity among African Americans
- Issues of Identity and Group Identification Terms
- Stereotypes and Cross-Racial Perceptions
- The African American Family
- Language and Communication
- Key Issues in Law Enforcement
- Summary
- Discussion Questions and Issues

INTRODUCTION

> There is no point in telling blacks to observe the law . . . It has almost always been used against them.
>
> —*Senator Robert Kennedy After Visiting the Scene of the Watts Riot, 1965*

The impact of slavery, racism, and discrimination plays a significant role in black/white relations. A history of intimidation of African Americans by police continues to affect the dynamics of law enforcement in some black communities even today; however, cultural differences also play a role. Understanding both the history and culture of African Americans is especially important for criminal justice agencies and their employees as they work toward improving relations and changing perceptions. Most African Americans are fourth- and fifth-generation Americans. Aspects of black culture are heavily influenced by African culture, and those of white culture by European culture. Cultural differences are seldom acknowledged, even though they can cause communication problems between citizens and police officers. Failing to recognize the distinctiveness of black culture, language, and communication patterns, in addition to history, can lead to misunderstandings, conflict, and even confrontation.

HISTORICAL INFORMATION

Many African Americans or blacks (terms used interchangeably) in the United States trace their roots to western or interior Africa. For some, African relatives had been kidnapped originally by Europeans, especially in the earliest days of the slave trade; others were prisoners of war due to tribal conflicts; yet others had been surrendered by their families or traded off by mercenary tribal leaders. They were torn from their cultures of origin between the seventeenth and the nineteenth centuries when they were brought to the U.S. as slaves. Blacks represent the only migrants to have come to the Americas, North and South, against their will. This experience has made African Americans, as a group, very different from immigrants who chose to come to the United States to better their lives, and different from refugees who fled their homelands to escape religious or political persecution. Slavery is the centerpiece of many of the societal dynamics we see today among blacks and whites; law enforcement bears a particular burden because of the role it has played in the treatment of African Americans.

Historically, in the United States, slaves were considered "inferior" beings; a slave is by definition entirely under the domination of some influence or person. While most slave owners likely understood that treating people as animals to be owned, worked, and sold was immoral, they wanted to think of themselves as good, religious, moral people. Hence they had to convince themselves that their slaves were not really human, but a lower form of life. They focused on racial differences (skin color, hair texture, etc.) as "proof" that black people were not really people after all. Racism began, then, as an airtight alibi for a horrifying injustice. A slave was counted as three-fifths of a person during census-taking as dictated by the Constitution, that is, the foundation of the U.S. judicial system. Many slave owners routinely and brutally raped their female slaves, often before puberty, as well as forcing their healthiest slaves to couple and breed regardless of the slaves' own attachments and preferences. (The fact that many African Americans' genetic background is part Caucasian is testimony to the slave owners' "tendencies" to violate slave girls and women.)

This historical notion of the slave, and by extension, any African American, as less than human has created psychological and social problems for succeeding generations of black citizens. Slavery and the system of apartheid that followed (i.e., Jim Crow laws) led to legalized discrimination—inferior housing, schools, health care, and jobs for black people—the impact of which is still felt today.

Although the institution of slavery formally ended in 1863, many racist ideas borne of slavery persisted. These ideas continue even now to leave deep scars on many African Americans from all socioeconomic classes. The psychological heritage of slavery, as well as current discrimination, continues to prevent equal opportunity and protection in many realms of life.

The history taught in American educational institutions has tended to present a distorted, incomplete picture of black family life, emphasizing familial breakdown during the slave era. This version of history has generally ignored the moral strength of the slaves and the community solidarity and family loyalty that arose after emancipation. There is no doubt that these attributes have positively affected the rebuilding of the African American community.

Despite many slave owners' attempts to destroy black family life, most slaves managed to form lasting families headed by a mother and a father, and slave couples typically enjoyed long marriages. Although white slave masters would often do everything possible to pull families apart (including the selling of slaves), there is evidence that slaves maintained their family connections as best as they could and produced stable units with admirable values. According to U.S. historian Char Miller, "Despite the fact that slavery tore apart many families, blacks maintained links, loves, and relationships just as anyone else would under these circumstances" (Miller, 2013).

African American survival, and consequently, African American contributions to U.S. society, testify to a people's great strength and thus deserve a high level of respect. It is not within the scope of this chapter to discuss African American contributions to society, but suffice it to say that the perceptions of some people in law enforcement are conditioned by exposure to the black underclass, for whom crime is often a way of life.

Law Enforcement Interaction with African Americans: Historical Baggage

> Many of the police and African-American problems in our communities today go way back and stem from history. Some of the issues can be traced directly from the Civil War reconstruction era, in slavery days, when police and the military were required to return runaway slaves. (Patton, 2013)

In the United States during the late seventeenth and eighteenth centuries, prior to and following slave uprisings in a number of colonies, the colonists created strict laws to contain slaves. Even minor offenses were punished harshly, setting a negative tone between law enforcement and blacks. American police were called on to form "slave patrols" and to enforce racially biased laws (Williams & Murphy, 1990). In many areas of the country, police were expected to continue enforcing highly discriminatory laws including those setting curfews for blacks and barring blacks from many facilities and activities.

Most police officers have had some exposure to the historical precedents of poor relationships between police and minority communities. The damages of the past give us no choice but to make greater effort today with groups such as African Americans for whom contact with law enforcement has long been problematic.

DEMOGRAPHICS: DIVERSITY AMONG AFRICAN AMERICANS[*]

As of 2010, blacks comprised about 13.6 percent of the U.S. population, or approximately 42 million people (U.S. Census Bureau, 2012). Originally living mostly in the southeastern United States, the First Great Migration involved the movement northward and westward of

---

[*]Refer back to Chapter 1, section on "Changing Population," for information about individuals who do not "neatly" fit into one demographic category such as black.

over 1.3 million blacks and took place between 1916 and 1930. The Second Migration occurred between 1941 and 1970, and involved 5 million blacks who migrated initially to the north and then to the west coast, largely seeking better job opportunities (Lemann, 1991). Although this was one of the primary reasons for such a mass exodus from the South, it was not the main reason. Many blacks left the South for the sole purpose of escaping racism and discrimination.

Historically, over 50 percent of the black population has lived in urban areas. The rural black population has decreased, in large part because of the great migrations; the shifting flow has contributed to the increase in numbers in suburban areas (some rural blacks may migrate directly into the inner city while others may move to more suburban areas; the flow is not actually known). In any case, urban cores experience cycles of repopulation, mainly by blacks, Latinos, and various new immigrant groups such as "asylum-seekers from Central Africa" (Bidgood, 2013). One of the most vivid examples is the city of Detroit, where over 84 percent of the population is black (U.S. Census Bureau, 2012) while most whites and immigrant groups have settled in outlying areas. Similarly, other cities such as Washington D.C., St. Louis, Chicago, and Cleveland, are populated mainly by blacks and new immigrants, creating layers of tension when diverse groups with conflicting values and customs suddenly find themselves crowded into the same urban settings.

Although many African Americans are among the lower socioeconomic class, they are represented in all the socioeconomic classes, from the underclass to the upper class, and have moved increasingly into the suburban middle class. Nevertheless, and despite the rise to the middle class, a 2012 survey concerning discrimination and race indicated that 50 percent of the respondents believed that there is "some" or "a lot of" discrimination against blacks, limiting their chances to get ahead. (See Exhibit 6.1.)

As with all racial/ethnic groups, there are significant class-related differences among blacks that affect values and behavior. However, color, more than class, tends to determine how the larger society reacts to and treats blacks. Therefore, the racial experience of many African Americans in the United States is similar, regardless of an individual's level of prosperity or education.

> We mistakenly believe that blacks who achieve economic success in this country are shielded from racism and discrimination and that the color of their skin is somehow neutralized by money. This could not be further from the truth. Many successful blacks have reported being on the receiving end of racially motivated discriminatory behavior, and this includes treatment by law enforcement. (Johnson, 2013)

Despite the commonalities of the racial experience, there is a great deal of cultural diversity among African Americans. Over the past 400 years, black families have come from many different countries (e.g., Jamaica, Trinidad, Belize, Haiti, and Puerto Rico). By far the largest group's

---

Percentage answering "some" or "a lot" to the question, "How much discrimination [against each group] do you feel there is in the United States today, limiting their chances to get ahead?

Immigrants	59%
Hispanics	52%
Blacks	50%
Women	49%
Whites	26%
Asians	26%
Men	19%

EXHIBIT 6.1 Racial Attitudes Survey

Source: Associated Press, Racial Attitudes Survey, October 29, 2012

• **Protestant**	**78%**

| –Historically Black Churches (59%) |
| Baptist (40%) |
| Methodist (5%) |
| Pentecostal (6%) |
| Holiness (1%) |
| –Evangelical Protestant Churches (15%) |
| –Mainline Protestant Churches (4%) |

• **Catholic**	**5%**
• **Jehovah's Witness**	**1%**
• **Muslim**	**1%**
• **Unaffiliated**	**12%**
• **Other***	**3%**

*Mormon, Orthodox, other Christian, Jewish, Buddhist, Hindu, other world religions, other faiths, "don't know".

EXHIBIT 6.2   Religious Affiliation among African Americans
Source: Pew Forum, 2008. Retrieved on July 15, 2013 from religions.pewforum.org

forebears came directly to the United States from Africa. In addition, there are cultural differences among African Americans related to the region of the United States in which they have lived longest. As with whites, there are "southern" and "northern" characteristics as well as urban, suburban, and rural characteristics.

Religious backgrounds vary, but the majority of American-born blacks are Protestant, and specifically Baptist. The first black-run, black-controlled denomination in the country was the African Methodist Episcopal church. It was created because churches in the North and South either banned blacks or required them to sit apart from whites. Another percentage of African Americans belongs to the black Muslim religions, including the Nation of Islam and American Muslim Mission. There are also sizable and fast-growing black populations among members of the Seventh-Day Adventists, Jehovah's Witnesses, Pentecostals (particularly Spanish-speaking blacks; see Exhibit 6.2), and especially among religions of Caribbean origin—Santeria, Candomble, Voudun, and similar sects—blending Catholic and West African (mainly Yoruba) beliefs and rituals. Rastafarianism has spread far beyond its native Jamaica to become an influential religious movement among immigrants from many other English-speaking Caribbean nations.

New immigrant groups from Africa continue to arrive. Of 40 million foreign-born residents living in the United States, 4 percent are from Africa—and of those, over 50 percent entered in 2000 or later (Grieco et al., 2012). The largest groups of new immigrants come from Ethiopia, Egypt, and Nigeria, with most of them settling in the states of California, New York, Texas, Maryland, and Virginia. Some have an easier time than others.

Black African immigrants generally fare well on integration indicators. Overall, they are well educated, with college completion rates that greatly exceed those for most other immigrant groups and US natives. . . Black African immigrants' earnings are on par with other immigrants and lag those of natives, despite their higher levels of human capital and their strong English skills. The underemployment of highly skilled African immigrants has been documented, and may be explained by factors such as a recent date of arrival, difficulty in transferring home-country credentials, and labor market discrimination. Cape Verde has the longest history of any African nation in sending migrants to the United States, almost all of whom enter through family reunification channels, but educational attainment, employment, and earnings are the lowest for immigrants from Cape Verde as well as several refugee-source countries—most notably Somalia. Refugees from Somalia have among the lowest levels of formal education and most difficulties integrating of any US immigrant group. (Capps, McCabe, & Fix, 2011)

ISSUES OF IDENTITY AND GROUP IDENTIFICATION TERMS

In the 1960s and 1970s, the Civil Rights Movement and the Black Pride Movement marked a new direction in black identity. The Civil Rights Movement resulted in improved educational and employment opportunities as well as active political involvement. Some adults marched in the Civil Rights Movement knowing that they themselves might never benefit directly from its advances; they hoped that their efforts in the struggle would better the lives of their children. Many middle-class youths who attended community churches and black colleges became leaders in the movement for equal rights (McAdoo, 1992).

Both American-born and Caribbean-born blacks, inspired by a growing sense of community identification and increased pride in racial identity, have also placed an emphasis on learning more about and identifying with African cultures. Despite the great differences in culture between African Americans and Africans, blacks throughout the western hemisphere are discovering that they can take pride in the richness of their African heritage, including its ethical values and community cohesiveness. Examples of African cultural values that have influenced American black culture or are held in high esteem by many African Americans are (Walker, 1992):

- Cooperative interdependence among and between peoples (focus on the group), in contrast with Western individualism (focus on the individual)
- Partnership with nature and with the spirit world reflected in the approach to ecology and communication with the spirit world, similar to Native American beliefs
- Balance and harmony among all living things, reflected in the placing of human relations as a priority value—as contrasted with the Western view of "doing" (achievement) as a priority over the nurturing of human relations
- Joy and celebration in life itself
- Time as a spiral and focused on "now," which can be contrasted with the Western view of "time is money" and time running away from us
- Giving of self to community
- Renewed interest in respecting elders

The combination of the Black Pride Movement of the 1960s and 1970s and the more current focus on cultural roots has freed many African Americans from the "slave mentality" that haunted the African American culture long after emancipation. Pride in race and heritage has, for some, replaced the sense of inferiority fostered by white racial supremacist attitudes.

Several ethnic groups, including African Americans, in a positive evolution of their identity and pride, have initiated name changes for their group. Although it can be confusing, it represents, on the part of group members, growth and a desire to name themselves rather than be labeled by the dominant society. Until approximately the early 1990s, the most widely accepted term was *black,* having replaced *Negro* (which, in turn, replaced *colored people*). *Negro* has been out of use for several decades, although some older blacks still use the term (as do some younger African Americans among themselves). To many, the term *Negro* symbolizes what the African American became under slavery. The replacement of *Negro* with *black* came to symbolize racial pride. Exceptions to the avoidance of the terms *Negro* and *colored* can be found in titles such as United Negro College and National Association for the Advancement of Colored People (NAACP). *African American*, a term preferred by many, focuses on positive historical and cultural roots rather than on race or skin color.

In the 1990s, the use of the term *African American* grew in popularity. (It is the equivalent of, for example, Italian American or Polish American.) Many feel that the word *black* is no more appropriate in describing skin color than is white. Yet, some Americans who are black do not identify with African American because it does not fully represent their background, which may be Caribbean or Haitian. Since the 1980s and early 1990s, the term *people of color* has sometimes been used, but this catchall phrase has limited use for police officers because it is used to describe anyone who is not white and can include Asian/Pacific Americans, Latino/Hispanic Americans, and Native Americans. Indeed, there is much controversy and history associated with broad, collective terms created in an attempt to categorize people.

The use of racial epithets is never acceptable, especially in crime fighting and peacekeeping, no matter how tense a situation might become. Although it is not uncommon for blacks to use a particular racial epithet in normal conversations among themselves, it is absolutely taboo for outsiders; especially for outsiders wearing badges. Law enforcement officers who do not like to be called "pigs" can likely relate to a person's feelings about being referred to in animal terms, such as "monkey." Officers must develop the professionalism to not only refrain from using derogatory terms, but also to inform their peers of the prejudice that such terms convey.

STEREOTYPES AND CROSS-RACIAL PERCEPTIONS

Many of the impressions people in society and law enforcement form about African Americans come from their exposure to messages and images in the media. Here the phenomenon of stereotyping is as much at work as when citizens see all police officers as repressive and capable of brutality. Police officers know that their kind will take a beating nationwide whenever there is publicity about an instance of police brutality against blacks or reports of racial profiling.

The white majority's view of blacks reflects the same problem. Those who are bent toward prejudice may feel that their racism is justified whenever a crime involving an African American makes the evening news. A suburban African American mother addressing a community forum on racism pointed out: "Every time I hear that there has been a murder or a rape, I pray that it is not a black who committed the crime. The minute the media reports that a black person is responsible for a crime, all of us suffer. When something negative happens, I am no longer seen as an individual with the same values and hopes as my white neighbors. I become a symbol, and even more so my husband and sons become feared. People treat us with caution and politeness, but inside we know that their stereotypes of the worst criminal element of blacks have become activated" (Personal communication; source wishes to remain anonymous).

Even the fact of a crime rate that is disproportionately high among young black males does not justify sweeping statements about all African Americans. Certainly, 42 million African Americans cannot be judged by a statistic about the criminal element. Unfortunately for the vast majority of the African American population, some whites do base their image of blacks largely on the actions of America's criminal class. Officers have been known to stop blacks and question them simply for not "looking like they belong to a certain neighborhood." Frequent depictions of black criminals in the media, particularly television and movies, further reinforce this image.

> This belief contributes to a police officer's decision to pull over Black motorists in nice cars or in affluent neighborhoods; the pedestrian's decision to cross the street or clutch her purse when approaching a Black male; the salesperson's decision to follow a Black customer throughout the store for fear of theft; and the politician's decision to use a Black face to kindle fears that crime is out of control. (Johnson, 2008)

Harboring unreasonable fears about black people is a result of the prevalence of stereotypes associated with criminality. In the chapter section entitled Children/Adolescents/Youth, an example is provided of a demeaning conversation between a law enforcement representative and an innocent young black man. Stereotypes indeed give way to the labels that people assign to others (Johnson, 2013). This consequence of stereotyping is a common phenomenon known in the

Black Male	White Male
Arrogant	Confident
Chip on shoulder	Self assured
Aggressive	Assertive
Dominant personality	Natural leader
Violence prone	Wayward
Naturally gifted	Smart
Sexual prowess	Sexual experimentation

EXHIBIT 6.3   Are People Viewed in Equal Terms?

fields of both sociology and criminology, and has clear implications for law enforcement behavior. (See Chapter 13 on Racial Profiling.)

The Trayvon Martin tragedy in 2013 was one in which an unarmed 17-year-old black teenager was shot and killed by a neighborhood watch "volunteer" in a suburban neighborhood. While George Zimmerman, the volunteer, was not a police officer, and the Trayvon case is not a specific example of *police stereotyping,* it is an illustration of what many believe to be a common cross-racial perception, characterizing conscious and subconscious stereotypical beliefs. The critical learning from the Trayvon case is the understanding of the relationship between stereotypes, bias (defined in Chapter 1), and subconscious decision-making that in turn influences action and behavior.

Prejudice, lack of contact, and ignorance lend themselves to groups' developing perceptions about the "other" that are often based on biased beliefs. Unfortunately, perceptions are then seen as reality or "the truth," whether or not they are valid. Exhibit 6.3 illustrates differing images that some members of the dominant society have toward black and white males.

Likewise, African Americans have attached certain negative connotations to the actions of police officers, even though many officers no longer exhibit racism. The description of perceptions listed in Exhibit 6.4 was presented to Northern California police officers in the

Police Action	Black Perception
Being stopped or expelled from so-called "white neighborhoods."	Whites want blacks to "stay in their place."
Immediately suspecting and reacting to blacks without distinction between dope dealer and plain-clothes police officer.	Police view black skin itself as probable cause.
Using unreasonable force; beatings; adding charges.	When stopped, blacks must be submissive or else.
Negative attitudes; jokes; body language; talking down to people.	Officers are racists.
Quick trigger; take-downs; accidental shootings.	Bad attitudes will come out under stress.
Slow response; low priority; low apprehension rate.	Black-on-black crime not important.
Techniques of enforcing local restrictions and white political interests.	Police are the strong arm for the status quo.
Police stick together, right or wrong.	Us-against-them mentality; they stick together, so we have to stick together.

EXHIBIT 6.4   Perceptions of Police Officers' Actions by Some Blacks

early 1990s by the then vice president of the Alameda, California, NAACP chapter (the late Al Dewitt). When Dewitt presented this list to police officers, he explained that, over time, African Americans had formed perceptions about police behavior that led to riots, race problems, and a lack of trust. According to Greg Patton (an African American and former Washington State Patrol Trooper), the items presented in Exhibit 6.3 are still entirely valid today. Improving and preventing racial misperceptions will take time and effort on the part of officers but will inevitably benefit all concerned by way of increased cooperation and safety (Patton, 2013).

THE AFRICAN AMERICAN FAMILY

African American families generally enjoy very strong ties among extended family members, especially among women. Female relatives often substitute for each other in filling family roles; for example, a grandmother or an aunt may raise a child if the mother is unable to do so. Sometimes several different family groups share one house. When a problem occurs (such as an incident that has brought an officer to the house), extended family members are likely to be present and wanting to help. An officer may observe a number of uncles, aunts, brothers, sisters, cousins, and boyfriends or girlfriends who are loosely attached to the black household. Enlisting the aid of any of these household members, no matter what the relationship, can be beneficial.

The Roles of Men and Women

In some urban core areas of the United States, and in particular housing projects, it is not uncommon to find that a majority of African American women lives alone with children; thus the widespread view that African American families are matriarchies in which women are typically the heads of the household. Over time, a variety of theories have been formulated to explain this. Some point to evidence that certain tribes in Africa were (and/or currently are) matriarchies, influencing modern African American culture. In the United States, during the days of slavery black women played a crucial role in the family because of repeated attempts by slave owners, police, and others to break down "black manhood" (Bennett, 1989). Yet an additional explanation is that the "system" of women running the household has mostly come about by default because of the absence of fathers.

> African American women are considered by mainstream America to be less threatening than their male counterparts. As a result, they are able to be more assertive in public situations and receive fewer negative consequences. This perception also holds true when it comes to contacts with law enforcement. However, unlike African American females, African American males often feel that they are at risk for arrest or some form of mistreatment if they exhibit anything other than passive behavior toward the police. (Johnson, 2013)

African American fathers usually view themselves as heads of the household; therefore, when a father is present, decisions regarding the family should include the father's participation. It is insulting and disrespectful for officers to direct questions to and focus on the mother when both parents are present. A mother's assertiveness does not mean that the father is passive or indifferent and thus should be ignored; nor does a father's silence indicate agreement with the officer's action. It is always worthwhile to get his view of the situation first.

The Single Mother

The single mother, particularly in the inner city, does not always receive the respect that she is due; outsiders may be critical of the way she lives—or the way they think she lives. She is often stereotyped by officers who doubt their own effectiveness in the urban black community. For instance, in theory, an unmarried African American mother on welfare who has just had a fight with her boyfriend should receive the same professional courtesy that a married white suburban mother is likely to receive from an officer; however, in practice this is not always the case. A common complaint made by African American women is that white officers in general treat them poorly. According to these complaints, officers feel comfortable using profanity and other obscenities in the presence of black women, something that is less likely to occur with white women.

Ondra Berry, retired Deputy Police Chief, Reno, Nevada, and an African American, offers advice regarding relations between the peace officer and the single African American mother. He advises officers to go out of their way to establish rapport and trust. Following are his suggestions for assisting the single mother (Berry, 2013):

- Offer extra assistance to low-income mothers, for example, connect them with community resources.
- Proactively engage youth and encourage them to participate in organized social activities.
- Give your business card to the mother to show that you are available for further contact.
- Make follow-up visits when there are no problems so that the mother and the children can associate the officer with good times.
- Make sure that you have explained to the mother her rights.
- Use the same discretion you might use with another minor's first petty offense (e.g., shoplifting); consider bringing the child home and talking with the mother and child rather than sending the child immediately to juvenile hall.

All of these actions will build a perception on the part of the African American single mother and her children that you can be trusted and that you are there to help. "Since you are dealing with history, you have to knock down barriers and, at times, work harder with this group than with any other group" (Berry, 2013).

Children/Adolescents/Youth

Because there are so many black households, especially in the inner city, in which the father is absent, young boys in their middle childhood years (ages seven to eleven) are at risk for serious behavioral problems, and school is often where these problems show up. According to Berry, many single mothers unwittingly place their young sons in the position of "father," giving them the message that they have to take care of the family. These young children can get the mistaken impression that they are the heads of the household, and in school situations may try to control the teacher—who is often female and often white. Officers who refer these children to agencies that can provide role models, even on a limited-time basis, stand better chances of gaining the family's and community's trust and respect. Eventually, cooperation will be earned from community members.

Among older African American male children, especially in inner cities, statistics indicate a disproportionately high crime rate, most likely stemming from the difficult economic conditions of their lives. Officers have to remind themselves that most African American teenagers are law-abiding citizens. African American teens and young adults report being stopped on a regular basis by police officers when they are in predominantly "white neighborhoods" (including those where they happen to live). For example, a 19-year-old African American male living in an upper-middle-class suburban neighborhood in Fremont, California, reported that he was stopped and questioned four times in two weeks by different officers. On one occasion, the conversation went this way:

OFFICER: What are you doing here?

TEEN: I'm jogging, sir.

OFFICER: Why are you in this neighborhood?

TEEN: I live here, sir.

OFFICER: Where?

TEEN: Over there, in that big house on the hill.

OFFICER: Can you prove that? Show me your I.D.

Racial profiling is discussed further in this chapter and covered in depth in Chapter 13.

LANGUAGE AND COMMUNICATION

Racial conflicts between African Americans and other citizens can cover up communication style differences, which until the 1990s had been largely ignored or minimized. Yet many would acknowledge that cultural differences between, for example, a white officer and a Vietnamese citizen could potentially affect their respective communication styles as well as their perceptions of each other. Similarly, language comes into play when looking at patterns of communication among many African Americans.

"Ebonics," or African American Vernacular English

Many African Americans use, or have used at least some of the time, what has been called *Black English, African American Vernacular English* (AAVE), *African American English, Black Vernacular,* or *Black English Vernacular.* Colloquially, it is known as *Ebonics.* While some African Americans speak only this version of English, many enjoy the flexibility and expressiveness of speaking Ebonics among peers and switching to "standard English" when the situation calls for it (e.g., at work; in interviews; with white friends).

African American Vernacular English   A recognized language and a dialect of English that meets all of the requirements of a language; it possesses a coherent system of signs; it has a grammar of elements and rules; and it is used for communication and social purposes (Patrick, 2006).

Many people cling to an unscientific and racist view of the language varieties spoken among African Americans. Ebonics has been ridiculed by people, including educators, who have no understanding of its foundation and legitimacy. "The use of [what has been called] black language does not represent any pathology in blacks . . . The beginning of racial understanding is the acceptance that difference is just what it is: different, not inferior. And equality does not mean sameness" (Weber, 1991). There are many varieties of English that are *not* "substandard," "deficient," or "impoverished" versions of the language. Instead, most have a complete and consistent set of grammatical rules and may represent the rich cultures of the groups that use them. For example, Asian Indians speak a variety of English that can be unfamiliar to Americans, while people in England speak numerous dialects of British English, each containing distinctive grammatical structures and vocabulary not used by Americans. Similarly, some African Americans speak a version of English that historically has been labeled substandard because of a lack of understanding of its origins.

Linguists have done years of research on the origins of Ebonics, and have made significant findings in the past 20 to 30 years. Black English evolved as slaves "learned" English from their masters and as they communicated amongst themselves despite their many tribal language differences. Thus, Ebonics appears to be derived from the early varieties of English spoken in the United States, mixed together with certain grammatical patterns common to several West African tribal languages (Wolfram & Torbert, 2005). For example:

Ebonics:	You be looking good.
Standard English:	You usually look good.

That is, the presence of the word *be* indicates a general condition and not something related only to the present. Apparently, some West African languages have grammatical structures expressing these same concepts of time. According to Dr. John R. Rickford, Stanford University Linguistics Professor and AAVE specialist, "This example captures a distinction that was missed by many of those who tried to poke fun of Ebonics in cartoons and columns during the [late 1990s] Ebonics controversy" (Rickford, 2009).

> One [view] says that there was African influence in the development of the language and the other says that there was not. Those who reject African influence believe that the African arrived in the United States and tried to speak English. And [according to this first view], because he lacked certain intellectual and physical attributes, he failed. This hypothesis makes no attempt to examine the . . . structures of West African languages to see if there are any similarities . . . when the German said "zis" instead of "this," America understood. But, when the African said "dis" [instead of "this"], no one considered the fact that [the sound] *th* may not exist in African languages. (Weber, 1991)

Many people still assume that Ebonics is "bad" English, and they display their contempt either nonverbally or through an impatient tone of voice. Acceptance of another person's variety of English can go a long way toward establishing rapport. People interacting with blacks who do not use "standard" English should realize that blacks are not necessarily speaking poorly. In fact, verbal skill is a highly prized value in most African-based cultures. On the other hand, it can be challenging for African Americans to juggle their "bilingualism."

> Speech style is one of the dimensions on which African Americans experience conflict about their cultural identity and self-concept. They often react to the stigma attached to their dialect and speech style with ambivalence, having received messages from their in-group *supporting* its use and from mainstream culture *rejecting* Black English as incorrect and deviant speech. (Hecht, Jackson II, & Ribeau, 2003)

Finally, when attempting to establish trust and rebuild relations with a race of people who historically have had few reasons to trust the police, white officers should not try to imitate black accents, dialects, or styles of speaking. These imitations can be viewed as very insulting and may give blacks the impression that they are being ridiculed—or that the officer is seriously uncomfortable with them. (See Chapter 4 for more information.) Being authentic and sincere when communicating with all African Americans, while remaining aware and accepting differences, is key to building better relations.

Nonverbal Communication: Style and Stance

Social scientists have been studying aspects of African American nonverbal communication that have often been misunderstood by people in positions of authority. A psychologist, as well as founder and former editor of the Journal of African American Studies, Richard Majors, termed a certain stance and posturing as the "cool pose," which is demonstrated by many young black men from the inner city. This form of nonverbal communication may include certain movements and postures (e.g., walking, standing, talking, and having aloof facial expressions) designed to emphasize the youth's masculinity. "While the cool pose is often misread by teachers, principals and police officers as an attitude of defiance, psychologists who have studied it say it is a way for black youths to maintain a sense of integrity and suppress rage at being blocked from usual routes to esteem and success" (Goleman, 1992).

Majors explains that while the cool pose is by no means found among the majority of black men, it is commonly seen among inner-city youth as a tactic for psychological survival to cope with everyday rejections (Goleman, 1992). The goal of the pose is to give the appearance of being in control. As Majors points out, it is a way for black youths to say, "[I'm] strong and proud, despite [my] status in American society" (Goleman, 1992). Problems, however, may occur when others, particularly police officers, misread this nonverbal communication. For example, when questioning a black male who is engaged in a cool pose, a white police officer may mistakenly interpret the body language as a sign of apathy or an act of defiance. This can cause an otherwise benign situation to turn into a hostile encounter. Communication styles across cultures have the potential of being misinterpreted; the "cool pose" is generally not intended to be a threatening or rude stance.

Eye contact during conversation is another area in which African American and mainstream styles can differ and have the potential to lead to miscommunication. In one research study, it was found that, ". . . while speaking, European Americans look less and African Americans look more, and while listening, African Americans look less and European Americans look more. When these patterns are combined, we can anticipate that when an [sic] European American is speaking the interactants will not be looking at each other frequently" (Hecht et al., 2003). Thus, a white police officer may misinterpret the listening style of a black citizen, incorrectly inferring that less eye contact during listening equates to a lack of engagement. Likewise, the steady gaze of an African American who is talking with a police officer could be misinterpreted as a display of confrontation.

Verbal Expressiveness and Emotionalism

> The Ebonics vernacular style of speech emphasizes emotional response—being "real" is the term. This means it is okay to express one's indignation, to be emotional, and to express to someone how you feel. Many African Americans perceive that the mainstream culture is taught to be reserved and to temper their emotions. This is a cultural difference that can be misread by law enforcement. (Patton, 2013)

Linguist and sociologist Thomas Kochman has devoted his professional life to studying differences in black and white culture that contribute to misunderstandings and misperceptions. Of historical significance, Chicago's African American mayor Harold Washington passed out copies of Kochman's book *Black and White Styles in Conflict* (1981) to the city hall press corps because he believed that he was seriously misunderstood by the whites of the city. According to Kochman, "If a person doesn't know the difference in cultures, that's ignorance. But if a person knows the difference and still says that mainstream culture is best, that 'white is right,' then you've got racism" (Kochman, 1981).

In his book, Kochman explains that blacks and whites have different perspectives and approaches to many issues, including conversation, public speaking, and power. This notion is supported in the following advice given to police officers by former Reno Assistant Police Chief Ondra Berry: "Don't get nuts when you encounter an African American who is louder and more emotional than you are. Watch the voice patterns and the tone. Blacks can sound militant [even when they are not]. Blacks have been taught (i.e., socialized) to be outwardly and openly emotional. Sometimes we are emotional first and then calm down and become more rational" (Berry, 2013). Berry went on to say that often whites are rational at first but express more emotion as they lose control. This cultural difference has obvious implications for overall communication, including how to approach and react to angry citizens.

Kochman explains that many "whites [are] able practitioners of self-restraint [and that] this practice has an inhibiting effect on their ability to be spontaneously self-assertive." He also states that, "the level of energy and spiritual intensity that blacks generate is one that they can manage comfortably but whites can only manage with effort" (Kochman, 1981). The problems in interaction come about because neither race understands that there is a cultural difference between them. Kochman states: "Blacks do not initially see this relative mismatch, because they believe that their normal animated style is not disabling to whites . . . Whites are worried that blacks cannot sustain such intense levels of interaction without losing self-control [because that degree of 'letting go' of emotions for a white would signify a lack of control]" (Kochman, 1981). In other words, a nonblack person, unaware of the acceptability in black culture of expressing intense emotion (including anger) might not be able to imagine that he himself could express such intense emotion without losing control. He may feel threatened, convinced that the ventilation of such emotion will surely lead to a physical confrontation.

While racism may also be a factor in communication breakdowns, differing conventions of speech contribute in ways that are not always apparent. In several cultural awareness training sessions, police officers have reported that white neighbors, upon hearing highly emotional discussions among African Americans, called to report fights. When the police arrived on the scene of the "fight," the individuals involved responded that they were not fighting, just talking. While continuing to respond to all calls, officers can be aware of different perceptions of what constitutes a fight. The awareness of style differences should have an impact on how officers approach citizens: Pastor Ronald Griffin, a prominent African American leader in Detroit who later joined the Detroit Police Department Board of Commissioners, recalled a communication style that was common among friends and neighbors as they got together and played cards. He said, "If anyone was listening from the outside, they would have heard us, at times, laughing, and, at times, talking loudly and pounding the table. These were intense moments of fellowship, and if you had been there you would have understood" (Griffin, 2009).

Berry illustrated how a white police officer can let his or her own cultural interpretations of black anger and emotionalism influence judgment. He spoke of a fellow officer who made the statement: "Once they [i.e., blacks] took me on, I wanted to take control." This officer, working in a predominantly black area for a three-month period, made 120 stops and 42 arrests (mainly petty offenses such as prowling and failure to identify). He then worked in a predominantly white area for the same period of time, made 122 stops and only 6 arrests. The officer went on to say that "one group will do what I ask; the other will ask questions and challenge me." His need to "take control" over people whom he perceived to be 'out of their place" was so extreme, it resulted in his being sued (Berry, 2013). His perception of the level of threat involved was much higher in the black community than in the white. One of the factors involved was, arguably, the officer's inability to deal with having his authority questioned or challenged. If he had used appropriate communication skills, he might have been able to work situations around to his advantage rather than creating confrontations. Listening professionally, instead of engaging in shouting matches with citizens of other backgrounds, can require a great deal of self-control, but it will usually bring the best results. As one African American police officer said in a media interview, "I make sure that whatever the 'perp' says I don't pay attention to. Most police brutality cases arise from cops who can't control their emotions in the face of insults" ("Black Police Officer Talks Police Brutality, Racism in Interview," 2010).

Threats and Aggressive Behavior

Kochman, who has conducted cultural awareness training sessions nationwide (for police departments as well as corporations), asks the question, "When does a fight begin?" Many whites, he notes, believe that "fighting" has already begun when it is "obvious" that there will be violence ("when violence is imminent"). Therefore, to whites, a fight begins as soon as the shouting starts. According to whites, then, the fight has begun whenever a certain intensity of anger is shown, along with an exchange of insults. If, in addition, the shouting includes threats, many whites would tend to agree that violence is surely on its way (Kochman, 2013).

Kochman explains that while verbal confrontation and threats may indeed be a prelude to a fight, they may also be a surrogate or substitute for a fight. Many blacks tend to make a clear distinction between what may appear to be verbal threats and physical confrontations. Kochman explains that fighting, for some blacks, does not begin until one person does something physically provocative (Kochman, 2013). Thus, loud conversation, *accompanied by* nonverbal signs (such as a hand going into a pocket or closer interpersonal distance) can indicate more of a threat.

Officers who are trained to think about officer safety, however, might have a problem believing that they "got nothing to worry about" when encountering two belligerent individuals of a different culture than their own. Similarly, a threat in today's society, where anyone may be carrying semiautomatic weapons, may be just that—a very real threat that will be carried out. A threat must always be taken seriously by officers. However, there can be instances when cultural differences are at work, and extreme anger can be expressed without accompanying physical violence. When this is the case, an officer can actually escalate hostilities with an approach and communication style that demonstrates a lack of understanding of culturally/racially different modes of expression.

KEY ISSUES IN LAW ENFORCEMENT

Differential Treatment

The results of a national survey entitled "Police Attitudes toward Abuse of Authority" showed race to be a divisive issue for American police. In particular, black and nonblack officers had significantly different views about the effect of a citizen's race and socioeconomic status on the likelihood of police abuse of authority (Weisburd & Greenspan, 2000).

"I am not prejudiced. I treat all citizens fairly." This type of statement by police officers can be heard around the country. Inevitably, this statement holds true for some officers, although explicit utterance of this type of statement usually signals prejudice. In the wake of many publicized allegations of differential treatment of minority groups, officers who hold prejudices have to face them and recognize when the prejudices result in action.

> My partner and I several years ago went to an all-white nightclub. He found cocaine on this white couple. He poured it out and didn't make an arrest. Later we were at an all-black nightclub. He found marijuana on one individual and arrested him. I was shocked, but I didn't say anything at the time because I was fairly new to the department. He had told me on two occasions that he "enjoyed" working with black officers and "has no difficulty" with the black community. (African American police officer; wishes to remain anonymous.)

Dr. James Johnson, researcher on criminal justice and minority group issues, reacted to the above-noted incident: "This officer validated and legitimized his white partner's discriminatory behavior by exercising the Blue Code of Silence.[*] Because the black officer did not say anything, the white officer will see no need to face or recognize his racially biased behavior" (Johnson, 2013).

Some officers have encountered the allegation, "You stopped me because I am black." The truth most likely lies between the categorical denial of some police officers and the statement, "We're always being stopped only because we're black." Undoubtedly, there are police procedures of which citizens are unaware, and they do not see all the other people whom an officer stops in a typical day. However, the citizen is not getting paid to be professional, truthful, or even reasonable with the officer. We know that some officers feel that they are doing "good policing" when they stop citizens whom they feel will be guilty of a crime. However, this "feel" for who may be guilty can actually be a reflection of a bias or an assumption that substitutes for real "data." Observing and selecting "guilty-looking" motorists can be the result of subconscious biased thinking. (Refer to Chapter 13 for an explanation of the "Ladder of Inference" with respect to racial profiling.)

---

[*]For an opportunity to discuss the above example, and the commentary, see Discussion Question 3 at the end of the chapter.

Racial Profiling in the African American Community

The Trayvon Martin case, mentioned earlier in this chapter, is not an example of police racial profiling, but it escalated discussions of racial profiling to the highest office in the land. One week after the verdict, President Obama shared with the nation that he was not immune to the stigma of "suspiciousness" associated with his black skin. President Obama acknowledged, "Trayvon Martin could have been me 35 years ago." Before becoming a senator, like many African American men, he too experienced ". . . being followed . . . in a department store . . . getting on an elevator [with] a woman clutching her purse . . . hearing the locks click on the doors of cars . . ." (FNS, 2013).

Dr. James Johnson, Social Science Analyst for the Administrative Office of the U.S. Courts, lives in Washington, D.C. He and other black men he knows, both professional and nonprofessional, have had the experience of being stopped by the police and subjected to the following line of questioning: "Do you have any ID? Where are you going? Do you have any drugs on you?" The justification for these stops, according to Johnson, is "we fit a description." Officers will typically say, "There have been some robberies in this neighborhood and you fit the description of one the suspects." Johnson expounds, "When this happens, we are being treated as if we have already committed a crime. Officers treat suspects differently than they treat persons whom they believe are innocent of any wrongdoing. We don't get the benefit of the doubt. It is assumed that we don't belong in a particular neighborhood merely because of our skin color, so we are profiled as "suspects." When asked if police officers have made progress in managing racial biases over the years, Johnson replies, "We as black Americans would like to believe so, but some of our experiences remind us that we have a long way to go. It seems like whenever this nation takes one step forward, something happens that causes it to take two steps back. You can roll off the names of African Americans who have been unjustly profiled and injured or even killed because of the color of their skin. That's not progress" (Johnson, 2013).

In essence, the freedom for black Americans to travel to any neighborhood is denied when officers' biases "kick in" and they stop minorities based on their color rather than their behavior. Johnson suggests that officers slow down their thinking process and challenge some of their personal biases and prejudices, particularly when there are no obvious signs of wrongdoing. Officers would be well advised to go through the following mental steps before acting on racial biases and prejudices (clearly, this does not suggest that all officers act on racial biases and prejudices):

- If I see an individual simply walking down the street, let me first acknowledge to myself that I am not sure whether there is any reason to stop this person.
- I will ask myself the following questions:

  "Why do I think this person should be stopped?"

  "What is this person doing that makes me think he/she is suspicious?"

  "Could this person be lost or in the need of help?"

  "Is this person's race a part of the reason why I want to stop them?"

- If I decide that I should, for whatever reason, stop this individual, would there be merit in my saying something like:

  "There has been a robbery in the neighborhood and I want you to be aware of the potential dangers. You look a little lost, so I was wondering if you need any help or directions." *This only applies if there have actually been recent robberies in the neighborhood. If the person lives in that neighborhood, being dishonest can negatively affect the officer's credibility* (Johnson, 2013).

In the process of slowing down one's mental processes, the officer makes a conscious decision to recognize potential bias if it is there, and refrains from making inferences or jumping

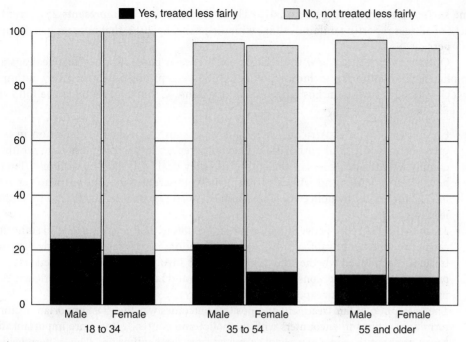

EXHIBIT 6.5   Black Perceptions of Police Treatment in Last Thirty Days

to conclusions based on racial bias or prejudice. Officers can increase cooperation with respectful communication, and, at the same time, assess the *behavior* of the person they are stopping.

Perceptions of Police/Authority Treatment

Exhibit 6.5 shows the results of a 2013 Gallup Poll in which the following question was asked: "Can you think of any occasion in the last thirty days when you felt you were treated unfairly in dealings with the police, such as [in] traffic incidents?" Nearly 4,400 adults were surveyed; 24 percent of young black men under the age of 35 reported that their dealings with police were unfair (results were similar for black men between the ages of 35–54). Responses by gender and age differed, with men and women 55 and older reporting significantly fewer unfair dealings with police (10% and 11%, respectively). Exhibit 6.6 shows results for the

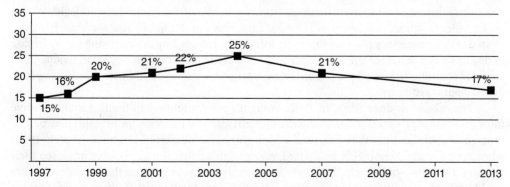

EXHIBIT 6.6   Black Perceptions of Police Treatment in Last Thirty Days (1997–2013)

same survey question from 1997 to 2013. The high point in 2004 represents 25 percent of blacks of all ages reporting unfair dealings with the police. By 2013, that number had dropped to 17 percent.

Older survey results show the relationship between perceptions of fair dealings and compliance with authority, including police. Ethnic perceptions of treatment by authority, surveying 1,500 residents in Los Angeles, and Oakland, California, revealed the following (Huo & Tyler, 2000):

- Compared to whites, African Americans report lower levels of satisfaction in their interactions with legal authorities. They also report less willingness than whites to comply with the directives of the authorities they deal with. This pattern of difference between minorities and whites was especially apparent among those who reported interactions with the police compared to those who reported interactions with authorities in court.
- Much of the difference between minorities and whites in their reactions to legal authorities can be accounted for by differences in their perceptions of how fairly or unfairly they were treated. When asked whether the legal authorities involved in their encounters used fair procedures to make decisions, African Americans (and Latinos) reported experiencing less procedural fairness than experienced by whites.
- The perception of fair treatment and positive outcomes was the most important factor in forming reactions to encounters with the police and courts. It was more important than concerns about the outcomes people received from legal authorities. This pattern held up across different situations and ethnic groups.

In other words, African Americans (and Latinos) continued to report more negative treatment from legal authorities than reported by whites. These perceptions on the part of minorities are significant in that they directly relate to compliance rates with authority among members of minority groups (Huo & Tyler, 2000). The study indicated that all groups were equally satisfied with their experiences in court and that, as a result, there was compliance with court directives. However, African Americans (and Latinos) were less willing to comply with directives from police (Huo & Tyler, 2000).

Excessive Force and Brutality

A controversial and complex issue is the use of excessive force by police, which is a problem heavily concentrated in minority communities. The International Association of Chiefs of Police defines excessive force as "the application of an amount and/or frequency of force greater than that required to compel compliance from a willing or unwilling subject" (IACP, 2001). When excessive force is used by a police officer, the conduct of the police often comes under public scrutiny and will receive attention from the media, the community, and legislators. A police officer's actions can result in lawsuits if members of the public feel someone has been treated with unnecessary physical or deadly force (e.g., initiated by the surviving family in case of deadly force). Whether the use of excessive force is aberrant behavior by an individual officer or is common practice by a law enforcement agency, public opinion can erode the police department's credibility.

The case of Rodney King, in 1992, brought public attention to the fact that excessive force and brutality were serious problems in America. The existence of brutality has been a problem that blacks and other racial and ethnic groups have asserted, but until the early 1990s when several cases were highly publicized, many whites either did not believe or closed their eyes to this reality—or thought these were an anomaly when considering the number of arrests made without brutality across the nation. Nearly a decade after the Rodney King event, in 1997, Americans and citizens worldwide witnessed another incidence of brutality against a black American, Abner Louima, a Haitian immigrant who was arrested and sodomized with a broomstick inside a restroom at the 70th Precinct station house in Brooklyn. "The case became a national symbol of police brutality and fed perceptions that New York City police officers were harassing or abusing young black men as part of a citywide crackdown on crime" (Chan, 2007).

On November 25, 2006, Sean Bell, an African American, died in a "hail of 50 bullets fired by a group of five officers. The shooting shocked the city and brought back memories of the deaths in other high-profile police shootings . . . it prompted unsettling questions about the changes in police procedures adopted in recent years, and about whether black men remained unfairly singled out for aggressive police action" ("Sean Bell," 2009).

In the San Francisco Bay Area on New Year's Day in 2009, a fatal shooting took place of an unarmed African American, on a train platform, by transit police officer Johannes Mehserle. Much of the tragedy was recorded on cell phones by other passengers, including the utterance of a racial epithet by one of the police officers. Mehserle was convicted of involuntary manslaughter and at least one other officer who was involved in the incident was fired for misconduct.

Clearly, most police officers around the nation do not use excessive force, and there have been great strides made between law enforcement and minority communities. Nevertheless, we know from examples that continue to occur that police brutality is not yet a phenomenon of the past.

As U.S. Attorney Jenny Durkan commented during an investigation into allegations of excessive force by the Seattle Police Department, "Police officers are taught how to win fights but not how to avoid them" (Pulkkinen, 2011). Methods of peacefully containing heated situations must be a priority training issue in all police departments across the country. Police departments also need to recognize that stress-reduction techniques must be addressed as frequently and effectively as are traditional topics such as self-defense. Finally, the individual officer must remember that even though abusive behavior from citizens constitutes one of the worst aspects of the job, it is not the citizens who must behave like professionals.

Law Enforcement Interaction with African American Communities

Many police officers feel that they are putting their lives in danger when they go into certain African American communities where the crime rate is high. As a result, some African Americans feel as though the police are not providing adequate protection to their communities. Increases in drug use and the availability of firearms in the black community contribute to defensive reactions among both the police and the African Americans. There is a vicious cycle that escalates and reinforces hostilities. Police are not expected to solve the social ills of society, and do not always have access to either the resources or the training to deal with problems rooted in historical, social, political, and economic factors. But they are expected to devote the same amount of time and resources to serving and protecting all communities equally.

African Americans and police officers are often frustrated with each other, and barriers seem insurmountable. While the following quote comes from a source in the early 1970s, officers have validated that the dynamic described is still operative:

> Many policemen find themselves on the alert for the slightest sign of disrespect. One author [McNamara] has shown that the police [officer] is often prepared to coerce respect and will use force if he feels his position is being challenged. Likewise, the attitudes and emotions of the black citizen may be similar when confronted with a police [officer]. Police intervention is often seen as oppression and an infringement on blacks' rights. Consequently many blacks are on the alert for the slightest sign of disrespect that might be displayed by the police [officer]. (Cross & Renner, 1974; Patton, 2013)

Cross and Renner (1974) explain that fears of belittlement and danger operate for both the African American citizen and the officer, and that these fears cause both sides to misinterpret what might otherwise be nonthreatening behavior. In other words, the problem often arises not from the reality of the situation but as the result of mutual fears. Johnson adds that, "Black men are more concerned about being respected, rather than fearing belittlement, and treated like men and not 'boys'" (Johnson, 2013). He also points out that, "The 'power distance' between an officer and an African American usually *only* leads to a verbal protest or the filing of a formal complaint if he or she senses that the officer is about to or has resorted to the use of force. In this case, the citizen is unlikely to use physical force as a response so he or she resorts to verbal means which the officer, then, interprets as belligerence" (Johnson, 2013).

Victimization: Offenders and Incarceration

The following data is from the Bureau of Justice Statistics' 2011 report on homicide trends:

- Based on the data from 1976 to 2008, blacks were disproportionately represented as both homicide victims and offenders. The victimization rate for blacks in 2008 was six times higher than that for whites. The offending rate for blacks in the same year was seven times higher than the rate for whites (US DOJ, 2011).

The following is from the Bureau of Justice Prison Statistics report for mid-year 2009:

- As of June 30, 2009, there were approximately 2,297,400 prisoners in federal, state, or local prisons or jails across the United States. There were 4,749 black males in the U.S. prisons per 100,000 U.S. residents as compared to 1,822 Hispanic male inmates and 708 white male inmates (per 100,000 U.S. residents, respectively) (US DOJ BJS, 2010).

Of interest, Clinton's Council of Economic Advisors found that "Discriminatory behavior on the part of police and elsewhere in the criminal justice system may contribute to blacks' high representation in arrests, convictions, and prison admissions . . ." (Council of Economic Advisors, 1998). At the time of the writing of this sixth edition, Clinton was the last U.S. president to conduct a study on the disproportionate representation of African Americans in the criminal justice system.

Hate Crimes against African Americans

U.S. law enforcement agencies reported over 6,000 hate crime incidents in 2011, according to the FBI *Hate Crime Statistics Report* (FBI, 2011). Based on this report, more than a third of all hate crime victims were African Americans though they account for only 13.6 percent of the U.S. population. Racist hate crimes are often vicious, and are intended to intimidate individuals based on a key dimension of their identity such as skin color. Hate crimes can trigger racial conflict that extends deep into communities and has repercussions nationwide (e.g., riots and civil disturbances). Not only must criminal justice professionals deal extremely sensitively and carefully with an individual hate crime victim (from any background), they must also be prepared for community backlash.

> From lynching, to burning crosses and churches, to murdering a man by chaining him to a truck and dragging him down a road for three miles, anti-black violence has been and still remains the prototypical hate crime, intended not only to injure and kill individuals but to terrorize an entire group of people. Hate crimes against African Americans have an especially negative impact upon society for the history they recall and perpetuate, potentially intimidating not only African Americans, but other minority, ethnic, and religious groups. (LCCREF, 2009)

When a member of one ethnic or racial group is the perpetrator of a hate crime against someone from another group, community organizations and law enforcement would be well advised to try to work together to help reduce the broader social impact of the crime. (Chapters 11 and 12 provide extensive information on victim needs and response strategies.)

African American Women and Police

While certain specific issues concerning African American women and their interactions with police were mentioned earlier in the section on families, one additional area is particularly worthy of attention. Historically, the sexual assault of an African American woman has not been considered as serious by law enforcement as the sexual assault of a white woman; past and current perceptions and experiences may contribute to lower reporting rates. The Department of Justice estimates that Black women refrain from reporting rapes at significantly higher rates than white women. According to Brooke Axtell, a writer and advocate for survivors of sexual assault and domestic violence, there are multiple reasons for this—by seeking help after a rape, some African American women may wish to avoid compromising their community, and particularly African American men about whom society has held stereotypical beliefs related to sexuality. Additionally because of police injustice, historically against Black communities, some African American women are more reluctant to report sexual assault. (Axtell, 2012)

As previously mentioned, law enforcement officials alone cannot solve social ills but should realize that African Americans in disadvantaged communities desperately need excellent police protection. The perception that whites in middle-class communities are better served by the police forces naturally reinforces existing antipolice attitudes among the lower class.

Addressing the Needs of the Inner City

"Black-on-black crime seems to be tolerated and even accepted as inevitable" ("Black on Black Crime," 1991). This statement, made by an African American chief of police in 1991, is as true today as it was then. African Americans and other racial and ethnic groups have criticized law enforcement for underpolicing their communities; however, progress has been made to improve relations between police and community members. There are increasing numbers of African American officers and police executives who are influencing and changing policy that directly affects police/black relations. Many departments have put into writing strict rules regarding discourtesy, racial slurs, racial profiling, use of excessive force, and aggressive patrol techniques.

While, ideally, there should not be a need to put the requirements for basic human decencies in writing, the reality is different.

Efforts toward a Positive Relationship between Police and Community

Communities and police departments differ widely in the way they build positive relationships with each other. Chapter 14 discusses the option of community policing and provides specific models of successful programs that have been implemented in various law enforcement agencies across the nation. Ideally, every law enforcement agency would pursue personal and face-to-face opportunities for building trust; especially with community groups that have not had a history of positive relations with law enforcement. However, community policing is not an absolute guarantee of positive community relations, though effort should always go first toward making it successful. Many inappropriate police actions within African American communities have resulted in the implementation of "consent decrees." Some police leaders believe that a consent decree is not a symbol of a positive relationship; at the same time, many community leaders have supported

Consent decree An out-of-court settlement whereby the accused party agrees to modify or change behavior rather than plead guilty or go through a hearing on charges brought to court (CSIS, 2003).

them. In any case, the aim of consent decrees is to force a change of prejudicial or unjust behavior or actions by legal means.

In a Harvard study of a consent decree imposed in Los Angeles, "We found the LAPD much changed from eight years ago, and even more so in the last four or five years. Public satisfaction is up, with 83 percent of residents saying the LAPD is doing a good or excellent job; the frequency of the use of serious force has fallen each year since 2004. Despite the views of some officers that the consent decree inhibits them, there is no objective sign of so-called "de-policing" since 2002; indeed, we found that both the quantity and quality of enforcement activity have risen substantially over that period. Our analysis confirmed what others have previously reported: that serious crime is down substantially in Los Angeles over this same period. A majority of Los Angeles residents no longer rate crime as a big problem, substantially down from only four years ago, and that is true among Black and Hispanic as well as White and Asian residents." (Stone, Foglesong, & Cole, 2009)

While there is controversy around consent decrees, and some officers complain that they add too much paperwork and bureaucracy to their already demanding jobs, they serve a purpose. Consent decrees are an attempt, on the part of the federal government as well as local and state police departments and communities, to try to improve community/police interaction in a quick and dramatic manner. Some outcomes can be influenced informally and others by consent decrees. However, the key to improved relationships deeply rests on all of the following:

- Leadership
- Vision
- Respect
- Goals
- Strategies
- Mutual benefits for police and community
- Effective communication and practices of both law enforcement agencies and the community
- Developing positive police/youth relationships early in a child's life, especially in inner city or impoverished areas

A model program is the Police Athletic League (PAL) of Jacksonville, Inc., one of the oldest police/citizen partnerships in the U.S. The driving force behind PAL is, ". . . the conviction that young people—if they are reached early enough—can develop strong positive attitudes towards police officers in their journey through life toward the goal of maturity and good citizenship. The PAL program brings youth under the supervision and positive influence of a law enforcement agency and expands public awareness about the role of a police officer and the reinforcement of the responsible values and attitudes instilled in young people by their parents."

Further, PAL's philosophy is that, ". . . if a young person respects a police officer on the ball field, gym or classroom, the youth will likely come to respect the laws that police officers enforce. Such respect is beneficial to the youth, the police officer, the neighborhood and the business community." Lieutenant Matt Nemeth is the executive director of PAL in Jacksonville, Florida, an institution that has served a majority of African American youth in much of Jacksonville for more than forty years. In many cases, police officers work as teachers, mentors and coaches, becoming surrogates for those parents who are incapable of or unwilling to fulfill their parental responsibilities. The program serves children and youth in areas of the city that have the highest rate of violence, crime and high school drop-out rates. Children as young as five years old through 17-year-old teens participate in programs including sports, after-school mentoring, and homework classes. Lieutenant Nemeth cites many cases in which young adults return ten years after participating in PAL with a "grateful heart." He describes the PAL partnership with Jacksonville's minority and non-minority community members as a "long-term investment in prevention. PAL provides opportunities to youth who are at a fork in the road. It provides them with direction that they would not have otherwise had." (Nemeth, 2013)

In addition to the above examples, personal means—one-on-one and face-to-face interaction—as well as goodwill—need to be relied upon by community members, leaders, and police officers to improve community/police relations. Pastor Ronald Griffin, a prominent leader in the Detroit African American community, echoes these sentiments:

> Face-to-face contact opens up dialogue where we have a chance to listen and to be heard. We as human beings really say we listen, but we often don't, and instead we come prepared to respond. So sometimes we put up our defenses and get into attack mode. We're already predisposed and most of us, then, are willing and ready for battle. This leads to a lot of pointless negative action even if both sides have a lot in common. We have had executive officers come to church activities to encourage the members and to help the members see officers in another light. So we're building on this and learning to trust each other. There's nothing I can't ask of the precinct, and the same from them of me. (Griffin, 2009)

Summary

- The experiences of both slavery and racism have shaped African American culture and continue to leave psychological scars on many African American communities and individuals. Law enforcement officials, in particular, represent a system that has oppressed African Americans and other minorities. To protect and serve in many African American communities across the nation necessarily means that officers will need to go out of their way to establish trust and win cooperation.

- African Americans are represented in all socioeconomic classes, from the underclass to the upper class, and have moved increasingly into the middle class. As with all racial and ethnic groups, there are significant class-related differences among blacks affecting values and behavior. However, color, more so than class, determines how the larger society reacts to and treats blacks. Therefore, the racial experience of many African Americans in the United States is similar, regardless of an individual's level of prosperity or education.

- The Civil Rights and Black Pride Movements, along with positive identification with African culture, have for some replaced the sense of inferiority fostered by white racist supremacist attitudes. The changing terms that African Americans have used to refer to themselves reflect stages of racial empowerment and cultural growth.

- The single mother, particularly in the inner city, does not always receive the respect that she is due. A respectful officer who takes the time to establish rapport and make appropriate and helpful referrals will stand a good chance of gaining the family's, and community's trust, respect and cooperation.

- Many African Americans switch back and forth between language styles or use what is commonly referred to as *Ebonics* or *African American Vernacular English*. Acceptance of another person's variety of English can go a long way toward establishing rapport. People interacting with blacks who do not use "standard" English should realize that blacks are not necessarily speaking poorly.

- Regarding communication style, within African American cultural norms it is acceptable to be highly expressive and emotional in speech. This is in contrast to an unspoken white mainstream norm that discourages the open and free expression of emotion; especially anger. Therefore, officers from different backgrounds should not overinterpret a style, which may differ from their own, as being aggressive and leading to violence. Similarly, people in positions of authority can misinterpret certain ways of walking, standing, and dressing, and perceive these styles as defiant.

- The issues of differential treatment, racial profiling, excessive force, and brutality are still realities in policing and interaction with African Americans in the United States. When acts of bias and injustice occur, everyone suffers, including officers and entire police departments. An additional challenge is addressing the needs of the inner city, and the need for increased police protection. Bridging the gap that has hindered relationships between the police and African Americans involves radical changes in attitudes toward police/community relations.

Discussion Questions and Issues

1. *Racism: Effects on Blacks and Whites.* Under the "Historical Information" section in this chapter, the authors state that slavery has created great psychological and social problems for succeeding generations of black citizens. How does the legacy of slavery continue to impact both blacks and whites? What are the implications for law enforcement?

2. *Offensive Terms.* Officers are advised to refrain from using racial epithets at all times, even when there are no African Americans present. Give two practical reasons for this.

3. *Blue Code of Silence.* Discuss the example that is provided (p. 169) in which an African American officer fairly new to a department did not speak up when it came to his partner's differential treatment of black citizens in a nightclub. What do you think held this officer back from speaking up? What might the consequences of his silence be with respect to the ongoing relationship between black and white officers? How should this example of differential treatment have been handled? After you have answered these questions, discuss how departments, in community-policing forums with African American and other ethnic communities, can convey their commitment to police professionalism and ethics—a step that is crucial in rebuilding trust with communities that have historically not had positive relations with law enforcement.

4. *Inner Cities: Officers' and Citizens' Reactions.* Toward the end of the chapter, the authors mention the vicious cycle that is created in urban areas, especially where citizens have become increasingly armed with highly sophisticated weapons and officers, consequently, have to take more self-protective measures. Each views the other with fear and animosity and approaches the other with extreme defensiveness. Obviously, there is no simple answer to this widely occurring phenomenon, and police alone cannot solve it. Discuss your observations of the way officers cope with the stresses of these potentially life-threatening situations and how the coping or lack thereof affects relations with African Americans and other minorities. What type of support do police officers need to handle this aspect of their job? Do you think police departments are doing their job in providing the support needed?

5. *When Officers Try to Make a Difference.* Many young African American children live without a father in the household. This means that they do not have a second parental figure as a role model and are consequently deprived of an important source of adult support. No one can take the place of a missing parent, but there are small and large things a police officer can do to at least make an impression in the life of a child. Compile a list of actions officers can take to demonstrate their caring for children in this type of environment. Include in your first list every gesture, no matter how small; your second list can be more realistic and include actions that can be taken given the resources available. Select someone to compile both sets of suggestions (i.e., the realistic and ideal suggestions). Post these lists as reminders of how officers can attempt to make a difference in their communities not only with African American children but with other children as well.

References

Associated Press. (2012, October 29). *Racial Attitudes Survey.* Conducted by GfK.

Axtell, Brooke. (2012, April 25). "Black Women, Sexual Assault and the Art of Resistance." *Forbes.*

Bennett, Lerone Jr. (1989, November). "The 10 Biggest Myths about the Black Family." *Ebony.* pp. 1–2.

Berry, Ondra. (2013, July). Retired Assistant Police Chief, Reno, Nevada, Police Department, personal communication.

Bidgood, Jess. (2013, March 6). "Helping Immigrants Warm to Winter." *The New York Times.*

"Black on Black Crime." (1991, April 24). *USA Today.*

"Black Police Officer Talks Police Brutality, Racism in Interview." (2010, August 13). *NewsOne.*

Capps, Randy, Kristen McCabe, and Michael Fix. (2011). *New Streams: Black African Migration to the United States.* Washington, D.C.: Migration Policy Institute.

Chan, Sewell. (2007, August 9). "The Abner Louima Case, 10 Years Later." *The New York Times* (New York/Region section).

Council of Economic Advisors. (1998, September). *Changing America: Indicators of Social and Economic Well-Being by Race and Hispanic Origin.* Chapter 7, Crime and Criminal Justice. President's Initiative on Race. National Center for Health Statistics, Bureau of Justice Statistics.

Cross, Stan, and Edward Renner. (1974). "An Interaction Analysis of Police-Black Relations." *Journal of Police Science Administration, 2*(1), 55–61.

CSIS. (2003). Consumer Services Information Systems Project—Glossary. Retrieved July 24, 2013, from http://csisweb.aers.psu.edu

FBI (2011). Hate Crime Statistics. Retrieved August 29, 2013, from www.fbi.gov/about-us/cjis/ucr/hate-crime/2011 (accessed August 29, 2013).

FNS: Federal News Service. (2013, July 19). "Transcript: Obama's Remarks on Trayvon Martin Case, Race in America." *The Wall Street Journal.*

Goleman, Daniel. (1992, April 21). "Black Scientists Study the 'Pose' of the Inner City." *New York Times.*

Grieco, Elizabeth, Yesenia Acosta, G. Patricia de la Cruz, Christine Gambino, Thomas Gryn, Luke Larsen, . . . Nathan Walters. (2012, May). "The Foreign-Born Population in the United States: 2010." Washington, D.C.: U.S. Census Bureau, *American Community Survey Reports*.

Griffin, Ronald Pastor. (2009). Detroit-based Pastor and Community Leader, Vice Chair of Detroit Board of Police Commissioners, personal communication.

Hecht, Michael, Ronald Jackson II, and Sidney Ribeau. (2003). *African American Communication: Exploring Identity and Culture*. Mahwah, NJ: Lawrence Erlbaum Associates, Inc.

Huo, Yuen, and Tom Tyler. (2000). *How Different Ethnic Groups React to Legal Authority*. San Francisco: Public Policy Institute of California.

IACP: International Association of Chiefs of Police. (2001). *Police Use of Force in America 2001*. Alexandria, VA: IACP.

Johnson, James L., Ph.D. (2013, July). Social Science Analyst, Administrative Office of the U.S. Courts, personal communication.

Johnson, James L., Ph.D. (2008). "The Construction of Mass Incarceration as a Means of Marginalizing Black Americans." *Dissertation Abstract International, 69*(3), 130A. (UMI No. AAT 3305791.)

Kochman, Thomas. (1981). *Black and White Styles in Conflict*. Chicago: University of Chicago Press, p. 121.

Kochman, Thomas. (2013, July). Founder and Chief Operating Officer of KMA Associates; internationally known diversity specialist; personal communication.

LCCREF: Leadership Conference on Civil Rights Education Fund. (2009). *Confronting the New Faces of Hate: Hate Crimes in America, 2009*.

Lemann, Nicholas. (1991). *The Promised Land: The Great Black Migration and How it Changed America*. New York: Vintage Books.

McAdoo, Harriet Pipes. (1992). "Upward Mobility and Parenting in Middle Income Families." *African American Psychology*. Newbury Park, CA: Sage.

Miller, Char. (2013, February). (Former) Professor of History, Trinity College, San Antonio, Texas, personal communication.

Nemeth, Matt, Lieutenant. (2013, July). Executive director, PAL, Jacksonville, Florida, personal communication.

Newport, Frank. (2013, July 16). "In U.S., 24% of Young Black Men Say Police Dealings Unfair." *Gallup Politics*.

Patrick, Peter L. (2006). *Answers to some Questions about Ebonics*. University of Essex, U.K.

Patton, Greg. (2013, May). Criminal Justice Cultural Diversity Instructor at Portland Community College, personal communication.

Pew Forum. (2008). "U.S. Religious Landscape Survey." Retrieved July 15, 2013, from http://religions.pewforum.org

Pulkkinen, Levi. (2011, December 16). "Feds: Seattle police show 'pattern of excessive force.'" *Seattlepi.com*.

Rickford, John Russell. (2009, June). Linguistics Professor; specialist in African American Vernacular English, personal communication.

"Sean Bell." (2009, April). *The New York Times* (Times Topics Section).

Stone, Christopher, Todd Foglesong, and Christine Cole. (2009, May). *Policing Los Angeles Under a Consent Decree: The Dynamics of Change at the LAPD*. Harvard Kennedy School.

U.S. Census Bureau. (2012, January 4). *Black (African-American) History Month*. Profile America: Facts for Features. CB12-FF.01.

US DOJ: U.S. Department of Justice. (2011). *Homicide trends in the U.S.* Office of Justice Programs, Bureau of Justice Statistics.

US DOJ: U.S. Department of Justice. (2010, June). *Prison Inmates at Midyear 2009—Statistical Tables*. Office of Justice Programs, Bureau of Justice Statistics. NCJ 230113.

Walker, Samuel. (1992). *The Police in America*. New York: McGraw-Hill.

Weber, Shirley. (1991). "The Need to Be: The Socio-Cultural Significance of Black Language," in *Intercultural Communication: A Reader*, 6th ed. Larry Samovar and Richard Porter (Eds.). Belmont, CA: Wadsworth Press.

Weisburd, David, and Rosann Greenspan. (2000, May). *Police Attitudes toward Abuse of Authority: Findings from a National Study*. National Institute of Justice Research in Brief.

Williams, Hubert, and Patrick Murphy. (1990, January). *The Evolving Strategy of Police: A Minority View*. Washington D.C.: U.S. Department of Justice, Office of Justice Programs, National Institute of Justice.

Wolfram, Walt and Benjamin Torbert. (2005). *The Linguistic Legacy of the African Slave Trade*. PBS, American Varieties: African American English.

7 Law Enforcement Contact with Latino/Hispanic Americans

LEARNING OBJECTIVES

After reading this chapter, you should be able to:

- Discuss the implications of group identification terms for Latino/Hispanic Americans.
- Describe the historical background of the Latino/Hispanic American community in the United States.
- Highlight the demographic features and diversity of the Latino/Hispanic community.
- Identify myths and stereotypes applied to Latino/Hispanic Americans.
- Explain the importance of family structure of Latino/Hispanic Americans for law enforcement.
- Discuss communication styles used by Latino/Hispanic Americans.
- Highlight key law enforcement issues related to Latino/Hispanic Americans.

OUTLINE

- Introduction
- Latino/Hispanic Americans Defined
- Historical Information
- Demographics: Diversity among Latino/Hispanic Americans
- Myths and Stereotypes
- The Latino/Hispanic American Family
- Communication Styles of Latino/Hispanic Americans
- Key Issues in Law Enforcement
- Summary
- Discussion Questions and Issues

INTRODUCTION

Most police officers have little knowledge of Latino/Hispanic people, communities, language, or culture. There is little to no training in police academies on these subjects. Academy trainers, field training officers, and instructors of advanced officer courses should understand and teach about the cultural attributes of Latino/Hispanic peoples, especially because

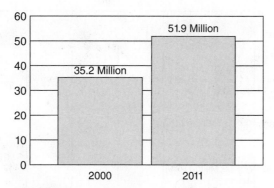

EXHIBIT 7.1 Increase in U.S. Hispanic Population from 2000–2011

Source: Hispanic Population Trends, 2013 "Hispanic Population Trends." Used by permission of Pew Research Center. Retrieved February 15, 2013, from www.pewhispanic.org/topics/population-trends/

in the United States, many cities and towns are experiencing an increase in the number of Latino/Hispanic residents. Officers must understand how assimilation of Latino/Hispanic people into the U.S. culture varies according to immigrant generation and also to country of origin.

Latino/Hispanic Americans are the fastest growing cultural group in the United States in terms of overall numbers of people. The Hispanic population reached 52 million as of 2011 (see Exhibit 7.1), according to Pew Research Hispanic Center tabulations, making people of Hispanic origin the largest ethnic or racial minority (17%). (See Exhibit 7.2.) According to the same report, 33.5 million (65%) of Hispanic-origin people in the United States self-identified as being of Mexican origin. Another 4.9 million (9%) residing in the U.S. were of Puerto Rican background, with an additional 3.7 million residing in Puerto Rico itself. (Because Puerto Rico is a U.S. territory, those born there are American citizens.) Pew Research further found that 2 million (4%) identified as Salvadoran, 1.9 million (4%) as Cuban, and 1.5 million (3%) as Dominican. The remainder were made up of other Central American, South American or other Hispanic or Latino origin. (See Exhibit 7.3.) The projected Hispanic population of the United States by July 2050 is 132.8 million, which will constitute 30 percent of the nation's population ("Hispanic Population Trends," 2013).

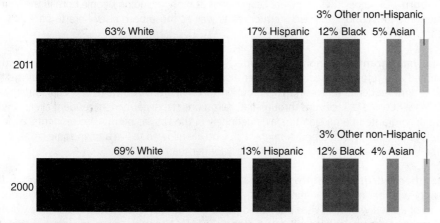

EXHIBIT 7.2 Percentage Changes in U.S. Racial/Ethnic Populations from 2000 to 2011

Source: Hispanic Population Trends, 2013. Used by permission of Pew Research Center. Retrieved from www.pewhispanic.org/topics/population-trends/

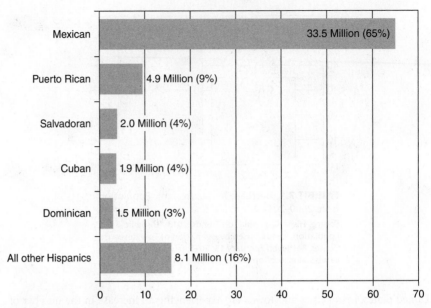

EXHIBIT 7.3   Two-thirds of the U.S. Hispanic population is of Mexican Origin "Hispanic Population Trends"

Source: Hispanic Population Trends, 2013. Used by permission of Pew Research Center. Retrieved from www.pewhispanic.org/topics/population-trends/

Terminology

In this text, we use "Latino" and "Hispanic" interchangeably as well as "Latino/Hispanic." Following are additional definitions from the U.S. Census Bureau, the Department of Homeland Security, and academic researchers (refer also to Chapter 1 for additional related definitions).

Foreign-born   Refers to an individual who is not a U.S. citizen at birth or who is born outside the U.S., Puerto Rico, or other U.S. territories, and whose parents are not U.S. citizens. The terms *foreign-born* and *immigrant* are used interchangeably.

U.S.-born   Describes those who are U.S. citizens at birth, including people born in the United States, Puerto Rico, or other U.S. territories, as well as those born elsewhere to parents who are U.S. citizens.

Legal immigrant   An individual granted legal permanent residence; granted asylum; admitted as a refugee; or admitted under a set of specific authorized temporary statuses for longer-term residence and work. This group includes "naturalized citizens," legal immigrants who have become U.S. citizens through naturalization; "legal permanent resident aliens," who have been granted permission to stay indefinitely in the U.S. as permanent residents, asylees, or refugees; and "legal temporary migrants," who are allowed to live and, in some cases, work in the U.S. for specific periods of time (usually longer than one year).

Unauthorized/Undocumented immigrants   All foreign-born noncitizens residing in the country who are not "legal immigrants" and who entered the country without valid documents or arrived with valid visas but stayed past their visa expiration date or otherwise violated the terms of their admission. (Passel & Cohn, 2011). (Although the term *unauthorized immigrant* is increasingly in use, it has not entirely replaced the term *undocumented immigrant*, which is used periodically in this text. See Chapter 1.)

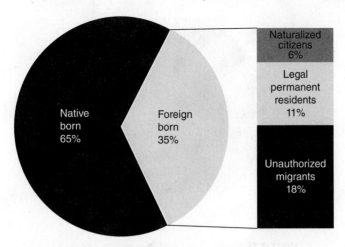

EXHIBIT 7.4   Nativity and Legal Status of Mexican-Origin Population in the U.S., 2011

Source: Ana Gonzalez Barrera and Mark Hugo Lopez from A Demographic Portrait of Mexican-Origin Hispanics in the United States, 2013. Used by permission of Pew Research Center. Retrieved from www.pewhispanic.org/2013/05/01/a-demographic-portrait-of-mexican-origin-hispanics-in-the-united-states/

Unauthorized Immigrants

Chapter 1 presented general issues related to unauthorized immigrants. The Pew Hispanic Center estimated that the total number of unauthorized immigrants in the United States as of March 2010 was 11.2 million, which represented a two-year decline from the peak of 12 million in 2007. It was the first significant reversal in a two-decade pattern of growth (Passel & Cohn, 2011). In 2011, more than half (55 percent) of these unauthorized immigrants were from Mexico (Gonzalez-Barrera & Lopez, 2013). The nativity and legal status of the Mexican-origin population as of 2010 is shown in Exhibit 7.4 (Gonzalez-Barrera & Lopez, 2013). Major factors explaining this trend are that "the U.S. economy is no longer flush with jobs. The border is more secure than ever. And in Mexico the birthrate has fallen precipitously" ("In Mexico, heading north has lost luster," 2013).

Across the country, law enforcement agencies vary as to whether or not to partner with the U.S. Immigration and Customs Enforcement (ICE) agency of the Department of Homeland Security in enforcing immigration laws. The same is true of participation in the Secure Communities program. Some states, cities, and county agencies refuse to participate, believing that involvement with ICE or Secure Communities corrodes their relationship with immigrant communities, who are already less likely to cooperate with law enforcement agencies or report crimes. See Chapter 10 for information about ICE and Secure Communities.

As of September 2013, the U.S. Congress was considering legislation dealing with unauthorized immigration. Democrats and Republicans, and factions within each, present different approaches to the issue, especially pertaining to the timeline in which those in the United States without authorization could qualify for permanent residency, a green card, and/or citizenship. In the public at large, there has been a backlash against unauthorized immigration, and even against Latino/Hispanic people, including those who were born in the U.S. or who immigrated legally. A Pew Hispanic Center survey in 2010 (see Exhibit 7.5), shows a marked division on the topic, even among Latinos/Hispanics (Lopez, Moran, & Taylor, 2010).

LATINO/HISPANIC AMERICANS DEFINED

The word *Hispanic* does not describe a racial group; for example, a person can be white, black, or Asian and still be considered Hispanic. *Hispanic* is a generic term referring to all Spanish-surname and Spanish-speaking people who reside within the United States and Puerto Rico. *Latino* is generally the preferred label on the West Coast, parts of the East Coast, and the Southeast.

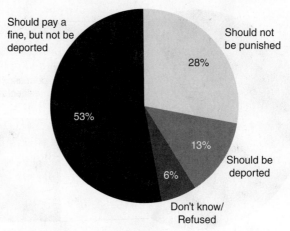

EXHIBIT 7.5 Latinos Are Divided over What to do about Unauthorized Immigrants

Source: Mark Hugo Lopez, Rich Morin and Paul Taylor from Illegal Immigration Backlash Worries, Divides Latinos, 2010. Used by permission of Pew Research Center. Retrieved from www.pewhispanic.org/2010/10/28/illegal-immigration-backlash-worries-divides-latinos

The term *Latino* is a Spanish word indicating a person of Latin American origin, and it reflects the gender-specific nature of its Spanish-language derivation: Latino, for men, and Latina, for women. Hispanic is generally preferred on the East Coast, specifically within the Puerto Rican, Dominican, and Cuban communities (although individual members within each of these communities may prefer the specific term referring to their country of heritage). Objections to the use of the term *Hispanic* include the following: (1) *Hispanic* is not derived from any culture or place (i.e., there is no such place as "Hispania") and (2) the term was primarily invented for use by the U.S. Census Bureau. In recent decades, many Latino/Hispanic Americans, inspired by a growing sense of community identification, high-profile and successful role models, and increased pride in their ethnic and cultural identity, have embraced the use of *Hispanic* and *Latino/Latina* for self- and group reference. A new and dynamic pride, confidence, and self-esteem in the Latino/Hispanic culture and heritage have emerged for many (especially among the younger generations) and have replaced some of the past negative associations with the terms *Latino* and *Hispanic*, often fostered by negative stereotypes related to unauthorized immigration status, migrant work roles, educational underachievement, and impoverished communities.

Sometimes, the term *Spanish-surnamed* may be used to recognize that one may have a Spanish surname but may not speak Spanish (which is the case for a large number of Latino/Hispanic Americans). *La Raza* is another term used, primarily on the West Coast and in the Southwest, to refer to all peoples of the Western Hemisphere who share a cultural, historical, political, and social legacy of the Spanish and Portuguese colonists, and the Native Indian; it has its origins within the political struggles of this region and the mixing of the races, *el mestizaje*; the word *raza* means "race." Like La Raza, *Chicano* is another term that grew out of the ethnic pride and ethnic studies movement in the late 1960s. Chicano refers specifically to Mexican Americans, and it is used primarily on the West Coast, in the Southwest, and in the Midwest. It is also commonly used in college communities across the United States that provide an ethnic studies curriculum.

United States Census—Hispanic and Latino Survey Category

In 1976, Congress passed Public Law 94-311, which required the inclusion of a self-identification question on Spanish origin or descent in government surveys and censuses. As such, *Hispanic* is the official term used in federal, state, and local governmental writings and for demographic references. Federal standards implemented in 2003 allow the terms *Latino* and *Hispanic* to be used interchangeably (Office of Management and Budget, 1997). As of 2013, the U.S. Census

Bureau has proposed a change of wording from "Hispanic" to "Hispanic Race" for the census that will take place in 2020 (Ayala & Huet, 2013). The reason for the change of wording is that many Hispanics do not identify with or see themselves fitting into the standard racial categories from which to select. For example, when it comes to race, according to a Pew Hispanic survey, half (51%) of Latinos identify themselves as "some other race" or volunteer "Hispanic/Latino." Meanwhile, 36 percent identify their race as white, and 3 percent say their race is black. Those completing the survey were able to mark one or more race, but only one Hispanic ethnicity category. One of the purposes of the proposed change is to reduce the number of nonresponses to the survey question and, thus, improve accuracy of the census pertaining to the numbers of Hispanic/Latino in the U.S. population (Taylor, Lopez, Martinez, & Velasco, 2012).

Labels and Terms

As noted earlier, the term *Latino/Hispanic* American is a convenient summarizing label to achieve some degree of agreement in referring to a very heterogeneous group of people. As with Asian/Pacific Americans, the key to understanding which terms to use is based on the principle of self-preference. Sensitivity is warranted in the use of the term *Hispanic* with the Latino/Hispanic American community. For those who have origins in the Caribbean (e.g., Puerto Rican, Cuban, Dominican), the term *Latino* may be equally problematic for self-designation and self-identification.

Until 2003, federal and other governmental designations used only Hispanic; Latino and Hispanic are now used interchangeably. The governmental designations are used in laws, programs, and regulations, and in most reports and publications. According to a PEW Research Center report, over 51 percent of those surveyed described themselves as "Mexican," "Cuban," "Puerto Rican," "Argentinean," "Salvadorian," or "Dominican," depending on the country from which their family came. Only 24 percent used the terms *Hispanic* or *Latino* to describe their identity. Twenty-one percent said they use the term *American* most often (Taylor et al., 2012). "Spanish speakers may take offense if law enforcement officials describe them as Latino[s] or Hispanic[s] or categorize them with citizens from countries other than their own." It is incorrect to assume that all Spanish speakers hold the same political views, especially if they are from different countries and don't "share the same identity, whether cultural or national. On the contrary, they often feel great pride in their local, provincial, or national identities to the point that they may resent being grouped with those from other parts of the Spanish-speaking world" (Natella & Madera, 2008). For law enforcement officers, the best term to use in referring to individuals is the term that those individuals prefer to be called. It is perfectly acceptable to ask people what nationality they are.

The use of slurs like "wetback," "Mex," "spic," "greaser," or other derogatory ethnic slang terms is never acceptable by law enforcement officers, no matter how provoked an officer may be. These and other stereotypic terms do not convey the kind of professionalism and respect for community diversity important to law enforcement and peacekeeping, and must be avoided in law enforcement work. Officers hearing these or similar words used in their own departments (or with peers or citizens) should provide immediate feedback about the inappropriateness of the use. Officers who may, out of habit, routinely use these or other derogatory terms may find themselves or their superiors in the embarrassing situation of explaining to offended citizens and communities why they used the term and how they intended no bias, stereotype, or prejudice.

HISTORICAL INFORMATION

The historical background of Latino/Hispanic Americans contains key factors that affect their interactions with and understanding of law enforcement personnel. Clearly, this brief historical and sociopolitical overview can only highlight some of the commonalities and diverse cultural experiences of Latino/Hispanic Americans. Our historical review focuses primarily on the larger Latino/Hispanic communities in the United States (those with Mexican, Puerto Rican, and Cuban ethnic and historical roots).

In the 1800s, under the declaration of Manifest Destiny, the United States began the expansionist policy of annexing vast territories to the south, north, and west. As Lopez y Rivas (1973) noted, the United States viewed itself as a people chosen by "Providence" to form a larger union through conquest, purchase, and annexation. With the purchase and annexation of the Louisiana Territories in 1803, Florida in 1819, Texas in 1845, and the Northwest Territories (Oregon, Washington, Idaho, Wyoming, and Montana) in 1846, it seemed nearly inevitable that conflict would occur with Mexico. The resulting Mexican–American War ended in 1848 with the signing of the Treaty of Guadalupe Hidalgo, in which Mexico received $15 million from the United States for the land that is now Texas, New Mexico, Arizona, and California, with more than 100,000 Mexican people living in those areas. As is obvious from this portion of history, it makes little sense for many Mexican Americans to be stereotyped as "unauthorized immigrants," especially since more than a million Mexican Americans can trace their ancestry back to families living in the southwestern United States in the mid-1800s. Moreover, for Latino/Hispanic Americans (especially Mexican Americans), the boundaries between the United States and Mexico are seen as artificial. "The geographic, ecological, and cultural blending of the Southwest with Mexico is perceived as a continuing unity of people whose claim to the Southwest is rooted in the land itself" (Montiel, 1978).

While one-third of Mexican Americans can trace their ancestry to families living in the United States in the mid-1800s, the majority of this group migrated into the United States after 1910 because of the economic and political changes that occurred as a result of the Mexican Revolution.

Puerto Rico, on the other hand, was under the domination of Spain until 1897, at which time it was allowed the establishment of a local government. The United States invaded Puerto Rico and annexed it as part of the Spanish–American War (along with Cuba, the Philippines, and Guam) in 1898. Although Cuba (in 1902) and the Philippines (in 1949) were given their independence, Puerto Rico remained a territory of the United States. In 1900, the U.S. Congress passed the Foraker Act, which allowed the president to appoint a governor, to provide an Executive Council consisting of 11 presidential appointees (of which only five had to be Puerto Rican), and to elect locally a 35-member Chamber of Delegates. In reality, the territory was run by the U.S. president-appointed governor and the Executive Council. The Jones Act of 1917 made Puerto Ricans citizens of the United States. It was not until 1948 that Puerto Rico elected its first governor, Luis Munoz Marin. In 1952, Puerto Rico was given Commonwealth status, and Spanish was allowed to be the language of instruction in the schools again (with English taught as the second language). Following World War II, large numbers of Puerto Ricans began migrating into the United States. With citizenship status, Puerto Ricans could travel easily, and they settled in areas on the East Coast, primarily New York City (in part because of the availability of jobs and affordable apartments).

Cubans immigrated into the United States in three waves. The first wave occurred between 1959 and 1965 and consisted of primarily white, middle-class or upper-class Cubans who were relatively well educated and had business and financial resources. The federal government's Cuban Refugee Program, Cuban Student Loan Program, and Cuban Small Business Administration Loan Program were established to help this first wave of Cuban immigrants achieve a successful settlement (Bernal & Estrada, 1985). The second wave of Cuban immigrants occurred between 1965 and 1973. This wave resulted from the opening of the Port of Camarioca, allowing all who wished to leave Cuba to exit. Those who left as part of the second wave were more often of the working class and lower middle class, primarily white men and women. The third wave of immigrants leaving Cuba from Mariel occurred from the summer of 1980 to early 1982. This wave was the largest (about 125,000 were boat-lifted to the United States) and consisted primarily of working-class persons, more reflective of the Cuban population as a whole than were previous waves. Most immigrated into the United States with hopes for better economic opportunities. Within this group of Marielitos were many antisocial, criminal, and mentally ill persons released by Fidel Castro (Gavzer, 1993).

In addition to the three major groups that have immigrated to the United States from Mexico, Puerto Rico, and Cuba, there are immigrants from 21 countries of South and Central America, as well as the Caribbean. Arrival of these immigrants for political, economic, and social reasons began in the early 1980s and has added to the diversity of Latino/Hispanic American communities in the United States. The total number of some groups, such as the Dominicans (a rapidly growing group on the East Coast), is difficult to determine because of their unauthorized entry status within the United States.

DEMOGRAPHICS: DIVERSITY AMONG LATINO/HISPANIC AMERICANS

The historical background illustrates the heterogeneity of Latino/Hispanic Americans. Composed of many different cultural groups, this broad label encompasses significant generational, educational, and socioeconomic differences; varying relocation experiences; and many other varieties of life experience. Although the Spanish language may provide a common thread among most Latino/Hispanic Americans, there are cultural and national differences in terms and expressions used, including nonverbal nuances. Moreover, the language of Brazil is Portuguese, not Spanish, and thus the language connection for Brazilian Latino/Hispanic Americans is unique. Some of the key demographics information about this population includes what follows. The implications of some of these demographics are presented in the "Key Issues in Law Enforcement" section of this chapter.

1. *Age:* The Latino/Hispanic American population tends to be younger than the general U.S. population. The median age is 27 years, in contrast to 37 for the rest of America (Motel & Patten, 2012). (See Exhibit 7.6.)

2. *Birthrate:* Among women ages 15 to 44 in 2011, nearly a quarter of all births nationwide were to Hispanics ("Hispanic Population Trends," 2013). (See Exhibit 7.7.) Although historically Hispanic women in the United States generally had the highest fertility rates, "both immigrant and native-born Latinas had steeper birthrate declines from 2007 to 2010 than other groups, including non-Hispanic whites, blacks, and Asians" (Saulny, 2012). The overall birth rate in the United States declined 8 percent from 2007 to 2010 to its lowest level ever recorded by 2011. "The birth rate for U.S.-born women decreased 6 percent during these years, but the birth rate for foreign-born women plunged 14 percent.... The birth rate for Mexican immigrant women fell even more, by 23 percent," ("U.S. Birth Rate Falls to New Lows," 2013). The decrease, according to some demographers and sociologists, has been linked to changes in the views of many Hispanic women about motherhood, size of family, desire to have a career, and use of contraception. Another factor suggested was the prolonged recession, which, historically, results in drops in birthrates.

3. *Language:* Latino/Hispanic American self-identification is most strongly demonstrated in the knowledge and use of Spanish. The Spanish language is often the single most important cultural aspect retained by Latino/Hispanic Americans. The 2010 U.S. Census indicated that of the 52 million Latino/Hispanics in the United States, 37 million 5 years and older, spoke Spanish at home. The same Census data indicated that over 50 percent of those who spoke Spanish in the home also spoke English "well" or "very well." (U.S. Census, 2010).

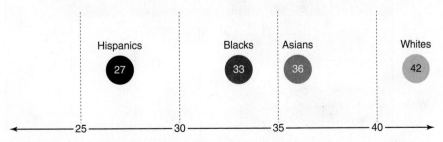

EXHIBIT 7.6   The Hispanic population is the nation's youngest major racial or ethnic group
Source: Hispanic Population Trends, 2013. Used by permission of Pew Research Center. Retrieved from www.pewhispanic.org/topics/population-trends/

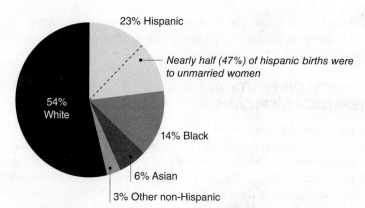

EXHIBIT 7.7 Nearly a quarter of all births nationwide last year were to Hispanic women

Source: Hispanic Population Trends, 2013. Used by permission of Pew Research Center. Retrieved from www.pewhispanic.org/topics/population-trends/

A Pew Research Center report in 2012, based on their tabulations from the 2010 American Community Survey, established that:

- The Hispanic origin groups with the highest rates of English proficiency are Puerto Ricans (82%), Mexicans (64%), Colombians (59%) and Peruvians (59%).
- Guatemalans (41%), Hondurans (42%) and Salvadorans (46%) have the lowest rates of English proficiency and are the only groups in which less than half of the population ages five and older is proficient in English. (Motel & Patten, 2012)

Eighty-seven percent of Hispanics surveyed say adult immigrants need to learn English to succeed in the United States and fully 95 percent want future generations to be able to speak Spanish (Taylor et al., 2012).

4. *Poverty rate:* The poverty rate among Hispanics was 6.1 million (26%) in 2011, which was higher than the U.S. poverty rate (16%) overall ("Hispanic Population Trends," 2013). (See Exhibit 7.8.) A recent Pew Hispanic Center report showed that more Latino

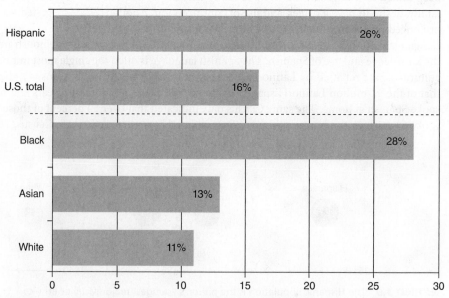

EXHIBIT 7.8 The Hispanic poverty rate is higher than the U.S. poverty rate overall

Source: Hispanic Population Trends, 2013. Used by permission of Pew Research Center. Retrieved from www.pewhispanic.org/topics/population-trends/

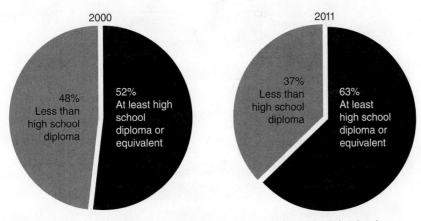

EXHIBIT 7.9 Percent of Hispanic Adults Ages 25 and Older with High School Diplomas 2000 and 2011

Source: Hispanic Population Trends, 2013. Used by permission of Pew Research Center.

children are living in poverty than any other major racial or ethnic group (Lopez & Velasco, 2011). The research covered the period that many call the Great Recession of 2007–2009.

5. *Education:* In 2011, the percentage of Hispanics 25 years and older that had
   - at least a high school education was 63 percent compared to 52 percent in 2000.
   - at least a bachelor's degree or higher was 13 percent compared to 10 percent in 2000.

(see Exhibits 7.9 and 7.10)

Nativity and Regional Distribution of Latino/Hispanic Origin Groups in the U.S.

The nativity of foreign-born among the U.S. Latino/Hispanic groups, according to a Pew study, is shown in Exhibit 7.11. According to the study,

Nearly two-fifths (37 percent) of all Hispanics are foreign born, compared with 13 percent of the overall U.S. population

The groups with the largest foreign-born shares are Guatemalans, Hondurans and Peruvians (all 67 percent)

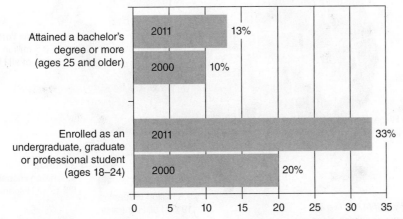

EXHIBIT 7.10 Rates of College Attainment and Enrollment of Hispanics—2000 and 2011

Source: Hispanic Population Trends, 2013. Used by permission of Pew Research Center.

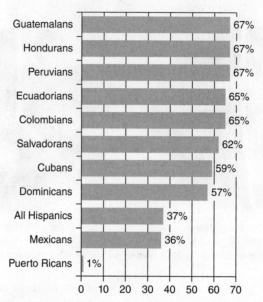

EXHIBIT 7.11 Share of Foreign Born among the U.S. Hispanic Population, by Origin, 2010

Source: Seth Motel and Eileen Patten from The 10 Largest Hispanic Origin Groups: Characteristics, Rankings, Top Counties, 2012. Used by permission of Pew Research Center. Retrieved from www.pewhispanic.org/2012/06/27/the-10-largest-hispanic-origin-groups

Mexicans and Puerto Ricans are the only Hispanic origin groups with majority native-born shares. Only 36 percent of Mexicans and 1 percent of Puerto Ricans are foreign born. (Motel & Patten, 2012)

As far as the regional distribution of Latino/Hispanic origin groups in the United States, two-thirds of Hispanics live in just five states—California, Texas, Florida, New York, and Illinois (see Exhibit 7.12).

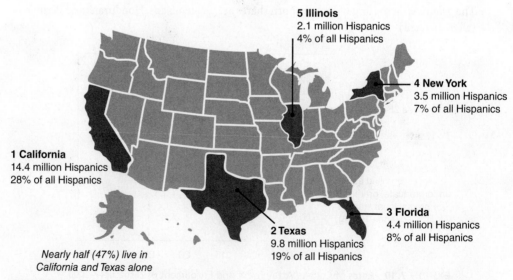

5 Illinois
2.1 million Hispanics
4% of all Hispanics

4 New York
3.5 million Hispanics
7% of all Hispanics

1 California
14.4 million Hispanics
28% of all Hispanics

3 Florida
4.4 million Hispanics
8% of all Hispanics

2 Texas
9.8 million Hispanics
19% of all Hispanics

Nearly half (47%) live in California and Texas alone

EXHIBIT 7.12 Two-thirds of Hispanics live in just five states

Source: Hispanic Population Trends, 2013. Retrieved from www.pewhispanic.org/topics/population-trends/

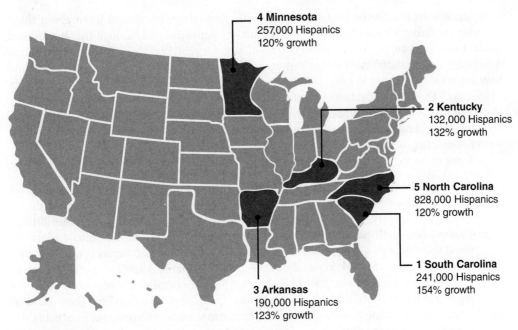

EXHIBIT 7.13   Five States with fastest growth since 2010

Source: Hispanic Population Trends, 2013. Used by permission of Pew Research Center. Retrieved from www.pewhispanic.org/topics/population-trends/

The five states that have seen the fastest growth of Hispanics, South Carolina, Kentucky, Arkansas, Minnesota, and North Carolina are shown in Exhibit 7.13. The same report indicates:

- Among the 10 largest Hispanic origin groups, all have their largest populations in just three states: California (Mexicans, Salvadorans and Guatemalans), Florida (Cubans, Colombians, Hondurans and Peruvians) or New York (Puerto Ricans, Dominicans and Ecuadorians).
- The largest single Hispanic origin group population in a state is the Mexican population in California at 11.8 million people. Texas is home to another 8.4 million Mexicans. Together, these two states contain 61 percent of the total Mexican population in the U.S. (Motel & Patten, 2012).

Typology of Latino/Hispanic Americans

In Chapter 1 of this text, we present a seven-part typology that is designed to deepen understanding of some of the differences between individuals (e.g., refugees and immigrants) within one broad ethnic label or category.

Our typology suggests that focusing on key differences within each of the typological groups will increase effectiveness as law enforcement, criminal justice, and public safety organizations personnel prepare and train their personnel to work with ethnic communities. Please refer to the description of the typology in Chapter 1 as a convenient framework for discussing how the motivational components within each of the groups may affect the way people respond in a law enforcement situation.

MYTHS AND STEREOTYPES

Knowledge of and sensitivity to Latino/Hispanic Americans' concerns, diversity, historical background, and life experiences will facilitate the crime-fighting and peacekeeping mission of law enforcement officers. It is important to have an understanding about some of the myths and stereotypes of Latino/Hispanic Americans that contribute to the prejudice, discrimination, and bias this population encounters. Many law enforcement officers do not have much experience with the diversity of Latino/Hispanic American groups and learn about these groups only through stereotypes (often perpetuated by movies) and through the very limited contact involved in their law enforcement duties. Stereotypic views of Latino/Hispanic Americans reduce individuals within this group to simplistic, one-dimensional characters and have led many Americans to lump members of these diverse groups into one stereotypic group: "Mexicans." The key to effectiveness with any ethnic or racial group is not that we completely eliminate myths and stereotypes, but that we are aware of these stereotypes and can monitor our thinking and our behaviors when the stereotypes are not true of those persons with whom we are interacting.

Some of the stereotypes that have affected Latino/Hispanic Americans include the following:

1. *Viewing all Latino/Hispanic Americans as "illegal aliens":* Although many may argue over the number of unauthorized immigrant Latino/Hispanic people in the United States, most do not fall into this category; the vast majority are U.S. citizens or legal residents (U.S. Census, 2010).

2. *Viewing Latino/Hispanic Americans as lazy and as poor workers:* It is difficult to understand why some people continue to hold this stereotype or what factors continue to perpetuate it, given what we know about the Latino/Hispanic American workforce in the United States and globally. Latino/Hispanic American community advocates make the argument that it is difficult to imagine anyone being labeled as "lazy" or "poor workers" when they are willing to work as laborers from dawn to dusk in the migrant farm fields, day in and day out, year after year.

3. *Perceiving Latino/Hispanic Americans as uneducated and uninterested in educational pursuits:* According to the previously mentioned 2010 Census, 63 percent of Hispanics 25 and older had at least a high school education; 13 percent of the Hispanic population 25 and older had a bachelor's degree or higher; and 6.2 percent of full-time college students (both undergraduate and graduate) were Hispanic (Hispanic Population Trends, 2012).

4. *Seeing Latino/Hispanic American young males as gang members and drug dealers:* Some hold the stereotype, especially about young males in inner cities, that Latino/Hispanic Americans are commonly involved in gangs and the illegal drug trade. Latino/Hispanic cultures are group oriented, and people, young and old, tend to congregate and be identified as groups rather than as individuals or couples. "Hanging out" as a group tends to be the preferred mode of socialization. However, given the stereotype of Latino/Hispanic American young males as being gang members, it is easy to perceive five young Latino/Hispanic males walking together as constituting a "gang." Such stereotypes have resulted in suspicion, hostility, and prejudice toward Latino/Hispanic Americans and have served to justify improper treatment (e.g., routine traffic stops) and poor services (e.g., in restaurants and stores). Such stereotypes can also lead law enforcement officers to unfairly associate Latino/Hispanic Americans with criminal activity.

5. *Assuming that all Latino/Hispanic Americans speak Spanish:* Mentioned previously is that over 50 percent of Latino/Hispanics 5 to 17 years of age who spoke Spanish in the home also spoke English "well" or "very well." (Hispanic Population Trends, 2012). Additionally, for many Latino/Hispanic Americans, their ancestors have been in the United States for six generations or more—longer than many other ethnic groups—and English is the only language they speak and write. Therefore, it could be considered both insulting and ignorant to comment on the use of English by Hispanic Americans.

THE LATINO/HISPANIC AMERICAN FAMILY

Names

Non-Latino/Hispanic persons, including police officers, are often confused when people from Spanish-speaking countries use two last names in contrast to those from English-speaking countries in which the last name is the family name and name of record. For example, a person named Octavio Chavez Hernandez may use Chavez as his last name of record rather than

Hernandez, which is his mother's last name. Some Latino/Hispanics may inadvertently mislead criminal justice authorities by telling them that the second of their two names is their name of record; some may do this intentionally. This confusion can result in a having to initiate a records check, issuing a citation, or even charging an individual using the wrong name. Another source of confusion is the fact that Latino/Hispanic married women may add their husbands' last name to their maiden name. They would add the Spanish word *de* (which means "of") before their married name, thus Octavio's wife, Ana Maria, would become Ana Maria de Chavez.

Importance of Family

Understanding the importance of family for Latino/Hispanic Americans might be of significant value in community peacekeeping and crime fighting. Obviously, with over 25 different cultural groups that make up the Latino/Hispanic American category, many differences exist among the groups in their family experiences. We would like to address some family characteristics that many of the different cultural groups share.

La familia is perhaps one of the most significant considerations in working and communicating with Latino/Hispanic Americans. (In places where we use the Spanish term, we have done so to indicate the additional cultural meanings that are not captured in the English term *family*.) The Latino/Hispanic American family is most clearly characterized by bonds of interdependence, unity, and loyalty, and includes nuclear and extended family members as well as networks of neighbors, friends, and community members. Primary importance is given to the history of the family, which is firmly rooted in the set of obligations tied to both the past and the future. In considering the different loyalty bonds, the parent–child relationship emerges as primary, with all children owing *respeto* to parents (*respeto* connotes cultural meanings beyond those in the English term *respect*).

Traditionally, the role of the father has been that of the disciplinarian, decision maker, and head of the household. The father's word is the law, and he is not to be questioned. The father tends to focus his attention on the economic and well-being issues of the family and less on the social and emotional issues. The mother, on the other hand, is seen as balancing the father's role by providing for the emotional and expressive issues of the family. Extended family members such as grandmothers, aunts and uncles, and godparents (*compadrazgo*) may supplement the mother's emotional support. In the Latino/Hispanic American family, the oldest son is traditionally the secondary decision maker to the father and the principal inheritor (*primogenito*) of the family. Because of the central nature of the Latino/Hispanic American family, it is common for police officers to come into contact with members of nuclear and extended families in the course of working with the Latino/Hispanic American community.

One key to the success of law enforcement officers in working with the Latino/Hispanic American extended network is the knowledge of how best to communicate within the family context and an understanding of whom to speak with for information, observations, and questions.

The Role of the Man and the Woman in a Latino/Hispanic American Family

Despite appearances, however, in many Latino/Hispanic American families, the father may appear to be the sole decision maker, but many other individuals may come into the picture. Generally, if there are grandparents in the household, the father may consult them, and also his wife, on major decisions.

In the case of law enforcement matters, it may be of great importance if officers can provide the father and the family with some privacy to discuss key issues. With central values like *respeto* and *machismo* (see later) in the Latino/Hispanic American culture, it is critical for the father and other family members to demonstrate control in family situations. Thus, law enforcement officers may find that the best way to maintain control in a situation is by allowing the citizen to think through a decision, come to the same conclusion as that of the officer, and exercise self-control in behaving in the best interests of all parties concerned.

Within the Latino/Hispanic American family, the sex roles are clearly defined; boys and girls are taught from childhood two different codes of behavior (Comas-Diaz & Griffith, 1988). Traditional sex roles can be discussed in the context of the two codes of gender-related behaviors: *machismo* and *marianismo*. *Machismo* literally means maleness, manliness, and virility. Within the Latino/Hispanic American cultural context, *machismo* means that the male is responsible for the well-being and honor of the family and is in the provider role. Machismo is also associated with having power over women, as well as responsibility for guarding and protecting them. Boys are seen as strong by nature and do not need the protection that is required by girls, who are seen as weak by nature.

Women are socialized into the role of *marianismo*, based on the beliefs about the Virgin Mary, in which women are considered spiritually superior to men and therefore able to endure all suffering inflicted by men (Stevens, 1973). Women are expected to be self-sacrificing in favor of their husbands and children. Within the context of the Latino/Hispanic American family, the role of the woman is as homemaker and caretaker of the children. In the current U.S. context, the traditional gender roles of women and men in the Latino/Hispanic American community have undergone much change, which has resulted in conflicts. Since women have begun to work, earn money, and have some of the financial independence men have (e.g., they can go out and socialize with others outside of the family), they have started pursuing many experiences inconsistent with the traditional Latino/Hispanic female role.

Because of these changes, there are no clear-cut rules as to whether law enforcement officers should go to the male head of the household or to the female family member; however, officers would probably be more correct if they address the father first in law enforcement inquiries.

Children, Adolescents, and Youth

Within the Latino/Hispanic American family, the ideal child is obedient and respectful of his or her parents and other elders. Adults may at times talk in front of the children as if they are not present and as if the children cannot understand the adults' conversations. Children are taught *respeto*, which dictates the appropriate behavior toward all authority figures, older people, parents, relatives, and others. If children are disrespectful, they are punished and scolded. In many traditional families, it is considered appropriate for parents (and other relatives) to physically discipline a disrespectful and misbehaving child.

In Latino/Hispanic American households, there is a high reliance on family members (older children and other adults) to help care for younger children. Both parents often work. As such, it is not uncommon for Latino/Hispanic American families to have latchkey children or have children cared for by older children in the neighborhood. In homes where English is a second language, often children have a special role in being the intermediaries for their parents on external community matters because of the ability of the younger individuals to learn English and the American ways of doing things. Children often serve as translators and interpreters for peace officers in their communication and relations with Latino/Hispanic American families involved in legal matters, immigration concerns, and community resources.

Although the use of children and family members as translators is viewed as professionally and culturally inappropriate, often it is the only means available to the law enforcement officer. In such situations, it is suggested that the officer review what role is expected of the youthful member of the family. The officer needs to see how sensitive a topic might be for different family members. Moreover, the consequence of an incorrect translation must be evaluated. For example, asking a juvenile to translate to his or her parents, who speak no English, that the juvenile has been involved in drinking and riding in a stolen vehicle may result in significantly changed content. Because of the embarrassment and fear of punishment on the part of the juvenile, and possibly a sense of shame or embarrassment to the parents, the message may be altered by the child to avoid negative ramifications. In all cases, when a child is acting as a translator for parents, the officer should direct all verbal and nonverbal communication to the parents. Otherwise, the parents may view the officer's lack of attention to them as an insult. Such sensitivity by the peace officer is particularly important for Latino/Hispanic Americans because of the cultural value of *personalismo*, which emphasizes the importance of the personal quality of any interaction. This cultural concept implies that relationships occur between particular individuals as persons, not as representatives of institutions (e.g., law enforcement), or merely as individuals performing a role (e.g., as a person who enforces the law).

COMMUNICATION STYLES OF LATINO/HISPANIC AMERICANS

Although we do not wish to create stereotypes of any kind, key features of Latino/Hispanic American verbal and nonverbal communication styles necessitate explanation. Misunderstanding resulting from style differences can result in perceptions of poor community services from police agencies, conflicts resulting from such misunderstandings, and safety and control issues for the peace officer.

1. Latino/Hispanic Americans' high cultural value for *la familia* results in a very strong family and group orientation. As such, officers should not view the frequently seen behavior of "eye checking" with other family members before answering and the lack of the use of "I" statements and/or self-reference as Latino/Hispanic Americans' not being straightforward about themselves or their relationships. The officer may be concerned because a Latino/Hispanic American witness may wish to use the pronoun "we" when the situation may call for a personal observation involving an "I" statement. For example, a Latino/Hispanic American family member who witnessed a store robbery may first nonverbally check with other family members before describing what he or she saw. Such verbal and nonverbal behavior is consistent with the family and group orientation of Latino/Hispanic Americans.

2. Speaking Spanish to others in the presence of a law enforcement officer, even though the officer requested responses in English, should not automatically be interpreted as an insult to or an attempt to hide information from the officer. In times of stress, such as a law enforcement situation, those who speak English as a second language automatically revert to their first language, which is the more accessible and comfortable language for them. Moreover, speaking Spanish gives the individual a greater range of expression (to discuss and clarify complex issues with other speakers and family members), thus yielding clearer, more useful information to law enforcement personnel about critical events.

3. It is important for officers to take the time to get information from witnesses, victims, and suspects even if the individuals have limited skills in speaking English (the use of officers who speak Spanish, translators, and language bank resources will help). Often Latino/Hispanic Americans have not been helped in crime-fighting and peacekeeping situations because officers could not or did not take information from nonnative English speakers.

4. Although Latino/Hispanic Americans may show respect to law enforcement officers because of police authority, they do not necessarily trust the officers or the organization. *Respeto* is extended to elders and those who are in authority. This respect is denoted in the Spanish language by the use of *usted* (the formal you) rather than *tu* (the informal you). Showing respect, however, does not ensure trust. The cultural value of *confianza* (or trust) takes some time to develop. Like many from ethnic minority communities, Latino/Hispanic Americans have experienced some degree of prejudice and discrimination from the majority community, and citizens with such experiences need time to

develop trust with law enforcement officers, who are identified as being a part of the majority community.

5. The cultural value of *personalismo* emphasizes the importance of the person involved in any interaction. Latino/Hispanic Americans take into strong consideration not only the content of any communication but also the context and relationship of the communicator. This means, for effective communications, it is important for the officer to provide information about why questions are asked, who is the person asking the question (i.e., information about the officer), and how the information will be used in the context. In addition, context for Latino/Hispanic Americans means taking some time to find out, as well as to self-disclose, some background information (e.g., living in the same neighborhood, having similar concerns about crime). Additional contextual elements, such as providing explanations and information to Latino/Hispanic Americans about procedures, laws, and so forth before asking them questions or requesting their help, will ease the work of the officer. By providing background information and establishing prior relationships with community members, law enforcement agencies and officers build a context for cooperation with Latino/Hispanic American individuals.

6. Officers should recognize nonverbal and other cultural nuances that may detract from effective communication. Many Latino/Hispanic Americans, especially younger individuals, find it uncomfortable and sometimes inappropriate to maintain eye contact with authority figures such as police officers. Strong eye contact with someone who is of higher position, importance, or authority is considered a lack of *respeto* in Latin/Hispanic American cultures. As such, many citizens from this background may deflect their eyes from police officers. It is important that officers not automatically read this nonverbal behavior as indicative of a lack of trust or as a dishonest response.

7. Latino/Hispanic Americans may exhibit behaviors that appear to be evasive, such as claiming not to have any identification or saying that they do not speak English. In some of the countries from which many Latino/Hispanic Americans have emigrated, the police and law enforcement agencies are aligned with a politically repressive government. The work of the police and of law enforcement in those countries is not one of public service. Therefore, many Latino/Hispanic Americans may have similar "fear" reactions to law enforcement officers in the United States. It is suggested that officers take the time to explain the need for identification and cooperation, and that they acknowledge the importance of comprehension on the part of the Latino/Hispanic American individual(s) involved.

8. Latino/Hispanic people from Latin America and Spain can be extremely expressive in their body language and facial expressions and tend to converse in close proximity to others. Officers should not, in most cases, believe that the expressive gestures are a threat to their personal safety. (Natella & Madera, 2008).

KEY ISSUES IN LAW ENFORCEMENT

Machismo

The term *machismo*, discussed earlier in the chapter, comes from the Spanish word *macho*. It refers to a strong sense of masculine pride or exaggerated sense of power or strength, a combination of attitudes basic to the Spanish-speaking world (Webster's New World Dictionary). Criminal justice officers, especially those in law enforcement, need to be aware of this potential trait found in Latino/Hispanic males they encounter. Criminal justice trainers (academies and in-field) should prepare students and probationary employees for the possibility that they may encounter a higher degree of resistance from Latino/Hispanic men due to machismo. It can be difficult to deal with individuals manifesting this trait or attitude. For example, in domestic violence incidents in which the man is the responsible party, he might not understand that hurting his spouse constitutes a criminal offense and is not just a matter of family, but a matter of civil control (Natella & Madera, 2008).

Underreporting of Crimes and Cooperation with Law Enforcement

Law enforcement officials may encounter difficulty getting cooperation from Latino/Hispanic American crime victims. (See Chapter 1 for an expanded discussion on this.) To some degree, this lack of cooperation relates to the fear of retaliation within the Latino/Hispanic community. Their past experiences with some law enforcement agencies in their countries of origin (e.g., repressive military force in their native country) may result in a reluctance to report crimes. Because of perceived "unresponsiveness" by police, they may not seek police assistance or help. Many people bring with them memories of how police within their home countries have brutalized and violated them and others. In addition, many immigrants and refugees are simply not knowledgeable about the legal system of the United States and may try to avoid any contact with law enforcement personnel. Another reason for lack of reporting or cooperation with the criminal justice system is the stereotype of law enforcement agencies as discriminatory. Outreach and community policing efforts will enhance relationships with Latino/Hispanic American communities and may help alleviate the underreporting of crimes and improve relationships and cooperation.

Hate Crimes against Latino/Hispanics

In the five-year period between 2003 and 2007, there was a 40 percent increase (from 426 hate bias crimes in 2003 to 595 in 2007) of hate bias crimes in which the victims were Latino/Hispanics. Official hate crime tracking showed increases through 2010 (the most recent year for which data are available). "Some groups that monitor hate crimes in the United States see the problem as part of a broader pattern, driven by anti-immigrant rhetoric and extremist groups looking for a scapegoat as the economy continues to shed thousands of jobs" (Hoffet, 2009).

However, between 2010 and 2011, anti-Latino hate crimes fell 31 percent, from 534 in 2010 to 405 in 2011. "It's not clear what might be behind that drop, other than an apparent diminution in anti-Latino and anti-immigrant propaganda as negative attention focused on Muslims." (Potok, 2012). It should be noted that when hate crimes targeting Latino/Hispanics were up, so were reports of discrimination against them. Mark Hugo Lopez and colleagues at the Pew Hispanic Center wrote that

> the national political backlash against illegal immigration has created new divisions among Latinos and heightened their concerns about discrimination against members of their ethnic group—including those who were born in the United States or who immigrated legally. . . . Today, more than six in ten (61 percent) Latinos say that discrimination against Hispanics is a "major problem," up from 54 percent who said that in 2007. Asked to state the most important factor leading to discrimination, a plurality of 36 percent now cites immigration status, up from a minority of 23 percent who said the same in 2007. (Lopez et al., 2010)

Racial Profiling of Latino/Hispanic Americans

Racial profiling, discussed in Chapter 13, is a major concern for people within many minority groups, but is particularly the case for African Americans, Arab Americans, and Latino/Hispanic Americans. A widespread belief among many Latino/Hispanic community members is that a significant determining factor as to whether peace officers exercise discretion in stopping a vehicle is race and ethnicity. In a February 2009 report, an immigration rights group called, "Casa de Maryland," alleged that ICE agents deliberately arrested, two years earlier, 24 individual of Hispanic/Latino background because they had been advised to increase their quota of 1,000 arrests per team ("bring more bodies"). This event took place at a 7-Eleven store where day laborers were known to convene. Advocates from Casa de Maryland claimed that Hispanics only were targeted without cause, and that other customers were ignored. (CASA de Maryland, 2009).

As this example suggests, racial profiling of Latino/Hispanic Americans by law enforcement still takes place. (For a complete discussion of racial profiling, see Chapter 13.) Yet like all people, Latino/Hispanic Americans must be able to trust that they will be treated fairly and protected as part of their involvement and association with local law enforcement and public safety. This is of particular importance when there might be some perceptions, assumptions, and/or stereotypes among community residents as to who might be reported to and questioned by ICE (with the possibility of deportation and detention because of real or suspected immigration status). In Chapter 10, recommendations are made for local law enforcement agencies that network with ICE and participate in the Secure Communities program on how they can maintain a good partnership with the Latino/Hispanic American community.

Increasing Police Services to the Latino/Hispanic American Community

The Police Neighborhood Resource Center, started in 1991 in the largely Hispanic community of Rolling Meadows, Illinois, showed positive results of cooperation among the police department, the Latino/Hispanic American community, and local and regional businesses. When it lost its funding in 2009, the program was terminated, and the crime rate began rising. During the years of operation, crime rates in Rolling Meadows, in particular East Park Apartments, were significantly reduced and much of the reduction was believed to be associated with the center. After it closed, the number of reported shootings, stabbings, robberies, aggravated batteries, and crimes against persons in the East Park Apartments increased. In 2008, the Police Department received 73 calls for such crimes; that number rose to 86 in 2009, 94 in both 2010 and 2011, and 119 in 2012. However, when the department hired a bilingual social worker in 2013 whose job it was to work with families in the neighborhood, the crime rate dropped once again. Rolling Meadows Police Chief David Scanlan noted that "we've been working very hard to establish communication, get the program up and running, mitigate crime problems in that area and make it a place where families want to live and where kids can play comfortably" (Owens-Schiele, 2013).

The outreach approach of using bilingual community service officers (CSOs) who are non-sworn officers (i.e., they hold badges and wear uniforms) to serve the ethnic communities in San Diego, California, provides yet another viable and effective model for the Latino/Hispanic American community as a whole. The CSOs provide many of the informational, referral, educational, and crime-reporting services available through the police department. Likewise, the use of Latino/Hispanic American police outreach coordinators is successfully used in some communities to liaison and outreach with residents of the community.

Law enforcement should be aware of the need to bridge the service gap and to reinforce the Latino/Hispanic American community with local and statewide law enforcement and public safety agencies. To this end, meetings between police executives and Latino/Hispanic American leaders of community-based and advocacy agencies have been found to be helpful when there are issues to resolve or there are allegations of misconduct by officers. Other efforts to build Latino/Hispanic police-community relationships include Durham, North Carolina's a Spanish-language version of their Citizens Police Academy. The classes, free and open to the public, meet twice each week to give residents first-hand knowledge of the operations of the police department ("Citizens Police Academy," 2013). Another way to bridge the gap is to have officers learn Spanish; some officers will attest that even "survival" Spanish-language training and crash courses in minority community relations have some degree of effectiveness. The use of everyday greetings and courteous phrases in Spanish indicates officers' respect and positive attitude and is seen favorably by members of the Latino/Hispanic American community. (See Chapter 4 for a discussion of language training in police departments.)

Increasing the Number of Latino/Hispanic American Police Officers

> Racial/ethnic minority police officers, including Latino/a police officers, support policing in our democratic society as representatives of a substantial proportion of the population in the United States. In addition, like other racial and ethnic minority police officers, Latino/a police officers can increase police effectiveness through the specific knowledge, skills, experience, and image that they bring to their departments. (Barlow & Barlow, 2013)

In the past decade, the number of Latino/Hispanic Americans has significantly increased in federal, state, and local law enforcement positions. Chapter 2 provides details of this increase at every level. Despite these improving numbers, Latino/Hispanic Americans are still underrepresented in local police departments and sheriffs' offices. Local law enforcement's attempts to effectively serve states, cities, and community neighborhoods with large Latino/Hispanic American populations are hampered by the proportionately small number of Latino/Hispanic American officers, given the dispersion of the Latino/Hispanic American population within the United States. A variety of reasons exist for such underrepresentation, including (1) the history of law enforcement relationships with Latino/Hispanic American communities; (2) the limited interest in and lack of knowledge about careers in law enforcement among Latino/Hispanic Americans; (3) the image that many in Latino/Hispanic American communities hold of law enforcement personnel; (4) the concerns that members of the community have regarding background checks and immigration status, physical requirements, and the application process; (5) ineffective and misdirected law enforcement recruitment and outreach efforts within the Latino/Hispanic American community; and (6) the lack of role models and advocates for law enforcement careers for Latino/Hispanic Americans. Law enforcement agencies have clearly seen the need for increasing their ability to serve the Latino/Hispanic American community with more bilingual/bicultural personnel and more visible role models.

Summary

- The label Latino/Hispanic American encompasses over 25 diverse ethnic, cultural, and regional groups from North, Central, and South America. Law enforcement officials must be aware of the differences between these groups (e.g., nationality, native cultural and regional differences and perceptions, and language dialects), as well as the within-group differences that may result from individual life experiences (e.g., sociopolitical turmoil). Since key stereotypes of Latino/Hispanic Americans by mainstream Americans are regarded as more negative than positive, it is important that police officers make a special effort to extend respect and dignity to this community of proud people with a culturally rich heritage.

- The preferred term for referring to Latino/Hispanic Americans varies with the context, group, and experiences of Latino/Hispanic American individuals. However, Pew research survey results indicate that the majority prefer to be identified with their family's country of origin rather than with pan-ethnic terms. When in doubt and a designation is required, officers should ask individuals which term they prefer. Spanish speakers and people from Latino/Hispanic backgrounds may take offense if law enforcement officers describe them as a Latino or Hispanic or incorrectly associate them with a country other than their own.

- Officers are advised to provide feedback to their peers whenever offensive terms, slurs, labels, and/or actions are used with Latino/Hispanic Americans. Such feedback will help reduce the risk of misunderstanding and improve the working relationships of officers within the Latino/Hispanic American communities.

- The experience of Latino/Hispanic Americans with law enforcement officers in the United States has been complicated by their perceptions of immigration law enforcement against undocumented or unauthorized immigrants, by the discriminatory treatment they have received in the United States, and by perceptions of police ineffectiveness and unresponsiveness. Some citizens may still remember this history and carry with them stereotypes of police services as something to be feared and avoided.

- The number of unauthorized immigrants (also referred to as undocumented, illegals, and illegal aliens) in the United States has fluctuated from a peak in 2007 of 12 million to an estimated 11.2 million in 2010. The reasons cited for the decrease were the poor economy in the U.S., a more secure border, and fewer births among Latino/Hispanic women. Within the public at large, there has been a political backlash against illegal immigration and even against Latino/Hispanic people, including those who were born in the U.S. or who immigrated legally.

- It is important to have an understanding about some of the myths and stereotypes of Latino/Hispanic Americans that contribute to the prejudice, discrimination, and bias this population encounters. The key to effectiveness with any ethnic or racial group is to be aware of these stereotypes and to monitor our thinking and behaviors when the stereotypes do not fit the persons with whom we are interacting.

- Many differences exist among the groups collectively described as Latino/Hispanic. However, *la familia* is perhaps the most significant concept to understand in working and communicating with these communities. The Latino/Hispanic American family is often characterized by bonds of interdependence, unity, and loyalty, and includes nuclear and extended family members as well as networks of neighbors, friends, and community members. To interact effectively with Latino/Hispanic individuals, law enforcement personnel should understand traditional gender roles in the family structure.

- Between 2003 and 2007, hate bias crimes against Latino/Hispanics increased by 40 percent. The increase of hate crime was attributed to the poor economy in the U.S. and anti-immigrant rhetoric. Between 2010 and 2011, anti-Latino hate crime fell 31 percent.

- Some Latino/Hispanic Americans may be concerned with their inability to communicate clearly or about possible reprisal from the police, based on their experiences in politically repressive countries. To communicate effectively, peace officers should maintain contact, provide extra time, use translators, and be patient with speakers. Officers must recognize the nonverbal aspects of some Latino/Hispanic Americans' communication styles, such as eye contact, touch, gestures, and emotionality. As in all cases when English is the second language, it is important to remember that listening and comprehension skills are usually better than speaking skills.

- For a variety of reasons, Latino/Hispanic Americans may be reluctant to report crimes and may not seek police assistance and help. It is important for law enforcement departments and officials to build relationships and working partnerships with Latino/Hispanic American communities using strategies such as community offices, bilingual officers, and participation by officers in community activities. Law enforcement officials need to go out of their way to establish trust, provide outreach efforts, and win cooperation to effectively serve Latino/Hispanic Americans. Building partnerships focused on community collaboration in the fight against crime is key to effectiveness.

Discussion Questions and Issues

1. *Latino/Hispanic Americans Viewing Law Enforcement as Not Sensitive.* In the historical information section of this chapter, we noted many associations made about immigration law enforcement that may leave Latino/Hispanic Americans with the view that law enforcement agencies are not sensitive, effective, and responsive. Suggest ways to improve such possible negative points of view.

2. *Diversity among Latino/Hispanic Americans.* Latino/Hispanic Americans comprise more than 25 diverse regional, national, ethnic, and cultural groups. Which groups are you most likely to encounter in crime fighting and peacekeeping in your work? Which groups do you anticipate encountering in your future work?

3. *Choice of Terms.* Use of the terms *Latino, Hispanic, Chicano, Mexican, La Raza, Puerto Rican,* and so forth is confusing for many people. How might you find out which term to use when referring to an individual if ethnic and cultural

information of this kind is necessary? What would you do if the term you use seems to engender a negative reaction?

4. *Offensive Terms and Labels.* Offensive terms should not be used in law enforcement work at any time. Give three practical reasons for this perspective. How would you go about helping other officers who use such terms in the course of their work to become aware of their offensiveness?

5. *Effects of Myths and Stereotypes.* Describe some of the Latino/Hispanic American stereotypes that you have heard of or encountered. What effect might these stereotypes have on Latino/Hispanic Americans? Suggest ways to manage these stereotypes in law enforcement. In what ways can you help an officer who uses stereotypes about Latino/Hispanic Americans to become aware of the effects of such stereotypes?

6. *Verbal and Nonverbal Communication Style Variations among Cultures.* How do you think the information in this chapter about verbal and nonverbal communication styles

can help officers in their approach to Latino/Hispanic American citizens? Does understanding the cultural components of the style and behaviors help you to become more sensitive and objective about your reactions? In what ways might you use your understanding about Latino/Hispanic American family dynamics in law enforcement?

7. *Avoidance of Law Enforcement and Underreporting of Crimes.* Why do you think that many Latino/Hispanic

Americans keep to their own communities and underreport crimes of violence? How can police agencies be of greater service to Latino/Hispanic American communities in this regard?

8. *The Future of Latino/Hispanic Americans and Law Enforcement.* The Latino/Hispanic American population is the fastest-growing segment of the U.S. population. What implications do you see for law enforcement in terms of services, language, recruitment, and training?

References

Ayala, Elaine and Ellen Huet. "Hispanic May Be a Race on 2020 Census." (2013, February 4). *San Francisco Chronicle.* Retrieved August 29, 2013, from www.sfgate.com/nation/article/Hispanic-may-be-a-race-on-2020-census-4250866.php

Barlow, David E., and Melissa H. Barlow. (2013). "Hiring Latino/a Police Officers: What Police Administrators Need to Know." Unpublished paper submitted to the Academy of Criminal Justice Sciences conference in 2013.

Bernal, G., and A. Estrada. (1985). "Cuban Refugee and Minority Experiences: A Book Review." *Hispanic Journal of Behavioral Sciences, 7,* 105–128.

CASA de Maryland. (2009). "New report shows ICE Agents were ordered to indiscriminately target immigrant communities in Baltimore in order to reach quota." Retrieved January 6, 2014, from www.casademaryland.org/index.php?id=666&option=com_content&task=view

Comas-Diaz, L., and E. E. H. Griffith (Eds.). (1988). *Cross-Cultural Mental Health.* New York, NY: Wiley.

"Citizens Police Academy." (2013). City of Durham, North Carolina, Police Department. Retrieved August 28, 2013, from http://durhamnc.gov/ich/op/DPD/Pages/CPA.aspx

Gavzer, G. (1993, March 21). "Held without Hope." *Parade.*

Gonzalez-Barrera, Ana and Mark Hugo Lopez. (2013, May 1). "A Demographic Portrait of Mexican-Origin Hispanics in the United States." Pew Hispanic Center. Retrieved August 21, 2013, from www.pewhispanic.org/2013/05/01/a-demographic-portrait-of-mexican-origin-hispanics-in-the-united-states/

"Hispanic Population Trends." (2013, February 15). Pew Hispanic Center. Retrieved August 21, 2013, from www.pewhispanic.org/2013/02/15/hispanic-population-trends/ph_13-01-23_ss_hispanics1/

"Hispanic Population Trends." (2013, February 15). Pew Research Hispanic Center. Retrieved August 17, 2013 from www.pewhispanic.org/topics/population-trends/

Hoffet, Nastassja. (2009, January 27). "Immigrants Scapegoated as Economy Teeters." Retrieved July 29, 2013, from www.alternet.org/story/122863/immigrants_scapegoated_as_economy_teeters

"In Mexico, Heading North Has Lost Luster." (2013, April 3). *Contra Costa* (Calif.) *Times.* p. A6.

Lopez y Rivas, Gilberto. (1973). *The Chicanos: Life and Struggles of the Mexican Minority in the United States, trans. Elizabeth*

Martinez and Gilberto Lopez y Rivas. New York, NY: Monthly Review Press.

Lopez, Mark Hugo and Gabriel Velasco. (2011, September 28). "Childhood Poverty Among Hispanics Sets Record, Leads Nation." Pew Hispanic Center. Retrieved August 8, 2013, from www.pewhispanic.org/2011/09/28/childhood-poverty-among-hispanics-sets-record-leads-nation/

Lopez, Mark Hugo, Rich Moran, and Paul Taylor. (2010, October 28). "Illegal Immigration Backlash Worries, Divides Latinos." Pew Hispanic Center. Retrieved August 29, 2013, from www.pewhispanic.org/2010/10/28/illegal-immigration-backlash-worries-divides-latinos

Montiel, Miguel. (1978). *Hispanic Families: Critical Issues for Policy and Programs in Human Services.* Washington, D.C.: National Coalition of Hispanic Mental Health and Human Services Organizations.

Motel, Seth and Eileen Patten. (2012, June 27). "The 10 Largest Hispanic Origin Groups: Characteristics, Rankings, Top Counties." Pew Hispanic Center. Retrieved August 8, 2012, from www.pewhispanic.org/2012/06/27/the-10-largest-hispanic-origin-groups-characteristics-rankings-top-counties/

Natella, Arthur, Jr. and Pablo Paul Madera. (2008, December). "Law Enforcement Training: Factors in the Spanish-Speaking Community." *FBI Law Enforcement Bulletin. 77*(12), 12–15.

Office of Management and Budget. (1997, October 30). "Revisions to the Standards for the Classification of Federal Data on Race and Ethnicity." *Federal Register, 62*(280), 58782–85790.

Owens-Schiele, Elizabeth. (2013, May 30). "Crime Drops at Apartment Complex after Police Hire Social Worker." Chicago Tribune. Retrieved August 28, 2013, from http://articles.chicagotribune.com/2013-05-30/news/ct-tl-nw-rolling-meadows-social-services-outreach-20130530_1_east-park-apartments-scanlan-social-worker

Passel, Jeffrey S. (2005, June 14). *Unauthorized Migrants: Numbers and Characteristics.* Washington, D.C.: Pew Hispanic Center.

Passel, Jeffrey S. and D'Vera Cohn. (2011, February 1). *Unauthorized Immigrant Population: National and State Trends, 2010.* Washington D.C.: Pew Hispanic Center.

Potok, Mark. (2012, December 10). "FBI: Anti-Muslim Hate Crimes Still Up." Retrieved July 30, 2013, from www.salon.com/2012/12/10/fbi_anti_muslim_hate_crimes_still_up/

Saulny, Susan. "Hispanic Pregnancies Fall in U.S. as Women Choose Smaller Families." (2012, December 31). *New York Times.* Retrieved August 21, 2013, from www.nytimes.com/2013/01/01/health/us-birthrate-dips-especially-for-hispanics.html

Stevens, E. (1973). "Machismo and Marianismo." *Transaction-Society, 10*(6), 57–63.

Taylor, Paul, Mark Hugo Lopez, Jessica Martinez, and Gabriel Velasco. (2012, April 4). "When Labels Don't Fit: Hispanics and Their Views of Identity." Pew Hispanic Center. Retrieved June 26, 2013, from www.pewhispanic.org/2012/04/04/when-labels-dont-fit-hispanics-and-their-views-of-identity/

"U.S. Birth Rate Falls to New Lows." (2013, January 9). Pew Research Center. Retrieved August 21, 2013, from www.pewresearch.org/daily-number/u-s-birth-rate-falls-to-new-lows/

United States Census (2010). U.S. Census Bureau. Retrieved June 26, 2013, from www.census.gov/2010census/

Law Enforcement Contact with Arab Americans and Other Middle Eastern Groups

LEARNING OBJECTIVES

After reading this chapter, you should be able to:

- List the groups belonging to the category "Middle Easterners," define "Arab" and "Muslim," and identify the non-Arabic-speaking Middle Eastern groups.

- Describe the reasons for Arab/Middle Eastern immigration to the United States and indicate where the largest populations of Arab Americans reside in the United States.

- Provide examples of differences among Middle Eastern groups as well as common basic Arab values.

- Explain the impact of Arab/Middle Eastern stereotypes on law enforcement and on Arab Americans and other Middle Easterners.

- Identify basic ways in which law enforcement can show respect toward the religion Islam.

- Understand select characteristics of traditional Arab American/Middle Eastern extended family structure as it relates to law enforcement contact.

- Define characteristics of traditional Arab/Middle Eastern communication styles and cultural practices, including taboos.

- List and discuss key issues associated with law enforcement contact with Arab American and other Middle Eastern groups.

OUTLINE

- **Introduction**
- **Middle Easterners and Related Terminology Defined**
- **Historical Information and Arab American Demographics**
- **Differences and Similarities**
- **Stereotypes**
- **Islamic Religion**
- **Family Structure**
- **Communication Styles and Cultural Practices**

- Key Issues in Law Enforcement
- Summary
- Discussion Questions and Issues

INTRODUCTION

Middle Easterners come to the United States for numerous reasons: to gain an education and begin their careers, to escape unstable political situations in their countries of origin, and to invest in commercial enterprises with the goal of gaining legal entry into the country. Most people in law enforcement have contact with Middle Easterners from a number of different countries, and thus would benefit from having basic knowledge about past and present world events that impact stereotypes of and dynamics among Middle Easterners. Attitudes among Americans toward Middle Easterners, as well as geopolitical events in the Middle East, can have ongoing implications for law enforcement.

Established Americans of Arab origin are sometimes treated as if they had just arrived from the Middle East and might be potential terrorists. This perception increased significantly after the terrorist attacks of 9/11, and continues to the present. Stereotypes, which have long been imprinted in people's minds, can and do significantly affect people's perceptions of Arab Americans, whether they are second- or third-generation American citizens or recent refugees.

MIDDLE EASTERNERS AND RELATED TERMINOLOGY DEFINED

Among the general population of the United States there is considerable confusion as to who Middle Easterners are and, specifically, who Arabs are. Although commonly thought of as Arabs, Iranians and Turks are not Arabs. Many people assume that all Muslims are Arabs, and vice versa. In fact, many Arabs are also Christians, and the world's Muslim population is actually composed of dozens of ethnic groups. (The country with the largest Muslim population is Indonesia, which is located in Southeast Asia—not in the Middle East.) Nevertheless, the predominant religion among Arabs is Islam, and its followers are called *Muslims*. They are also sometimes called *Moslems*, but *Muslim* is the preferred term because it is closer to the Arabic pronunciation.

The following excerpt is from *100 Questions You Have Always Wanted to Ask about Arab Americans,* compiled in 2001 by the Detroit Free Press staff in consultation with Arab American community members. (To date, the Detroit Metropolitan area still has the largest Arab American population in the United States.)

SHOULD I SAY ARAB, ARABIC, OR ARABIAN?

Arab is a noun for a person and is used as an adjective as in "Arab country." Arabic is the name of the language and generally is not used as an adjective. Arabian is an adjective that refers to Saudi Arabia, the Arabian Peninsula, or the "Arabian horse." When either ethnicity or nationality is relevant, it is more precise and accurate to specify the country by using Lebanese, Yemeni, or whatever is appropriate.

What all Arabs have in common is the Arabic language, even though spoken Arabic differs among countries (e.g., Algerian Arabic is different from Jordanian Arabic). The following countries are generally considered to constitute the Middle East and all are Arab countries with the exception of three:

- Aden
- Bahrain
- Egypt

- Iran (non-Arab country)
- Iraq
- Israel (non-Arab country)

- Jordan
- Kuwait
- Lebanon
- Oman
- Palestinian Authority (also referred to as Palestine)
- Qatar
- Saudi Arabia
- Syria
- Turkey (non-Arab country)
- United Arab Emirates
- Yemen

There are other Arab countries that are not located in the Middle East (e.g., Algeria, Tunisia, Morocco, Libya), in which the majority population speaks Arabic and adheres to the religion Islam. In this chapter we primarily cover information on refugees and immigrants from Arab countries in the Middle East. They constitute the majority of Middle Eastern newcomers who bring cultural differences and special issues requiring clarification for law enforcement. Issues related to the established Arab American community (i.e., people who began arriving in the United States in the late nineteenth century) are covered as well. We begin with a brief description of the populations from the three non-Arab countries.

Iranians and Turks

Iranians use a variation of the Arabic script in their writing but for the most part speak Farsi (Persian) and not Arabic. Turks speak Turkish, although there are minority groups in Turkey that speak Kurdish, Arabic, Greek, and Armenian. About 98 percent of Iranians and Turks are Muslim. Armenians, who are largely Christian, were a persecuted minority in Turkey. The Armenian genocide, between 1915 and 1923, claimed the lives of between 1 and 1.5 million people. Animosity still exists between some Armenians and Turks. Turkey continues to deny that the Armenians were the victims of genocide during World War I (Today's Zaman, 2012).

Many Iranians in the United States are Jewish or Bahai, both of which groups are minorities in Iran. Of the Muslim population in Iran, most belong to the Shi'a sect of Islam, which is the state religion. Persians are the largest ethnic group in Iran, making up about 61 percent of the population (World Factbook, 2013), but there are other ethnic populations, including Kurds and Arabs. Many Iranian Americans and Turkish Americans came to the United States in the 1970s and were from upper-class professional groups such as doctors, lawyers, and engineers. During the Iranian hostage crisis in 1979, Iranians in the United States were frequently targets of hate crimes and anti-Iranian sentiment; the same attitudes prevailed against other Middle Easterners (Arabs) and South Asians (Indians from India) who were mistakenly labeled as Iranian. Many Jewish Iranians who now live in the United States left Iran after the fall of the Shah; there are large Iranian Jewish populations in the San Francisco Bay Area, Los Angeles, and New York. Also, populations of Muslim Iranians are found in major U.S. cities, such as New York, Chicago, and Los Angeles. Although Iranians and Turks are not Arabs, some of their family values with respect to pride, dignity, and honor are similar to those in the traditional Arab world.

Israelis

Israel is the only country in the Middle East in which the majority of the population is not Muslim. Approximately 20 percent of the population in Israel is made up of Arabs, both Christian and Muslim. Approximately three-quarters of the Israeli population is Jewish (World Factbook, 2013), with the Jewish population divided into two main groups: Ashkenazim and Sephardim. The Ashkenazim are descended from members of the Jewish communities of Central and Eastern Europe. The majority of Israeli Jews are Ashkenazi, while the minority of Israeli Jews (by an increasingly small margin) are Sephardim, having come originally from Spain, other Mediterranean countries, and the Arab countries of the Middle East. Israeli immigrants in the United States may be either Ashkenazi or Sephardic; their physical appearance will not indicate to an officer what their ethnicity is. An Israeli may look like an American Jew, a Christian, or a Muslim Arab—or none of these.

Most Arabs who live within the borders of Israel are Palestinians whose families stayed in Israel after the Arab–Israeli war of 1948, following the birth of Israel as a nation. The Six-Day War in 1967 resulted in the occupation of lands that formerly belonged to Egypt, Syria, and Jordan, in which the majority of the population was Palestinian. Thus, until the signing of the Oslo 1993 peace accords between Israel and the Palestine Liberation Organization (PLO), Israel occupied territories with a population of approximately 1 million Palestinians. The Palestinian/Israeli situation in the Middle East has created a great deal of hostility on both sides. In the fall of 2000, failure to reach a negotiated settlement agreement required by the Oslo peace accords of 1993 resulted in a period of increased hostilities. The tension continued and intensified during what is referred to as the second *intifada* or Palestinian "uprising," which took place between approximately 2000 and 2005. Hostilities continued in 2006 with the outbreak of war involving Israel and Lebanon, associated with the rocket attacks by Hezbollah and Hamas into Israel proper. Similarly, violence in Gaza, which began in December 2008, was also associated with rocket attacks into Israel and had repercussions around the world, including in the United States. These political tensions have definite implications for law enforcement officials in the United States, especially in communities that contain large populations of Jews and Arabs, or where Israelis and Palestinians reside in large numbers (e.g., Los Angeles, New York, Chicago). All law enforcement agencies should become knowledgeable about individuals and groups with extremist views who operate in their jurisdictions or regions.

Public events such as Israeli Independence Day celebrations and Israeli or Palestinian political rallies have the potential for confrontation, although most of these events have transpired peacefully. Police presence is required at such events, but as with other situations, excessive police presence can escalate hostilities. Law enforcement officials need to be well informed about current events in the Middle East, as conflicts there often have a ripple effect across the world.

The impact of the "Arab Spring" in Arab-majority countries in the Middle East and North Africa at the end of 2010 was also felt in major cities around the world via demonstrations and other various forms of protest. For the most part, U.S. cities experienced only minor protests. However, it appeared that the 2011 Occupy Wall Street protestors modeled their demonstrations on those of the Arab Spring (Knafo, 2011).

The monitoring of world events and community trends will help police officers take a preventive posture that can ultimately avoid confrontation among various Middle Eastern ethnic groups in this country. Chapter 11 goes into more depth on the importance of such monitoring.

HISTORICAL INFORMATION AND ARAB AMERICAN DEMOGRAPHICS

Although many recent Middle Eastern immigrants and refugees in the United States left their countries due to political reasons, not all Arab Americans did so. There have been two major waves of Arab immigration to the United States. The first wave came between 1880 and World War I, and was largely from Syria and what is known today as Lebanon (at the time these areas were part of the Turkish Ottoman Empire). Of the immigrants who settled during this wave, approximately 90 percent were Christian. Many people came to further themselves economically (thus they were immigrants, and not refugees forced to leave their countries); but in addition, many of the young men wanted to avoid military service for the Ottoman Empire (Samhan, personal communication, August 2006). A substantial percentage of these immigrants were farmers or artisans, and they became involved in the business of peddling their goods to farmers, moving from town to town. In the way of crime statistics, not much is reported, partly because in the Arab immigrant community, people took care of their own (Samhan, personal communication, August 2006).

In sharp contrast to the first wave of immigrants in terms of motivation and compositional characteristics, the second wave of Arab immigration to the United States, beginning after World War II, came in large part as students and professionals. They came seeking to escape economic instability and political unrest in their home countries. As a result, these groups brought a "political consciousness unknown to earlier immigrants" (John Zogby, personal communication, August 2013). The largest group of second-wave immigrants was made up of Palestinians, many of whom came around 1948 (the time of the partition of Palestine which resulted in Israel's independence). In the 1970s, after the Six-Day War among Israel, Egypt, Syria, and Jordan, another large influx of Palestinians was witnessed by the United States. In the 1980s, a large group of Lebanese came as a result of the civil war in Lebanon. Yemenis (from Yemen) have continued to arrive throughout the twentieth century; also many Syrians and Iraqis have made the United States their home since the 1950s and 1960s because of political instability in their countries (John Zogby, personal communication, August 2013). Thus, these second-wave immigrants came largely because of political turmoil in their respective home countries and have been instrumental in changing the nature of the Arab American community in the United States.

The most dramatic example of how immigration from the Middle East has affected the United States is the Detroit area in Michigan. Arabs began to arrive there in the late nineteenth century, but the first huge influx was between 1900 and 1924, when the auto industry attracted immigrants from all over the world (Woodruff, 1991). Today the Detroit/ Dearborn area has the largest Arab community in the United States, with Arab Americans constituting about 30 percent of the population of Dearborn. In addition, a large percentage of the Detroit area's Middle Eastern population is Chaldean, Christian Iraqis who speak the Chaldean language. While they are from the heart of the Middle East, most do not identify themselves as Iraqi, and some are deeply offended if referred to as Arab (Haddad, personal communication, July 2006).

Select Arab American Demographics

Immigrants from all over the Arab world continue to settle in the United States. The greatest numbers of Middle Eastern immigrants come from Iraq, Egypt, and Lebanon. According to the Migration Policy Institute, which does research based on U.S. Census and U.S. Department of Homeland Security data, the number of Iraqi immigrants rose from approximately 32,000 in 1980 to 154,220 in 2009 (Terrazas, 2011). The U.S. war in Iraq began in 2003, and it took several years for the surge of Iraqi refugees or asylees to reach the United States.

Although in 2010 the U.S. Census Bureau estimated the Arab American population of the United States at under 2 million people, the Arab American Institute Foundation suggests that a more accurate estimate is over 3.6 million (AAIF, 2012). The communities with the largest Arab American populations are located in Los Angeles, Detroit, the greater New York area, Chicago, and Washington, D.C. According to Zogby International research, the five states with the largest Arab American populations in 2010 were California, Michigan, New York, Florida, and Texas (AAIF, 2012).

DIFFERENCES AND SIMILARITIES

There is great diversity among Arab American groups. Understanding this diversity will assist officers in not categorizing Arabs as homogeneous and will encourage people to move away from thinking in stereotypes. As previously mentioned, Arabs from the Middle East come from at least 13 different countries, many of which are vastly different from each other. The governments of Arab countries also differ, ranging from monarchies to emirates to republics (World Factbook, 2013). Arab visitors such as students, tourists, businesspeople, and diplomats to the United States from the Gulf countries (e.g., Saudi Arabia, Qatar, Oman, Bahrain,

United Arab Emirates) are typically wealthy, but their Jordanian, Lebanese, and Palestinian brethren do not generally bring wealth to the United States; in fact, many are extremely poor. Another area of difference is clothing. In a number of countries in the Middle East, many older men wear headdresses, but it is less common among young men. Similarly, young women in the Middle East may choose not to wear head coverings and long dresses that cloak them from head to toe.

The younger generation of Arab Americans, much to the disappointment of some of their parents and grandparents, may display entirely different behavior from what is expected of them (which is typical in most immigrant and refugee groups). In addition, as with other immigrant groups, there are Arab Americans who have been in the United States for generations and have completely assimilated into American culture. Consequently, they may not identify in any way with their roots. Others, although they have also been in the United States for generations, consciously try to keep Arab traditions alive and pass them on to their children. (See the section "Typology of Immigrants and Refugees" on pages 15–25 in Chapter 1.) Officers should not treat established Arab Americans as if they were newcomers.

There are broad differences among Arab American groups in terms of social class and economic status. Although many Arab Americans living in the United States are educated professionals—more than 50 percent of foreign-born adults from Saudi Arabia, Egypt, and Kuwait have bachelor's degrees (Terrazas, 2011)—a percentage comes from rural areas (e.g., peasants from southern Lebanon, West Bank Palestinians, Yemenis), and they differ in outlook and receptiveness to modernization. On the other hand, despite holding traditional values, many newcomers are modern in outlook. For example, although people in the United States tend to have a stereotypical image of the Arab woman, many women of Arab descent do not adhere to this image. John Zogby, president of Zogby International, describes the modern Arab women who defy the stereotype: "Among the upper-class, educated Palestinian population, for example, you can find many women who are vocal and outspoken. You might see the young husbands wheeling the babies around in strollers while the women are discussing world events" (John Zogby, personal communication, August 2013).

On the other hand, certain Arab governments (e.g., that of Saudi Arabia) place restrictions on women, mandating that they do not mix with men, they must always be veiled, and they cannot travel alone or drive a car. Women from less restrictive Arab countries (e.g., Lebanon and Jordan) might exhibit very different behavior from those whose governments grant them fewer freedoms. Nevertheless, women in traditional Muslim families from any country typically have limited contact with men outside their family and wear traditional dress. Some implications of these traditions, as they relate to Arab women and male police officers in the United States, are discussed further in this chapter.

Examining people's motivation for coming to the United States can help to avoid stereotyping. There is a distinction between immigrants (who have "few problems adjusting to the United States") and refugees. Some refugees, having been forced to leave their country of origin, believe that they are here temporarily, because they are waiting for a conflict to end. As a result, they may be hesitant to change their traditional ways, and relationship building by law enforcement personnel may take extra time.

Similarities

Despite many differences, whether apparent in socioeconomic status, levels of traditionalism, or motivation for coming to the United States, there are values and beliefs associated with Arab culture that law enforcement officials should understand in order to establish rapport and trust. Officers will recognize that some of the information listed later does not apply only to Arab cultures. At the same time, the following will help officers understand deeply held beliefs that many Arab Americans would agree are keys to understanding traditional Arab culture.

BASIC ARAB VALUES

1. Traditional Arab society upholds honor (in Arabic, *ayb*); the degree to which an Arab can be shamed publicly is foreign to the average Westerner. Officers recognize that dignity and respect should be shown to all individuals, but citizens from cultures emphasizing shame (*sharam*) and loss of honor (e.g., Middle Eastern, Latin American) may react even more severely to loss of dignity and respect than do other individuals. People will go so far to avoid shame that they will not report crimes. "It is often difficult to get members of Arab communities to be full-fledged complainants, because they either don't complain in the first place, or do not follow through. Therefore, because of their primary concern to avoid shame and maintain harmony, it becomes more difficult to gain successful prosecution" (Haddad, personal communication, July 2006). Keep in mind that some "shame" cultures have sanctioned extreme punishments for loss of honor (e.g., death if a woman loses her virginity before marriage).
2. Loyalty to one's family takes precedence over other personal needs. A person is completely intertwined with his or her family; protection and privacy in a traditional Arab family often overrides relationships with outsiders. Members of Arab families tend to avoid disagreements and disputes in front of others, preferring to resolve issues on their own (Haddad, personal communication, July 2006).
3. Communication is expected to be courteous and hospitable, and harmony between individuals is emphasized. Too much directness and candor can be interpreted as extremely impolite. From a traditional Arab view, it may not be appropriate for a person to give totally honest responses if they result in a loss of honor, especially for self or family members (this may not apply to established Arab Americans). This aspect of cross-cultural communication is not easily understood by most Westerners and is often criticized. Certainly, officers will not accept anything but the whole truth, despite arguments rationalized by cultural ideals of honor. However, this should not lead officers to draw attention explicitly to an indirect communication style. Officers would be well advised to work around this style rather than insinuating that a citizen is not being honest.

STEREOTYPES

The Arab world has been perceived in the West in terms of negative stereotypes, and these have been transferred to Americans of Arab descent. As with all distorted information about ethnic groups, it is important that police officers recognize how stereotypes interfere with true understanding.

Movies and Television

Perhaps the most offensive Arab stereotypes come from the media; television programs, video games, and movies routinely portray Arabs in a negative light. Even films and programs aimed at children propagate the stereotype of Arabs as villains. Because many Americans do not know Arabs personally, media images become embedded in people's minds. In a talk at the Levantine Cultural Center in Los Angeles in late 2012, Jack Shaheen, author of *Reel Bad Arabs: How Hollywood Vilifies a People*, recounted how in his research he "has found the same stereotypes repeated since the early days of Hollywood—the belly dancer, the terrorist, the dangerous but incompetent Arab, the lecherous sheikh, the submissive woman . . . the constant repetition of negative images of Arabs, even in fictional movies or television shows, has a tendency to desensitize the public and entrench harmful stereotypes" (Lohmann, 2013).

Shaheen has argued that the atmosphere created by Hollywood contributed to the recorded 326 hate crimes against Arab Americans in the first month alone following the terrorist attacks in 2001. Though military retaliations after the attacks were labeled "antiterrorist" rather than "anti-Islamic," the movie industry has continued the negative stereotyping of Arabs and Muslims.

In Shaheen's view, "There certainly should be movies based on what happened, but if [images of Arabs as terrorists] are the only images we see from now on, if we continue to vilify all Muslims and all Arabs as terrorists instead of making clear this is a lunatic fringe, what are we accomplishing?" (Shaheen, 2001).

While some filmmakers and studios have become more sensitive to the potential they have in terms of perpetrating stereotypes, a number of Muslim and Arab American organizations feel that there is room for improvement.

The "Terrorist" Stereotype, Post-9/11 Backlash, and Ongoing Challenges

Even prior to the attacks of 9/11, Arabs had often been stereotyped as terrorists. A most convincing example of the persistence of discrimination against Arabs occurred after the Oklahoma City bombing in April 1995. Immediately following the bombing, many journalists and political leaders said that the tragedy appeared to be the work of Muslim terrorists. This was an initial conclusion made without any supporting evidence; the arrest and conviction of Timothy J. McVeigh proved them wrong. The paranoia that had led to that conclusion gave way to Arab-bashing, including many hate calls to Arabs; scapegoating of Arabs spread pervasively across the country.

The rage that ensued after 9/11 turned into general Arab and Muslim bashing. Within the first nine weeks following the attacks, there were more than 700 reported violent crimes against Arab Americans and Muslim Americans, or those who were perceived to be. Even Sikhs, who may have simply been dark-skinned and wore turbans but were neither Muslim nor Middle Eastern, were targets and victims of hate crimes in the aftermath of the attacks. (Sikhs continue to be the targets of hate crimes, such as in the 2012 shootings at a Sikh temple in Wisconsin. Chapter 5 includes discussion on Hate Crimes against Sikhs.)

The attacks of 9/11 were a pivotal point in the history of Arab Americans in this country. The impact, more than a decade later, is no less important to understand as it was immediately following the attacks:

> What remained [after the attacks] was primarily a heightened self-consciousness (including a heightened sense of vulnerability) on the part of Arab Americans, and a much more widespread cognition in the rest of American society of the existence of these communities (although this recognition was . . . accompanied by a degree of antipathy). Arab American individuals and organizations would, for the foreseeable future, be placed under a microscope of intense scrutiny for disloyalty and covert sympathy with those who attacked the United States. (ADC Research Institute, 2008)

Law enforcement needs to be aware of the heightened risk of threats and hate crimes toward Arab Americans when criminal acts around the world are committed by terrorists in the name of Islam. The ADC report cited above includes two examples of global news and its impact on hate crimes against those perceived to be Arab Americans in the United States.

- Under his leadership, the late terrorist leader in Iraq, Abu Musab Al Zarqawi, oversaw beheading atrocities; this resulted in a rise of hate incidents around this period.
- The July 7, 2005, bombings in London by Islamists were linked to a similar increase in hate crimes.

When global events occur, fear and anger can be ignited among some highly intolerant individuals who then lash out at people who appear to be Middle Eastern. This leads to "an ongoing anxiety that Arab Americans have been and are continuing to live with" (ADC Research Institute, 2008).

Increased understanding will benefit all concerned. Arab contributions to civilization have been significant in numerous areas, including mathematics, astronomy, medicine, architecture, geography, and language. High-profile Arab Americans participate in all sectors of the professional world—organizations such as the National Arab American Medical Association and the Michigan Arab American Legal Society have highly respected and substantial membership (Haddad, personal communication, July 2006). Since the first edition of this book in 1995, sizeable percentages of Arab Americans have moved out of marginal urban areas and into the suburbs (James Zogby, 2013).

ISLAMIC RELIGION

Misunderstanding between Americans and Arab Americans can often be traced, in part, to religious differences and to a lack of tolerance of these differences. Islam is practiced by some Muslim newcomers to the United States as well as by Muslim African Americans. Many Muslims in the United States *identify* culturally with their religion, but this does mean that they are "religious." The reader should keep in mind that the term "Islamic" is not necessarily connected to culture or ethnicity. Muslims, or those who practice or identify with Islam, come from all over the world. "Islamic" does not mean "Arabic;" nor does it mean "Middle Eastern" (demographic groups were explained earlier in the chapter). "Islamic" is merely an adjective referring to the religion of Islam. The majority of Muslims in the United States are African American (see Chapter 6), not Arab or Middle Eastern. Many Arab Americans (especially those from the first wave of Arab immigration) are Christian, although non-Arab Americans tend to assume that they are Muslim simply because they are Arabs. *Muslims* refer to those who practice the religion, Islam. (In a later chapter section [pp. 213–214], further terms such as "Islamist" and related distinctions are defined.)

By and large, most Americans do not understand what Islam is and, because of stereotyping, wrongly associate Muslims with terrorists or fanatics. Many, but by no means all, Arab Muslims in the United States continue to practice traditional aspects of their religion, which are intertwined with daily life. However, some Muslims attend mosques only on holy days. Some do not have any "official" affiliation at all.

Islam means submission to the will of God, and for traditional, religious Muslims, the will of God (which is somewhat similar to the Western notion of fate) is a central concept. Islam has been called Mohammedanism, which is an incorrect name for the religion because it suggests that Muslims worship Mohammed[*] rather than God (Allah). It is believed that God's final message to man was revealed to the prophet Mohammed. *Allah* is the shortened Arabic word for the God of Abraham, and it is used by both Arab Muslims and Arab Christians.

The Qur'an (Koran) and the Pillars of Islam

The Qur'an is the holy text for Muslims, and is regarded as the word of God. There are five Pillars of Islam, or central guidelines, that form the framework of the religion:

1. Profession of faith in God
2. Prayer five times daily
3. Giving of alms (concern for the needy)
4. Fasting during the month of Ramadan (sunrise to sunset)
5. Pilgrimage to Mecca (in Saudi Arabia) at least once in each person's lifetime

There are several points where law enforcement officials can show respect for a Muslim's need to practice his or her religion. The need to express one's faith in God and to be respected for it is one area. Usually, people pray together as a congregation in a mosque, which is the Islamic equivalent of a church or synagogue. People, however, can pray individually if a congregation is not present. Religious Muslims in jails, for example, will continue to pray five times a day and should not be ridiculed for or prevented from doing so. Remember that prayer, five times a day, is

---

[*]An alternate spelling is Muhammad, which is closer to the Arabic pronunciation of the name.

a "pillar" of Islam and that practicing Muslims will want to uphold this "command" no matter where they are. Call to prayer takes place at the following times:

- One hour before sunrise
- At noon
- Midafternoon
- Sunset
- Ninety minutes after sunset

Taboos in the Mosque

Police officers convey respect to the Muslim community if they can avoid, where possible, entering mosques and interrupting prayers (emergencies may occasionally make this impossible). Religion is vital in Arab life; one of the quickest ways to build rapport with the Muslim community is to show respect for Islamic customs and beliefs. Thus, other than in emergency situations, officers are advised to:

- Never step on a prayer mat or rug with shoes on.
- Avoid walking in front of people who are in the midst of prayer.
- Speak softly while people are praying.
- Dress conservatively (both men and women are required to dress conservatively; shorts are not appropriate).
- Invite people out of a prayer area to talk to them.
- Never touch a Qur'an, place it on the floor, or put anything on top of it.

Proper protocol in a mosque (also referred to as a *masjid*) requires that people remove their shoes before entering, but this must be left to the officer's discretion. Officer safety, of course, comes before consideration of differences.

Ramadan: The Holy Month

One of the holiest periods in the Islamic religion is the celebration of Ramadan, which lasts for one month. There is no fixed date because, like the Jewish and Chinese calendars, the Islamic calendar is based on the lunar cycle, related to the phases of the moon, with dates varying from year to year. During the month of Ramadan, Muslims do not eat, drink, smoke, or satisfy certain other "physical needs" from sunrise to sunset. Muslims fast during Ramadan in order to practice self-discipline and to experience and demonstrate unity with Muslims all over the world who identify with their religion. On the 29th night of Ramadan, when there is a new moon, the month of fasting is officially over. The final fast is broken and for up to three days people celebrate with feasting and other activities. Throughout the month of Ramadan, Muslim families tend to pray in mosques more often than during other parts of the year.

For Muslims, Ramadan is as important and holy as Lent and Christmas are for Christians; this fact is appreciated when others who are not Muslim recognize its importance. One city with a sizable Arab American population (Dearborn, Michigan) puts up festive lights in its business district during Ramadan as a gesture of acceptance and appreciation for the diversity that Arab Americans bring to the city. The Arab American community has reacted favorably to this symbolic gesture.

Knowledge of Religious Practices

Knowledge of religious practices, including what is considered holy, will help officers avoid creating problems and conflicts. One belief that is part of the Islamic religion that may occasionally come to the fore in the course of police work will illustrate this point. In a suburb of San Francisco, California, police officers and a group of Muslims from Tunisia were close to violence when police entered a morgue to obtain a hair sample from a person who had just been killed in a car accident. Apparently, the body had already been blessed by an *Imam* (a religious leader) and, according to the religion, any further contact would have been a defilement of the body that had already been sanctified and was ready for burial. The police officers were merely doing what they needed to do to complete their investigation and were unaware of this taboo. This, together with a language barrier, created an extremely confusing and confrontational situation in which officers lost necessary control. A better course of action would have been to explain what had to be done and request permission to handle a body that had already been sanctified. If the citizens had not granted permission, the police would then have had to decide how to proceed. Most members of the Arab American community would comply with the wishes of police officers. As in many other situations involving police/citizen communication, the initial approach sets the tone for the entire interaction.

Similarities between Christianity, Judaism, and Islam

When reading the above tenets of the Muslim faith, notice that certain practices and aspects of Islam are also found in Christianity and Judaism. All three religions are monotheistic, that is, each believes in only one God. Followers of these religions believe that God is the origin of all, and is all-knowing as well as all-powerful. Because God is merciful, it is possible for believers to be absolved of their sins, though the practices for obtaining absolution vary in the different ideologies. All three religions have a Holy Book central to the faith: Judaism has the Torah (the first five books of the Old Testament), Christianity the Bible, and Islam the Qur'an (Koran). All three religions regard their texts to be either the direct word of God or inspired by the word of God. There are similarities between the three books. For example, the concept of the Ten Commandments is present in each. All three contain stories about many of the same people, such as Adam, Noah, Abraham, Moses, David, and Solomon. Also, both the Bible and the Qur'an contain stories about Mary, Jesus, and John the Baptist. The oral reading or recitation of each book constitutes part of regular worship.

Prophets exist in each tradition and are revered as those who transmit the word of God to people. Chronologically, Judaism became a religion first, followed by Christianity and then Islam. Islam builds upon the foundations of Judaism and Christianity and believes in the authenticity of the prophets of earlier books. For example, Islamic belief sees both Moses and Jesus as rightful prophets and as precursors to Mohammed, who is believed to be the final prophet of God. As there are different interpretations of Christianity and Judaism, so do followers of Islam, too, interpret the religion in different ways. Differing readings of the Qur'an can lead to more (or less) tolerance within the religion. Lastly, both the Islamic and the Judeo-Christian traditions are said to stem from the same lineage; Abraham was father to both Isaac, whose progeny became the people of Israel, and Ishmael, who started the Arab lineage.

Definition of Further Terms: "Islamist" and "Jihad"

The term "Islamist" refers to Muslims who identify with the religion and believe its tenets should directly influence political life. "Islamist" does not automatically equate to "terrorist," which is a common misconception. There are many degrees of Islamism or political affiliation, as well as many nuanced definitions (Khan, personal communication, August 2013).

One way to understand "Islamist" (the person) and "Islamism" (the ideology) is to think about some Christian political coalitions. There are political Christian movements that may be considered fundamentalist or conservative in their religious beliefs, but they are certainly not terrorists. Members of Christian political organizations in the United States identify religiously and have political agendas which vary among Christian political coalitions just as they do among Islamists (Khan, personal communication, August 2013).

The media frequently uses the word "Islamist" to mean "fundamentalist," or extremist, and often the two words (Islamist extremist) are used together. According to Humera Khan, an expert on preventing radicalization and violent extremism in the American Muslim community and who also consults to the Federal Bureau of Investigation (FBI) and the Justice Department on counter-terrorism:

> The word "Islamist" is always political—but that word does not indicate how conservative or extreme a particular group or individual is; Islamist conveys a political position. In contrast with the word "Islamic," Islamist is not about a way of life—that is, rather, "Islamic." Your personal identity as a Muslim is related to Islam, and you identify with things "Islamic," but politically you could still be very secular. (Khan, personal communication, August 2013)

Another term that is frequently linked with extremism is *jihad*, which means "struggle" in Arabic. ("Jihadi" or "jihadist" are adjectives, as in "Jihadist movement," or can pertain to an individual, as in "a jihadist.") Jihad refers to both the notion of an inner spiritual religious struggle as well as to an external struggle against oppression and enemies of Islam. The latter concept is sometimes described in mainstream American media as a "holy war," and is a distorted variation of the ideological foundation for terrorist organizations such as al-Qaida. Because of widespread media coverage of terror groups, many people are probably aware only of the notion of violent jihad (which is inaccurately used as a synonym for terrorism), though the internal personal struggle is often referred to as the more significant jihad and physical conflict as the lesser jihad.

Fundamentalism

Some attribute the acts of radical Muslims to "different readings" of the Qur'an—which often entail literal interpretations of certain passages. For example, one scholar points to certain modern writings or interpretations of the Qur'an, such as "The Way of a Muslim," which is used to indoctrinate young men in fundamentalism (Wallace & Effron, 2010). However, other religions and sects have also produced extremists who commit violence under the rubric of faith, such as the Ku Klux Klan. Islamic fundamentalism or extremism is not synonymous with terrorism. Humera Khan has observed:

> In fact, scholars from different schools of Islamic thought sometimes associated with "extremism," such as Wahabism and Salafism, have issued *fatwas* (opinions or rulings on points of Islamic law by a recognized authority) condemning terrorism. Wahabis and Salafis, for example, may be more conservative in their leanings and practice, but this does not mean that the way they practice Islam directly leads to terrorism. Terrorism is a deviation from Islam. (Khan, personal communication, August 2013)

Khan emphasizes that law enforcement officials should not infer that a visibly religious person has terrorist tendencies. "Law enforcement sees the outer veneer of what a person practices, and then stereotypes can often play out" (Khan, personal communication, August 2013). She further explains that people who don't know much about Islam are often the ones who are more likely to join terrorist groups. "We are seeing a younger and younger age group involved. They don't know what religion is to start with, and when they learn about a deviant ideology, they can't filter out what Islam truly is and what it is not" (Khan, personal communication, August 2013).

FAMILY STRUCTURE

Arab Americans typically have close-knit families in which members have a strong sense of loyalty and fulfill obligations to all members, including extended family (aunts, uncles, cousins, grandparents). Traditionally minded families also believe strongly in the family's honor, and members try to avoid behavior that will bring shame or disgrace to the family. The operating unit for Arab Americans (which may be less true for people who have been in the United States for generations) is not the individual but the family. Hence, if a person behaves inappropriately, the entire family is disgraced. Similarly, if a family member is assaulted in the Arab world, there would be some type of retribution. For police officers, three characteristics of the Arab family will affect their interaction with family members:

- Extended family members are often as close as the "nuclear family" (mother, father, children) and are not seen as secondary family members. If there is a police issue, officers can expect that several members of the family will become involved in the matter. Although officers might perceive this as interference, from an Arab cultural perspective, it is merely involvement and concern. The numbers of people involved are not meant to overwhelm an officer.
- Family loyalty and protection is seen as one of the highest values of family life. Therefore, shaming, ridiculing, insulting, or criticizing family members, especially in public, can have serious consequences.
- Newer Arab American refugees or immigrants may be reluctant to accept police assistance. Because families are tightly knit, they can also be closed "units" within which members prefer to keep private matters or conflicts to themselves. As a result, officers will have to work harder at establishing rapport if they want to gain cooperation.

There is an important point of contact between all three of these characteristics and law enforcement interaction with members of Arab American families. Berro (personal communication, February 2013) explains: "When we respond to a call at a home, the police car is like a magnet. Every family member comes out of the house and everyone wants to talk at once. It can be an overwhelming sensation for an officer who doesn't understand this background" (Berro, 2013).

Police officers who are not trained in understanding and responding appropriately and professionally to cultural differences could alienate the family by: (1) not respecting the interest and involvement of the family members and (2) attempting to gain control of the communication in an authoritarian manner. The consequences are likely to be that the officers would have difficulty establishing the rapport needed to gain information about the conflict at hand and would not be trusted or respected. To do their jobs effectively, law enforcement officials must demonstrate respect for Arab family values, along with communication style differences (the latter will be discussed shortly).

Head of the Household

As in many cultures with a traditional family structure, the man in the Arab home is overtly the head of the household and his role and influence are strong. The wife has a great deal of influence, too, but it can more often be "behind the scenes." An Arab woman does not always defer to her husband in private as she would in public. However, as mentioned earlier in the chapter, there are many women who have broken out of the traditional mold and tend to be more vocal, outspoken, and assertive than were their mothers or grandmothers. A Middle Eastern woman's country of origin might also be a factor in determining her public behavior.

> In Syria, women are free to drive cars, to purchase property, or to own a business. Women keep their family name when they marry. The government does not restrict women's right to cover or not cover themselves in public. Many Syrian women pursue a discrete existence centered on work, school, home, family, and mosque. Yet others choose to participate in civic affairs and to entertain themselves in restaurants, theaters, sporting arenas, and nightclubs—just as women do in Europe and the United States. Syrian women have had the right to vote since 1949, three years after independence (Shora, 2009).

Traditionally, in many Arab countries, fathers maintain their status by being strict disciplinarians and demanding absolute respect, thus creating some degree of fear among children and even among wives. Once again, Arab Americans born and raised in this country have, for the most part, adopted a middle-class "American" style of child raising whereby children participate in some of the decision-making and are treated in an egalitarian manner. In addition, as with changing roles among all kinds of families in the United States, the father as traditional head of the household and the mother as having "second-class" status is no longer prevalent among established Arab Americans in the United States. Wife abuse and child abuse are not considered respectable practices by educated Arab Americans, but the practices still occur, just as they do in mainstream American society.

In traditional Arab society, displays of power and influence are common among males. While this can be viewed in a negative light from certain Western perspectives, this trait can be helpful in securing the compliance of the family in important matters. The husband or father can be a natural ally of authorities. Officers would be well advised to work with both the father and the mother, for example, in matters where children are involved. On family matters the woman frequently is the authority, even if she seems to defer to her husband. Communicating with the woman, even if indirectly, while still respecting the father's need to maintain his public status, will win respect from both the man and the woman.

Children and Americanization

Americanization, the process of becoming "American" in behavior, attitudes, and beliefs, has always been an issue with refugees/immigrants and their children. Typically, children are better able than their parents to learn a language and pick up the nuances of a culture. In addition, peer influence and pressure in American society begin to overshadow parental control, especially beginning in the preteen years. Arab children, who are cherished by their parents, face an extremely difficult cultural gap with their parents if they reach a stage where they are more "American" than "Arab." Children in Arab families are taught to be respectful in front of parents and to be conscious of family honor. Middle Eastern parents do not consider certain aspects of Americanized behavior, in general, to be respectful or worthy of pride. When children exhibit certain behavior that is believed to bring shame to the family, discipline can indeed be harsh.

In extreme and infrequent cases, shame to the family can result in crimes against children that involve violence. A police officer in a Midwest police department described a case in which a father shot his daughter because she had a boyfriend (Arab women are not allowed to associate freely with men before marriage and are expected to remain virgins). This case does not suggest that violent crime, in the Arab cultural context, is an appropriate response. Mental problems or drugs and alcohol accompany most violent acts. However, when a child's (and especially a girl's) behavior involves what is seen as sexual misconduct, the family's honor is ruined. When this happens, *all* members of the family suffer. Culturally, when a family member commits a crime, there is great shame that colors the reputation of the entire family (Ismail, personal communication, July 2013).

There is very little that police officers can do to change the attitudes of parents who oppose their children's behavior. However, if officers respond to calls during which they notice that the family has become dysfunctional because of children's behavior, it would be a service to the family to initiate some sort of social service intervention or make a referral. If a family is already at the point of needing police assistance in problems involving children and their parents, then, more likely than not, they need other types of assistance as well. At the same time, newer immigrants and refugees will not necessarily be open to social service interventions, especially if the case workers do not speak Arabic. According to Lobna Ismail, President of Connecting Cultures, a Washington, D.C., firm specializing in Arab American cross-cultural understanding, some individuals may reveal more information to people outside their own community than to people within. Refugees and immigrants are concerned about shaming the family if personal information were to be disclosed to people from their own cultural, religious, or ethnic group (Ismail, personal communication, July 2013).

COMMUNICATION STYLES AND CULTURAL PRACTICES

As with all other immigrant groups, the degree to which people preserve their cultural practices varies. The following descriptions of everyday behavior will not apply equally to all Arab Americans, but they do not necessarily apply only to newcomers. Immigrants may preserve traditions and practices long after they come to a new country by conscious choice or sometimes because they are unaware of their cultural behavior (i.e., it is not in their conscious awareness).

Greetings, Names, Approach, Touching

Most Arab American newcomers expect to be addressed with a title and their last name (e.g., Mr. or Miss followed by the last name), although in many Arab countries people are addressed formally by a title and their first name. Most Arab women do not change their names after they are married or divorced. They therefore might not understand the distinction between a maiden name and a married name. The usual practice for an Arab woman is to keep her father's last name for life (Ismail, personal communication, July 2013.) An Arabic name may be spelled in several different ways in English. If you see "ibn" in the middle position of a name, it means "son of," and if you see "bint" in the same position, it means "daughter of."

Many Arab Americans who have retained their traditional customs shake hands and then place their right hand on their chest near the heart, which signifies warmth, deep respect, and gratitude. When visiting the Middle East, Americans are advised to reciprocate whenever they observe this gesture. Officers can decide whether they are comfortable using this gesture—most people would not expect it from an officer, but might appreciate the gesture as long as the officer was able to convey sincerity. Generally, when Arabs from the Middle East shake hands, they do not shake hands briefly or firmly. (The expression "He has a dead fish handshake" is unfamiliar to many cultural groups!) Traditional Arab style is to hold hands longer than other Americans do and shake hands more lightly. Older children are taught to shake hands with adults as a sign of respect. Many Arabs would appreciate an officer shaking hands with their older children. With a recent immigrant or refugee Arab woman, it is generally not appropriate to shake hands unless she extends her hand first. This would definitely apply to women who wear head coverings.

Many Arabs of the same sex greet each other by kissing on the cheek. Two Saudi Arabian men, for example, might greet each other by kissing on both cheeks a number of times. Public touching of the opposite sex is forbidden in the traditional Arab world, and male officers should make every effort not to touch Arab women, even casually—unless, as noted above, a woman extends her hand first for a handshake.

Police officers should be aware that some Arab American citizens (e.g., Lebanese) who are new to the United States may react to a police officer's approach in unexpected ways. For example, an officer who has just asked a person to give his driver's license may find the person getting out of his car to be able to talk to the officer. From the person's perspective, he or she is simply trying to be courteous (because this is how it is done in the person's home country). An officer, always conscious of safety issues, may simply have to explain that in the United States, officers require citizens to remain in their cars.

Hospitality

Hospitality is a byword among Arabs, whatever their station in life. Guests are generally treated to the kindest and most lavish consideration. Hospitality in the Arab culture is not an option; it is more of an obligation or duty. In some parts of the Arab world, thanking someone for hospitality might be answered with a common expression meaning, "Don't thank me. It's my duty." (Here the word *duty* has a more positive than negative connotation.) To be anything but hospitable goes against the grain of Arab culture. Officers need to understand how deeply ingrained the need to be hospitable is and should not misinterpret this behavior. Whether in the home or in a business owner's shop or office, when an officer enters, an Arab American may very well offer coffee and something to eat. This is not to be mistaken for a bribe and, from the Arab perspective, carries no negative connotations. According to Berro (2013), most people would be offended if officers did not accept their offers of hospitality. The period of time spent socializing and extending hospitality gives Arab Americans a chance to get to know and gauge the extent to which the other person should be trusted. Obviously, on an emergency call, there is no time for such pleasantries. However, with the trend toward increasing community policing practices, officers may find that they are involved in more situations in which they may decide to accept small gestures of hospitality, within departmental policy.

Verbal and Nonverbal Communication

Arabs in general are very warm and expressive people, both verbally and nonverbally, and appreciate it when others extend warmth to them. There are some areas in the realm of nonverbal communication in which Americans, without cultural knowledge, have misinterpreted the behavior of Arab Americans simply because of ethnocentrism (i.e., the tendency to judge others by one's own cultural standards and norms).

CONVERSATIONAL DISTANCE   Acceptable conversational distance between two people is often related to cultural influences. Officers are very aware of safety issues and keep a certain distance from people when communicating with them. Generally, officers like to stand about an arm's length or farther from citizens to avoid possible assaults. This distance is similar to how far apart "mainstream Americans" stand when in conversation. When this distance is "violated," officers can feel threatened (either consciously or subconsciously). Many Arabs, especially if they are new to the country, tend to have a closer acceptable conversational distance than do Americans. In Arab culture, it is not considered offensive to "feel a person's breath." Yet many Americans, unfamiliar with this intimacy in regular conversation, have misinterpreted the closeness. While still being conscious of safety, law enforcement officers can keep in mind that this closer-than-normal behavior (i.e., "normal" for the officer) does not necessarily constitute a threat.

When Americans travel to the Middle East, they often notice this tendency for people to stand closer to each other as compared to mainstream U.S. cultural norms. This is relevant to police officers in the United States, especially in the context of communicating with recent immigrants and refugees. (It is recommended not to back away when an Arab stands very close while speaking to you in order to maintain rapport.) Some Arabs may stare into other people's eyes, watching the pupils for an indication of the other person's response (e.g., dilated pupils mean a positive response). Male police officers, however, should avoid staring directly into a woman's eyes.

GESTURES   There are some distinct gestures and body language in some Arab countries that first generation immigrants may exhibit. For example:

- *Indicating that something is not understood.* The right hand is held up, with the palm up, and is twisted back and forth.
- *Indicating to someone to hold on or to wait.* Fingers and thumb are touching with the palm up.
- *Indicating, "Never."* The right forefinger is pointed up and moved from left to right quickly and repeatedly.

---

*The names of individuals and departments have been omitted even though permission has been granted to quote. The purpose of including these incidents is not to put undue attention on any one department or individual but rather to provide education on police professionalism in interethnic relations.

- *Saying, "No."* The head moves back slightly, eyebrows are raised as is the chin; there is also a sound that may be made by clicking the tongue on the roof of the mouth.
- *Motioning to someone to leave.* The right hand is held out with the palm down and moved as if pushing something away from you.

As with many other cultural groups, pointing a finger directly at someone is considered rude and can be taken as a sign of contempt. Arab immigrants, especially older ones, will often use their entire hand to point. The "OK" or "thumbs-up" gesture is considered obscene. Again, this applies only to people who have not yet been acculturated to mainstream America.

Emotional Expressiveness

> When I came to my brother's house to see what the problem was [i.e., with the police], I asked, "What the hell is going on?" I held my hands out and talked with my hands as I always do. I repeated myself and continued to gesture with my hands. Later (i.e., at trial) the police officer said that the Arab woman was yelling and screaming and acting wild, waving her arms and inciting observers to riot by her actions.*

The Arab American involved in the above situation explained that Arab women, in particular, are very emotional and that police sometimes see this emotionalism as a threat. She explained that upon seeing a family member in trouble, it would be most usual and natural for a woman to put her hands to her face and say something like, "Oh, my God" frequently and in a loud voice. While other Americans can react this same way, it is worth pointing out that in main-stream American culture, there is a tendency to subdue one's emotions and not to go "out of control." What some Americans consider "out of control," Arabs (like Mexicans, Greeks, Israe-lis, and Iranians, among other groups) consider perfectly "normal" behavior. In fact, the lack of emotionalism that Arabs observe among mainstream Americans can be misinterpreted as lack of interest or involvement.

Although a communication-style characteristic never applies to all people in one cul-tural group (and we have seen that there is a great deal of diversity among Arab Americans), there are group traits that can apply to many. Arabs, especially the first generation of relatively recent newcomers, tend to display emotions when talking (as seen in the previous example). Unlike many people in Asian cultures (e.g., Japanese), Arabs have not been "taught" to sup-press their emotions. Arabs, like other Mediterranean groups such as Israelis or Greeks, tend to shout when they are excited or angry and are very animated in their communication. They may repeatedly insert expressions into their speech such as "I swear by God." This is simply a cultural mannerism.

Westerners, however, tend to judge this "style" negatively. To some Westerners, the emo-tionalism, repetition, and emphasis on certain statements can give the impression that the person is not telling the truth or is exaggerating for effect. An officer unfamiliar with these cultural mannerisms may feel overwhelmed, especially when involved with an entire group of people. It would be well worth it for the officer to determine the spokesperson for the group, and to refrain from showing impatience or irritation at this culturally different style. An Arab American community member made the following comment about police reactions toward Arab Americans:

> Police see Arab emotionalism as a threat. They see the involvement of our large families in police incidents as a threat. They don't need to feel overwhelmed by us and try to contain our reactions. We will cooperate with them, but they need to show us that they don't view us as backward and ignorant people who are inferior just because we are different and because we express ourselves in a more emotional way than they do. (Arab American community member)

SWEARING, OBSCENITIES, AND INSULTS Officers working in Arab American communities should know that for Arabs, words are extremely powerful. If an officer displays a lack of professionalism by swearing at an Arab (using even words like "damn"), it will be nearly impossible to repair the damage.

In one case of documented police harassment of several Arab Americans (names have been omitted in order not to single out this department), witnesses attest to officers' saying, "Mother-f_____ Arabs, we're going to teach you. Go back home!" One of the Arab American citizens involved in the case reported that officers treated him like an animal and were very insulting by asking in a demeaning tone questions such as, "Do you speak English? Do you read English?" (The man was a highly educated professional who had been in the United States for several years.) In asking him about his place of employment—he worked at an Arab American organization—the man reported that they referred to his place of employment as "the Arab Islamic sh__ or crap? What is that?"

Officers who understand professionalism are aware that this type of language and interaction is insulting to all persons. The choice to use obscenities and insults, especially in conjunction with one's ethnic background, however, means that officers risk never being able to establish trust within the ethnic community. This can translate into not being able to secure cooperation when needed. Even a few officers exhibiting this type of behavior can damage the reputation of an entire department for a long period of time.

ENGLISH LANGUAGE PROBLEMS   If time allows, before asking the question "Do you speak English?" officers should try to assess whether the Arab American is a recent arrival or an established citizen who might react negatively to the question. A heavy accent does not necessarily mean that a person is unable to speak English (although that may be the case). There are specific communication skills that can be used with limited-English-speaking persons (see Chapter 4), which should be applied with Arab Americans. Officers should proceed slowly and nonaggressively with questioning and, wherever possible, ask open-ended questions. An officer's patience and willingness to take extra time will be beneficial in the long run.

KEY ISSUES IN LAW ENFORCEMENT

Perceptions of and Interactions with Police

It is not possible to generalize Arab Americans' perception of the police, but it is fair to say that a large part of the Arab American community has great respect for law enforcement. On the other hand, some immigrants, such as Jordanians and Palestinians, do not understand the American system and have an ingrained fear of police because of political problems in their own region of the world (James Zogby, personal communication, August 2013). Given that they distrust the government, they are more likely to reject help from the police, and this puts them at a decided disadvantage in that they can more easily become victims. Their fear, in combination with the interdependence and helpfulness that characterize the extended family, results in families not wanting assistance from the police. Thus, police will encounter some families that would prefer to handle conflicts on their own even when police intervention is clearly needed. Some of the newer immigrants and refugees feel that it is dishonorable to have to go outside the family (e.g., to police and social service providers) to get help, and, if given a choice, they would choose not to embarrass themselves and their families in this manner.

Within the Arab world of the Middle East, there are major differences among countries in the institution of policing and the manner in which citizens are required to behave with police. Immigrants from Iraq, for example, have complained that "Saddam's enforcers robbed them of their jewelry, even if it meant cutting off their fingers to get it" (Haddad, personal communication, July 2006). Similarly, in Saudi Arabia there is more fear of police than in some other countries because the punishments are stricter. For example, repeat offenders who are caught stealing will have a hand removed. A Saudi Arabian woman caught shoplifting in a San Francisco Bay Area 7-11 store begged a police officer on her knees not to make the arrest because she feared being sent back to Saudi Arabia and did not know what would happen to her there. As it turned out, the officer did let her go because it was her first offense. He felt that he had some discretion in this case and decided to consider the woman's cultural background and circumstances. When it comes to interpreting cultural influences on police incidents and crimes, especially those of a minor nature, each officer has to decide for himself or herself. (This aspect of law enforcement is discussed in Chapter 1.)

Modesty, Women's Dress, and Diversity among Women

In many parts of traditional Arab society, women do not socialize freely with men and tend to dress modestly. However, as previously mentioned, everyday practices in the various Arab countries differ greatly. In countries such as Lebanon and Jordan, women sometimes dress in a contemporary and modern manner and may, at the same time, cover their hair with headscarves.

In Saudi Arabia, strict rules are maintained about public dress. The "morals police" might tap women on the ankle with a stick if their dresses are too short. How some Arab women perceive the norms around their attire can differ greatly from how that same attire is perceived in the United States. For example, one of this text's coauthors (DL) spoke with several women in Algeria who appreciated the anonymity they could achieve with the *sefsari* (i.e., clothing that completely covered them). The contrasts in women's attire in the Middle East are striking. Lobna Ismail of Connecting Cultures described the cover of a book publication entitled *Teen Life in the Middle East*:

> Two young women are talking to each other. One is wearing a black cloak or *abaya* and her hair is covered with a black scarf. The other is also wearing a black cloak, but it is open and you can see that the young woman is wearing ripped jeans and her kneecap is exposed, she has a tight shirt, and she is smoking a cigarette. (Ismail, personal communication, July 2013)

More than a decade later than the above-noted book's publication, one can see even more Westernization of attire in the Middle East. Ismail points out the tremendous diversity among women in the various Arab countries and the need to stay away from stereotypes based on an image of a woman in traditional Arab dress. She adds that it is not possible to draw conclusions about a woman's degree of religiosity, political affiliation, or education level based solely on how she dresses. She has also observed that people often assume that an American Muslim woman who covers her hair is a newcomer to the United States and cannot speak English well. This can be quite contrary to the reality (Ismail, personal communication, July 2013).

Similarly, according to Ismail, there is a great deal of diversity in the United States as to how people interpret the religious preference for dressing modestly (Ismail, personal communication, July 2013). What a woman chooses to do differs among families. Some traditional families, even in the United States, may encourage their daughters and wives to dress modestly. In some cases, young women themselves choose to dress more modestly than their parents expect. For example, in the United States, some young women cover their hair even if their mothers do not (Ismail, personal communication, July 2013). In the Middle East, women might or might not wear head coverings; the choice depends on multiple factors, such as age, background, and family or personal preferences.

Modesty for a traditional Arab Muslim woman may include the need to cover her head so that men will not see her hair. In some traditional societies, a man must not see a woman's hair, and male officers should understand that asking a woman to remove her head covering (e.g., for the purpose of searching her or getting a photo identification) is analogous to asking her to expose a private part of her body. Former Dearborn Police Department Corporal Berro, an Arab American, would give this advice to officers: "Approach this matter sensitively. Don't overpower the woman, intimidate her, or grab her head cover. Ask her to go into a private room and have her remove it or get a female officer to help with the procedure" (Berro, personal communication, February 2013).

American officers may have difficulty understanding the violation that a traditional Arab woman feels when her head covering is taken away forcibly. Even if a woman is arrested for something like disorderly conduct, she will be offended by any aggressive move on the part of the officer to remove her head cover or touch her in any way. When police procedures require that a head cover be removed, the officers should explain the procedure and offer some kind of an apology to show respect. Having dealt with this same issue, the department of U.S. Citizenship and Immigration Services (USCIS) states its regulations in the following way: "Every applicant . . . shall clearly show a three-quarter profile view of the features of the applicant with head bare (unless the applicant is wearing a headdress as required by a religious order of which he or she is a member)" (Code of Federal Regulations, 8 C.F.R. 333.1(a), 2003). Thus, USCIS officials accept photographs of Muslim women with their head coverings on. Because police departments deal with safety issues (such as concealed weapons), they may not have the liberty to accommodate this particular cultural difference in the same way that USCIS does. The matter of women and head coverings must be handled with extreme sensitivity. Similar to Berro's advice, Lobna Ismail's suggestion is that if a woman has to remove her head covering for an extensive search, the officer should first ask her to remove it herself in a private area with a female officer in attendance. Moreover, this should be done out of view of any unrelated male (Ismail, personal communication, July 2013). It is recommended that law enforcement officers and corrections personnel use good judgment in this matter and not compromise their individual safety in the performance of their duties.

Arab Small Business Owners

Racial and ethnic tensions exist between Arab grocers and liquor store owners in low-income areas and members of other minority groups. The dynamics between Arab store owners and African Americans are similar to those between Koreans and African Americans in inner cities. The non-Arab often views the Arab as having money and exploiting the local residents for economic gain. Dr. James Zogby explains that this perception is reinforced because, in some locales, one rarely sees a non-Arab working in an Arab-owned store. The local resident, according to Zogby, does not understand that the Arabs, for the most part, are political refugees (e.g., Palestinians) and have come to the United States for a better life. Despite stereotypes that these store owners have connections to "Arab money" (i.e., oil money), when they first arrive, the only work that they can do is to operate small "marginal" businesses. Most of the small Arab-run grocery stores, liquor stores, and gas stations are family-operated businesses where two brothers, or a father and two sons, for example, are managing the operation. It would not be economically possible for them to hire outside the family (James Zogby, personal communication, August 2013). Police officers, in the midst of conflicts between store owners and residents, can attempt to explain the position of the refugees, but of course, the explanation by itself cannot take care of the problem. Many poor American-born citizens harbor a great deal of animosity toward immigrants and refugees because of scarce resources.

Alcohol is forbidden in the Muslim religion, yet Arab liquor store owners sell it to their customers. There has been a debate in the Arab American community as to whether Muslim immigrants and refugees should go into this type of business. For the majority of newcomers, however, the choices are very limited. Members of other ethnic groups have also owned mom-and-pop stores throughout the years.

Finally, there is another dimension to the problem of Arab store owners in inner cities. Many inner-city residents (Arab Americans and African Americans included) do not feel that law enforcement officials take the needs of the inner city as seriously as they do elsewhere. A pattern has emerged in the Arab American community whereby Arab American store owners feel that they themselves have to take on problems of crime in their stores (John Zogby, personal communication, August 2013). If an Arab store owner is robbed and is treated in an unsupportive or harsh way by police, he feels that he has to defend himself and his store all by himself. In some cases, Arab store owners have assaulted shoplifters in their stores, potentially risking becoming victims themselves. Like many other minority group members, some Arab shop owners in the inner city have given up on the police. Police officers cannot solve the social ills that plague the inner city, but, at a minimum, need to instill the confidence that they will be as supportive as possible when dealing with the crimes that immigrant/refugee store owners experience. In addition, Arab shop or gas station owners often assist their more recently arrived relatives in opening similar businesses. Many of these recent immigrants do not know the system or all the regulations for running a business. There have been instances of store owners being chastised for running "illegal" businesses, when in fact they were not familiar with the complete process required for proper licensing (Haddad, personal communication, July 2006).

Hate Crimes against Arab Americans

In August 2013, the Department of Justice announced that a number of additional groups would be included in the national program that tracks hate crime, i.e., the Uniform Crime Reporting Program , discussed in Chapters 11 and 12. These groups include Arab Americans as well as individuals from South Asia, such as Sikhs and Hindus (also, Buddhists who are from all parts of Asia). As of the writing of this text's sixth edition, there were no published DOJ statistics on hate crimes against "Arab Americans."

The weeks and months following the 9/11 attacks were accompanied by a huge spike in unofficial (i.e., non-DOJ) reporting of hate crimes directed at Arab Americans, Muslim Americans, and those thought to be of the same background. There were more than 700 violent crimes against Arab Americans reported within the first nine weeks after the tragedy of 9/11, and 165 reported hate crimes from January 1, 2002, through October 11, 2002, a figure higher than most years in the previous decade (ADC Research Institute, 2003). However, the American-Arab Anti-Discrimination Committee (ADC) emphasized that this did not represent the actual total number of hate crimes; many cases were not made public because victims feared additional violence against them. Dearborn, Michigan, Police Chief Ronald Haddad points out that fear is a universal human emotion when one is victimized, and this fear factor plays an important role in why many hate crimes go unreported. In explaining the lack of reporting to police, it is also important to recognize the Arab value of honor and maintaining harmony whenever possible (Haddad, personal communication, July 2006).

Prior to the terrorist attacks of 9/11, "single-bias" hate crimes (with a single motivation) against people from one ethnic or national group were the second *least* reported of the hate crimes. The initial spike in post-9/11 hate crimes against Arab Americans or those perceived to be Arab or Muslim has declined significantly as community members and law enforcement officers work together to curb the number of incidents.

Weeks before the war with Iraq, the FBI warned of a similar potential surge in hate crimes. Top FBI officials met with Arab and Muslim leaders in the United States to assure them of the FBI's priority to prevent and investigate hate crimes. This was a step that they had *not* initially taken in the aftermath of 9/11. The targeted interviews of thousands of Iraqis living in the United States were also organized in part to reassure the Iraqi community that law enforcement officials would not tolerate any ethnic backlash in the case of a war ("FBI: War Could . . .," 2009).

In 2008, the ADC reported on hate crimes and discrimination against Arab Americans between the years 2003 and 2007. While the actual number of hate crimes was down as compared to the immediate post-9/11 period, there were nevertheless significant numbers of hate crimes, acts of discrimination (especially at airports and at the workplace), and border and customs issues targeted toward Arab Americans (ADC Research Institute, 2008). Vandalism and destruction of property at mosques and Islamic centers were on the rise during the years 2003–2007 (ADC Research Institute, 2008). Nevertheless, in the ADC's report of hate crimes during this period, praise was given to law enforcement authorities:

> Hate crimes have for the most part been thoroughly investigated by law enforcement authorities, particularly the civil rights division of the Department of Justice (DOJ). ADC commends local, state and federal law enforcement for their efforts to ensure that Arab Americans and those perceived to be Arab Americans are protected from such abuses and hate crimes. (ADC Research Institute, 2008)

Unfortunately, increases were seen again beginning in 2010. The Southern Poverty Law Institute summarized FBI data by reporting "that there were 157 anti-Muslim hate crimes in 2011, down very slightly from the 160 recorded in 2010. The 2011 crimes occurred during a period when Islam-bashing propaganda, which initially took off in 2010, continued and even intensified" (SPLI, 2013). In 2013, Arab Americans were once again the targets of violence after the highly publicized Boston Marathon bombings.

Relations between Law Enforcement and Arab Americans Post-9/11

According to a study released by the Vera Institute of Justice in 2006, "In the aftermath of September 11, Arab Americans have a greater fear of racial profiling and immigration enforcement than of falling victim to hate crimes." Nearly 100 Arab Americans and over 100 law enforcement personnel (FBI agents and police officers) participated in the study, which was conducted from 2003 to 2005. Interviewees in the study, both from the Arab American community and from the law enforcement agencies, felt that cooperation and trust post-9/11 had deteriorated. Arab Americans reported an "increasing sense of victimization, suspicion of law enforcement, and concerns about protecting their civil liberties" (Henderson, Ortiz, Sugie, and Miller, 2006). Interview inquiries confirmed that:

> September 11 had a substantial impact on Arab American communities. In every site, Arab Americans described heightened levels of public suspicion exacerbated by increased media attention and targeted governmental policies (such as special registration requirements, voluntary interviews, and the detention and deportation of community members). Although community members also reported increases in hate victimization, they expressed greater concern about being victimized by federal policies and practices than by individual acts of harassment or violence. Among law enforcement, the most notable change was a new pressure to incorporate counterterrorism into their work. Local police and FBI participants alike reported that this pressure had frequently resulted in policies that were poorly defined or inconsistently applied. (Henderson et al., 2006)

The findings of the Vera Institute Study support the recommendations of the ADC that were published soon after 9/11. To build trust, the ADC recommends that law enforcement agencies and Arab Americans work closely with one another especially to foster a safe environment where citizens feel comfortable reporting hate crimes. The ADC recommends that law enforcement officials avoid stereotyping as suspects those involved in lawful political and religious activities, with the reminder that racial profiling is neither effective nor acceptable (ADC, 2002).

Summary

- There is some confusion as to who Arabs and Middle Easterners are; although commonly thought of as Arabs, Iranians and Turks are not Arabs, and they do not speak Arabic. Many people assume that all Muslims are Arabs, and vice versa. Many Arabs are also Christians, and the world's Muslim population is actually composed of dozens of ethnic groups. Nevertheless, the predominant religion among Arabs is Islam, and its followers are called Muslims. Israel is the only country in the Middle East in which the majority of the population is Jewish; there are also Arabs living in Israel who are Christians or Muslims.

- The first wave of Arab immigrants, largely from Syria, came between 1880 and World War I to further themselves economically. The second wave of Arab immigrants to the United States, beginning after World War II, came in large part as students and professionals seeking to escape economic instability and political unrest in their home countries. The communities with the largest Arab American populations are in Los Angeles/Orange County, Detroit, the greater New York area, Chicago, and Washington, D.C. California has the largest "cluster" of Arab American communities.

- There is great diversity among Arab American groups. Understanding this diversity will assist officers in not categorizing Arabs as homogeneous and will encourage people to move away from thinking in stereotypes. Nevertheless, there are several basic Arab cultural values that officers should keep in mind when interacting with Arab American citizens, and these are shared across the various cultural groups. The cultural value of honor is of paramount importance. Family loyalty often takes precedence over other needs. Communication should be courteous and hospitable; honor and the avoidance of shame govern interpersonal interactions and relationships.

- Arab Americans have been wrongly characterized and stereotyped by the media; as with all stereotypes, inaccurate perceptions have affected people's thinking about Arab Americans. Officers should be aware of stereotypes that may influence their judgment. The terrorist stereotype deepened after 9/11, and scapegoating against Arabs spread pervasively across the country.

- Officers can demonstrate to Muslim Arabs a respect for their religion by refraining from interrupting people in the mosque, and during prayers, unless absolutely

necessary; maintaining courteous behavior in mosques, such as not stepping on prayer mats, not walking in front of people who are praying, and not touching a Qur'an. Finally, officers should attempt to work out solutions with community members regarding such issues as noise and parking associated with religious celebrations.

- The basic unit for Arab Americans, especially for recent arrivals and traditional families, is not the individual but the family, including the extended family. If a family member is involved in a police incident, officers should expect that other family members will become actively involved; this is not an attempt to interfere with police affairs. Traditionally and outwardly, the father is the head of the household and much of the conversation should be directed toward him; this does not mean that the officer should ignore any women who are present.

- There are a number of specific cultural practices and taboos that officers should consider when communicating with Arab Americans who have preserved a traditional lifestyle. Be respectful of the preference of some Arab women to be modest. Male officers should not touch a woman at all, and should be mindful of her modesty in front of male officers. Traditional Arabs deeply value hospitality; it is a hallmark of culture in the Middle East. There are cultural differences in communication style that can affect officers' judgment and reactions. Becoming highly emotional (verbally and nonverbally) and speaking loudly is not looked down upon in the Arab world.

- Law enforcement needs to be continually vigilant as to the potential for hate crimes against Arab Americans and other Middle Eastern groups. In addition, some Middle Eastern immigrants bring negative perceptions of the police from their own experiences, and these contribute to difficulty in trusting the police.

Discussion Questions and Issues

1. *Police/Ethnic Community Relations.* Discuss the following incident that took place at the end of the holy month of Ramadan in a city close to Detroit: officers ticketed many cars parked across the street from a mosque. According to community people, the stores adjacent to the parking lots were closed, and although parking was technically for customers only, Arab Americans did not anticipate that there would be a problem utilizing the parking lot after hours. From a community relations point of view, the mass ticketing created some very negative feelings and a collective perception that

"They (meaning the police) don't respect us; they don't want to understand us." What is your opinion regarding the way things were handled? Do you have any suggestions as to how this situation could have been avoided? Comment on what both the community and the police could have done to prevent the problem.

2. *Who Is the Head of the Household?* The stated head of the household in most traditional Arab families is the father, although the mother actually has a great deal of power within the family. Although in public many Arab women will defer

decision-making to their husbands, a police officer should not discount what the woman might have to offer in various police-related situations. How can the police officer, while respecting the status of the father, still acknowledge the mother and get input from her?

3. *Nonverbal Variations across Cultures.* When Arab Americans greet each other, they sometimes shake hands and then place their right hand on their chest near their heart. This is a sign of sincerity. In your opinion, should officers greet Arab Americans using this gesture if a person greets them in this way? What would be the pros and cons of doing this?

4. *Hospitality toward Officers: A Cultural Gesture.* Hospitality is a virtue in Arab culture and also functions to help people get to know (and see if they can trust) others with whom they are interacting. Given this cultural emphasis on being hospitable, what should an officer do if offered a cup of coffee and something to eat? Should department policy regarding the acceptance of hospitality be reexamined in light of this cultural tendency? Would your answer be different for departments that have adopted a community-based policing philosophy?

5. *"But It's the Custom in My Country."* In January 1991, the Associated Press reported that a Stockton, California, man originally from Jordan was arrested for investigation of "selling his daughter into slavery" because he allegedly accepted $25,000 for her arranged marriage. After police officers had taken the girl to a shelter, a police lieutenant reported on the father's protest claiming that "he was within his rights to arrange his daughter's marriage for a price." The father contacted the police and explained that it was the custom in his country and was perfectly acceptable. The police explained that he couldn't do that in this country: "It is slavery. . . ." The father then went to the shelter where the daughter was being held and was arrested for creating a disturbance. If you were investigating this case, how would you proceed? How might you assess the validity of what the father was saying? If you found out that the act was indeed "perfectly acceptable in his country," how would you explain practices in the United States? Comment on the statement that the police made ("It is slavery"). From the perspective of needing cooperation from this man, what type of approach should be taken?

6. *Officer Discretion: To Let Her Go?* In the section on the perceptions of police, the authors mention an incident involving a Saudi Arabian woman who was caught shoplifting in a 7–11 store. She begged the officer to let her go because she feared being sent home, and there she would receive a harsh punishment (typically, in Saudi Arabia, a person's hand is cut off if he or she steals). The officer decided that since this was her first offense, he would let her go. What is your reaction to the officer's decision? What would you have done?

References

ADC: American-Arab Anti-Discrimination Committee. (2002). *ADC Fact Sheet, Condition of Arab Americans Post-9/11*. Washington, D.C.: ADC Research Institute.

ADC Research Institute. (2003). *Report on Hate Crimes and Discrimination against Arab Americans: The Post-September 11 Backlash, Tracking Crimes from September 11, 2001 through October 11, 2002*. Washington, D.C.: American-Arab Anti-Discrimination Committee.

ADC Research Institute. (2008). *2003–2007 Report on Hate Crimes and Discrimination against Arab Americans*. Washington, D.C.: American-Arab Anti-Discrimination Committee.

AAIF: Arab American Institute Foundation. (2012). *Demographics*.

Berro, Mohammed. (2013, February). Former Corporal, Dearborn, Michigan, Police Department, personal communication.

Code of Federal Regulations. (2003). *Title 8, Aliens and Nationality*. Washington, D.C.: Office of the Federal Register, U.S. Government Printing Office.

Detroit Free Press. (2001). *100 Questions and Answers about Arab Americans: A Journalist's Guide*. Detroit, Michigan.

"FBI: War Could Trigger Hate Crimes." (2009, February 11). Retrieved August 30, 2013, from www.cbsnews.com/2100-500164_162-543781.html

Haddad, Ronald. (2006, July). Police Chief, Dearborn, Michigan, Police Department, personal communication.

Henderson, Nicole, Christopher Ortiz, Naomi Sugie, and Joel Miller. (2006, June). *Law Enforcement and Arab American Community Relations after September 11, 2001: Engagement in a Time of Uncertainty*. New York: Vera Institute of Justice.

Ismail, Lobna. (2013, July). President of Connecting Cultures, Washington, D.C., personal communication.

Khan, Humera. (2013, August). Executive Director of Muflehun, personal communication.

Knafo, Saki. (2011, September 18). "Occupy Wall Street: Protesters Gather for Demonstration Modeled on Arab Spring." *Huffington Post*.

Lohmann, Ashley. (2013, January 24). "Sheikhs and Stereotypes in American Media." *Fair Observer*.

Terrazas, Aaron. (2011, March). "Middle Eastern and North African Immigrants in the United States." *Migration Policy Institute*.

Samhan, Helen. (2006, August). Executive Director, Arab American Institute, Foundation, Washington, D.C., personal communication.

Shaheen, Jack. G. (2001). *Reel Bad Arabs: How Hollywood Vilifies a People*. New York: Olive Branch Press.

Shora, Nawar. (2009). *The Arab-American Handbook: A Guide to the Arab, Arab-American, and Muslim Worlds*. Seattle: Cune Press.

SPLI: Southern Poverty Law Institute. (2013, Spring). FBI: Bias Crimes against Muslims Remain at High Levels. *Intelligence Report*, 149.

Today's Zaman. (2012, January 29). *Turkish minister: I deny the Armenian genocide, come arrest me*. Retrieved July 23, 2013, from www.todayszaman.com/news-269907-turkish-minister-i-deny-the-armenian-genocide-come-arrest-me.html

Wallace, Rob, & Lauren Effron. (2010, October 1). "Does the Koran Advocate Violence?" *ABC News*.

Woodruff, D. (1991, February 4). "Letter from Detroit: Where the Mideast Meets the Midwest—Uneasily." *Business Week*, p. 30A.

The World Factbook. (2013). Washington, D.C.: Central Intelligence Agency.

Zogby, James, Ph.D. (2013, August). Director, Arab American Institute Foundation, Washington, D.C., personal communication.

Zogby, John, Ph.D. (2013, August). President, Zogby International, New York, personal communication.

9 Law Enforcement Contact with Native Americans

LEARNING OBJECTIVES

After reading this chapter, you should be able to:

- Describe the historical background of Native Americans, especially as it relates to the dynamics between law enforcement representatives and Indians today.
- Define the terms *reservation, Indian country*, and *federally recognized tribe.*
- Understand cultural commonalities shared by most traditional Indian tribes.
- Recognize characteristics of traditional Native American communication styles, including aspects of verbal and nonverbal interaction.
- Provide examples of terms, labels, and stereotypes that have been used to refer to or disparage Native Americans.
- Identify select characteristics of the traditional Native American extended family, as well as assimilation problems of those who lack cultural and family support.
- List and discuss key issues associated with law enforcement contact with Native Americans.

OUTLINE

- Introduction
- Historical Information and Background
- Native American Populations, Reservations, Tribes, and Identity
- Similarities among Native Americans
- Language and Communication
- Offensive Terms, Labels, and Stereotypes
- Family and Acculturation Issues
- Key Issues in Law Enforcement
- Summary
- Discussion Questions and Issues

INTRODUCTION

"It's just a bunch of Indians—let them go!"

Retired Chief Jim Cox, a Comanche Indian formerly with the Midwest City Police Department in Oklahoma, heard a police officer utter these words in the context of a traumatic moment he experienced as a youth in Oklahoma. He was riding with other Native American teenagers in an old Nash automobile. Police officers stopped the car and discovered that the teens had been drinking. Instead of taking appropriate action, which would have been to arrest the young people or at least to call the parents to pick up the kids, the officers let them go. Cox recalls to this day his feeling that Indians were not worth the time or bother: he interpreted the officer's statement to mean that if the young people had killed themselves, it did not matter because they were "just Indians" (Cox, personal communication, May 2009). This impression of biased and prejudicial treatment of Indians[*] remained with him even after he had become a police officer. Dr. Peggy Bowen, Native American and Assistant Professor of Criminal Justice, expressed the sentiment that "as distasteful as the remark was then, it is absolutely still the reality today" (Bowen, personal communication, August 2013).

JOSE RIVERA, NATIVE AMERICAN CALIFORNIA STATE PEACE OFFICER (RETIRED)

When an officer contacts an Indian person, there is often 500 years of frustration built up. . . . Officers should be aware of the "baggage" that they bring to the encounter. (Rivera, personal communication, August 2013)

SITTING BULL [LAKOTA], IN THE SPIRIT OF CRAZY HORSE

What treaty that the whites have kept has the red man broken? Not one. What treaty that the white man ever made with us have they kept? Not one. When I was a boy the Sioux owned the world; the sun rose and set on their land; they sent ten thousand men to battle. Who slew [the warriors]? Where are our lands? Who owns them? What white man can say I ever stole his land . . . ? Yet, they say I am a thief. What white woman, however lonely, was ever captive or insulted by me? Yet they say I am a bad Indian. What white man has ever seen me drunk? Who has seen me . . . abuse my children? What law have I broken? Is it wicked for me because my skin is red? (Matthiessen, 1992)

HISTORICAL INFORMATION AND BACKGROUND

Recorded history disputes the origins of the first "Indians" in America. Some researchers claim that they arrived from Asia more than 40,000 years ago; others claim that they arose spontaneously. Recent DNA research indicates that Native Americans came to North America in waves from Siberia; anthropological findings estimate the timing at 15,000 years ago (Powell, 2012). In any case, despite their long history in North America and the fact that they were the first "Americans," traditional U.S. history books simply mentioned their existence upon the arrival of Christopher Columbus in 1492. The depiction of native peoples as insignificant reflects an ethnocentric and Eurocentric view of history.

Even the word *Indian* is not a term that Native Americans originally used to designate their tribes or communities. Because Columbus did not know that North and South America

---

[*]The authors use the terms *Native American, American Indian*, and *Indian* interchangeably. *Native American* is often preferred as the generic name; however, government agencies often break down this overly broad category into American Indian and Alaska Native. In modern usage, the term *Native Americans* can also include Native Hawaiians, Chamorros (native people of Guam), and American Samoans. This chapter does not include information about these cultural groups.

existed, he thought he had reached the Indies, which then included India, China, the East Indies, and Japan. In fact, when he arrived in what is now called the West Indies (in the Caribbean), he referred to the people he met as *Indians* (*Los Indios*). Eventually, this became the name for all the indigenous peoples in the Americas. However, before white settlers came to North and South America, almost every "Indian" tribe had its own name, and despite some shared cultural values, Native Americans did not see themselves as one collective group or call themselves *Indians*. Over the years, most tribes have referred to themselves in their own languages as "The People," "The Allies," or "The Friends." Some of the terms that whites use for various tribes are not even authentic names. For example, the label *Sioux*, which means enemy or snake, was originally a term given to that group by an enemy tribe and then adopted by French traders.

Traditionally, rather than being described as part of the American people's common legacy, Native American cultural heritage has often been presented as bits of colorful "exotica." Genocide, or the killing of entire tribes, is not a feature of U.S. history on which people have wanted to focus. The reality is that Euro-American and Indian relations have long been characterized by hostility, contempt, and brutality. Native peoples have generally been treated by Euro-Americans as less than human or as "savages," and their rich cultures have been ignored or crushed. For this reason, many American Indians do not share in the celebrations of Thanksgiving or Christopher Columbus Day. To say that Columbus discovered America implies that Native Americans were not considered "human enough" to be of significance.

Ignoring the existence of Native Americans before 1492 constitutes only one aspect of ethnocentrism. American Indians' experience with the "white man" has largely been one of exploitation, violence, and forced relocation. This historical background has shaped Native American views of Euro-Americans and their culture. While most people in the United States have a sense that Native Americans were not treated with dignity in U.S. history, many are not aware of the extent of current societal prejudices against them. Overall, the American Indian and Alaska Native grouping is a small and traditionally "forgotten minority" in the United States, constituting approximately 5.2 million people or only 1.7 percent of the overall population (U.S. Census Bureau, 2012).

It would not be accurate to say that no progress at all has been made in the United States with respect to the awareness and rights of our nation's first Americans. Today in public schools across the United States, some educators are beginning to discuss the realistic nature of the contact with Native Americans in early American history. At the government level, former President Bill Clinton renewed his commitment to tribal sovereignty by issuing Executive Order 13175 on consultation with tribal governments. The purpose of the Order was "to establish regular and meaningful consultation and collaboration with tribal officials in the development of Federal policies that have tribal implications, to strengthen the United States government-to-government relationships with Indian tribes, and to reduce the imposition of unfunded mandates upon Indian tribes" (Federal Register, 2000). President Obama's speech to the Crow Indian Nation on their reservation in Montana acknowledged the failure of the U.S. government to keep its promises to Native Americans, referring to a "tragic history."

> Few have been ignored by Washington for as long as Native Americans—the first Americans . . . I understand the tragic history . . . Our government has not always been honest or truthful in our deals. (Zeleny, 2008)

In 2013, President Obama signed an executive order establishing the White House Council on Native American Affairs "as a means of promoting and sustaining prosperous and resilient tribal communities" (White House, 2013).

The U.S. government has not always acted in good faith toward its Native American citizens, instead seriously and repeatedly disregarding Indian rights that have been guaranteed in the form of binding treaties. Consequently, individuals and tribes are reluctant to trust the words of the government or people representing "the system." Whether they are aware of it or not, law enforcement agents are perceived in the same light and carry this "baggage" into encounters with Native Americans. Historically, the police officer from outside the reservation has been a symbol of rigid and authoritarian governmental control that has affected nearly every aspect of Indian life. Officers, like most citizens, have only a limited understanding of how the government, including the criminal justice system, caused massive suffering by not allowing Indians to preserve their cultures, identities, languages, sacred sites, rituals, and lands. Because of this, officers have a responsibility to educate themselves about the history of the treatment of Indian peoples in order to deal with them effectively and fairly today. Law enforcement officers must understand Indian communities and put forth extra effort to establish rapport. Doing so will increase the possibility of success in gaining cooperation and respect from people who never before had any reason to trust any representative of the government.

One example of a process of building trust between Native Americans and law enforcement occurred in Seattle after an Indian wood carver was shot on the street by a police officer for not putting his small carving knife down quickly enough. As tensions rose in the community, a mediated discussion was held among family members of the deceased, other Native Americans, and local law officials. "The [wood] carvers expressed anger over what they perceived to be a lack of respect shown by many newer officers for First Nations/Native American people, other minorities, and the homeless, as well as about the way the 'command and control' approach demands obedience and escalates quickly and unnecessarily into use of force to punish those the police don't like or who don't obey. As [the deceased man's brother] asked bluntly: 'Who gives you the right to play God?'" (Brenneke, 2012). While this discussion and others held later were mostly successful at calming community tensions, the City of Seattle Police Department was nevertheless put under investigation by the Department of Justice for "a pattern and practice of unconstitutional excessive use of force and a need for serious structural reform in training, supervision, and discipline" (Brenneke, 2012). It was a painful situation for all concerned; a situation that could have been avoided if ample levels of trust had existed on all sides.

Native Americans and Military Service

For some American Indians, an additional phenomenon aggravates the repeated breach of trust by the federal government. There is a very proud tradition of American Indians serving in the armed services. For more than 200 years, they have participated with distinction in U.S. military actions. American military leaders, beginning with George Washington in 1778, have recognized American Indians to be courageous, determined, and as having a "fighting spirit" (CEHIP, 1996). American Indians contributed to military efforts in the 1800s and participated on an even larger scale beginning in the 1900s. In World War I, it is estimated that 12,000 American Indians served in the military.

> More than 44,000 American Indians, out of a total Native American population of less than 350,000, served with distinction between 1941 and 1945 in both European and Pacific theaters of war. Native American men and women on the home front also showed an intense desire to serve their country, and were an integral part of the war effort. More than 40,000 Indian people left their reservations to work in ordnance depots, factories, and other war industries. American Indians also invested more than $50 million in war bonds, and contributed generously to the Red Cross and the Army and Navy Relief societies. . . . The Native American's strong sense of patriotism and courage emerged once again during the Vietnam era. More than 42,000 Native Americans, more than 90 percent of them volunteers, fought in Vietnam. (CEHIP, 1996)

No description of Native American participation in war would be complete without mentioning the Navajo Code Talkers, whose efforts on behalf of the U.S. Marine Corps completely stumped expert Japanese code breakers during World War II. Kept secret for over two decades due to security concerns, the service of these Navajo veterans was revealed to the public in the late 1960s, and finally honored in a moving ceremony held at the White House (Jevec, 2001).

In Desert Storm, Bosnia, and the wars in Afghanistan and Iraq, Native Americans continued to serve in the U.S. Armed Forces with the estimated number having exceeded 12,000 American Indians ("First American . . ." 2003).

NATIVE AMERICAN POPULATIONS, RESERVATIONS, TRIBES AND IDENTITY

According to Bureau of Indian Affairs (BIA) figures, there are 566 federally recognized tribal governments in the United States (the words *tribe* and *nation* may also be used), and these include native groups of Alaskans such as Aleuts (BIA, 2013). The three states with the largest Native American populations in 2010 were, in descending order, California, Oklahoma, and Arizona (U.S. Census Bureau, 2012).

Each federally recognized tribe has a distinct history and culture and often a separate language. Each has its own government, schools, and law enforcement and economic systems. The previously mentioned executive order signed by President Obama underscores this issue: "The United States recognizes a government-to-government relationship, as well as a unique legal and political relationship, with federally recognized tribes" (White House, 2013). However, there are still many tribes that, for historical and political reasons, do not benefit from federally recognized status. Members of such tribes are not necessarily eligible for special benefits under federal Indian programs. On the other hand, fraud in this area is quite rampant whereby people falsely claim Indian ancestry to take unfair advantage of governmental benefits and other perceived opportunities. Some tribes may be state recognized or in the process of seeking federal recognition, while others may not seek recognition at all. The issue of increasing rivalry among some Indian groups seeking recognition is reflected in the sentiment that some Indian tribes are pitted against each other over government benefits and resources.

Indian tribe   Any Indian or Alaska Native tribe, band, nation, pueblo, village, or community that the Secretary of the Interior acknowledges to exist as an Indian tribe (U.S. Code, 2012b).

Indian Country   "All land within the limits of any Indian reservation under the jurisdiction of the United States Government . . ., all dependent Indian communities within the borders of the United States whether within the original or subsequently acquired territory thereof, and whether within or without the limits of a state, and all Indian allotments, the Indian titles to which have not been extinguished . . ." (U.S. Code, 2012a).

An Indian reservation is land that a tribe has reserved for its exclusive use through statutes, executive order, or the course of treaty-making. It may be on ancestral lands or on the only land available when tribes were forced to give up their original territories through federal treaties. A reservation is also land that the federal government holds in trust for the use of an Indian tribe. The BIA administers and manages over 56 million acres of land that are held in trust for American Indians, Indian tribes, and Alaska natives. Census results for 2010 show over 1.1 million Indians and Alaska natives living on reservations (U.S. Census, 2012). It should be noted, however, that a total of 4.6 million people live on American Indian reservations or in Alaska Native villages; thus, 76 percent of these residents are *not* American Indian or Alaska Natives (Perry, 2012).

The largest of the American Indian reservations is that of the Navajo Nation which extends into three states—Arizona, New Mexico, and Utah. Indians are not forced to stay on reservations, but many who leave have a strong desire to remain in touch with and be nourished by their home cultures. For this reason and because of culture shock experienced in urban life, many later return to reservations.

In general, the Indian population is characterized by constant movement between the reservation and the city, and sometimes relocation from city to city. In urban areas, when officers encounter American Indians, they will not necessarily know how acculturated to city life those individuals are. In rural areas it is easier for officers to get to know the culture of a particular tribe. In the city, one's tribal background may be less significant than the fact that the person is an American Indian.

Since the early 1980s, more than half of the Native American population has been living outside of reservation communities; many have left to pursue educational and employment opportunities, as life on some of the reservations can be very bleak. Although a large number returns home to the reservation to participate in family activities and tribal ceremonies, many attempt to remake their lives in urban areas. A percentage of Indians does adjust to mainstream educational and occupational life, but the absolute numbers are still disproportionately low.

As with other culturally or ethnically defined categories of people (e.g., Asian, African American), it would be a mistake to lump all Native Americans together and to assume that they are homogeneous. For example, in Arizona alone, one finds a number of different tribes with varying traditions: there are Hopis in the northeast, Pimas and Papagos in the south, Apaches in the north-central region, and Yuman groups in the west. All of these descend from people who came to what is now called *Arizona*. The relative "newcomers" are the Navajos and Apaches, who arrived about 1,000 years ago. Overall, these six tribes represent differences in culture, with each group having its own history and life experiences.

Broadly speaking, in the United States there are distinct cultural groups among Native Americans. Every tribe has evolved its own sets of traditions and beliefs, and each sees itself as distinct from other tribes despite some significant broad similarities. However, since the governmental removal of entire tribes from their homelands, tribes ended up spread out across the country as forced migrants from their homes. For example, as a result of the Indian Removal Act of 1830, five tribes—Cherokee, Choctaw, Chickasaw, Creek, and Seminole—were forced to relocate to Oklahoma in an area designated as Indian Territory. Some of these tribes were traditional enemies, though in current times, they have learned to coexist peacefully.*

Law enforcement officials may find themselves confused about who an American Indian is. The issue of identity is important for law enforcement because of jurisdictional laws governing which police departments, tribal or state/local, may arrest and prosecute criminals (i.e., whether Indian or non-Indian; jurisdiction is discussed later in this chapter). Individuals may claim to have "Indian blood," but tribes have their own criteria for determining tribal membership. Because the determination of tribal membership is a fundamental attribute of tribal sovereignty, the federal government generally defers to tribes' own determination when establishing eligibility criteria under special Indian entitlement programs.

---

*Some readers may have heard of the "Trail of Tears," the Cherokee nation's description of their forced migration in 1838 and 1839 from Georgia, Tennessee, and North Carolina to an area in present-day Oklahoma. They called this journey the "Trail of Tears" because of the tragic effects of hunger, disease, and exhaustion on the forced march during which several thousand Cherokee men, women, and children died. The bitterness remains today among some descendents of the original people of the "Trail of Tears." While no records have been kept, there are also many stories of people who refused to go on the forced march and were killed by federal authorities.

In the reverse, individuals may claim to be Indian when they are not. When a tribal member leaves the reservation, he or she is subject to the laws of the surrounding county and state as anyone else would be. But the question of Indian identity arises when an Indian is in "Usual and Accustomed" (U&A) places where Native Americans may exercise treaty rights such as hunting or fishing. If, for example, hunting season is not open for non-Native Americans, and a state wildlife officer sees someone with a rifle, the officer might question that individual and request identification. Non-Native Americans may claim to be Indian when they are not in order to take advantage of Native Americans' rights on U&A lands. If officers have any doubt, about whether the individual they encounter is truly an Indian, they should ask to which tribe the person belongs and then contact the tribal headquarters to verify that person's identity. Every tribe has its own administration and authority, the members of which will be able to answer questions of this nature. By verifying information about the individual's identity with tribal authorities rather than making personal determinations of "Indianness," officers will help create good rapport between tribal members and law enforcement officials (Becker, personal communication, 2013).

In another potentially confusing area of identity determination, some Native Americans in the southwest have Spanish first or last names (because of intermarriage or because they adopted or were given these names by early *conquistadores*—conquerors—from Spain) and may "look" Hispanic or Latino (e.g., Hopis). Identification can be difficult for officers, so they should not assume that a person is Latino just because of the name or appearance. Many Native Americans do not want to be grouped with Latinos because (1) they are not Latinos; (2) they may resent that some Latinos deny their Indian ancestry and instead identify only with the Spanish part of their heritage; and (3) many tribes have a history of warfare with the *mestizo* (mixed ancestry) populations of Mexico. As an aside, the majority population in Mexico, Central America, and South America is of "Indian" ancestry. Many Latinos in U.S. border communities are really of Indian, not Spanish, heritage, or they may be a mixture of the two.

SIMILARITIES AMONG NATIVE AMERICANS

Significant differences exist among the cultures, languages, history, and socioeconomic status of Native American tribes, communities, and individuals. Yet, it is still possible to talk about general cultural characteristics of Native American groups without negating their diversity. The cultural characteristics described in the following sections apply to Native Americans, who are traditionally "Indian" in their orientation to life. While being aware of tribal differences, the law enforcement officer should also understand that there is a strong cultural link among the many worlds and tribes of Native Americans and their Indian counterparts throughout the American continent.

Philosophy toward the Earth and the Universe

"The most striking difference between . . . Indian and Western man is the manner in which each views his role in the universe. The prevailing non-Indian view is that man is superior to all other forms of life and that the universe is his to be used as he sees fit . . . an attitude justified as the mastery of nature for the benefit of man [characterizes Western philosophy]" (Bahti, 1982). Through its contrast with Western philosophy (that people have the capacity to alter nature), we can gain insight into the values and philosophies common to virtually all *identifying* Native Americans. While acknowledging the character of each Indian tribe or nation, there is a common set of values and beliefs involving the earth and the universe, resulting in a deep respect for nature and "mother earth." According to American Indian philosophy, the earth is sacred and is a living entity. By spiritual involvement with the earth, nature, and the universe, individuals bind themselves to their environment. Indians do not see themselves as superior to all else (e.g., animals, plants) but rather as part of all creation. Through religious ceremonies and rituals, Indians are able to transcend themselves to be in harmony with the universe and connected to nature.

The inclination of people who do not understand this philosophy might be to dismiss it as primitive and even backward. The costumes, the rituals, the ceremonies, and the dances are often thought of as colorful but strange. Yet from an Indian perspective, "It is a tragedy indeed that Western man in his headlong quest for Holy Progress could not have paused long enough to learn this basic truth—one which he is now being forced to recognize (with the spoilage of the earth), much to his surprise and dismay. Ever anxious to teach 'backward' people, he is ever reluctant to learn from them" (Bahti, 1982). Many non-Indians now embrace certain Native American beliefs regarding the environment; what people once thought of as primitive, they now see as essential in the preservation of our environment. Native Americans speak of "earth wisdom," a cultural legacy from their traditions that all people should embrace for the future of the environment.

An Indian prayer

Oh our Mother the earth, Oh our Father the sky,
Your children are we, and with tired backs
We bring you the gifts you love.
Then weave for us a garment of brightness . . .
May the fringes be the falling rain.
May the border be the standing rainbow.
That we may walk fittingly where birds sing . . . and where grass is green
Oh our mother earth, Oh our father sky. (Author unknown)

When law enforcement officers make contact with people who are in the midst of celebrating or praying, whether on reservations or in communities, it is vitally important to be as respectful as possible. Officers must refrain from conveying an air of superiority and ethnocentrism, or an attitude that "those rituals" are primitive. Native American prayers, rituals, and ceremonies represent ancient beliefs and philosophies, many of which have to do with the preservation of and harmony with the earth. Thus, officers should, at all costs, try to avoid interrupting prayers and sacred ceremonies, just as one would avoid interrupting church services. (Officers should also be aware that taking photographs during ceremonies would constitute an interruption and is forbidden. In general, officers should seek permission before taking photos of American Indians; this is true for many tribes. Visitors to some reservations are told that their cameras will be confiscated if they take pictures.)

In certain parts of the country, people are revitalizing Native American culture rather than letting it die. For some tribes and individuals, the result is a sense of "pan-Indianism" in which there is a growing pride around ethnic Indian identity. Members of tribes or communities with very different traditions identify as a group by following certain practices that are associated with Indians. Examples include males wearing long hair, a symbol of strength and power—if you shame yourself, you cannot have long hair (Bowen, personal communication, August 2013); the use of the sacred pipe (i.e., the pipestone pipe, sometimes called the *peace pipe*); and participation in rituals, sweat lodges, and the sacred sun dance for purification. Many tribes have these elements in their traditions, and tribes practice them to varying degrees, gravitating more toward one tradition over another (Rivera, personal communication, August 2013).

It should be noted that the pan-Indian movement is not necessarily viewed positively by all Indians; some believe that there is a strong possibility of misusing a tradition or diluting the meaning of a ritual. There are some tribes that are reviving their own identities by emphasizing their unique customs and strengths rather than identifying with the pan-Indian movement.

LANGUAGE AND COMMUNICATION

It is possible to make generalizations about the way a group of people communicates, even when there is great diversity within the group. The following contains information about nonverbal and verbal aspects of communication as well as tips for the law enforcement officer interacting with Native Americans. The paragraphs that follow describe patterns of communication and behavior as exhibited by some American Indians who are traditional in their outlook. No description of communication traits, however, would ever apply to everyone within a group, especially within one that is so diverse.

Openness and Self-Disclosure

Many Native Americans, in early encounters, use caution in their interactions with others in order to demonstrate humility and create harmony. Too much openness is to be avoided, as is disclosing personal and family problems. This often means that an officer has to work hard to establish rapport and gain trust. In contrast, within mainstream American culture, appearing friendly and open is highly valued—especially in certain regions such as the West Coast and the South. Because different modes of behavior are expected and accepted, non-Indians may view Indians as aloof and reserved. The Indian perception can be that Euro-Americans, due to their excessive openness, are superficial and thus untrustworthy. Mainstream American culture encourages open expression of opinions, while American Indian culture encourages calmness and emotional control.

Silence and Interruptions

The ability to remain quiet, to be still, and to observe is highly valued in Native American culture; consequently, silence is truly a virtue. (In mainstream American culture, it is said that "silence is golden," but this is probably more an expression of an ideal than a description of a fact.) Indians are taught to study and assess situations and only act or participate when one is properly prepared (Bowen, personal communication, August 2013). When law enforcement officials contact Native Americans, they may mistake this reticence to talk as sullenness or a lack of cooperation. The behavior must not be misinterpreted or taken personally. A cultural trait must be understood as just that: a behavior, action, or attitude that is not intended to be a personal insult. The officer must also consider that interrupting an Indian when he or she speaks is seen as very aggressive and should be avoided whenever possible. As a survival skill on the reservation, Dr. Peggy Bowen, as a child, learned to remain silent and especially to avoid speaking directly to a male. Direct communication was perceived as a challenge to authority. While this has changed to a certain extent because of the influence of the media, a reticence to talk directly to authority is still prevalent (ibid.).

Talking and Questions

Talking just to fill silence is not seen as important. The small talk that one observes in mainstream society ("Hi, how are you? How was your weekend?" and so on) is traditionally not required by Native Americans. Words are considered powerful and are therefore chosen carefully. This cultural trait may result in a situation in which Native Americans retreat and appear to be withdrawn if someone else is dominating a conversation. When law enforcement officials question Native Americans who exhibit this tendency (i.e., preferring formality and/or silence), the officer should not press aggressively for answers. Aggressive behavior, both verbal and physical, is traditionally looked down upon. Questions should be open-ended, and the officer willing to respect the silence and the time it may take to find out the needed information.

Nonverbal Communication: Eye Contact, Touching

With respect to American Indian cultures, people often make the statement that Indians avoid making direct eye contact. Although this is true for some tribes, it does not hold true for all. Some Indian tribes believe that looking directly into another person's eyes for a prolonged period of time is disrespectful, just as pointing at someone is considered impolite. Direct eye contact can be viewed as an affront or an invasion of privacy by some tribes. Navajo tribe members tend to stare at each other when they want to express anger. An Indian who adheres to the unspoken rules about eye contact may appear to non-Indians to be shifty and evasive. Officers and other law enforcement officials must not automatically judge a person as guilty or suspicious simply because that person is not maintaining direct eye contact. To put a person at ease, the officer can decrease eye contact if it appears to be inhibiting the Native American citizen. Avoidance of eye contact with the officer can also convey the message that the officer is using an approach that is too forceful and demanding. Where such norms about eye contact avoidance apply, and if an officer has to look at a person's eyes, it would help to forewarn the person (e.g., "I'm going to have to check your eyes").

With regard to their sense of space, most Native Americans are not comfortable being touched by strangers, whether a pat on the back or the arm around the shoulder. Either no touching is appropriate or it should be limited to a brief handshake. Married couples do not tend to show affection in public. In addition, people should avoid crowding or standing too close. Keep in mind that Indian relations with strangers are more formal than those of the mainstream culture; therefore, officers might be viewed as overly aggressive if they do not maintain a proper distance. Officers who are going to pat down or search a Native American should first explain the process.

Law enforcement officials may experience particular difficulty when trying to communicate with female Native Americans. Bowen recalls that until she left the reservation, she was unable to maintain direct eye contact with authority because it was never a behavior that was reinforced. As with speaking directly to males, girls and women could get into trouble if they attempted direct eye contact with men. This is still the case, to a certain extent, particularly on reservations that are relatively isolated (Bowen, personal communication, August 2013).

For law enforcement officials in the United States, holding back on judging Native American cultural styles of communication is key to establishing good rapport.

Language

Some Native Americans speak one or more of the 169 Native North American languages in use today (Siebens & Julian, 2011). English, for many, is a second language; those who do not speak English well may be inhibited from speaking. In addition, because many Native Americans tend to speak quietly and nonforcefully, law enforcement agents must demonstrate patience and allow extra time for discussions; interaction must not be rushed. The Native American who is not strong in English needs to spend more time translating from his or her own language to English when formulating a response (this is true of all second-language speakers who are not yet fluent). As with other languages, English words or concepts do not always translate exactly into the various Indian languages. Indian languages are rich and express concepts reflecting unique views of the world. It is mandatory that the utmost respect be shown when Native Americans speak their own languages; in other words, officers would do well to resist the temptation to force them to speak only English in public. Remember that Indians have a long history of forced assimilation into Anglo society, during which, among other things, many were denied the right to speak their native languages.

OFFENSIVE TERMS, LABELS, AND STEREOTYPES

> Native American Indians are a people in transition between history and contemporary America. The challenge for Native Americans is to maintain their heritage, erase a stereotype and adjust recognition in society. Native Americans are too often stereotyped by antiquated and discriminatory attitudes. . . . (Seven Fires Council, 2013)

In the interview cited in the opening of this chapter, retired chief of police Jim Cox, a Comanche Indian, described a situation in which police officers referred to him and his friends as "just a bunch of Indians" in his presence. Proud of his heritage, he was deeply offended by this insensitive communication. In addition, the use of racial slurs toward any group is never acceptable in crime fighting and peacekeeping, no matter how irritated an officer might become. When officers hear others use disrespectful terms and stereotypical statements about Native Americans, they should speak up about this lack of professionalism and disrespect for community diversity.

There are a number of words that are offensive to Native Americans: *chief* (a leader who has reached this rank is highly honored), *squaw* (extremely offensive), *buck*, *redskin*, Indian *brave*, and *skins*. (Some young Indians may use the word *skins* to refer to themselves but would be offended if others use the term.) Words such as *braves*, *chiefs*, *squaws*, and *papooses* are not native Indian terms, but have come about as mistranslations, mispronunciations, or as shortened terms, and are "perpetuated by non-Native Americans" (Seven Fires Council, 2013). In addition, the use of Indian tribal names or references as mascots for sports teams is highly objectionable to many Native Americans.

Other terms used to refer to Native Americans are *apple* (a slightly dated term referring to a highly assimilated Indian: "red" on the outside, "white" on the inside) and *the people* (more commonly used by some groups of Indians to refer to themselves). In some regions of the country, a reservation is called a *rez* by Indians, but this word would not be appreciated when uttered by those who are not Native Americans (Bowen, personal communication, August 2013). It is also patronizing when non-Indians use certain kinship terms, such as *grandfather* when talking to an older man, even though other Indians may use those terms. As a rule of thumb, it is advisable to ask Native Americans how *they* would like to be addressed, and then respect their preferences. The key is to avoid making assumptions about the names used to directly call or indirectly refer to an individual (Bowen, personal communication, August 2013).

Other offensive and commonly used terms include *sitting Indian style* to refer to sitting in a cross-legged position on the floor; *Indian giver* to characterize someone who takes back a present or an offer; *wild Indians* to describe misbehaving children; *powwow* to mean a discussion; or *bottom of the totem pole* to mean lowest ranking. In addition, it is worth noting that some American Indians deliberately choose not to reveal their ethnic identity in the workplace because of concerns about stereotypes about Indians. Coworkers may make comments about Indians or use offensive expressions because they do not "see one in the room." People can be deeply offended and hurt by "unintentional" references to American Indians.

Indians find it offensive when non-Indians make claims that may or may not be true about their Indian ancestry, such as "I'm part Indian—my great-grandfather was Cherokee." Although this may be an attempt to establish rapport, it rings of, "Some of my best friends are Indians" (i.e., to "prove" that one does not have any prejudice). People should not assume affinity with American Indians based on novels, movies, a vacation trip, or an interest in silver jewelry. These are among the most offensive, commonly made errors when non-Indians first encounter an American Indian person or family. Another is a confidential revelation that there is an Indian "princess" in the family tree—tribe unknown, identity unclear, but a bit of glamour in the family myth. The intent may be to establish rapport, but to the Indian these types of statements reveal stereotype images.

Many people growing up in the United States can remember the stereotypical depiction of an Indian as a wild, savage, and primitive person. In older textbooks, including history books recounting Native American history, Indians were said to "massacre" whites, whereas whites simply "fought" or "battled" the Indians (Harris, Moran, & Moran, 2004). Hollywood has to take some responsibility for the promotion of stereotypes as well. "Native Americans have a long history of one-sided portrayals in Hollywood, including such stereotypical characters as the war whooping savage or the grunting tribesman" (Bull, 2009).

Other common stereotypical or disparaging statements include "All Indians are drunks" (an argument has been put forth that the white man introduced "fire water" or alcohol to the Indian as a means of weakening him); "You can't trust an Indian;" "Those damn Indians;" and "The only good Indian is a dead one"—a remark that can be traced back to a statement made by a U.S. General in 1869 (Harris et al., 2004).

Despite the persistence of many social problems, progress has been made with respect to education and political participation among Native Americans. Law enforcement officials must not hold on to the stereotype of American Indians as being uneducated. There is a growing Native American population attending colleges and rising to high positions in education, entertainment, sports, and industry.

FAMILY AND ACCULTURATION ISSUES

Respect for Elders

"Nothing will anger an Indian more than them seeing [his or her] grandmother or grandfather being spoken to belligerently or being ordered around with disrespect. If that happens, that's a firecracker situation right there" (Rivera, personal communication, August 2013). Unlike mainstream American culture, Indian cultures value aging because of the respect they have for wisdom and experience. People do not feel that they have to cover up signs of aging because this phase of life is highly revered. The elders of a tribe or the older people in Native American communities must be shown the utmost respect by people in law enforcement. This includes acknowledging their presence in a home visit, even if they are not directly involved with the police matter at hand. In some tribes (e.g., the Cherokee), the grandmother often has the maximum power in the household and is the primary decision-maker. It is advisable for people in law enforcement to include elders in discussions so they can give their advice or perspective on a situation. The elders are generally respected for their ability to enforce good behavior within the family and tribe.

It should also be noted, however, that because of assimilation or personal preference among some Native Americans, the elders in any given household may tend to avoid interfering with a married couple's problems. And although the elders are respected to a higher degree than in mainstream American culture, they may withdraw in certain situations in which there is police contact, letting the younger family members deal with the problem. If in doubt, it is advisable to begin the contact more formally, deferring to the elders initially. Officers can then observe the extent to which the elders participate and whether the younger family members include them.

Extended Family and Kinship Ties

In mainstream American society, people usually think of and see themselves first as individuals, and, after that, they may or may not identify with their families or various communities and groups with which they are affiliated. In traditional Native American culture, a person's primary identity is related to his or her family and tribe (i.e., a group orientation). Some law enforcement agents may be in positions to make referrals when there is a problem with an individual (e.g., an adolescent) in a family. A referral for counseling for that person alone may be culturally alienating;

family counseling might be a more appropriate alternative. In other words, Western-style individual counseling or therapy is a foreign way to treat problems.

Today, some of this family and tribal cohesiveness has lessened because of forced assimilation, extreme levels of poverty, and lack of education and employment. However, many Native Americans still have large networks of relatives who are in close proximity to each other. It is not uncommon for children to be raised by someone other than the father or mother (e.g., grandmother, aunts). When law enforcement officials enter an Indian's home and, for example, ask to speak to the parents of a child, they may actually end up talking to someone who is not the biological mother or father. Various other relatives can function exactly as a mother or father would in mainstream culture. This does not mean that Indian "natural" parents are lazy about their child-rearing duties, even when the child is physically living with another relative (and may be raised by several relatives throughout childhood). The intensely close family and tribal bonds allow for this type of child raising. The officer must not assume that something is abnormal with this type of arrangement or that the parents are neglecting their children.

Children and Separation from Parents

It is crucial that police officers understand the importance of not separating children from family members if at all possible. Many Native American families in urban areas and on reservations have memories of or have heard stories from elder family members that involved the federal government's routine and systematic removal of Indian children from their homes; in many cases, children were placed in boarding schools operated by the BIA that were often hundreds of miles away. This phenomenon, including education for the children that stripped them of their language and culture, began in the late nineteenth century. The underlying premise was that Indians were savages and did not know how to treat children. Children were punished for speaking their own languages and for saying prayers from their own religious traditions. They were basically uprooted and placed in an alien environment in an attempt by the government to eliminate the Indian population (Bowen, personal communication, August 2013).

Although for many families the severe trauma of children's forced separation from parents took place years ago, the aftereffects linger (Rivera, personal communication, August 2013). In the early twentieth century, there was a famous case in which Hopi Indian fathers were sentenced to Alcatraz Island to hard labor. Their crime was hiding their children from BIA officials because they did not want the children to be taken to the BIA boarding schools. By hiding the children, the Hopi fathers violated federal law and were arrested and charged with sedition. This case is still talked about today (Rivera, personal communication, August 2013). The memory of a "uniform coming to take away a child" is an image that can be conjured up easily by some Indians. It is this "baggage" that law enforcement officers encounter today when interacting with Native Americans. Officers may be totally unaware of the power of Native Americans' memories of these deplorable actions.

Given that Native American parents can be very protective of their children, an officer is well advised to let the parents know about any action that needs to be taken with regard to a child. Law enforcement officers must become knowledgeable about the Indian Child Welfare Act (ICWA), passed by Congress in 1978. Prior to the passage of this Act, Indian children removed from their homes were placed with white foster parents. There were no Indian foster homes, and the tribes did not have any way to deal with cases involving children. With the passage of ICWA, the mandate exists to find viable homes in which to place the children, first with a tribal member, and, if that is not possible, then in a Native American home. How the ICWA works in practice is being tested in courts; the case of *Adoptive Couple v. Baby Girl* went all the way to the Supreme Court (Wolf, 2013). When officers go out on calls to pick up children, there can be serious consequences if officers are not aware of the ICWA and its implications. Law enforcement officials are likely to establish good rapport with Indian families if they treat the children well (i.e., in contact off the reservation), which includes understanding the legal rights of Indian children (Bowen, personal communication, August 2013).

Acculturation to Mainstream Society

People who are caught between two cultures and are successful in neither run the risk of contributing to family breakdown, often becoming depressed, alcoholic, drug dependent, and/or suicidal. However, Indian group members who have remained tightly identified with their culture and religion and who have close-knit extended families tend to exhibit this type of behavior less. With cultural and family support, their isolation from mainstream culture is not as pronounced as it is with individuals and families who lack this support (Bowen, personal communication, August 2013).

In studies on suicide and ethnicity in the United States, much has been written about patterns of what can be described as self-destructive behavior. This has been generalized to those Indian groups whose lives are characterized by despair, and, for many, a loss of ethnic identity. According to Psychologist Dr. Jon Perez, former director of the Behavioral Health Unit of the Indian Health Service (IHS):

> The intergenerational trauma, compounded by extreme poverty, lack of economic opportunity and widespread substance abuse has shattered these communities. Suicide is a single response to a multiplicity of problems. If you have these things going on, and you don't see any hope for the future, suicide seems like an option. (Meyers, 2007)

The national Centers for Disease Control and Prevention has reported that the rate of suicide for "American Indian/Alaska Native adolescents and young adults ages 15 to 34 . . . is 2.5 times higher than the national average for that age group," and that within that age group, "suicide is the second leading cause of death" (CDC, 2012). Various outreach efforts, such as "tribal listening sessions" conducted by the Indian Health Service together with other government agencies, aim to diminish the "ongoing tragedy of suicide in Indian Country" (IHS, 2010).

Mortality rates attributed to alcohol consumption are seven times higher for American Indians and Alaska Natives than for other races (Boyd, Milman, Stuart, Dekker, & Flaherty, 2008). Alcoholism continues to be the leading health and social problem of American Indians. The use of crystal methamphetamine (CM) on some reservations is an issue of epidemic proportions, creating tremendous problems associated with domestic violence and neglect of children. According to a 2006 report commissioned by the BIA, 96 law enforcement agencies in Indian Country were surveyed, and "74 percent said [CM] was the biggest drug threat they faced" (Evans, 2006). This was the most recent comprehensive study of this topic as of the writing of this text's edition. Following are a few of the key findings:

- 60 percent (of all 96 law enforcement agencies in Indian Country) said CM arrests had increased in 2005
- 43 percent said powdered methamphetamine was highly available on their reservations
- 46 percent said CM was highly available
- 64 percent said CM was responsible for an increase in both domestic violence and assault and battery incidents
- 48 percent said child abuse and neglect cases were up because of CM
- 90 percent said they want drug investigation training
- 75 percent said they were paying more overtime to their officers in order to deal with CM

It must be emphasized that the origins of the psychosocial problems that some Indians experience in mainstream society are not due to innate weaknesses or deficiencies. The cause of so many problems for Native Americans dates back to the way the government has handled and regulated Indian life. The dominant society in no way affirmed the cultural identity of

Indians; thus, many Indians have internalized the oppression that they experienced from the outside world. Furthermore, many young people feel the stresses of living between two cultural worlds. They are not fully part of the traditional Indian world as celebrated on the reservation or in a community that honors traditions; neither are they fully adapted to the dominant American culture. Many young people feel alienated when it comes to their native identity, and some older Native Americans complain bitterly that their grandchildren are not learning their tribal languages. The following quote reflects the sentiments of a Native American law enforcement officer in a Southern California police department: "I know very little about my roots. My mother and grandmother were denied the opportunity to learn about their culture [forced assimilation] and nothing was passed on. I feel empty and have intense anger toward those who held the power to decide that certain traditions were not worth preserving. Forced denial of our ethnicity has resulted in extremely high alcohol, illegal drug use and suicide rates as a collective response."

KEY ISSUES IN LAW ENFORCEMENT

Perception of Police

The general distrust of police held by Native Americans stems from a history of negative relations with "the system," which can refer to federal, state, and local governments. In the view of Native Americans, officers represent a system that has not supported Indian rights, tribes, or communities; most contact with law enforcement has been negative in nature. Thus, many Native Americans have never had a chance to build relationships of trust and cooperation with people in law enforcement.

Victimization Rates/Comparisons with Other Groups

According to a National Crime Victimization Survey, between 1992 and 2001, American Indians experienced violence at rates more than twice that of blacks, two and a half times that of whites, and four and a half times that of Asians (BJS, 2004). American Indians comprised 0.5 percent of the U.S. population but 1.3 percent of all violent crime victims. These crimes affected both males and females; victims were from all geographies, age groups, and economic levels.

Beginning in 2009, the issue of public safety for Native Americans was pronounced a priority by Attorney General Eric Holder and brought to the attention of congressional leaders. On July 29, 2010, President Obama signed the *Tribal Law and Order Act* to "address crime in tribal communities and [place] a strong emphasis on decreasing violence against American Indian and Alaska Native women." Early results show promise (see Exhibit 9.1), but violent victimization rates against American Indians and Alaska Natives are still woefully high. As

	2002	2010	2011
Whites	32.6	18.3	21.5
Blacks	36.1	25.9	26.4
American Indian/Alaska Native	62.9	77.6	45.4
Asian/Native Hawaiian/other Pacific Islander	11.7	10.3	11.2

EXHIBIT 9.1   Rate of violent victimization per 1,000 persons aged 12 or older
Truman, Jennifer L. and Michael Planty. (2012, October). *Criminal Victimization, 2011*. U.S. Department of Justice, Office of Justice Programs, Bureau of Justice Statistics.

reported in *The New York Times*, "The country's 310 Indian reservations have violent crime rates that are more than two and a half times higher than the national average, according to data compiled by the Justice Department. American Indian women are 10 times as likely to be murdered than other Americans" (Williams, 2012).

Native American Women and Rape

Concern had begun to build when a report was issued in the early 2000s citing that the rate of violent crime victimization for Native American women was at least twice as that of other women (BJS, 2004). Amnesty International picked up the thread in 2007 with its report titled, "Maze of Injustice," issuing a follow-up report one year later that cautioned, "this is not simply a public health or criminal justice issue, but a serious human rights issue, that the U.S. government is obligated to address under internationally recognized human rights standards (AI, 2008). A 2010 report showed that 26.9 percent of American Indian or Alaska Native women had "reported rape victimization in their lifetime," as opposed to 18.8 percent of white women (Black, Basile, Breiding, Smith, Walters, Merrick, Chen, & Stephens, 2011).

The epidemic of rape in Indian Country is due, in large part, to "a maze of archaic laws that prevent tribes from arresting and prosecuting offenders" (Sullivan, 2009). Chickasaw Nation Tribal Police Chief, Jason O'Neal explained that if a woman is Indian on Indian land and her attacker is Indian, he [O'Neal] can help her. If not, there is not much that he can do (Sullivan, 2009). O'Neal describes the attackers as almost "untouchable . . . 80% of victims describe their offenders from outside the reservation" (Sullivan, 2009).

> Two years ago, the Standing Rock Sioux Reservation, which straddles North and South Dakota, had five Bureau of Indian Affairs officers to patrol an area the size of Connecticut. Officials there, and on many reservations nationwide, described a rampant problem of rape where hundreds of cases were going unreported, uninvestigated and unprosecuted. According to the Justice Department, one in three Native American women will be raped in her lifetime. Tribal leaders say predators believe Native American land is almost a free-for-all, where no law enforcement can touch them. (Sullivan, 2009)

In 2013, the U.S. Congress passed the Violence Against Women Reauthorization Act, which will eventually allow Native American tribes "to exercise their sovereign power to investigate, prosecute, convict, and sentence both Indians and non-Indians who assault Indian spouses or dating partners or violate a protection order in Indian country" (USDOJ, 2013). President Obama stated, "Previously, tribes had no jurisdiction over non-tribal members, even if they are married to Native women or reside on native lands. But as soon as I sign this bill, that ends" (ICTMN, 2013). The Act, unfortunately, does not cover crimes between two strangers, including sexual assaults. Obviously, the need to serve and protect Native American women must be a priority for law enforcement officials at all levels in the years to come.

Hate Crimes against Native Americans

With the overall number of Native Americans being a tiny minority of the U.S. population, the total number of hate crimes appears to be small. However, many of these crimes are quite violent, and seem to be "misdirected" as crimes toward people of color, in general, rather than Native Americans specifically. In some cases, Native American victims have been referred to by their attackers using the "N—word," and in one case were mistaken for Pacific Islanders. The attacker wrote on his Facebook page, "Just laid the fists and boots to some 6' 5" Tongan dude" (Kain, 2011).

Many Native Americans feel that the crimes against them are not investigated in a fair or timely way. The previously mentioned victim who had been mistaken for a Tongan suffered a broken nose and sinus cavities after being hit with a baseball bat, yet was held in jail for six days with no medical treatment; his wife was told by a guard "that if he wanted to receive medical treatment he'd need to 'get his Indian doctor'" (Kain, 2011).

Jurisdiction

> Investigating crimes on native lands poses a unique challenge for FBI personnel and their law enforcement partners. Working in Indian Country, as we call it, often means operating in isolated, forbidding terrain where cultural differences abound. Some older Native American people, for example, do not speak English . . . On many reservations there are few paved roads or marked streets. Agents might be called to a crime scene in the middle of the night 120 miles away . . . (FBI, 2012)

The FBI, since its beginnings in 1908, has played an important role in the investigation of crimes committed on Indian Country lands. History dating even further back helps to explain the role of the U.S. government in law enforcement in Indian Country. In 1885, the Major Crimes Act was passed in the United States. This gave exclusive jurisdiction to the federal government on major crimes committed on reservations. The 1994 Crime Act expanded federal criminal jurisdiction in Indian Country because of the sovereign status of federally recognized Indian tribes, which precludes most states from exercising criminal jurisdiction in Indian Country over Indian persons. Jurisdiction resides with the tribes themselves, on a limited basis, or with the federal government. Federal criminal jurisdiction in Indian Country is derived from the U.S. Code, Title 18, USC 1152 (General Crimes Act) and Title 18, USC 1153 (Major Crimes Act). Due to changes enacted in 1953 under Public Law 280, however, certain matters fall under state (rather than federal or tribal) jurisdiction in places such as Alaska, California, Minnesota, Nebraska, Oregon, and Wisconsin. As noted in an issue of the FBI Law Enforcement Bulletin, "Confusion about jurisdiction in Indian country remains a problem. Jurisdiction still is a patchwork of tribal, state, and federal jurisdiction that varies depending on the crime, identity of the perpetrator, identity of the victim, and location of the offense" (Bulzomi, 2012).

Resources allocated by the FBI to various locations throughout the country are based on a number of factors, including identified crime problems; jurisdictional responsibilities; and the availability of non-FBI investigative resources. Also, by virtue of the Indian Gaming Regulatory Act (IGRA) enacted in 1988, the FBI has federal criminal jurisdiction over acts directly related to casino gaming in Indian Country gaming establishments, including those locations on reservations under state criminal jurisdiction.

Four Indian Country Field Divisions (Albuquerque, Minneapolis, Phoenix, and Salt Lake City) of the FBI typically account for 75 percent of all Indian Country case initiations. The FBI normally has over 100 full-time special agents assigned to Indian Country matters and funds 14 Safe Trails Task Forces in Indian Country to handle violent crime or miscellaneous issues that would otherwise go unaddressed (FBI, 2013). Despite these efforts, there is a feeling of bias against Indian Country in terms of follow-through on cases: "Federal prosecutors in 2011 declined to file charges in 52 percent of cases involving the most serious crimes committed on Indian reservations . . . The government did not pursue rape charges on reservations 65 percent of the time . . . and rejected 61 percent of cases involving charges of sexual abuse of children . . ." (Williams, 2012).

In terms of other areas of federal involvement in Indian Country law enforcement, occasionally the FBI joins forces with the BIA to hold regional training conferences for Indian Country officials. But since the mid-90s, most training has been held at the United States Indian Police Academy, which is co-located with the Federal Law Enforcement Training Center in Artesia, New Mexico. Specialized training for Indian Country includes "courses in the Indian Child Welfare Act, Indian Country jurisdictional issues, and the challenge of working alone without assistance of backup for an extended period of time due to the ruralness of where they work" (Wright, 2010).

Coordination of law enforcement effort is valuable. In a landmark drug case, cooperation among a wide range of tribal and federal law enforcement agencies led to multiple

Interview with Former Chief Jason O'Neal, Chief of Police Chickasaw Nation Lighthorse Police (Ada, Oklahoma) May 19, 2009*

Q. *What are the most important ways for civilian police to show respect on Indian lands?*

A. First, it is important for civilian police to understand tribal sovereignty as well as the tribes and their history. It's equally important for tribal police to understand the issues facing civilian police. This helps to build cooperation. Tribal police need to make it a priority to build relationships with all the agencies in their jurisdictions, including state and local.

Q. *What, in particular, should civilian police be learning about Indian culture?*

A. They should become familiar with religious practices, and should understand that every tribe is unique, and has its own customs and beliefs. They also need to get a basic understanding of Indian jurisdiction. We have worked with the state [of Oklahoma] to ensure that the state academy presents information of this kind. Civilian police have issues facing Indian Country, and require dedicated training in this area.

Q. *Is there anything that you can think of that Native Americans find frustrating when it comes to dealing with civilian police?*

A. It is frustrating for Native Americans and tribal police that some law enforcement agencies do not recognize tribal police as equal or even perceive tribal police as police. Many of our officers attend a Police Academy. We work with outside agencies to achieve common goals, and we have worked on cross-deputization agreements. We all need to recognize each other.

It can also be frustrating when civilian police are working operation in and around Indian Country, and do not coordinate with tribal police. Cooperation and mutual recognition are key. For example, we have cross-training with the Oklahoma Bureau of Narcotics and Dangerous Drugs; we have assigned an investigator to their office and vice versa.

Q. *What do Native Americans say about civilian police?*

A. We mainly receive calls from the Native public who have dealings with civilian police and who want our department to be part of the investigation. When civilian police are working in Indian Country, they should consult us during an operation. We might be able to assist them or come up with an even more effective alternative to a problem.

Q. *Is there a particular message you would like to be passed on to the readers of our text regarding law enforcement interaction with Native Americans?*

A. We have to be interconnected. There is a maze of jurisdictional rules in and around Indian Country. The only way to achieve public safety is through cooperative law enforcement efforts. It benefits everyone.

Communication is the key. During any calls for service, it is critical that officers take the time to communicate with the population they serve, and in this way officers also learn how to do their jobs more effectively.

*Jason O'Neal, Chickasaw Nation Lighthorse Police Chief, was recognized for his pioneering work in cooperative law enforcement as he was awarded Chief of Police of the Year . . . at the national conference of the National Native American Law Enforcement Association in Las Vegas ("Lighthorse Police Chief Named Police Chief of the Year," 2008).

arrests at Standing Rock reservation in the upper midwest. "Besides the FBI and BIA, the U.S. Marshal's Service, Homeland Security Investigations, Drug Enforcement Administration, Sioux County Sheriff's Department and U.S. Parole and Pre-Trial Services also were involved in the investigation and arrests . . . on the reservation that straddles North Dakota and South Dakota" (Michael, 2012).

Tribal and Civilian Police

Law enforcement activities in Indian Country are managed by the BIA, under which falls the Office of Justice Services (OJS). The problems these groups face are immense. "The OJS continues to address the issues prevalent in Indian communities which are diverse, dispersed, and spread over large geographic expanses. These communities often face socioeconomic challenges such as high levels of unemployment and drug abuse, which can cause severe challenges for emergency services personnel" (U.S. Department of the Interior, 2013). In addition, tribal police and criminal justice services are chronically short-handed. Exhibit 9.2 shows that while the situation is improving slightly due to diligent efforts in recruitment, training, and retention, still only 53 percent of tribal law enforcement agencies had adequate

2006	36%
2007	50%
2008	59%
2009	18%
2010	52%
2011	53%

EXHIBIT 9.2 Percent of BIA/tribal law enforcement agencies on par with recommended national ratio of staffing

Source: U.S. Department of the Interior. *Budget Justifications and Performance Information: Indian Affairs.* Figures for 2006 from Fiscal Year 2011 report; figures for 2008–2011 from Fiscal Year 2013 report.

levels of staffing in 2011. In that same year, a report was released by the U.S. Government Accountability Office that neatly summarized the plight:

> In [a DOJ] study, researchers estimated that there are fewer than 2 officers per 1,000 residents in Indian country compared to a range of 3.9 to 6.6 officers per 1,000 residents in non-tribal areas such as Detroit, Michigan and Washington, D.C. The challenge of limited law enforcement resources is exacerbated by the geographic isolation or vast size of many reservations. In some instances officers may need to travel hundreds of miles to reach a crime scene. For example, the Pine Ridge Indian Reservation in South Dakota has about 88 sworn tribal officers to serve 47,000 residents across 3,466 square miles, which equates to a ratio of 1 officer per 39 square miles of land . . . (GAO, 2011)

While tribal law enforcement obviously cannot handle everything given their manpower and geographic constraints, policing on tribal lands can also cause confusion and friction between tribal and civilian law enforcement. Jurisdiction of the tribal police may be limited, and the non-Indian is not always subject to Indian tribal law. Some tribes have decriminalized their codes and taken on civil codes of law (e.g., for basic misdemeanors, civil fines may go to the tribal court), yet still conduct a trial of the non-Indian in a tribal court.

Police officers can be put into an unusual situation when it comes to enforcing the law among Indians. They may make an arrest in an area that is considered to be "Indian land" (on which tribal police have jurisdiction). The land may be adjacent to non-Indian land, sometimes forming "checkerboard" patterns of jurisdiction. In the case of an Indian reservation on which tribal police usually have authority, civilian law enforcement agencies are challenged to know where their jurisdiction begins and ends. With the multijurisdictional agreements that many tribes have signed with local and state officials, nontribal police officers may have the right to enter reservations to continue business. It is not uncommon for a person suspected of a crime to be apprehended by a nontribal police officer on a reservation.

It is expected that civilian law enforcement agents inform tribal police or tribal authorities when entering a reservation, but this does not always happen. Going onto reservation land without prior notice and contacting a suspect or witness directly is an insult to the authority of the tribal police (Bowen, personal communication, August 2013). Civilian police should see themselves as partners with tribal police. Obviously, in dangerous or emergency situations, time may prevent civilian authorities from conferring with the tribal police. Where possible, it is essential that the authority of the reservation be respected. As we mentioned, on some reservations, it may not be clear who has jurisdiction, and it becomes all the more necessary to establish trusting relations.

Levels of cooperation and attitudes toward civil and tribal law enforcement partnerships differ from area to area. Retired Police Chief Cox, who also recently served as Executive Director of the Oklahoma Chiefs of Police, spoke of the progress his state has made with respect to legislation associated with jurisdictional issues and the cross-deputization of local, state, and tribal police officers (e.g., Sac and Fox, Cherokee, Creek, Comanche, and Chickasaw Nations). Most of the state's approximately 22 tribal police departments have been cross-deputized; some departments have a shared database for intelligence purposes. In the past several years, the increasing use of GPS devices has contributed to better identification of location, jurisdiction, and resources. This cross-training and cooperation are especially critical in the complex geography of the state (Cox, personal communication, May 2009). In Oklahoma, Indian Country spans approximately 8,000 miles, and there is no contiguous border (out of 77 counties, 63 are in Indian Country). The patchwork Indian land and non-Indian land, therefore, lends itself to an uneven system of arrests and prosecutions, depending on whether a crime takes place on Indian land, with an Indian victim, and/or with an Indian perpetrator. Cross-deputization, which is now fairly widespread in Oklahoma, enables both tribal and civilian police to make arrests in each other's jurisdiction. Retired Chief Cox hopes that the models and progress he has seen in Oklahoma will benefit other states as well (Cox, personal communication, May 2009).

Police departments around the country, such as in New Mexico and Washington State, have also been working intensively to form relationships with local Indian tribes. Tribal police officers in Oregon are federally commissioned and state-certified police officers with full law enforcement authority. In Oregon, if a tribal police officer arrests a non-Indian, the non-Indian will be lodged in the county jail and arraigned in the county circuit court. If the same tribal police officer arrests an Indian, the Indian will be lodged in the tribal jail, usually housed in the county jail, and arraigned in tribal court. If there is a will to work cooperatively, police departments and Indian tribal departments can be of tremendous benefit to each other. Initiating this type of effort means, for both Indians and non-Indians, putting aside history and transcending stereotypes. Furthermore, individual officers should be sensitive to their own potentially condescending attitudes toward tribal police and tribal law.

Finally, cross-cultural contact between civilian officers and tribal members can take place in another not uncommon scenario. Deputy Chief Larry Becker works with the Port Gamble S'Klallam Tribe, a small tribe consisting of 1300 members on a reservation of 8–10 square miles in Northwest Washington. This tribe is a sovereign, self-governing tribe with its own courts, laws, prosecutor, public defender, and police department. The county and the state have no authority over this small tribe's reservation, and thus its members are free to use or not use tribal law officers. Deputy Chief Becker explained that only civilian officers, that is, non-Native American officers, police the reservation. Because small tribes may consist primarily of family members, members have a higher level of comfort when police officers from outside the reservation are hired by the tribe to enforce laws. Deputy Chief Becker said that this scenario, that is, non-Native American officers' policing reservations, was common for many of Washington's 26 (of 32 total tribes) sovereign, self-governing tribes. (Becker, personal communication, 2013).

Racial Profiling of Native Americans

Just as other groups such as Latinos and African Americans have routinely been victims of profiling, so have Native Americans (see Chapter 13 for extensive information on racial profiling). If a group of Native Americans is riding in a poorly maintained car, there is the potential that they will be stopped simply because they are perceived as suspicious and because negative stereotypes are operating. Negative biases against Native Americans are strong and have persisted for generations. In one study conducted in Arizona, it was shown that "The highway patrol was 3.5 times more likely to search a stopped Native American than a White . . ." (The Leadership Conference, 2011). When there is no legitimate reason to stop a car, the next step is for officers to check their own stereotypes of whom they think is a criminal (See Chapter 6 for a reminder of the questions that officers should ask themselves before stopping an individual for no apparent reason). Like members of other ethnic groups, Indians have repeatedly reported being stopped for no reason, adding to their distrust of police.

Peyote

Many states have specific laws exempting the traditional, religious use of peyote by American Indians from those states' drug enforcement laws. Following is a definition of peyote:

> Peyote is a small turnip-shaped, spineless cactus [containing] nine alkaloid substances, part of which, mainly mescaline, are hallucinogenic in nature; that is, they induce dreams or visions. Reactions to peyote seem to vary with the social situation in which it is used. In some it may merely cause nausea; believers may experience optic, olfactory and auditory sensations. Under ideal conditions color visions may be experienced and peyote may be "heard" singing or speaking. The effects wear off within twenty-four hours and leave no ill aftereffects. Peyote is non-habit forming. (Bahti, 1982)

There have been a variety of uses associated with peyote: (1) as a charm for hunting, (2) as a medicine, (3) as an aid to predict weather, (4) as an object to help find things that are lost (the belief being that peyote can reveal the location of the lost object through peyote-induced visions; peyote was even used to help locate the enemy in warfare), and (5) as an object to be carried for protection. People have faith in peyote as a powerful symbol and revere its presence.

Dried peyote charms are carried in small bags or pouches, which are then typically placed inside a "peyote box." (Peyote boxes contain items for use in religious ceremonies, as well as personal objects. See Swan, 2010, for more information.) Peyote charms and other medicinal items can be "ruined" if touched.* Police officers may need to confiscate peyote but should do it in a way that is appropriate and respectful. It is far better to ask the Native American politely to remove a bag containing peyote rather than forcibly take it away.

In a 1990 freedom-of-religion case, the Supreme Court ruled that state governments could have greater leeway in outlawing certain religious practices. The ruling involved the ritual use of peyote by some American Indians who follow the practices of the Native American Church of North America (NACNA), which has an estimated membership of 250,000 people (Morris, 2010). Until that time, the U.S. government allowed for the religious use of peyote among Native Americans based on the Bill of Rights' Free Exercise of Religion guarantee; in other words, peyote use was generally illegal except in connection with bona fide American Indian religious rituals.

From a law enforcement perspective, if drugs are illegal, no group should be exempt, and indeed, officers have to uphold the law. From a civil rights perspective, religious freedom applies to all groups and no group should be singled out for disproportionately burdensome treatment. Historically, legal and illegal status of peyote has been complex. There have been many attempts to prohibit the use of peyote on the federal level, and many states passed laws outlawing its use. However, several states have modified such prohibitions to allow traditional American Indians to continue using peyote as a sacrament. Moreover, in some states, anti-peyote laws have been declared unconstitutional by state courts insofar as they burden the religious practice of American Indians.

This historic ambiguity on the state level, together with the 1990 ruling on the federal level, causes confusion and resentment on the part of many Native Americans. Recognizing that the existing Act of August 11, 1978 (42 USC 1996), commonly called the American Indian Religious Freedom Act, was no longer adequate in protecting Native Americans' civil rights in

---

*Native Americans from many tribes across the country wear small bags called medicine bags; these are considered to be extremely sacred. The medicine bags do not carry drugs or peyote, but hold symbols from nature (e.g., corn pollen, cedar, sage, tree bark), and are believed to have certain powers. If it becomes necessary, law enforcement officers should handle these as they would handle any sacred symbol from their own religion. Ripping into the bags would be an act of desecration. The medicine contained in the bags has often been blessed and therefore must be treated with respect.

their traditional and cultural religious use of peyote, Congress passed, and President Clinton signed into law, the American Indian Religious Freedom Act Amendments of 1994. Following are select portions of this federal law, namely, Public Law 103-344 of the 103rd U.S. Congress, October 6, 1994:

> Section 3. The Congress finds and declares, among other issues, that:
>
> 1. for many Indian people, the traditional ceremonial use of the peyote cactus as a religious sacrament has for centuries been integral to a way of life, and significant in perpetuating Indian tribes and cultures;
> 2. since 1965, this ceremonial use of peyote by Indians has been protected by Federal regulation;
> 3. while at least 28 States have enacted laws which are similar to, or are in conformance with, the Federal regulation which protects the ceremonial use of peyote by Indian religious practitioners, 22 States have not done so, and this lack of uniformity has created hardship for Indian people who participate in such religious ceremonies; and
> 4. the lack of adequate and clear legal protection for the religious use of peyote by Indians may serve to stigmatize and marginalize Indian tribes and cultures, and increase the risk that they will be exposed to discriminatory treatment.

The use of peyote outside the NACNA (established in 1918) is technically forbidden and generally regarded by church members as sacrilegious. Within the NACNA, there are very specific rules and rituals pertaining to its sacramental use. But within the judicial system, the issue eventually arose as to whether peyote use by non-Indian members of the NACNA would be legally allowed, such as in the Utah case of James "Flaming Eagle" Mooney (who is not a Native American). Some church members say that to limit peyote use to Native Americans constitutes racial discrimination. Officers who have regular contact with Native American communities should stay informed about court rulings as to whether NACNA membership or "Indianness" is the critical factor in allowing the use of peyote. Establishing respectful communication with the leaders of the NACNA can also assist officers in determining whether peyote is being abused in certain circumstances.

Law enforcement officials would do well to understand the importance and place of peyote in the culture from a Native American point of view. It is not the intent of the authors to recommend a particular course of action with regard to enforcement or lack thereof. When the use of peyote is understood from an Indian perspective, officers will be more likely to communicate a respectful attitude toward an ancient ritual that some researchers say dates back over 5,000 years. If police officers suddenly enter a prayer meeting or drumming ceremony where peyote is being used and aggressively make arrests, it will be very difficult to establish trust with the community. When peyote is an issue, officers must recognize their own ethnocentrism (i.e., subconsciously viewing other cultures or cultural practices as primitive, abnormal, or inferior). Law enforcement personnel working in communities where peyote use is an issue should anticipate the problems that will occur and should discuss it with members of the Indian community. Officers should also know the laws pertaining to peyote use in their jurisdictions and the policy of their agencies regarding enforcement if it is illegal. Historically, the federal government actively tried to suppress and change Native American cultures. The banning of peyote was and has been viewed by Native American groups as a failure of the Bill of Rights to truly guarantee the freedom to practice one's own religion.

Trespassing and Sacred Lands

In a number of states, traditional Indian harvest areas or sacred burial and religious sites are now on federal, state, and, especially, private lands. Indians continue to visit these areas just as their ancestors did to collect resources or to pray. The point of concern for law enforcement involves conflicts occurring among ranchers, farmers, and homeowners on what Indians consider their holy ground. How officers react to allegations of trespassing determines whether there will be an escalated confrontation (Rivera, personal communication, August 2013). When there is a dispute, officers can alienate Indians by choosing an authoritarian and aggressive method of handling the problem (e.g., "You're going to get off this land right now"). Alternatively, officers could show empathy and the Native American may very well be more supportive of efforts to resolve the immediate conflict. If there is no immediate resolution, the officers can, at a minimum, prevent an escalation of hostilities.

Given that police officers cannot solve this complex and very old problem, the only tool available is the ability to communicate sensitively and listen well. "The officer is put between a rock and a hard place. If the officer is sensitive, he could try to speak to the landowner and describe the situation, although often the landowners don't care about the history, claiming, 'It's my land now.' However, there have been some people who have been sensitive to the needs of the Native Americans and who have worked out agreements" (Rivera, personal communication, August 2013).

Native American Sites—Use of, Desecration, and Looting

The Native American Free Exercise of Religion Act of 1993 was an attempt by Senator Inouye and his cosponsors to return authority over religious sites on Indian lands to Native American tribes. A scaled-down version was signed that year by President Clinton, which mostly applied to the use of peyote (see previous section). It took two more years for an executive order to be signed concerning the protection of Native American heritage sites. Excerpts:

> SECTION 1. ACCOMMODATION OF SACRED SITES.
>
> **a.** In managing Federal lands, each executive branch agency with statutory or administrative responsibility for the management of Federal lands shall, to the extent practicable, permitted by law, and not clearly inconsistent with essential agency functions, (1) accommodate access to and ceremonial use of Indian sacred sites by Indian religious practitioners and (2) avoid adversely affecting the physical integrity of such sacred sites. Where appropriate, agencies shall maintain the confidentiality of sacred sites.
>
> **b.** For purposes of this order . . . (iii) "Sacred site" means any specific, discrete, narrowly delineated location on Federal land that is identified by an Indian tribe, or Indian individual determined to be an appropriately authoritative representative of an Indian religion, as sacred by virtue of its established religious significance to, or ceremonial use by, an Indian religion, provided that the tribe or appropriately authoritative representative of an Indian religion has informed the agency of the existence of such a site. (Federal Register, 1996)

Even more degrading to Native Americans than the violation of sacred lands is the taking of human remains (skulls and bones) from Indian reservations and public lands. Most often, this type of looting has been done to make a profit on Native American articles and artifacts. Vandalism to archeological sites often occurs without any criminal prosecution. Officers in certain parts of the country may enter non-Indian homes and see such remains "displayed" as souvenirs of a trip into Indian Country. The Native American Graves Protection and Repatriation Act of 1990, passed by Congress and signed by former President George H. W. Bush, resulted as a response to such criminal acts. When officers see human remains, they must investigate as to foul play. Officers should contact state agencies established to enforce laws that protect Indian relics to determine how to proceed in such situations.

Indian Casinos and Gaming

Native American reservations in the United States are considered to be sovereign nations, and as such, leaders are responsible for providing and securing financing in order to pay for basic infrastructure and services as leaders would in any city. To date, the most successful source of public funds for Indian reservations has been casinos and other types of gaming for profit. The legal wording on most documents referring to this industry uses the term *Indian gaming*.

Legalized gambling on reservations dates back to a landmark case in 1976 in which the Supreme Court ruled that states no longer could have regulatory jurisdiction over Indian tribes. Because of the lawsuits that followed, it was later ruled that states did not have the right to prohibit Native American tribes from organizing and participating in for-profit legalized gambling. The Indian Gaming Regulatory Act became law in 1988. For the first time, Native Americans were given the right to regulate all gaming activities on their sovereign lands.

There is a great deal of controversy around the Indian gaming industry. On the one hand, according to one research study, "Four years after tribes open casinos, employment [increases] by 26 percent, and tribal population [increases] by about 12 percent. . . . The increase in economic activity appears to have some health benefits in that four or more years after a casino opens, mortality [falls] by 2 percent." On the other hand, according to the same study, "bankruptcy rates, violent crime, and auto thefts and larceny are up 10 percent in counties with a casino" (Evans & Topoleski, 2002).

At the time, there were over 310 gaming operations of various types, run by more than 200 different tribes in the United States. About 220 of these gaming operations were Las Vegas-style casinos with slot machines, table games, or both (Evans & Topoleski, 2002). Until the end of 2007, the gaming industry, in general, performed well (Parmelee & Wong, 2008). American Indians made significant gains and progress through the gaming industry as it enabled a certain amount of economic self-reliance for some tribes. The recession beginning in 2008 brought some financial difficulties to the gaming industry, with analysts speculating on the impact for tribes and reservations that relied on the industry. Data eventually published by the National Indian Gaming Commission, however, showed overall steady gross revenues from 2008 through 2012 (NIGC, 2012).

Fishing

"If you ever want to get into a fight, go into a local bar [e.g., in parts of Washington State] and start talking about fishing rights. The fishing issue is a totally hot issue" (Rivera, personal communication, August 2013).

The wording of treaties with regard to the fishing rights of Native Americans is clear and unequivocal in English as well as in the languages of the specific tribes concerned. For example, the treaty with Indians of the Northwest regarding fishing rights on the rivers gives these rights to the Indians "for as long as the rivers shall flow." The rivers in the Northwest are still flowing, and Indians are still struggling with the state of Washington about the state's violations of the treaty's terms, even on Indian property.

Indians continue to say, "We have treaties with the government allowing us to fish here." Commercial and sports fishermen, on the forefront of trying to prevent Native Americans from exercising their treaty rights, claim that Indians are destroying the industry. From the Native Americans' perspective, they are providing sustenance to their families and earning extra money for themselves or their tribes to make it through the year. (For 150 years, there had been no industry on many, if not most, of the reservations.) Once again, the officer on the front line will be unable to solve a problem that has been raging for generations. The front-line officer's actions, in part, depend on the sensitivity of his or her department's chief executive. Admittedly, the commander is in a difficult position, caught between the state fish and game industry and the people trying to enforce federal treaties. Nevertheless, he or she can communicate to officers the need for cultural sensitivity in their way of approaching and communicating with Native Americans. The alternative could be dangerous, as illustrated by at least one situation when, in northern California, peace officers with flak jackets and automatic weapons resorted to pursuing Native Americans with shotguns up and down the river (Rivera, personal communication, August 2013).

Similar issues arise concerning hunting and general water use rights. After a decade of negotiations, a formal agreement meant to sort out water rights in western Montana was stalled by local farmers and ranchers. As reported in *The New York Times*, "A water war is roiling the Flathead Indian Reservation here in western Montana, and it stretches from farms, ranches and mountains to the highest levels of state government, cracking open old divisions between the tribes and descendants of homesteaders who were part of a government-led land rush into Indian Country a century ago. 'Generations of misunderstanding have come to a head,' said Robert McDonald, the communications director for the Confederated Salish and Kootenai Tribes. 'It's starting to tear the fabric of our community apart'" (Healy, 2013).

There are many complex dimensions to cases involving Native Americans "breaking the law" when, in parallel, the federal government is not honoring its historical treaties with them. Native Americans are frustrated by what they see as blatant violations of their rights. The history of the government's lack of loyalty to its American Indian citizens has caused great pain for this cultural group. Clearly, sensitivity and understanding on the part of law enforcement officials are required. Officers should demonstrate patience and tact, remembering that history has defined many aspects of the current relationships between law enforcement and American Indians. Being forceful and displaying anger will alienate Native Americans and will not result in the cooperation needed to solve issues that arise.

Summary

- Historically, the police officer from outside the reservation has been a symbol of rigid and authoritarian governmental control that has affected nearly every aspect of Indian life, especially on reservations. Officers, like most citizens, have only a limited understanding of how the government, including the criminal justice system, caused massive suffering by not allowing Indians to preserve their cultures, identities, languages, sacred sites, rituals, and lands.

- Each federally recognized tribe has a distinct history and culture, and often a separate language. Each has its own government, schools, law enforcement, and economic systems. Federal recognition means that a legal relationship exists between the tribe and the federal government. "Indian Country" refers to all land that is within the limits of an Indian reservation under the jurisdiction of the U.S. government, and to all dependent Indian communities within the borders of the United States. An Indian reservation is land that a tribe has reserved for its exclusive use through statutes, executive order, or treaty-making.

- Significant differences exist among the cultures, languages, history, and socioeconomic status of Native American tribes, communities, and individuals. Yet, there is a strong cultural link among the many worlds and tribes of Native Americans. There is a common set of values and beliefs involving the earth and the universe, resulting in a deep respect for nature and "mother earth." According to American Indian philosophy, the earth is sacred and is a living entity. Indians do not see themselves as superior to animals and plants, but rather as part of all of creation. Through religious ceremonies and rituals, traditional Native Americans are able to transcend themselves so that they are connected to nature and in harmony with the universe.

- Many American Indians who favor traditional styles of communication tend toward formality and slow building of rapport with strangers. Behavior that appears aloof or hostile may be part of a cultural style; police officers should not automatically attribute a lack of cooperation to the behavior observed. Aggressive questioning can result in withdrawal of responses. In addition, direct eye contact for some traditional tribal members is an affront or invasion of privacy. Holding back on judging cultural styles of communication is key to establishing good rapport.

- There are many offensive terms for and stereotypes of Native Americans. The terms *chief, redskin, buck, squaw, braves,* and *skins* are examples of these, especially when used by a non-Indian. The use of Indian tribal names or references as mascots for sports teams is highly objectionable to many Native Americans.

- The traditional extended family is close-knit and interdependent, and a great deal of respect is paid to the elderly. Police officers should remember to ask elders for their opinions or advice, as they are often the major decision-makers in the family. A particularly sensitive area in family dynamics relates to the separation of children from families. This can bring back memories of times when children were forcibly taken from their parents. Native Americans who have close-knit extended families, and who identify with their tribal cultures, tend to be better adjusted than those who lack family and cultural support. In the case of the latter, social and health problems can be severe, and include depression, alcoholism, drug use, and suicidal tendencies.

- Key issues for law enforcement with respect to Native Americans include jurisdiction, victimization, fishing, the use of peyote, allegations of trespassing, sacred sites violations, and Indian gaming and casinos. Some of these involve matters in which Native Americans feel they have been deprived of their rights: in the case of peyote, the right to religious expression; in the case of trespassing, the right to honor their ancestors; and in the case of fishing, the ability to exercise their rights as guaranteed by treaties made with the U.S. government.

Discussion Questions and Issues

1. *Popular Stereotypes.* List some of the commonly held stereotypes of Native Americans. What is your personal experience with Native Americans that might counter these stereotypes? How have people in law enforcement been influenced by popular stereotypes of Native Americans?
2. *Recommendations for Effective Contact.* If you have had contact with Native Americans, what recommendations would you give others regarding effective communication, rapport building, and cultural knowledge that would be beneficial for officers?
3. *The Government's Broken Promises to American Indians.* The famous Lakota chief, Sitting Bull, spoke on behalf of many Indians when he said of white Americans, "They made us many promises . . . but they never kept but one: They promised to take our land, and they took it." There was a time when many acres of land in what we now call the United States were sacred to Native American tribes. Therefore, today many of us are living on, building on, and in some cases destroying the remains of Indian lands where people's roots run deep. How would you deal with the problem of an Indian "trespassing" on someone's land when he or she claims to be visiting an ancestral burial ground, for example? What could you say or do so as not to alienate the Native American and thereby risk losing trust and cooperation?
4. *Jurisdiction.*
   a. What should law enforcement agents do when state law is in conflict with a federal law that has been based on treaties with Native Americans signed by the federal government? How can officers who are on the front line win the respect and cooperation of Native Americans when they are asked to enforce something that goes against the treaty rights of the Indians?
   b. A special unit in the early 1990s was established by the San Diego Sheriff's department to patrol Native American reservations, overrun from the outside by drugs and violence. Federal Public Law 280 transferred criminal jurisdiction and enforcement on reservations to some states. Conduct research on law enforcement jurisdiction issues and tribal lands in your region or state (if applicable); note whether there are still unresolved areas or areas of dispute.

References

AI: Amnesty International. (2008, Spring). *Maze of Injustice: The Failure to Protect Indigenous Women from Sexual Violence in the USA*. One Year Update.

American Indian Religious Freedom Act, Amendments of 1994, Public Law 103-344 [H.R. 4230]; October 6, 1994, 103rd Congress.

Bahti, Tom. (1982) *Southwestern Indian Ceremonials*. Las Vegas, Nev.: KC Publications.

Becker, Larry. (2013). Deputy Chief of S'Klallam Tribes in Kingston, Sequim, and Port Angeles, Washington, personal communication.

BIA: Bureau of Indian Affairs. (2013, May 6). Federal Register, *78*(87).

Black, Michele C., Kathleen C. Basile, Matthew J. Breiding, Sharon G. Smith, Mikel L. Walters, Melissa T. Merrick, Jieru Chen, and Mark R. Stephens. (2011). *The National Intimate Partner and Sexual Violence Survey: 2010 Summary Report*. Atlanta, GA: National Center for Injury Prevention and Control, Centers for Disease Control and Prevention.

Bowen, Peggy. (2013, August). Assistant Professor of Criminal Justice, Alvernia College, Reading, Pennsylvania, personal communication.

Boyd, David R., Karen Milman, Peter Stuart, Anthony Dekker, and Jim Flaherty. (2008, March). *Alcohol Screening and Brief Intervention (ASCI): Program Implementation and Operations Manual*. Indian Health Service, Emergency Services, Office of Clinical and Preventive Services.

Brenneke, Andrea. (2012, February 1). "A Restorative Circle in the Wake of a Police Shooting." *Tikkun*.

Bull, Brian. (2009, May 4). "For Native Americans, Old Stereotypes Die Hard." National Public Radio, *All Things Considered*.

Bulzomi, Michael J. (2012, May). "Indian Country and the Tribal Law and Order Act of 2010." *FBI Law Enforcement Bulletin*.

BJS: Bureau of Justice Statistics. (2004). *A BJS Statistical Profile, 1992–2002: American Indians and Crime*. Washington D.C.: Department of Justice.

CDC: Centers for Disease Control and Prevention. (2012). *Suicide: Facts at a Glance*. National Center for Injury Prevention and Control, Division of Violence Prevention.

CEHIP. (1996). "20th Century Warriors: Native American Participation in the United States Military." Washington, D.C.: CEHIP Incorporated, in partnership with Native American advisors Rodger Bucholz, William Fields, and Ursula P. Roach. Department of Defense. Retrieved August 29, 2013, from www.history.navy.mil/faqs/faq61-1.htm

Cox, Jim. (2009, May). Retired Police Chief, Retired Executive Director of Oklahoma Chiefs of Police, Midwest City, Oklahoma, personal communication.

Evans, Mark. (2006, April 12). *National Methamphetamine Initiative Survey: The Status of the Methamphetamine Threat and Impact on Indian Lands.* Las Cruces, NM: The New Mexico Investigative Support Center.

Evans, William N. and Julie H. Topoleski. (2002, September). *The Social and Economic Impact of Native American Casinos.* National Bureau of Economic Research, Working Paper 9198.

FBI: Federal Bureau of Investigation. (2012, June 1). *Journey through Indian Country—Part 1: Fighting Crime on Tribal Lands.* Retrieved August 29, 2013, from www.fbi.gov/news/stories/2012/june/indian-country_060112

FBI: Federal Bureau of Investigation. (2013). "Indian Country Crime." Retrieved August 1, 2013, from www.fbi.gov/about-us/investigate/vc_majorthefts/indian

Federal Register. (1996, May 24). "Executive Order 13007: Indian Sacred Sites." *61*(104).

Federal Register. (2000, November 9). "Executive Order 13175, Consultation and Coordination with Indian Tribal Governments." Vol. 65, No. 218.

"First American Female and Native Soldier Killed in Iraq War Is Remembered." (2003). *Indian Country Today,* Staff Reports.

GAO: Government Accountability Office, United States Government. (2011, February). *Indian Country Criminal Justice: Departments of the Interior and Justice Should Strengthen Coordination to Support Tribal Courts.* Report to Congressional Requesters.

Harris, Philip R., Robert T. Moran, and Sarah V. Moran. (2004). *Managing Cultural Differences: Global Leadership Strategies for the 21st Century,* 6th ed. Oxford, UK: Butterworth-Heineman.

Healy, Jack. (2013, April 21). "Water Rights Tear at an Indian Reservation." *The New York Times.*

ICTMN: Indian Country Today Media Network. (2013, March 7). *President Obama Signs Violence against Women Act into Law.*

IHS: Indian Health Services. (2010, November 14). *Federal Agencies to Collaborate with Tribes on Suicide Prevention.* Press Release.

Jevec, Adam. (2001, Winter). "Semper Fidelis, Code Talkers." *Prologue Magazine,* 33(4).

Kain, Erik. (2011, July 6). "Did Police Turn a Blind Eye to Attack on Native American Family in Nevada?" *Forbes.*

The Leadership Conference on Civil and Human Rights. (2011, March). *Restoring a National Consensus: The Need to End Racial Profiling in America.*

"Lighthorse Police Chief Named Police Chief of the Year." (2008, October 20). *The Ada News.*

Matthiessen, Peter. (1992). *The Spirit of Crazy Horse.* New York, NY: Penguin Books.

Meyers, Laurie. (2007, February). "A Struggle for Hope." *Monitor on Psychology,* p. 30. American Psychological Association.

Michael, Jenny. (2012, June 5). "FBI and BIA arrest 17 in 14-month investigation on Standing Rock." *The Bismarck Tribune.*

Morris, Nomi. (2010, October 30). "Rituals of Native American Church offer comfort, sustenance." *Los Angeles Times.*

NIGC: National Indian Gaming Commission. (2012). *2003–2012 Gross Gaming Revenue Trends.*

O'Neal, Jason (2009, May). Chief of Police, Chickasaw Nation Lighthorse Police, Ada, Oklahoma, personal communication.

Parmelee, Craig, and Donald Wong. (2008, October 3). *U.S. Gaming Defaults Reach Record Levels: What Happened To This 'Recession-Resistant' Industry?* Standard and Poor's.

Perry, Steven W. (2012, October). *Tribal Crime Data Collection Activities, 2010.* U.S. Department of Justice, Office of Justice Programs, Bureau of Justice Statistics. Technical Report NCJ 239077.

Powell, Alvin. (2012, July 24). "Mystery of Native Americans' arrival." *Harvard Gazette.*

Rivera, Jose. (2013, August). Retired California State Peace Officer, Manager of Audience Development and Community Partnerships of Bay Area Discovery Museum, personal communication.

Seven Fires Council. (2013). "Our People, Our Future." Kentucky Native American online Web site. Retrieved August 6, 2013, from www.merceronline.com/Native/native10.htm

Siebens, Julie and Tiffany Julian. (2011, December). *Native North American Languages Spoken at Home in the United States and Puerto Rico: 2006–2010.* U.S. Census Bureau. American Community Survey Briefs.

Sullivan, Laura. (2009, May 3). "Lawmakers Move to Curb Rape on Native Lands." *National Public Radio.*

Swan, Daniel C. (2010). "Objects of Purpose—Objects of Prayer: Peyote Boxes of the Native American Church." *Museum Anthropology Review.*

Truman, Jennifer L. and Michael Planty. (2012, October). *Criminal Victimization, 2011.* U.S. Department of Justice, Office of Justice Programs, Bureau of Justice Statistics.

U.S. Census Bureau. (2012, January). *The American Indian and Alaska Native Population: 2010.*

U.S. Code. (2012a, January 3). "Indian Country Defined." Title 18; Section 1151. Retrieved July 31, 2013, from uscode.house.gov.

U.S. Code. (2012b, January 3). "Indians. Definitions." Title 25; Section 479a. Retrieved July 31, 2013, uscode.house.gov

U.S. Department of the Interior. *Budget Justifications and Performance Information: Indian Affairs.* From Fiscal Years 2011 and 2013 reports.

U.S. Department of Justice. (2013). *Violence against Woman Act (VAWA) Reauthorization 2013.* Retrieved August 1, 2013, www.justice.gov/tribal/vawa-tribal.html

White House. (2013, June 26). "Executive Order: Establishing the White House Council on Native American Affairs." Office of the Press Secretary.

Williams, Timothy. (2012, February 20). "Higher Crime, Fewer Charges on Indian Land." *New York Times.*

Wolf, Richard. (2013, June 26). "Court rules for adoptive parents in Baby Veronica case." *USA Today.*

Wright, Joseph W. (2010, March 18). As transcribed in *Examining Bureau of Indian Affairs and Tribal Police Recruitment, Training, Hiring, and Retention.* Hearing before the Committee on Indian Affairs, United States Senate. Washington, D.C.: U.S. Government Printing Office.

Zeleny, Jeff. (2008, May 19). "Obama Adopted by Native Americans." *The New York Times:* The Caucus section.

Multicultural Law Enforcement Elements in Terrorism and Disaster Preparedness

Chapter 10 Multicultural Law Enforcement and Terrorism, Homeland Security, and
Disaster Preparedness

Part Three provides information on working with multicultural communities in the areas of domestic and international terrorism. Peacekeeping efforts of homeland security and disaster preparedness within our local, state, regional, national, and global multicultural communities are addressed. Generally speaking, acts of terrorism in the United States usually involve local law enforcement agencies and other public safety personnel as first responders. Part Three highlights law enforcement's prevention and response strategies related to the war on terrorism, homeland security, and disaster preparedness within multicultural communities. The chapter that follows contain (1) overview, background, and historical information with respect to law enforcement's changing roles in combating terrorism, in homeland security, and in disaster preparedness; (2) response strategies addressing local community, regional, national, and global issues; (3) goals for homeland security and disaster preparedness in multicultural communities; (4) key multicultural law enforcement communication issues in dealing with terrorism, homeland security, and natural disasters; and (5) relationships and processes inherent in multijurisdictional efforts and responses related to terrorism, homeland security, and natural disaster work. The chapter ends with key concerns relevant to officers and specific challenges involved in the changing roles and practices in dealing with terrorism, homeland security, and disaster preparedness within multicultural communities.

Multicultural Law Enforcement and Terrorism, Homeland Security, and Disaster Preparedness

LEARNING OBJECTIVES

After reading this chapter, you should be able to:

- Define *terrorism* and describe the two different types of *terrorism* that occur in the United States.
- Describe the role of the Department of Homeland Security and its six core missions within multicultural communities.
- Discuss the purpose and multicultural benefits of the National Incident Management System (NIMS) for local, state, and federal agencies.
- Describe the U.S. Patriot Act and the concerns of multicultural communities.
- Explain the purpose and value of Citizen Corps and its five federally sponsored programs that allow all multicultural citizens to get involved and help their communities.
- List and discuss key issues associated with law enforcement and other emergency services personnel in responding to terrorism and protecting homeland security within multicultural communities.

OUTLINE

- Introduction
- Multicultural Law Enforcement Roles in Terrorism and Homeland Security
- Myths and Stereotypes about Terrorists
- Response Strategies Addressing Local-Community, Regional, National, and Global Issues
- U.S. Patriot Act and Intelligence Communities
- Working with Multicultural Communities on Terrorism Prevention and Disaster Preparedness
- Key Issues in Law Enforcement
- Summary
- Discussion Questions and Issues

INTRODUCTION

This chapter provides specific information on the vital role that law enforcement plays in dealing with domestic and international terrorism, homeland security, and disaster preparedness within multicultural communities. Although crimes involving terrorism affect our nation as a whole (and thus are seen as national in scope), the immediate targets, outcomes, and results are local in effect. Local law enforcement personnel and agencies are called upon to respond, provide assistance, establish order, and protect the immediate and larger community from any additional harm and danger. Multicultural knowledge and the skills required to work within diverse communities are key resources in preventing and dealing with the aftermath of terrorism, investigation of crimes, required intelligence gathering, and disaster preparedness.

MULTICULTURAL LAW ENFORCEMENT ROLES IN TERRORISM AND HOMELAND SECURITY

In the entire history of crime fighting and public safety, law enforcement at the federal, state, and local levels has never before had a challenge of the scope and complexity that it faces today with terrorism and homeland security. Today's terrorists respect neither law nor community-established practices; they honor neither law enforcement personnel nor humanitarian-service professionals. Their sole goal and mission is to inflict maximum casualty, mass destruction, and public fear. This is illustrated by the following translated excerpt from an al-Qaida terrorist manual, located by the Manchester (England) Metropolitan Police in a computer file from a police raid of a cell member's home in May 2000 (U.S. Department of Justice, 2001):

> PLEDGE, O SISTER:
> . . . to make their women widows and their children orphans.
> . . . to make them desire death and hate appointments and prestige.
> . . . to slaughter them like lambs and let the Nile, al-Asi, and Euphrates flow with their blood.
> . . . to be a pick of destruction for every godless and apostate regime.
> . . . to retaliate for you against every dog who touches you with even a bad word.

Moreover, terrorists may not come to the attention of local law enforcement officers and agencies until they have committed their terrorist acts:

> Terrorism poses a fundamental challenge to the legal system. Terrorists often do nothing indictable until they commit the act. Ninety percent of the time, sleepers are absolutely legal, so you can't do anything about them even if you know who they are. Terrorism challenges our categories of what is legal and what is illegal. (Ford, 2002)

Although terrorists commit crimes to bring national and international attention to their causes and purposes, the response to terrorist attacks and the actions that might prevent them are usually accomplished in local cities, neighborhoods, and communities.

> In panel after panel, the same hard truths were expressed repeatedly: With the events of 9/11, the nation entered a new and sobering era. 9/11 shocked the nation with the chilling realization that foreign enemies from both within and without are bent on destroying our institutions, our lives, and our very civilization. Terrorist crime, though national in scope, is usually local in execution. In the war on terror, community police will therefore have to shoulder an increasingly heavy burden. (Bankson, 2003)

Law enforcement's knowledge and responsiveness to local and regional issues is central to the success in the war on terrorism and homeland security. Relationships with multicultural local and regional community leaders will be an essential resource in dealing with and preventing terrorism. Law enforcement personnel have the dual role of protecting the public from acts of terrorism by those terrorists who may be hiding in multicultural communities in the United

States, and protecting the members of multicultural communities who may have no ties to terrorists or criminals but are stereotyped, harassed, or discriminated against because of the biases and prejudices of others.

Definitions

As indicated in "Terrorism 2002–2005," there is no single, universally accepted, definition of terrorism (Federal Bureau of Investigation, 2010).

> **Terrorism** "Terrorism is defined in the *Code of Federal Regulations* as the unlawful use of force and violence against persons or property to intimidate or coerce a government, the civilian population, or any segment thereof, in furtherance of political or social objectives (28 C.F.R. Section 0.85)"(FBI, 2010).

The FBI defines two types of terrorism that occur in the United States:

> **Domestic terrorism** "The unlawful use, or threatened use, of force or violence by a group or individual based and operating entirely within the United States or Puerto Rico without foreign direction committed against persons or property to intimidate or coerce a government, the civilian population, or any segment thereof in furtherance of political or social objectives"(FBI, 2010).
>
> **International terrorism** "Involves violent acts or acts dangerous to human life that are a violation of the criminal laws of the United States or any state, or that would be a criminal violation if committed within the jurisdiction of the United States or any state. These acts appear to be intended to intimidate or coerce a civilian population, influence the policy of a government by intimidation or coercion, or affect the conduct of a government by assassination or kidnapping" (FBI, 2010).

The FBI further divides terrorist-related activities into two major categories:

> **Terrorist incident** "A violent act or an act dangerous to human life, in violation of the criminal laws of the United States, or of any state, to intimidate or coerce a government, the civilian population, or any segment thereof, in furtherance of political or social objectives" (FBI, 2010).
>
> **Terrorism prevention** "A documented instance in which a violent act by a known or suspected terrorist group or individual with the means and a proven propensity for violence is successfully interdicted through investigative activity" (FBI, 2010).

WEAPONS OF MASS DESTRUCTION (WMD) According to the FBI, the set of weapons referred to as "weapons of mass destruction" are: (1) chemical, (2) biological, (3) radiological, (4) nuclear, and (5) explosive. These weapons have a large-scale impact on people, property, and/or infrastructure (FBI, 2013). The subcategories of WMD include activities that may be labeled as "agro terrorism," which is to harm our food supply chain, and "cyber terrorism," which is to harm our telecommunications, Internet, and computerized processes and transactions.

The FBI's (2010) definition of terrorism tends to be too specific and narrow to be used by local and state law enforcement and with respect to other criminal justice objectives. For the purposes of this textbook, our definition of terrorism is broadened in scope to include all crimes involving terrorism, bombings, and weapons of mass destruction, whether domestic

Weapons of Mass Destruction (WMD) "Any weapon or device that is intended, or has the capability, to cause death or serious bodily injury to a significant number of people through the release, dissemination, or impact of (a) toxic or poisonous chemicals or their precursors; (b) a disease organism; or (c) radiation or radioactivity" (Title 50, US Code, Chapter 40, Section 2302).

or international. It is clear that criminals, who resort to terrorism and WMD, regardless of their motives, are usually not restricted by any definition and/or categories. Since the primary goal of law enforcement is to ensure public safety and security, a terrorist threat in itself is a public safety issue that can send a community into confusion and even chaos. In the case of the use of WMD or "Weapons of Mass Disruption" (such as "dirty bombs"), making prompt and accurate information available to all community members can help prevent mass confusion and panic. Law enforcement is called upon to respond to threats of terrorism as well as to actual incidents and acts of terrorism. Law enforcement's knowledge, skills, resources, and sensitivity to multicultural community issues and concerns will facilitate the effectiveness of its response in the three stages of a terrorism incident: before, during, and after an act of terrorism.

Dirty Bomb "Is one type of a radiological dispersal device (RDD) that combines a conventional explosive, such as dynamite, with radioactive material. The terms dirty bomb and RDD are often used interchangeably in the media. Most RDDs would not release enough radiation to kill people or cause severe illness—the conventional explosive itself would be more harmful to individuals than the radioactive material. A dirty bomb is not a 'Weapon of Mass Destruction' but a "Weapon of Mass Disruption," where contamination and anxiety are the terrorists' major objectives" (U.S. Nuclear Regulatory Commission, 2013a).

Historical Information and Background

Terrorism has always been a part of organized society (Hoffman, 2006). From the earliest history of establishing order through the enforcement of laws and government, extremist groups and individuals have used property damage and violence against people to generate fear and compel "change" in society and organizations. The FBI has been investigating and helping prevent terrorist attacks since the 1920s, and makes available on its Web site *Major Terrorism Cases: Past and Present*.

The targets and tactics of terrorists have changed over time (Hoffman, 2006). In the past, more often the targets of terrorists were individuals. The death of a unique, single individual such as a head of state, president, or prime minister would produce the major disruption that the terrorist desired. In modern times, governments and organizations have become far more bureaucratic and decentralized. Consequently, the targets of terrorists have included unique individuals, their surrounding networks, affiliated organizations and institutions, and any functions or processes associated with any targeted individual or groups. Today, terrorists attack not only prominent individuals and their organizations but also a wider range of targets that have been considered immune historically. For example, prior to modern times, terrorists had granted certain categories of people immunity from attack (e.g., women, children, elderly, disabled, and doctors). By not recognizing any category of people as excluded from attack, terrorists today have an unlimited number of targets for attack. The apparent randomness and unpredictability of terrorist attacks make the work of law enforcement and other public safety organizations extremely challenging, and solutions require a high level of sophistication.

Up through the attacks of 9/11, almost all of the homeland security efforts were seen as national in direction, leadership, and scope. The U.S. policies for counterterrorism were centered on dealing with enemies and events primarily outside of the United States. For example, Presidential Decision Directive (PDD-39) regarding terrorism included:

1. To deter, defeat, and respond vigorously to all terrorist attacks on U.S. territory and against U.S. citizens, or facilities, whether they occur domestically, in international waters or airspace or on foreign territory.
2. The United States regards all such terrorism as a potential threat to national security as well as a criminal act and will apply all appropriate means to combat it.
3. The United States shall pursue vigorously efforts to deter and preempt, apprehend and prosecute, or assist other governments to prosecute, individuals who perpetrate or plan to perpetrate such attacks.
4. The United States shall work closely with friendly governments in carrying out its counterterrorism policy and will support Allied and friendly governments in combating terrorist threats against them.
5. The United States shall seek to identify groups or states that sponsor or support such terrorists, isolate them, and extract a heavy price for their actions.
6. It is the policy of the United States not to make concessions to terrorists.
7. The FBI is the lead agency for crisis management during terrorist attacks and incidents.
8. Federal Emergency Management Agency (FEMA) is the lead agency for the consequence and recovery management during terrorist attacks.

Starting around the mid-1990s, national policies and procedures for dealing with terrorism and homeland security were enacted; however, the focus was still very much on leadership and direction on a national level with implementation by federal agencies (PDD-39). Involvement of local and regional law enforcement agencies was minimal in the planning, policy development, and implementation of the federal response to terrorism and homeland security. Subsequent inquiries following the terrorist attacks on 9/11 recommended coordinated and collaborative efforts of local public safety agencies and officers with federal departments and organizations.

Department of Homeland Security

In response to the 9/11 terrorist attacks against the United States that killed 2,973 innocent people on U.S. soil, the Department of Homeland Security (DHS) was created as a cabinet-level department on November 25, 2002. DHS became the third-largest federal department, bringing together 22 different federal agencies, each with a separate function. The role of DHS is one of facilitating and developing the avenues of communication between local, state and federal government public safety organizations to ensure viable and effective leadership, policies, and procedures for homeland security in the United States. Its six core missions are as follows (DHS, 2013a):

1. *Prevent terrorism and enhance security.* This means to prevent the unauthorized acquisition, importation, movement, or use of chemical, biological, radiological, and nuclear materials and capabilities within the United States. Enhanced security would apply to critical infrastructure and key resources.
2. *Secure and manage U.S. borders.* It is essential to secure U.S. air, land, and sea borders to prevent illegal activity. It is important to disrupt and dismantle transnational criminal and terrorist organizations.
3. *Enforce and administer U.S. immigration laws.* The focus is on streamlining and facilitating the legal immigration process. DHS has fundamentally reformed immigration enforcement,

prioritizing the identification and removal of criminal aliens who pose a threat to public safety and targeting employers who repeatedly break the law.

4. *Safeguard and Secure Cyberspace.* DHS works to analyze and reduce cyber threats and vulnerabilities; distribute threat warnings; and coordinate the response to cyber incidents to ensure that homeland computers, networks, and cyber systems remain safe.

5. *Build a resilient nation.* DHS provides the coordinated, comprehensive federal response in the event of a terrorist attack, natural disaster or other large-scale emergency while working with federal, state, local, and private sector partners to ensure an expedient and effective recovery effort. DHS provides communication and collaboration, grants, plans, and training to DHS and law enforcement partners. Part of this process involves facilitating the rebuilding and recovery of those areas that have been damaged.

6. *Mature and strengthen the DHS enterprise.* DHS has taken steps to create a unified department focusing on accountability, efficiency, transparency and leadership development.

Since the establishment of DHS, law enforcement agencies have been receiving a variety of intelligence information, advisories, and warnings on possible terrorist threats. More now than ever, studying the demographic background of terrorists and possessing multicultural knowledge and skills are important to every law enforcement officer. Further, these resources constitute critical elements in the (1) preparation of local communities for safety and security with regard to terrorism, (2) prevention of possible terrorists' crimes and incidents, (3) participation in emergency response to terrorism, (4) investigation and information gathering involving terrorists, and (5) follow-up actions and prosecution of crimes involving and/or resulting from terrorism.

MYTHS AND STEREOTYPES ABOUT TERRORISTS

Knowledge of the concerns, diversity, and historical backgrounds of various multicultural communities will facilitate the public safety and peacekeeping mission of law enforcement officers in dealing with terrorism. It is important to have an understanding about some of the myths and stereotypes that are held of groups associated with terrorism and how these stereotypes might contribute to prejudice, discrimination, and biased encounters with members of these populations. Stereotypic views of multicultural groups who might be potential terrorists reduce individuals within those groups to simplistic, one-dimensional caricatures and as either "incompetent cowards" who can't fight face to face or "suicidal bogey persons" who can't be stopped. It is important for law enforcement officers to be aware of the different stereotypes of potential terrorists. The key to effectiveness in multicultural law enforcement with any group is to intelligently discern the myths and stereotypes about that group. Further, we need to be aware of these stereotypes and be able to monitor our thinking and our behaviors when the stereotypes do not apply to the persons with whom we are interacting.

Some of the current stereotypes that might affect law enforcement officers' perceptions of terrorists include the following:

1. *Arab and Middle Eastern Nationality or Muslim Religious Background:* As a result of high-profile attention to terrorist incidents such as the 9/11 attacks by al-Qaida and the Boston Marathon bomb explosions on April 15, 2013, it is easy to stereotype terrorists as having Arab and Middle Eastern nationality or Muslim religious backgrounds. Terrorists can be foreign or domestic; clearly the majority of the domestic terrorist incidents and attacks in the United States have not originated from groups or individuals of Arab and Middle Eastern nationality or Muslim religious backgrounds. In "Terrorism 2002–2005," the FBI (2010) highlights the long-standing trend that the vast majority of

the terrorist attacks in the United States are conducted by Americans (domestic extremists) against other Americans. During the period covered in the report, 23 of the 24 recorded terrorism incidents were perpetrated by special interest extremist groups (i.e., 22 of the 24 incidents were by animal rights and environmental movement groups and one by a white supremacist group) (FBI, 2010). Corley, Smith, and Damphousse (2005), in their research on the Changing Face of American Terrorism, reviewed the files of the American Terrorism Study (ATS), a project that included demographic data on persons indicted under the FBI's Counterterrorism Program since the 1980s. In the 1980s, of the 215 terrorists indicted, 79 percent were Americans (48% in the right-wing category and 31% in the left-wing or environmental categories) and only 21 percent were international terrorists. Similar findings were noted for their 1990s findings: of the 231 terrorists indicted, 70 percent were Americans (45% in the right-wing groups and 25% in the left-wing or environmental groups) and 30 percent were in the international terrorist groups.

As of January 27, 2012, the National Counterterrorism Center (NCTC) reports at least 50 Foreign Terrorist Organizations (FTOs). The FTOs are designated by the Secretary of State in accordance with Section 219 of the Immigration and Nationality Act (INA). Exhibit 10.1 includes some examples of FTOs.

Any of the current terrorist organizations around the world could combine forces or utilize operatives from other organizations to "look different" than expected or stereotyped. As highlighted by Howard et al. (2008), "we have seen a threat posed by non-state actors spanning the globe that exploit open societies, porous borders and differences in state legal structures and international laws to perpetrate their acts."

2. ***Insane and/or Behave Like Automatons:*** Unlike the movie industry's portrayal of terrorists, these individuals are usually not insane, although their actions may appear insane or irrational (Dershowitz, 2002). According to Malcolm W. Nance, a retired U.S. Navy Senior Chief from the U.S. intelligence community's Combating Terrorism Program and author of *The Terrorist Recognition Handbook*, second edition, most terrorists are generally intelligent, rational, decisive, and clear-thinking. In the heat of an attack, terrorists may focus on and harness their energies to accomplish their mission with dedication, motivation, ruthlessness, and commitment that may appear to outsiders as "insanity" (Nance, 2008).

3. ***Not as Skillful or Professional as U.S. Law Enforcement Officers and Personnel:*** Terrorists are clearly not all similar in skills, training, and background. They vary in terrorist-training background, from foreign-government-trained professionals who make up the foreign intelligence agencies of countries such as Libya, Cuba, Iran, and North Korea to the novice, untrained civilian militia, vigilante, and criminals. The training and experience of some of the terrorists render them as skillful in their craft as any law enforcement professional in the United States. On the other hand, others have skill levels similar to petty criminals on the street. The use of intelligence information (i.e., not assumptions or stereotypes) to assess the skill and ability levels of terrorists or terrorist groups is central to homeland security. Howard et al. (2008) notes, "Al-Qaeda's training is very eclectic and comprehensive; its tacticians and trainers have taken much from the special operations forces of several nations, including the U.S., U.K., and Russia. Indeed, Al-Qaeda fighters are as well or better trained than those of many national armies."

Throughout this text, it has been emphasized that attitudes and skills required of law enforcement officials in a multicultural society include (1) respecting cultural behaviors that are different from one's own, (2) observing and understanding behaviors important to diverse communities, and (3) analyzing and interpreting diverse behaviors for application within multicultural communities. Similarly, multicultural skills and knowledge are also elements that can

1. Abdallah Azzam Brigades (AAB)	12. Revolutionary Organization 17 November (17N)
2. Abu Nidal Organization (ANO)	13. Revolutionary People's Liberation Party/ Front (DHKP/C)
3. Abu Sayyaf Group (ASG)	
4. Ansar al-Islam (AAI)	
5. Aum Shinrikyo (AUM)	14. Shining Path (Sendero Luminoso, SL)
6. Basque Fatherland and Liberty (ETA)	15. United Self-Defense Forces of Colombia (AUC)
7. Communist Party of the Philippines/New People's Army (CPP/NPA)	
8. Continuity Irish Republican Army (CIRA)	16. Harakat-ul Jihad Islami (HUJI)
9. Al-Qaida (AQ)	17. Tehrik-e Taliban Pakistan (TTP)
10. Real IRA (RIRA)	18. Jundallah
11. Revolutionary Armed Forces of Colombia (FARC)	19. Army of Islam (AOI)
	20. Indian Mujahideen (IM)

EXHIBIT 10.1   Examples of Foreign Terrorist Organizations
Source: National Counterterrorism Center (2013).

contribute to detecting and predicting terrorist actions and activities for homeland security when coupled with an intelligence-based approach. Just as it is important to understand one's own biases and stereotypes about multicultural communities in order to effectively serve those communities, law enforcement officers need to change their perceptions of who the terrorists are before they can effectively detect terrorist activities.

Tips to Detect Terrorist Behavior

1. *Anyone could be a Terrorist:* Law enforcement officers who start to look for specific groups may be blinded and may overlook a group or individuals who may actually be the real terrorists sought. For example, if one were going by Arab descent or nationality, one would have missed Richard C. Reid, the shoe bomber (i.e., who was of British citizenship), and Jose Padilla, the alleged plotter for releasing a "dirty bomb" in the United States (born in Chicago, of U.S. citizenship and Puerto Rican descent). If one thought that terrorists were inferior and not intelligent, one would have missed apprehending Theodore Kaczynski, the Unabomber, who was a former professor at the University of California at Berkley.

2. *Learn to Acknowledge the Terrorist's Motivation, Skills, and Capabilities:* Because of the actions of terrorists, law enforcement officers may view terrorists with contempt along with other negative stereotypic descriptors such as "crazies," "camel jockeys," "suicidal," "scum of the earth," and "rag heads." Such contempt and disdain for terrorists may indeed be the perspective that blinds law enforcement officers and others to the lethal actions and goals of terrorists. Law enforcement officers must, with clear insight and perceptions, acknowledge terrorists for what they are: motivated, ruthless human beings who use destruction, death, and deceit to meet their lethal goals. For example, prior to the bombing of the Alfred P. Murrah Federal Building in Oklahoma City, one law enforcement and intelligence stereotype held that U.S. domestic terrorists were not capable of mass destruction, but were merely a criminal nuisance element of society (Heymann, 2001).

3. *Analyze and Utilize Intelligence and Other Source Information:* Law enforcement officers are trained to gather and use information from various sources in a criminal investigation. For homeland security, key sources of information include, not only local, state, and federal intelligence sources, but also knowledge, relationships, and networks developed within the local multicultural communities. As noted by Nance (2008), "Terrorism against America

can only be defeated through careful intelligence collection, surveillance, cooperative efforts among law enforcement and intelligence agencies, and resolving the root complaints of the terrorist-supporting population."

4. ***Observe and Interpret Street-Level Behaviors:*** Law enforcement officers are trained to observe and interpret street-level criminal behaviors, and such skills are applicable to recognizing some of the behaviors of terrorists. Terrorists are not invisible "ghosts" (i.e., terrorists' behaviors and actions are usually visible to the trained observer); however, stereotypes based on race, ethnicity, gender, age, nationality, and other dimensions of diversity may inhibit a law enforcement officer from observing and correctly interpreting the actions and behaviors of possible terrorists. Racial profiling would be one of the actions that could hamper law enforcement efforts in detecting a terrorist's intent.

Without proper intelligence, it is almost impossible to effectively interpret behaviors that one observes. For example, three of the nineteen 9/11 terrorists were involved in traffic stops by the police for speeding on three separate occasions prior to the attacks:

- Mohammed Atta, the al-Qaida 9/11 skyjacker who piloted the American Airlines Flight 77 into the North Tower of the World Trade Center, was stopped in July 2001 by the Florida State Police for driving with an invalid license. A bench warrant was issued for his arrest because he ignored the issued ticket. Atta was stopped a few weeks later in Delray Beach, Florida, for speeding, but the officer was unaware of the bench warrant and let him go with a warning (Kleinberg & Davies, 2001)
- Ziad al-Jarrah, the al-Qaida 9/11 skyjacker who investigators believe was a pilot on United Airlines Flight 93, which crashed in an open field near Shanksville, Pennsylvania, was stopped and cited by the Maryland State Police on September 9, 2001, for driving 90 miles per hour in a 65-mph zone near the Delaware state line (a $270 fine). Trooper Catalano, who made the stop, reported that he looked over the car several times, videotaped the entire transaction, and said that the stop was a "regular, routine traffic stop" ("A Nation Challenged," 2002).
- Hani Hanjour, one of the al-Qaida 9/11 skyjackers aboard American Airlines Flight 77 that crashed into the Pentagon, was stopped for speeding within a few miles of the military headquarters 6 weeks before the attack and was ticketed by the Arlington, Virginia, police for going 50 miles per hour in a 35-mph zone. Hanjour surrendered his Florida driver's license to the police officer who stopped him but was allowed to go on his way (Roig-Franzia & Davis, 2002).

Lessons can be learned from historical events as in the case of Timothy McVeigh, the Oklahoma City bomber, when law enforcement officials properly interpreted information, which led to his arrest at a traffic stop. McVeigh was stopped by Trooper Charles Hanger of the Oklahoma Highway Patrol about 90 minutes after the bombing of the Alfred P. Murrah Federal Building. Trooper Hanger was looking for suspicious vehicles headed his way given the approximate travel distance to his location and time of the bombing.

Oklahoma Highway Patrol Trooper Charles Hanger pulled over McVeigh's yellow Mercury Marquis on I-35 about 63 miles north of Oklahoma City because his car was missing a rear license plate. Hanger told the jury he took shelter behind the door of his cruiser as McVeigh got out of the car and walked toward him. As McVeigh reached for his camouflage wallet, Hanger said he noticed a bulge under his light windbreaker. "I told him to take both hands and slowly pull back his jacket," Hanger said. "He said, 'I have a gun.' I pulled my weapon and stuck it to the back of his head." As Hanger searched and cuffed him, McVeigh told the trooper he was also carrying a knife and a spare clip of ammunition. In the chamber of the pistol, Hanger found a round of Black Talon ammunition, bullets designed to inflict maximum damage on a shooting victim. Hanger then arrested McVeigh for carrying a concealed pistol in a shoulder holster. Three days later, McVeigh was tied to the blast as he waited for a court hearing on the gun charge. ("Trooper Describes Arrest," 1997).

RESPONSE STRATEGIES ADDRESSING LOCAL-COMMUNITY, REGIONAL, NATIONAL, AND GLOBAL ISSUES

The targets and methods of terrorists have become more diverse and more difficult to predict. Howard et al. (2008) notes that "not only are targets selected to cause casualties without limit, they are selected to undermine the global economy."

> Whereas the violent global jihadist movement manifested itself primarily in terrorism preventions in the United States from 2002 through 2005, internationally the movement claimed major attacks against U.S. and Western targets that resulted in American casualties. Most of these incidents were perpetrated by regional jihadist groups operating in primarily Muslim countries, and included attacks committed by Indonesia-based Jemaah Islamiya and al-Qa'ida in the Arabian Peninsula. The coordinated suicide bombing of London's mass transit system by homegrown jihadists, however, brought the violent jihadist movement and the tactic of suicide bombing to a major European capital. (FBI, 2010)

Often, clues surrounding the terrorist incident and/or attack will reveal whether domestic or international terrorism was involved and will point toward possible motives and the perpetrators behind the incident. Clues that might be helpful, surrounding a terrorist event, include the following:

Timing of the event may be significant to the terrorist group or individual. For many years to come, 9/11 will be a day on which all U.S. facilities around the world will operate at a heightened state of security and awareness because of the al-Qaida's simultaneous terrorist attacks. Within the United States, April 19 will continue for some time to be a day of heightened alert because it is the anniversary of both the domestic terrorist bombing of the Alfred P. Murrah Federal Building in Oklahoma City and the fire at the Branch Davidian compound in Waco, Texas. The more law enforcement works with a community policing model to understand the makeup of a multicultural community, the greater the likelihood that officers will have the knowledge to anticipate potential terrorist targets within communities.

Potential Terrorist Targets

Occupancy, location, and/or purpose related to the target include the following types of elements:

- Controversial businesses are those that have a history of inviting the protest and dislike of recognized groups that include one or more components of extremist elements. For example, controversial businesses include abortion clinics, logging mills, nuclear facilities, and tuna fishing companies.
- Public buildings and venues with large numbers of people are seen by terrorist as opportunities for attention-getting with mass casualties and victims. For some terrorists, causing massive destruction and casualties in targeted public buildings or in venues containing large numbers of people is linked to the identity of the operator/owner of the building or venue. Examples of such targets are the World Trade Center (attacked by terrorists on 1993 and 2001), the World Bank, entertainment venues, athletic events, tourist destinations, shopping malls, airports, and convention centers.
- Symbolic and historical targets are links the terrorists make regarding the relationship of the target and the organization, event, and/or services that specifically offend extremists. Examples of symbolic and historical targets include the offices of the Internal Revenue Service (IRS) for tax resisters, the offices of the Bureau of Alcohol, Tobacco and Firearms (ATF) for those who oppose any form of gun control, and African American churches and Jewish synagogues for those who are members of white supremacist groups.
- Infrastructure systems and services include those structures and operations that are vital for the continued functioning of our country. Throughout the United States, these targets include communication companies, power grids, water treatment facilities, mass transit, telecommunication towers, and transportation hubs. Terrorists' attacks on any of these

targets have the potential for disabling and disrupting massive areas and regions, resulting in chaos, especially with respect to huge numbers of injuries and fatalities across large geographical areas. Law enforcement officers' and agencies' knowledge of possible targets linked to occupancy, location, and/or purpose of an organization within the local, multicultural communities will enhance the ability to prevent and to prepare for a terrorist incident. For any of the noted indicators of a terrorist incident or attack, law enforcement officers would nearly always be among the first responders to the scene (IACP, 2001).

The First-Response Challenge for Law Enforcement, Fire and Emergency Management System Personnel

Law enforcement officers, firefighters, and emergency management system (EMS) personnel as first responders to a terrorist attack confront tremendous challenge, risk, and responsibility. The terrorist attack or crime scene is complicated by confusion, panic, and casualties as well as residual effects of weapons of mass destruction in the case that they were used. Moreover, terrorists typically and deliberately target responders and rescue personnel at the crime scene. Terrorists have utilized "secondary devices" to target law enforcement and other public safety personnel responding to a terrorist's attack. For example, in the 1997 bomb attack at an Atlanta abortion clinic, a second bomb went off approximately one hour after the initial explosion and was very close to the command post established for the first bomb attack. In the 2013 Boston Marathon terrorist bomb attacks, two unexploded devices were later recovered in a crime scene search of the area. As in all hazardous law enforcement and emergency response situations, officer safety and self-protection are top priorities. However, the suicide terrorist attacks on 9/11 caused more law enforcement and firefighter line of duty deaths than any other single incident in American history. A total of 343 firefighters from the New York City Fire Department and 71 law enforcement officers from 8 different agencies were killed when the two World Trade Center buildings collapsed in New York City. The first responders died as they were attempting to rescue the victims trapped in the World Trade Center after both towers were struck by separate airplanes, hijacked by suicide terrorists. It should be noted the combined efforts of law enforcement officers along with fire and EMS personnel, saved over an estimated 25,000 people. In another state, one law enforcement officer from the U.S. Fish and Wildlife Service was killed when United Flight 93 crashed into a field in Shanksville, Pennsylvania, as he and other passengers attempted to retake control of the plane from terrorist hijackers ("Officer Down Memorial Page," 2013; "The 9/11 Commission Report,"2004). Exhibit 10.2 shows the agencies that reported law enforcement officers killed at the two World Trade Center buildings on 9/11.

Extract is from a prepared speech by former Department of Homeland Security Secretary Janet Napolitano to New York City First Responders (New York City, NY) September 10, 2010:

As first responders, you are the critical link in our nation's security and preparedness. You are often the first to identify a potential threat or recognize a larger trend that you're seeing in your communities. In a way, you are "first preventers" as well as first responders. And we have a responsibility get you the kind of tools and training you want and need to do your job.

The old view that "if we fight the terrorists abroad, we won't have to fight them here" is just that—the old view. It is abundantly clear that we have to fight them abroad; we have to fight them at home. We have to fight them, period. And you are as squarely in that fight as I am.

Accordingly, I felt that the Department needed to do more to support you, and also to do more to engage the private sector as partners in this effort. And, indeed, I felt we needed to do more to inform and empower citizens and communities to be the enormous assets they can be before, and during, a crisis or emergency have to fight them, period. (Napolitano, 2010)

Agency	Law Officers Killed
New York City Fire Department	1
New York City Police Department	23
New York State Office Of Court Administration	3
New York State Office of Tax Enforcement: Petroleum, Alcohol and Tobacco Bureau Revenue Crimes Bureau	1 4
Port Authority of New York and New Jersey Police Department	37
Federal Bureau of Investigation	1
United States Secret Service	1

EXHIBIT 10.2   Law Enforcement Officers killed at the Twin Towers, New York City on 9/11
Source: Officer Down Memorial Page (2013).

Law enforcement officers must understand the various types of danger and harm that may result from a terrorist situation not only for their own self-protection but in order to understand the reactions of affected victims and to be able to provide effective assistance to those affected by terrorist activities. Law enforcement personnel need to be aware that many people who are from multicultural communities may have had prior experiences (or have heard of prior experiences) with WMD incidents within their home countries (e.g., Vietnamese Americans' experience with thermal harm during the napalm bombing of their villages; Iraqi and Iranian Americans' experience with chemical harm from mustard gas attacks within their communities during the Iran–Iraq War). Law enforcement personnel, as first responders to terrorists' crimes, need to know that the forms of self-protection can be defined in terms of the principles of time, distance and shielding. The U.S. Nuclear Regulatory Commission (USNRC) addresses these three principles as they relate to radiation exposure, however, the principles are useful in all WMD incidents.

1. *Time* is used as a tool in a terrorist crime scene. Spend the shortest amount of time possible in the affected area or exposed to the hazard. The less time one spends in the hazard area, the less likely it is that one will become injured. Minimizing time spent in the hazard area will also reduce the chances of contaminating the crime scene.
2. *Distance* from the affected terrorist area or hazardous situation should be maximized. The greater the distance from the affected area while performing one's functions, the less the exposure to the hazard. Maintaining distance from the hazard areas will also ease the evacuation of the injured, allow for other emergency personnel requiring immediate access, and facilitate crowd control by law enforcement officers.
3. *Shielding* can be used to address specific types of hazards. Shielding can be achieved through buildings, walls, vehicles, body armor, and personnel protective equipment including chemical protective clothing, fire protective clothing, and self-contained breathing apparatus (U.S. Nuclear Regulatory Commission, 2013b).

Officers and EMS personnel must have sufficient cross-cultural and language skills to communicate the importance of time, distance, and shielding for effective action and response within all communities during a terrorist incident.

NATIONAL INCIDENT MANAGEMENT SYSTEM   Homeland Security Presidential Directive (HSPD)-5 (2003) established the National Incident Management System (NIMS) to be under the control of the Department of Homeland Security. The lessons learned from the 9/11 terrorist attacks and Hurricane Katrina (2005) highlighted the need to improve upon emergency management, incident response, and coordination processes across the United States. NIMS has incorporated those lessons learned as best practices and provides a consistent nationwide template to enable federal, state, tribal and local governments, nongovernmental organizations (NGOs), and the private sector to work together to prevent, protect against, respond to, recover from, and mitigate against threatened or actual natural disasters, acts of terrorism, or other manmade disasters. HSPD-5 requires all federal departments and agencies to adopt NIMS and to use it in their individual incident management programs and activities, as well as in their actions to assist state, tribal, and local governments. HSPD-5 mandates states, tribal, and local organizations to adopt NIMS as a condition for federal preparedness assistance through grants, contracts, and other activities. The benefits of NIMS are as follows (U.S. Department of Homeland Security, 2008):

1. A comprehensive, nationwide systematic approach to incident management, including the Incident Command System, Multiagency Coordination Systems, and Public Information
2. A set of preparedness concepts and principles for all hazards
3. Essential principles for a common operating picture and interoperability of communications and information management
4. Standardized resource management procedures that enable coordination among different jurisdictions or organizations
5. Scalable, so it may be use for all incidents (from day-to-day to large scale)

HELPING STATE AND LOCAL LAW ENFORCEMENT   The Office for State and Local Law Enforcement (OSLLE) was established in 2007 by Congress upon the recommendation of the 9/11 Commission within the Department of Homeland Security. OSLLE defined its two purposes as "(1) Lead the coordination of DHS-wide policies related to state, local, tribal, and territorial law enforcement's role in preventing, preparing for, protecting against, and responding to natural disasters, acts of terrorism, and other manmade disasters within the United States; and (2) Serve as the primary liaison between DHS and non-Federal law enforcement agencies across the country." The responsibilities of the OSLLE include (DHS, 2013b):

1. Serve as the primary Department liaison to state, local, tribal, and territorial law enforcement;
2. Advise the Secretary on the issues, concerns, and recommendations of state, local, tribal, and territorial law enforcement;
3. Keep the law enforcement community up-to-date on Department-wide activities and initiatives such as "If You See Something, Say Something, the Blue Campaign, Nationwide Suspicious Activity Reporting (SAR) Initiative (NSI), and the Department's efforts in Countering Violent Extremism;
4. Coordinate with the Office of Intelligence and Analysis to ensure the time coordination and distribution of intelligence and strategic information to state, local, tribal, and territorial law enforcement; and
5. Work with the Federal Emergency Management Agency to ensure that law enforcement and terrorism-focused grants to state, local, tribal, and territorial law enforcement agencies are appropriately focused on terrorism prevention activities.

Response Strategies: Detecting and Preventing Attacks of Terrorism

Law enforcement officers spend years studying criminal behaviors in order to prevent crimes and to capture and prosecute criminals. Public safety roles for law enforcement agencies now require the use of some of these same skills in identifying the criminal behaviors of potential terrorists. As noted by Hoffman (2006) and others, the most difficult and critical component of homeland security is to recognize and prevent a terrorist attack. As such, criminal justice officers need to be competent in recognizing the Terrorist Attack Pre-incident Indicators (TAPIs), a term used by the intelligence community to describe actions taken and behaviors exhibited by terrorists before they carry out an attack (Nance, 2008).Chapter 13 mentions one source of TAPIs, which includes the tools of "profiling" used in law enforcement today. For example, Secret Service officers are trained to watch for individual behaviors, compiled as a profile, which may serve as indicators for possible actions toward those whom the officers are protecting.

Law enforcement officers, trained in observing and working with cultural differences and diverse communities, can also apply some of these human behavior skills to recognizing terrorist behavior. As noted in Chapter 13, public safety officers must avoid a stereotype-based approach to detecting criminals; this holds equally true in detecting terrorists. Stereotypes alone do not help in the detection and prevention of terrorism regardless of whether they are based on race or on the notion of what constitutes a "terrorist." Stereotyping will obscure law enforcement officers' perceptions of the real dangers and issues in providing for our homeland security. For example, several of the 9/11 terrorists behaved in ways that threw off any surveillance based on cultural and religious stereotypes: more than one skyjacker was seen in nightclubs and strip bars. Such behaviors would be contrary to the American stereotype of devout Muslim fundamentalists who would be averse to alcoholic beverages, nightclub exotic dancers, and overt sexual behaviors of men and women at bars. It is beyond the scope of this chapter to detail the development of law enforcement skills for recognizing terrorists' behaviors. But what is important to understand, from a multicultural perspective, is the intergroup relationships where one group may be threatened by another, and to work proactively with community members and across agencies in helping to create safe environments. One such example of collaboration among law enforcement agencies was the successful operation of a police department, Homeland Security and the FBI; this multiagency effort, in 2009, resulted in the capture of Muslim terrorists plotting to bomb a Jewish community center in the Bronx. Unbeknownst to the terrorists, law enforcement had been monitoring the criminals for over a year. The terrorists "explosives" were actually duds, provided by authorities. Just as the terrorists had placed what they thought were explosives in cars parked next to the Community Center, the police arrested them (Weiss, Calabrese, & Fermino, 2009).

Multijurisdictional Action

In our discussion about coordinating efforts for terrorism prevention, homeland security, and disaster preparedness, a variety of diverse federal, state, and local agencies and organizations are involved in multijurisdictional actions for combating a terrorist incident or attack. Some of the key elements ensuring success for law enforcement agencies and officers in such incidents include the following:

1. Preparation and planning provide some of the best avenues for successful crisis management and subsequent recovery from a terrorist incident. The following planned steps are critical:
   - Develop pertinent plans and policies for terrorist incidents and attacks
   - Establish multijurisdictional plans/protocols and mutual-aid agreements
   - Ensure availability of multicultural law enforcement personnel with language expertise
   - Implement, as much as possible, preventive procedures and plans
   - Train law enforcement personnel as first responders and as members of multijurisdictional teams involved in a terrorist incident according to National Incident Management System (NIMS) and Incident Command System (ICS) standards
   - Provide background information about the makeup of the different multicultural communities and their prior experiences as victims of terrorism

- Rehearse possible events and incidents
- Acquire the necessary protective and communication equipment
- Establish multidiscipline community service teams (and, again, where possible, provide for the range of language expertise required by the community)
- Establish a network of multicultural leaders and communities for communication, intelligence, and response implementation

2. Cost and deployment of resources impact all local governments with respect to the degree of burden and expenditure needed to be borne by local law enforcement and by other public safety agencies involved in combating possible terrorist incidents.

    Since local tax-based funds are insufficient to address the enormity of costs involved in the planning, prevention, and deployment of resources to address terrorism concerns and issues, one of the key concerns within multicultural communities is the diversion of funds from community policing activities to the war on terrorism.

3. Access to intelligence and informational databases provides the information necessary for the prevention of and response to terrorist threats. The best prevention against terrorist incidents and acts at the local community level is to ensure coordination with federal and state intelligence sources and access to ongoing intelligence-gathering capacity from the federal level. On the local level, it is important that law enforcement officers and agencies develop critical relationships and networks with the local multicultural communities. Fusion Centers are an example of a collaborative effort between Department of Homeland Security (DHS), FBI Joint Terrorism Task Forces, FBI Field Intelligence Groups, DEA, Emergency Operation Centers, Protective Security Advisors, and tribal, state, and local government law enforcement agencies.

    > State and major urban area fusion centers serve as primary focal points within the state and local environment for the receipt, analysis, gathering, and sharing of threat-related information among federal, state, local, tribal, and territorial (SLLT) partners. Located in states and major urban areas throughout the country, fusion centers are uniquely situated to empower front-line law enforcement, public safety, fire service and private sector security personnel to lawfully gather and share threat-related information. They provide interdisciplinary expertise and situational awareness to inform decision-making at all levels of government. Fusion centers conduct analysis and facilitate information sharing, assisting law enforcement and homeland security partners in preventing, protecting against, and responding to crime and terrorism. Fusion centers are owned and operated by state and local entities with support from federal partners in the form of deployed personnel, training, technical assistance, exercise support, security clearances, and connectivity to federal systems, technology and grant funding. (DHS, 2013c)

4. Multijurisdictional training and rehearsals have been identified as critical elements in the successful implementation of terrorist incident management and recovery. Clearly, there are few opportunities to develop the relationships, awareness, communication, and processes required for a coordinated effort ahead of an incident's occurring. The involvement of multijurisdictional agencies and their personnel in rehearsals provide valuable lessons for any possible real terrorist incidents. The involvement of multijurisdictional agencies and their personnel in rehearsals provide valuable lessons for any possible real terrorist incidents. One such example is a simulation exercise led by the Department of Defense that took place in June 2013 in Harrisburg, Pennsylvania. It involved the Special Emergency Response Team (SERT) of the Pennsylvania State Police, Department of Health, the Harrisburg Capitol Police and the Dauphin County Emergency Services. The scenario to which police and various other first and second responders had to simulate involved overtaking terrorists and bringing them into custody; the drill involved a dirty bomb situation whereby SERT officers exchanged paintball fire with "terrorists" (Marroni, 2013).

Training for terrorist incidents that are multijurisdictional in nature would allow for the rehearsal and practices necessary for effective overall terrorism response efforts. As in any simulated practice exercise, not all components of a terrorist incident can be anticipated or incorporated. Nonetheless, such training and rehearsal would allow for a timelier implementation of the response strategies important to a terrorist incident, as will be noted in the next section. Training in responding to terrorism, to date, has included limited scenarios related to multicultural community elements. In time, emphasis upon language expertise, bilingual communications, and interpreter participation need to be added to training exercises.

Protecting Critical Infrastructure and Key Resources

Infrastructure and key resources are important to all of America's urban and rural communities. As noted in its National Infrastructure Protection Plan, DHS (2009), "Risk in the 21st century results from a complex mix of manmade and naturally occurring threats and hazards, including terrorist attacks, accidents, natural disasters, and other emergencies." While DHS and local law enforcement agencies cannot assume to be able to prevent all of these incidents, prevention, protection, and preparedness activities can help manage and reduce the most serious risks. Exhibit 10.3 lists the Sector-Specific Agency for the Critical Infrastructure and Key Resources Sector.

Sector-Specific Agency	Critical Infrastructure and Key Resources Sector
Department of Agriculture	Agriculture and Food
Department of Health and Human Services	
Department of Defense	Defense Industrial Base
Department of Energy	Energy
Department of Health and Human Services	Healthcare and Public Health
Department of the Interior	National Monuments and Icons
Department of the Treasury	Banking and Finance
Environmental Protection Agency	Water
Department of Homeland Security	Chemical
Office of Infrastructure Protection	Commercial Facilities
	Critical Manufacturing
	Dams
	Emergency Services
	Nuclear Reactors, Materials, and Waste
Office of Cyber security and Communications	Information Technology
	Communications
Transportation Security Administration	Transportation Systems
Immigration and Customs Enforcement, Federal Protective Service	Government Facilities

EXHIBIT 10.3 Sector-Specific Agency and Critical Infrastructure and Key Resources Sector
Source: Department of Homeland Security (2009).

U.S. PATRIOT ACT AND INTELLIGENCE COMMUNITY

U.S. Patriot Act

An important element of DHS, the U.S. Department of Justice and the FBI in their counterterrorism legal efforts, is the USA Patriot Act signed into law by President George Bush on October 26, 2001, to improve government coordination in law enforcement, intelligence gathering, and information sharing. The official title for this act was "the U.S.A. P.A.T.R.I.O.T. Act," in which the acronym stands for, "Uniting and Strengthening America by Providing Appropriate Tools Required to Intercept and Obstruct Terrorism." In this text, this is called as "the Patriot Act," which has ten Titles that provide for additional powers for government to use against terrorists. Key components of the Patriot Act that have raised concern within multicultural communities (especially Arab and Middle Eastern) include the power of law enforcement officers to (1) question, detain, and remove potential foreign terrorists within our borders; (2) enhance surveillance methods to track and intercept communications without customary court orders; and (3) increase information sharing for key infrastructure protection by allowing for cooperation between federal, state, and local law enforcement agencies through the expansion of the Regional Information Sharing System (RISS). The Patriot Act was last renewed by President Barack Obama in May 2011, with most of its components and titles intact.

The FBI and DHS have requested the assistance of state and local law enforcement and public safety agencies in data-gathering and interviewing efforts for homeland security purposes under the provisions of the Patriot Act.

Law enforcement agencies must be concerned about how they participate in homeland security data-gathering efforts in order to avoid adversely affecting their relationships with multicultural communities. Clearly, as the U.S. is a nation built on the rule of law, DHS must utilize federal laws to win the war on terrorism while always protecting the civil liberties of those individuals within multicultural communities and within the larger national communities as a whole. DHS uses our federal immigration laws and customs regulations to protect our borders and ensure uninterrupted commerce, and encourages state and local governments to strengthen their codes and regulations to protect our public welfare, to prosecute terrorists, and to be partners in countering the domestic and global threat of terrorism.

National Counterterrorism Center

The National Counterterrorism Center (NCTC) was established by Presidential Executive Order 13554 in August 2004 and later passed into law by the Intelligence Reform and Terrorism Prevention Act of 2004 (IRTPA). By federal law, "NCTC serves as the primary organization in the United States Government (USG) for integrating and analyzing all intelligence pertaining to counterterrorism (except for information pertaining exclusively to domestic terrorism)." Its services and functions include, but are not limited to (NCTC, 2013):

1. Integrates foreign and domestic analysis from across the Intelligence Community (IC) and produces a wide-range of detailed assessments designed to support senior policymakers and other members of the policy, intelligence, law enforcement, defense, homeland security, and foreign affairs communities.
2. Provides the President's Daily Brief (PDB) and daily the National Terrorism Bulletin (NTB).
3. Provides information on the Homeland Threat Task Force.
4. Leads the Intelligence Community (IC) in providing expertise and analysis of key terrorism-related issues, with immediate and far-reaching impact. For example, NTC's Radicalization and Extremist Messaging Group leads the IC's efforts on radicalization issues.
5. Evaluates the quality of Counterterrorism (CT) analytic production, the training of analysts working CT, and the strengths and weaknesses of the CT analytic workforce. NCTC created the Analytic Framework for Counterterrorism, aimed at reducing redundancy of effort by delineating the roles of the IC's various Ct analytic components. NCTC also

created a working group for alternative analysis to help improve the overall rigor and quality of CT analysis.

6. Is collocated with more than 30 intelligence, military, law enforcement and homeland security networks under one roof to facilitate information sharing.

7. Operates as a partnership of organizations to include: Central Intelligence Agency; Department of Justice/Federal Bureau of Investigation; Departments of State, Defense, and Homeland Security; and other entities that provide expertise to the Departments of Energy, Treasury, Agriculture, Transportation, and Health and Human Services; Nuclear Regulatory Commission; and the U.S. Capitol Hill Police.

National Security Agency

The National Security Agency (NSA) was established in 1952, by executive order of President Harry Truman. President Truman's decision to establish the NSA followed several studies on how to best continue the code breaking work in the post-war era that was successful in breaking German and Japanese codes during WWII. The Central Security Service (CSS) was established by President Richard Nixon's executive order in 1972 to form a combined partnership between NSA and the Service Cryptologic Components of the U.S. Armed Forces, in which the Director of NSA has the dual role as the Chief of CSS. The NSA operates under the direction of the Department of Defense and reports to the Director of National Intelligence. Following are key components from their mission statement (NSA, 2011):

- The NSA/CSS leads the U.S. Government in cryptology that encompasses both Signals Intelligence (SIGINT) and Information Assurance (IA) products and services, and enables Computer Network Operations (CNO) in order to gain a decision advantage for the Nation and our allies under all circumstances.
- The IA mission confronts the formidable challenge of preventing foreign adversaries from gaining access to sensitive or classified nation security information.
- The Signals Intelligence mission collects, processes, and disseminates intelligence information from foreign signals for intelligence and counterintelligence purposes and to support military operations.
- The Agency also enables Network Warfare operations to defeat terrorists and their organizations at home and abroad, consistent with U.S. laws and the protection privacy and civil liberties.
- Executive Order 12333, originally issued December 4, 1981, authorizes the Director, NSA/Chief, and CSS to collect (including through clandestine means), process, analyze, produce, and disseminate signals intelligence information and data for foreign intelligence and counterintelligence purposes to support national and departmental missions.
- Executive Order 12333 was amended on July 31, 2008, in order to: align with the Intelligence Reform and Terrorism Prevention Act of 2004; implement additional recommendations of the 9/11 and WMD Commissions; further integrate the Intelligence Community and clarify and strengthen the role of the DNI as the head of the Community; and maintain or strengthen privacy and civil liberties protections.

In an appearance before Congress, General Keith Alexander, Director of the NSA testified "that more than 50 potential terrorist attacks have been thwarted by two controversial programs tracking more than a billion phone calls and vast swaths of Internet data each day" (Parkinson, 2013). That said, a general challenge for individuals in law enforcement professions is to focus on developing positive relations and trust with community members who feel most vulnerable and fearful about such monitoring, especially including people from Middle Eastern and Muslim backgrounds.

On May 2, 2011, President Barack Obama announced on a nationally televised broadcast that Osama bin Laden, the leader of al-Qaida and mastermind of the 9/11 attacks, was killed by a team of U.S. Armed Forces. President Obama indicated through the U.S. intelligence community that Bin Laden was located in Abbottabad, Pakistan. To emphasize the need for sustained attention on terrorism, President Obama asserted, "There's no doubt that al Qaeda will continue to pursue attacks against us. We must—and we will—remain vigilant at home and abroad" (Obama, 2011). At the same time, mindful of the impact of his words on the American public, Obama reiterated that, "Our war is not against Islam. Bin Laden was not a Muslim leader; he was a mass murderer of Muslims." (Chapter 8 provides information on the impact of 9/11 on Hate Crimes and on stereotypes regarding Arab Americans and people perceived to be Muslim). In fighting the war on terrorism, criminal justice professionals must also protect communities from hateful backlash on innocent citizens.

WORKING WITH MULTICULTURAL COMMUNITIES ON TERRORISM PREVENTION AND DISASTER PREPAREDNESS

Since the establishment of DHS, law enforcement agencies have been receiving a variety of intelligence information, advisories, warnings, and other pertinent communications regarding efforts and activities to be implemented in local communities. Local law enforcement agencies and officers, because of their community knowledge and networks, have been called upon to aid in intelligence data gathering regarding possible terrorists. Such efforts have often sparked a mixed reception by law enforcement organizations. From one perspective, this puts a strain on the established relationships of community policing within multicultural communities. Public confidence and trust in law enforcement agencies are essential for the effective prevention of and response to terrorism and for homeland security. Residents in diverse communities must be able to trust that they will be treated fairly and protected as part of homeland security. This is of particular importance where there may be perceptions, assumptions, and/or stereotypes among community residents as to who might be suspected of being a terrorist in the multicultural community. When local law enforcement agencies and officers are called upon to provide assistance, the tasks of information gathering and interviewing possible terrorist suspects within multicultural communities involve the following critical steps:

1. *Contact with Community Leaders:* Law enforcement officers need to work closely with community leaders in order to establish a cooperative plan for gathering necessary information. Community leaders can effectively inform their multicultural communities as to why information gathering is taking place and what the associated processes are. In addition, community leaders can, for example, work with the community relations offices of law enforcement agencies to develop a communication plan for the effective dissemination of information.

2. *Utilize a Communication Plan:* It is essential to have a well-developed and pilot-tested communication plan to ensure that the proper messages are disseminated to multicultural communities. This is particularly important when language translations and interpretation are necessary. A carefully pre-tested core message regarding data-gathering procedures and interviews has more chance of success than on-the-spot messages: unplanned messages would be subject to the momentary interpretation of those who first hear such information.

3. *Clearly Explain the Implications of Participation in the Data-Gathering Process:* When it comes to accusations of terrorism and/or fears related to homeland security, members of multicultural communities who might be stereotyped as "terrorists," or have experienced prejudice by others in this regard, would naturally be quite cautious of any contact with law enforcement agencies and officers. Clearly defined procedures and information about data gathering and interviews are extremely important. In addition, if there are federal-agency consequences (e.g., being reported to the ICE for a visa violation), these elements should be clearly stated to ensure an ongoing relationship of trust with the community.

4. ***Utilize Law Enforcement Personnel, Interpreters from Similar Backgrounds:*** Use, whenever possible, law enforcement personnel (and interpreters) from the same or similar ethnic/cultural background as that of the communities involved; this contributes to relationship building and the trust necessary for information-gathering attempts. Clearly, the availability of bilingual personnel can make a significant difference to speakers of other languages.

Building Community Networks and Resources

In order to detect and deter terrorist incidents and attacks, and foster natural disaster preparedness, the development of strong community networks, relationships, and resources is critical. Developing such relationships requires both ongoing efforts and constant renewal of relationships through clear communication and trust between local law enforcement and multicultural community members. Outreach to such organizations and communities include, but are not limited to:

1. Local immigrant and refugee groups
2. Cultural, religious and ethnic groups (e.g., Black Family Associations, Muslim Community Associations, Samoan Community Councils, Tribal Councils)
3. Lesbian Gay Bisexual Transgender (LGBT) organizations; since historically the LGBT community has been excluded
4. Homeless organizations and shelters

Citizen Corps

After the tragic events of 9/11, state and local governments have increased opportunities for citizens to be more active in protecting their communities and supporting local first responders. Citizen Corps was created to help coordinate volunteer activities that will make local communities safer and better prepared to respond to any emergency situation. It provides opportunities for all people to participate in a variety of measures to make their families, homes, and multicultural communities safer from the threats of crime, terrorism, and all types of disasters. Citizen Corps is coordinated nationally by the Department of Homeland Security's Federal Emergency Management Agency (FEMA). In this capacity, FEMA works with other federal agencies, state and local governments, first responders and emergency managers, the volunteer community, and the Corporation for National and Community Service. Citizen Corps has five partner programs that allow citizens to get involved. These five federally sponsored programs help support first responders through volunteer programs and activities (DHS, 2013d):

1. Community Emergency Response Team (CERT) educates people about disaster preparedness and provides basic disaster response training.
2. Fire Corps (FC) promotes the use of citizen advocates to enhance the capacity of resource constrained fire and rescue departments.
3. USAonWatch—Neighborhood Watch works to provide information, training, and resources to citizens and law enforcement agencies throughout the country.
4. Medical Reserve Corps (MRC) program strengthens communities by helping medical, public health, and other volunteers offer their expertise during local emergencies and year-around.
5. Volunteers in Police Service (VIPS) works to enhance the capacity of state and local law enforcement to utilize volunteers.

Using Multicultural Media as a Resource

For any terrorist and homeland security incident or community disaster, law enforcement agencies must help to provide a constant flow of credible information to the local community. Clearly, if positive relationships have been formed with the diversity of residents and the multicultural community leaders, the law enforcement agency's credibility would not be suspect and/or in question. Media sources used for the release of information should include the ones used by most populations, as well as those used by specific multicultural groups, especially those broadcast or print in the languages of the key multicultural groups of the community. Some public safety agencies may be concerned about not having their information already prepared and translated into the language of the diverse ethnic and cultural groups; however, given the nature and importance of the information, most ethnic media will do the translation in order to provide critical information to their audiences.

Policies, procedures, and mechanisms need to be in place for releasing information to enable the safety and security of all community residents. This means that the involvement of multicultural media is critical. The ready availability of translated literature is key in ensuring appropriate responses, alleviating any unnecessary fears or concerns, and providing assurances that public safety agencies and officers are in control of the situation. The media have been shown to be the most efficient and reliable means to disseminate information rapidly to the community regarding a terrorist or emergency incident and to notify community residents of the subsequent response by the public safety agencies. Strategic media events should be held to continuously inform the public that the incident is well under control, the personnel are well prepared and trained to handle the incident, and the community's recovery is fully expected.

Whether dealing with a terrorist incident or an everyday event, the basis for effective communications with the community through the media is a strong partnership and established positive relationships with the media. Law enforcement agencies need to understand that whether in crisis management or in daily peacekeeping, the media have a dual role: to obtain information, stories, and perspectives on the incident for news-reporting objectives and to inform the community efficiently of impending dangers and threats stemming from the incident. Good media relations allow for the strategic communication of critical incident information to the communities served by the law enforcement and other emergency management agencies. To reach multicultural communities, police officers must go beyond the conventional and mainstream media sources and become familiar with all media, in English and in other languages that will reach the broadest populations in the shortest amount of time.

Racial Profiling within the Context of Homeland Security

The issue of racial profiling, as will be noted in Chapter 13, is a major problem and concern for African Americans, Arab Americans, and Latino/Hispanic Americans, and for members of other groups as well. Individuals from different cultural and racial backgrounds believe that the determining factor in whether peace officers exercise their discretion in stopping a vehicle has to do with the driver's race and ethnicity. In the area of homeland security, current federal policy prohibits the use of racial profiling except under narrow circumstances. Law enforcement officers should be cautious in the use of racial profiling for detecting terrorists and in homeland security matters. Hoffman (2006) has documented that terrorists will "do whatever it will take" to avoid detection and accomplish a mission. Even though the use of racial profiling in circumstances involving terrorism is legal and justifiable, its use may not actually result in detecting the terrorist because the terrorist is knowledgeable about the racial profiling used.

Immigration and Customs Enforcement and Secure Communities

In Chapter 1, the controversy surrounding "The ICE 287 (g) Program: A Law Enforcement Partnership" is addressed as it relates to state and local law enforcement agencies, allowing officers to perform immigration law enforcement functions. Further, Chapter 1 provides the status on ongoing reforms enacted upon 287 (g) by ICE; in addition to describing ICE's program "Secure Communities." As previously mentioned in Chapters 1 and 7, law enforcement agencies vary whether or not to partner with ICE in enforcing immigration laws. The same is true of participation in the Secure Communities program in regard to unauthorized immigrants from all backgrounds. Some states, cities, and counties refuse to participate, believing involvement with ICE or Secure Communities corrodes their relationship with immigrant communities.

One of the key situations for a law enforcement agency involves decision-making whereby the local public safety agencies and departments become involved in enforcing and working with the Immigration and Customs Enforcement (ICE) section, now a part of the Department of Homeland Security. The ramifications for immigrant community relationships and network building are significant. The decision-making and strategic responses to the enforcement of ICE efforts are not clear cut, nor "givens," for any law enforcement agency. However, the general argument in support of leaving undocumented immigrants alone (unless they have committed a criminal act or are creating a disturbance) is based on the perspective that tracking down and deporting them is technically the job of the ICE and not the police. Central to the clarity of roles required by the officer in the field is the delineation by police agencies of specific policies related to determining, reporting, and turning in such immigrants to ICE. Sometimes the trust of the entire community (undocumented and documented) is at stake, as for example, with the Latino/Hispanic American community. Many police departments across the country have clearly made it known to immigrant community members the circumstances under which the decisions are made not to contact and/or to turn in unauthorized immigrants to ICE. In San Antonio, Texas, community activists protested against the Balcones Heights Police Department in early 2009, alleging that police officers were guilty of racial profiling people from Hispanic/Latino background, which included entering homes and inquiring as to whether individuals were authorized immigrants or not. These protests resulted in a decision on the part of the police department to cease its collaboration with the U.S. Immigration and Customs Enforcement in the identification of unauthorized immigrants. Although city management representatives denied the allegations, it was clear that they wanted to make a statement against and take action to prevent differential treatment going forward (Zarazua, 2009).

Recommendations for Local Law Enforcement Agencies Working with ICE

All immigrants must be able to trust that they will be treated fairly and protected as part of their involvement and association with local law enforcement and public safety. This is of particular importance when there might be some perceptions, assumptions, and/or stereotypes among community residents as to who might be reported to and questioned by ICE (with the possibility of deportation and detention because of real or suspected immigration status). The following recommendations are made for local law enforcement agencies working with all immigrant communities, concerning legal and undocumented immigration status:

1. *Develop agency and departmental policies with regard to reporting and working with ICE:* Law enforcement agencies must have clear policies and procedures to address the circumstances in reporting to ICE. The policy must include (1) the circumstances under which a person will be reported to ICE and (2) that no person will be reported or referred to ICE where no laws have been violated.

2. *Maintain contact with the Multicultural Leaders:* Law enforcement officers need to work closely with community leaders to establish a cooperative plan to inform them of the agency's policies and their implementation. Often, announcements made by multicultural community leaders to inform their respective communities of any fears associated with reporting crimes and/or assistance to the police department have been very helpful. Community leaders could, for example, work with law enforcement agencies' community relations officers to develop a communication plan for the effective dissemination of information about their policies in working with ICE.

3. *Utilize a communication plan:* It is essential to have a well-developed and pilot-tested communication plan to ensure that proper messages are provided to the community when it involves a person who may or may not be reported or referred to ICE. This is particularly important when language translations and interpreting are necessary. A carefully pretested "core message" regarding the department's procedures will usually work better than on-the-spot messages subject to the momentary interpretation of those who first hear such information.

4. *Clearly define the implications for any contact with the law enforcement agency and possible reporting to ICE:* When it comes to the possibility that a contact with the local police department may result in a person being questioned by ICE and/or being involved in deportation procedures, members from multicultural communities tend to be quite cautious. The fear that they might be stereotyped as "illegal" (or having experienced prejudice by others in this regard) would naturally make any contact with law enforcement agencies and officers tenuous. It is essential to provide clearly defined procedures and information as to how any contact would normally be reported or not be reported to ICE. In addition, if there are possible consequences of such reporting, these elements should be clearly stated to ensure an ongoing relationship of trust with members of the multicultural community involved.

5. *Train all sworn and nonsworn personnel with respect to the agency or departmental policy for working with ICE:* Law enforcement agencies need to provide training and education to enable officers to effectively utilize legal enforcement tools so that they can perform their work professionally and effectively within today's multicultural communities. Clearly, most law enforcement officers know not to act based on the prejudices and stereotypes that they might hold. However, the nature of prejudice is such that some people are not aware of their prejudices or biases. Therefore, they make inferences and take actions toward certain groups based upon these biased perceptions, such as who might or might not be an unauthorized migrant and/or an undocumented immigrant. Establishing training that provides accurate information concerning groups for which officers might have prejudices and stereotypes is one of the approaches police departments should use to ensure implementation of the department's policy in working with ICE.

6. *Utilize law enforcement personnel and translators/interpreters from the same or similar communities:* To the extent possible, the use of law enforcement personnel from the same or similar ethnic communities can potentially add great value to sustaining relationships and trust within multicultural communities.

7. *Ensure community outreach services:* Every police and community interaction requires a strong, ongoing link to community groups and advocacy organizations. A link is established when community task forces are assembled to address issues, especially issues involving possible police interactions with undocumented immigrants and/or unauthorized migrants. These steps demonstrate respect for the multicultural community and create shared responsibility for whatever action is taken. The police hold primary responsibility for community outreach on every level, but the community is also responsible for becoming involved in activities that form positive relationships with the police. Policing within the community can function only in an environment of mutual engagement and respect.

8. *Provide real-time linkage and referral to multicultural community-based advocacy services:* Police departments may want to provide real-time linkage and referral to the resources and community-based advocacy services available to facilitate knowledge dissemination regarding any police interactions that might involve people with undocumented immigration issues. In this way, multicultural citizens would have a third-party opinion and support for their actions. Law enforcement's referral of multicultural citizens to these services would facilitate and support the trust building and relationships necessary to work effectively in the American community.

ICE cooperation by local law enforcement agencies is of particular concern for all multicultural communities where there has been a history of legal as well as undocumented immigration.

Indeed, some multicultural community members will be prosecuted and deported. However, where no wrong has been committed, then law enforcement must keep a check on potential stereotyping and the prejudicial act of singling out individuals based on those stereotypes.

Emergency Preparedness and Response

Regional and local law enforcement and public safety agencies must prepare to minimize the damage and to recover from any future terrorist attacks that may occur despite our best efforts at prevention. Past experience has shown that preparedness efforts are important in providing an effective response to major terrorist incidents and natural disasters. As previously mentioned, DHS developed the National Incident Management Systems (NIMS), which is a comprehensive national system to bring together and command all necessary response assets quickly and effectively. DHS has been building on the strong foundation already laid by the FEMA, and continues to improve upon leading our national efforts to employ a system that is responsive to all disasters—manmade and natural.

Following some of the past concerns raised by multicultural groups, FEMA has implemented its Diversity Outreach Program. For example, as part of the Diversity Outreach Program, the State of Florida and FEMA have proactively worked with affected families and individuals to provide assistance for damages caused by the four major hurricanes that devastated the state in prior hurricane seasons (FEMA, 2004). An extraction from a news release (2009) shows the Diversity Outreach Program as follows:

> One aspect of this comprehensive effort is the established relationship with Native American tribal associations in the declared counties. FEMA and state officials met with 21 tribes across the declared counties, from the Lummi and Nooksack in Whatcom County in the northern part of the state, to the Cowlitz in Cowlitz County in the south, to the Jamestown S'kallam, Lower Elwha Klallam, Makah and Quileute in Clallam County in the west. There are also several teams of multi-lingual representatives prepared to meet with members of these particular communities. These representatives have the ability to speak 8 languages: Vietnamese, Laotian, Cambodian, Thai, Hmong, Spanish, Korean, and Chinese. Many flyers have been printed up in not only these languages but also in Croatian, Ukrainian, Arabic, Japanese, Russian and Tagalog. Multilingual members have also been invited to speak at various forums, from Spanish speaking radio stations to Buddhist congregations. (FEMA, 2009)

Following Hurricane Katrina in 2005, FEMA made some major changes in its philosophy of service. In congressional testimony to the U.S. House Transportation and Infrastructure Committee, Subcommittee on Economic Development, on March 30, 2011, FEMA Administrator Craig Fugate said "Government can and will continue to serve disaster survivors. However, we fully recognize that a government-centric approach to disaster management will not be enough to meet the challenges posed by a catastrophic incident. That is why we must fully engage our societal capacity." To illustrate his point, Administrator Fugate implemented *A Whole Community Approach to Emergency Management: Principles, Themes, and Pathways for Action* and brought together diverse members from across the country to comprise a core working group. The group reviewed and validated the principles and themes; and included their local experiences in the document (FEMA, 2011). In the fall of 2012, FEMA applied its *Whole Community Approach* in its response to Hurricane Sandy, which had struck several Northeastern states. FEMA received positive reviews from public officials and disaster experts.

Training Law Enforcement Agencies in Multicultural Community Homeland Security Issues

Law enforcement professionals have recognized that prejudices left unchecked, and actions based on them, can result in not only humiliation and citizen complaints, but also missed opportunities for building long-term police community relationships important for homeland security. Social scientists have noted that stereotypes and prejudices become more pronounced when fear, danger, and personal threat enter the picture, as may happen in possible terrorist incidents. Law enforcement officers would benefit in completing all training sponsored by DHS and FEMA on Homeland Security issues. Moreover, the U.S. Department of Justice Office of Community Oriented Policing (COPS) offers ongoing training and resources to state, local, and tribal law enforcement agencies. Some of the training modules available are (COPS, 2013):

1. Law Enforcement Intelligence: A Guide for State, Local and Tribal Law Enforcement Agencies
2. Enhancing the Law Enforcement Intelligence Capacity: Recommendations from the IACP's Strategic Planning Session
3. National Summit on Intelligence: Gathering, Sharing, Analysis, and Use after 9/11
4. Policing Terrorism: An Executive's Guide
5. Protecting Your Community from Terrorism (Five Volumes: Volume 1—Local-Federal Partnerships; Volume 2—Working with Diverse Communities; Volume 3—Preparing for and Responding to Bioterrorism; Volume 4—The Production and Sharing of Intelligence; and Volume 5—Partnerships to Promote Home Security.

Educating Multicultural Communities on Homeland Security

Most cities and states currently host Web sites and online information on homeland security for their communities. Similarly, DHS provides a Web site and online information and education regarding homeland security–specific actions for the prevention of terrorism and how to report suspicious activity. Workshops on homeland security and the Citizen Corps program would benefit many multicultural communities with recent immigrants and refugees (including those from South and Central America, Asia, Eastern Europe, and the Middle East). The role of law enforcement officers in providing such information offers another viable avenue for developing positive relationships with multicultural communities and for community-policing efforts. Clearly, all communities are interested in acquiring specific information regarding activities of homeland security.

Law enforcement agencies may also want to include in their Citizen's Police Academies' curriculum information regarding homeland security and ways that the multicultural communities could participate and provide assistance to the public safety departments. In addition, law enforcement agencies should encourage all sworn and nonsworn personnel, including reserves, cadets, and volunteers to provide such information in a bilingual mode to ensure proper information to communities with large populations of immigrants and refugees. Community-based presentations at familiar neighborhood centers, associations, churches, mosques, and temples may facilitate greater multicultural population attendance and participation. Likewise, collaborative programs of law enforcement agencies and community-based organizations have resulted in positive dissemination of information and an ongoing building of trust with multicultural communities (e.g., see IRCO, Police and Emergency Services in Chapter 1 and Spanish Police Academy in Chapter 7).

Worldwide Caution

The U.S. Department of State has issued a "Worldwide Caution" on the continuing threat of terrorist actions and violence against U.S. citizens and interests throughout the world. The following information is provided (U.S. Department of State, 2013):

1. U.S. citizens are reminded to maintain a high level of vigilance and to take appropriate steps to increase their security awareness.
2. Current information suggests that al-Qaida, its affiliated organizations, and other terrorist organizations continue to plan terrorist attacks against U.S. interests in multiple regions, including Europe, Asia, Africa, and the Middle East.

3. These attacks may employ a wide variety of tactics including suicide operations, assassination, kidnapping, hijackings, and bombings.

4. Extremists may elect to use conventional or nonconventional weapons, and target both official and private interests. Examples of such targets include high-profile sporting events, residential areas, business offices, hotels, clubs, restaurants, and places of worship, schools, public areas, and other tourist destinations both in the United States and abroad where U.S. citizens gather in large numbers, including during holidays.

5. U.S. citizens are reminded of the potential for terrorists to attack public transportation systems and other tourist infrastructure. Extremists have targeted and attempted attacks on subway and rail systems, aviation, and maritime services. In the past, these types of attacks have occurred in cities such as Moscow, London, Madrid, Glasgow, and New York City.

6. The Department of State encourages U.S. citizens living overseas or planning to travel abroad to enroll in the Smart Traveler Enrollment Program (STEP).

7. As the Department of State continues to develop information on potential security threats to U.S. citizens overseas, it shares credible threat information through its Consular Information Program documents, including Travel Warnings, Travel Alerts, Country Specific Information, and Emergency Messages, all of which are available on the Bureau of Consular Affairs Web site.

KEY ISSUES IN LAW ENFORCEMENT

1. *Reluctance to Report Crimes and Participate in Homeland Security Efforts:* Multicultural groups that have been stereotyped as possible terrorists (e.g., individuals from Arab and other Middle Eastern backgrounds as well as people of South Asian, Central Asian, and Eastern European ancestry) may be reluctant to report crimes related to these stereotypes and may not seek police assistance and help for violations of their civil rights. Moreover, many may avoid contact with law enforcement agencies entirely with respect to homeland security efforts. Many of the multicultural groups may come from countries with extensive terrorism problems and may remember how police and the military in their home countries have brutalized and violated them and others (in quelling terrorism). Sensitivity to the experiences of these multicultural groups and knowledge of their history of being victimized by terrorists will be of positive value in gaining participation and cooperation in homeland security efforts. Another key challenge to effective cooperation with multicultural communities on homeland security issues is to help allay the fears and concerns expressed by community members with regard to their multiple interactions with law enforcement officers. Inquiries relating to homeland security, for example, may coexist with the investigation into other crimes and code enforcements such as immigration, health, sanitation, housing, and welfare.

2. *Victimization:* Law enforcement agencies protect the safety and security of citizens in multicultural communities where harassment and discrimination resulting from being stereotyped as a terrorist may lead to victimization. Documentation of such crimes against Asian/Pacific Americans and Arab and Middle Eastern Americans are provided in Chapters 5 and 8, respectively, and in Chapter 13 in this text. Some victims are harassed and attacked because of their attire or their appearance. Victimization also includes unfair accusations of being a terrorist. Those accused, or so identified, must have the trust that the police and other public safety personnel are not against them. Furthermore, they must believe that their well-being and safety are just as important as those of others who are not subject to these perceptions, assumptions, or stereotypes. Moreover, residents who are discriminated against or stereotyped as terrorists must be able to trust that prosecutors, judges, parole, and probation will utilize their full armamentarium to deter and jail terrorists, as well as

those who unjustly terrorize, discriminate, and/or harass other citizens who are unfairly stereotyped as terrorists.

3. *Differential Treatment:* In this chapter, as well as in the culture-specific chapters, we have provided examples of how members of multicultural communities have been treated unfairly because of law enforcement officers' perceptions that they are threats to homeland security or possible terrorists. Especially if a target is a possible terrorist, expressions of bias and prejudice by law enforcement agencies may go unchallenged because of the tremendous fear of the potential terrorist threat, as well as the need to rally around the issues of homeland security. Often such bias and prejudice are expressed via inappropriate language and disrespectful terms such as, "rags," "suicidal rag-heads," "A-rabs," "Arab-bombers," and "Muslim fanatics." Under such circumstances, both law enforcement executive leadership and officers' professionalism will determine whether such bias and prejudices go unchecked or whether the treatment of a possible terrorist suspect will be fair and justifiable. Clearly, should the suspect not be a terrorist; then an act of injustice had occurred because of differential treatment. Moreover, the multicultural community of which the suspect is a member will begin to question their trust and reliance on the police agency that shows such bias and prejudice. Should the suspect indeed have been correctly identified as a possible terrorist, then any stereotypic and differential treatment may compromise the prosecution of the case as well.

4. *False Tips from Informants:* As with any information-gathering and intelligence operations, there will always be the need to determine the validity, reliability, and trustworthiness of information received. Law enforcement agencies have always depended on informants as sources of critical information as part of any investigative process. In a terrorism incident, some of these informants would be very much connected with the criminal and often the most notorious elements within the community. Likewise, some of these informants may be keenly aware of what is "on the street" but may have ulterior or personal motives for providing information. Both standard interviewing and incident interview skills and tools need to be used to sort out false information and to confirm the credibility of sources important to the facts of a terrorist incident.

5. *Training to Heighten Awareness:* Until 9/11, issues of terrorism and weapons of mass destruction were primarily the domain of the federal law enforcement agencies, with minor involvement of local law enforcement personnel. The awareness of terrorism cues, situations, and warnings of possible acts were not part of the everyday experience of local law enforcement personnel and their agencies. With the establishment of DHS, terrorist-related awareness training has been used as an approach to heighten the awareness and skill levels of local law enforcement officers.

6. *Extension of Community Policing Approaches:* Community policing has been proven to be a valuable approach to working with multicultural community groups and to learning about their needs, concerns, and problems (Oliver, 2008). Chapter 14 discusses some of the key concepts, principals, and practices for community policing within multicultural communities. In this chapter, we highlight the importance of using those same community-policing concepts, tools, and practices for information gathering as well as for information dissemination following a terrorism incident.

The process of and learnings from community policing could benefit those charged with the responsibility for the war on terrorism. Community policing emphasizes prevention by problem solving and partnerships involving law enforcement and community members. It can involve other government agencies such as social services and immigration centers as well as business and the media. Such an approach is a holistic one in which the community is understood to be a whole system with interdependent segments. Similarly, homeland security—as part of the criminal justice system—can apply and implement aspects of a community policing orientation in its War on Terror.

Summary

- Terrorism is defined in the Code of Federal Regulations as "the unlawful use of force and violence against persons or property to intimidate or coerce a government, the civilian population, or any segment thereof, in furtherance of political or social objectives." The FBI identifies and describes two different types of terrorism as Domestic Terrorism and International Terrorism.

- The role of the Department of Homeland Security (DHS) is one of facilitation and development of communication among local, state, and federal government public safety organizations with its core missions to: (1) Prevent terrorism and enhance security; (2) Secure and manage U.S. borders; (3) Enforce and administer U.S. immigration laws; (4) Safeguard and secure cyberspace; (5) Build a resilient nation; and (6) Mature and strengthen the DHS enterprise.

- The lessons learned from the 9/11 terrorist attacks and Hurricane Katrina highlight the need to improve emergency management, incident response, and coordination processes among all communities and across the United States.
  The National Incident Management System (NIMS), under the control of the Department of Homeland Security, benefits agencies and multicultural communities with: (1) A comprehensive nationwide systematic approach to incident management, including the Incident Command System, Multiagency Coordination Systems, and Public Information; (2) A set of preparedness concepts and principles for all hazards; (3) Essential principles for a common operating picture and interoperability of communications and information management; (4) Standardized resource management procedures that enable coordination among different jurisdictions or organizations; and (5) Scalable, so it may be used for all incidents (from day-to-day to large scale).

- An important element of DHS, the U.S. Department of Justice, and the FBI in their counterterrorism legal efforts is the USA Patriot Act, designed to improve government coordination in law enforcement, intelligence gathering, and information sharing. Key components of the Patriot Act have raised concerns with multicultural community members, including the power of law enforcement officers to (1) question, detain, and remove potential foreign terrorists with our borders; (2) enhance surveillance methods to track and intercept communications without customary court orders; and (3) increase information sharing for key infrastructure protection by allowing for cooperation between federal, state, and local law enforcement agencies through the expansion of the Regional Information Sharing System (RISS).

- After 9/11, state and local governments increased opportunities for citizens to be more active in protecting their communities and supporting local first responders. Citizen Corps was created to help coordinate volunteer activities that result in increased community safety and preparedness to respond to any emergency situation. It provides opportunities for all people to participate in a variety of measures to make their families, homes, and multicultural communities safer from the threats of crime, terrorism, and all types of disasters.

- Five key issues concern law enforcement and other emergency services personnel when responding to terrorism and protecting homeland security within multicultural communities: (1) Reluctance to report crimes and participate in Homeland Security efforts; (2) Victimization; (3) Differential treatment; (4) False tips from informants; (5) Training to heighten awareness; and (6) Extension of community policing approaches. As law enforcement and emergency services agencies develop the knowledge, skills, and abilities to respond to these five issues, improved multicultural relationships should follow.

Discussion Questions and Issues

1. *Terrorist Targets in Your Local Community:* The chapter provided the types of elements for potential targets. Review the possible terrorist targets in your community and list the special challenges involved in protecting them. List some of the unique challenges in working with multicultural communities in this regard (either within your community or in a nearby community with multicultural neighborhoods).

2. *Multicultural Media as a Resource:* The chapter identified media resources as an effective way to communicate and disseminate information to community residents. What media resources might you use for communicating a potential terrorist incident involving Weapons of Mass Destruction (WMD) materials in your city or town? Provide some examples of multicultural media resources that might be used in your area. What approaches might you use to develop positive

and effective relationships between these media resources and your local law enforcement agency?

3. ***Utilizing Law Enforcement Personnel from Similar Backgrounds:*** Select an area in your city or town that would have the greatest diversity of languages spoken. How would you plan for and ensure adequate bilingual personnel or other language resources to assist these community residents in the case of a terrorist incident?

4. ***Working with Multicultural Groups on Homeland Security and Disaster Preparedness:*** Under the section, entitled "Building Community Networks and Resources," five partner programs under the Citizen Corp are listed. Select one of the partner programs and research its features.

Next, identify one or more multicultural groups that are part of your community and discuss how you would encourage leaders in those groups to become involved in this program.

5. ***Victimization including being unfairly accused or identified as a possible terrorist:*** What are ways to prevent and to help multicultural communities so members would not be the recipients of unjust accusation and victimization? What approach would you recommend for your local law enforcement agencies to prevent such victimization? What would you suggest that your multicultural communities do to prevent discrimination and harassment for those who are unfairly stereotyped?

References

"A Nation Challenged: The Terrorists; Hijacker Got a Speeding Ticket." (2002, January 9). *New York Times*, p. A12.

Bankson, R. (2003). "Terrorism: National in Scope, Local in Execution." *Community Links*. Washington, D.C.: Community Policing Consortium.

Community Oriented Policing Services (COPS). (2013). "Homeland Security through Community Policing." Retrieved August 19, 2013, from www.cops.usdoj.gov/Default.asp?Item=2487

Corley, Sarah. H., Brent. L. Smith, and Kelly. R. Damphousse. (2005). "The Changing Face of American Terrorism."

Dershowitz, Alan. M. (2002). *Why Terrorism Works: Understanding the Threat, Responding to the Challenge*. New Haven, Conn.: Yale University Press.

Federal Bureau of Investigation. (2010, October). *Terrorism 2002–2005*. Washington, D.C.: U.S. Department of Justice.

Federal Bureau of Investigation. (2013). "Weapons of Mass Destruction: Frequently Asked Questions." Retrieved August 4, 2013, from www.fbi.gov/about-us/investigate/terrorism/wmd/wmd_faqs

Federal Emergency Management Agency (FEMA). (2004, December 7), "FEMA's Diversity Outreach Program a Success." News Release Number: 1539-303.

Federal Emergency Management Agency (FEMA). (2009, March 9), "Reaching Washington's Many and Diverse Communities." News Release Number: 1817-047.

Federal Emergency Management Agency (FEMA). (2011, December). "A Whole Community Approach to Emergency Management: Principles, Themes, and Pathways for Action." FDOC 104-008-1. Retrieved August 30, 2013, from www.fema.gov/media-library-data/20130726-1813-25045-0649/whole_community_dec2011__2_.pdf

Ford, Peter. (2002, March 27). "Legal War on Terror Lacks Weapons." *Christian Science Monitor*, Section 4, p.1.

Heymann, Philip. B. (2001). *Terrorism and America: A Commonsense Strategy for a Democratic Society*. Cambridge, MA: MIT Press.

Hoffman, Bruce. (2006). *Inside Terrorism*. New York, NY: Columbia University Press.

Howard, Russell D., Reid L. Sawyer, and Natasha E. Bajema. (2008. *Terrorism and Counterterrorism: Understanding the New Security Environment*, 3rd ed. New York, NY: McGraw-Hill.

International Association of Chiefs of Police (IACP). (2001). *Leading from the Front: Project Response: Terrorism*. Alexandria, VA: Author.

Kleinberg, Eliot and D. Davies. (2001, October 19). "Delray Police Stopped Speeding Terror Suspect." *Palm Beach Post* (Florida), p. A1.

Marroni, Steve. (2013, June 19). "Police, military work together in mock terrorist-plot exercise at the Farm Show Complex." *The Patriot News* (Pennsylvania). Retrieved August 15, 2013, from www.pennlive.com/midstate/index.ssf/2013/06/police_military_work_together.html

Nance, Malcom. W. (2008). *The Terrorist Recognition Handbook*, 2nd ed. Boca Raton, FL: CRC Press.

Napolitano, Janet. (2010, September 10). "Remarks as Prepared by Secretary Napolitano to New York City First Responders." Retrieved August 7, 2013, from www.dhs.gov/news/2010/09/10/remarks-prepared-secretary-napolitano-new-york-city-first-responders

National Counterterrorism Center (NCTC). (2012). "Foreign Terrorist Organizations." Retrieved August 6, 2013, from www.nctc.gov/site/other/fto.html

National Counterterrorism Center (NCTC). (2013). "About the National Counterterrorism Center." Retrieved August 16, 2013, from www.nctc.gov/about_us/about_nctc.html

National Security Agency (NSA). (2011). "Mission." Retrieved August 16, 2013, from www.nsa.gov/about/mission/index.shtml.

Obama, Barack. (2011, May 2). "Remarks by the President on Osama Bin Laden." Retrieved August 18, 2013, from www.whitehouse.gov/the-press-office/2011/05/02/remarks-president-osama-bin-laden

Officer Down Memorial Page (2013). "Fallen Officers from 9/11 Terrorist Attacks." Retrieved August 11, 2013, from www.odmp.org/search/incident/september-11-terrorist-attack

Oliver, Willard M. (2008). *Community-Oriented Policing: A Systemic Approach to Policing*, 4th ed. Upper Saddle River, NJ: Prentice-Hall.

Parkinson, John R. (2013, June 18). "NSA: Over 50 Terror Plots Foiled by Data Dragnets." Retrieved August 18, 2013, from abcnews.go.com/Politics/nsa-director-50-potential-terrorist-attacks-thwarted-controversial/story?id=19428148

Roig-Franzia, Manuel and P. Davis. (2002, January 9). "For Want of a Crystal Ball; Police Stopped Two Hijackers in Days before Attacks." *Washington Post*, p. A13.

U.S. Department of State. (2013, February 13). "Worldwide Caution." Retrieved August 19, 2013, from www.travel.state.gov/travel/cis_pa_tw/pa/pa_4787.html

The 9/11 Commission Report. (2004). Retrieved April 15, 2014, from http://www.9-11commission.gov/report/index.htm

"Trooper Describes Arrest 90 Minutes after Bombing." (1997, April 28). *Deseret News* (Salt Lake City), p. A2.

U.S. Department of Homeland Security. (2008, December). "National Incident Management System." Retrieved August 30, 2013, from www.fema.gov/pdf/emergency/nims/NIMS_core.pdf

U.S. Department of Homeland Security. (2009). "National Infrastructure Protection Plan: Partnering to enhance protection and resiliency, 2009." Retrieved August 16, 2013, from www.dhs.gov/xlibrary/assets/NIPP_Plan.pdf

U.S. Department of Homeland Security. (2013a). "Mission." Retrieved August 3, 2013, from www.dhs.gov/mission

U.S. Department of Homeland Security. (2013b). "The Office for State and Local Law Enforcement." Retrieved August 16, 2013, from www.dhs.gov/office-state-and-local-law-enforcement

U.S. Department of Homeland Security. (2013c). "National Network of Fusion Centers Fact Sheet." Retrieved August 15, 2013, from www.dhs.gov/national-network-fusion-centers-fact-sheet

U.S. Department of Homeland Security. (2013d). "Citizen Corps." Retrieved August 15, 2013, from www.dhs.gov/citizen-corps.

U.S. Department of Justice. (2001). "al Qaeda Training Manual." Retrieved August 3, 2013, from www.au.af.mil/au/awc/awcgate/terrorism/alqaida_manual/

U.S. Nuclear Regulatory Commission (NRC). (2013a). "Background on Dirty Bombs." Retrieved April 15, 2014, from www.nrc.gov/reading-rm/doc-collections/fact-sheets/fs-dirty-bombs.html

U.S. Nuclear Regulatory Commission (NRC). (2013b). "Minimize Your Exposure." Retrieved August 10, 2013, from www.nrc.gov/about-nrc/radiation/protects-you/protection-principles.html

Weiss, M., E. Calabrese, and M. Fermino. (2009, May 21). "Chilling Terror Plot Thwarted–4 Set to 'Bomb' Synagogues; Eyed Plane 'Shootdown' Upstate." *New York Post*, p. 7.

Zarazua, Jeorge (2009, March 5). "Suburb's Cops Won't Call Feds for ID Check," *San Antonio Express-News*, p. B1.

Response Strategies for Crimes Motivated By Hate/Bias and Racial Profiling

Part Four provides a detailed explanation of strategies for preventing, controlling, reporting, monitoring, and investigating crimes that are based on hate or bias caused by the victim's race, ethnicity, national origin, religion, gender, gender identity, or sexual orientation. Criminal cases of these types have come to be known as bias or hate crimes; noncriminal cases are referred to as incidents. Some agencies refer to these acts as civil rights violations. The next two chapters contain policies, practices, and procedures for responding to these types of crimes or incidents. We recognize that other groups, such as women, the elderly, the homeless, and the disabled, are sometimes victimized. However, in this book we focus primarily on hate crimes and incidents wherein the motivation was related to the victim's race, ethnicity, national origin, religion, or sexual orientation. The reasons for collecting data on crimes and incidents motivated by hate/bias committed by individuals or organized groups are included in Chapter 12. The end of that chapter provides examples to help students, members of the criminal justice system, and the community to develop sensitive and workable programs for handling these crimes and incidents. The recommended policies, training, practices, and procedures outlined in this text are currently in operation in most law enforcement agencies across the nation and are based on studies and recommendations by the U.S. Department of Justice's Community Relations Service. The Commission on Peace Officer Standards and Training, found in all states of the nation, is another major source of materials. The final chapter in Part Four provides information about racial profiling for members of the criminal justice system. The type of policing reviewed in this unit is a civilizing process that will contribute to multicultural coexistence and cooperation. All law enforcement professionals should have a good working knowledge of the guidelines that follow.

11 Hate/Bias Crimes

Victims, Laws, Investigations, and Prosecutions

LEARNING OBJECTIVES

After reading this chapter, you should be able to:

- Describe the scope of the hate crime problem, including historical perspectives.
- Define as well as differentiate between hate crimes and hate incidents.
- Explain hate crime and incident source theories.
- Discuss response strategies to hate crimes and appropriate victim assistance techniques.
- Identify hate crimes related to anti-Semitism, sexual orientation, race, ethnicity, and national origin.
- Explain hate crime laws, investigative procedures, and offender prosecution.

OUTLINE

- Introduction
- The Hate/Bias Crime Problem
- Definition of Hate Crime and Hate Incident
- Hate Crime Source Theories
- Jews and Anti-Semitism
- Lesbian, Gay, Bisexual, and Transgender Victimization
- Hate Crime Laws Specific to LGBT
- Hate/Bias Crime and Incident Investigations
- Hate/Bias Crime Prosecution
- Hate/Bias Crime and Incident Victimology
- Summary
- Discussion Questions and Issues

INTRODUCTION

A relatively new term, "hate crime" was introduced in the mid-1980s to identify crimes motivated by hate or bias (Jacobs & Potter, 1998). Crimes motivated by hate/bias have occurred in the United States for generations. Most of the immigrant groups that have come to America, including the Irish, Italians, Chinese, Polish, and Puerto Ricans, to name a few, have been victimized. Even though they are indigenous peoples, Native Americans also have not been immune to hate crimes. The descendents of African Americans continue to be victims of bias, discrimination, and crimes motivated by hate. This chapter primarily addresses crimes motivated by hate in which the victims are Jewish or gay, lesbian, bisexual, or transgender individuals. Please find additional information on hate crimes against other groups in Chapters 5 through 9.

THE HATE/BIAS CRIME PROBLEM

The criminal justice system as well as communities whose members are victims must address the problem of hate/bias crimes and incidents. Victims of hate/bias crimes are particularly sensitive and unsettled because they feel powerless to alter the situation, since they cannot change their color, racial, ethnic, religious background, gender, gender identity, or sexual orientation. Furthermore, the individual involved is not the sole victim, because often fear of similar crimes can affect an entire group of citizens. A physical attack on a person because of race, religion, ethnic background, sexual orientation, gender, or gender identity is a particularly insidious form of violent behavior. Verbal assaults on persons because of others' perceptions of their "differences" are equally distressing to both the victim and to society. The ripple effect of bias crime is shown in Exhibit 11.1.

And, unfortunately, these kinds of incidents can also occur in the law enforcement workplace among coworkers. When law enforcement treats such occurrences seriously, it sends a message to community members that the local police agency will protect them. Doing the same within the law enforcement organization and correctional system sends a vitally important message to all employees. The criminal justice system, and especially local law enforcement agencies, will become the focus of criticism if attacks are not investigated, resolved, and prosecuted promptly and effectively. A hate/bias crime can send shock waves through the community at which the act was aimed. Law enforcement and corrections personnel must have some perspective on both the global and the local situation when it comes

EXHIBIT 11.1   The Ripple Effect of Bias Crime

Source: "Responding To Hate Crime: A Multidisciplinary Curriculum." National Center for Hate Crime Prevention. U.S. Department of Justice. Retrieved from www.hhd.org/sites/hhd.org/files/Responding%20to%20 hate%20crime%20-%20A%20multidisciplinary%20 curriculum.pdf

to hatred and bias within the population they serve or within which they work. Criminal justice professionals must be trained to counteract hate crimes and violence as well as to address their impact. The importance of local law enforcement officials' monitoring of world events that may provoke local reactions is discussed in Chapter 12. This is a major undertaking, as there are ongoing conflicts in many countries that have had and still have repercussions in the United States.

Many studies over the years have determined that a large number of perpetrators of hate crimes are youthful thrill-seekers motivated by the desire for excitement, and that as many as 60 percent of offenders commit crimes for the thrill associated with victimization ("What Motivates Hate Offenders," 2008). The second most common group responsible for hate crimes is reactive offenders who feel that they are responding to an attack by their victims. The least common perpetrators, according to reports, are hard-core fanatics who are driven by racial or religious ideology or ethnic bigotry ("What Motivates Hate Offenders," 2008). These individuals are often members of or potential recruits for extremist organizations (discussed in Chapter 12). Some perpetrators of hate crimes live on the U.S. borders and are extremely fearful of Mexicans, South and Central Americans, Cubans, and Haitians who enter the United States both legally and illegally. They feel that if they cease their militant rhetoric and violence toward these immigrants, the country will be inundated with immigrants. Mexicans are the largest immigrant group in the country, and their visibility makes them a magnet for anti-immigrant sentiment, including discrimination and hate crimes.

Community awareness of hate violence grew rapidly in the United States during the late 1980s and the 1990s. Many states commissioned special task forces to recommend ways to control such violence, and new legislation was passed. Despite the abundance of rhetoric deploring acts of bigotry and hate violence, however, few communities have utilized an integrated approach to the problem. Typically, efforts to prevent and respond to such crimes by local agencies have not been coordinated. Indeed, there are many effective programs that deal with a particular aspect of bigotry or hate in a specific setting; however, few models weave efforts to prevent hate violence into the fabric of the community.

Hate crimes are the most extreme and dangerous manifestation of racism. Criminal justice professionals, including neighborhood police officers (a key source of intelligence information) must be aware of the scope of the hate/bias crime problem from both historical and contemporary perspectives. The same is true of the correctional officers who work directly with the inmate population. During the 2008 presidential campaign, and continuing into the presidency of Barack Obama, the nation witnessed what has been described as a backlash against the election of the first black president in U.S. history. Across America, law enforcement agencies documented a range of alleged hate crimes and incidents, ranging from threats, verbal insults, and vandalism to physical attacks. Most of these crimes were committed not by gangs or hate groups, but by individuals motivated by their biases. "There have been 'hundreds' of incidents since the election, many more than usual, said Mark Potok, director of the Intelligence Project at the Southern Poverty Law Center, which monitors hate crimes" (Washington, 2008). Potok adds that an increase in the number of antigovernment "patriot" groups, which includes paramilitary hate organizations, "reached an all-time high of 1,360 in 2012," in part because of the reelection of President Obama and the focus on gun control legislation and immigration reform (Potok, 2013). In Virginia, the Ku Klux Klan used Obama's reelection as a recruiting tool to find new members (Strasser, 2013).

The Scope of Hate Crimes Nationally

The federal Hate Crime Statistics Act of 1990 encourages states to collect and report hate crime data to the Federal Bureau of Investigation (FBI). The FBI, in partnership with state and local law enforcement agencies, began collecting data in 1992 on hate/bias incidents, offenses (see later in this chapter definitions of hate/bias incidents and offenses), victims, offenders, and motivations. Congress amended the Act in 1994 to include bias against persons with disabilities and again in 2010 to include hate crimes based on gender and gender identity prejudices as well as hate crimes committed by/directed against juveniles ("Hate Crime Data Collection Guidelines and Training Manual," 2012). The change adding gender and gender identity, which took effect in 2013, was added to hate crime data collection as a result of the Matthew Shepard and James Byrd, Jr., Hate Crimes Prevention Act.

The FBI publishes an annual report as part of the Uniform Crime Reporting (UCR) Program, which collects data for crimes motivated by biases against race, religion, sexual orientation, ethnicity/national origin, gender and gender identity, and disability. Each bias type is then broken down into more specific categories. For example, when a law enforcement agency determines that a hate crime was committed because of bias against an individual's race, the agency may then classify the bias as antiwhite, antiblack, anti-American Indian/Alaskan Native, anti-Asian/Pacific Islander, or antimultiple races, which describes a group of victims in which more than one race is represented. Most hate/bias crime statistics are, by definition, "single-bias incidents" (that is, those that involve one type of bias). Multiple-bias incidents are those that involve two or more offense types motivated by two or more biases. In August 2013, the Department of Justice announced that a number of additional groups would be included in the national program that tracks hate crime. These groups include individuals from South Asia who are living in the United States, such as Arabs, Sikhs, and Hindus, as well as Buddhists, who are from all parts of Asia. (As of the writing of the sixth edition of this text, hate crimes against Asian/Pacific Americans did not include these new categories, thus there are no data available.)

The UCR Program is a nationwide cooperative statistical effort of city, county, state, federal, tribal, university, and college law enforcement agencies. The collection of hate crime information reported in the UCR is voluntary, however, and not all agencies gather or submit data to the FBI. During 2011 (the most recent year for which data are available), 1,944 law enforcement agencies active in the UCR Program documented 6,222 hate crime incidents involving 7,254 offenses of which 6,216 were single-bias incidents that involved 7,240 offenses, 7,697 victims, and 5,224 offenders. Of the 6,216 single-bias incidents, 46.9 percent were racially motivated; 20.8 percent resulted from sexual-orientation bias; 19.8 percent were motivated by religious bias; 11.6 percent stemmed from ethnicity/national origin bias; and 0.9 percent were prompted by disability bias (see Exhibit 11.2). Of the 3,465 racial bias offenses, 72 percent were motivated by antiblack bias; 16.7 percent stemmed from antiwhite bias; 4.8 percent resulted from anti-Asian/Pacific Islander bias; 4.7 percent were a result of bias against groups of individuals comprising more than one race; and 1.9 percent were motivated by anti-American Indian/Alaskan Native bias (see Exhibit 11.3). Of the 1,318 religious bias offenses, 62.2 percent were anti-Jewish; 13.3 percent were anti-Islamic; 5.2 percent were anti-Catholic; 4.8 percent were antimultiple religions, 3.7 percent were anti-Protestant; 0.3 percent were anti-atheist/agnosticist/etc.; and 10.5 percent were anti-another religion (see Exhibit 11.4). Of the 1,508 sexual-orientation bias offenses, 57.8 percent were classified as antimale homosexual bias; 28.4 percent were reported as antihomosexual bias; 11.1 percent were prompted by antifemale homosexual bias; 1.5 percent were classified as antibisexual bias; and 1.1 percent were the result of antiheterosexual bias (see Exhibit 11.5). Of the 891 ethnicity/national origin bias offenses, 56.8 percent were anti-Hispanic and 43.2 percent were anti-other ethnicity/national origin bias ("Hate Crime Statistics, 2011," 2013).

THE FBI UCR PROGRAM VERSUS THE NATIONAL CRIME VICTIMIZATION SURVEY (NCVS) The FBI's annual hate crime report is an essential tool for understanding our nation's hate crime problem; however, it alone does not provide a clear picture of the extent and nature of this type of crime. This is because of the voluntary nature of the reporting system on the part of law enforcement agencies and the failure of many victims to report crimes to police. Thus, although the report gives some

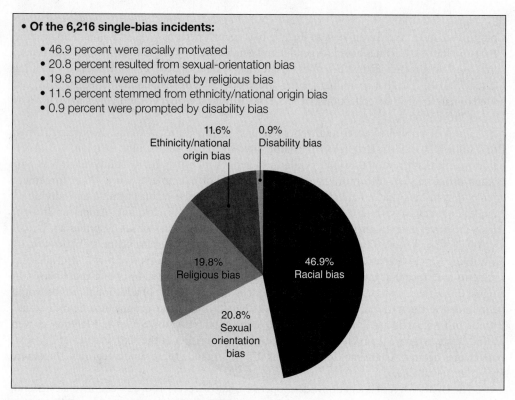

• Of the 6,216 single-bias incidents:

- 46.9 percent were racially motivated
- 20.8 percent resulted from sexual-orientation bias
- 19.8 percent were motivated by religious bias
- 11.6 percent stemmed from ethnicity/national origin bias
- 0.9 percent were prompted by disability bias

EXHIBIT 11.2   Hate Crime: Bias Motivated Percentage 2011

Source: "Hate Crime Statistics, 2011." (2013, December). Federal Bureau of Investigation. Retrieved from www.fbi.gov/about-us/cjis/ucr/hate-crime/2011

insight into the trends in hate crimes, it does not entirely reflect the total problem. The data in the FBI annual report also provide little information about the characteristics of crimes, victims, offenders, or arrests. Recognizing these deficiencies, the FBI created the National Incident-Based Reporting System (NIBRS). NIBRS staff interview individuals about their experience with crime, both reported and not reported, which results in more details on additional categories of crime, including concurrent offenses, weapons, injury, location, property loss, and characteristics of the victims, offenders, and arrestees, including their gender, race, and age. The information is analyzed annually and becomes the NCVS report. The information is combined with the statistics collected by the FBI as part of the UCR Program and results in a more thorough report and analysis of the data. To make the data comparable between the UCR Program and the NCVS, only those crimes in which an individual was the victim are included. A comparison of UCR and NCVS data reveals some striking similarities but also some major differences between the two.

Underreporting of Crime

Nearly two of three hate crimes go unreported to the police, according to the U.S. Department of Justice. A report by that agency indicates that "[t]he percentage of all hate crime victimizations reported to police declined from 46 percent in 2003-06 to 35 percent in 2007-11" ("Hate Crime Victimization, 2003-2011," 2013). The report indicates that despite growing awareness of hate crimes, reporting has decreased over the years because victims of violent attacks doubt the police can or will help. The study determined the following:

- From 2007 to 2011, 24 percent of hate crime victims said they did not report the crime because they believed that the police could not or would not help, compared to 14 percent between 2003 and 2006.

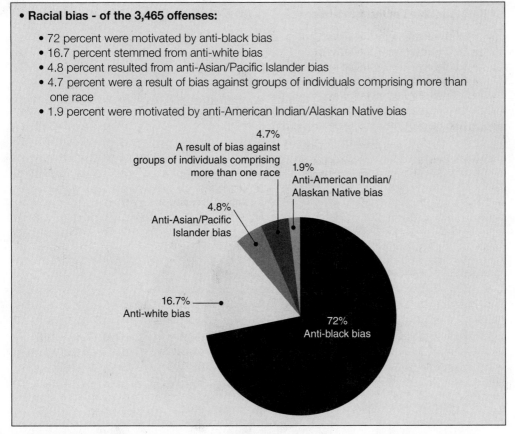

• Racial bias - of the 3,465 offenses:

- 72 percent were motivated by anti-black bias
- 16.7 percent stemmed from anti-white bias
- 4.8 percent resulted from anti-Asian/Pacific Islander bias
- 4.7 percent were a result of bias against groups of individuals comprising more than one race
- 1.9 percent were motivated by anti-American Indian/Alaskan Native bias

EXHIBIT 11.3   Hate Crime: Racial Bias Motivated Percentage 2011

Source: "Hate Crime Statistics, 2011." (2013, December). Federal Bureau of Investigation. Retrieved from www.fbi.gov/about-us/cjis/ucr/hate-crime/2011

- During that period, 15 percent of hate crime victims stated that fear of reprisal or getting the offender in trouble was the reason not to report the crime to police, compared to 9 percent from 2003 to 2006.
- From 2007 to 2011, 23 percent of hate crime victims did not report the crime because they felt it was a private or personal matter or dealt with the crime in another way, compared to 35 percent from 2003 to 2006 ("Hate Crime Victimization, 2003-2011," 2013)

Another study by a task force of the Crime Victims Center involved feedback from and interviews with victims of hate crimes. The finding was that victims do not report due to:

- Lack of knowledge about what constitutes a hate crime, how the laws are applied, and the overall criminal justice process;
- Lack of knowledge of crime victims' rights and available support services;
- Fear of retaliation by the perpetrator for reporting;
- Fear of being revictimized by the criminal justice process, especially by those immigrants who had been terrorized at the hands of military personnel and/or corrupt police in their countries of origin;
- Lack of English language proficiency or knowledge of the mechanisms available to report hate crimes;
- Fear of being identified as an undocumented immigrant and being deported;
- A belief, whether real or perceived, that law enforcement does not want to address hate crimes;

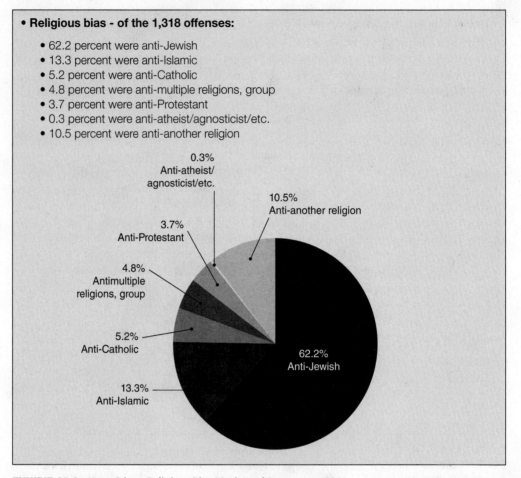

• **Religious bias - of the 1,318 offenses:**

  • 62.2 percent were anti-Jewish
  • 13.3 percent were anti-Islamic
  • 5.2 percent were anti-Catholic
  • 4.8 percent were anti-multiple religions, group
  • 3.7 percent were anti-Protestant
  • 0.3 percent were anti-atheist/agnosticist/etc.
  • 10.5 percent were anti-another religion

EXHIBIT 11.4   Hate Crime: Religious Bias Motivated Percentage 2011

Source: "Hate Crime Statistics, 2011." (2013, December). Federal Bureau of Investigation. Retrieved from www.fbi.gov/about-us/cjis/ucr/hate-crime/2011

• Shame or embarrassment for being a victim of any crime, especially a hate crime;
• Cultural or personal beliefs that one should not complain about misfortunes and handle problems on one's own;
• Fear of being exposed as gay, lesbian, bisexual or transgendered to one's family, employer, friends, or the general public and the potential ramifications of exposure;
• Fear of retaliation on the part of the elderly or persons with disabilities who have emotional and/or life-supporting dependence upon someone who has or is committing hate crimes against them;
• The inability of some persons with disabilities to articulate that they have been victims of hate crimes (Ahearn, 2011).

Growth of Online Racism

Racial insults and epithets are generally not as overt as in the days of the Civil Rights era, and now, on the Internet, bigots are able to express their intolerance and prejudice more insidiously and anonymously. The worldwide web has no scarcity of racist Web sites; furthermore, readers can freely comment on articles with race-related content. It is not difficult to find vicious remarks about a multitude of targeted groups, including immigrants, gays, blacks, and Muslims. Such comments may or may not end up removed from chat threads; their existence suggests

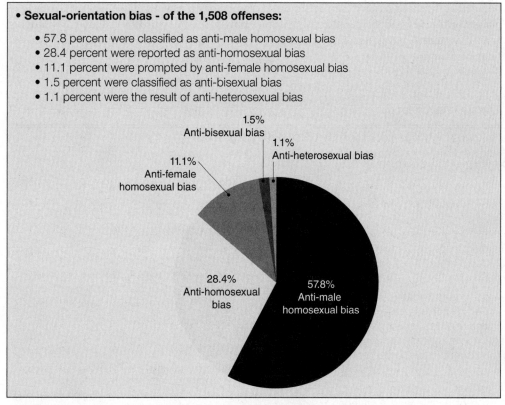

• Sexual-orientation bias - of the 1,508 offenses:

- 57.8 percent were classified as anti-male homosexual bias
- 28.4 percent were reported as anti-homosexual bias
- 11.1 percent were prompted by anti-female homosexual bias
- 1.5 percent were classified as anti-bisexual bias
- 1.1 percent were the result of anti-heterosexual bias

1.5%
Anti-bisexual bias

1.1%
Anti-heterosexual bias

11.1%
Anti-female
homosexual bias

28.4%
Anti-homosexual
bias

57.8%
Anti-male
homosexual bias

EXHIBIT 11.5 Hate Crime: Sexual-Orientation Bias Motivated Percentage 2011

Source: "Hate Crime Statistics, 2011." (2013, December). Federal Bureau of Investigation. Retrieved from www.fbi.gov/about-us/cjis/ucr/hate-crime/2011

that while racial progress has been made, the abundance of hate speech on the Internet reveals a different reality. (Online Racism, 2010). Society struggles with the fine line between freedom of speech and the censorship of such discourse on Web sites. The apparent growth of online racism remains a major race relations challenge where, intolerance expressed, can incite violence.

DEFINITION OF HATE CRIME AND HATE INCIDENT

Hate Crime

Under Title 18 U.S.C. Section 249, a hate crime is "a criminal offense committed against a person, property, or society that is motivated, in whole or in part, by the offender's bias against a race, religion, disability, sexual orientation, or ethnicity/national origin" (U.S. Department of Justice, 2010). Definitions of hate crime often incorporate not only violence against individuals or groups but also crimes against property, such as arson or vandalism, in particular those directed against government buildings, community centers, or houses of worship. As it is sometimes difficult to determine the offender's motivation, bias is to be reported only if an investigation establishes sufficient objective facts "to lead a reasonable and prudent person to conclude that the offender's actions were motivated, in whole or in part by bias" ("Hate Crime Data Collection Guidelines and Training Manual," 2012).

Hate Incident

Hate incidents involve behaviors that, though motivated by bias against a victim's race, religion, ethnicity, gender, gender identity, disability, or sexual orientation, are not criminal acts. Hostile or hateful speech, or other disrespectful or discriminatory behavior, may be motivated by bias, but is not illegal. Such incidents become crimes only when they directly incite perpetrators to commit violence against persons or property or if they place a potential victim in reasonable fear of physical injury.

Definitions for Hate Crime Data Collection

To ensure uniformity in reporting, the following have been adopted by the FBI Uniform Crime Report Program:

Bias—A preformed negative opinion or attitude toward a group of persons based on their race, religion, disability, sexual orientation, ethnicity, gender, or gender identity.

Bisexual—Of or relating to people who are physically, romantically, and/or emotionally attracted to both men and women.

Disability Bias—A preformed negative opinion or attitude toward a group of persons based on their physical or mental impairments, whether such disability is temporary or permanent, congenital or acquired by heredity, accident, injury, advanced age, or illness.

Ethnicity Bias—A preformed negative opinion or attitude toward a group of people whose members identify with each other, through a common heritage, often consisting of a common language, common culture (often including a shared religion), and/or ideology that stresses common ancestry. The concept of ethnicity differs from the closely related term *race* in that "race" refers to grouping based mostly upon biological criteria, while "ethnicity" also encompasses additional cultural factors.

Gay—Note: Generally this word is used to refer to gay men, but may also be used to describe women; the term "gay" is preferred over the term "homosexual." For FBI UCR Program purposes, however, if reporting an antigay bias, the victim should be a male.

Gender—This term is used synonymously with *sex* to denote whether a newborn is male or female at birth, for example, "it's a boy" or "it's a girl."

Gender Bias—A preformed negative opinion or attitude toward a person or group of persons based on their actual or perceived gender, for example, male or female.

Gender Identity—A person's internal sense of being male, female, or a combination of both; that internal sense of a person's gender may be different from the person's gender as assigned at birth. Note: A transgender person may express their gender identity through gender characteristics, such as clothing, hair, voice, mannerisms, or behaviors that do not conform to the gender-based expectations of society.

Gender Identity Bias—A preformed negative opinion or attitude toward a person or group of persons based on their actual or perceived gender identity, for example, bias against transgender or gender nonconforming individuals.

Gender Nonconforming—Describes a person who does not conform to the gender-based expectations of society, for example, a woman dressed in traditionally male clothing or a man wearing makeup. Note: A gender nonconforming person may or may not be a lesbian, gay, bisexual, or transgender person but may be perceived as such.

Hate Group—An organization whose primary purpose is to promote animosity, hostility, and malice toward persons of or with a race, religion, disability, sexual orientation, ethnicity, gender, or gender identity that differs from that of the members or the organization. Examples include the Ku Klux Klan and the American Nazi Party.

Heterosexual—Of or relating to people who are physically, romantically, and/or emotionally attracted to people of the opposite sex. Note: The term *straight* is a synonym.

Homosexual—Of or relating to people who are physically, romantically, and/or emotionally attracted to people of the same gender. Note: Some people consider this to be an outdated and derogatory term, but it depends on the context in which it is used. Current journalistic standards restrict the usage of this term. "Lesbian" and/or "gay" are the currently accepted terms for referring to people who are attracted to others of the same sex.

Lesbian—Of or relating to women who are physically, romantically, and/or emotionally attracted to other women. Note: Some lesbian women prefer to be described as gay women. For FBI UCR Program purposes, however, if reporting an antigay bias, the victim should be a male.

LGBT—Common initialism for "lesbian, gay, bisexual, and transgender," used here to refer to community organizations or events that serve lesbian, gay, bisexual, transgender, and allied people.

Racial Bias—A preformed negative opinion or attitude toward a group of persons who possess common physical characteristics, such as color of skin, eyes, and/or hair, facial features, and so forth, genetically transmitted by descent and heredity, which distinguish them as a distinct division of humankind, for example, Asians, blacks or African Americans, and whites.

Religious Bias—A preformed negative opinion or attitude toward a group of persons who share the same religious beliefs regarding the origin and purpose of the universe and the existence or nonexistence of a supreme being, for example, Catholics, Jews, Muslims, Protestants, and atheists.

Sexual Orientation—The term for a person's physical, romantic, and/or emotional attraction to members of the same and/or opposite sex, including lesbian, gay, bisexual, and heterosexual (straight) individuals. Note: Avoid the offensive terms "sexual preference" or "lifestyle."

Sexual-Orientation Bias—A preformed negative opinion or attitude toward a person or group of persons based on their actual or perceived sexual orientation.

Transgender—Of or relating to a person who identifies as a different gender from their gender as assigned at birth. Note: The person may also identify himself or herself as "transsexual." Note: A transgender person may outwardly express his or her gender identity all of the time, part of the time, or none of the time; a transgender person may decide to change his or her body to medically conform to his or her gender identity. Note: Avoid the following terms: "he-she," "she-male," "tranny," "it," "shim," "drag queen," "transvestite," and "cross-dresser."

Source: ("Hate Crime Data Collection Guidelines and Training Manual," 2012).

HATE CRIME SOURCE THEORIES

Introduction

Hate crime has been studied over the past three decades by criminologists, sociologists, and others, but there is no single conclusion about its causes. Although the reader should understand there are sometimes social forces, described later, that are offered as the reason for hate crime, the individual committing such a crime is still responsible for his or her action and should be punished. Among the community characteristics that have been cited as contributing to hate crime are density and overcrowding, clustering, move-in violence, inequality, and economic deprivation, each of which will be discussed more fully later in this chapter. The intent of providing the following descriptions of hate crime source theories is that by understanding them, there is the potential for government and community agencies to change the social conditions that have the potential to breed hate.

Urban Dynamics and Other Theories

IMMIGRANT CLUSTERING   It is important to understand that hate incidents and crimes often do not occur in a vacuum but are part of a larger social and economic interchange, one aspect of which is immigration. Studies have shown that newly arrived immigrants who are not trained professionals (e.g., those in the high-tech field) tend to locate or cluster where people of their own ethnic or racial background are already established. They tend to congregate in the same areas of the country or within a city to be near relatives or friends, to have assistance in finding housing and jobs and in coping with language barriers, and to find the security of a familiar religion and social institutions. This is true of unauthorized as well as authorized immigrants. According to Steven Wallace, Chair of the Department of Community Heath Sciences at the UCLA School of Public Health, for the first generation or two, ethnic communities are helpful because they provide a sense of continuity for immigrants while easing subsequent generations into American values and society. The existence of an ethnic or immigrant community is obvious evidence that a group has not assimilated. He explains that a community represents a place where immigrants are able to associate with others like themselves. An immigrant community provides a safe place to engage in those activities that deviate from dominant norms such as speaking a language other than English, honoring "foreign" symbols of pride, and exhibiting other non-Anglo behavior. It is common for the ethnic (and especially first-generation immigrant communities) to live in low-rent districts where they can afford to work (Wallace, personal communication, 2013).

These core areas are typically where low-socioeconomic-class whites, blacks, Hispanics, and established immigrants live, because housing is cheap (or government subsidized), employment or welfare services are available, and there is a measure of comfort derived from living with people of one's own race or culture. These areas are often impoverished ghettos, with substandard, older housing, and they are frequently overcrowded, with a high incidence of social conflict and crime, including drug and gang activity. As new immigrants and members of varied racial and cultural groups move into the core area, they come into conflict with existing members of that community—a phenomenon that has been going on for generations. The newcomers and the established community members compete for housing, jobs, financial resources (such as welfare or food stamps), and education. When there is a collapse of affordable health services, lack of affordable housing, and reductions in benefits (cuts in social programs by federal and state authorities), as occurred in the 1990s, 2003, and again from 2008 to 2013, conflicts escalate between racial and ethnic groups. As these circumstances intensify, incidents of discrimination, bias, and hate violence increase. Those who are more established want to move out, not just to improve their lot but also to escape the conflict.

Wallace indicates that the rewards of better education and jobs tend to come with assimilation into mainstream society. Some groups of immigrants can be seen as "temporary inhabitants" of the inner city; they work toward and achieve their goal of moving into the suburbs as they improve their economic situation. As they gain wealth and education, they acquire the same economic and educational advantages as long-time Americans (Wallace, personal communication, 2013).

Although Wallace published his initial findings in the 1980s, he does not think that "the basic theories [about social causes] have changed much over the past 30 years, though the details have" (Wallace, personal communication, 2013). Among those details are the characteristics of the more recent victims of hate crime, including Sikhs and Muslims after 9/11, and LGBT persons.

THE ECONOMY AND HATE VIOLENCE   A poor economy contributes greatly to hate violence. In many areas of the country, when major industries have downturns, go out of business, or relocate, the likelihood of economic distress among low-skilled and unskilled workers increases. Between 2007 and 2013, several large American cities even filed for bankruptcy, including Detroit, which "became the biggest U.S. city to file for bankruptcy [July 18, 2013], its finances ravaged and its neighborhoods hollowed out by a long, slow decline in population and auto manufacturing" ("Detroit Becomes Largest U.S. City to File for Bankruptcy," 2013). Crime there has skyrocketed and the city has experienced the highest murder rate since the 1970s ("Detroit Becomes Largest U.S. City to File for Bankruptcy," 2013). The distress that accompanies unemployment is often directed toward immigrants and minorities and manifests itself as harassment and violence.

> Poverty and concentrations of diverse populations in one area often lead to conflict in these neighborhoods, not just in inner cities but in suburbs as well. From 2000 to 2011, "the percentage of people living in poverty in the suburbs rose ... 64 percent nationwide. ... [P]overty during the past decade grew twice as fast in the suburbs as cities. By 2011, 3 million more poor people lived in suburbs of the nation's major metropolitan areas than in its big cities" (Newman, 2013).

The stresses associated with these economic challenges can give rise to increased incidents of violence.

MOVE-IN VIOLENCE   Move-in violence can occur when people of one ethnicity or race move into a residence or open a business in a neighborhood composed of people from a different race or ethnicity. Changing demographics can have a significant impact on a community because of hostility based on both perceived and real group differences. However, the presence of new migrants or immigrants in a racially or ethnically different neighborhood does not automatically result in intergroup conflict or violence.

Historically, most cases of move-in violence have involved black, Hispanic, or Asian victims who locate housing or businesses in previously all-white suburbs or neighborhoods. Whites have not been the sole perpetrators, however; they have also been victims. According to the U.S. Department of Justice's Community Relations Service, there have been cases of Hispanic migration or immigration into communities that had been presided over for many years by black leaders; a case in point is Los Angeles' South Central neighborhood, once the site of the Rodney King riots and now a predominantly Hispanic area (Medina, 2012). Other cases of conflict have involved communities with new immigrants from the Middle East and South Asia. In some of these new mixed neighborhoods, community members have perceived that their concerns are being ignored.

Targets of Hate Crimes

The psychocultural origin of hate crimes stems from human nature itself. People can be culturally conditioned to hate those who are different from them because of their places of origin, looks, beliefs, or preferences. As the musical *South Pacific* says, "You've got to be taught to hate and fear/ You've got to be taught from year to year." Crimes and acts of hate serve as frightening reminders to vulnerable citizens that they may not take safety for granted. Collectively, they begin to develop a mentality that hate crimes can take place anywhere—in streets, in neighborhoods, at workplaces, and even in their homes. Not all crimes motivated by prejudice or bias involve hate per se. Many nonviolent incidents are committed impulsively, or as acts of conformity, or as deliberate acts of intimidation designed to achieve the specific ends of the perpetrator.

There are innumerable examples of hate/bias crimes that have victimized blacks, Asians, and Hispanics. Clearly, such hate goes back for many generations. Examples of these are included in Part Two, "Cultural Specifics for Law Enforcement." The following sections address Jews and lesbian, gay, bisexual, and transgender people as victims of hate or bias crimes.

JEWS AND ANTI-SEMITISM

Jews

As of 2012, American Jews comprised approximately 1.8 percent of the adult American population or between 6.4 and 6.6 million people (Zeveloff, 2013). Jews belong to a religious and cultural group, although they have sometimes been incorrectly labeled as constituting a racial group. Jews have experienced discrimination, persecution, and violence throughout history because their religious beliefs and practices often set them apart from the majority. Even when they were totally assimilated (integrated into society), as was true in Germany in the early twentieth century, they were still not accepted as full citizens and eventually experienced the ultimate hate crime—genocide. The term *anti-Semitism* means "against Semites," which literally includes Jews and Arabs. Popular use of this term, however, refers to anti-Jewish sentiment.

European anti-Semitism had religious origins: Jews did not accept Jesus Christ as the son of God and were portrayed as betrayers and even killers of Christ. This accusation gave rise to religious anti-Semitism and what Christians saw as justification for anti-Jewish acts. In the past half century, there have been great strides made by religious leaders to eliminate centuries of prejudice. For example, a 1965 Roman Catholic decree (the *Nostra Aetate*) stated that the church did not hold Jews responsible for the death of Christ. The decree, written by the Second Vatican Council under the leadership of the pope, encouraged people to cease blaming Jews and instead work for stronger links and increased understanding between the religious groups. But despite some progress in ecumenical relations, there are still individuals who, 2,000 years after the birth of Christ, believe that Jews of today are responsible for Christ's death, even though he was a Jew himself. Abraham Foxman, national director of the Anti-Defamation League (ADL) since 1987, has expressed his great concern about two different types of "insidious anti-Semitism." One emanates from the incorrect belief that Jews are more loyal to Israel than to the U.S. The other relates to the belief that Jews killed Christ (Foxman, 2005). No other group in the history of humankind has been accused of killing the God of another religious group; this religious dimension may explain the virulence and long history of anti-Semitism.

A nationwide survey in 2011 by the ADL found that 15 percent (nearly 35 million adults) of American people had "deeply" anti-Semitic attitudes, which was an increase from 12 percent in 2009. However, this was a dramatic decline since their initial survey in 1964, when 29 percent of Americans were found to hold anti-Semitic attitudes. The ADL attributed the increase from 2009 to 2011 to the "the impact of broader trends in America—financial insecurity, social uncertainty, the decline of civility and the growth of polarization" ("ADL Poll Finds Anti-Semitic Attitudes on Rise in America," 2011). The report suggests that in times of high unemployment and economic problems, age-old myths and/or stereotypes about Jews and money, influence, and power in business become even more prevalent and negative. Jews remain the religious group most likely to be targeted in hate crimes, according to statistics. They are targeted more often than those of Islamic faith.

Another type of anti-Semitism falls under what some would label as anti-Zionism (i.e., against the establishment of the state of Israel as a homeland for Jews). Although politically oriented, this type of anti-Semitism still makes references to "the Jews" and equates all Jews with the suppression of the Palestinian people. Police officers must be aware of the potential fallout in the United States when conflicts arise in the Middle East, particularly between Israelis and Palestinians. Anti-Israel attitudes are sometimes expressed as anti-Zionist and anti-Jewish sentiments, despite the fact that Jewish political identification with Israel varies greatly. For example, in January 2009, five Chicago Jewish institutions were tagged with anti-Israel and anti-Semitic graffiti, in apparent response to the conflict in Israel and Gaza. Lonnie Nasatir, Chicago ADL Regional Director, issued a statement:

> These acts of anti-Semitic vandalism against our local Jewish institutions are despicable and cowardly and clearly have no place in Chicago. We applaud law enforcement for taking these incidents seriously and treating them as hate crimes, and we hope that the perpetrators will be brought to justice. Together, we must send a message that our community stands united against the haters and that acts of intimidation will not be tolerated. We saw a similar spike in anti-Israel and anti-Semitic incidents in Chicago and across the country during the Lebanon campaign in 2006 and following the outbreak of the second Palestinian intifada in 2000. It is a sad statement that events taking place across the globe can reverberate in acts of hate in our local community. ("ADL Decries the Anti-Semitic Vandalism of Five Jewish Institutions in Chicago," 2009)

Prevalence of Anti-Semitic Crimes

The ADL produces an annual report on the number of anti-Semitic incidents, which is compiled from official crime statistics from all states and the District of Columbia as well as information provided to ADL's regional offices by victims, law enforcement officials, and community leaders. The numbers consistently exceed those collected by the FBI for the UCR report produced each year, and identify both criminal and noncriminal incidents of harassment and intimidation, including distribution of hate literature, threats, and slurs. It includes incidents such as physical and verbal assaults, harassment, property defacement, vandalism, and other expressions of anti-Jewish sentiment.

In 2013, the Anti-Defamation League's annual audit of Anti-Semitic incidents recorded 927 in the United States in 2012, representing a 14 percent decrease from the 1,080 incidents reported in 2011. These included the following:

- 17 physical assaults on Jewish individuals;
- 470 cases of anti-Semitic harassment, threats, and events;
- 440 cases of anti-Semitic vandalism ("ADL Audit: U.S. Anti-Semitic Incidents Declined 14 Percent in 2012," 2013).

Anti-Semitic Groups and Individuals

Several types of groups in the United States have exhibited anti-Semitic attitudes, and some of the most extreme groups have committed hate crimes against Jews. These organizations include white supremacist groups, such as the Ku Klux Klan (KKK), Aryan Nations, White Aryan Resistance

(WAR), Posse Comitatus, and neo-Nazi skinheads (discussed further in Chapter 12). These groups tend to hate all who are different from them but focus a great deal of attention on blacks and Jews.

Those who argued that it was the United States' support of Israel that led to the 9/11 attacks have demonstrated another aspect of anti-Semitism. Some hate groups used this argument to stir up anti-Jewish feelings and to erode sympathy and support for Jews and for Israel at their organizations' rallies and within the general public. In addition, those who are vehemently pro-Arab and anti-Israel may exhibit strong anti-Jewish attitudes. While it is not as common for anti-Zionist attitudes to result in acts of violence against Jews in the United States as it is in Europe, Jewish Americans, like Arab Americans, can nevertheless become targets during Middle Eastern crises. Finally, in times of recession, Jews are often blamed for the economic decline, and the notion of Jewish "influence" (that is, the baseless charge that Jews control the media, the banks, and even the world economy) provides a convenient scapegoat. It is not within the scope of this section to delve into these myths; however, there is widespread harmful misinformation about Jews that anti-Semites continue to spread.

In May 2009, four men were arrested after a year-long investigation by the FBI and the New York Police Department in connection with an alleged plot to bomb two synagogues in the River-dale section of the Bronx. All were convicted and sent to prison in October 2010. The four men were all Muslim, one of Afghan descent and three who had converted to Islam in prison. James Cromitie, identified as the leader of the group, stated "that he was upset about the war in Afghanistan and that that he wanted to 'do something to America' (Baker and Hernandez, 2009). Conversations with the men, recorded secretly by an informant, "included plans for mass violence and anti-Semitic comments" (Fahim, 2010).

> The arrests illustrate how law enforcement continues to play a critical role in ensuring the safety and security of the Jewish community and in protecting all of its citizens from terrorism. We have long known that Jews remain a prime target for would-be terrorists, and we must always remain vigilant in the face of this threat. The bombing plot uncovered by law enforcement is another reminder of the extreme lengths violent anti-Semites will go to act on their hatred. According to the police complaint, the suspects in the attempted Riverdale bombings were motivated by a deep-seated hatred of Jews, and were so determined to attack synagogues that they allegedly engaged in surveillance of the potential targets, and sought for nearly a year to obtain the weapons and bombs to bring the attack to fruition. ("ADL Applauds Law Enforcement for Arrests of Homegrown Terrorists in Plot to Blow Up New York City Synagogues," 2009)

Synagogues are not the only targets of anti-Semites. In 2011, for example, "an Oregon white supremacist and his girlfriend, linked to four slayings in three states, were driving to Sacramento to 'kill more Jews' when they were arrested by police" ("Couple suspected in slayings planned to 'kill more Jews,'" 2011).

Jewish Community Concerns

Around the holiest days of the Jewish year (Rosh Hashanah and Yom Kippur, usually occurring in the early fall), there may be heightened anxiety among some community members regarding security. Indeed, many synagogues hire extra security during times of worship over this 10-day holiday period. Acts of defilement can occur in synagogues and other Jewish institutions at random times as well. These acts and manifestations of prejudice bring back painful memories for Jews who experienced violent expressions of anti-Semitism in other countries, especially for those who lived through the Holocaust; some of the memories and fears have been passed on to subsequent generations. A swastika painted by teenagers on a building does not necessarily precede any acts of anti-Jewish violence, yet it can evoke fear among many Jewish community members, especially older Jews, because of the historical significance of the symbol.

Police officers must understand that different segments of the Jewish community feel vulnerable to anti-Semitism, and therefore officers are advised to listen to and take seriously community members' expressions of concern and fear. At the same time, officers can explain that acts of vandalism are sometimes isolated or random, and are not targeting any group in particular. Finally, police officers should be aware that anti-Semitism has a long and active history, and even if some fears appear to be exaggerated, they have a basis in reality. Therefore, officers who take reports from citizens should reassure those citizens that their local law enforcement agency views hate crimes and incidents seriously and that extra protection will be provided if the need arises.

What Law Enforcement Can Do

Officers can take some steps to establish rapport and provide protection in Jewish communities when the need arises:

1. When an officer hears of an act that can be classified as a hate crime toward Jews, it should be investigated, tracked, and dealt with as such. Dismissing acts of anti-Semitism as petty crime will result in a lack of trust on the part of the community.
2. When hate crimes and incidents are perpetrated against other groups in the community (e.g., gay, African American, Asian American groups), officers should alert Jewish community leaders immediately. Their institutions may be the next targets.
3. Officers should be aware of groups and individuals who distribute hate literature on people's doorsteps or vehicle windshields. Even if no violence occurs, the recipients of such hate literature become very fearful.
4. In cooperation with local organizations such as Jewish community relations councils or regional offices of the ADL, officers can provide information through joint meetings on ways that individuals can heighten the security of Jewish institutions (such as information on nonbreakable glass, lighting of facilities in evenings).
5. Law enforcement officials should be familiar with the important dates of the Jewish calendar, especially when the High Holidays (Rosh Hashanah and Yom Kippur) occur. (Note that the Jewish holiday cycle is based on the lunar calendar, thus the holiday dates vary from year to year.) Some people are concerned about safety and protection during events at which large groups of Jews congregate.
6. Finally, officers should contact Jewish umbrella organizations in the community and ask for assistance in sending necessary messages to local Jewish institutions and places of worship. Two organizations in particular are worth noting: the national JCRC (Jewish Community Relations Council) and the ADL. The JCRC has representative organizations in almost every major city in the United States. The JCRC, regional ADL organizations, and Jewish Federations can greatly assist law enforcement in disseminating information to community members.

Because of Jewish history, anti-Semitic incidents do not come as a surprise to many Jews. An officer's ability to calm fears as well as to investigate threats thoroughly will result in strong relations between law enforcement officials and Jewish community members.

LESBIAN, GAY, BISEXUAL, AND TRANSGENDER VICTIMIZATION

According to Mitchell Grobeson, a retired LAPD sergeant who is gay,

> When members of the gay community sought respectability within society, there was no word that did *not* carry a derogatory connotation for non-heterosexuality. The term "homosexual" carried negative connotations because the American Psychiatric Association used this as a medical diagnosis for a psychiatric illness until 1993. As such, various gay leaders tried to replace this with the term "homophile" and subsequently, "gay." Because "lesbians" sought distinctiveness, the phrase "gay and lesbian" became more common. Other discriminated classes sought out their own unique identification, so the terms "bisexual" and "transgender" were added as these persons sought recognition within the larger community. (Grobeson, personal communication, 2013)

A related term that is important to understand is *phobia*, which is defined "as an irrational, excessive, and persistent fear of some particular thing or situation," *Homophobia* is an "irrational hatred or fear of homosexuals or homosexuality" (Collins English Dictionary online). Sometimes, homophobia results in homophobic acts, which can run the full spectrum from antigay jokes to physical battery resulting in injury or death. In this text, as in government reporting systems, homophobic acts are referred to as antisexual orientation or gender identity bias incidents and offenses. LGBT is an initialism or acronym referring collectively to lesbian, gay, bisexual, and transgender people. The authors use those initials throughout this textbook.

Hate crimes targeting LGBT individuals are distinct from other bias crimes because they target a group made up of every other category discussed in this textbook. In the United States today, there are organizations whose membership includes gay, lesbian, bisexual, and transgender Jews, Catholics, Mormons, Buddhists, Armenians, Latinos/as, African Americans, Asians or Pacific Islanders, as well as nearly every other ethnic, racial, and religious group.

Hate Crime Laws Specific to LGBT Persons as Victims

Every year in the United States, thousands of LGBT persons are harassed, beaten, or murdered solely because of their sexual orientation or gender identity. As of June 2013, 45 states and the District of Columbia have hate crime statutes criminalizing various types of bias-motivated violence or intimidation ("State Hate Crimes Laws," 2013). Fifteen states have created laws specific to crimes directed against LGBT persons because of their sexual orientation or gender expression. An additional 15 states have enacted hate crime laws that are based only upon sexual orientation, and do not include gender identity or expression. On October 28, 2009, legislation, known as the "Local Law Enforcement Hate Crimes Prevention Act" (LLEHCPA), was signed into law after many years of debate. The Act is the first federal law to extend legal protections to transgender people. The federal law is also known as the "Matthew Shepard and James Byrd, Jr., Hate Crimes Prevention Act" after the 21-year-old Wyoming student who was tortured and murdered because of his sexual orientation. The Act provides for the following:

- Extend existing federal protections to include "gender identity, sexual orientation, gender, and disability"
- Allow the Justice Department to assist in hate crime investigations at the local level when local law enforcement is unable or unwilling to fully address these crimes
- Mandate that the FBI begin tracking hate crimes based on actual or perceived gender identity, sexual orientation, gender, and disability
- Remove limitations that narrowly define hate crimes as violence committed while a person is accessing a federally protected activity, such as voting or going to school
- Require the FBI to track statistics on hate crimes against transgender people ("H.R. 1913, Local Law Enforcement Hate Crimes Prevention Act of 2009, 2009")

LGBT Persons as Victims of Hate/Bias Incidents and Offenses

Supporters of the expansion of hate crime laws to include LGBT persons argued that hate crimes are worse than regular crimes. They maintain that because this type of crime "targets" an entire group of persons rather than an individual, and because of the prejudiced motivation, it takes hate crime victims almost twice as long as victims of a non-hate-related crime to recover psychologically and emotionally. This leads to a higher incidence of depression, anxiety, and post-traumatic stress disorder for LGBT individuals (Noelle, 2002).

THE SCOPE OF LGBT VICTIMIZATION   The FBI-UCR hate crime report covering 2011, previously mentioned, indicates that there were 6,216 single-bias incidents reported, of which 1,508 (20.8 percent) were based on sexual orientation ("Hate Crime Statistics, 2011," 2013). However, the UCR statistics, as in previous years, continue to fall well short of the number of incidents and offenses reported to the National Coalition of Anti-Violence Programs (NCAVP) and other such organizations. The NCAVP is a network of over 35 antiviolence organizations that monitor, respond to, and work to end incidents of hate and domestic violence and other forms of violence affecting LGBT communities. The coalition produces a report each year documenting the number of bias-motivated incidents targeting LGBT individuals in the United States.

Because the number of LGBT victims reporting bias-motivated incidents to the NCAVP is significantly higher than to the FBI, researchers and gay rights groups question the validity, findings, and implications of the FBI-UCR reports. Recall that law enforcement compliance with the Hate Crime Statistics Act of 1990 is voluntary and many agencies in the United States do not report hate bias incidents and offenses to the FBI.

Increases in bias crimes based on sexual orientation occurred during the years when gays and lesbians were trying to gain marriage and adoption rights, which resulted in movements in some states to block these efforts. Because of the prominence of these issues, LGBT persons and communities gained more visibility, both positive and negative. Both statistical and anecdotal evidence have demonstrated that when LGBT issues are in the limelight, LGBT communities and individuals are more likely to be targeted for violence. It should be noted that since "same-gender" marriage received formal recognition from both the Executive and Judicial branches of the federal government in 2013, data on "retaliatory" bias crimes has not as yet been evaluated.

LGBT VICTIM PROFILES   According to the NCAVP, across various demographics, whites represented the largest proportion of LGBT victims of hate crimes (45%). The race/ethnicity of victims for the year 2011 is displayed in Exhibit 11.6.

Anti-LGBT murders are often distinguishable from other murders by the level of brutality involved. See Exhibit 11.7 for a year-to-year analysis of known anti-LGBT murders in the years 1998 through 2011 according to the NCAVP ("Hate Violence Against Lesbian, Gay, Bisexual, Transgender, Queer, and HIV-affected Communities in the United States in 2011," 2012). Hate violence murders increased from 27 in 2010 to 30 in 2011, an 11 percent increase. It is the highest number of murders ever recorded by the NCAVP.

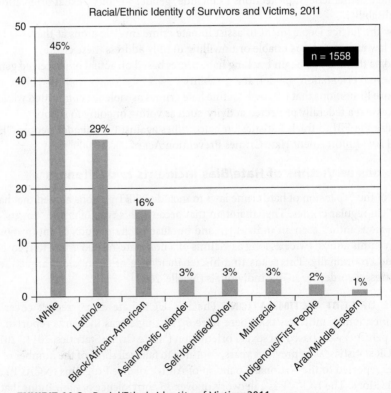

EXHIBIT 11.6   Racial/Ethnic Identity of Victims 2011

Source: "Hate Violence Against Lesbian, Gay, Bisexual, Transgender, Queer and HIV-affected Communities in the U.S. in 2011." Retrieved from www.avp.org/storage/documents/Reports/2012_NCAVP_2011_HV_Report.pdf

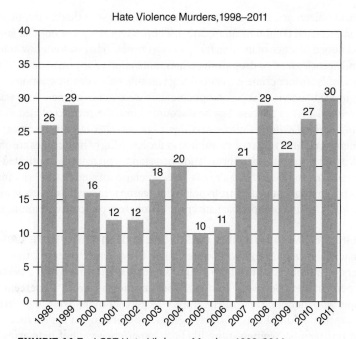

Hate Violence Murders, 1998–2011

EXHIBIT 11.7 LGBT Hate Violence Murders 1998–2011

Source: "Hate Violence Against Lesbian, Gay, Bisexual, Transgender, Queer and HIV-affected Communities in the U.S. in 2011." Retrieved from www.avp.org/storage/documents/Reports/2012_NCAVP_2011_HV_Report.pdf

Victims of anti-LGBT bias hesitate to report their experiences, either to police or to organizations within their own community. The reasons for this include the possibility that the victim:

a. fears reprisal from the offender(s)
b. fears embarrassment or abuse from police
c. anticipates ostracism from family, friends, or coworkers and would possibly lose employment, custody of children, or housing
d. has been urged by family members, friends, and coworkers not to report the incident
e. is so emotionally impacted by the experience that he or she wishes to "forget" it and "move on"
f. blames himself or herself for being in the "wrong" place, saying the "wrong" thing, or acting or dressing in the "wrong" way
g. either does not believe anything can be done or believes the police will not do anything
h. dismisses hate incidents (versus hate offenses/crimes) as not being serious enough to report.
i. is not aware of national or local antiviolence organizations and intake centers (such as Lesbian and Gay Community Centers) or other programs that provide alternatives to the police, or believes the organizations will not help if he or she does not make an official police report (Grobeson, personal communication, 2013).

Differences in culture and language, along with gender, age, and class, often lead to perceptions that advocacy organizations may not be sensitive to the victim's own background. The NCAVP strongly believes that the incidence of anti-LGBT bias crime affecting younger and older people, immigrants, people of color, people in the military, and those within other marginalized populations is grossly underreported ("Hate Violence against Lesbian, Gay, Bisexual, Transgender, Queer, and HIV-affected Communities in the U.S. in 2011," 2012).

Reasons for antisexual orientation crimes being underreported:

a. ***Mixed Motive or Pick-Up Crimes.*** According to Grobeson, although victims' advocates believe that a crime in which bias was a *primary* motivation should be classified as a hate crime, law enforcement officers are often unwilling to do so if there is any other motive in addition to bias (Grobeson, personal communication, 2013). These advocates point out that law enforcement personnel have a practice of looking for "pick-up crimes." That is, some law enforcement personnel and agencies tend to drop the hate/bias motivation of any incident or offense in which an element of *any* other crime is involved (e.g., assault with a deadly weapon or robbery). For example, in a situation in which homophobic slurs were used, but the victim was also robbed, the hate crime aspect of the case may be discounted, and the crime classified as a robbery.

   b. *Conflicting Police Training Policies and Practices.* Another facet underreporting is that law enforcement personnel who receive training in the handling of hate crimes are often instructed *not* to ask about a person's sexual orientation, so assaults and batteries motivated by homophobia are often not classified as hate crimes. The reluctance of some LGBT victims to reveal the homophobic component of a crime to police, for reasons already discussed, leads to low criminal justice figures on homophobic hate crime (Grobeson, personal communication, 2013).

TRANSGENDER PERSONS AS VICTIMS OF SEXUAL ORIENTATION HATE CRIMES   Significantly, while hate violence incidents within the United States have decreased, the overall number of hate murders of members of the LGBT community has increased by 11 percent. Of those murdered, 87 percent were people of color, showing an increase from 70 percent in 2010. Furthermore, people who identify as transgender were 28 percent more likely to experience physical violence than gay men and lesbians who were gender conforming in appearance (Bolles, 2012). Not only were transgender women more likely to experience violent hate crimes, those hate crimes were more likely to result in their death. In a 2011 study, transgender women made up 44 percent of murders while representing only 11 percent of all victims of violent hate crimes ("New Studies Examine Violence Directed at Transgender People of Color," 2011).

   It is important that hate crime reports document the perspective of the perpetrator as well as of the victim in attacks on transgender individuals. Most homophobic incidents targeting transgender individuals include epithets such as "You f___ queer." Critical to reporting, investigating, and collecting accurate statistical data, these incidents must be documented as targeting persons because they are gay, transgender, or both (Grobeson, personal communication, 2013). It is recommended that large police agencies have personnel specifically assigned to investigate hate crimes against LGBT individuals. Most agencies assign hate crimes to investigators of other offenses, often to those assigned to handle "crimes against persons," as a corollary duty. "If you assign a robbery detective to investigate hate crimes, you will wind up with a robbery filing," says Grobeson. At the very least, agencies should ensure that those who investigate hate crimes receive appropriate training by the FBI, district attorneys who prosecute hate crimes, and LGBT and transgender organizations that provide legal services or do intakes of LGBT/transgender hate crimes and incidents from victims (Grobeson, personal communication, 2013).

Perpetrators of Crime Related to Sexual Orientation

Grobeson suggests that many suspects in crimes related to sexual orientation fit specific profiles, such as being a gang member or member of a white supremacist group. Sometimes gangs incorporate "gay-bashing" into their new-member initiation. It is important to note that those who engage in homophobic acts almost always engage in actions that discriminate against other groups as well. However, studies have also determined that perpetrators are sometimes ordinary young adults who are not members of a gang or hate group but fall into the category of "thrill seekers," "moral ideologues," or "turf defenders," and most of them do not know the victim (Schafer & Navarro, 2003).

Sexual Orientation Hate/Bias Crimes and the Military

On September 20, 2011, the ban on gays in the military was eliminated, which meant that service members were now able to openly acknowledge their sexual orientation. Up to that date, the military had written policy that did not permit them to recruit or retain persons who were known to be homosexual.

It is important that FBI agents, military police, and law enforcement agencies that have adjacent military installations become familiar with organizations such as Servicemembers Legal Defense Network (SLDN) and the Palm Center, the updated policies issued by the Department of Defense (DoD) pertaining to investigations of hate crimes against LGBT persons. Military police officers should have an action plan to address relevant (anti-LGBT) issues, including eliminating mistreatment, harassment, and inappropriate comments or gestures; training; reporting of harassment; enforcement of policies prohibiting harassment; measurement of antiharassment program effectiveness, and, significantly, "environmental audits" to determine on a regular basis if there exists a hostile work environment. One simple way of checking for a supportive work environment is to include relevant questions in exit interviews when servicemembers leave the unit they are working in or reach the end of their contractual enlistment period. This is a time when servicemembers are most likely to be candid (Grobeson, personal communication, 2013).

Sexual Orientation Hate/Bias Crimes and School Campuses

Every two years, the Gay, Lesbian, & Straight Education Network (GLSEN) surveys schools to assess the experience of LGBT students from 50 states and the District of Columbia. Some of the key findings from its 2011 report include the following:

- 81.9 percent of LGBT students reported being verbally harassed, 38.3 percent reported being physically harassed, and 18.3 percent reported being physically assaulted at school in the past year **because of their sexual orientation**.
- 63.9 percent of LGBT students reported being verbally harassed, 27.1 percent reported being physically harassed, and 12.4 percent reported being physically assaulted at school in the past year **because of their gender expression** (Ford, 2012).

Campus police need to be aware that many states have enacted "Safe Schools" laws mandating environments that are free of harassment, bullying, and discrimination, where no student is subjected to abuse or a hostile learning environment. There are a number of cases nationwide wherein students who were not protected by administrators or were subjected to unequal restrictions have sued their schools. Many court decisions found school administrators liable for failing to provide an environment free of hostility, which resulted in expensive verdicts. Bullying, discrimination, and assaults for any reason are a serious problem in today's schools and society. Not only do LGBT children not feel safe in such a school environment, the effects of such actions can be detrimental to a child's self-esteem and social and academic success.

The U.S. Department of Health and Human Services reports that gay and lesbian teens are two to six times more likely than heterosexual teens to attempt suicide. They account for 30 percent of all reported suicides in the country, 28 percent of all dropouts, and 40 percent of homeless teens ("LGBT Homeless," 2012).

"Cyberbullying," which is the use of the Internet and social media to harm other people, primarily fellow students, in a deliberate, repeated, and hostile manner, has become so common that it is one of the most frequent issues being addressed by school administrators and legislators. Due to several high-profile LGBT teen suicides, many LGBT advocacy organizations, particularly those whose focus is on campus environments, have begun campaigning for intervention by law enforcement. Advocates want legislation passed to protect young people and raise awareness to combat the harm caused by misuse of these modern communication systems ("Cyberbullying FAQs for Teens," n.d.).

It is also important that parents, as well as law enforcement entities involved in campus safety, be aware of resources and applicable laws for their communities ("Working to Halt Online Abuse," n.d.)

Although federal law prohibits "any interactive computer service, or any facility of interstate or foreign commerce to engage in a course of conduct that causes substantial emotional distress," no federal statute specifically applies to bullying, unlike harassment, which violates federal civil rights law because it is a form of unlawful discrimination ("Working to Halt Online

Abuse," n.d.). A proposed federal bill, titled the Bullying Prevention and Intervention Act of 2011 (H.R. 83), died in committee in the 112th Congress.

There are numerous state and local laws and ordinances that address the issues of bullying and cyberbullying, however ("Working to Halt Online Abuse," n.d.). These laws establish that allegations of discrimination, bullying, or harassment are to be investigated and disciplinary action imposed, if warranted, by the school district. As of 2013, 49 states (Montana being the exception) have enacted legislation requiring school districts to adopt policies regarding bullying. Of those states, only nine require school administrators, under certain circumstances, to report incidents of bullying to the law enforcement agency in their district (Sacco, Silbaugh, Corredor, Casey, & Doherty, 2012). Though traditionally authority over such allegations of bullying has fallen to the school system, the trend in a number of states is to incorporate antibullying provisions into their criminal and juvenile justice codes. Often these bullying laws are in conjunction with harassment laws, and the terms are sometimes used interchangeably in the laws and policies in many states.

Because of this trend, law enforcement agencies, particularly campus police, are becoming more involved in campus situations such as sexual-orientation bias crimes and bullying. They are expected to complete official documentation regarding alleged violations and physical assaults based on a student's perceived or actual sexual orientation or gender identity. It is particularly important for campus police to be vigilant because most LGBT teens do not report that they are victims of bias incidents or crimes at school, for such reasons as fearing that school officials will tell their parents about their real or perceived sexual orientation and/or that school officials will not do anything to stop the abusers.

Carolyn Laub, executive director of the Gay-Straight Alliance Network, commenting on the murder of an Oxnard (California) student shot while at school, said that "with young people coming out at younger ages, our schools—especially our junior highs and middle schools—need to be pro-active about teaching respect for diversity based on sexual orientation and gender identity" ("Gay Killing Draws Call for Change," 2008). It is obvious that school officials, including campus police and school resource officers, where they exist, must take steps to alter the negative experiences of LGBT students, so they are not harassed, bullied, or assaulted while attempting to get an education.

Police Relations with Gay and Lesbian Communities

> Improved policing comes from having a diverse police force. So if you want to be able to address some of the unique issues—whether they be hate crimes or some other issue—within the gay community, it's good to have officers who are at least culturally competent. And if you can get gay and lesbian officers, all the better. (Colvin, 2013)

Historically, in most cities and counties in the United States, relations between the police and the gay and lesbian communities have been strained, sometimes as a result of how the community members, as individuals or as a group, have been mistreated or abused by law enforcement officers. Many LGBT persons believe that the police regard them as deviants, criminals, and second-class citizens who are unworthy of protection or equal rights. Because of this perception, many gay and lesbian victims do not report the crimes to the police or cooperate with investigations. Even though negative attitudes and stereotypes will probably continue, progressive police agencies and law enforcement officers who are professionals have found that communication and mutual respect between the department and gay and lesbian communities are in the best interests of all concerned.

Examples of police departments in which outreach and communication have resulted in cooperation between the agencies and the gay community include San Francisco, San Diego, Portland, and Boston (Grobeson, personal communication, 2013). These departments have observed a noticeable difference in such things as increased reporting of hate crimes and incidents by lesbian and gay crime victims, fewer complaints of police abuse, and a general improvement in relations between law enforcement and gay and lesbian communities. It is also important that community-based policing principles and protocol be utilized in LGBT communities. Officers should recognize issues and concerns not only about sexual-orientation bias crimes but also about domestic violence within the LGBT community. According to Grobeson, domestic violence, although virtually invisible in LGBT communities, is commonplace and should be investigated following the same guidelines and policies as those used for heterosexual relationships.

One of the keys to good relations between law enforcement agencies and the LGBT community, according to Roddrick Colvin, associate professor at John Jay College of Criminal Justice, is regular, institutionalized communication at the department, in committees and councils, and in public forums. In addition, he mentions the following:

1. The creation of task forces and councils to establish ongoing dialogue and networking on important issues.
2. Public forums that allow police officials to meet the LGBT community and help officials to recognize that they are a constituency with legitimate needs and concerns.
3. The appointment of a police official to be a liaison with the LGBT community to respond to complaints and requests.
4. The involvement of prosecutors in the development of policies, procedures, communications, and awareness training to improve relations between the criminal justice system and LGBT groups and individuals. (Colvin, 2013)

Almost every community has extremists, and the LGBT community is no exception. Some activists or activist groups may require additional attention and special interaction with local law enforcement. The goal of the agency liaison and management should be to avoid costly litigation and to communicate effectively with persons representing such groups. Departments should have the assigned liaison officer meet with these groups in an attempt to agree on acceptable behavior before any public demonstration occurs. Some groups obtain press coverage by orchestrating arrests by the police; in such cases, liaison and close monitoring by field supervisors, a press relations officer, a police video unit, and a department manager would be an absolute necessity. This methodology has been successful with agencies in the San Francisco Bay Area, resulting in no physical confrontation with groups, no negative press or photos, and no legal action. However, even the best police outreach efforts may prove ineffective. For example, some activist groups have refused to communicate with police during their "actions." Nevertheless, police officers should not permit negative publicity from previous incidents with any group to stop them from attempting to make positive contact prior to scheduled public events. The willingness of the police to work with any community group, particularly LGBT activist groups, always results in positive publicity for law enforcement agencies and the cities or counties they serve (Grobeson, personal communication, 2013).

The handling and investigation of hate crimes require specialized and unique expertise. The epidemic of hate crimes will continue unabated as long as law enforcement management does not address it proactively. For example, just as law enforcement agencies commit plainclothes personnel to "Vice" assignments, in areas where there are hate incidents, plainclothes officers can make arrests and management can publicize these responses, which in turn will likely prevent escalation to hate crimes. It is equally important for law enforcement administrators to realize that they can be subjected to litigation and even punitive damages for the actions of their subordinates if they fail to provide proactive policies or take affirmative stances in regard to officer training or discipline (vicarious liability). Military and campus police officers must also know the laws and establish protocol for preventing and investigating crimes motivated by hate against anyone within their jurisdictions, including LGBT individuals.

HATE CRIME LAWS SPECIFIC TO LGBT

Federal Laws

Federal laws provide criminal and civil causes of action for victims of hate crimes in the United States, regardless of whether they are citizens. Federal law does not prohibit all acts of hate violence, however. Federal statutes forbid violence by private parties only when there is intent to interfere with a federally protected right—that is, one specifically guaranteed by a federal statute or by the U.S. Constitution. Such activity includes voting, serving on a jury, going to work, or enrolling in or attending public school. Nevertheless, these rights are broadly interpreted when a perpetrator's motive is tainted by racial hatred. For additional information pertaining to federal laws, see previous discussion of the Matthew Shepard Act in this chapter under the heading "Hate Crime Laws Specific to LGBT Persons as Victims."

A victim of a hate/bias crime that violates a federal law can initiate criminal prosecution by reporting the crime to a local office of the FBI. That office then assigns an investigator to the case. A victim may also contact the local U.S. attorney's office or the criminal section of the Civil Rights Division at the U.S. Department of Justice in Washington, D.C. In addition to criminal prosecution, a victim can pursue a civil suit if the facts support a civil action under the federal statutes. The victim can seek both damages and injunctive relief in civil action against the perpetrator of violence that is motivated by racial, sexual orientation, gender, or disability hatred.

In general, the federal criminal statutes are intended to supplement state and local criminal laws. Procedurally, the U.S. Department of Justice (DOJ) will not become actively involved in prosecuting a particular action until local authorities have concluded their case. After a person is convicted or acquitted in state courts, the DOJ evaluates the result before determining whether to prosecute under federal statutes. There is no set time within which the Justice Department makes its decision.

State Laws

As noted earlier in the chapter, as of June 2013, 45 states and the District of Columbia have hate crime statutes criminalizing various types of bias-motivated violence or intimidation. However, a significant number of those statutes do not include coverage of crimes based on sexual orientation or gender identity. In 2013, California, and some other state legislatures, introduced legislation to amend or repeal criminal laws that single out HIV-positive people. Thirty-two states and two U.S. territories have laws that criminalize exposing others to HIV even if the virus isn't actually transmitted. Thirty-six states reported at least 350 cases in recent years in which HIV-positive people have been arrested or prosecuted for consensual sex, biting and spitting, according to the Center for HIV Law and Policy (Richmond, 2013). In those states, it is a felony to expose someone to HIV if you know you're infected at the time you have unprotected sex with that partner, haven't disclosed your status to that partner, and act with specific intent to infect that partner. The penalty upon conviction could result in three, five, or eight years in prison. Some argue that such laws are based on bias, not science, and that our federal and state laws should not discriminate against people who are living with HIV ("Bill targets HIV Criminal laws," 2013). Federal legislation calling for an end to federal and state HIV-specific criminal laws and prosecutions has been introduced before but has not passed, as it is very controversial.

Many states have enacted "penalty-enhancements" statutes, which were upheld unanimously by the U.S. Supreme Court in June 1993 in its decision in *Wisconsin* v. *Mitchell* (508 U.S. 476, 1993). Penalty enhancements are legal when the defendant intentionally selects his or her victim based on the victim's race, religion, national origin, sexual orientation, gender, or disability. Many states have also enhanced criminal penalties for vandalism aimed at houses of worship, cemeteries, schools, and community centers.

Violence against Women Act (VAWA)

Chapter 1 presents information on VAWA primarily in the context of violence against immigrant women; Chapter 9 provides more detail with respect to Native American women. VAWA also provides protection for LGBT individuals. The legislation was reauthorized twice (in 2000 and 2005) with little resistance, but was allowed to expire by Congress in 2011 due to an election-year clash over expanding protections for gay, lesbian, bisexual, transgender, and Native American individuals. However, in 2013, the legislation was renewed with those protections included ("Obama Signs Expanded Violence against Women Act," 2013).

Why Special Laws and Penalty Enhancements?

There are those, including some law enforcement leaders, who argue that there is no need for special laws dealing with hate/bias crimes because there are already statutes covering specific crimes. For example, an assault by one person on another is prosecutable in all jurisdictions. Therefore, the argument runs, why would such an assault be prosecuted differently even if it is motivated by a person's hate or bias toward victims because of their color, ethnic background, religion, sexual orientation, gender, or disability?

There are several responses to this critique. First, if incidents were not classified by racial, ethnic, sexual orientation, disability, or religious motivation, it would be virtually impossible to tabulate acts of hate violence, spot trends, perform analyses, or develop response strategies. Second, an inaccurate characterization of certain types of hate violence crimes would occur. For example, in the past, cross burnings were variously classified as malicious mischief, vandalism, or burning without a permit, and swastikas painted on buildings were often classified as graffiti incidents or malicious mischief.

There are also some key differences that make hate/bias crimes more serious than standard offenses, justifying the establishment of special laws and sentence enhancements. "Hate crimes differ from other forms of interpersonal violence in three important ways. They are more vicious, extremely brutal, and frequently perpetrated at random on total strangers, commonly a single victim by multiple offenders and predominately male teenagers and young adults (Christie, Wagner, & Winter, 2001). Crimes of this sort deny the free exercise of civil rights, sometimes frightening the victim out of exercising freedom of speech, association, and assembly. Often, the attacks are acts of terrorism intended to punish the victim for being visible (i.e., a person who looks or acts different from others is easy for a bigoted person to single out). Finally, these acts against individuals are also often meant to terrorize entire communities.

Hate/bias crimes require more police resources for investigation, community response, and victim assistance than most other crimes. There is a national consensus that such crimes justify special laws and enhanced penalties for offenders. They send a clear message to the perpetrator and the public that these crimes will not be tolerated and will be treated as serious offenses.

HATE/BIAS CRIME AND INCIDENT INVESTIGATIONS

Criminal justice agencies must make hate/bias crimes a priority for response, from the initial report through prosecution. To ensure that all personnel treat such crimes seriously, each agency must have written policies and procedures that establish protocol for a quick and effective response. Only when such policies and procedures, as well as feasible community programs, are in place, will society begin to control and reduce hate crimes.

Law enforcement agencies must provide investigators with training that includes such critical elements as understanding the role of the investigator, identifying a hate/bias crime, classifying an offender, interviewing a victim, relating to a community, and prosecuting an offender. When hate/bias crimes occur, they require investigators' timely response, understanding, and vigilance to ensure a careful and successful investigation. Investigators must have a comprehensive knowledge of the general elements and motivations behind hate/bias crimes and must recognize the potential of these crimes to affect not only the primary victim, but also the victim's family, other members of the victim's group, and the larger community.

There are general and specific procedures and protocols that should be used in response to crimes and incidents motivated by the victim's race, religion, ethnic background, or sexual orientation (RRES). These include actions to be taken by each of the following categories of personnel:

- Assigned officer/first responder
- Patrol field supervisor
- Watch commander
- Assigned investigator or specialized unit

- Crime prevention, community relations, or specialized unit
- Training unit

The actual guidelines may vary among jurisdictions, but the basics are the same. Specific guidelines are available from federal and state organizations or police and sheriffs' departments. Some law enforcement agencies have model protocols that could be secured and used in the classroom or by departments who have not developed their own procedures.

Models for Investigating Hate/Bias Crimes

The following are suggested guidelines for law enforcement agencies without standardized protocol for follow-up of hate/bias crimes and incidents. The suggested formats are based on the size of the department. However, regardless the size of the department, it is recommended that there be an established protocol between law enforcement and emergency medical services personnel who respond to the crime scene. This will benefit the victim and the overall outcome of the investigation.

SMALL DEPARTMENT (AGENCIES OF 1 TO 100 SWORN)   A small department may not have the staffing depth to have a specialized unit or investigator who can deal solely with hate crimes. Officers in small departments are usually generalists, meaning that they carry any type of case from the initial report through the investigation and submission to the district attorney. Therefore, all personnel should receive awareness training on cultural and racial issues and learn the requirements of handling crimes and incidents motivated by hate. The officer who takes the crime or incident report must have it approved by his or her supervisor. Some small departments have allowed patrol officers to specialize in the investigation of certain crimes; they might be involved in either providing advice and direction or actually taking the case and handling it to its conclusion. These officers are usually the ones allowed to attend training and conferences that will teach and update them on the investigations of these crimes and incidents. Some departments have a patrol supervisor perform the follow-up investigation and submit the case to the prosecutor's office. It is important that the officer and his or her supervisor keep command officers informed of major cases. Small agencies with a detective follow-up investigations unit must make sure that unit members are trained in aspects of dealing with crimes motivated by hate.

MEDIUM-SIZED DEPARTMENT (AGENCIES OF 100 TO 500 SWORN)   The following is a model suggested for a medium-sized department with a crimes-against-persons investigations unit and an administration unit responsible for community relations or affairs. The format follows this protocol: The responding patrol officer takes the initial report, decides if what occurred could be considered a crime or incident motivated by hate or bias, and then completes a preliminary investigation. Then the officer documents the findings on the department offense report form and follows the policy and procedure as established by the agency. The officer's supervisor and watch commander approve the report (which may or may not already be classified as a hate/bias or civil rights violation, depending on department policy). Then it is forwarded to the investigations unit that follows up on such cases (usually the crimes against persons unit). The investigations unit supervisor reviews the report and again evaluates whether a hate/bias crime or incident took place. If it is decided that it is a hate/bias crime, the report is assigned to a crimes against persons investigator *who specializes in this type of investigation.*

A copy of the report is also forwarded (through the appropriate chain of command) to the administration or community relations unit for follow-up. The staff of the latter unit is also trained to handle hate/bias and civil rights violations investigations and to provide victim assistance. The administrative follow-up includes:

- Investigations required
- Referrals and support for the victim
- Conducting of public meetings to resolve neighborhood problems

- Conflict resolution
- Liaison with the diverse organizations in the community and victim advocates

Some cases may require that the criminal investigator and the administrative officer work jointly to resolve the crime or incident under investigation.

LARGE DEPARTMENTS (AGENCIES OF 500-PLUS SWORN) Most large departments have enough staff that they can have a specialized unit that focuses on crimes motivated by hate/bias or civil rights violations. There are many advantages to having such a unit. The investigators become familiar and experienced with the law and special procedures required and can handle more complex, sensitive cases. Investigators who are allowed to specialize can form networks with victim advocate organizations, other police agencies, and community-based agencies. They work closely with the district attorney's office (probably with a special bias unit within that agency), establishing the working relationships and rapport important to successful prosecutions. The investigators develop a sense of pride in their efforts and a commitment to provide a competent investigative and victim assistance response. Since the primary function of the unit is hate/bias crime investigations, officers can sometimes develop knowledge of individuals and groups that commit such offenses and become more aware of where the incidents occur.

Detectives who handle a multitude of cases do not have the time to track and monitor these crimes and therefore may not spot trends. Specialized units can evaluate the field performance of the patrol officers who have handled such crimes and can provide suggestions for improvement or commendations when the response has been effective or innovative.

There are also disadvantages to specialized units. Often, when there is a specialized unit, patrol officers believe that what is happening in the neighborhood in which they work is not their problem—it is the problem of the specialized unit. The officer takes reports and then transfers responsibility for resolution of problems. Patrol officers may be unaware of a problem or its magnitude or even what resources are being marshaled to resolve it unless there is good communication between them and the members of the specialized unit. These disadvantages are surmountable, however, especially if the department uses community-oriented policing strategies, which usually involve a higher degree of communication among agency units and with the community.

Hate crimes that fit certain criteria are investigated at the federal level by the FBI's Bias Crimes Unit, the Bureau of Alcohol, Tobacco and Firearms (ATF), and church arson and explosives experts. ATF investigators also focus on regulating the illegal sale to and possession of firearms by potential perpetrators of hate crimes.

HATE/BIAS CRIME PROSECUTION

District Attorneys' or Prosecutors' Offices

Many district attorneys' offices in the United States now have attorneys and/or units that specialize in hate crime prosecution. These agencies have established policies and procedures designed to prosecute such crimes effectively and efficiently. There are compelling reasons for district attorneys to devote special attention and resources to these crimes. A prosecutor has discretion to influence, if not determine, what might be called the public safety climate that citizens in the communities he or she serves will experience. Establishing a public safety climate that fosters the full enjoyment of civil and political rights by the minority members of our communities requires a focused political will directed to that end, as well as resources and capacity. The most effective and successful approaches to building a climate of public safety have been those that:

- established specialized hate crimes or civil rights violations units
- standardized procedures to prosecute hate crime cases
- appointed attorneys to be liaisons with various ethnic, racial, religious, and sexual orientation groups in the community

- provided all attorneys on staff with cultural awareness or sensitivity training
- provided alternative sentencing programs aimed at rehabilitating individuals who commit hate-motivated crimes.

District attorneys can play a major role in educating judges on the nature, prevalence, and severity of hate crime and in encouraging effective sentences for this offense. They can also be very effective in their working relationships with and encouragement of police officers investigating these crimes. The effort involves each member of the criminal justice system, but the prosecutor has one of the most important roles.

Special Problems in Prosecuting Hate/Bias Crimes

Prosecutors confront an array of issues when considering a potential hate crime. Ascertaining the real motivation for someone's behavior is difficult, and actually proving that a person took an action because of hate can be an arduous task. Hate crime charges are the only ones for which proving motive becomes as important as proving modus operandi. Juries can often find it impossible to conclude with certainty what was going on in a defendant's mind during the crime. Attorneys who handle hate/bias crimes indicate that there are four potential obstacles to successful prosecutions:

1. Proving the crime was motivated by bias
2. Uncooperative, complaining witnesses
3. Special defenses
4. Lenient sentences

Given these obstacles, prosecutors sometimes have difficulty deciding whether to file hate crime charges. It is often difficult to accurately identify hate-motivated crimes or incidents. Usually, no single factor is sufficient to make the determination, and sometimes the perpetrator disguises the incident so that it does not appear to be a hate/bias crime. Even cases that have been well investigated may lack sufficient evidence to prove that the crime was motivated, beyond a reasonable doubt, by hate or bias. Generally, prosecutors follow established guidelines for determining whether a crime was bias-related. Their criteria include the following:

- Common sense
- Perceptions of the victim(s) and witnesses about the crime
- Language used by the perpetrator
- Background of the perpetrator
- Severity of the attack
- Lack or presence of provocation
- History of similar incidents in the same area
- Absence of any apparent motive

The American Prosecutor's Research Institute (APRI) developed a comprehensive desk manual for prosecutors for identifying, responding to, and preventing hate violence. The desk manual, entitled *A Local Prosecutor's Guide for Responding to Hate Crimes*, contains information about working with outside agencies and organizations, case screening and investigation, case assignment and preparation, victim and witness impact and support, trial preparation, sentencing alternatives, and prevention efforts. The manual could be useful in the development of a training curriculum specifically designed for prosecutors.

Objective Evidence: Bias Motivation

It is important that first responders and investigators properly identify and classify bias-motivated crimes. Officers unsure about identifying a potential hate/bias crime should consult with a supervisor or internal or external expert on the topic. To help investigators determine whether an incident meets sufficient objectively determined criteria to be classified as a hate/bias crime, the U.S. Department of Justice (DOJ) developed a document, "Hate Crime Data Collection Guidelines and Training Manual" (U.S. Department of Justice, 2012), which contains a series of examples related to the reporting of hate crime incidents. These examples are intended to ensure uniformity in reporting data to the state and the FBI's UCR Section. The following are a few examples of guidelines:

- The offender and the victim were of different racial, religious, ethnic/national origin, or sexual orientation groups. For example, the victim was black and the offenders were white.
- Bias-related oral comments, written statements, or gestures were made by the offender that indicated his or her bias. For example, the offender shouted a racial epithet at the victim.
- Bias-related drawings, markings, symbols, or graffiti were left at the crime scene. For example, a swastika was painted on the door of a synagogue.
- The victim was visiting a neighborhood where previous hate crimes had been committed against other members of his or her racial, religious, ethnic/national origin, or sexual orientation group and where tensions remain high against his or her group.
- Several incidents have occurred in the same locality, at or about the same time, and the victims are all of the same racial, religious, ethnic/national origin, or sexual orientation group.
- A substantial portion of the community where the crime occurred perceives that the incident was motivated by bias (U.S. Department of Justice, 2012).

Because of the difficulty of knowing with certainty that a crime is motivated by bias, the Hate Crimes Statistics Act stipulates that "bias is to be reported only if the investigation reveals sufficient objective facts that would lead a reasonable and prudent person to conclude that the offender's actions were motivated, in whole or in part, by bias" (U.S. Department of Justice, 2012).

The specific types of bias to be reported are as follows

Race:

Antiwhite

Antiblack or African American

Anti-American Indian or Alaskan Native

Anti-Asian

Anti-Native Hawaiian or Other Pacific Islander

Antimultiple Races, Group

Religion:

Anti-Jewish

Anti-Catholic

Anti-Protestant

Anti-Islamic (Muslim)

Anti–Other religion (Buddhism, Hinduism, Shintoism, etc.)

Antimultiple Religions, Group

Anti-Atheism/Agnosticism

Ethnicity:

Anti-Hispanic or Latino

Anti–Not Hispanic or Latino

Sexual Orientation:

Antigay (Male)

Antilesbian

Antilesbian, gay, bisexual, or transgender (Mixed Group)

Antiheterosexual

Antibisexual

Disability:

Antiphysical Disability

Antimental Disability

Gender:

Antimale

Antifemale

Gender Identity:

Antitransgender

Antigender nonconforming

Training is available from the U.S. Department of Justice to help criminal justice agency personnel make decisions regarding hate/bias crimes. Following are a few of those sources:

- Office for Victims of Crime (OVC)
- Bureau of Justice Assistance (BJA)
- Office of Juvenile Justice and Delinquency Prevention (OJJDP)

All three sponsor grants to agencies to fund the development of programs and to provide training seminars and technical assistance to individuals and local agencies regarding hate crimes. OVC is working to improve the justice system's response to victims of hate crimes; OJJDP funds agencies to develop training for professionals and to address hate crimes through preventive measures and community resources. BJA has a training initiative for law enforcement agencies designed to generate awareness and to help in identifying, investigating, and taking appropriate action for bias crimes, as well as arming agencies with tools for responding effectively to incidents.

Mini Case Study #1

It is Halloween 2008, and you are a police officer who receives 60 calls from different persons offended by an effigy showing the likeness of Republican vice presidential nominee Sarah Palin. The effigy is hanging by a noose from a tree on the front lawn of a home. (This occurred in October 2008, in West Hollywood, California).

You decide: Are federal, state, or local laws violated in this incident? Can officials order the offending effigy to be taken down? Could this be considered a hate crime? Is the display protected by the First Amendment? Apply what you learned in this chapter and discuss in class how the incident should be handled. Would this case be handled differently if the effigy were of a black person?

(Source: Kim and Abdulrahim, 2008).

Mini Case Study #2

Unknown persons enter a synagogue overnight and destroy many religious objects, draw swastikas on a door, and write "Death to Jews" on a wall. There are many items of value in the synagogue, but none are stolen.

You decide: How should the investigating officer report this incident, using the UCR Hate Crime Data Collection Guidelines?

Mini Case Study #3

A woman, who is transgender, is walking in a park when two men approach her. One says, "Hey, what are you doing here?" She continues walking, trying to avoid them, when the other man says, "We don't want no queers in our neighborhood," and hits her, knocking her to the ground.

You decide: How should the investigating officer report this incident, using the UCR Hate Crime Data Collection Guidelines?

Mini Case Study #4

Two white, gay men are walking through a neighborhood where a number of gay bars and businesses are located. Four Latino men approach them and hit one of them in the face, rendering him unconscious. The assailants then hurl antigay slurs at the men and demand their money and cell phones.

You decide: How should the investigating officer report this incident, using the UCR Hate Crime Data Collection Guidelines?

Sources 2, 3, and 4: U.S. Department of Justice, "Hate Crime Data Collection Guidelines and Training Manual" (2012).

Answers can be found in this chapter after the Summary.

HATE/BIAS CRIME AND INCIDENT VICTIMOLOGY

Meaningful assistance to victims of major crimes became a priority only in the 1980s. The growth of a body of "victimology" literature (President's Task Force on Victims of Crime created by President Ronald Reagan in 1982; the Omnibus Victim and Witness Protection Act of 1982; and the Comprehensive Crime Control Act of 1984, to name a few) and the emergence of numerous victim advocate and rights organizations began at about that time, reflecting a growing concern about crime, the victims of crime, and their treatment by the criminal justice system. The perception was that the defendant's rights were a priority of the system, while the victim was neglected in the process. As a result of the task force recommendations, state and federal legislation, and research by public and private organizations (most notably the National Institute of Justice), improvements were made in victim services and treatment as well as in the criminal justice system.

Law Enforcement and the Victim

In the law enforcement field, courses in recruit academies and advanced in-service officer programs typically include training about victimization that covers such topics as sociopsychological effects of victimization, officer sensitivity to the victim, victim assistance and advocacy programs, and victim compensation, restitution criteria, and procedures for applying. Classes normally stress the importance of keeping victims informed of their case status and of the criminal justice process. How patrol officers and investigators of such crimes interact with victims affects the victims' immediate and long-term physical and emotional recovery. Proper treatment of victims also increases their willingness to cooperate in the total criminal justice process. Because of such training programs, the victims of hate crimes began receiving special attention and assistance in progressive cities and counties all over the country.

Victims of hate/bias violence generally express three needs: (1) to feel safe, (2) to feel that people care, and (3) to get assistance. To address the first two needs, law enforcement agencies and all personnel involved in contacts with victims must place special emphasis on victim assistance to reduce trauma and fear. Such investigations sometimes involve working with people from diverse ethnic backgrounds, races, and/or sexual orientation. Many victims may be recent immigrants with limited English and unfamiliar with the American legal system, or may have fears of the police, courts, or government rooted in negative experiences from their countries of origin.

Therefore, the officer or investigator must be not only a skilled interviewer and listener but also sensitive to and knowledgeable about cultural and racial differences and ethnicity. He or she must have the ability to show compassion and sensitivity toward the victim and his or her plight while gathering the evidence required for prosecution. As when dealing with other crime victims, officers involved in the investigation must:

- approach victims in an empathic and supportive manner and demonstrate concern and sensitivity;
- attempt to calm the victim and reduce the victim's alienation;
- reassure the victim that every available investigative and enforcement tool will be utilized by the police to find and prosecute the person or persons responsible for the crime;
- consider the safety of the victim by recommending and providing extra patrol and/or providing prevention and precautionary advice;
- provide referral information to entities such as counseling and other appropriate public support and assistance agencies;
- advise the victim of criminal and civil options.

The stress experienced by victims of hate/bias crime or incidents may be heightened by a perceived level of threat or personal violation. Just like the victims of rape or abuse, many become traumatized when they have to recall the details of what occurred. Sometimes victims even transfer their anger or hostility to the officer—a psychological reaction called *transference*. The officer must be prepared for this reaction and must be able to defuse the situation professionally without resorting to anger. It is imperative that investigators and officers make every effort to treat hate crime victims with dignity and respect so that they feel that they will receive justice. Insensitive, brash, or unaware officers or investigators may not only alienate victims, witnesses, or potential witnesses, but also create additional distrust or hostility and cause others in the community to distrust the entire police department.

Addressing the victim's need to get assistance requires that the community provide resources that can assist the victim and the victim group. Few communities have the resources necessary to offer comprehensive victim services. Even where resources are available, victims are often unaware of them because of poor public awareness programs or the failure of the criminal justice system to make appropriate referrals because of a lack of training or motivation. A key resource is the availability of interpreters for non-English-speaking victims and witnesses. Ideally, jurisdictions with large populations of non-English-speaking minorities should recruit and train an appropriate number of bilingual employees. If the jurisdiction does not have an investigator who speaks the same language, an interpreter system should be in place for immediate callout.

Readers wishing additional information about how to deal with victims can refer to *The Victims of Crime*, by Jerin and Moriarty (2009)—a well-developed book. Another resource for first responders, *Bringing Victims into Community Policing*, was developed by the National Center for Victims of Crime (NCVC) and the Police Foundation. The publication, available on the NCVC Web site, provides guidelines for dealing with specific types of crime victims.

Law Enforcement and the Community

When it comes to hate/bias crimes, it is essential that law enforcement work with the community to:

- Reduce fears
- Stem possible retaliation
- Prevent additional bias incidents
- Encourage other victimized individuals to come forward and report crimes
- Condemn the bigotry that leads to violence
- Provide an outlet for collective outrage
- Create public awareness of the scope of bias crimes and prevention strategies
- Control rumors

(Source: National Center for Hate Crime Prevention, DOJ, 2000)

Summary

- The federal Hate Crime Statistics Act of 1990 encouraged states to collect and report hate crime data to the Federal Bureau of Investigation. The FBI, in partnership with local law enforcement agencies, collects data on hate/ bias incidents, offenses, victims, offenders, and motivations and publishes an annual report as part of the Uniform Crime Reporting (UCR) Program.
- In the United States, crimes motivated by hate have historically been directed against immigrant groups. Other victims include Native Americans, African Americans, and Jews; as well as Arabs, Muslims from multiple geographic regions, East Asians, South Asians such as Sikhs, as well as gays, lesbians, and bisexual and transgender individuals, and they continue to be victims of bias, discrimination, and crimes motivated by hate.

- The federal definition of hate crime falls under Title 18 U.S.C. Section 249. Although state definitions and statutes vary, in general a hate crime is considered to be a criminal act, or attempted act, against a person, institution, or property, that is motivated in whole or in part by the offender's bias against a race, color, religion, gender, ethnic/national origin group, disability status, gender or gender identity, or sexual orientation group.
- The prevalence of hate/bias crimes and incidents is often attributed to changing national and international conditions, immigration, and demographic changes translated to a local environment. Various theories attempt to explain hate crime and hate incidents as occurring due to the relationships among the clustering of new immigrant groups, the economy, and move-in violence.

- Jews belong to a religious and cultural group that has experienced discrimination, persecution, and violence throughout history because their religious beliefs and practices often set them apart from the majority.
- The acronym or initials LGBT refers to lesbian, gay, bisexual, and transgender people. Hate crimes targeting LGBT individuals are distinct from other bias crimes in that they target a group made up of every other category discussed within this textbook. Every year, in the United States, thousands of LGBT persons are harassed, beaten, or murdered solely because of their sexual orientation or gender identity.
- Criminal justice agencies must make hate/bias crimes a priority for response, from the initial report through prosecution. Law enforcement agencies must provide all responders and investigators with training on the various protocols relating to hate/bias crimes. It is often necessary for the agency to establish liaisons with diverse organizations in the community and with victim advocates.
- District attorneys' offices have established policies and procedures designed to prosecute hate/bias crimes effectively. This is necessary in order to establish a public safety climate that fosters the full enjoyment of civil and political rights by minority members of communities.
- Meaningful assistance to victims of hate/bias crimes should be a priority for members of the criminal justice system that investigate and prosecute perpetrators. Perpetrators of hate crimes commit them to intimidate a victim and members of the victim's community. Criminal justice agency employees dealing with the victims of hate/bias crimes must be aware of and sensitive to the sociopsychological effects of victimization.

Answers to Mini Case Studies:

1 What did you decide? In the actual incident, the mayor of West Hollywood appealed to the individuals who had hanged the effigy of Sarah Palin to take it down, and they ultimately did. Officials of the Secret Service, Los Angeles County Sheriff's Department, and Los Angeles city Code Enforcement Division each ruled the effigy violated no laws. A spokesman for the Sheriff's Department said, "This is a country that has freedom of speech, and we protect that right even when we think it's idiotic and stupid and in bad taste" (Kim & Abdulrahim, 2008). Others in the community who did not think the effigy was appropriate said if it was another presidential candidate hanging from a noose, or another ethnicity, it would have been treated as a hate crime. "But Peter Scheer, executive director of the California First Amendment Coalition and a free-speech expert, said the same display with Obama also would probably fall under protected speech, as long as it was not made with the intent of inciting violence" (Kim & Abdulrahim, 2008).

2 This incident should be reported with an Anti-Jewish Bias because the offenders destroyed religious objects and left anti-Semitic words and graffiti behind, and theft did not appear to be the motive for the burglary.

3 Even though an antigay slur was used during the attack, this incident should be reported with an Anti-Transgender Bias because the victim was attacked for presenting as a female despite having been born biologically male.

4 An antigay bias should be reported with this incident. The bias was evident in the attack, through the use of slurs, and in the selection of a gay area as the site of the attack, even though robbery was also a motive. Race should not be identified as the bias because there was no evidence of racial or ethnic animosity.

Discussion Questions and Issues

1. *Hate/Bias Crimes and Incident Reduction.* Make a list of important elements in the design of a community-based program to reduce the number of hate/bias crimes and incidents in your area.
2. *Move-In Violence.* Discuss, in a group setting, what strategies might be used by a community to reduce the impact of move-in violence on a new immigrant.
3. *Victims of Hate/Bias Crimes or Incidents.* Have you been the victim of a hate/bias crime or incident? Share the experience with others in a group setting: the circumstances, the feelings you experienced, how you responded, and what action was taken by any community-based agency or organization.
4. *Victim Resources.* Find out what resources exist in your community to assist victims of hate/bias crimes.

a. Which groups provide victim assistance?
b. Which coalition groups exist, and what types of community outreach programs are offered?
c. What types of pamphlets or other written materials are available?
d. Which groups have speakers' bureaus?
e. Which groups are working with local law enforcement agencies with regard to response programs or cultural awareness training?
f. Which groups are working with the district attorney's office?
g. What types of legislative lobbying efforts are taking place, and who is championing the work?

References

"ADL Applauds Law Enforcement for Arrests of Homegrown Terrorists in Plot to Blow up New York City Synagogues." (2009, May 21). Anti-Defamation League. Retrieved May 27, 2009, from www.adl.org/PresRele/ASUS_12/5532_12.htm

"ADL Audit: U.S. Anti-Semitic Incidents Declined 14 Percent in 2012." (July 22, 2013). Anti-Defamation League. Retrieved August 26, 2013, from www.adl.org/press-center/press-releases/anti-semitism-usa/adl-audit-us-anti-semitic-incidents-declined-14-percent.html

"ADL Decries the Anti-Semitic Vandalism of Five Jewish Institutions in Chicago." (2009, January 12). Anti-Defamation League. Retrieved April 20, 2009, from archive.adl.org/PresRele/ASUS_12/5442_12.htm

"ADL Poll Finds Anti-Semitic Attitudes on Rise in America." (2011, November 3). Anti-Defamation League. Retrieved August 22, 2013, from archive.adl.org/PresRele/ASUS_12/6154_12.htm

Ahearn, Laura. "Why are Hate Crimes Not Reported in the United States and in Suffolk County?" (2011, April). Crime Victims Center Hate Crime Task Force Recommendations. Retrieved August 2, 2013, from www.parentsformeganslaw.org/export/sites/default/Megans_proj/jsp/public/CRIMEV_x007E_2.PDF

Baker, Al and Javier Hernandez. (20 May 2009). "Four Accused of Bombing Plot at Bronx Synagogues." *The New York Times.* Retrieved August 22, 2013, from www.nytimes.com/2009/05/21/nyregion/21arrests.html

Bolles, Alexandra. (2012, June 4). "Violence Against Transgender People and People of Color is Disproportionately High, LGBTQH Murder Rate Peaks," GLAAD Organization. Retrieved August 27, 2013, from www.glaad.org/blog/violence-against-transgender-people-and-people-color-disproportionately-high-lgbtqh-murder-rate

Christie, Daniel J., Richard V. Wagner, and Deborah D. Winter (Eds.). (2001). *Peace, Conflict, and Violence: Peace Psychology for the 21st Century.* Englewood Cliffs, NJ: Prentice-Hall. Retrieved August 27, 2013, from academic.marion.ohio.state.edu/dchristie/Peace%20Psychology%20Book.html

Collins English Dictionary online. Retrieved July 26, 2013 from www.collsdictionary.com/dictionary/english.

Colvin, Roddrick A. (2013). *Gay and Lesbian Cops: Diversity and Effective Policing.* Boulder, Colorado: Lynne Rienner Publishers.

"Couple suspected in slayings planned to 'kill more Jews.'" (2011, October 12), *Contra Costa* (Calif.) *Times*, p. A7.

"Cyberbullying FAQs for Teens." National Crime Prevention Council. Retrieved July 25, 2013, from www.ncpc.org/topics/cyberbullying/cyberbullying-faq-for-teens

"Detroit Becomes Largest U.S. City to File for Bankruptcy." (2013, July 19). *Contra Costa* (Calif.) *Times*, p. A1, A9.

Fahim, Kareem. (2010, October 18). "4 Convicted of Attempting to Blow Up 2 Synagogues." *The New York Times.* Retrieved August 22, 2013, from www.nytimes.com/2010/10/19/nyregion/19plot.html

Foxman, Abraham H. (2005, April 22). "After 350 Years, Still a Lot to Do." *Haaretz.* Retrieved April 20, 2009, from www.haaretz.com/print-edition/opinion/after-350-years-still-a-lot-to-do-1.156780

Ford, Zack. (2012, September 5). "GLSEN Releases New School Climate Report: 82 Percent Of LGBT Students Still Encounter Verbal Harassment." *Think Progress.* Center for American Progress. Retrieved July 24, 2013, from thinkprogress.org/lgbt/2012/09/05/797501/glsen-releases-new-school-climate-report-8

"Gay killing draws call for change." (2008, March 29). *Contra Costa* (Calif.) *Times*, p. A7.

Grobeson, Mitchell. (2013). Sergeant (Ret.), Los Angeles Police Department, personal communication.

"Hate Crime Data Collection Guidelines and Training Manual." (2012, December 19). U.S. Department of Justice FBI Criminal Justice Information Services Division Uniform Crime Reporting Program. Retrieved April 15, 2013, from www.fbi.gov/about-us/cjis/ucr/hate-crime/data-collection-manual.

"Hate Crime Statistics, 2011." (2013, December). Federal Bureau of Investigation. Retrieved May 8, 2013, from www.fbi.gov/about-us/cjis/ucr/hate-crime/2011

"Hate Crime Victimization, 2003-2011." (2013, March). U.S. Department of Justice, Bureau of Justice Statistics Special Report. Retrieved May 8, 2013, from www.bjs.gov/content/pub/pdf/hcv0311.pdf

"Hate Violence Against Lesbian, Gay, Bisexual, Transgender, Queer, and HIV-affected Communities In the United States in 2011." (2012). The National Coalition of Anti-Violence Programs. Retrieved May 8, 2013, from www.avp.org/storage/documents/Reports/2012_NCAVP_2011_HV_Report.pdf

"H.R. 1913, Local Law Enforcement Hate Crimes Prevention Act of 2009." (2009). *Legislative Digest.* Digest for H.R. 1913, 111th Congress, 1st Session. Retrieved July 24, 2013, from www.GOP.gov/bill/111/1/hr1913

Jacobs, James B. and Kimberly Potter. (1998). *Hate Crimes: Criminal Law & Identity Politics.* New York, NY: Oxford University Press.

Jerin, Robert A. and Laura J. Moriarty. (2009, January 21). *The Victims of Crime.* Upper Saddle River, NJ: Prentice Hall.

Kim, Victoria and Raja Abdulrahim. (2008, October 29). "Uproar Continues over Palin Effigy" *Los Angeles Times.* Retrieved August 9, 2013, from articles.latimes.com/2008/oct/29/local/me-palineffigy29

"LGBT Homeless." (2012, February 21). National Coalition for the Homeless. Retrieved July 24, 2013, from www.national-homeless.org/factsheets/lgbtq.html

Medina, Jennifer. (2012, April 24) "In Years Since the Riots, a Changed Complexion in South Central." *The New York Times.* Retrieved August 22, 2013, from www.nytimes.com/2012/04/25/us/in-south-los-angeles-a-changed-complexion-since-the-riots.html?pagewanted=all&_r=0

Newman, Bruce. (2013, May 21). "Poverty Continues to Rise in Suburbs." *Contra Costa* (Calif.) *Times*, p. B4.

"New Studies Examine Violence Directed at Transgender People of Color." (2011, September 29). Basic Rights, Oregon.

Retrieved August 27, 2013, from www.basicrights.org/news/trans-justice-news/new-studies-examine-violence-directed-at-transgender-people-of-color/.

Noelle, Monique. (2002). "The Ripple Effect of the Matthew Shepard Murder: Impact on the Assumptive Worlds of Members of the Targeted Group." *American Behavioral Scientist, 46*(1), 27–50.

"Obama Signs Expanded Violence Against Women Act." (2013, March 7). *Fox News.* Retrieved March 11, 2013, from www.foxnews.com/politics/2013/03/07/obama-signs-expanded-violence-against-women-act/

"Online Racism." (2010, September 26). *Contra Costa* (Calif.) *Times*, pp. AA, AA2.

Potok, Mark. (2013). "The Year in Hate and Extremism." *Southern Poverty Law Center.* Intelligence Report, Spring 2013, Issue 149. Retrieved August 20, 2013, from www.splcenter.org/home/2013/spring/the-year-in-hate-and-extremism

"Responding to Hate Crime: A Multidisciplinary Curriculum." (2000, February). The National Center for Hate Crime Prevention Education Development Center, Inc. Retrieved May 8, 2013, from https://www.ncjrs.gov/ovc_archives/reports/responding/files/ncj182290.pdf

Richmond, Josh. (2013, May 9). "Barbara Lee bill would push states to roll back criminal HIV laws." *San Jose (Calif.) Mercury News.* Retrieved August 30, 2013, from www.lee.house.gov/barbara-lee-bill-would-push-states-roll-back-criminal-hiv-laws. . .

Sacco, Dena T., Katharine Silbaugh, Felipe Corredor, June Casey, and Davis Doherty. (2012, February 22). "An Overview of State Anti-Bullying Legislation and Other Related Laws." Berkman Center for Internet & Society at Harvard University. Retrieved July 29, 2013, from cyber.law.harvard.edu/publications/2012/state_anti_bullying_legislation_overview

Schafer, John R. and Joe Navarro. (2003, March 1). "The Seven-Stage Hate Model: The Psychopathology of Hate Groups." *FBI Law Enforcement Bulletin,* Number 72. Retrieved July 30, 2013, from www.au.af.mil/au/awc/awcgate/fbi/7stage_hate_model.pdf

"State Hate Crimes Laws." (2013, June 19). Human Rights Campaign. Retrieved July 29, 2013, from www.hrc.org/files/assets/resources/hate_crimes_laws_062013.pdf

Strasser, Annie-Rose. (2013, January 9)."Virginia KKK Uses Obama's Presidency As A Recruiting Tool." ThinkProgress, Center for American Progress. Retrieved August 3, 2013, from thinkprogress.org/justice/2013/01/09/1422471/virginia-kkk-obama-recruiting/

Washington, Jesse. (2008, November 16). "Obama Election Spurs Race Crimes Around Country." *USA Today.* Retrieved August 20, 2013, from usatoday30.usatoday.com/news/nation/2008-11-15-2960000388_x.htm

"What Motivates Hate Offenders." (2008, January 9). *National Institute of Justice.* Retrieved August 3, 2013, from www.nij.gov/topics/crime/hate-crime/motivation.htm

"Working to Halt Online Abuse." Retrieved July 29, 2013, from www.haltabuse.org/resources/laws/

Zeveloff, Naomi (2012). "U.S. Jewish Population Pegged at 6 million." The Jewish Daily Forward. Retrieved August 30, 2013, from forward.com/articles/149492/us-jewish-population-pegged-at--million/

12 Hate/Bias Crimes
Reporting, Monitoring, and Response Strategies

LEARNING OBJECTIVES

After reading this chapter, you should be able to:

- Discuss the nationwide reporting system for hate crime data collection.
- Explain the need for standardized and comprehensive statistics for the analysis of trends related to hate crimes and bias.
- Identify extremist hate groups and organizations that monitor them.
- Develop community response strategies to reduce hate crimes and incidents.
- Understand the scanning methodology and approaches for hate/bias crimes in multicultural communities.

OUTLINE

INTRODUCTION

Changing demographics in almost every part of the United States require that all localities deal with issues of inter-group relations. The ideal of harmony in diversity is offset by increased stress on the social fabric of a community, stress that often leads to bigoted or violent acts. Newspaper headlines across the country provide convincing examples of disharmony on a daily basis. Hate/bias crimes are not a new phenomenon; they have been present for generations. It is crucial for law enforcement to maintain accurate and thorough documentation of such crimes.

Data must be collected at local levels and sent in a standardized fashion to state and national clearinghouses so that proper resources may be allocated to hate/bias crime investigations, prosecutions, and victim assistance. Such a system provides information necessary not only to the criminal justice system, but also to public policymakers, civil rights activists, legislators, victim advocates, and the general public. The data, if comprehensive and accurate, provide a reliable statistical picture of the problem. Agencies collecting data have also been able to use the statistics to strengthen their arguments and rationale for new hate crime penalty enhancements. In addition, the information is used in criminal justice training courses and in educating communities on the impact of the problem. Another, and possibly the most important, rationale for expending energy on tracking, analyzing, investigating, and prosecuting these crimes is that a single incident can be the tragedy of a lifetime to its victim and may also be the spark that disrupts an entire community.

Increased public awareness of and response to such crimes have largely been the result of efforts by community-based organizations and victim advocate groups. By documenting and drawing public attention to acts of bigotry and violence, these organizations laid the groundwork for the official action that followed. It is extremely important that hate groups across the United States be monitored by criminal justice agencies. Documenting and publicizing a problem does not guarantee it will be solved, but is a critical part of any strategy to create change. It also raises consciousness within the community and the criminal justice system. It is a simple but effective first step toward mobilizing a response.

HATE/BIAS CRIMES REPORTING

Purpose of Hate/Bias Crime Data Collection

Establishing a good reporting system within public organizations (e.g., human relations commissions) and the justice system is essential in every area of the country. Hate/bias crime data are collected to help police:

- Identify current and potential problems (i.e., trends)
- Respond to the needs of diverse communities
- Recruit a diverse force
- Train criminal justice personnel on the degree of the problem and the reasons for priority response

When police have information about crime patterns, they are better able to direct resources to prevent, investigate, and resolve problems pertaining to them. Tracking hate/bias incidents and crimes allows criminal justice managers to deploy their resources appropriately when fluctuations occur. Aggressive response, investigation, and prosecution of these crimes demonstrate that police are genuinely concerned and that they see such crimes as a priority. As departments show their commitment to addressing hate/bias crime, the diverse communities they serve will be more likely to see police as responsive to their concerns. A secondary benefit for a responsive agency is that blacks, Asians, Hispanics, lesbians, gays, and women would be more apt to consider law enforcement as a good career opportunity.

The Boston Police Department began recording and tracking civil rights violations in 1978, when it created its Civil Disorders Unit. Boston was probably the first law enforcement agency in the United States to record and track such crimes. The Maryland State Police Department was also a forerunner when it began to record incidents on a statewide, systematic basis as part of a pioneering government-wide effort to monitor and combat hate violence in 1981. Agencies that implemented policies and procedures to deal with hate/bias crimes during the 1980s proved to be leaders in the field; in addition to Boston and Maryland, New York, San Francisco, and Los Angeles had forward-looking programs. The policies and procedures of these agencies have been adopted as models by other organizations.

Congressional Directive: Federal Hate Crime Legislation

In response to a growing concern and in an attempt to understand the scope of the hate crime problem, the U.S. Congress enacted the federal Hate Crimes Statistics Act (HCSA) of 1990. The Act and subsequent legislation pertaining to hate crime is discussed in detail in Chapter 11. The Act requires the attorney general to establish guidelines, and to collect and publish data on the prevalence of crimes that "manifest evidence of prejudice based on race, religion, sexual orientation, or ethnicity" (1990). The U.S. Attorney General delegated his agency's responsibilities under the Act to the FBI. The Uniform Crime Report (UCR) section of the FBI was assigned the task of developing the procedures for and managing the implementation of the collection of hate crime data. The national clearinghouse for hate/bias crime data enables the criminal justice system to monitor and respond to trends in those localities that voluntarily submit the information.

As part of the UCR Program, the FBI publishes statistics annually in *Hate Crime Statistics*. However, most states lack a central repository for police intelligence on hate crimes. That means an investigator working in one city might not even know about a critical piece of information gathered in another location within the same state during a different incident. In 2000, California unveiled what it called the first high-tech database in the country aimed at combating hate crimes. The state implemented a computer system allowing police departments statewide to call up names, mug shots, and even the types of tattoos that identify particular individuals or groups linked to hate crimes.

HATE/BIAS CRIMES MONITORING

Monitoring Hate Groups

Monitoring extremist groups is an important obligation of law enforcement. A nationwide criminal justice reporting system tracks these groups, and their activities are also monitored through nongovernmental organizations such as:

> *Southern Poverty Law Center (SPLC):* The nonprofit Southern Poverty Law Center, located in Montgomery, Alabama, monitors and investigates organizations and individuals whom it deems "hate groups" and "extremists" and publishes a quarterly *Intelligence Report*. The organization considers the monitoring of white supremacist groups on a national scale and the tracking of hate crimes among its primary responsibilities. The SPLC also offers free legal services to victims of discrimination and hate crimes. The organization publishes e-mail newsletters "Hatewatch Weekly," "Mix It up Monthly," "Tolerance.org," and "Teaching Tolerance," and, in 2006, added "Immigration Watch" to report on and monitor hate and extremism in the anti-immigration movement. The Center, which began as a small civil rights law firm in 1971, is now internationally known for its publications about hate/bias, tolerance education programs, legal victories against white supremacist groups, and tracking of hate groups.
>
> Over the years, SPLC has won lawsuits against many supremacist groups, including White Aryan Resistance, Church of the Creator, Christian Knights of the KKK, Aryan Nations, and Imperial Klans of America (IKA). The legal actions resulted in the taking of those groups' assets, which crippled or ended their operations. In some cases, the assets have included homes of white supremacists and the land and/or compounds they used for meetings. A court action against IKA, the second-largest Klan organization in America, was brought in November 2008. The suit was brought against five members who

committed an unprovoked attack on a 16-year-old boy of Panamanian descent at the Meade County Fairgrounds in Brandenburg, Kentucky ("No. 2 Klan Group on Trial in KY Teen's Beating," 2008).

Anti-Defamation League (ADL): The Anti-Defamation League was founded in 1913 "to stop the defamation of Jewish people and to secure justice and fair treatment to all citizens alike." The ADL has been a leader of national and state efforts in the development of legislation, policies, and procedures to deter, investigate, and counteract hate-motivated crimes. The organization is also respected for its research publications and articles dealing with such crimes. The ADL developed a recording system that has served as a model of data collection nationwide since its launch in 1979.

National Gay and Lesbian Task Force (NGLTF) **and** ***NGLTF Policy Institute:*** The NGLTF works to eradicate discrimination and violence based on sexual orientation and Human Immunodeficiency Virus (HIV) status. The NGLTF was founded in 1973 to serve its members in a manner that reflects the diversity of the lesbian and gay community. In 1991, the task force was restructured into two organizations—the NGLTF and the NGLTF Policy Institute—to improve its lobbying efforts and expand its organizational and educational programs.

Simon Wiesenthal Center: The Simon Wiesenthal Center, based in Los Angeles, is a human rights group named after the famed Nazi hunter. It monitors the Internet worldwide for tactics, language, and symbols of the high-tech hate culture. The center shares its information with affected law enforcement agencies. The organization, in some states, also operates Holocaust exhibits that are used as shocking examples of atrocities committed against Jewish people during World War II. Police academies and in-service, advanced officer training courses often use the exhibits for training on hate violence.

ORGANIZED HATE GROUPS

Knowledge of hate groups is essential when policing in a multicultural society. It is imperative for the criminal justice system to investigate (using methods including informants, surveillance, and infiltration), monitor, and control organized hate groups. Aggressive prosecution and litigation against these groups are also critical.

THE WHITE SUPREMACIST MOVEMENT   "The white supremacist movement is composed of dozens of organizations and groups, each working to create a society totally dominated by white Christians, where the human rights of lesbians and gay men and other minorities are denied. Some groups seek to create an all 'Aryan' territory; others seek to re-institutionalize Jim Crow segregation" (Center for Democratic Renewal, 1992). While most of these organizations share a common bigotry based on religion, race, ethnicity, and sexual orientation, they differ in many ways. They range from seemingly innocuous religious sects or tax protesters to openly militant, even violent, neo-Nazi skinheads and Ku Kluxers. No single organization or person dominates this movement. Frequently, individuals are members of several different groups at the same time. An SPLC Intelligence Report asserts that for the last several years white supremacist groups have focused their attention on Latino immigrants, and in particular on those who are in the country illegally. The supremacists had historically targeted blacks and Jews. These hate groups have exploited the controversy surrounding illegal immigration in order to recruit more members, especially in the states bordering Mexico.

NUMBERS OF HATE GROUPS IN THE UNITED STATES   The SPLC, as previously mentioned, tracks active hate groups in the United States. They identify groups by gathering information from hate group publications, citizens' reports, law enforcement agencies, field sources, and news reports. The number of groups known to be active fluctuates and is determined by surveying marches, rallies, speeches, meetings, leafleting, Web sites, published literature, and criminal acts. Some white supremacist groups consist of only a few members, while others have tens of thousands. In 2012, the Southern Poverty Law Center reported that there were 1,007 active hate groups in the United States and 602 in 2000. This is an increase of 69 percent since 2000 (see Exhibit 12.1). California had the most hate groups, with 82, followed by Texas with 62 and Florida with 59 (Southern Poverty Law Center, 2012). According to the SPLC, these hate groups in 2012 included:

- 186 separate Ku Klux Klan groups with 52 Web sites
- 196 neo-Nazi groups with 89 Web sites
- 111 white nationalist groups with 190 Web sites
- 98 white power skinhead groups with 25 Web sites
- 39 Christian Identity groups with 37 Web sites
- 93 neo-Confederate groups with 25 Web sites
- 113 black separatist groups with 40 Web sites
- 90 additional groups of various categories such as antigay, Holocaust denial, and others.

These numbers are likely due to high illegal immigrant populations in these states, a circumstance that historically has contributed to a rise in hate groups. In addition to immigration issues, the SPLC report ascribes the increase in the number of hate groups to the economic recession and the election of the first African American president. The report explains that bigoted extremists emerge in greater numbers during bad economic times, and they focus blame for the downturn on specific groups of people. The SPLC points out that President Barack Obama received more threats than any president in history, and that there were numerous cases of beatings, graffiti, and threats toward other African American citizens following his election.

Hate groups are categorized by the SPLC as Ku Klux Klan (KKK), Neo-Nazi, Racist Skinhead, Christian Identity, Black Separatist, Neo-Confederate, Patriot, and Other. The "Other" category includes groups, vendors, and publishing houses endorsing a hodgepodge of racist doctrines. Although the numbers of white supremacists in the United States are small in comparison with the total population, Loretta Ross, formerly program research director of the Center

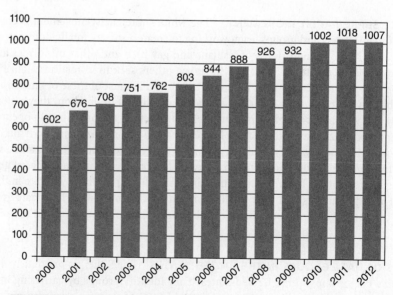

EXHIBIT 12.1   Hate Groups 2000–2012

Source: The Year in Hate and Extremism, Intelligence Report, Issue 149. Copyright © 2013 by Southern Poverty Law Center. Used by permission of Southern Poverty Law Center.

for Democratic Renewal, a now-closed organization that tracked hate groups, explains why they should be taken seriously:

> Because the percentage of whites who actually belong to white supremacist groups is small, there is a general tendency to underestimate their influence. What is really significant is not the number of people actually belonging to hate groups, but the number who endorse their messages. Once known primarily for their criminal activities, racists have demonstrated a catalytic effect by tapping into the prejudices of the white majority. (Ross, 1995)

The following is a partial list of hate groups with brief descriptions and ideology. Over the years, each group's membership and activities have fluctuated, for many reasons.

Neo-Nazis and Klans

The reason for concern about the activities of neo-Nazis and Klans is obvious from their history of criminal activities, and their plots to launch race wars and kill officials who oppose them.

The largest of the neo-Nazi and Klan groups include the following:

Neo-Nazi-Type Groups	**Klan-Type Groups**
Aryan Nations	Alabama White Knights of the KKK
Knights of Freedom	America's Invisible Empire Knights of the KKK
National Alliance	American Knights of the KKK
Nationalist Socialist Movement	Imperial Klans of America
World Church of the Creator (Creativity Movement)	Invincible Empire Knights of the KKK
	Knights of the White Kamellia
	New Order Knights of the KKK
	White Shield Knights of the KKK

The ideology of Klan members, neo-Nazis, and other white supremacists has been clear since the formation of these groups. They commonly advocate white supremacy, anti-Semitism, homophobia, racism, and an anti-illegal-immigrant philosophy.

The most violent groups are the neo-Nazis, and their movements are growing in the United States and in countries such as Germany and Austria. Young people in the age group of 13 to 25 years who wish to join these organizations are required to commit a hate crime as part of the induction process. They openly idealize Hitler, and have committed murders and hundreds of assaults as well as other violent crimes; most of their victims are African Americans, Latinos, Asian Americans, gays, lesbians, bisexuals, transgender individuals, and even the homeless.

WORLD CHURCH OF THE CREATOR OR CREATIVITY MOVEMENT The World Church of the Creator (WCOTC), classified as a neo-Nazi-type group, was founded in 1973 by Ben Klassen, who wrote the organization's manifesto, *The White Man's Bible*. The organization's existence ended in mid-1990 following the suicide of Klassen and the imprisonment of other leaders. In 1996, however, the WCOTC was reborn under the leadership of Matt Hale. The group's rallying cry is "Rahowa," which stands for Racial Holy War. The group is also violently anti-Christian. A judge of the U.S. District Court in Chicago ruled in December 2002 that the WCTOC, founded in Illinois, would have to surrender the name because an Oregon-based religious group already had a trademark on it. The group now calls itself the Creativity Movement and makes a concerted effort to encourage women and children to become members. The organization has been tough to control because of its quasi-religious facade, which allows its members to gather for meetings in prison.

ARYAN NATIONS The group Aryan Nations was formed in the early 1970s by Richard Butler. The organization virtually collapsed when he died in 2004, but under his leadership it was America's most notorious neo-Nazi group. Although there are still small factions in some states, Aryan Nations is no longer considered powerful as it was. The organization preaches that God's creation of Adam marked "the placing of the White Race upon this earth," that all nonwhites are inferior, and that Jews are the "natural enemy of our Aryan (white) race" (Anti-Defamation League, 2009).

THE NATIONAL ALLIANCE The neo-Nazi group National Alliance (NA) believes it is subject to nature's laws only; therefore, members are able to determine their own destiny regardless of laws imposed by the government. They profess that those who believe in a divine control over mankind absolve themselves of responsibility for their fate. They also believe they are members of the Aryan (or European) race and are superior to other races. The NA is headquartered in Hillsboro, West Virginia. For many years, it was the largest and best-organized neo-Nazi group in the United States. The group owns a white power music company that sells racist music and paraphernalia primarily to skinheads (Anti-Defamation League, 2009). On January 17, 2011, hundreds of people had come together to celebrate Martin Luther King, Jr. Day in Spokane, Washington. Kevin Harpham, a member of the National Alliance and former artilleryman in the U.S. Army, had hidden a homemade bomb in a backpack along the parade route. A city worker found it and alerted authorities, who changed the parade route, disarmed the bomb, and ultimately arrested Harpham. He was convicted and sentenced to 32 years in prison for a hate crime plus offenses related to the attempted bombing. FBI Special Agent Frank Harrill, who supervised the investigation, said that Harpham "targeted those who were attempting to celebrate an event meant to unite society and he was prepared to indiscriminately kill men, women, and children" ("MLK Parade Bomber: Horrific Hate Crime Prevented; Case Solved," 2012).

Racist Skinheads

According to the Anti-Defamation League, "racist skinheads are among the most dangerous radical-right threats facing law enforcement today" (Anti-Defamation League, 2009). It is important that law enforcement and corrections become familiar with these groups' history, ideology, insignias, tattoos, apparel, and means of operation. They are known for being hard to track because they are organized into small, mobile "crews" which move around frequently and without warning. They can act independently of other members or network in their verbal and physical attacks, sometimes violent, upon the persons or property of Jews, blacks, Hispanics, immigrants, gays, lesbians and others.

Membership of young adults, both men and women, in racist skinhead groups has grown considerably since 1986. According to a 2009 report by the ADL, the United States has seen a "significant and troubling" resurgence of racist skinhead activity (Anti-Defamation League, 2009).

The ADL report cites several factors for this resurgence:

- Alienated white youth have found a welcome reception on the Internet from white supremacists hungry for new recruits. The Internet has made it very easy for young people to be exposed to online message forums and social networking Web sites prevalent in the racist skinhead subculture.
- The white power music industry, around which the racist skinhead subculture revolves, has experienced a substantial growth in online promotion and sales.
- Racist skinhead groups such as Hammerskin Nation and Blood & Honor have expanded globally using the Internet to create a network of international white supremacist sites and giving haters in different parts of the country—indeed, the world—the ability to connect online.

- Less competition from the major established white supremacist groups, whose activity has diminished due to the arrests or deaths of leaders and serious factional infighting. (Anti-Defamation League, 2009)

Racist skinheads are often easily recognized because a significant part of their subculture is their dress and appearance. They typically have closely shaven heads, many visible tattoos and piercings, and skinhead-related garb such as work boots (with red laces) and suspenders. It should be noted, however, that some influential white supremacists have advocated that their members try to blend in more with the community. Some followers heeded the advice and regrew their hair, covered or removed their tattoos, and acquired legitimate jobs, thus enabling them to carry out their racist activities more covertly. As a result of this "revolutionary action," not every skinhead fits the profile (Anti-Defamation League, 2009). Some skinheads are transient and do not join groups. Because of this, the SPLC indicates that their numbers are hard to assess. Law enforcement and corrections officers should also be aware, however, that "the skinhead subculture was not originally racist—and, in fact, today around the world there remain many non-racist or explicitly anti-racist skinheads (often called sharps, for 'skinheads against racial prejudice)" (Anti-Defamation League, 2009).

The influence of adult white supremacist groups on racist skinheads and neo-Nazi skinheads has been substantial, since the adult hate groups seek to replenish their membership ranks from the younger groups.

In October 2008, two men from a rural county in Tennessee, described as neo-Nazi skinheads, were arrested by federal authorities. They were charged with possessing an unregistered firearm, conspiring to steal firearms from a federally licensed gun dealer, and, more seriously, plotting to kill 88 people with plans for beheading 14 of them. The killing spree was to have included a black school and ultimately targeted the Democratic candidate for president, Barack Obama. According to a newspaper account of the incident, "the numbers 14 and 88 are symbols in skinhead culture . . . referring to a 14-word phrase attributed to an imprisoned white supremacist: 'We must secure the existence of our people and a future for white children' and to the eighth letter of the alphabet, H. Two '8's or 'H's stand for 'Heil Hitler.'" Authorities stated that "there did not appear to be any formal assassination plan, [but the authorities] took the threats seriously" ("Obama Assassination Plot Foiled," 2008). These numeric codes are sometimes used by neo-Nazis to avoid the use of Nazi symbols, such as the *swastika*, so they can attend events and not stand out except to others who identify with their racist beliefs. The number 28, for example, is a symbol that signifies "BH" (the 2nd and 8th letter of the alphabet), which stands for "Blood and Honor." According to the ADL, "These symbols might be found on the outside walls of synagogues, churches, schools; depicted on fliers and literature distributed in communities; tattooed on the bodies of white supremacists, or proudly displayed as jewelry or on clothing" (Anti-Defamation League, 2005).

There are many skinhead groups, but the **American Front**, described as a militia-style organization, is known for domestic terrorism. Eleven members were arrested in May 2012 in Florida for planning acts of violence and preparing for "an inevitable race war" (Morlin, 2012).

Christian Identity

Christian Identity describes a movement that is fundamentally racist, anti-Semitic, and antihomosexual. According to the SPLC, the active Identity groups across the United States are organized under different names but with similar ideologies. The goal of these groups is to broaden the influence of the white supremacist movement under the guise of Christianity. They form their views of diverse people based on a particular interpretation of the Bible. The movement takes the position that white Anglo-Saxons—not Jews—are the real biblical "chosen people," and that blacks and other nonwhites are "mud people" on the same level as animals and therefore are without souls ("Hate Crime on the Internet," 1999). Identity followers believe that the Bible commands racial segregation, interpreting racial equality as a violation of God's law.

POSSE COMITATUS   Another Identity group is Posse Comitatus, which means "power of the country" in Latin. The group is antitax and anti–federal government. Members of the Posse believe that all government power is vested in the county rather than at the federal level.

Black Separatists

The SPLC has identified black separatist groups active in the United States under two different names: the House of David and the Nation of Islam. Black separatist groups are organizations whose ideologies include tenets of racially based hatred. Black separatist followers share the same agenda as white supremacists: racial separatism and racial supremacy. The two movements also share a common goal of racial purity and a hatred of Jews.

Despite the differences between black extremist and white supremacist groups, and their mutual contempt, these groups are able to join rhetorical forces to demean and slander Jews.

Patriot Groups

According to the SPLC annual "Hatewatch" publication, there has been "very significant growth of the radical right . . . [anti-government] 'Patriot' groups, what we used to call militia groups. There were 149 of these groups in 2008. . . . That number as of 2012 was 1,360. That's 813% growth in four years" (Fallon, 2013). The SPLC report states that gun control is one of the main issues leading to the growth of this movement, both in the 1990s and again in 2012–2013. It should be noted, however, that some of the Patriot groups listed by the SPLC deny that they are antigovernment or manifest hate toward anyone.

RESPONSE ALTERNATIVES TO ORGANIZED HATE GROUPS

Law enforcement agencies must actively work to fight and control organized hate groups, tracking their activities, establishing when they are responsible for crimes, and assisting in their prosecution. Intelligence gathering is crucial to the efforts to reduce and prevent hate/bias crimes. Equally important is networking and sharing hate group information with other criminal justice agencies. Many have called this approach a cross-disciplinary coalition against racism. It involves statewide and regional commitments by criminal justice agencies to work with other public and private entities, including the Internal Revenue Service. All the institutions jointly develop and implement components of multitiered intervention strategies targeting enforcement, education, training, victim assistance, media relations, political activism and advocacy, and ongoing self-evaluation.

The fight begins with an assessment of the size and scope of the various supremacist groups, their movements, their leaders, and their publications. When hate crimes are perpetrated against one group in the community, law enforcement must immediately alert any other organizations that are potential targets. For example, if a synagogue is the object of an arsonist, law enforcement should notify not only other synagogues and Jewish organizations, but also the National Association for the Advancement of Colored People (NAACP), National Council of La Raza, and other minority organizations in the region, state, and adjoining states. The investigating agency should also notify other law enforcement agencies (city, county, state, and federal) in their county and region of the incident as well.

TRENDS AND PREDICTIONS FOR ORGANIZED HATE GROUPS

Some experts predict that white supremacists will continue to commit traditional crimes (such as cross-burnings and vandalism) but will also venture into high-tech activities such as computer system infiltration and sabotage. Their political activism will include "white rights" rallies, protests, and demonstrations; election campaigns by racist candidates; and legislative lobbying.

These activities are expected to incite counter movements and will create very labor-intensive situations for law enforcement to handle.

Observers of hate groups have also noted the shift in tactics of white supremacists in the United States. Discovering that supremacists could no longer effectively recruit members using the ideology of open racism with the focus on persons of color, Jews, immigrants, and the like, they are now targeting lesbians and gays. According to those who study hate groups, supremacists find that while many whites may share their racial, religious, and ethnic prejudices, most are no longer willing to act on them openly. Thus a new strategy is being employed that combines old hatreds with new rhetoric. This new approach does not imply that supremacists no longer hate people of color, Jews, and so on. Rather, it means they are refocusing their energies; they are exploiting white fear of change; and they have adopted as a prominent part of their new agenda not only homophobia but also antiabortion, anti-immigration, and the so-called pro-family and pro-American values, in addition to their traditional racist and anti-Semitic beliefs. Ross says the broadening of issues and the use of conservative buzzwords have attracted the attention of whites who may not consider themselves racist but do consider themselves patriotic Americans concerned about the moral decay of "their" country (Ross, 1995).

Organizations and officials tracking hate groups have offered other predictions on the evolution and future of hate groups. These experts believe groups that have traditionally shunned or actively opposed each other for ideological reasons will join forces against their "common enemies." For one example among many, although neo-Nazis have long despised Arabs and Muslims, they have increasingly allied with Arab and Muslim extremists against common enemies, most often Jews. American neo-Nazis have also been increasingly cooperating with their counterparts in Europe.

The Internet and Hate Groups

One disturbing trend is observed in the age and gender of new members of supremacist groups: there are more younger members than in the past (including teenagers), and many are young women. Organized hate is no longer the exclusive domain of white men over 30 years of age. As noted previously, the Internet, including Facebook, Twitter, and the like, has become the medium of choice for recruiting young members to hate groups and for disseminating hate dogma and racist ideology. The Internet enables people to spread hate around the world instantaneously, in a cheap, easy, and anonymous manner. The medium provides hate groups the ability to send unsolicited mass e-mailings simultaneously into millions of homes, some of them seeking to recruit today's affluent and educated youth to their cause. Their hundreds, or possibly thousands, of Web sites entice viewers with online games, comic strips, and music, or simply a friendly pitch from another kid. College and university sites are being bombarded with messages and lures from hate groups. In some areas the Internet is also being used to provide tips on how to target groups' opponents with violence. Internet providers must work with the police, within the realm of freedom-of-speech requirements, to enforce their own standards and to block hate dogma Web sites or hate e-mail within their system.

First Amendment versus Hate Speech

The sight of members of the Westboro Baptist Church of Topeka (Kansas) picketing outside many military funerals has provoked outrage across the United States. The unaffiliated church, which consists primarily of the members of one family, believes that military deaths are God's punishment for U.S. tolerance of homosexuality. The members hold signs with offensive, antigay messages such as "God Hates You" and "God Hates Fags" not only at funerals, but also at other events that attract a lot of people, such as football games and concerts. Members travel nationally to picket funerals of LGBT victims of murder or those who have died from AIDS. The church has been described as a hate group and is monitored by the SPLC and the ADL. The United States Supreme Court, in a free-speech ruling that challenged popular opinion, ruled that even deliberately obnoxious funeral protests were protected by the First Amendment ("Hate Speech Still Free Speech," 2011).

HATE/BIAS CRIME AND INCIDENT CONTROL

Hate/bias crimes and incidents can be controlled only through the combined efforts of the community (schools, private organizations, government agencies, churches, service organizations, and families), federal and state legislatures, and the criminal justice system—a holistic approach. It is important to profile communities to determine whether they are at risk of strife or conflict caused by the social, economic, and environmental conditions that can result in hate crimes and incidents.

Identifying Communities at Risk

COMMUNITY PROFILING Law enforcement agencies experiencing demographic changes in their communities are well advised to perform an analysis of what is taking place: community profiling. It is important to know if the numbers of any group are increasing and why. The assessment should include estimates of the number of those who might be in the country illegally. Such a profile must include a sense of timing: what can the community and law enforcement personnel expect from profiled groups with regard to the observance of holidays and religious or cultural ceremonies?

> **Community Profiling** Demographic analysis of a community with regard to the ethnicity/national origin, race, religion, and sexual orientation of groups whose members work or reside there.

Progressive agencies send their patrol officers lists of religious and cultural holidays and world crisis events that could affect the area they serve. If officers wait to identify at-risk communities until after hate crimes are committed, they are not fulfilling their professional responsibilities. Knowing how to identify at-risk communities and then committing resources to resolve problems before they escalate is proactive police work, which is crucial to preventing conflict. While this involves more departmental time and personnel initially, the ultimate savings through the prevention of community disruption is well worth the effort.

NEIGHBORHOOD AND POLICE PARTNERSHIP Neighborhoods (citizens and all those local institutions encompassed by the term) working together with the police provide the best means of identifying communities at risk. How does a city determine if a neighborhood is at risk? Who is responsible for the assessment? What strategies can be utilized to mitigate the at-risk status? The best approach is community policing, described in Chapter 14, whereby police help the community protect itself and enhance the quality of life of its members. Officers and citizens meet to discuss the neighborhoods' most serious problems and work together to resolve them.

> **At-Risk Communities** Communities having a high level of criminal activity or disorder and usually a higher number of incidents of civil rights violations—hate/bias crimes, discrimination, racism, and bigotry.

Community policing encourages officers to delve into observations and feelings to determine not only what is happening, but also who is involved, what their motivation is, and where they are from. Officers should consider themselves as first-line intelligence assets for their community. For example, they should watch for graffiti and/or other materials posted on walls, fences, telephone poles, and buildings. These markings could signal a racist operation in progress or a locally active hate group. In addition, to be effective, officers who patrol highly diverse areas must have some degree of cultural awareness and ability to engage in cross-cultural communication. It has been said that if officers are scrambling to understand communities only after a crime is committed, it is a terrible indictment of their lack of professionalism.

In addition, officers must know neighborhood leaders and ways to locate them quickly if they are needed to provide general assistance or to help control rumors or people. Neighborhood leaders can also provide invaluable help when it comes to dealing with victims who distrust police. A problem-focused approach provides officers with a solid understanding of social, economic, and environmental problems in the community. There are limits to what the police can do without community help. In many communities, however, police first have to overcome their traditional role identification as crime fighters independent of the community before they can become an integral part of a team that works together to solve local problems. When officers patrol neighborhoods daily, they can interact with citizens to engender trust and can monitor their activities. Herman Goldstein, University of Wisconsin law professor and the architect of the problem-oriented policing (POP) concept, said that "the police department, more than any other agency of government, must have a bird's eye view of the dynamics within its community, including the demographics, agendas of various groups, and an in-depth understanding of the hopes, aspirations and frustration of various groups. This will give the police a feel for the mood and tensions that exist within a community" (Parker, 1991).

ROLE OF HUMAN RELATIONS COMMISSIONS (HRCS) Many cities and counties nationwide have established community HRCs. Created as independent agencies, they are responsible for fostering equal opportunity and eliminating all forms of discrimination. These objectives are accomplished by means of investigating, mediating, and holding public hearings on problems that arise from discrimination prohibited by federal, state, and local laws. Most HRCs will not investigate incidents of discrimination where such a function is preempted or prohibited by state or federal legislation. In cases where there is a violation of state or federal law, the HRC refers the complainant to the appropriate agency. It then monitors the progress of the complaint. Each HRC has established procedures that govern how it receives, investigates, holds hearings on, and mediates and resolves complaints. Confidentiality is a protected right of the complainant in discrimination cases reported to HRCs. As established by state or federal law, the names of the parties may not be made public, with a few exceptions, without the written consent of both parties involved. Human relations commissions should also be part of the community–police partnership, in which they all take responsibility for educating their community about its diversity. This includes serious and sustained efforts to bring people together for dialog.

COMMUNITY RELATIONS SERVICE (CRS) The CRS, an arm of the U.S. Department of Justice, is a specialized federal conciliation service available to state and local officials to help prevent and resolve racial and ethnic conflict, violence, and civil disorder. When governors, mayors, police chiefs, and school superintendents need help to defuse racial or ethnic crises, they turn to CRS. This service helps local officials and residents tailor locally defined resolutions when conflict and violence threaten community stability and well-being. Created by the Civil Rights Act of 1964, CRS is the only federal agency dedicated to preventing and resolving racial and ethnic tensions, incidents, and civil disorders. CRS gathers data in seven areas: demographic balance, administration of justice (particularly police–community relations), employment, education, housing, health and welfare, and community relationships. The statistical data is then used to assess six critical factors:

1. Relationship of minorities to the administration of justice system
2. Impact of the economy
3. Level of minorities' inclusion in and/or exclusion from the system, and the number of minorities serving as elected officials
4. Quality of intergroup relationships
5. Current level of violence in the community/neighborhood and/or city
6. Basic demographic influences

It is time consuming to perform this type of analysis and to develop a program based on the findings. Police departments have access to the same kind of data and they possess a great deal of the experience and expertise necessary to complete the same type of analysis within neighborhoods, if they choose to do so.

TRENDS TO MONITOR: STEEP TYPOLOGY

Trend Monitoring in Multicultural Communities

Monitoring conditions in a community provides useful information for forecasting potential negative events and preparing accordingly. The framework for evaluating any predictions should include an analysis of economic circumstances, social and cultural conditions, as well as the political environment within the community.

The acronym STEEP stands for social, technological, environmental, economic, and political. There is often a connection between the economy, social conditions, and politics and the numbers of hate/bias crimes that occur. This relationship is explained in Chapter 11. It is important for agency personnel and officers involved in community-oriented policing to understand the basic economic, social, and political issues contributing to social unrest.

Economic Circumstances

Crime, social unrest, riots, and disturbances have often occurred during depressed economic times, as mentioned in Chapter 11. Waves of immigrants (both legal and illegal) also add to the scramble for available jobs and services. Internationally, poverty, overcrowding, and wars have been pressuring more people to migrate than ever before, laying the conditions for what the United Nations called "the human crisis of our age." In Florida, for example, refugees from Cuba and Haiti flooded the state in the 1980s and 1990s. Many areas experienced real conflict as established residents who were already struggling now had masses of people competing with them for services and jobs. California continually experiences legal and illegal immigration from Mexico and Central and South America. The new immigrants (the weakest group) become the target for people's frustrations as their own sense of well-being decreases. The established ethnically and racially mixed groups in neighborhoods see what they perceive as preferential treatment for the newcomers and react accordingly.

Federal decisions that lead to settlement of immigrants into economically depressed communities have frequently been made without regard to the adequacy of local resources to handle the influx. Subsequent polls reflect an increase in anti-immigrant attitudes. Eventually, police and community problems evolve as a consequence of these well-meaning national policies that have not been thoroughly worked through. Tracking influxes of immigrants into communities, plus an awareness of political decisions, should keep law enforcement executives and officers alert to relocation and acculturation problems of newcomers in their communities. Tracking also provides an opportunity to work with the community to develop transition management plans as well as preventive programs for keeping the peace. National immigration policies and politics have a tremendous impact on cities and counties, and therefore criminal justice agencies must monitor them and plan accordingly.

Henry DeGeneste and John Sullivan wrote the following in *Fresh Perspectives*, a Police Executive Research Forum publication in 1997, and clearly it is still true today:

> Urban tensions are fueled by a combination of . . . wealth disparity and the pressures of large scale migration, which are present not only in American cities, but in cities worldwide. . . . [Robin] Wright [a journalist for the *Los Angeles Times*] notes, "[T]ensions in cities are often complicated by another dimension—racial or ethnic diversity." Minorities are increasingly left stranded in urban outskirts— slums or squatter camps—and excluded politically and financially. Their ensuing frustrations contribute to the volatility of urban life.
>
> Conflict (such as riots) resulting from urban decay, overcrowding, poor social services and ethnic tension has occurred in cities worldwide and can be expected to continue, particularly as swelling migrant populations flock to cities. (DeGeneste and Sullivan, 1997)

A survey by the Pew Research Center, described in *The New York Times*, determined that "conflict between rich and poor now eclipses racial strain and friction between immigrants and native-born as the greatest source of tensions in American Society. . . . About two-thirds of Americans believe there are 'strong conflicts' between rich and poor in the United States" (Tavernise, 2012).

Political Environment

Executives of criminal justice agencies must monitor legislation, sensitive court trials, and political events that affect not only the jurisdictions they serve, but also the nation and the world. Often what goes on outside of the United States has an impact on local populations. Law enforcement must be aware of foreign political struggles and their potential to polarize ethnic and racial groups in the local community, leading to conflict. Police must have the ability to recognize potential problems and strive to prevent or mitigate intergroup conflict. Only by acknowledging their primary role in preventing and mediating conflict in the community can peace officers begin to remediate long-standing and emerging tensions. The criminal justice system cannot operate in a vacuum.

Social and Cultural Conditions

Typically, poverty and frustration with the system, the perception of racism, and unequal treatment are conditions for social unrest. Diverse peoples living in close proximity can also create potentially unstable social conditions. Furthermore, on the familial level, a decline in the cohesiveness of the nuclear family (including divorce) adds to stresses within micro units in society. Unemployment, especially among youth, is another social condition with potentially dangerous consequences.

Finally, gangs and the use of illegal drugs and their impact on neighborhoods lead to social and cultural conditions ripe for explosive events. None of these elements alone, however, account for community violence. But all these factors, in combination with political and economic conditions, contribute to discontent. Officers frequently are frustrated because they cannot undo decades of societal precursors that set the stage for upheavals.

LAW ENFORCEMENT RESPONSE STRATEGIES

Public confidence and trust in the criminal justice system, and law enforcement in particular, are essential for effective response to hate/bias crimes. Residents in communities where people of a race, ethnic background, religion, or sexual preference different from their own reside must be able to trust that they will be protected. They must believe that the police are not against them, that the prosecutors are vigorously prosecuting, that the judges are invoking proper penalties, and that parole, probation, and corrections are doing their share to combat crimes motivated by hate or bias. If people believe they have to protect themselves, tensions build, communication breaks down, and people try to take the law into their own hands.

Community Programs to Reduce and Control Hate Crimes

Some solutions to reduce hate/bias crimes involve going back to basics, involving grassroots institutions such as families, schools, workplaces, and religious organizations. Partnerships between the criminal justice system and these institutions are often more successful in instituting crime reduction programs than is the criminal justice system alone. However, some institutions that once built positive values or exercised some control over people are no longer working or have diminishing influence. The broken or dysfunctional family, for example, contributes significantly to society's problems, including the increase in criminal activity.

An effort must be made to reinstitute values that reinforce noncriminal behavior; law enforcement must be an integral part of that movement. The status quo policing approach (reactive) will not work anymore. "People have clearly begun to recognize that our strict law enforcement arrest approach isn't getting the job done," notes Darrel Stephens (2006), former executive director of the Police Executive Research Forum. Progressive criminal justice executives and communities realize that crime has multiple and complex causes and that police departments are neither the first nor the only line of defense. If crime is to be controlled, there must be a community alliance or partnership and the causes must be attacked on multiple fronts.

Generic Community Resources and Programs

Community resources and programs that are available or can be established include:

- *Victims' Hotline:* Similar to those available for domestic violence and rape victims, and suicide prevention. The staff is trained to provide victim assistance in terms of compassion, advice, referrals, and a prepared information package.
- *Human Relations Commission:* The staff provides assistance to victims of hate crimes or incidents, holds hearings, and provides recommendations for problem resolution.
- *United States Department of Justice Community Relations Service:* The CRS, with headquarters in Washington, D.C., has 14 regional and field offices and provides services to every state. The Justice Department has trained staff who, when notified of a problem, will participate in and mediate community meetings in an attempt to resolve conflicts. Many states have similar justice agencies that perform these services.
- *Conflict Resolution Panels:* Specially trained staff of a city or county who can assist agencies and/or victims (including groups) in the resolution of conflict, such as that caused by hate or bias.
- *The Media:* Cooperation in building public awareness of the problem of hate/bias violence via articles on causes and effects, resources, and legal remedies is essential.
- *Multilingual Public Information Brochures:* These can be provided by government agencies on the rights of victims, services available, and criminal and civil laws related to hate and bias.
- *Police Storefronts:* Police substations, established in the neighborhoods of communities with high concentrations of ethnic minorities, which are staffed by bilingual officers and/or civilians. The staff takes reports and provides assistance to the members of that community.
- *Community Resource List:* List of organizations that specialize in victim assistance. Examples are the Anti-Defamation League, Black Families Associations, Japanese American Citizens Leagues, the NAACP, and the Mexican American Political Association, to name a few. The importance of establishing networks with minority leaders and organizations

cannot be overstressed. These networks are extremely important for criminal justice agencies and should be identified and cultivated in advance so the leaders will be available and willing to assist in a timely fashion with investigations, training, victim aid, and/or rumor control. If an agency experiencing serious hate/bias problems does not react quickly and effectively, victims and their community groups gain media attention when they publicly question an inadequate response or resolution. If a system involving trust and respect is already in place, such a network proves its worth when violence occurs in the agency's community. A good relationship with representatives of diverse communities is essential because it can help broaden the department's understanding of different cultures, ethnicities, and races. The same is true of members of gay and lesbian groups. When community members are utilized within departments, they can also help convince reluctant victims and/or witnesses to cooperate with investigators. Furthermore, they can encourage more victims to report incidents.

The key to a successful law enforcement response to hate crimes is building a partnership with victimized communities. There are many components and processes in building such a partnership. Other activities and events characterizing such a joint effort would include educating the public at large, providing organizational networking opportunities, monitoring the media, and implementing federal, state, and county programs. The activities for each are described in the following sections.

EDUCATING THE PUBLIC AT LARGE   Prejudice and bias, which can ultimately lead to violence, are often the result of ignorance. In many cases the biased individual has had little or no firsthand exposure to the targeted group; thus the bias may be due to learned stereotypes and negative media images.

One key to combating ignorance is to educate the public as well as criminal justice system employees about the history, diversity, cultures, languages, and issues of concern of the various groups within the community. This can be accomplished through neighborhood forums, workshops, and speakers' bureaus. The speakers' bureaus should be composed of people who are well versed on the issues and are available to speak at community meetings, schools, and other forums. Criminal justice employees, of course, would be trained in the workplace and/or through in-service or academy-based training courses. Most cities and counties have organizations that represent community groups that can assist in developing and implementing such education at local elementary and secondary schools, in churches, and on college and university campuses. To check the accuracy of material presented, organizers of educational programs should have at least two or three minority community members provide input on the content of the program to be delivered. Preferably, they would represent the different subgroups within the community. Neighborhoods and community residents should be encouraged to observe their various heritages through the celebration of holidays and other special days via fairs and festivals. Calendars show that there are more holidays for different religions and cultures in the United States than anywhere else in the world.

ORGANIZATIONAL NETWORKING   National and local organizations must network to share information, resources, ideas, and support regarding crimes motivated by hate. The list of potential organizations would include the NAACP, the ADL, the Committee against Anti-Asian Violence, the NGLTF, and the SPLC.

Such advocacy organizations can construct an invaluable bridge to victim populations and assist in urging citizens to come to the police with information about hate crimes. Most of these organizations have publications and reports covering such topics as how to respond to bigotry, trends in racism, and community organizing. Through networking, organizations or groups learn who their allies are, increase their own resources and knowledge about other minority groups, and form coalitions that make a greater impact on the community and the criminal justice system. They can also assist criminal justice agencies in dealing with community reactions to hate violence and help the victims of violence cope with the experience.

The Phoenix (Arizona) Police Department offers a good example of organizational networking. In 1994, a hate crimes advisory board with representation from most of Phoenix's ethnic groups was created. The knowledge that members shared about their communities, cultures, and potential hot spots was highly beneficial. Such partnerships between human rights groups, civic leaders, community leaders, and law enforcement can advance police–community relations by demonstrating a commitment to be both tough on those responsible for hate crimes and aware of the special needs of hate crime victims.

MONITORING THE MEDIA   Minority organizations and the criminal justice system must monitor the media, which can be a foe or an ally. The media must be used strategically for education and publicity about hate/bias crimes and incidents, about multicultural and multiracial workshops, and about festivals and other cultural events. They must be monitored in terms of accuracy of reporting and must be asked to publish corrections when warranted. Negative editorials or letters to the editor pertaining to an affected group should be countered and rebutted by an op-ed piece from within management of the involved criminal justice agency. Organization leaders or their designated spokespersons should make themselves available as the primary sources of information for reporters to contact.

FEDERAL, STATE, AND COUNTY PROGRAMS   Police executives should seek out every source of federal, state, and county law enforcement assistance programs and make the information available to investigators and/or task forces investigating or preventing hate crimes.

CHURCHES, MOSQUES, AND SYNAGOGUES   Where the usual support organizations (such as the ACLU, NAACP, and ADL) do not exist, and sometimes even where they do, churches, mosques, and synagogues often are advocates for people facing discrimination and/or who are victims of a hate incident or crime.

Communities with Special Programs

Some jurisdictions have used a community approach to decrease the numbers of crimes and incidents of all types, including those motivated by hate/bias. Some exemplary programs include the following:

- *Town Watch:* Operation Town Watch is an organization located in the City of Philadelphia which is dedicated to the development and promotion of organized, law enforcement-affiliated crime and drug prevention programs. Members include: Neighborhood, Crime, Community, Town and Block Watch Groups; law enforcement agencies; state and regional crime prevention associations; and a variety of businesses, civic groups and concerned individuals working to make their communities safer places to live and work. The organization promotes neighborhood safety through community policing and support services.
- *Task Force on Police–Asian Relations:* In localities that have large Asian populations, task forces have been created that consist of criminal justice professionals, educators, victim/refugee advocates, volunteer agency representatives, and representatives from each Asian group living or working in the community. The purposes are several: to train criminal justice employees on communication techniques that improve relations and make them more effective in dealing with the Asian community; to prepare Asians on what to expect from the various criminal justice components, especially the police; to open lines of communication between law enforcement and Asians; and to encourage Asians to report crimes and trust the police. These task forces could certainly be

adapted to other ethnic and racial groups as well. The city of Boston and other cities have effectively used the task force approach to resolve neighborhood problems, and have found them to be effective for exchanging information and curtailing rumors; identifying problems and working on solutions; and, perhaps most important, allowing citizens to help with and approach problems on a joint basis. Boston also has the Asian Task Force Against Domestic Violence, which provides resources, a newsletter, tips, and links to receive assistance.

- **_School Programs:_** The Maine Office of the Attorney General's Civil Rights Team Project, created in 1996 with the help of a U.S. Department of Justice, Bureau of Justice Administration grant, uses teams of students and faculty members to promote awareness of bias and prejudice in its public high schools, middle schools, and elementary schools. Their stated mission is that no students in the state should have to experience anxiety, fear, or terror in school because of their color of the skin, religion, gender, sexual orientation, or disability, or any other aspect of themselves that makes them different from other students. Law enforcement works together with teachers and administrators to empower students to stand up for civility and respect. The teams are made up of three or four students per grade, plus two or three faculty advisers. The teams have two formal responsibilities: (1) to promote awareness of bias and prejudice within their schools and (2) to organize forums for students to talk about harassment. If a team receives information about harassment, it is charged with forwarding that information to a responsible teacher or administrator. The Attorney General's office assigns a community adviser to each team to serve as liaison between the team and the Office. Annually, the Attorney General's office provides full-day training for new and returning civil rights teams and for faculty and community advisers. This training includes:

  - a presentation on the type of hate crimes committed in Maine schools
  - interactive exercises on the role of degrading language and slurs in escalating a situation to serious harassment and violence
  - a presentation by a Holocaust survivor or a victim of bias and prejudice
  - role-playing exercises on how to run effective civil rights team meetings
  - small-group work using real-life scenarios

  All participating schools agree to host Attorney General's office staff for a half-day workshop for faculty, administrators, and staff. The workshop gives teachers and other school staff a better understanding of the destructive impact of degrading language and bias-motivated harassment and teaches them how to intervene when students engage in such behavior. A similar project within the schools was created in Massachusetts.

Such community models, including those of churches and synagogues, can play a vital role in reducing violence in neighborhoods, schools, and the workplace. Successfully implemented programs can reduce individual violence, ranging from street crime to domestic abuse to drug-related crimes. Civil unrest, which can often include gang violence and open confrontations between various segments of society, can also be reduced. Building bonds of trust between the police and the community also allows community-oriented policing to contribute to the goal of promoting color-blind policing, where citizens and their police form new partnerships that offer the promise of reducing the potential for civil unrest.

Stephen Wessler, for the Bureau of Justice Administration (BJA), prepared a research paper, "Addressing Hate Crimes: Six Initiatives That Are Enhancing the Efforts of Criminal Justice Practitioners" that describes six BJA-funded projects that involve efforts of local, state, and federal law enforcement agencies in combating bias-motivated crime. The paper identifies projects that support police and prosecutorial agencies in responding to hate crimes and supplies sources for additional information. The monograph (NCJ 179559), can be found on the Web site of the National Criminal Justice Reference Service.

Mini Case Study: Lewiston, Maine, 2001 to the Present

The ongoing, changing relationship between the people of Lewiston, Maine, and its Somali population can be used as a case study, illustrating the strategies suggested in this text.

After reading the case study below, consider these questions:

1. What other methods could be employed in Lewiston to address the tensions and ease the Somalis' assimilation into that community?
2. Could Lewiston have predicted the arrival of more Somalis and prepared for them? What strategies have you learned that could be used?

In the year 2000, the census of the small city of Lewiston, Maine, counted approximately 35,000 people, including 361 black residents, none of whom were Somali. Then refugees from that African country began to arrive to escape civil war, poverty, and political or religious persecution. Many had been waiting for years in refugee camps in Kenya for an opportunity to come to America. Some of the newcomers came to Lewiston from Somali communities elsewhere in the United States, looking for cheaper housing, better schools, and a better social environment. They were also seeking more generous government assistance programs than those in the metropolitan areas from which they moved. The Somalis wanted to protect their children from exposure to gangs, drugs, and violence as well as racial prejudice they found in the big cities. After September 11, 2001, however, the Somalis' decision to move to Maine became easier when employers and the general public in the big cities became suspicious of them and many lost their jobs.

At first these immigrants were welcomed to Lewiston. Over the years, as their numbers increased, tension at times ran high. Friction occurred as the city's resources (jobs, schools, welfare, housing) were overwhelmed and competition for them increased; language problems were

also a factor. Some in the community began to react in racist and discriminatory ways toward the Somalis.

In early 2003, the World Church of the Creator (WCOTC) and the National Alliance planned a rally at a local college to exploit these reactions to the growing Somali community. These two groups saw the friction in Lewiston as an opportunity to organize the community against the Somalis. But the city and its police department responded by creating a steering committee for a new group, the "Many and One Coalition," which had 200 members. Taking advice from the SPLC (especially its publication *Ten Ways to Fight Hate: A Community Response Guide*) and other local and national human rights groups, they planned the community's response to the impending rally. An outreach coordinator for the SPLC Tolerance Project came to Lewiston days prior to the rally to help the town organize its efforts. The day before the rally, the college hosted a forum on issues of tolerance and diversity. The following day, about 5,000 townspeople showed up for a separate rally in support of diversity and the Somali community. Only 30 people turned out for the hate rally.

As of the beginning of 2009, Lewiston had the largest percentage of Somalis of any U.S. city—approximately 3,500. Although not every problem associated with the Somalis has been resolved, over the years the city has made many accommodations. The city hired an English-speaking Somali to work as a liaison officer and added an AT&T language translation line for Somali callers. Schools implemented adult education and "English as a second language" programs. Cultural exchange programs were established in which residents could learn about the Somali culture, and Somalis, about American. Most Somalis have assimilated into the community and are accepted by the local population.

Sources: Southern Poverty Law Center, 2003; Martin, 2005; "Tensions Flare over Somalis in Lewiston," 2007; "Tension over Somali Refugees in Maine," 2007.

Mini Case Study: Immigrants from Asia Settle in Long-Established Neighborhoods

After reading about what occurred in San Francisco, California, respond to these questions:

1. Should the San Francisco Police Department have foreseen and planned response strategies for what took place in this neighborhood?
2. What community programs might be utilized to reduce crimes against seniors in this neighborhood for both groups?
3. How could community networking between the police department and national, regional, state and/or local organizations and the neighborhood have been employed?
4. How could community educational programs via the media and schools have been used?
5. What other steps would you take if it were your responsibility to plan strategies to bring harmony to and fewer attacks against the citizens of the neighborhood?

6. What community policing resources could be used to prevent, investigate, and resolve the issue of any citizen in the neighborhood becoming the victim of crime?

Attacks in 2010 against elderly and vulnerable Asians in an affordable area of San Francisco, which had been historically a primarily black neighborhood, resulted in a wedge that divided the two minorities. Asian immigrants held rallies at City Hall complaining that they were targets of racially motivated violence. In all cases, according to police investigations, the perpetrators were black teenagers. Many black residents of the area and activists expressed their displeasure at the outcries of the Asian immigrants, saying that this sort of violence had been happening to African American seniors for a long time; and thus that anyone moving into a neighborhood where there is violence can become a victim. These tensions were exacerbated by economic stresses at the time as well as deep language and cultural barriers between the Asian immigrants and black members of the neighborhood.

Summary

- The U.S. Congress enacted the federal Hate Crimes Statistics Act (HCSA) of 1990. The collection of hate/bias crime data enables the criminal justice system to monitor and respond to trends in those localities that voluntarily submit the information.
- Standardized and comprehensive statistics for hate/bias crimes provide information to law enforcement agencies so they can monitor and respond to trends. The tracking of these crimes allows criminal justice managers to deploy their resources appropriately when fluctuations occur. Aggressive response, investigation, and prosecution demonstrate that police are genuinely concerned and that they see such crimes as a priority.
- The criminal justice system must be proactive and react swiftly to crimes by hate groups. It will let the hate groups know that their actions will result in apprehension and prosecution. A result of proactive enforcement is that other members of the community will also become sensitive to the impact of hate/bias crimes on victims and how the criminal justice system responds. A secondary benefit is that blacks, Asians, Hispanics, Native Americans, lesbians, gays, women and any other victimized group would be more apt to consider law enforcement as a good career opportunity.
- Knowledge of hate groups is essential when policing in a multicultural society. It is imperative within the criminal justice system that organized hate groups be investigated, monitored, and controlled. Aggressive prosecution of these groups is also critical. It is equally important that criminal justice agencies develop a method for networking in order to share information about hate groups.

- Extremist hate groups are categorized as Ku Klux Klan, Neo-Nazi, Racist Skinhead, Christian Identity, Black Separatist, Neo-Confederate, and Other. The "Other" category includes groups, vendors, and publishing houses that endorse racist doctrines.
- Hate/bias crimes and incidents can be controlled only through the combined efforts of the community. This includes schools, private organizations, government agencies, churches, service organizations, families, federal and state legislatures, and the criminal justice system. It is important to profile communities to determine whether they are at risk of strife or conflict caused by the social, economic, and environmental conditions that can result in hate crimes and incidents. Monitoring conditions in a community provides useful information for forecasting potential negative events and for preparing accordingly.
- The framework for evaluating any predictions should include an analysis of economic circumstances, social and cultural conditions, as well as the political environment within the community. Some solutions for reducing hate/bias crimes involve grassroots institutions such as families, schools, workplaces, and religious organizations. Partnerships between the criminal justice system and these institutions are often more successful in instituting crime reduction programs than is the criminal justice system alone.
- Progressive criminal justice executives and communities realize that crime has multiple and complex causes and that police departments are neither the first nor the only line of defense. The key to a successful law enforcement response to hate crime is a strong partnership between law enforcement and the victimized communities.

Discussion Questions and Issues

1. *Hate Crimes Monitoring Systems:* Does your law enforcement agency have a system in place for monitoring hate/bias crimes and incidents? If yes, obtain a copy of the statistics for at least the past five years (or for as many years as are available) of the hate/bias crimes and determine the following:
   a. What trends are noticeable in each category?
   b. Do the categories measure essential information that will assist your law enforcement agency in recognizing trends?
   c. What would improve the data collection method to make it more useful in measuring trends and making predictions?
   d. Has your law enforcement agency actually used the data to track the nature and extent of such crimes and incidents? Did it deploy resources accordingly? Provide the class with examples.

2. *Trend Monitoring:* Make a list of specific community social, economic, and political conditions and events occurring within the law enforcement jurisdiction in which you work or live. Which ones, if any, could potentially be connected to crimes motivated by hate? For each condition listed, make a "Comments" column. Suggest what specific factors a peace officer or criminal justice practitioner should look for in the community that would assist the agency in forecasting trends and events.

3. *Resources:* Find out what resources exist in your community to assist victims of hate/bias crimes.
   a. Which groups provide victim assistance?
   b. Which coalition groups exist, and what types of community outreach programs are offered?
   c. What types of pamphlets or other written materials are available?
   d. Which groups have speakers' bureaus?
   e. Which groups are working with local law enforcement agencies with regard to response programs or cultural awareness training?
   f. Which groups are working with the district attorney's or prosecutor's office?

4. *Role of Your District Attorney's Office:* Assess the role of your district attorney's or prosecutor's office by determining the following:
   a. Does it have a special hate crimes or civil rights unit?
   b. Do hate crime cases receive special attention?
   c. Are misdemeanor and felony hate crimes prosecuted differently?
   d. How does the office determine if it will prosecute a hate crime case?
   e. What types of training do assistant district attorneys receive regarding hate crimes?
   f. What types of community outreach does the district attorney's office provide regarding hate crimes?

5. *Victim Assistance:* Identify avenues of victim assistance in your area. Research and document the following:
   a. Does your state have a crime victims' assistance program? Does it offer victim compensation? What about a victim's bill of rights?
   b. What services does the local department of mental health staff offer?
   c. Do any community groups, rape crisis centers, or crime victim services agencies in the area offer counseling to hate crimes victims?
   d. Are any mental health care professionals willing to donate their services to victims of hate crimes?

6. *Human Relations Commission:* What is the role of the human relations commission, if one exists in your area?
   a. Does it have a specific task force on hate crimes?
   b. Does it have any type of tracking system for recording statistics on hate crimes?
   c. What is its relationship with local law enforcement agencies and district attorneys' offices regarding hate crimes?
   d. What is its relationship with community organizations concerned with hate crimes? Has it produced any brochures, pamphlets, or other materials on hate crimes?
   e. Does it provide multicultural workshops or sensitivity training regarding different ethnic, racial, and lifestyle groups?
   f. Have there been occasions when the HRC has gone beyond the scope of its charter or stated goals that resulted in negative exposure or media attention? Describe the circumstances.

References

Anti-Defamation League. (2005). "Hate on Display: About the Symbols." Retrieved April 15, 2013, from www.archive.adl.org/hate_symbols/about.asp

Anti-Defamation League. (2009). *Racist Skinhead Project.* Retrieved April 20, 2013, from www.archive.adl.org/racist_skinheads/ (accessed April 20, 2013).

Center for Democratic Renewal. (1992). *When Hate Groups Come to Town: A Handbook of Effective Community Responses.* Atlanta, Georgia: Center for Democratic Renewal.

DeGeneste, Henry I., and Sullivan, John P. (1997, July). "Policing a Multicultural Community." *Fresh Perspectives.* Washington D.C.: Police Executive Research Forum.

Fallon, Kevin. (2013). "Southern Poverty Law Center: Right-Wing Hate Rises Along With Obama." *The Daily Beast.* Retrieved April 15, 2013, from www.thedailybeast.com/articles/2013/03/09/southern-poverty-law-center-right-wing-hate-rises-along-with-obama.html

Federal Bureau of Investigation. (2007). *Hate Crime Statistics, 2007.* Retrieved April 15, 2013, from www.fbi.gov/about-us/cjis/ucr/hate-crime/2007

Hate Crime on the Internet: Hearing Before the Committee on the Judiciary, United States Senate, 106th Cong. (1999) (statement of Howard Berkowitz, national chair, Anti-Defamation League).

Hate Crimes Statistics Act (HCSA) of 1990. Public law 101-274, 101st Congress. (April 4, 1990).

"Hate Speech Still Free Speech." (2011, March 3). *Contra Costa* (Calif.) *Times,* pp. AA, AA2.

Martin, Susan Taylor. "A Collision of Cultures Leads to Building Bridges in Maine." (2005, March 13). *St. Petersburg Times,* p. 1A. Retrieved April 15, 2013, from www.sptimes.com

"MLK Parade Bomber: Horrific Hate Crime Prevented; Case Solved," (2012, January 13). Retrieved April 15, 2013, from www.fbi.gov/news/stories/2012/january/hatecrime_011312

Morlin, Bill. (2012, May 14). "Court Documents: American Front was Planning Violence." *Hatewatch Blog.* Retrieved April 15, 2013, from www.splcenter.org/blog/2012/05/14/court-documents-american-front-was-planning-violence/

"No. 2 Klan Group on Trial in KY Teen's Beating." (2008, November 11). *New York Examiner,* p. 2.

"Obama Assassination Plot Foiled." (2008, October 28). *Contra Costa* (Calif.) *Times,* p. 1, 13.

Parker, Patricia A. (1991, December). "Tackling Unfinished Business: POP Plays Valuable Position in Racial Issues." *Police,* 19, 5–9.

Potok, Mark. (2013, Spring). Southern Poverty Law Center. "The Year in Hate and Extremism." Intelligence Report, Issue 149. Retrieved April 15, 2013, from www.splcenter.org/home/2013/spring/the-year-in-hate-and-extremism

Ross, Loretta. (1995). "White Supremacy in the 1990s." *Public Eye (Political Research Associates).* Retrieved April 15, 2013, from www.publiceye.org/eyes/whitsup.html

Southern Poverty Law Center. (2003, March). "Maine Town's Diversity Rally Outdraws Hate-Group Gathering." Vol. 33, No. 1, p. 8.

Southern Poverty Law Center. (2012). "Hate Map." Retrieved April 15, 2013, from www.splcenter.org/get-informed/hate-map

Stephens, Darrel W. (2006). Personal communication.

Tavernise, Sabrina. (2012, January 12). "Survey Finds Rising Perception of Class Tension." *The New York Times.* Retrieved April 15, 2013, from www.nytimes.com/2012/01/12/us/more-conflict-seen-between-rich-and-poor-survey-finds.html

"Tensions Flare over Somalis in Lewiston." (2007, May 13). *Contra Costa* (Calif.) *Times,* p. A18.

"Tension over Somali Refugees in Maine." (2007, May 11). *Vail Daily.* Retrieved May 11, 2009, from www.vaildaily.com

13 Racial Profiling

LEARNING OBJECTIVES

After reading this chapter, you should be able to:

- Explain the historical background of the term *racial profiling* in law enforcement.
- Define *racial profiling* and explain the problems associated with using inconsistent definitions.
- Explain the challenges involved in the use of profiling in the war on terrorism.
- Identify seven approaches used by police departments to prevent racial profiling.
- Discuss the rationale for and against collection of racial profiling data.
- Explain the differences between "racial profiling" and the legitimate use of "profiling" in law enforcement.

OUTLINE

- Introduction
- Definitions
- Historical Background of the Term *Racial Profiling*
- Profiling Challenges in the War on Terrorism
- Police and Citizen Perceptions of Racial Profiling
- Profiling as a Legal Tool of Law Enforcement
- Is Racial Profiling Justified by the War on Terrorism?
- Prevention of Racial Profiling in Law Enforcement
- Professional Police Traffic Stops
- Data Collection on Citizens' Race/Ethnicity
- Summary
- Discussion Questions and Issues

INTRODUCTION

Actual or perceived racial profiling by law enforcement officers affects blacks, Hispanics, Arab Americans, and other minority groups from every walk of life, every vocation, and every level of the socioeconomic ladder. The extent to which race, ethnicity, and/or national origin can be used as factors in targeting suspects for stops, searches, and arrests has been a concern of citizens and law enforcement for some time. The controversy over racial profiling is compounded by the unsupported assumption that the officer making traffic and field-interrogation stops of nonwhite citizens is making a race-based decision rooted in racial prejudice. These concerns became even more critical since the "War on Terrorism" began on September 11, 2001.

DEFINITIONS

Since the issues of biased policing came to the attention of the public and to law enforcement in the 1990s, racial profiling has been discussed and defined in hundreds of articles and publications. However, no single definition dominated the national conversation about this issue. The debate troubled not only those involved in the criminal justice system, but also concerned citizens and communities, scholars, researchers, civil rights organizations, and legislators. With no agreed-upon criteria for what does or does not constitute racial profiling, it was difficult to clarify, address, and develop approaches to prevent the practice. Variation among definitions means interested parties are often talking at cross-purposes, unwittingly discussing different types of police practices, behavior, and stops. For this reason, proposals to prohibit racial profiling were difficult to develop and carry out. Eventually, the U.S. government, federal and state legislatures, law enforcement organizations, and community advocacy institutions addressed the problem of definition and reached some agreement.

Racial Profiling

The authors will use the definition developed by the U.S. Department of Justice and the National Organization of Black Law Enforcement Executives (NOBLE). According to these organizations, racial profiling is any police-initiated action that relies on the race, ethnicity, or national origin rather than on the behavior of an individual or on information that leads the police to a particular individual who has been identified as being, or having been, engaged in criminal activity. Racial profiling, also known as "Driving While Black or Brown" (DWB), has been ruled illegal by the courts and is considered improper police practice by law enforcement officers and agencies.

Profile: Formal and Informal

A *formal profile* is typically a document containing explicit criteria or indicators issued to officers to guide them in their decision-making. It is often based on data collected and interpreted to signify a trend or suggest that given behavioral or situational commonalties, a person could believe that something may result. It can be an outline or short biographical description, an individual's character sketch, or a type of behavior associated with a group. Officers use behavioral or situational indicators to develop reasonable suspicion or probable cause to stop subjects. A profile is a summary of data that also relies upon expert advice about "average" or "typical" appearance that can *potentially* identify perpetrators of criminal activities. An *informal profile* represents the "street sense," personal experiences, and strongly held beliefs that officers use to evaluate people or situations. Informal profiles are more common in law enforcement than formal ones.

Profiling

The term *profiling* refers to any police-initiated action that uses a compilation of the background, physical, behavioral, and/or motivational characteristics for a type of perpetrator to identify a particular individual as being, having the potential to be, or having been engaged in criminal activity.

Minority

The terms *minority* or *minorities* are used within the text to describe groups of individuals who represent a numeric minority within a racial or ethnic population.

Reasonable Suspicion

A police officer may briefly detain a person for questioning or request identification only if the officer has what is called a "reasonable suspicion" that the person's behavior is related to criminal activity. Reasonable suspicion requires that the officer have specific facts that must be articulated to support his or her actions; a mere suspicion or "hunch" is not sufficient. Reasonable suspicion can be based on the observations of a police officer combined with his or her training and experience, and/or reliable information received from credible outside sources. A police officer possesses reasonable suspicion if he or she has enough knowledge to lead a reasonably cautious person to believe that criminal activity is occurring and that the individual played some part in it. Reasonable suspicion is a level of belief that is less clear-cut than probable cause.

Probable Cause

Probable cause is a higher level of reasonable belief, based on facts that can be articulated, that is required to arrest a person and prosecute him or her in criminal court. Also, before a person or a person's property can be searched, police must possess probable cause, with some exceptions to be discussed later. All states have similar constitutional prohibitions against unreasonable searches and seizures.

Suspect-Specific Incident

An incident in which an officer is lawfully attempting to detain, apprehend, or otherwise be on the lookout for one or more specific suspects who have been identified or described in part by national or ethnic origin, gender, or race is called a "suspect-specific" incident.

HISTORICAL BACKGROUND OF THE TERM *RACIAL PROFILING*

During the 1990s, concerns about police use of racial profiling as a pretext to stop, question, search, and possibly arrest people became a major focus of minority individuals and communities, politicians, law enforcement administrators, scholars, and researchers. National surveys during that period revealed that the majority of Americans, white as well as black, believed racial profiling was commonly used in the United States, but 80 percent of those surveyed opposed the practice. They believed that police were routinely guilty of bias in their treatment of racial and ethnic minorities, and also that such behavior had been going on for a long time.

What is the source of racial profiling as both a term and as a law enforcement practice? Before addressing that question, it is useful to examine how people use prior events or information to make decisions in everyday life.

People routinely form mental images or tentative judgments about others and the surrounding circumstances or situation, both consciously and subconsciously, which is also a form of stereotyping. This sort of stereotyping, or looking for what one perceives to be indicators, provides a preliminary mental rating of potential risk to a person encountering a particular event or person.

This mental activity involves conscious and unconscious thought processes whereby an individual: (1) makes observations and selects data born out of that person's past experiences, (2) adds cultural and personal meaning to what he or she observes, (3) makes assumptions based on the meanings that he or she has attributed to the observation, (4) draws conclusions based on his or her own beliefs and, finally, (5) takes action (see Senge's "Ladder of Inference" discussed later in this chapter). This process comprises, for all people, basic decision making in their lives, and it guides a person's interpretation of events. A person's socialization, including the person's upbringing by his or her parents, plays a major role in determining decisions and the actions taken as a result of these decisions in both professional and personal settings.

Profiling in law enforcement is used by officers to look for characteristics that indicate the probability of criminal acts, or factors that tend to correlate with dangerous or threatening behavior. For officers, most of these characteristics have been internalized based on experience and training. If they have had dangerous encounters while on duty, such experiences prepare them for similar future events—as the old saying goes, *better safe than sorry!* The professional training that leads to the development of indicators or common characteristics comes from many sources, beginning with the police academy and in-service training under the supervision of a field-training officer. Informal education may include mentoring by an older partner and pressure from peers on how to do the job, and more formal training continues via advanced officer courses on various subjects. All of these help establish the common practice of profiling. If an official profile of a suspect is used by an agency, and the perpetrator is caught, we say, "He or she fits the profile," thus validating this perspective. When serial bombing suspect Eric Robert Rudolph was finally apprehended in June 2003, for example, FBI profiling experts immediately confirmed that the notorious fugitive did indeed "fit their profile." Training and experience provide officers with indicators to look for, not only to prevent harm to themselves, but also to identify those people or events that are suspicious and warrant closer attention. This attention then helps civilians and police officers decide what action is prudent to take when confronted by a similar person or situation. This does not necessarily mean the person using profiling in this way is biased or prejudiced. Writer Ira Straus, in a commentary for United Press International that is still valid today, suggests that some degree of profiling can be appropriate and even necessary as long as it is not abusive. In the article, he is using the term *profiling* chiefly to mean stereotyping:

> Profiling is universal. Every person relies on it for a preliminary rating of their risks with each person they run into. If people do not profile explicitly, they do it implicitly. If they do not do it consciously, they do it unconsciously. . . . Do police do it too? Of course they do. All police and investigative efforts involve working from two ends, direct and indirect. The direct end means following the trail of specific leads and informants. The indirect end means profiling; that is, finding a social milieu or pool to look in and ask around in—a milieu where there are more likely to be informants, leads, and criminals answering to that crime.
>
> To profile is morally risky. . . . The dangers of unfair and unreasonable profiling—that is, profiling based on unfounded prejudices such as racism—are well known. (Straus, 2002)

Straus implies that profiling is not always based on accurate information or data. When the meanings placed on observations are faulty or biased, the assumptions and conclusions, therefore, may be incorrect, thereby leading to inappropriate attitudes, behavior, and actions.

Law enforcement officers, airport security personnel, customs and border patrol agents, and members of some other occupations use profiles. In the absence of conclusive or specific details, it is the only way to narrow the amount of information from which to make decisions, including whether or not to stop a person for further investigation.

Although there are other historical examples of racial profiling, the first use of the term appears to have occurred in New Jersey, where troopers were trying to stem the flow of illegal drugs and other contraband into and across their state. In the early 1990s, the Drug Enforcement Administration (DEA) and the New Jersey State Police (NJSP) developed a relationship: the DEA provided training to the NJSP on what it had determined to be common characteristics of drug couriers along Interstate 95 from Miami through New Jersey. The characteristics included the types of cars preferred (Nissan Pathfinders), the direction of travel, and the use of rental vehicles from another state. In addition, it was common to find that a third party had rented the vehicle, that the driver was licensed in a state different from the one in which the rental took place, and that there were telltale behavioral cues (such as nervousness or conflicting stories). The profile also noted that the national origin of those involved in drug trafficking organizations was predominantly Jamaican, thus implying dark skin.

The NJSP used "pretextual stops" (i.e., using some legal pretext, such as failing to signal a lane change or having a missing license plate or faulty brake light) on I-95 to determine the potential criminality of a car's driver and occupants. The officer(s) would then attempt to establish a legal basis to search for illegal drugs. Many argued, and the courts agreed, that these pretextual stops were also based on the fact that the cars' drivers and occupants were black or dark-skinned. In other words, they had been racially profiled—targeted because of the color of their skin. The resultant studies determined that blacks and Hispanics on I-95 were stopped with a frequency disproportionate to their numbers on that road. Due to the controversy, and the subsequent court decision and punitive judgment against the NJSP, that organization no longer distributes a typical felony offender profile to their officers "because such profiles might contribute to what the state's attorney general calls 'inappropriate stereotypes' about criminals" (Will, 2001). New Jersey, like other states, has also created legislation making racial profiling illegal, with criminal sanctions for officers practicing it.

PROFILING CHALLENGES IN THE WAR ON TERRORISM

Prior to September 11, 2001, the use by law enforcement agencies of profiles that included race, ethnicity, or national origin, or the act of profiling using the same criteria, had come to be generally frowned upon, or even condemned, in the United States. But an attitude change occurred after the horrendous attacks on the World Trade Center in New York City and the Pentagon. One outcome of that event was the establishment of the U.S. Department of Homeland Security (DHS) and the attempt to coordinate law enforcement agencies and the military in defense of the nation's citizenry and infrastructure. The scope of the state of emergency created by the hijackers altered both public opinion and government policy concerning profiles and profiling based on national origin and ethnicity, especially regarding both the legitimacy and necessity of the practices. Given the ongoing and complex conflicts in the Middle East, plus the global terrorist threat from al-Qaida, the Taliban, and other Islamist extremists, the issue became more charged and complicated. Police at the national and local level had to develop strategies for detecting and apprehending terrorists. Tentative profiles were quickly developed on the basis of obvious characteristics and experience.

Since all the terrorists involved in the 9/11 incidents were Islamic males from the Middle East, the issue became whether law enforcement and security personnel could target or profile suspicious men with similar backgrounds for stops, searches, or increased questioning. Profiling, using those criteria, began to be employed on the basis of several factors common to these particular terrorists, who were:

- young males, Arab in appearance
- primarily citizens of Saudi Arabia
- trained in fundamentalist religious and/or al-Qaida training camps in Afghanistan or Pakistan

- adherents of Islam who had been inspired to religious extremism by fundamentalist clergy, especially with regard to **Al-jihad**
- harboring a deep hatred, in general, of Western decadence, materialism, and immorality, which they perceived as undermining the values and stability of their societies, and, in particular, of America for its interference in Middle Eastern affairs.

> **Al-jihad or Jihad**   Struggle (literal translation of Arabic). The term has also been used by some to mean "holy war" against infidels or nonbelievers.

This subject is covered in more detail in Chapter 8, Law Enforcement Contact with Arab Americans and other Middle Eastern Groups.

Initially there was little outcry among the general public against these actions. Recall that prior to 9/11, 80 percent of Americans opposed racial profiling. Polls taken soon after the attack showed that 70 percent of Americans believed that some form of profiling was necessary, and acceptable, to ensure public safety. A McClatchy-Ipsos poll in 2009, eight years after 9/11, determined that 51 percent of Americans agreed that "it is necessary to give up some civil liberties in order to make the country safe from terrorism" after an attempted terrorist attack set off a debate regarding full-body scans by the Transportation Security Administration (TSA) at airports ("War on Terrorism: Trade Liberties for Safety?" 2010). It is apparent that the public was willing to give up certain freedoms in exchange for helping the government reduce the opportunity for terrorists to operate in the United States. Members of the American Association for Public Opinion Research, at a May 2002 meeting, offered a historical perspective. They said that while civil liberties usually have broad public support, the public has been willing to tolerate substantial limits on those freedoms when there are serious threats to security and safety within the United States and to Americans abroad. Their report cited the decline in support for civil liberties after Pearl Harbor and again at the height of the Cold War. Other than the American Civil Liberties Union (ACLU) and the National Association of Arab Americans, there were few who spoke out against detentions of Middle Easterners and South Asians at security areas in airports and elsewhere after 9/11. These organizations questioned the use of what appeared to them to be racial profiling and abuse of civil rights, generally and specifically. However, many citizens argued that proactive law enforcement and enhanced security measures at airports were necessary to prevent or reduce opportunities for terrorist acts and to investigate and bring to justice those involved. Discovering terrorists and their missions, prior to another attack, became a matter of urgency. The researchers added, however, that support for civil liberties has always resumed when the threat subsided. This certainly was the case as time passed after 9/11 without additional terrorist acts in the United States.

The use of profiles and profiling in law enforcement requires a balancing of morality, legality, efficiency, equality, liberty, and security concerns. It has the potential to affect millions of innocent people in the United States who are or may appear to be of Muslim, Arab, Middle Eastern or South Asian descent, or Sikh. It is important that law enforcement officials and security agents avoid hasty judgments and not condemn all Muslims or Middle Easterners for the crimes of a few. Officers, agents, and those who protect airports and other public facilities should seek to learn more about both Islam and Arab civilization.

POLICE AND CITIZEN PERCEPTIONS OF RACIAL PROFILING

Myth, Misperception, or Reality?

There are some police officers, government administrators, and others who maintain that racial profiling is a myth or a misperception. They argue that the majority of officers does not stop or detain people based on their race, ethnicity, or national origin, but on their behavior, location, circumstances, and other factors. Officers contend that those who are stopped often do not understand police procedures or are overly sensitive, or are using the allegation that bias was involved in their stop, questioning, search, and/or arrest to cast aspersions on the action taken in an attempt to nullify it.

There have been over two decades of reform measures by agencies to eliminate racial profiling or the perception thereof. Sometimes the reforms were compelled by a class action lawsuit or legislation. Regardless of the motivations for reform, have these measures resulted in perceptible change? Are law enforcement agencies still being accused of racial profiling? Some examples from across the country illustrate the continued concern with this issue:

- *Oregon:* The fifth edition of this text indicated that in 2006, the Portland Police Bureau was accused by local media, based upon an ACLU complaint, of stopping Latinos and African Americans at a rate disproportionate to their numbers in the community. African Americans represented 6 percent of the city's population, but 14 percent of all traffic stops that year. Latinos represented 6 percent of the population, but 9 percent of traffic stops.

In 2009, the Portland Police Bureau actively worked with the community to develop a plan to address the issue of racial profiling. The plan, which can be seen on the agency's Web site, emphasizes the following strategic priorities:

- Work with the Human Rights Commission and Office of Human Relations, among others, to create opportunities for officers to engage with communities of color.
- Develop a plan to reduce the number of unsuccessful searches by improving officers' ability to accurately identify individuals likely to carry weapons and/or contraband (i.e., improving their "hit" rate on searches)—thereby reducing disparate treatment among Caucasians, African Americans, and Latinos.
- Inventory the Bureau's training and supervision on issues of professionalism and respect, with the goal of improving customer service.
- Develop and improve partnerships with other agencies engaged in reducing racial disparities in our work. ("Plan to Address Racial Profiling," 2009)

As of 2012, however, data show that minorities in that city continue to be disproportionately pulled over in traffic stops ("Portland's Racial Profiling Reality," 2012).

- *Missouri:* To address concerns about allegations of racial profiling, the state of Missouri passed a law in 2000 mandating the collection of data on traffic stops. According to an analysis of the data, the disparity index for African American drivers continued to be of concern, rising from 1.49 in 2006 to 1.63 in 2011. The index is a measure that compares a racial or ethnic group's proportion of total vehicle stops to its proportion of the driving-age population. Values above 1 indicate overrepresentation. In 2011, African Americans represent 10.7 percent of Missouri's population, yet account for 16.9 percent of all vehicle stops. There are many who question the "yardstick" Missouri is using to determine if racial profiling is taking place. A benchmark that compares the race of drivers stopped with the racial makeup of the community, to be discussed later in this chapter, presumes that the driving population in Missouri accurately mirrors the driving-age census population. Critics of this system say that highways and major destinations, such as amusement parks, sports stadiums, malls, schools, and major employers, can skew the numbers dramatically, making the data unreliable.
- *Arizona:* In 2008, the Arizona Department of Public Safety implemented policies requiring highway patrol officers to document their reasons for searching vehicles they stop and to obtain motorists' consent for a search. Consent was to be verified by the driver's signature on a form or by using a video or audio recording of the driver giving permission. Department policy and training now also state that "officers must have a 'reasonable suspicion of

criminal activity' before requesting consent for a search" ("Ariz. DPS Tightens Search Rules to Avoid Profiling," 2008). The changes were recommended by an advisory board created by the governor as a result of a class action suit brought by the ACLU in 2001 alleging racial profiling on northern Arizona interstate highways.

- *New York:* The New York Police Department (NYPD) was criticized in 2009 by civil rights groups because officers had stopped, questioned, and frisked more than a half a million people the previous year. The contention, based on data collected and released by the NYPD, was that a disproportionate number of these individuals were African Americans and Latinos. According to the Center for Constitutional Rights, the raw data indicated that more than 80 percent of those stopped were young African American or Latino men ("NYCLU Analysis Reveals NYPD Stopped Nearly 2 Million Innocent New Yorkers; Most are Black & Latino," 2009). Civil rights advocates had sued the NYPD in 2006 over the same issue, a year when the department data also indicated they had stopped over 500,000 persons. Despite these figures, however, the RAND Corporation, an independent research agency hired to analyze the same data, found no racial profiling in its examination, and "warned against the kind of simplistic comparisons made by the civil rights groups" ("New York: Analysis of Racial Disparities in the New York City Police Department's Stop, Question, and Frisk Practices," 2007). Requests to dismiss the case by New York City were rejected in 2011 and again in 2012 as, according to the judge, there was enough evidence to raise questions; the number of stops continue to "display a measurable racial disparity: black and Hispanic people generally represent more than 85 percent of those stopped by police, though their combined populations make up a small share of the city's racial composition" (Baker, 2011). In August 2013, a U.S. federal district court judge ruled that "police [in New York City] have intentionally and systematically violated the civil rights of tens of thousands of people by wrongly targeting black and Hispanic men." (Long, 2013)

Although these anecdotes highlight departments that still need improvement, there have been success stories as well. For example, the *New York Times* reported in 2007 that federal monitors from the U.S. Department of Justice had found that the New Jersey State Police had made so much progress in eliminating racial profiling that it no longer needed their supervision. This was only eight years after that agency acknowledged that troopers were focusing on black and Hispanic drivers at traffic stops (Chen, 2007).

It appears that despite laws, court orders, and agency policies and procedures that prohibit officers from using race or ethnicity as a decision-making factor, the practice still takes place. However, it is difficult to analyze the degree to which this is the case, because the data collected by law enforcement agencies are often fraught with methodological problems. This is discussed later in this chapter.

As indicated, most police officers and city or county administrators deny the existence of racial profiling. They claim that those who believe they have been the victims of profiling may not be aware of other factors that the officer took into consideration. A traffic stop is the most common situation leading to complaints of racial profiling. A 2008 nationwide survey regarding police contact with the public established that speeding was the most common reason for being pulled over, representing about half of driver stopped. The survey determined that "about 73.8% of black drivers believed police had a legitimate reason for stopping them compared to 86.3% of white and 82.5% of Hispanic drivers"("Contacts between the Police and the Public, 2008," 2011). Black drivers (12.3%) were about three times as likely as white drivers (3.9%) and about two times as likely as Hispanic drivers (5.8%) to be searched ("Contacts between the Police and the Public, 2008," 2011).

Researchers studying allegations of racial profiling must also explore discretionary decision-making of individual officers, a subject that has long been the object of study by those doing research in the criminal justice field.

Most of the research on criminal justice has documented that the impact of racial prejudice on criminal justice agents' decision-making has been decreasing in prevalence and importance for at least 30 years. Prior to the 1970s, racial prejudice was still the basis for many state and local laws. Since that time, police departments have made continuing serious managerial efforts to reduce and eliminate prejudicial behavior by police officers, and . . . research is no longer consistent with earlier research on the extent to which race per se directly influences police decisions. This . . . research suggests that police officers' behavior is predicted primarily by legal and situation-specific factors and that the influence of race and other extra-legal factors is diminishing. (Engel, Calnon, & Bernard, 2002)

Police Perceptions

What are the police officers' perceptions of allegations that all race-based decision-making by them is motivated by their own prejudice?

Most law enforcement officers would maintain that they are not biased, prejudiced, or using racial profiling in their policing methods. Proactive policing sometimes involves using legitimate profiling based on officer experience and training or using profiles provided by their agency. Sometimes, however, officer experience can mean a lot of things. If the experience leads to faulty assumptions and conclusions, then the officer might engage in inappropriate behavior and take the wrong action. (See the section "Education and Training" of this chapter for a discussion of the sources of officers' beliefs and attitudes.)

Officers use profiling (behavioral commonalities or indicators) or written profiles to identify those whom they should investigate to determine if they are committing or about to commit a crime. Profiling is done on a daily basis by police officers, not just in high-crime areas where gangs congregate or highway corridors where drug runners operate, but in all communities. It also takes place in predominantly white communities when officers see out-of-place or suspicious-looking members of minority groups. The officer in this situation would argue that he or she would find reason to check out anyone, regardless of color, who did not seem to fit the area or time of day, especially if he or she were acting suspiciously. Profiling also takes place when an officer sees a white person in a predominantly minority area, especially if the area is one in which drug sales or prostitution takes place. The officer checks out the individual if reasonable suspicion is present that a crime might be taking place. Most officers would emphatically deny they are biased or prejudiced when using such profiling.

Officers also insist that both their agency and the community in which they work pressure them to reduce crime in the neighborhoods, and that profiling (not racial profiling) is a tool to accomplish a reduction in some crimes. For example, the *New York Times* reported that on November 11, 2008, a young man was shot and killed not far from the Queens home of Dennis Walcott, Deputy Mayor of New York. Residents in the predominantly Caribbean neighborhood demanded what the *Times* described as "a vigorous police presence." Soon there were complaints about young men being stopped, but at the same time, street violence diminished. "We struggle with the duality of wanting a safe neighborhood and police who are respectful of our children," the deputy mayor said. "It's an inherent challenge and I'm not sure there is an easy answer" (Powell, 2009).

Also, if officers believe that their agency supervisors and managers want them to be aggressive on the streets by stopping vehicles and pedestrians to determine if there is potential criminal activity, officers will do so, especially if this behavior is rewarded within their organization. Reward structures within agencies include such things as favorable evaluations, shifts, and assignments, and even promotions. Unfortunately, if officers come to believe that minority citizens are more likely to be involved in criminal activity of some sort and that aggressively stopping their vehicles will result in more searches and arrests, they are more likely to stop them (referred to as the expectancy theory), especially if the department encourages and rewards the practice.

The Police Executive Research Forum (PERF) undertook an extensive study of racial profiling. They chose to avoid the term *racial profiling*, preferring *racially biased policing*. They indicate in their report that racial profiling was defined so restrictively that the term does not fully capture the concerns of both police and citizens. For example:

> Racial profiling is frequently defined as law enforcement activities (e.g., detentions, arrests, searches) that are initiated *solely* on the basis of race. Central to the debate on the most frequently used definitions is the word "solely." In the realm of potential discriminatory actions, this definition likely references only a very small portion. Even a racially prejudiced officer likely uses more than the single factor of race when conducting biased law enforcement. For example, officers might make decisions based on the neighborhood and the race of the person, the age of the car and the race of the person, or the gender and the race of the person. Activities based on these sample pairs of factors would fall outside the most commonly used definition of racial profiling. (Fridell, Lunney, Diamond, & Kubu, 2001)

Using this common definition of racial profiling, then, makes the term less useful, since when the practice is defined "so narrowly (i.e., race as the only reason for stopping, questioning or arresting someone), . . . we can imagine only the most extreme bigots engaging in it. Using such a definition, racial profiling is easy to both denounce and deny" (Barlow & Barlow, 2002).

In the PERF study, staff conducted meetings around the country with citizens and police line and command staff regarding occurrences and perceptions of biased policing. The subsequent report, "Racially Biased Policing: A Principled Response," revealed that the police in the study were using the narrow definition of racial profiling (stops based *solely* on race or ethnicity) and thus could declare vehemently that police actions based solely on race, national origin, or ethnicity were quite rare. The citizens in the study, however, were using a broader definition, one that included race as one among several factors leading up to the stop of the individual.

> Many of our law enforcement participants did express skepticism that "racial profiling" was a major problem, exacerbating some citizens' frustration. It became clear to staff that these differing perceptions among citizens and police regarding racial profiling's pervasiveness were very much related to the respective definitions they had adopted. The citizens equated "racial profiling" with all manifestations of racially biased policing, whereas most of the police practitioners defined "racial profiling" as stopping a motorist based *solely* on race. Presumably, even officers who engage in racially biased policing rarely make a vehicle stop based *solely* on race (often ensuring probable cause or some other factor is also present). (Fridell et al., 2001)

OTHER FACTORS IN POLICE STOPS   Those concerned about racial profiling must also recognize that when a stop or detention by officers is not self-initiated, it was most likely to have been initiated because a witness or victim had provided a description of a person or event that they felt required police action—a suspect-specific incident or one due to computer-generated information. This is the case in the majority of contacts police make with citizens. If the complainant describes a suspect of a certain race, ethnicity, or national origin, that is what the officer will search for. For example, if police receive a report of possible criminal activity, and reliable information indicates that he is 5 foot 8 inches, lean, long-haired, and Asian, then "Asian" may be considered, along with the other demographics, in developing reasonable suspicion or probable cause to detain. If, however, the citizen is reporting the activity of a minority because of his or her own biases, the police should attempt to ensure the legitimacy of the complaint and not be an agent of what might be racially charged paranoia. In Brooksfield, Wisconsin, dispatchers are trained to gather more information from callers to determine if the call is legitimate. If not, they then can explain this fact to the caller and not trigger a potentially volatile police–citizen encounter.

Some allegations of racially motivated stops are clearly not reasonable. In some cases, officers cannot discern the race or ethnicity of the driver and/or occupant(s) prior to the stop. For example, some cars have tinted or darkened windows or a head rest on the back of the seat, making it impossible to determine the race, ethnicity, or even gender of the occupant(s). When officers use radar, it is the electronic device that determines which vehicle to stop, and not the race, ethnicity, or national origin of the driver. Obviously at nighttime, it is challenging to identify drivers or passengers in detail. (Readers of this textbook should try to describe the occupants of a vehicle in front of them, especially at night, to test these arguments.)

Policing during the 1990s and into the present day has been driven by two forces: (1) data developed and analyzed by specialists (crime analysts) that provide officers with predictions on where crimes might occur (including time of day and even generalized suspect information) and (2) POP or COP approaches, wherein neighborhood representatives tell officers about problems, including potential suspects, in their communities. In the latter case, members of the community demand that officers take enforcement action against drug dealers, prostitutes, gang members, those disturbing the peace, and suspicious persons, regardless of their race or ethnicity.

Another example of urban policing using race-neutral, data-driven technology and methods is New York's innovative **CompStat**—or COMPSTAT—(short for **Comp**uter **Stat**istics or COMParative STATistics) program. CompStat is the New York Police Department's personnel and resource management system, the purpose of which is crime reduction. It uses Geographic Information Systems (GIS) technology to map crime and identifies problems in the city. Crime data are forwarded every week to the chief of the department's CompStat Unit. Based on this information, precinct commanders and members of top management deploy manpower and resources to most effectively reduce crime and improve police performance.

Officers are held accountable for reducing specific crime in targeted areas. If robberies are up in a certain precinct, officers are deployed to locate and arrest those responsible. If the neighborhood to which officers are assigned is a minority part of the city, then the people they contact will likely be members of that minority group. Race is irrelevant to this sort of policing. When Russian immigrants in New York dominated the Ecstasy trade, law enforcement efforts targeted (profiled) them, and ultimately their illegal activities were reduced. Arrests are most often the result of criminal intelligence, computer-generated data, and good police work, not racism. The CompStat system, which began in 1994, has since been replicated in many other police agencies across the nation, sometimes under different names or acronyms ("The Growth of Compstat in American Policing," 2004).

There are some who argue that the use of racial profiling is justified and should be legal because the demographics of crime demonstrate a relationship between the numbers of blacks and Hispanics stopped, searched and arrested, and incarcerated, and the numbers of crimes committed—that is, members of those minority groups do commit more crime than do whites or Asians (MacDonald, 2001). Others argue this sort of rationalization perpetuates the problem through a vicious cycle. Studies have been used both to prove and to disprove this hypothesis. It is open to question whether officers stop minorities because they believe this hypothesis, because they are biased, or both.

Victim and Civil Rights Advocates' Perceptions

The claims and counterclaims about the existence and prevalence of racial profiling have been made for years, and they should not be dismissed as misperceptions or misunderstandings. We have to regard them as indicators of a very real social phenomenon.

Recent court and U.S. Department of Justice decisions have upheld claims of targeting, harassment and intimidation by law enforcement officers in various jurisdictions in the United States. For example:

> U.S. Department of Justice officials have demanded that Los Angeles County, Lancaster, and Palmdale pay a total of $12.5 million to residents who the federal government found were victims of harassment and intimidation in the Antelope Valley. (Leonard & Winton, 2013)

The Department of Justice accused the Alamance County, North Carolina Sheriff's Office in a Tuesday letter of violating the Constitution by racially profiling and targeting Latinos. ("Feds Accuse N.C. Sheriff of Discriminatory Policing," 2012)

Police search African American and Hispanic Missouri drivers at a notably higher rate than white drivers–despite the fact that these minority groups are actually less likely to have contraband on them. (Levin, 2013)

In a 2013 Gallup's Minority Rights and Relations poll,

Overall, 17% of black adults say the police treated them unfairly within the 30 days prior to the interview. That number is down from Gallup's measures of the question between 1999 and 2007, including the high point in 2004, when 25% of all blacks said they had been treated unfairly within the past month. (Newport, 2013)

Blacks are not the only Americans who say they have been the targets of racial or ethnic profiling by law enforcement. Studies have concluded that Hispanic men report being more likely than white men to question why they were stopped and how they were treated. Just as "DWB" (Driving While Black/Brown) has been used by civil rights advocates to demonstrate racial profiling of African Americans or Hispanics, in recent years, "flying while Arab" has been used to describe the targeting of Arabs, South Asians, and Middle Easterners. These complaints of racial profiling are most often heard at airports and other places where there is a concern about the potential for terrorist attack. Civil rights advocates say that Arabs, South Asians, and Middle Easterners, most of them loyal American citizens, have become victims of the new war on terrorism. It is a difficult issue and one in which officers and security agents are damned if they do and damned if they don't. Minorities complain that they are not only more likely to be stopped than whites, but they are also often pressured to allow searches of their vehicles.

There are many accounts by people who have been stopped by police on questionable grounds and subjected to disrespectful behavior, intrusive questioning, and disregard for their civil rights. The newspaper coverage of such allegations and court findings were mentioned earlier in this chapter. A study by Amnesty International (AI), United States, published in 2004, estimates that there are 32 million victims of racial profiling and that 87 million individuals are at high risk of victimization during their lifetimes (Amnesty International, 2004). The study involved a series of nationwide hearings and public testimony from individuals alleging to be victims of racial profiling while driving, walking, shopping, traveling through airports, and during other activities. These accounts lend credibility to the reality of the practice. Data collected by police departments to refute such claims often reveal that, without further analysis and interpretation, minority drivers are stopped in numbers out of proportion to their presence on the road. A 2009 follow-up by the ACLU to the 2004 AI report maintains that

Indeed, data and anecdotal information from across the country reveal that racial minorities continue to be unfairly victimized when authorities investigate, stop, frisk, or search them based upon subjective identity-based characteristics rather than identifiable evidence of illegal activity. Victims continue to be racially or ethnically profiled while they work, drive, shop, pray, travel, and stand on the street. The disproportionate rates at which minorities are stopped and searched, in addition to the often high concentrations of law enforcement in minority communities, continue to have a tremendous impact on the over-representation of minorities (and especially members of African American, Latino, and Native American communities) in the American criminal justice system. (The American Civil Liberties Union and The Rights Working Group, 2009)

It is not uncommon for white officers to downplay the existence and scope of racial profiling during departmental training programs on the topic. However, upon hearing fellow officers describe their own experiences as members of a minority group, the white officers typically respond with surprise, but are then more receptive to the suggestion that there is a problem (Fridell et al., 2001). In a 2002 study, the findings of which are still relevant today, David and Melissa Barlow surveyed African American police officers in Milwaukee to determine whether they felt they had ever been racially profiled, and, if so, to what extent. The researchers wanted to learn how black officers felt about the legality of the circumstances under which they had been

	Yes (%)	No (%)
Stopped	69	31
Questioned	52	60
Searched	19	81
Ticketed	21	79
Arrested	7	93

EXHIBIT 13.1 Racial Profiling Survey

Question: In your professional opinion, do you believe you have ever been stopped, questioned, searched, ticketed, or arrested as a result of racial profiling?

Source: Barlow and Barlow, 2002, p. 14.

stopped by police. Because the subjects of the survey were themselves police officers, their views could not be easily dismissed.

The survey defined racial profiling as "when race is used by a police officer or a police agency in determining the potential criminality of an individual" (Barlow & Barlow, 2002). Of the 2,100 sworn personnel of the Milwaukee Police Department, 414 were designated as black. The response rate to this survey was 38 percent (158 officers). Over 99 percent were over 25 years of age and had been sworn police officers for at least 1 year. The percentage of male respondents was 83.5, while the percentage of female respondents was 16.5.

Exhibit 13.1 shows that the majority of those who responded to the survey believed that they had been racially profiled. Note that the percentages drop off rapidly as the survey proceeded from questions about being stopped and questioned to questions about being arrested. The researchers suggest that the numbers fall off rapidly because the officers would have identified themselves as such upon being stopped and thus avoided further action. It should be noted that some of those surveyed reported that they were on duty but in plain clothes when they were stopped. From their findings, the Barlows conclude that black men are more likely to be the victims of racial profiling than black women by a ratio of three to one.

In their research, the Barlows also asked the sworn police officers of the Milwaukee Police Department whether they personally used racial profiling in the performance of their job. They found that most (90%) of the respondents said that they do not use racial profiling nor believe it is a necessary or legitimate tool for law enforcement. The researchers concluded: "Although many white Americans, members of law enforcement, and government officials deny the existence of racial profiling or racially biased policing, the findings from the study suggest it is a reality" (Barlow & Barlow, 2002).

The following mini case studies involve descriptions of fictional events but are based upon actual occurrences. The issues and implications of each should be discussed in class, especially the question of whether the police behavior is proper, justified, legal, or necessary.

Mini Case Studies: Culture and Crime

You Decide—Racial Profiling?

Mini Case Study 1

A well-dressed young Hispanic male is driving through a predominantly white community early in the morning on his way to work in a new BMW. He is pulled over for speeding and the officer, instead of simply asking for a driver's license and writing a speeding ticket, calls for backup and is joined by another officer. The young man is told to leave his vehicle and the officers search it. "Hey, where did you get the money for something like this?" one officer asks mockingly as he starts going through every inch of the BMW. One of the officers pulls off an inside door panel, and more dismantling of the vehicle follows. They say they are looking for drugs, but in the end find nothing. After ticketing the driver for speeding, the two officers drive off.

1. While Hispanic officers might have stopped the same speeding driver, do you think they would have treated the driver in the same manner?
2. Is there any indication of probable cause in the example that would lead the officers to such a search?
3. Do you believe police officers do in fact pull over and search the vehicles of minorities disproportionately to their numbers?
4. Should profiling only include the actions, behavior, and activities of the person(s) observed by the officer?
5. How can law enforcement leadership and trainers teach officers to distinguish between behavioral profiling and racial profiling?
6. Are those who argue that the "demographics of crime" justify racial profiling using data that are biased? Does this sort of rationalization perpetuate the problem through a vicious cycle?

Mini Case Study 2:

An Arab American was traveling from Washington, D.C. to Detroit. At the airport, he was pulled out of the security line, questioned, and searched. He reported that this was done in front of everyone else in line and was humiliating. He thought that the authorities at the airport were doing this so non-Arab Americans could see that something was being done about security. He felt he had been racially profiled.

1. Passengers who appear "Arab-looking," a category that has included South Asians and Latinos, have been asked by airline officials to leave airplanes because fellow passengers and crew members refuse to fly with them. How can airline security and management justify these actions?
2. Should Sikh men be denied the right to board aircraft because they refuse to fly without their turban, which equates to asking an individual to fly without a basic article of clothing?
3. Has the war on terrorism or the conflicts in the Middle East provided the opportunity for officers and security personal to use racial profiling tactics?
4. What options are available for officers and security personnel to provide security and safety to the public they serve?

PROFILING AS A LEGAL TOOL OF LAW ENFORCEMENT

How does law enforcement balance the need to reduce crime, and especially terrorism, against the potential for accusations of discrimination, race-biased policing, and stereotyping? It is a challenging and complex problem for officers, especially for those strongly committed to nonbiased practices who believe in proactive policing. The real questions associated with any type of law enforcement profiling are as follows:

1. Who is doing the profile construction and on what basis?
   - Does that person have some expertise (e.g., in behavioral science)?
   - Is the profile creator objective, unbiased, and nonjudgmental in formulating a particular profile?
2. Who is interpreting the profile?
   - Is that person sufficiently trained in its application?
3. Is the officer who is using profiling doing so legally?
   - Is it based on departmental policy rather than on his or her personal biases, attitudes, and beliefs?

Criminal justice agencies face major challenges regarding the issue and impact of the use of profiles and profiling. Law enforcement personnel are entrusted with (1) protecting the rights of those who are the subject of stereotyping, harassment, and discrimination (i.e., those who are *misidentified* as a result of profiles or profiling); (2) identifying and bringing to justice those who are terrorists or criminals (i.e., those who are *correctly identified*); (3) identifying terrorists and/or criminals who do *not* fit a particular profile or stereotype; and (4) not being so hampered by their personal stereotypes, attitudes, beliefs, perceptions, and knowledge (or lack thereof) that innocent people are detained and terrorists are not apprehended in the course of law enforcement.

Profiling and profiles have long been used as legitimate law enforcement tools to look for signs of potential criminal activity in almost every country in the world, although the people profiled will vary by country. In Israel, for example, the police have profiles of Palestinian terrorists. Now the criminal justice community in many parts of the world is using profiles to locate and arrest members of al-Qaida and allied radical Islamist groups. In the United States, a potential terrorist's profile used by airport and homeland security agents might include such factors as (1) a man in his 20s or 30s who comes from Saudi Arabia, Egypt, or Pakistan (2) who is probably living in one of six states: Texas, New Jersey, California, New York, Michigan, or Florida; and (3) who is likely to have engaged in some sort of suspicious activity, such as taking flying lessons, traveling in areas of possible targets, or getting a U.S. driver's license. Meeting some of these criteria—not necessarily having a certain skin color—is enough to instigate questioning by law enforcement authorities.

The Police Executive Research Forum (PERF) created policy intended for adoption by police departments across the nation that clearly delineates what is legal profiling. Because the Fourth Amendment to the Constitution protects citizens against unreasonable search and seizure, the policy mandates that officers shall *not consider* race/ethnicity to establish reasonable suspicion or probable cause except under specific circumstances. The policy:

- disallows use of race as a general indicator for criminal behavior
- disallows use of stereotypes/biases
- allows for the consideration of race *as one factor* in making law enforcement decisions if it is based on trustworthy and locally relevant information that links specific suspected unlawful activity to a person(s) of a particular race/ethnicity
- relies on *descriptions* of actual suspects, not general *predictions* of who may be involved in a crime.

For example, an officer observes the following: (1) the tail light is burned out on a vehicle with a white driver; (2) it is midnight; (3) the car is in a minority neighborhood where drugs are known to be sold; (4) the driver pulls up to the curb and talks briefly to someone standing there; (5) an exchange takes place; (6) the driver drives away; (7) the driver makes furtive movements as if hiding something under the seat when police pull him over. Although not a representative example because the driver is white, race was used as only part of the decision to pull the driver over.

PERF recommends that the following principle be applied: "Race/ethnicity should be treated like other demographic descriptors. Police can use race/ethnicity as one factor in the same way that they use age, gender and other descriptors to establish reasonable suspicion or probable cause." The organization recommends that the best test for officers to use includes two questions: (1) Would I be engaging this particular person but for the fact that this person is white? (2) Would I be asking this question of this person but for the fact that this person is [fill in the demographic descriptor] (Fridell et al., 2001)?

What is necessary in assessing the use of profiles and profiling is a combination of common sense and fairness, a balance between effective law enforcement and protection of civil liberties. The authors believe that profiles and profiling will not upset such a balance if they are used judiciously, fairly, and within the law. Most officers understand that profiling, not racial profiling, is an acceptable form of proactive law enforcement, and the courts agree. The U.S. Customs Service, the U.S. Border Patrol, and the DEA have long used profiles as a tool to detain and investigate persons fitting the "drug courier profile." Such a profile is based on behaviors, actions, traits, demeanor, intelligence information, carrier routes, statistical evidence, and other factors—not just a single characteristic like race or ethnicity. The U.S. Border Patrol obviously links ethnicity to incidence of crime on the border with Mexico. It is only logical to assume that most people attempting to enter the country illegally from Mexico are of Hispanic/Latino or Mestizo descent. The use of profiles in this context appears to be legal and acceptable. A border patrol profile, however, not only includes the ethnicity of the individual but also such factors as their proximity to the border, erratic driving, suspicious behavior, and the officers' previous experience with alien traffic.

A discussion of the 2009 U.S. Immigration and Customs Enforcement (ICE) 287 (g) program can be found in Chapter 7. The 287 (g) program amended the Illegal Immigration Reform and Immigrant Responsibility Act of 1996 wherein the federal government can enter into agreements with state and local law enforcement agencies to enforce immigration laws and receive training to do so. The ACLU and other civil rights organizations argue that such a policy "continue[s] to contribute significantly to the persistence of racial profiling" (The American Civil Liberties Union and The Rights Working Group, 2009).

IS RACIAL PROFILING JUSTIFIED BY THE WAR ON TERRORISM?

Airport police and security agents [Transportation Security Administration (TSA)], and other officials within the Department of Homeland Security (DHS) use profiles to try to identify those who might be a threat to security in their respective jurisdictions. Airport police and security agents first used the CAPPS system (CAPPS I), implemented in 1998, which relied on what is known as a Passenger Name Record (PNR). CAPPS stands for Computer Assisted Passenger Prescreening System. It was first implemented and administered by the FBI and the Federal Aviation Administration (FAA) in response to terrorist incidents in the United States and abroad. When a person books a plane ticket, certain identifying information is collected by the airline, including name, birth date, address, and phone number. If an international flight is involved, a passport number is also required. This information is checked against other data such as the TSA's No-Fly list and the FBI's 10 most wanted fugitive list. The traveler is then assigned a terrorism "risk score." High scores require the airline to conduct extended baggage and/or personal screening, and, where appropriate, to contact law enforcement. In November 2001, control of the CAPPS I system was transferred from the FBI and FAA to the TSA. The CAPPS I system also screened passengers based on their destination and how they purchased their tickets—not on how they looked. None of the profile information specifically involves the race, ethnicity, or national origin of the persons checked.

In 2003, the TSA presented a proposal for an expanded system to be called CAPPS II, but because of opposition from Congress and civil liberties groups, it was never implemented. TSA immediately announced a successor program called Secure Flight which ultimately passed tests for accuracy and privacy protection. All flights into, out of, or within the U.S. had the Secure Flight program in place by December 2010 (Martin, 2010).

TSA also uses race- and ethnicity-neutral techniques to screen passengers. That is, everyone boarding an airplane in the United States is treated the same way, regardless of age, disability, appearance, nationality, race, or ethnic group. If metal detector, full-body scan, or pat-down discovers a discrepancy, extra scrutiny is triggered. Some flyers have voiced resentment to this intrusion. Some argue that TSA should be allowed to profile travelers, as their resources are wasted on screening low-risk passengers. Unfortunately, there have been examples of United States-born, non-Arab-appearing persons who planned terrorist attacks. Until the Boston Marathon bombings in April 2013, almost all domestic terrorist plots have been thwarted, mostly due to good work by government agencies watching for threats.

Legitimate Use of Race/Ethnicity

An important question is whether race can *ever* be a valid consideration when conducting law enforcement activity. In the *United States v. Travis* opinion, the Sixth Circuit Court of Appeals ruled that "race or ethnic background may become a legitimate consideration when investigators have information on this subject about a particular suspect" (*U.S. v. Travis*, 62 F.3d 170, 1995). Simply put, the suspect described and being sought is of a certain race or ethnicity (refer to the definition of suspect-specific incident in this chapter). Court decisions have allowed officers to consider the totality of the circumstances surrounding the subject of their attention in light of their experience and training, which may include "instructions on a drug courier profile" (*Florida v. Royer*, 460 U.S. 491, 1983). Actually, many courts have upheld the use of drug courier profiles as the sole determinant of a stop or cause for suspicion. Therefore, profiles combined with other facts and circumstances can establish reasonable suspicion or probable cause. Race or color may be a factor to consider during certain police activity (*U.S. v. Brignoni-Ponce*, 442 U.S., 837, 887, 1975). The *Whren* (*Whren v. United States - 517 U.S. 806*, 1996) decision by the Supreme Court enhanced the already extensive power of police to detain individual citizens under the banner of the war on drugs by allowing pretext stops through the "objective" standard test.

Some see the *Whren* decision "objective" standard (defined as a standard that is based on factual measurements, in the absence of a biased judgment or analysis) ruling as opening the door for police abuse. They argue that in the *Whren* case, it did not matter to the court that the officers lied about their intent, that they were violating departmental policy to make the stop, or that they really wanted to stop the car because it contained two African American men who sat at a stop sign for 20 seconds in an area known for drug dealing. They are concerned that the *Whren* decision clearly opens the door for racial profiling because it allows police officers to stop anyone without reasonable suspicion or probable cause, thus providing a mechanism for circumventing the Fourth Amendment requirements of the U.S. Constitution. Because minor traffic violations are numerous, they argue, to limit stops to the observation of traffic violations is no limitation at all. If a police officer wants to stop a car but does not have the legal authority to do so, all the officer has to do is to follow it until the driver gets nervous and at some point turns right without a turn signal, drifts across the center line, or simply fails to come to a complete stop at a stop sign. Upon observing a minor traffic violation, the police officer can stop the driver and attempt to pressure him or her into giving consent for the car to be searched. Under this "objective" standard, the motivation of the officer and previous enforcement patterns become irrelevant (Barlow & Barlow, 2002). It is important to note that the Court's decision in *Whren* did not create the practice of pretextual stops. Instead it validated this long-standing police practice that is even encouraged by police administrators. Neither was the *Whren* decision unpredictable. It is the result of more than a decade of decisions wherein the courts were unwilling to consider the legality of the use of race in law enforcement decision-making (Withrow, 2006).

The courts said the burden that "brief detentions" place on law-abiding minority citizens is a minor and necessary inconvenience in the war on crime, suggesting that little damage is done by the practice of profiling. However, those who advocate making the standard for brief detentions more restrictive insist that these court decisions have failed to acknowledge that these detentions grow into regular occurrences, breeding resentment and anger both in the citizens stopped and in the police officers who confront hostile persons of color. Police officers who use race, ethnicity, gender, sexual orientation, or national origin as a factor in criminal profiling based on presumed statistical probabilities then contribute to the very statistics upon which they rely.

The Supreme Court has made it clear that as long as the government can show that police searches and seizures are objectively reasonable (i.e., based on probable cause or reasonable suspicion, defined earlier in this chapter), they do not violate the Fourth Amendment (see shaded area), regardless of the officer's subjective (actual) motivation for the search or seizure. That does not mean, however, that objectively reasonable searches and seizures can never violate the Constitution. Officers motivated by prejudice who lawfully search or seize only members of certain racial, ethnic, religious, or gender groups are still subject to claims of constitutional violations (i.e., racial profiling).

> "The right of the people to be secure in their persons, houses, papers, and effects against unreasonable searches and seizures shall not be violated, and no warrants shall issue but upon probable cause supported by oath or affirmation, and particularly describing the place to be searched, and the persons or things to be seized." United States Constitution, Amendment IV

Police officers who undertake searches of persons or vehicles not incident to an arrest must have reasonable suspicion or probable cause to perform such a search. An officer who does not have reasonable suspicion may ask for a consent to search (except in those states or localities where it is illegal) and even have the motorist sign a waiver to that effect. Sometimes, however, evidence of racial bias may be discovered when there is a repeated pattern of minorities being subjected to consent searches much more often than whites. Law enforcement agencies must monitor the data they collect on discretionary consent searches to ensure that the discretion is not applied more often to minorities. One explanation for the disparity, according to some researchers, is that minorities may be more nervous around police and officers may misinterpret that as suspicious behavior.

Far-reaching authority for searches was granted to law enforcement when, in 2001, President George W. Bush signed the USA Patriot Act (USAPA) into law. The law gave sweeping new powers to both domestic law enforcement and international intelligence agencies. The provisions of the law, aimed at terrorism, expanded surveillance capabilities (in effect, searches) and allowed for nationwide wiretaps under certain circumstances. Many aspects of the new law were questioned by those concerned about the potential for government intrusion into the lives and civil rights of innocent people. The Patriot Act was renewed by congress in 2006, following an intense debate regarding protection of civil liberties. Proponents were able to show that in the four years since the Act was passed, there were no verified civil-liberties abuses, and the new bill added more than 30 new significant civil liberties safeguards. In 2011, the 112th Congress passed and the president signed Senate Bill 291, which extended the Patriot Act another four years. The USAPA is discussed more fully in Chapter 10.

There are exceptions to the general rules that require that searches must be based on reasonable suspicion or probable cause. Courts have ruled in favor of routine searches at airports, mass transit sites and entrances to courts and other official buildings. These screenings or searches are called the "special needs" exception to the Fourth Amendment requirements, and are permitted only in limited circumstances or situations. The purpose of such searches or screening is not primarily to detect weapons or explosives or to apprehend those who carry them, but to deter such persons from carrying banned items into the area being protected. The court considers such screening a legitimate means of implementing counterterrorism measures while at the same time expecting that the intrusion to the public and their privacy is minimal. It is also expected that such administrative programs are an effective deterrent to a terrorist attack or the bringing of contraband or restricted items into a controlled area.

Illegitimate Use of Race/Ethnicity

Courts have held that matching a profile *alone* is not the equivalent of the reasonable suspicion or probable cause necessary to conduct an investigative detention or arrest (see, for example, *Reid v. George*, 448 U.S. 438, 1980, and *Royer* at 525, note 6). There are no circumstances under which officers may stop citizens based solely on their race, ethnicity, gender, religion, national origin, or any other demographic feature. Officers must base their stops of persons, whether in a vehicle or on foot, on reasonable suspicion or probable cause that a violation of the law has been or is about to be committed based on facts and information that they can articulate.

Some states, via legislation, have banned consent searches where there is no clear reason for suspicion. The mere nervousness of the motorist or occupant(s) is not sufficient reason to ask for a consent search. The Fourth and the Fourteenth (equal protection under the law) Amendments to the U.S. Constitution provide a framework for the protection of drivers from being indiscriminately targeted by the police via traffic stops. To prove an allegation of being indiscriminately targeted, the claimants must produce facts or statistics showing that they were targeted solely because of their race, ethnicity, gender, religion, or national origin. The burden then shifts to the police to provide evidence that they did not act solely on the basis of any of these factors.

In 2003, the U.S. Department of Justice banned all racial profiling by federal agents in a directive entitled "Guidance Regarding the Use of Race by Federal Law Enforcement Agencies."

Critics of the directive complain that it is inadequate and ineffective because it does not provide criteria that define racial profiling, is merely advisory and not legally binding, and contains no legal remedies for those who think they have been racially profiled.

The United States Congress has considered various pieces of legislation that would ban state and local law enforcement agencies from using racial profiling. Senate bill S.1038 (and its corresponding House bill, H.R. 2851), introduced in 2013 and entitled the "End Racial Profiling Act of 2013," were in committee at the time of publication of this text; the legislation has little likelihood of becoming law in the foreseeable future. The proposed legislation would allow the United States, or individuals injured by racial profiling, to bring civil actions for declaratory or injunctive relief. It would require federal law enforcement agencies to maintain policies and procedures for eliminating racial profiling and to end existing practices that permit racial profiling. It would require state, local, and Indian tribe governments applying for federal law enforcement assistance grants to certify that they have done the same, and to establish an administrative complaint procedure and independent auditor program for addressing complaints (United States Senate, 2013).

As of 2009, which was the most recent study, 25 states had enacted laws that require law enforcement agencies to develop and enforce policies to prevent racial profiling (see Exhibit 13.2). Twenty-one of those 25 states require the collection of data on the race and gender of each driver stopped by police and what actions were taken; 21 states collect data voluntarily; four states do not collect any data ("Jurisdictions Currently Collecting Data," 2009). Weeding out the illegitimate uses of profiles or profiling by police officers is the only way law enforcement can maintain credibility

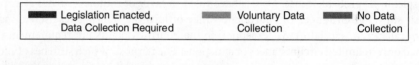

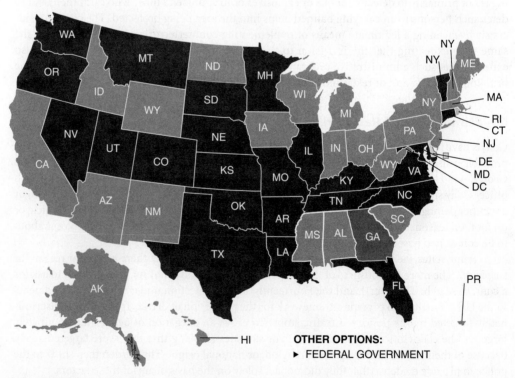

EXHIBIT 13.2 Jurisdictions Currently Collecting Data
Source: Data Collection Resource Center, 2009

within the communities they serve. The authors believe that the majority of officers know not to base their actions on any prejudices they might hold.

PREVENTION OF RACIAL PROFILING IN LAW ENFORCEMENT

To formulate measures to prevent the practice of racial profiling and inappropriate behavior and actions on the part of officers, the criminal justice system should consider the following seven areas:

- Accountability and supervision
- Agency policy to address racial profiling
- Recruitment and hiring
- Education and training
- Minority community outreach
- Professional traffic stops
- Data collection on citizens' race/ethnicity

Accountability and Supervision

Preventing the use of racial profiling or biased policing in law enforcement is critical. Police executives must reflect seriously on this and respond to both the reality and the perceptions of biased policing. Law enforcement executives, managers, and supervisors must send a clear message to all personnel that using race, ethnicity, or national origin alone as the basis for any investigative stop is not only unacceptable conduct, but also illegal. It can lead to termination from employment and possibly to prosecution. If convicted, the officer(s) could be fined and/or incarcerated depending on the laws of the particular state.

Police managers and supervisors, in order to identify officers who might be biased, should monitor such indicators as: (1) high numbers of minority citizen complaints; (2) high numbers of use-of-force or resisting incidents involving minorities; (3) large numbers of arrests not charged because prosecutors find improper detentions and/or searches; (4) perceptible negative attitude toward minorities; (5) negative attitudes toward training programs that enhance police–community relations or cultural awareness.

Prevention of racial profiling also involves other components of the criminal justice system, such as prosecutors and courts. Legislators are also an integral part of the process. For example, in New Jersey it is a crime for the police to use race as the primary factor in determining whom to stop and search, punishable by five years in prison and a $15,000 fine. Supervision, legislation, and documentation of the race/ethnicity of drivers stopped alone will not root out rogue officers who use racial profiling tactics. A program that reviews other contacts officers have with residents should also be instigated to help reduce such incidents. Law enforcement agencies must convey to their communities that they, the citizens, will be protected from such abuses and that abuse is not tolerated or advocated. Preventing the use of racial profiling by law enforcement officers not only is crucial to maintaining credibility within the community, but also reduces exposure to civil liability on the part of the departments and officers. Law enforcement managers might use the following self-assessment to evaluate their agency's policies and practices to determine if any of them could lead to a negative image of the department in the community or possible civil liability.

Self-Assessment

1. Has your law enforcement agency taken a proactive stance regarding bias-based traffic law enforcement?
2. How many civil rights complaints has your department received during the past year? What percentage is related to traffic stops?

3. Has your department been negatively portrayed in the media regarding community relations or bias-based traffic enforcement?
4. Do you collect data on the race, ethnicity, gender, and national origin of those your agency's officers have stopped, detained, searched, and arrested?
5. Have you authorized department-wide use of in-car video systems?
6. Is there an effective citizen complaint system in place and is the department responsive?
7. Do you have supervisory control that can identify (early alert) officers who may have patterns of bias-based traffic enforcement?
8. Does your agency have disciplinary policies and training established for officers with patterns of bias-based traffic enforcement?
9. Has your agency instituted proactive measures to build positive relations with the minority community (e.g., meetings with community leaders and neighborhood associations) before problems surface? ("Understanding Bias-Based Traffic Law Enforcement," 2003)

The authors of this text believe the majority of law enforcement officers, supervisors, and managers within agencies across the country are hardworking men and women who are committed to serving all members of our communities with fairness and respect. These professionals know racial profiling is unacceptable and conflicts with the standards and values inherent in ensuring all people are treated equally regardless of their race or ethnicity. They know racial profiling can expose a police department to costly lawsuits and ruin minority relations. They are intolerant of the use of racial profiling and willingly partner with their communities to address the issues involved. These professionals develop approaches to eradicate both confirmed acts of racial profiling and the perception that it is taking place within their agency or jurisdiction.

Agency Policies to Address Racial Profiling

Law enforcement agencies must have clear policies and procedures to address racial profiling and the perceptions thereof. Many departments in the United States have developed such general orders to cover not only traffic stops, but also the temporary detentions of pedestrians and even bicyclists. The policies usually address the Fourth Amendment requirement that investigative detentions, traffic stops, arrests, searches, and property seizures by officers must be based on a standard of reasonable suspicion or probable cause that officers can support with specific facts and circumstances. The policy must include the following: (1) no motorist, once cited or warned, shall be detained beyond the point where there exists no reasonable suspicion of further criminal activity and (2) no person or vehicle shall be searched in the absence of probable cause, a search warrant, or the person's *voluntary* consent. The policy should specify that in each case where a search is conducted, this information shall be recorded, including the legal basis for the search and the results. It is strongly recommended that consent searches be conducted only with written consent utilizing the agency forms provided. Some agencies now require that an officer's verbal request for consent to search an individual or vehicle be documented by a video or audio recording at the scene. According to Professor Brian Withrow, "Some police chiefs are considering imposing Miranda-like restrictions on the consent search. This will make the consent search process more onerous (i.e., expensive) so that hopefully the police will be more judicious in its use" (Withrow, 2009).

According to the International Association of Chiefs of Police (IACP), departments without a policy should look at as many models addressing racial profiling as possible before they create one that meets their needs. Agencies should also involve community members, especially minorities and civil rights advocates, in the development and implementation of the policy. The policy must communicate a clear message to law enforcement personnel and the people they serve that racial profiling and other forms of bias-based policing are not acceptable practices. The statement should include what discipline (including criminal prosecution where such laws exist) could result if officers violate the provisions of the policy.

The San Francisco Police Department created a general order that outlines their policy for policing without racial bias. It states that the department has always "striven to gain the trust of the community. To maintain that trust, it is crucial for members of our Department to carry out their duties in a manner free from bias and to eliminate any perception of policing that appears racially biased." The general order clarifies the circumstances under which officers can consider race, color, ethnicity, national origin, gender, age, sexual orientation, or gender identity when making law enforcement decisions.

> *Policy:* Investigative detentions, traffic stops, arrests, searches, and property seizures by officers will be based on a standard of reasonable suspicion or probable cause in accordance with the Fourth Amendment of the U.S. Constitution. Officers must be able to articulate specific facts and circumstances that support reasonable suspicion or probable cause for investigative detentions, traffic stops, arrest, nonconsensual searches, and property seizures. Department personnel may not use, *to any extent or degree*, race, color, ethnicity, national origin, age, sexual orientation or gender identity in conducting stops or detentions, or activities following stops or detentions *except* when engaging in the investigation of appropriate suspect-specific activity to identify a particular person or group. Department personnel seeking one or more specific persons who have been identified or described in part by any of the above listed characteristics may rely on them in part only in combination with other appropriate identifying factors. The listed characteristics should not be given undue weight:
>
> - Except as provided above, officers shall not consider race, color, ethnicity, national origin, gender, age, sexual orientation, or gender identity in establishing reasonable suspicion or probable cause.
> - Except as provided above, officers shall not consider race, color, ethnicity, national origin, gender, age, sexual orientation, or gender identity in deciding to initiate even those consensual encounters that do not amount to legal detentions or to request consent to search. (San Francisco Police Department General Order 5.17, 2011)

In 1979, the IACP, NOBLE, the National Sheriffs' Association, and the PERF created the Commission on Accreditation for Law Enforcement Agencies (CALEA). The primary purpose of the Commission is to improve law enforcement service by creating a national body of standards developed by law enforcement professionals. Furthermore, it recognizes professional achievements by establishing and administering an *accreditation* process through which a law enforcement agency can demonstrate that it meets those standards. "Participation in the CALEA accreditation program is voluntary, but successful completion provides a law enforcement agency with a nationally recognized award of excellence and professional achievement. Additional benefits of obtaining CALEA accreditation may include more favorable liability insurance costs and increased governmental *and community support*" (see CALEA Web site: www.calea.org).

CALEA in 2001 issued Standard 1.2.9 regarding bias-based profiling. The standard requires that CALEA-accredited agencies have a written policy governing bias-based profiling and, at a minimum, include the following provisions: (1) a prohibition against bias-based profiling in traffic contacts, in field contacts, and in asset seizures and forfeiture efforts; (2) training agency enforcement personnel in bias-based profiling issues including legal aspects; (3) corrective measures if bias-based profiling occurs; and (4) an annual administrative review of agency practices, including citizen concerns. CALEA does not require mandatory collection of traffic stop data even though there is a growing demand for such action. The Commission's position is that not all law enforcement agencies must collect traffic stop data when other successful measurement systems are in use and/or the situation in the community served does not indicate that there is a concern about police bias.

Recruitment and Hiring

Police agencies can reduce racial bias by recruiting and hiring officers who can police in a professional way. Within legal parameters, the department should hire a workforce that reflects the community's racial and ethnic demographics. Those hired should be expected to carry out their duties with fairness and impartiality. Having such a workforce increases the probability that, as a whole, the agency will be able to understand the perspectives of its racial/ethnic minorities and communicate with them effectively.

The officers that departments should be recruiting are those who are aware of and capable of managing their own ethnic, racial, and cultural stereotypes and biases in a professional way. These qualities are essential to reducing bias in policing. The multiple testing stages that applicants for law enforcement positions go through help weed out those who are unable to control their biases. Interviews, polygraphs, psychological tests, and background investigations are all intended to identify those who are biased to the point that they might act based on their prejudices (see Chapters 1 and 3). It should be noted that the possibility of bias is not limited to white officers. Members of minority groups can have biases against white people, against members of other minority groups, or even against members of their own race/ethnic group. There have been numerous studies that have determined that minority officers can be just as tough as whites on minority drivers, and sometimes tougher. Police recruitment messages, verbal and written, must emphasize that those who are prejudiced, regardless of their race or ethnicity, and who cannot distinguish between appropriate and inappropriate behavior and actions, will not be hired. As mentioned earlier in this chapter, no one is completely free of bias, but the recruitment effort should be targeted at those who understand and control their biases.

Education and Training

Law enforcement agencies need to provide training and education to enable officers to utilize legal enforcement tools so they can perform their work professionally and effectively within today's multicultural communities. Some departments have used interactive simulation training exercises to train officers on professional traffic stop procedures, especially those involving agitated citizens. Clearly, most law enforcement officers know not to act based on the prejudices and stereotypes they might hold. However, the nature of prejudice is such that some people are not aware of their own prejudices or biases. Therefore, they make inferences and take actions toward certain groups based on these unrecognized biased perceptions. Training that provides accurate information concerning groups about which officers might have prejudices and stereotypes is one of the approaches police departments should use to prevent racial profiling.

What is the mental process that takes place when an officer makes a stop based on race, ethnicity, or national origin? Officers who have a biased belief system observe and collect certain data that in turn reinforce that belief system. Meanings are added to make sense of the observations ("I notice minorities more and stop them more because of my biased beliefs about them"). Based on these meanings, assumptions are made that fill in for missing data ("This motorist is carrying drugs on him"). The officer draws conclusions (based on beliefs) and then takes action (decides to stop African American and Hispanic motorists much more frequently than whites). These steps in our thinking take place very quickly. Most of us are not aware that this process goes on all the time (see the section in Chapter 1 on "Prejudice in Law Enforcement").

In their book *The Fifth Discipline Fieldbook: Strategies and Tools for Building a Learning Organization*, management specialist Peter Senge and his coauthors provide a clear and simple model called the "Ladder of Inference," which illuminates most people's typical patterns (and flaws) of thinking. Using the ladder, the authors discuss thinking and decision-making processes to describe, from the bottom up, how people select data, add meanings, make assumptions, draw conclusions, adopt beliefs, and ultimately take action (see Exhibit 13.3). They maintain that:

> We live in a world of self-generating beliefs that remain largely untested. We adopt those beliefs because they are based on conclusions, which are inferred from what we observe, plus our past experience. Our ability to achieve the results we truly desire is eroded by our feelings that:
>
> • Our beliefs are the truth.
> • The truth is obvious.

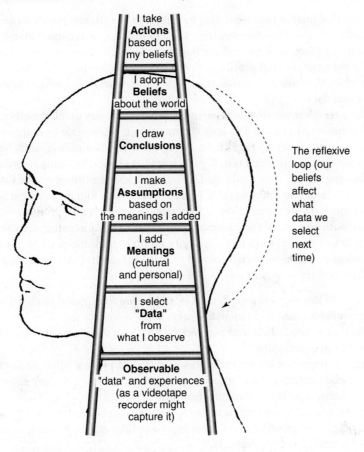

I take
Actions
based on
my beliefs

I adopt
Beliefs
about the world

I draw
Conclusions

I make
Assumptions
based on
the meanings I added

I add
Meanings
(cultural
and personal)

I select
"Data"
from
what I observe

Observable
"data" and experiences
(as a videotape
recorder might
capture it)

The reflexive
loop (our
beliefs
affect
what
data we
select
next
time)

EXHIBIT 13.3 Ladder of Inference.
Source: Senge et al., 1994, pp. 242–246. Reproduced with permission of
Peter Senge.

- Our beliefs are based on real data.
- The data we select are the real data. (Senge, Kleiner, Roberts, Ross, & Smith, 1994)

The authors explain that most people no longer remember where their attitudes and beliefs came from (i.e., what data or experiences led to their assumptions and conclusions). Therefore, they may not understand the basis of the actions they take. Senge and his coauthors discuss "leaps of abstraction" in which:

> our minds literally move at lightning speed . . . because we immediately "leap" to generalizations so quickly that we never think to test them. . . . [L]eaps of abstraction occur when we move from direct observation (concrete "data") to generalization without testing. Leaps of abstraction impede learning because they become axiomatic. What was once an assumption becomes treated as a fact. (Senge et al., 1994)

The authors go on to say that we then treat generalization as fact.

> How do you spot leaps of abstraction? First, by asking yourself what you believe about the way the world works. . . . Ask "what is the 'data' on which this generalization is based?" Then ask yourself, "Am I willing to consider that this generalization may be inaccurate or misleading?" It is important to ask this last question consciously, because, if the answer is no, there is no point in proceeding. (Senge et al., 1994)

In intensive training conducted by Senge, police and other corporate executives are able to learn about the models above and relate them to issues and challenges in their own organizations.

The models provide insight into what may be going on in officers' minds as they stop members of minority groups. Thus the models can help officers better understand their actions vis-à-vis racial profiling. It is natural for people to substitute assumptions for what is not known, but in the case of racial profiling, this is a very dangerous proposition. Officers have to recognize when they are converting their biases into "facts" and when their assumptions substitute for real data.

Training and education provide departments an opportunity to inform officers of the penalties for not adhering to policies and laws on the subject. Many state legislatures have created laws barring law enforcement officers from engaging in racial profiling. Such legislation also requires that every law enforcement officer participate in expanded training regarding racial profiling. This training is typically coordinated, monitored, and controlled by the Commission on Peace Officer Standards and Training (POST), an agency that is found in every state. These state commissions should, if they haven't already, integrate the topic of racial profiling into their diversity training for both entry-level and in-service programs. Law enforcement agencies should consult local chapters of their community's minority group organizations to obtain accounts and examples of actual or perceived racially biased policing for use in training programs. Such programs should also cover:

1. Definitions of key terms involved, such as *profile, profiling, racial profiling, racially biased policing, probable cause*, and *reasonable suspicion.*
2. Identification of key indices and perspectives that signal cultural differences among residents in a local community.
3. The negative impact of biases, prejudices, and stereotyping on effective law enforcement, including examination of how historical perceptions of discriminatory enforcement practices have harmed police–community relations.
4. History and role of the civil rights movement and its impact on law enforcement.
5. Specific obligations of officers in preventing, reporting, and responding to discriminatory or biased practices by fellow officers.
6. Various perspectives of local groups and race relations experts regarding cultural diversity and police–community relations.

Training should also involve constitutional law and ethics. Every state will have different requirements, but here is an example from the Commission on POST of Missouri:

1. All commissioned, licensed peace officers, who have the authority to enforce vehicle/traffic laws, must attend a minimum of one hour of racial profiling training each year.
2. Individuals who have *no authority* to make traffic stops are *exempt* from this annual requirement.
3. All racial profiling training used to meet the requirement must be obtained from a licensed training center, an approved provider of continuing education, or a course approved by POST.

The law enforcement community is more capable now than ever before of effectively addressing biased policing. In the past few decades, there has been a revolution in the quality and quantity of police training, the standards for hiring officers, and accountability.

Minority Community Outreach

Every police–community interaction requires a strong, ongoing link to community groups and civil rights organizations. Links might be established when community policing, which became popular in the 1990s, is used to address neighborhood problems. A link is also established when community task forces are assembled to address issues, especially of racial profiling and the perception thereof. These steps demonstrate respect for the minority community and create shared responsibility for whatever action is taken. The police hold primary responsibility for community outreach on every level, but the community is also responsible for becoming involved in activities that form positive relationships with the police. Policing within the community can function only in an environment of mutual engagement and respect. In the context of racial profiling or biased policing, outreach to the community is imperative. For constructive dialog to take place, therefore, police executives must remain open to discussions of racial profiling or the perception thereof within their jurisdictions. Sometimes, data on traffic stops and people searched can be used as a springboard for dialog and communications between law enforcement and the community. It is an opportunity for the clarification and open discussion of the raw data. An individual who has been trained in the analysis of such data and the use of appropriate statistical benchmarks should moderate the discussions.

Although there are many examples of police departments collaborating with the minority community to discuss and resolve issues pertaining to racial profiling or racially biased policing, the Chicago Police Department could serve as a positive example. Since 2000, Chicago's police superintendent has sponsored a series of meetings between the police and residents of the minority community to address racial tensions and concerns about police racial bias. The forums have included community activists, and staff of all ranks represented the police department. Prior to the first meeting, participants were surveyed for their opinions, perceptions, and observations about racial profiling and racially biased policing. The survey also asked them to rate the department's strengths and weaknesses regarding minority outreach and solicited their ideas about how to improve police–minority relations and resolve issues. The forums were moderated by an independent facilitator. At the first meeting, community members shared their thoughts, experiences, and concerns, and police staff listened but did not respond. Later in the day, the police shared their thoughts and reactions to the morning session, and the citizens were instructed to listen and not respond. During the final session of the day, all participants joined in a discussion of the issues and ideas raised earlier. The meetings continued over a period of time until the participants identified specific actions to be taken by both the police and community members to address the issues that had been raised (Fridell et al., 2001).

PROFESSIONAL POLICE TRAFFIC STOPS

The reason for every stop made by a law enforcement officer must be legally defensible and professional. Professional traffic stops involve four key elements:

- *Organizational/agency policy.* Agencies must develop a well-structured policy concerning professional traffic stops, outlining the conduct of officers and the prohibition of discriminatory practices.
- *Officer training.* Agencies should include a component on racial profiling into existing in-service training programs. Special workshop discussions on the issue of racial profiling can also be scheduled.
- *Data collection.* Agencies must collect traffic stop data when the situation in the community served indicates that there is a concern about police bias.
- *Accountability/supervision.* Law enforcement supervisors and managers must hold officers accountable for adhering to the policy. Managers must personally take the message to employees, as well as to the public, that biased policing will not be tolerated and could result in discipline, possibly including prosecution or termination. Managers, supervisors, and the entire workforce must embrace and adhere to the policy.

Deputy Chief Ondra Berry (Reno, Nevada, Police Department), now retired, in diversity training he conducts nationwide (and as he formerly did in communications with his own officers), offers the following advice: "When contemplating stopping a motorist, ask yourself, 'Is there a possibility that I may be making an assumption about this driver based on race? Am I moving from my own personal 'data' and making a leap of extraction about this vehicle or about this person?'" Officers must recognize that this is a possibility. Berry further advises, "Do not take race into account when deciding who to stop. Use your good policing skills. Again, if you are normal, you have unbalanced views about people who are different from you" (Berry, 2013).

In the context of Chapter 6, Law Enforcement Contact with African Americans, we emphasize the need for officers to slow down their thinking processes and challenge some of their personal biases when considering stopping an individual when there are no obvious signs of wrongdoings. To review, officers would be well advised to go through the following mental steps before acting on racial biases and prejudices (clearly, this does not suggest that all officers act on racial biases and prejudices):

> If I see an individual simply walking down the street, let me first acknowledge to myself that I am not sure whether there is any reason to stop this person. I will ask myself the following questions:
>
> "Why do I think this person should be stopped?"
>
> "What is this person doing that makes me think he/she is suspicious?"
>
> "Could this person be lost or in the need of help?"
>
> "Is this person's race a part of the reason why I want to stop them?"
>
> > If I decide that I should, for whatever reason, stop this individual, would there be merit in my saying something like:
> > "There has been a robbery in the neighborhood and I want you to be aware of the potential dangers. You look a little lost, so I was wondering if you need any help or directions." (This only applies if there have actually been recent robberies in the neighborhood. If the person lives in that neighborhood, being dishonest can negatively affect the officer's credibility.) (Johnson, 2013)

In the process of slowing down one's mental processes, the officer makes a conscious decision to recognize potential bias if it is there, and refrains from making inferences or jumping to conclusions based on racial bias or prejudice. Officers can increase cooperation with respectful communication, and, at the same time, assess the **behavior** of the person they are stopping.

The IACP, after significant study, identified the components that constitute a "professional traffic stop." The organization's publication "Recommendations from the First IACP Forum on Professional Traffic Stops" should be referred to for additional information.

DATA COLLECTION ON CITIZENS' RACE/ETHNICITY

When racial profiling became an issue throughout the United States, many law enforcement jurisdictions began collecting data on the race/ethnicity of people stopped and/or searched by police. Some did so voluntarily while others did so because of court decrees or community pressure. The purpose of collecting data is to address racially biased policing and the perceptions thereof and to determine whether it is taking place. The use of data collection requires officers to complete a form following each traffic stop.

Research by PERF examined the arguments for and against data collection:

Arguments in Favor of Data Collection

Data collection helps agencies:

1. Determine whether racially biased policing is a problem in the jurisdiction
2. Convey a commitment to unbiased policing
3. "Get ahead of the curve"
4. Effectively allocate and manage department resources

Collecting data and interpreting them, if done correctly, reflects accountability and openness on the part of the agency. The process helps to improve police–community relations. Departments doing so identify problems and search for solutions. The data can be informative to department management about what types of stops and searches officers are making. Managers and supervisors can then decide not only whether these practices are the most efficient allocation of department resources, but also whether biased policing is taking place. Without the collection and analysis of data, departments can have a difficult time defending their practices if challenged in court.

Arguments against Data Collection

1. Data collection does not yield valid information regarding the nature and extent of racially biased policing.
2. Data could be used to harm the agency or its personnel.
3. Data collection may impact police productivity, morale, and workload.
4. Police resources might be used to combat racially biased policing and the perceptions thereof in more effective ways (Fridell et al., 2001).

Many departments still resist record keeping. They argue, for one, that the mere collection of "racial" statistics may imply that biased policing is taking place. These agencies maintain that the raw data, when first collected and before analysis and comparison with benchmarks, could reinforce or increase the public's negative perceptions of the agency at the cost of both the morale and the effectiveness of officers. At the same time, some departments have expressed concern that any data they do collect could be used against them in court. These law enforcement executives question the ability of data collection systems to provide valid answers about the nature and extent of racially biased policing within their departments. The simple collection of data will neither prevent racial profiling nor accurately identify if it is taking place. The process alone does not protect agencies from public criticism, scrutiny, and litigation because the data collected are open to interpretation. The raw data collected represent meaningless numbers unless put into a relevant context using statistical benchmarks (discussed later) to provide a legitimate means of comparison. Standing alone, the data collected can be used to make or defend any position that someone may adopt about racial profiling. Law enforcement agencies, therefore, must take additional steps to ensure that the numbers they collect accurately reflect reality. Each department must evaluate its specific circumstances. For agencies that have had no community complaints and/or already closely monitor officer behavior in other ways, undertaking data collection may not be the most efficient use of resources.

Another argument used against data collection has been the observation that, within some law enforcement agencies, officers discontinued or reduced the number of self-initiated traffic stops and pedestrian contacts they made when data collection became a requirement. Officers resentful or concerned about being monitored ceased to initiate stops in order to avoid the possibility of being perceived as racially biased. Some agencies do not require the officer to reveal his or her identity on the data form. The identity of the individual(s) detained is never documented on the form. Some city/county administrators and law enforcement executives are also concerned about the time and costs associated with the collection and analysis of data.

Thus, data collection has its advantages, disadvantages, and limitations. PERF recommends that police agency executives, in collaboration with citizen leaders, review the pros and cons of the practice. They must factor in the agency's political, social, organizational, and financial situation to decide whether or not to either initiate data collection or allocate available resources to other approaches to address racially biased policing and the perceptions thereof.

DATA COLLECTION ELEMENTS   The basic elements for data collection that both the U.S. DOJ Resource Guide and PERF recommend to law enforcement agencies are:

- Date/time/location
- Characteristics of the individual(s): Age/gender, race/ethnicity/national origin

- Reason for stop: penal or vehicle code violation or infraction; reactive (call for service) or self-initiated
- Search or no search: if search, the search authority (including consent, if consent involved) and results (what, if anything, was recovered)
- Disposition: arrest, citation, verbal warning, written warning, or no action

There is a rationale and justification behind each of the recommended elements. They are designed to determine not only whom the police are stopping, but also the circumstances and context of the stops. "In effect, we are trying to collect 'circumstantial' data to tell us the real reasons citizens are being stopped—which should reflect the motivations of the officers and/or the impact of agency policies and practices" (Fridell et al., 2001). In completing the section of the form pertaining to race, ethnicity, or national origin, officers are expected to use their best judgment, based on their observations, training, and experience, and not ask the person detained. PERF, COPS, and the U.S. Department of Justice have developed protocols and guidelines for the collection, analysis, and interpretation of vehicle stop data. These detailed how-to guides should be referred to by those involved in developing a system or method of tracking vehicle stops and trying to measure racial bias in policing. The materials available from these agencies provide information on what activities to target for data collection.

Most agencies collect data only on traffic stops (moving or mechanical violations) because of their frequency and also because that is where there is the greatest potential for police racial bias (or perception thereof) to occur. Another source of data is vehicle stops or general investigative stops of drivers. This sort of stop involves officer discretion (wherein the officer should have reasonable suspicion or probable cause to conduct an investigative stop) and is also an important source of information to analyze. Collecting data on *detentions* encompasses not only traffic and vehicle stops, but also pedestrian or bicyclist stops. A fourth source of data is *nonconsensual encounters*, in which an officer is not detaining the citizen, but is questioning him or her. PERF recommends that agencies collect data on all vehicle and traffic stops. Their recommendation does not include pedestrian stops or nonconsensual encounters that do not amount to detentions.

Data collection would be different for municipal and highway policing. The job of city police and county sheriffs is mostly responsive in nature in that they answer to calls for service from victims or witnesses to events. The officers' enforcement patterns depend on the character of the neighborhoods in which they serve, and thus the race/ethnicity of the persons they contact will vary accordingly. This must be taken into account during data analysis and interpretation. Comparative benchmarks must be utilized for each differing community and area of the city or county. Highway policing, in contrast, involves more self-initiated activity and more discretion on the part of officers. The Bureau of Justice Statistics (BJS) reported that, as of October 2004, 29 of the nation's 49 state law enforcement agencies, whose primary duties include highway patrol, required their officers to record the race or ethnicity of motorists stopped for traffic violations. Twenty-two state agencies required officers to record race or ethnicity data for all officer-initiated stops, and seven did so in more limited circumstances. The report indicates that most agencies (27) relied on their officers' observations of the driver's race or ethnicity as the method of determining the race or ethnicity of the motorist (Hickman, 2005). There has been no BJS study of state law enforcement agencies' reporting requirements since.

The Montgomery County (Maryland) Police Department, as part of an agreement with the Fraternal Order of Police and the Department of Justice in 2000, began to collect data on all traffic stops, using electronic media rather than paper. The agency continues to collect traffic stop data today, and Maryland state law now mandates that all agencies (127) in the state do so also. The intent of the legislation is to provide information about the pervasiveness of racial profiling. All law eligible traffic stops (defined as all stops made that are eligible to issue traffic violations) result in the officers' entering specific information into a handheld computer with specialized software; the information is later downloaded into the department's central database and forwarded to the Maryland Statistical Analysis Center. The officers use a "Traffic Stop Data Format Guide" with fields that include codes for (1) agency, (2) gender, (3) race, (4) stop reason, (5) registration (state; out of state), (6) search conducted or not, (7) search reason, (8) disposition of search, (8) outcome (warning, citation, repair order, arrest), and (9) arrest reason. The Governor's Office of Crime Control and Prevention is the clearinghouse for all of the data collected, and the office generates a report each year that includes an analysis of the results for the entire state. The report issued for calendar year 2011 contains the following conclusions:

- The descriptive statistics suggest that traffic stops and the characteristics of traffic stops were generally consistent with regard to race/ethnicity.
- With the exception of Asian men and women and African American men, the most likely reason for all other drivers to be stopped was for vehicle equipment violations.
- Searches of drivers and their vehicles were not conducted very often by police officers during traffic stops (less than 3% of all stops).
- The majority of each group stopped had nothing confiscated, regardless of their race/ethnicity.
- Once stopped, drivers were most likely to receive either a written or verbal warning, excluding Hispanic males, who were more likely to receive a citation.
- Hispanic males were also the most likely to be arrested after a traffic stop had been conducted.
- The majority of all arrests made by law enforcement during traffic stops were based on the initial reason for the stop.

The report indicates that

> The major limitation of the current study pertains to the possibility of omitted variables that may account for any differences observed between race/ethnicities. . . . [N]o statistical conclusions can be drawn from this report regarding the effect of race/ethnicity on the frequency or characteristics associated with traffic stops. ("Ninth Report to the State of Maryland Under TR 25-113," 2012)

There is no mention in the Maryland report of the use of any statistical benchmarks against which to analyze, interpret, and compare the race/ethnicity distribution of stopped drivers to test for racial profiling. Thus, it appears to be only a descriptive analysis, and although it suggests there is no racial profiling, it is impossible to be conclusive.

STATISTICAL BENCHMARKS Statistical benchmarks are the comparative populations or groups against which the data collected are going to be analyzed and interpreted. In other words, they are the estimates of the proportions of individuals available to be stopped by race or ethnicity within the area studied. Racial profiling analysis requires developing and using an appropriate benchmark. The selection and development of benchmarks is a very complicated process often requiring the assistance of specialists in the field so the correct interpretation of the data is achieved. There are different types of benchmarks, but three are most common:

1. *Resident population or census of the community* that is policed by the department under consideration; that is, the demographics of the geographic area to be studied. This method is probably the most commonly used.
2. *Field observation of drivers* at randomly selected sites during randomly selected times. Normally field observers attempt to identify the race or ethnicity and approximate age of each driver.
3. *Accident records for not-at-fault drivers* to estimate the qualitative features (e.g., racial composition) of actual roadway users. Information arising from accident statistics is commonly used by traffic engineers to develop qualitative benchmarks of actual road users.

There are advantages and disadvantages to each type of benchmark, and there is no agreement among experts on which is the most reliable. None of these benchmarks is universally adaptable to every racial profiling evaluation, and the positive and negative aspects of each must be taken into consideration when deciding which one to use. However, one criminal justice researcher, Brian Withrow, maintains that:

> A benchmark comparison alone cannot measure the factors that influence a police officer's decision to initiate a traffic stop. We cannot even determine whether or not the officer even knew the race of the individual prior to the stop. In other words, benchmark comparisons only tell us who gets stopped, not why. (Withrow 2004)

The benchmarks selected must be able to help measure whether individuals are being stopped on the basis of their race, ethnicity, or national origin. One question to be asked is, in a similar situation, would a person who was not a member of a minority group have been stopped? In other words, the correct comparison is not to the people living in the neighborhood or driving on the highway who did not engage in the same conduct as the person stopped, but to those who did engage in the same conduct but were not stopped because they were not of a minority race (U.S. Department of Justice, 2000). One can see how difficult a task it is to develop statistical benchmarks.

Unfortunately, most research and analysis of collected data on traffic and field interrogation stops (detentions) does not take into consideration the decision-making processes of the officers involved. Distinguishing between low- and high-discretion stops may prove useful for data collection and analysis. Most data collection efforts have neglected the need to explain how and why officers make decisions pertaining to traffic or other stops when studying racial profiling. Research designs should allow for the investigation of officers' decision-making after stops have been initiated (Engel et al., 2002). One strategy recently developed to do this is the Internal Benchmarking method, which involves conducting routine, ongoing racial profiling surveillance of certain law enforcement officers and comparing their behavior or performance with similarly situated peers. The term *similarly situated* refers to officers who work the same assignment (e.g., patrol), in the same geographical area, and during the same time period. The method was developed by Professor Samuel Walker (Walker, 2003) from the University of Nebraska, and tested using data collected at the Wichita (Kansas) Police Department in 2001 by Professor Withrow. The goal was to construct an internal benchmark that would identify officers on an individual level who actually stop substantially higher numbers of racial minorities. The method is a "data-driven administrative tool for identifying employees with performance problems and providing some kind of intervention to correct the problematic behavior" (Withrow, 2009).

An agency using the Internal Benchmark strategy to determine if a suspected officer is using racial profiling practices would also incorporate other performance indicators into the investigation. For example, is the officer receiving an above-average number of citizen complaints or excessive-force allegations? Professor Walker describes performance indicators as part of what can be a comprehensive early warning system that agencies can use to evaluate the behaviors of their officers. According to Professor Withrow, however, although the Internal Benchmark method is an encouraging strategy, it is not a panacea. He indicates that

> the number of variables necessary to define similarly situated officers may be problematic. It is because policing is a dynamic process. When properly developed, however, the advantages of an early warning system for racial profiling surveillance can be substantial. The analysis based on these data is free from the error known to exist within the traditional benchmarking strategies. The results are more credible and less subject to conjecture or debate. Also, the information provides insight into officer performance at the individual level. This allows the department to focus its attention on the individual officers who appear to be performing errantly or at the very least ineffectively. (Withrow, Dailey, & Jackson, 2008)

Unfortunately, no benchmarking strategy has proven to be universally acceptable, and there is considerable disagreement amongst practitioners, scholars, and researchers on their reliability and validity. In general, benchmarking strategies fail to completely measure the population of individuals who are actually observed by the police but not stopped. At best, benchmarks estimate the population of individuals who *might* or *should* be observed by the police, and thus available to be stopped (Withrow, 2007). The benchmark sets the stage for responding to the most important question asked in a racial profiling study: Do the police stop a disproportionate number of racial and ethnic minorities? "Inevitably, the answer to this question comes from comparing a numerator (the proportion of individuals actually stopped by race or ethnicity) with a denominator (the proportion of individuals estimated to be available to be stopped by race or ethnicity)" (Withrow et al., 2008).

An example of the use of benchmarks is found in a 2006 study by the RAND Corporation. The New York City Police Department (NYPD) had stopped half a million pedestrians for suspected criminal involvement. The RAND report indicated that the raw statistics for these encounters suggested large racial disparities—89 percent of the stops involved nonwhites. The report asked the following questions:

1. Do these statistics point to racial bias in police officers' decisions to stop particular pedestrians?
2. Do they indicate that officers are particularly intrusive when stopping nonwhites?

The NYPD asked the RAND Corporation to help it understand this issue and come up with recommendations for addressing potential problems. Researchers analyzed data on all street encounters between NYPD officers and pedestrians in 2006. They compared the racial distribution of stops to external benchmarks. Using these benchmarks, the researchers attempted to construct what the racial distribution of the stopped pedestrians would have been if officers' decisions had been racially unbiased. They then compared each officer's stopping patterns with an internal benchmark constructed from stops in similar circumstances made by other officers. Finally, they examined stop outcomes, assessing whether stopped white and nonwhite suspects had different rates of frisk, search, use of force, and arrest. They found small racial differences in these rates, and made communication, recordkeeping, and training recommendations to the NYPD for improving police–pedestrian interactions ("New York: Analysis of Racial Disparities in the New York City Police Department's Stop, Question, and Frisk Practices," 2007).

DATA ANALYSIS AND INTERPRETATION   Once data have been collected, what do they show? The most difficult part of the process is the analysis and interpretation of the statistics compiled. As researcher Robin Engel and her colleagues reported:

> Ultimately, the problem with interpreting results is that the traffic and field interrogation data have been collected without the guidance of any theoretical framework. Researchers have simply counted things—the number of traffic stops, citations, and searches conducted by police against white and nonwhite suspects. Instead, the research should be conducted under the larger theoretical context of *explaining* behavior. Problems with the interpretation of empirical data are due partially to data collection efforts that have not addressed *why* officers might engage in decision-making based on citizens' race. (Engel et al., 2002)

Engel and her coauthors suggest that research on racial profiling should include consideration of three dependent variables:

1. *The behavior of the individual police officer:*
   a. Why do police officers in general stop more black citizens than white citizens? How and why do officers make decisions?
   b. Why do some officers exhibit more racial disproportionality, while others exhibit less?
   c. Have there been changes in racial disproportionality over time?

2. *The behavior of different police departments:* Do some police departments have high rates of racial profiling and others have low rates? If so, what explains these differences?
3. *The aggregate rates of officer and departmental behavior:* Has race-based decision-making been transformed in the past 40 years from one based primarily on individual racial prejudice to one based mainly on race-based departmental policies? (Engel et al., 2002)

As explained, statistical benchmarks must be developed for comparison with the raw data collected by agencies. Among the decisions that must be made are:

1. Are the statistics collected compared with the city's racial makeup as determined by the nationwide census?
2. Are they compared with licensed drivers living in the city's jurisdiction?
3. Are they compared with the racial composition of the drivers on the roads, if that could be determined?
4. Are situational characteristics (e.g., suspects' characteristics, characteristics of the police–citizen encounter, and legal characteristics) considered and collected?
5. Are officers' characteristics (e.g., sex, race, experience, and attitudes) considered and collected?
6. Are organizational characteristics (e.g., formal and informal policies and attitudes and preferences of administrators and first-line supervisors) considered and collected?
7. Are community characteristics (e.g., demographic, economic, and political) considered and collected?

Data interpretation can be done internally by the law enforcement agency involved if the community political climate is good and there is trust that the analysis will be credible. However, since a positive community political climate is not usually the case, and to avoid the perception that the findings are suspect, most agencies obtain the services of an independent analyst. It is important that the analyst not only have some general knowledge of law enforcement procedures, but also be knowledgeable on the selection and development of statistical benchmarks or base rates. COPS, in conjunction with the Department of Justice (DOJ), has produced a document entitled "How to Correctly Collect and Analyze Racial Profiling

CASE STUDY—The San Angelo (Texas) Police Department

The Texas legislature in 2002 addressed the issue of racial profiling in policing when they passed Senate Bill 1074, the Texas Racial Profiling Law, which was amended by House Bill 3389. The purpose of the legislation was to address concerns regarding such practices among the state's police forces. Due to the statute, the San Angelo Police Department adopted a detailed written policy on racial profiling which:

1. Defines acts constituting racial profiling
2. Strictly prohibits peace officers from engaging in racial profiling
3. Implements a process by which an individual may file a complaint with the San Angelo Police Department if he or she believes that a San Angelo peace officer has engaged in racial profiling

4. Provides public education relating to the agency's complaint process
5. Requires appropriate corrective action to be taken against a peace officer who, after an investigation, is shown to have engaged in racial profiling
6. Requires collection of information relating to motor vehicle stops in which a citation is issued and to arrests made as a result of those stops, including information relating to:
   a. the race or ethnicity of the individual detained;
   b. whether a search was conducted and, if so, whether the individual detained consented to the search; and
   c. whether the peace officer knew the race or ethnicity of the individual detained before detaining that individual

7. Requires the agency's chief administrator of the agency to submit an annual report of the information collected to the Commission on Law Enforcement Officer Standards and Education and the governing body of San Angelo. (Texas Code of Criminal Procedure, 2001)

From 2002 to 2006, statistical data on traffic stops was gathered by the San Angelo Police Department and the findings reported as required. However, racial profiling experts and civil rights activists questioned the results, claiming that the findings were inconclusive because they were limited to only a descriptive analysis. In other words, they believed that the statistical benchmarks used were questionable.

The Police Department then hired an assistant professor of Criminal Justice at Angelo State University, an expert in the field of racial profiling, to perform the study required by the statute. Throughout 2006, data on traffic stops were collected and analyzed and compared to the baseline population data derived from the U.S. Census Bureau and to the citation-based contact data collected from both the City of San Angelo Police Department and the City of San Angelo Municipal Court. The analyses suggested that there was "no evidence that the San Angelo police officers, especially White, did differentially target minority resident drivers." ("The San Angelo Police Department Annual Racial Profiling Report," 2006)

Similar reports since 2006 have had the same findings. The department now has what is called a "Tier One - Partial Exemption Racial Profiling Report" because their patrol units that conduct vehicle stops are equipped with video and audio equipment. The department is required to maintain the videos for 90 days. Shift supervisors randomly pull patrol car videotapes to review and look for evidence of one race being targeted (taking into consideration the area the officer works in) and to determine whether corrective action is necessary. Tier One requires the collection of data only on people who were issued citations and searched. Tier Two requires information on the race of individuals involved in any law enforcement-initiated action, including those who were stopped but not issued a citation or searched.

In-service officers are required to take a four-hour training course on racial profiling and are instructed how to handle traffic stops, searches and arrests. The course includes U.S. Supreme Court decisions about procedures in traffic stops.

Data: Your Reputation Depends on It." This provides recommendations on the methodology for data collection and analysis. This 2002 document can be downloaded from the COPS Web site. Another helpful document, published by PERF in 2005 in collaboration with COPS and DOJ, is "Understanding Race Data from Vehicle Stops: A Stakeholder's Guide," by Lorie Fridell.

COMMUNITY TASK FORCES FOR DEVELOPMENT AND IMPLEMENTATION   Citizen input is critical to the success of data collection and interpretation. Community group representatives reflecting the diversity of the community must be involved with police personnel of all ranks to form a task force. The task force members, including in most cases an independent analyst, work together to decide: (1) if data will be collected about the race/ethnicity of persons contacted by officers, (2) the design of benchmarks to utilize in the interpretation of the data, and (3) the response or action to be taken based on the interpretation. Police departments should take the input of the task force and implement the appropriate recommendations in subsequent phases of the project. Task forces and community policing are beneficial to a department's efforts to investigate and solve problems associated with allegations of racial profiling. Task forces not only help ensure that the process addresses specific concerns of the community, but also help improve police–community relations. PERF suggests how to get started:

1. Unless mandated, decide, with citizen input, whether data collection should be one component of the jurisdiction's overall response to racially biased policing and the perceptions thereof.
2. Communicate with agency personnel as soon as a decision is made to start collecting data. The executive should provide a rationale for data collection and address anticipated concerns.

3. Set up a process for listening to the concerns of personnel, and have personnel help to develop constructive ways to address them.
4. Develop a police–citizen group to serve in an advisory capacity.
5. Develop the data collection and analysis protocol. Ensure that the interpretations will be responsible, based on sound methodology and analysis.
6. Field test the data collection system for 3 to 6 months, and use that test to make modifications before implementing the system jurisdiction-wide. (Fridell et al., 2001)

UNINTENDED RESULTS OF DATA COLLECTION In some agencies, when mandatory data collection was instituted, the number of traffic tickets dropped precipitously as officers, wary of being accused of racial profiling, stopped fewer people. This occurred, for example, in Houston and Cincinnati. In some other agencies, officers refused to fill out the forms or made mistakes, which made the data unusable. The officers complained that the collection process was a waste of time and that the data collected might be used against them. Some argued that officers who use racial profiling because they are prejudiced will never fill out the form. There are examples of cities in which police officers are so fearful of the possibility of being accused of being racist if they stop a person of color that they avoid making contact even if a violation or minor crime is being committed. If accusations begin to control policing, public safety suffers. Some agencies have equipped their patrol vehicles with video cameras and audio recording devices to provide evidence of the actions of their officers in the event of complaints.

Summary

- Although the term *racial profiling* was first used in association with the New Jersey State Police stopping individuals along Interstate 95 in the early 1990s, there have been complaints about this practice for decades in the United States.
- When the issue of racial profiling came to the attention of the public and of law enforcement in the 1990s, there was no agreement on a definition, so it was difficult to develop approaches to prevent the practice.
- Prior to September 11, 2001, use of profiles that included race, ethnicity, or national origin were condemned by most U.S. citizens, but this attitude changed after the attacks on the World Trade Center and the Pentagon, and after subsequent attempted attacks. As time has passed since those events, profiling has again become controversial. This has become a challenge in the national response to terrorism.
- Some police officers, government administrators, and others maintain that racial profiling is a myth or a misperception. An abundance of anecdotes and government reports, organizational studies, and statistics indicate that the racial profiling of African Americans, Latinos, Native Americans, Arabs, Sikhs, and some other races and ethnicities persists, however, despite efforts to end the phenomenon.
- Many police and sheriffs' departments across the nation as well as federal law enforcement agencies have adopted policies that address racial profiling. These policies cover accountability and supervision; recruitment and hiring; education and training; outreach to the minority community; professional traffic stops; and data collection on race and ethnicity.
- To be legally defensible and professional, traffic stops must be part of a well-structured organizational policy that prohibits discriminatory practices; officer training must include a component on racial profiling; traffic stop data must be collected if there is a community concern about police bias; and officers must be held accountable by their supervisors. Any data collected must be analyzed using appropriate benchmarks.
- Citizen discontent and lawsuits can originate as a result of racial profiling or the use of any profiling that appears to have been based on bias. Law enforcement professionals must be critical and introspective when analyzing the problem of racism and prejudice in the profession, and must be aware of the strong feelings the topic of profiling engenders.

Discussion Questions and Issues

1. *Law Enforcement Agency Policy on Racial Profiling.* The student can determine if a police department in the area meets recommended standards regarding policies pertaining to racial profiling in the following manner:

   a. Does the policy clearly define acts constituting racial profiling using the definition provided at the beginning of this chapter?

   b. Does the policy strictly prohibit peace officers employed by the agency from engaging in racial profiling?

   c. Does the policy provide instructions by which individuals may file a complaint if they believe they were victims of racial profiling by an employee of the agency?

   d. Does the agency provide public education relating to the complaint process?

   e. Does the policy require appropriate corrective action to be taken against a peace officer employed by the agency who, after an investigation, is shown to have engaged in racial profiling in violation of the agency's policy?

   f. Does the agency require the collection of data relating to traffic stops in which a citation is issued and to arrests resulting from those traffic stops, including information relating to:

      1. The race or ethnicity of the individual detained?

      2. Whether a search was conducted and, if so, whether it was based on the consent of the person detained?

   g. Does the agency's policy require it to submit a report on the findings and conclusions based on the data collected to a governing body of the county or state for review and monitoring purposes? What benchmarks are utilized and who interprets the data?

2. *Actual Incident for Discussion.* In a city in Indiana, an African American police officer driving an unmarked police car was pulled over by an officer not from his agency. The officer was wearing his uniform at the time, but he was not wearing his hat, which would have identified him as a police officer when viewed from outside the car. According to a complaint filed, the trooper who pulled the man over appeared shocked when the officer got out of the car. The trooper explained that he had stopped the man because the stopped officer had three antennas on the rear of his car. Discuss the following:

   a. Do you think the officer who pulled over a colleague was guilty of racial profiling?

   b. Do you think the officer was being honest when he said the reason for the stop was the multiple antennas? Is having multiple antennas a crime?

   c. Can complaints of being racially profiled be dismissed as the exaggerations of hypersensitive minorities or people who do not understand the job of a police officer?

References

The American Civil Liberties Union and The Rights Working Group. (2009, August). "The Persistence of Racial and Ethnic Profiling in the United States: A Follow-Up Report to the U.N. Committee on the Elimination of Racial Discrimination," p. 12. Retrieved February 28, 2013, from www.aclu.org/files/pdfs/humanrights/cerd_finalreport.pdf

Amnesty International. (2004). *Threat and Humiliation: Racial Profiling, Domestic Security, and Human Rights in the United States.* Retrieved August 6, 2013, from www.amnestyusa.org/pdfs/rp_report.pdf

"Ariz. DPS tightens search rules to avoid profiling." (2008, December 30). My Fox Phoenix Local News online. Retrieved January 13, 2009, from www.myfoxphoenix.com

Baker, Al. (2011, August 31). "Judge Declines to Dismiss Case Alleging Racial Profiling by City Police in Street Stops." *The New York Times*, p. A1. Retrieved February 23, 2013, from www.nytimes.com/2011/09/01/nyregion/racial-profiling-case-against-new-york-police-is-allowed-to-proceed.html

Barlow, David E., and Melissa Hickman Barlow. (2002). "Racial Profiling: A Survey of African American Police Officers." *Police Quarterly*, 5, 334–358.

Berry, Ondra. (2013). Retired deputy chief, Reno (Nev.) Police Department, personal communication.

Chen, David W. (2007, September 6). "New Jersey Police Win Praise for Efforts to End Profiling." *The New York Times*, p. C13.

"Contacts between the Police and the Public, 2008." (2011, October 5). U.S. Department of Justice, Bureau of Justice Statistics, NCJ 234599. Retrieved January 13, 2009, from www.bjs.ojp.usdoj.gov/index

Engel, Robin S., Jennifer M. Calnon, and Thomas J. Bernard. (2002). "Theory and Racial Profiling: Shortcomings and Future Directions in Research." *Justice Quarterly*, 19(2), 249–273.

"Feds Accuse N.C. Sheriff of Discriminatory Policing." (2012, September 18). *Police Patrol - The Law Enforcement Magazine.* Retrieved July 29, 2013, from www.policemag.com/channel/patrol/news/2012/09/18/feds-accuse-n-c-sheriff-of-discriminatory-policing.aspx

Fridell, Lorie, Robert Lunney, Drew Diamond, and Bruce Kubu. "Racially Biased Policing: A Principled Response." (2001). Police Executive Research Forum. Washington, D.C.

"The Growth of Compstat in American Policing," (2004). Police Foundation Reports, Washington D.C., p. AA. Retrieved February 26, 2013, from www.policefoundation.org/content/growth-compstat-american-policing

Hickman, Matthew J. (2005, June 1). "Traffic Stop Data Collection Policies for State Police, 2004." U.S. Department of Justice, Bureau of Justice Statistics Fact Sheet, NCJ 209156. Retrieved August 6, 2013, from www.bjs.gov/content/pub/pdf/tsdcp04.pdf

Johnson, James L. PhD. (2013, July). Social Science Analyst, Administrative Office of the U.S. Courts, personal communication.

"Jurisdictions Currently Collecting Data." (2009). Racial Profiling Data Collection Resource Center. Retrieved January 19, 2013, from www.racialprofilinganalysis.neu.edu/background/jurisdictions.php

Leonard, Jack and Richard Winton. "Payment Ordered to Bias Victims." (2013, July 2). *Los Angeles Times*. Retrieved July 29, 2013, from http://articles.latimes.com/2013/jul/02/local/la-me-sheriff-civil-rights-20130702

Levin, Sam. "Report: Black, Hispanic Missouri Drivers Face Disproportionate Number of Police Searches." (2013, June 3). *Riverfront Times, St. Louis*. Retrieved July 29, 2013, from http://blogs.riverfronttimes.com/dailyrft/2013/06/chris_koster_racial_disparity_police_searches.php

MacDonald, Heather. (2001, Spring). "The Myth of Racial Profiling." *City Journal*, 11(2), 1–5.

Martin, Hugo. (2010, December 6). "All Airline Passengers are Now Checked Against Watch Lists, Homeland Security Says," *Los Angeles Times*, p. 1.

"New York: Analysis of Racial Disparities in the New York City Police Department's Stop, Question, and Frisk Practices." (2007). RAND Corporation. Retrieved April 16, 2013, from www.rand.org/content/dam/rand/pubs/technical_reports/2007/RAND_TR534.sum.pdf

Newport, Frank. (2013, July 16). "In U.S., 24% of Young Black Men Say Police Dealings Unfair." Retrieved July 29, 2013, from www.gallup.com/poll/163523/one-four-young-black-men-say-police-dealings-unfair.aspx

"Ninth Report to the State of Maryland Under TR 25-113." (2012, August 28). Retrieved April 16, 2013, from www.goccp.maryland.gov/msac/documents/TSDReport2012.pdf

"NYCLU Analysis Reveals NYPD Stopped Nearly 2 Million Innocent New Yorkers; Most are Black & Latino." (2009, February 11). New York Civil Liberties Union. Retrieved April 16, 2013, from www.nyclu.org/news/nyclu-analysis-reveals-nypd-stopped-nearly-2-million-innocent-new-yorkers-most-are-black-latino

Long, Colleen. (2013, August 13) "NYC Mayor Lambastes Stop-and-Frisk Ruling - Breitbart." Associated Press. Retrieved August 30, 2013, from www.breitbart.com/system/wire/DA854M6G0

"Plan to Address Racial Profiling." (2009, August). Retrieved April 23, 2013, from www.portlandoregon.gov/police/article/230887

"Portland's Racial Profiling Reality." (2012, July 18). *The Portland Observer*. Retrieved April 23, 2013, from www.portlandobserver.com/2012/07/portlands-racial-profiling-reality/

Powell, Michael. (2009, January 4). "Police Polish Image, but Concerns Persist." *New York Times*, p. 21.

"Recommendations from the First IACP Forum on Professional Traffic Stops." (2001). International Association of Chiefs of Police. Retrieved January 19, 2009, from www.theiacp.org/PublicationsGuides/ResearchCenter/Publications/tabid/299/Default.aspx?id=119&v=1

"The San Angelo Police Department Annual Racial Profiling Report." (2006). Retrieved August 7, 2013, from www.criminaljusticecoalition.org/files/userfiles/2007_racial_profiling_report.pdf

San Francisco Police Department General Order 5.17. (2011). Retrieved August 6, 2013, from www.sf-police.org/modules/ShowDocument.aspx?documentid=14774

Senge, Peter, Art Kleiner, Charlotte Roberts, Richard Ross, and Bryan J. Smith. (1994). *The Fifth Discipline Fieldbook: Strategies and Tools for Building a Learning Organization*. New York, NY: Currency Doubleday.

Straus, Ira. (2002, October 19). "Commentary: Profile to Survive." United Press International. Retrieved January 19, 2004, from www.upi.com/Top_News/2002/10/19/Commentary-Profile-to-Survive/UPI-41611035051600/

Texas Code of Criminal Procedure (2001). Title 1, Chapter 2, Article 2.132. Retrieved August 6, 2013, from www.statutes.legis.state.tx.us/Docs/CR/htm/CR.2.htm#2.131

"Understanding Bias-Based Traffic Law Enforcement." (2003, July). National Highway Traffic Safety Administration. Retrieved January 19, 2009, from www.nhtsa.gov/people/injury/enforce/biasbased03/trafficenforcement.htm

United States Senate. (2013). Text of S.1038 retrieved August 6, 2013, from www.gpo.gov/fdsys/pkg/BILLS-113s1038is/pdf/BILLS-113s1038is.pdf

U.S. Department of Justice. (2000). *A Resource Guide on Racial Profiling Data Collection Systems: Promising Practices and Lessons Learned*. Washington, D.C.

U.S. v. Brignoni-Ponce, 442 U.S., 837, 887. (1975). Retrieved April 14, 2009, from www.supreme.justia.com/us/422/873/

Walker, S. (2003, March 8–9). "Internal Benchmarking for Traffic Stop Data: An Early Intervention System Approach." Presented at Racial Profiling in the 21st Century: New Challenges and Implications for Racial Justice. Northeastern University, Boston, Mass.

"War on Terrorism: Trade Liberties for Safety?" (2010, January 13). *Contra Costa* (Calif.) *Times*, p. AA.

Will, George F. (2001, April). "Exposing the 'Myth' of Racial Profiling." *Washington Post*, p. A19.

Withrow, Brian L. (2004, March). "A Comparative Analysis of Commonly Used Benchmarks in Racial Profiling: A Research Note." Unpublished paper submitted to the Academy of Criminal Justice Sciences, Wichita State University, School of Community Affairs, Wichita, Kansas.

Withrow, Brian L. (2006). *Racial Profiling from Rhetoric to Reason*. Upper Saddle River, NJ: Pearson-Prentice Hall.

Withrow, Brian L. (2007). "When *Whren* Won't Work: The Effects of a Diminished Capacity to Initiate a Pretextual Stop on Police Officer Behavior." *Police Quarterly*, 10(4), 351–370.

Withrow, Brian L., (2009, February), personal communication.

Withrow, Brian L., Jeffrey D. Dailey, and Henry Jackson. (2008). "The Utility of an Internal Benchmarking Strategy in Racial Profiling Surveillance." *Justice Research and Policy* 10(2), 19–47.

Cultural Effectiveness for Law Enforcement

Chapter 14 Community Policing and Multicultural Response Strategies for Gangs, the Homeless, and the Mentally Ill

Part Five concludes this text, highlighting some of the themes from previous chapters and presenting broad concepts on the emerging role of peace officers within a twenty-first-century multicultural society.

Chapter 14 discusses community policing and multicultural response strategies for officers and agencies in their dealings and interactions with gangs, the homeless, and the mentally ill—groups represented in the majority of America's multicultural cities and communities. This chapter raises awareness of the problems and issues that arise with gangs, the homeless, and the mentally ill, and provides officers with insight into dealing with these groups effectively.

In addition to the Instructor's Manual for this text, Appendix D, Listing of Gangs and Identifying Characteristics, includes further resource material on Part Five.

Community Policing and Multicultural Response Strategies for Gangs, the Homeless, and the Mentally Ill

LEARNING OBJECTIVES

After reading this chapter, you should be able to:

- Assess the relevance of community policing to all multicultural communities.
- Describe the three types of major gangs and their level of criminal activity.
- Describe a youth gang and causation.
- Identify strategies law enforcement can use to reduce the gang problem.
- Define homelessness and its impact on homeless people and multicultural peacekeeping.
- Identify response strategies law enforcement can use to mitigate the homelessness problem in multicultural communities.
- Define mental illness and the challenges for people with mental illness in multicultural communities.
- Explain police protocol for encounters with mentally ill people and appropriate response strategies for managing these encounters.

OUTLINE

- Introduction
- Community Policing
- Types of Gangs and Criminal Activity
- Gang Causation
- Law Enforcement Strategies to Reduce Gang Problems
- Homelessness and Its Impact on Peacekeeping
- Peacekeeping Strategies to Mitigate the Homelessness Crisis
- Mental Illness Challenges in Multicultural Communities
- Police Protocol in Encounters with People Who Have Mental Illness
- Response Strategies between Police and People with Mental Illness
- Summary
- Discussion Questions and Issues

INTRODUCTION

Gangs, homeless persons, and people with mental illness are groups that are represented in the majority of America's multicultural cities and communities. Law enforcement officers have continual contact with these groups for various reasons: gangs—suspected criminal activity; homelessness—loitering complaints by businesses; and people with mental illness—public nuisance complaints. Police officers need to recognize that there is a great amount of diversity among gangs, the homeless, and people with mental illness. Learning about the backgrounds of these groups can safeguard against negative stereotypes and biases, which can often lead to prejudicial law enforcement treatment.

Law enforcement's responsiveness to gang problems and the challenges of homelessness and people with mental illness is an essential component of developing strategies for peacekeeping in a diverse society. Ongoing relationships with multicultural community leaders, nonprofit organizations, and other government entities are needed resources in dealing with these societal issues. How community policing interplays with these multicultural groups and communities is pivotal to the success or failure of every police department's stated mission.

COMMUNITY POLICING

A. L. "Skipper" Osborne, former Portland Chapter President of NAACP, states:

> The police must meet with the community on a regular basis—not when there is a crisis but before there is a crisis. It is important that the police and community are honest and accountable to each other and build a relationship of trust. The police and community must share common goals of respect, cooperation and justice for all if community policing is to work in a free and multicultural society. (Osborne, personal communication, July 2013)

Community policing is one of several terms that police agencies across the nation use to refer to working partnerships with communities. Other commonly used terms are problem-oriented policing (POP), community-based policing (CBP), service-oriented policing (SOP), and community-oriented policing (COP). The concept of and practices associated with community policing are central to any discussion on multicultural groups and immigrant populations. The legislative basis of what became known as Community Oriented Policing Services (COPS, Title 1 of the Violent Crime Control and Law Enforcement Act of 1994) became law under the Clinton Administration and directed the U.S. Department of Justice to create the Office of Community Oriented Policing Services. The primary purpose of COPS is to support the efforts of all law enforcement agencies in the United States in dealing with community problems and public safety issues. From 1995 to 2013, the COPS Office funded the hiring of more than 124,000 police officers to over 13,000 state, local, and tribal law enforcement agencies (COPS Office, 2013a). The major goals of the COPS Office are as follows:

1. Awarding grants to tribal, state, and local law enforcement agencies to hire and train law enforcement officers
2. Awarding grants to tribal and local law enforcement agencies to purchase and use crime reduction technologies
3. Awarding grants to tribal and local law enforcement agencies to develop and test innovative policing strategies
4. Providing training and technical assistance to advance community policing to all levels of law enforcement and to other criminal justice components
5. Providing training and materials to state and local government leaders and the citizens in those communities to foster problem solving and police officers' interaction with communities

> **Community policing** A partnership between the police and the local community that identifies strategies to reduce crime, increase traffic safety, and deal with all other public safety problems.

Today's police officers are increasingly comfortable with contemporary community policing, described as a problem-solving approach. Community policing enables police officers to work with citizens outside the conventional channels by meeting with community groups and learning of their concerns. It also allows community members to understand the "culture" of law enforcement and helps them grasp the reasons police officers make the decisions they do. It encourages new strategies and creative ways of dealing with crime and peacekeeping at the neighborhood level and allows for a change of image of the traditional law enforcement officer. This is especially true in certain immigrant neighborhoods or ethnic conclaves where citizens have traditionally feared the police.

A great deal of literature is available to law enforcement agencies on community policing. Community policing depends on a strong partnership with the various communities that make up a city or jurisdiction. The partnership ensures dialogue and provides the mechanism that allows a police department to be aware of current and relevant issues in the community as they relate to crime, public safety, public nuisance, and the use of "order maintenance." The following description of a police department without a community-policing approach, though dated, is a graphic example of how world events and the influx of refugees have to be monitored in a community policing partnership approach.

> **Order maintenance** The police handling of incidents that are not crimes but public nuisance matters about which the police officer uses discretion to decide a course of action.

This dramatic example involves the case of a medium-sized police department in Garden Grove, California, that exemplifies the problems associated with community policing. Neither the management of the department nor the city was aware that the ethnic community had been changing significantly. Only two years after startling events began to take place did patrol officers begin to pay attention to the changes, most of which occurred suddenly following the fall of Saigon in 1975. After the withdrawal of American forces from Vietnam, the United States changed its immigration policy to relocate people in jeopardy from Southeast Asia. Police officers were performing their "crime fighter" role, but, because there was no partnership with the community, there was no reason or incentive to monitor and report the changes they were noticing. This particular community, therefore, was not prepared for the increase in racial disputes and violence on the streets and in the schools, nor was it prepared for the increasing needs in government, infrastructure, and social services. Police officers recognized that it took much longer to answer calls involving Vietnamese citizens because of language and cultural differences. Police officer and management frustrations resulted. Community policing would have had a plan in place for that neighborhood transition. Why? Had community policing been in place, the department, including all local government institutions, and the neighborhoods would have been working together closely.

Community policing allows for collaboration with the community. The police are unable to know the community as well as the community knows itself (Berry, personal communication, July 2013). Community policing represents a more democratic style of policing, allowing for openness and dialogue between the police and citizens to deal with strategies to combat crime. The following information, for example, illustrates how the implementation of community policing in Chicago, Illinois, was the definitive factor in the overall decrease of violent crimes and property crimes in a 10-year period.

Similar to other major cities and communities in the early 1990s, Chicago also witnessed a rise in crime rates; however, the Chicago Police Department acted differently from most other police departments when it decided to initiate a new experiment known as "community policing" in April 1993. The experiment was called CAPS—Chicago Alternative Policing Strategy. It was based on the hypothesis that if the police, residents, and other city agencies work together, they can reduce crime. This was a mammoth-sized project and required a long-term commitment, but the decision to embrace the mechanics of community policing paid off immediately and continues to do so today. In the 10 years from 2001 to 2010, the Chicago Police Department reported that the overall decline in violent crimes, such as murder, criminal sexual assault, robbery, and aggravated assault/battery, and property crimes, such as burglary, theft, motor vehicle theft, and arson, was 23.7 percent (Chicago Police Department, 2011). Noteworthy to the success of CAPS are the ongoing meetings and activities with citizens and the following organizational details:

> Chicago is divided into 25 police districts. Each police district contains between 9 and 15 police beats, with a total of 285 beats throughout the city. It is at the beat level that the Department's strategy of police–community partnership and problem-solving is carried out. Each police district is led by a district commander. In addition to uniformed beat and rapid response officers, each district has teams of civilian-dressed tactical officers. Each district also offers a Community Policing Office which helps coordinate police–community partnership and problem-solving at the beat level and provides special services to senior citizens (Chicago Police Department, 2011).

Storefront Offices and Other Temporary Offices

Minority groups, neighborhoods, schools, and businesses appreciate the outreach efforts of the police to build and maintain positive relationships. However, the police must remind themselves that, in order to maintain goodwill relationships with citizens in their communities, they must have ongoing contact with the people they are sworn to protect and to serve. Different types of temporary offices known as "storefront," "schoolfront," and "neighborhood" offices afford this ongoing contact.

Storefront office   A temporary office located in a business office or shopping center where the police officer conducts routine business.

Schoolfront office   A temporary office located in a school where the police officer conducts routine business. Schools that have a regular police school resource officer are not considered schoolfront offices.

Neighborhood office   A temporary office located in a neighborhood, usually an apartment/business office complex where the police officer conducts routine business.

Each temporary office has a unique purpose for businesses, schools, and neighborhood multicultural communities, but they also possess similar characteristics and benefits:

- In the storefront office, for example, which is not a new concept, police work at a desk in an office inside a business location during a day or swing shift. Schoolfront and neighborhood offices serve the same function.
- When police officers show up at any of the facilities (business, school, or apartment complex) and park their patrol cars, they provide visibility to the public. Inside, the officer completes reports, returns telephone calls, or visits with the facility's staff or occupants.
- At the storefront, schoolfront, or neighborhood office, people in the community see the police on a frequent basis. This interaction creates a more positive and personal relationship.

- The police at storefront, schoolfront, and neighborhood offices provide interventions for problem business customers and school students, resources for school counselors, and safety-related classes to students and neighborhood organizations.

The Police Executive Research Forum (PERF) looked for commonalities among various community-policing programs across the country and conducted thorough research on community policing. The researchers outlined four major categories of community-policing activities within agencies throughout the United States. These are still applicable today (PERF, 2004).

1. *Citizenship participation:* This involves citizens attending police–community meetings and helping police identify and resolve problems; attending citizen police academies; and participating in Neighborhood Watch programs and other volunteer programs.
2. *Police partnership outreach:* Police conduct regularly scheduled meetings with community groups; sponsor youth programs; work with victim assistance programs; and reach out to other special needs organizations.
3. *Police problem solving:* Police collaborate with external resources such as community groups, other police departments, businesses, nonprofit organizations, and government agencies; enforce criminal and traffic laws; and work with other nonpolice code enforcement agencies.
4. *Police organizational change:* The organization uses different styles of leadership and empowerment; uses scientific methods for assignment to patrol areas or beats; reviews classification and prioritization of calls; uses crime analysis and crime solvability; uses progressive methods for recruiting sworn and nonsworn personnel; and uses citizen participation, partnership outreach, and different methods of problem solving.

All of these activities and tasks require opening a dialogue between the police and diverse community groups so that groups can identify their peacekeeping concerns and the police can respond to them. Departments typically mix a variety of community-policing activities together; however, the common thread within all tasks is that the police assist the community in policing and protecting itself in many societal ways. To do so, the police must engage the community in the duty of policing. The police are dependent on a relationship and partnership with the community to perform these important tasks. This is sometimes referred to as "building bridges." The community identifies problems with the encouragement, direction, and ongoing participation of the police.

Even with the attention community policing has been receiving in Criminal Justice College programs and police departments throughout the United States, more instruction on this topic would benefit everyone. For example, from the most current reporting period in 2006, the majority of state and local law enforcement training academies offered only eight hours of community policing in their basic police training programs to new police officers (U.S. Department of Justice, 2009a).

The focus on community policing not only encompasses ethnic, racial, and national groups, but also all other subcultural groups as well. The more knowledge and familiarity officers have

---

Mini Case Study: What Would You Do?

You are a patrol sergeant, and an apartment manager, who also serves as the community leader for new immigrants from Nigeria, approaches you at a community meeting. He requests your police department open up a neighborhood office in his apartment complex. He indicates that there are at least 40 families with small children and teenagers from Nigeria in the large complex. He asks you to provide, in addition to the police presence at the neighborhood front office, some workshops on crime prevention and traffic laws for the 12 new families who just arrived in the United States one month ago. Further, he tells you that there are at least 10 children in the apartment complex who need bicycle helmets. Describe what steps you will take to establish a neighborhood office and how you will operate it. Also, outline how you will organize and present your workshops to these new immigrants, and obtain bicycle helmets for the children who need them.

with all groups in our diverse society, the more skilled they will be in using the right kind of communication and response strategies. Gangs, the homeless, and the mentally ill represent significant community diversity. We now look at gangs, including their multicultural facets.

TYPES OF GANGS AND CRIMINAL ACTIVITY

In 1982, only 27 percent of U.S. cities with populations of 100,000 or more had a reported gang problem (Miller, 1982/1992). In the mid-1980s, criminal gangs started expanding from urban cities to suburban areas to rural America. The following information provided by the U.S. Department of Justice National Gang Intelligence Center's (NGIC) National Gang Threat Assessment shows the more recent relative increases in gang numbers (NGIC, 2011):

- In 2011, more than half of state and local law enforcement agencies reported that criminal gangs were active in their jurisdictions over the last two years.
- Approximately 1.4 million gang members, belonging to more than 33,000 gangs across all the 50 states and the District of Columbia, were criminally active in 2011.
- From 2009 to 2011, there was a 400,000 person (40%) increase in gang membership; 1.17 million gang members reside in local communities and 230,000 are incarcerated in local, state, and federal correctional facilities.
- Hybrid gangs are nontraditional gangs with multiple affiliations and ethnicities. They are a new and a growing phenomenon. They are present in at least 25 states.
- The NGIC attributes the increase in gang membership to improved law enforcement reporting, aggressive recruitment efforts by gangs, formation of new gangs, expanded drug trafficking, collaboration with rival gangs and drug trafficking organizations (DTOs), gangster rap culture, internet and social media, proliferation of generational gang members, and limited resources to combat gangs.

In law enforcement, these numbers represent the three most common types of gangs: street gangs, prison gangs, and outlaw motorcycle gangs (OMGs). To help mitigate the growth of gangs and their criminal activity, the Federal Bureau of Investigation (FBI), at the direction of Congress, facilitated creation of the National Gang Intelligence Center (NGIC) in 2005. The NGIC compiles gang intelligence from federal, state, and local law enforcement on the growth, migration, criminal activity, and association of gangs, which pose a significant threat to the United States. The NGIC consists of representatives from the FBI, U.S. Drug Enforcement Administration (DEA), U.S. Bureau of Alcohol, Tobacco, Firearms, and Explosives (ATF), U.S. Bureau of Prisons (BOP), U.S. Immigration and Customs Enforcement (ICE), U.S. Department of Defense (DOD), National Drug Intelligence Center (NDIC), and U.S. Customs and Border Protection (CBP). Its mission is to support law enforcement by disseminating timely information and by providing strategic/tactical analysis of intelligence. Another invaluable resource for criminal justice agencies is the National Gang Center (NGC). It is part of the Office of Juvenile Justice and Delinquency Prevention, under the control of the Bureau of Justice Assistance of the U.S. Department of Justice. The NGC features the latest research about gangs; descriptions of evidence-based, antigang programs; and links to tools, databases, and other resources to assist in developing and implementing effective community-based gang prevention, intervention, and suppression strategies (NGC, 2011).

Definition of Gang

The definition of a gang varies among most law enforcement agencies and jurisdictions at the federal, state, and local levels in the United States. The NGC promotes a functional definition for criminal justice professionals and educators, used in this section. The following five criteria are widely accepted and recognized among researchers for classifying groups as gangs; however, there is flexibility in these criteria (Decker & Curry, 2003; Esbensen, Winfree, He, & Taylor, 2001; Klein, 1995; Miller, 1982/1992; Spergel, 1995):

1. The group has three or more members, generally aged 12–24.[*]
2. Members share an identity, typically linked to a name, and often have shared symbols, typically including style of clothing, graffiti, tattoos, and hand signs.
3. Members view themselves as a gang, and are recognized by others as a gang.
4. The group has some permanence and a degree of organization.
5. The group is involved in an elevated level of criminal activity.

Criminal Activity

Gang criminal activities and threats reported by NGIC for criminal justice study and review describe the following information (NGIC, 2011):

- Gang-related crime and violence continues to rise. Gang members are responsible for an average of 48 percent of violent crime in most jurisdictions.
- Gang members are moving from urban areas to suburban and rural communities for a variety of reasons, including expanding drug distribution territories, increasing illicit revenue, and recruiting new members.
- In many communities, up to 90 percent of the crimes are committed by gangs. Crimes include alien smuggling, human trafficking, prostitution, armed robbery, assault, burglary, vehicle theft, drug trafficking, extortion, debt collection, money laundering, counterfeiting, fraud, home invasions, identity theft, murder, and weapons trafficking.
- Gang members are the primary retail-level distributors of most illicit drugs. They distribute wholesale-level quantities of marijuana and cocaine in most urban and suburban communities.
- Some gangs traffic illicit drugs at the regional and national levels; several are capable of competing with U.S.-based Mexican drug trafficking organizations.
- Gang members illegally cross the U.S–Mexico border for the purpose of smuggling illicit drugs and illegal aliens from Mexico into the United States.
- Many gangs use the Internet to recruit new members and to communicate with members in other parts of the United States and in foreign countries.
- Street gangs and outlaw motorcycle gangs pose a threat to law enforcement along the U.S. borders of Canada and Mexico. They associate with Canadian- and Mexican-based gangs and criminal organizations to facilitate various criminal activities.

Mexican Drug Trafficking Organizations

United States law enforcement officials at federal, state, and local levels have been combating the flow of illegal drugs from Mexico's drug cartels or drug trafficking organizations (DTOs) across the border into the U.S. border states of California, Arizona, New Mexico, and Texas for years. It remains an ongoing problem, and U.S. law enforcement agencies have responded by using drug interdiction and other practices, which have netted in countless arrests and drug seizures. Drug trafficking, human trafficking, and, most noticeably, the violence from these criminal activities have spilled over into local U.S. communities across the Mexico border and beyond.

Since establishing the specialized home invasion unit in 2008, the city police department of Tucson, Arizona, has investigated more than 200 home invasions, with more than three-quarters of the invasions linked to the drug trade. One incident involved intruders breaking into the wrong house, shooting and injuring a woman. Another incident involved a man who was suspected of being a drug dealer, who was kidnapped from his home at gun point and has not been found since. The increased violence from drug cartel gang wars has spread from Mexico throughout the United States and even into Canada. Law enforcement officials suspect Mexican drug cartels were responsible for

---

[*]More common with street gangs.

numerous shootings in Vancouver, British Columbia; kidnappings in Phoenix, Arizona; aggravated assaults in Birmingham, Alabama; and many more violent crimes in other states and communities (Archibold, 2009). Law enforcement officials in Mexico and the United States agree that the United States is the primary source of the guns used in the violent drug cartel wars in Mexico. In one of the many strategic responses to this crisis in 2009, the Obama administration increased security measures at the border with the goal of detecting firearms being smuggled in cars from the United States into Mexico. The increased searches of vehicles at the border have resulted in more weapons being seized; however, gun smugglers are still getting illegal guns into Mexico by changing their tactics. A few examples of these tactics are weapons being dismantled and the components being placed in separate vehicles and families with children in minivans transporting smuggled firearms (Carcamo, 2013).

National and Regional Gangs

The NGIC has identified the approximate number of gangs in seven regions of the United States where there are thousands of gang members, some of whom operate in multiple regions. (See Exhibit 14.1.) State, county, and city law enforcement agencies are more aware of local gangs in their multicultural jurisdictions. See Appendix D for a listing of national and regional gangs and their specific characteristics, for the three major types of gangs.

Region	Gangs	Members	Gangs with Significant Activity
New England: VT, NH, ME, MA, CT, and RI	640	17,250	Hells Angels, Latin Kings, Tiny Rascal Gangster Crips, Sureños 13, Trinitarios, and United Blood Nation
East: NY, PA, NJ, DE, MD, DC, WV, and VA	2,900	73,650	Black Guerilla Family, Crips, Latin Kings, MS13, Ñeta, and United Blood Nation
Central: ND, SD, NE, KS, MN, IA, MO, WI, IL, MI, IN, OH, and KY	5,800	222,400	Bandidos, Chicago-Based Gangster Disciples, Latin Kings, Native Mob, Outlaws, Vice Lords, and Black P. Stones
Southeast: AR, LA, TN, MS, AL, GA, NC, SC, and FL	9,871	172,360	Bandidos, Crips, Gangster Disciples, Latin Kings, and M13
Southwest: UT, CO, OK, AZ, NM, and TX	5,297	111,000	Aryan Brotherhood, Bandidos, Barrio Azteca, Hermanos de Pistoleros Latinos, Latin Kings, Mexican Mafia, Mexikanemi, Tango Blast, and Texas Syndicate
Pacific: CA, NV, and HA	6,900	237,000	Aryan Brotherhood, 18th Street, Bandidos, Black Guerrilla Family, Bloods, Crips, La Eme, Mexican Mafia, Nuestra Familia, Hells Angels, and M13
Northwest: WA, OR, ID, MT, and WY	2,093	36,650	Bloods, Brown Pride, Crips (74 Hoover and Rolling 60s), Florencia 13, Gangster Disciples, La Eme, Norteños, Surenos, and Varrio Locos 13

EXHIBIT 14.1 Gangs By Region, 2009

Source: NGIC (January 2009). (Latest data available as of the writing of this text's sixth edition.)

Gangs in the Military

It is not uncommon to find gang membership among military personnel and their dependents in the U.S. Armed Forces. As of April 2011, the NGIC had identified at least 53 gangs whose members have served in or are affiliated with the U.S. military. According to the NGIC, members from nearly every major street gang, as well as prison gangs and OMGs have been identified in the U.S. military on both foreign and domestic installations. Even though the actual numbers are unknown, military personnel and military veterans who are gang members pose a risk to law enforcement, particularly if these gang members, trained in weapons and tactics, pass this instruction on to other gang members. Due to transfers and deployments, these gang members have the ability to expand their culture and operations both regionally and worldwide (NGIC, 2011).

Street Gangs

National, regional, and local street gangs are the largest and control the greatest geographic area. They are represented in urban and rural communities and Indian Country. Street gangs are active in crime and violence. A number of juveniles join street gangs and actively participate in criminal behavior and violence. However, 65 percent of gang members identified by law enforcement agencies are 18 years or older compared to 35 percent who are under 18 years of age (NGC, 2011). Exhibit 14.2 shows a listing of national and regional street gangs.

Gang (National or Regional)	Region	Primary Race/Ethnicity
18th Street (National)	44 cities in 20 states	Mexican
Almighty Latin King and Queen Nation (National)	15 cities in 5 states	Mexican and Puerto Rican
Asian Boyz (National)	28 cities in 14 states	Asian
Black P. Stone (Regional)	Chicago	African American
Bloods (National)	123 cities in 33 states	African American
Crips (National)	221 cities in 41 states	African American
Florencia 13 (Regional)	5 states	Mexican
Fresno Bulldogs (Regional)	California	Hispanic
Gangster Disciples (National)	110 cities in 31 states	African American
Latin Disciples (Regional)	Chicago	Puerto Rican
Mara Salvatrucha (National)	5 states	Hispanic
Sueños and Norteños (Regional)	California	Hispanic
Tango Blast (Regional)	Texas	Hispanic
Tiny Rascal Gangsters (National)	Southwest, Pacific, and Eastern states	Asian
United Blood Nation (Regional)	West Coast	African American
Vice Lord Nation (National)	74 cities in 28 states	African American

EXHIBIT 14.2 National and Regional Street Gangs, 2009

Source: NGIC, (January 2009). (Latest data available as of the writing of this text's sixth edition.)

Juvenile Gangs

The terms *youth* and *street gang* are commonly used interchangeably; however, the use of the term *street gang* for *youth gang* often results in confusing youth gangs with adult criminal organizations (NGC, 2011). To eliminate the confusion, it is important to remember that street gangs are composed of juveniles and young adults. Gangs have traditionally recruited juveniles because of their underage status, vulnerability, and the likelihood of their not serving long sentences in correctional facilities. Such groups as Gangster Rap gangs, often composed of juveniles, are being used to launder drug money through decoy legitimate businesses (NGIC, 2011).

Gangs in Indian Country

Most street gangs that operate on reservations are local gangs and are primarily composed of Native American youth. Some Indian Country street gangs are regional, such as the Native Mob, located on and off reservations. According to the NGIC, the Native Mob is identified as one of the largest and most violent Native American street gangs for criminal activity and has gangs operating in Minnesota, Michigan, Wisconsin, North Dakota, and South Dakota. Similar to other gangs, the Native Mob is involved with the retail-level distribution of illegal drugs (primarily marijuana and methamphetamine) and its members commit crimes such as auto theft, assault, robbery, drive-by shootings, and homicide (NGIC, 2009). NGIC data shows that national-level gangs such as the Barrio Azteca, Bloods, Crips, Mexican Mafia, and Norteños are operating on a number of reservations. In addition, due to the proximity of some reservations to Canada and Mexico, there is an ongoing problem of cross-border drug trafficking (NGIC, 2011).

Prison Gangs

National, regional, and local prison gangs are prevalent throughout the federal and state prison system in the United States. They are highly structured and organized networks, having an influence in prison operations and in street gang crime. According to the NGIC, national-level prison gangs pose a major crime threat since most maintain some form of relationship with DTOs. Prison gangs are controlled by established internal rules and codes of conduct that are strictly enforced by gang leaders. Incarcerated gang members communicate to gang members on the street through family, friends, lawyers, corrections personnel, legal mail, and smuggled cellular devices to direct criminal activities such as drug distribution, assault, and murder (NGIC, 2011). Moreover, prison gangs are structured along racial and ethnic lines and are more powerful within state correctional facilities compared to federal correctional facilities (U.S. Department of Justice, 2013a). See Appendix D for the listing of prison gangs and their specific characteristics.

Outlaw Motorcycle Gangs

According to the NGIC, there was a significant increase of outlaw motorcycle gangs (OMGs) from 20,000 members in 2008, to an estimated 44,000 members nationwide in 2011, comprising approximately 3,000 gangs. OMGs are highly structured and organized networks whose members commit such criminal acts as violent crimes, weapons trafficking, and drug trafficking. Outlaw Motorcycle Gang chapters in the United States range in size with hundreds of chapters and thousands of members worldwide. There are over 300 active OMGs in the United States and a number of these chapters pose a serious domestic threat because of their strong associations with transnational DTOs and other criminal enterprises. OMG chapters such as the Hell's Angels, Mongols, Bandidos, Outlaws, and Sons of Silence have been identified, performing the majority of cross-border (Canada and Mexico) drug smuggling operations with major international DTOs (U.S. Department of Justice, 2013b). The NGIC also reports that national-level OMGs maintain criminal networks of regional and local motorcycle clubs, commonly referred to as "support," "puppet," or "duck" clubs, whose members conduct criminal activities in support of the larger OMGs, and who are a source for new members. It is reported that some members of support

Year	Hispanic or Latino	Black or African American	White	Other
1996	45.2%	35.6%	11.6%	7.5%
1998	46.5%	33.6%	11.8%	8.0%
1999	47.3%	30.9%	13.4%	8.4%
2001	49%	33.7%	10.3%	7%
2002	47%	35.7%	10.4%	6.9%
2004	48.7%	37.8%	7.9%	5.7%
2005	50.1%	32.6%	9.5%	7.7%
2006	49.5%	35.2%	8.5%	6.8%
2008	50.2%	31.8%	10.5%	7.6%
2011	46.2	35.3%	11.5%	7.0%

EXHIBIT 14.3 Race/Ethnicity of Gangs, 1996–2011
Source: NGC (2011).

clubs have obtained employment with private businesses or government agencies, which allows them to provide national-level OMGs with business, government, and financial information that can be used to protect their criminal enterprises (NGIC, 2009). See Appendix D for the listing of OMGs and their specific characteristics.

Racial and Ethnic Composition of Gangs

From 1996 to 2011, race and ethnicity of gang members were assessed in ten National Youth Gang Surveys (NGC, 2011). The report findings showed stability in gang members' race and ethnic composition across survey years; however, the percentages were disproportionately high for the general population of Hispanic/Latino Americans and African Americans, and extremely low for white Americans in the United States (see Exhibit 14.3). Examine Appendix D for the racial and ethnic characteristics of all three types of gangs. Readers need to keep in mind that even though the numbers are reported to be low for white membership in these three major types of gangs, white membership is among the highest in hate/bias groups in the United States as referenced in Chapter 12.

Gangs and Gender

In 2010, the majority of gang members were males with slightly over 92 percent compared to females at just over 7 percent (NGC, 2011). The NGC reports that these percentages have remained somewhat constant over the last twelve years with a slight variance. The National Youth Gang Survey Analysis shows that nearly half of the gangs outside larger cities are reported to have female gang members, compared with approximately one in four in the larger cities (NGC, 2011). Also noteworthy is the expansion of hybrid gangs that comprise multi-ethnic and mixed-gender gangs in at least 25 states (NGIC, 2011).

Females leave gang membership at an earlier age than do the majority of males (Gottfredson & Gottfredson, 2001; Thornberry, Krohn, Lizotte, Smith, & Tobin, 2003). Some observers attribute this early departure to maturity, and others, to pregnancy.

Gang-Related Homicides

Homicides by drive-by shooting and by other means have occurred in almost every city where there are criminal gangs. Multiple gang-related homicides usually occur more often in larger cities and suburban counties than in smaller cities and rural counties. The National Youth Gang Survey Analysis highlights gang-related homicides for the period of 2007 to 2011 (NGC, 2013):

1. The total number of gang homicides reported by law enforcement respondents in the NYGS sample averaged more than 1,900 annually from 2007 to 2011. During the same time period, more than 15,500 homicides were committed across the United States. These numbers suggest that gang-related homicides typically accounted for around 12 percent of all homicides annually.
2. Highly populated areas accounted for the vast majority of gang homicides: nearly 70 percent occurred in cities with populations over 10,000, and 19 percent occurred in suburban counties in 2011.
3. The number of gang-related homicides increased approximately 10 percent from 2009 to 2010 and then declined slightly (2%) in 2011 in cities with populations over 10,000.
4. In a typical year in the so-called "gang capitals" of Chicago and Los Angeles, around half of all homicides are gang-related; these two cities alone accounted for approximately one in five gang homicides recorded in the NGS from 2010 to 2011.
5. Among agencies serving rural counties and small cities that reported gang activity, more than 80 percent reported zero gang-related homicides. About 5 percent or less of all gang homicides occurred in these areas annually.

Gun Use by Gangs

Law enforcement officers know that firearms play a major role in gang violence and that gang members are more likely to carry guns and use them. In a five-year study that examined five cities with a high prevalence of gang homicides, the Centers for Disease Control and Prevention (CDC) analyzed data from the National Violent Death Reporting System (NVDRS) for firearms usage. The cities in the CDC study were Los Angeles, California; Oklahoma City, Oklahoma; Long Beach, California; Oakland, California; and Newark, New Jersey. The CDC findings showed that more than 90 percent of the gang-related homicides in each city involved firearms. Further, the majority of the shootings occurred in public places which would infer they were quick and retaliatory (CDC, 2012). Law enforcement officers must always be alert and watchful to the potential threat of violence directed against them and bystanders when encountering suspected and known gang members; however, they must be professional and not overreact in their contacts.

GANG CAUSATION

Risk Factors for Gang Membership

All criminal justice professionals should be aware of the risk factors that make young people vulnerable to gang membership. The following five risk factors were identified by the combined efforts of Thornberry (1998), Esbensen (2000); Hill, Lui, and Hawkins (2001), and Howell and Egley (2005):

- Prior delinquency in violence and alcohol/drug use.
- Poor family management and problematic parent–child relations.
- Low school attachment and academic achievement, and negative labeling by teachers.
- Association with peers who engage in delinquency.
- Disorganized neighborhoods where large numbers of youth are in trouble and where drugs and firearms are readily available.

LAW ENFORCEMENT STRATEGIES TO REDUCE GANG PROBLEMS

In 1992, the FBI developed a National Gang Strategy designed to incorporate the investigative and prosecutorial practices proven successful in the Organized Crime/Drug Program National Strategy. By promoting coordination and information sharing between federal, state, and local law enforcement agencies, the FBI's Safe Streets and Gang Unit is able to identify violent gang enterprises that pose a significant threat and to pursue these criminals with coordinated investigations that support successful prosecutions. The FBI's Safe Streets and Gang Unit administers 160 Violent Gang Safe Streets Task Forces throughout the United States (FBI, 2013). Likewise, state and local law enforcement agencies have been responding to the gang threat since their inception but have not always maintained a consistent level of responsiveness. This is owing to any one or a combination of several reasons, which are a lack of budget funding, lack of political support, and lack of effective resources, or dealing with a formidable and relentless gang threat.

U.S. Department of Justice Office of Community Oriented Policing

The COPS Office recognizes that street gangs can take on many forms and offers the COPS Gangs Toolkit that consists of resources for law enforcement officials, educators, and parents to address specific types of crimes committed by gangs. These resources provide details of community-policing solutions to youth crime and school violence. The COPS Office encourages law enforcement agencies to analyze their local gang problem and use these resources when appropriate. The following publications can be downloaded from the COPS Web site (COPS, 2013b):

1. Bullying in Schools
2. Disorderly Youth in Public Places
3. Drive-By Shootings
4. Drug Dealing in Open-Air Markets
5. Gang Reference Card for Parents (English, Spanish, Hmong, and Vietnamese)
6. Gun Violence Among Serious Young Offenders
7. Juvenile Runaways
8. Solutions to Address Gang Crime CD-ROM
9. Street Gangs and Interventions: Innovative Problem Solving with Network Analysis
10. Witness Intimidation

Largest Gang Arrest in U.S. History

On May 21, 2009, in the City of Hawaiian Gardens and nearby communities, just southeast of Los Angeles, California, approximately 1,400 federal, state, county, and city law enforcement officers arrested 88 Latino gang members. According to the Department of Justice, the multiagency operation was connected to the murder of a sheriff's deputy, racially motivated attacks on African Americans, and illicit drug trafficking. Called "Operation Knock Out," the largest gang arrest in the U.S. history led to federal indictments against 147 members and associates of the Latino gang Varrio Hawaiian Gardens, whose members have ties to the Mexican Mafia. The investigation of the gang began in 2005 after Los Angeles County Sheriff's Deputy Jerry Ortiz was fatally shot by Varrio Hawaiian Gardens' gang member Jose Orozco, while Deputy Ortiz was attempting to arrest Orozco in connection with the shooting of an African American male. After the shooting, Orozco was arrested for murder, convicted, and placed on death row. Prior to the massive arrests, 10 defendants were already in custody and 49 were still at large as fugitives or waiting to be located. Charges included violation of the federal RICO (Racketeer Influenced and Corrupt Organizations) Act, murder, attempted murder, drug trafficking, carjackings, extortion, kidnapping, and witness intimidation. Seventeen SWAT teams helped make the arrests, and police seized 105 firearms and 31 pounds of methamphetamines. Twenty-six children were taken into protective custody (FBI, 2009b; Glover & Winton, 2009).

This major multiagency gang operation illustrates the need for law enforcement officers, especially in certain regions of the country, to familiarize themselves with the cultural, racial, and ethnic dimensions of gangs. Training academies and department management must commit to sustaining a focus on cross-cultural gang activity, updating their training content on this topic on a regular basis.

Resources for Law Enforcement

Below are valuable resources and strategies to assist federal, state, and local law enforcement agencies to mitigate the gang threat in our multicultural nation. The following agencies are of key importance in this process:

BOYS & GIRLS CLUBS OF AMERICA GANG PREVENTION THROUGH TARGETED OUTREACH (GPTTO)   The Boys & Girls Clubs of America developed special gang prevention and intervention initiatives targeting youth ages 10 to 17. Through referrals from schools, courts, law enforcement, and community youth service agencies, the tested and proven Targeted Outreach Program identifies and recruits delinquent or at-risk youth into club programs and activities. The initiative is sponsored by the Office of Juvenile Justice and Delinquency Prevention (OJJDP) of the U.S. Department of Justice (BGCA, 2013).

GANG RESISTANCE EDUCATION AND TRAINING (G.R.E.A.T.) PROGRAM   The G.R.E.A.T. program is a school-based, law enforcement officer-instructed classroom curriculum. The program's primary objective is prevention, and it is intended as an immunization against delinquency, youth violence, and gang membership. G.R.E.A.T. develops partnerships with the Boys & Girls Clubs of America and the Police Athletic League. It also has five regional training centers to train police officers across the United States (G.R.E.A.T., 2013).

POLICE ATHLETIC LEAGUE (PAL)   The purpose of the National Police Athletics/Activities Leagues Inc. is to prevent juvenile crime and violence by providing civic, athletic, recreational and educational opportunities and resources to PAL Chapters. The National PAL provides its chapters with resources and opportunities to operate their own programs and enhance the quality of their employee and volunteer services (PAL, 2013). PAL's mission is introduced in Chapter 6, and references an example in Jacksonville, Florida.

Mini Case Study: What Would You Do?

You are a police officer who has just been reassigned to a new neighborhood. You are meeting with a group of parents in a multicultural neighborhood gathering this evening. The neighborhood has misgivings toward your agency because of some police officers' use of profanity toward citizens and disrespect toward African American teenage males at traffic stops. There are a few street gangs in the neighborhood, and one of the biggest complaints from parents is that, "Even good kids are being treated by the police as if they are gang members." What would you say at this meeting? How would you respond to the parents' allegations?

HOMELESSNESS AND ITS IMPACT ON PEACEKEEPING

Dealing with the homeless is not a new task for law enforcement in America. In repeated acts of humane and compassionate treatment, the Philadelphia Police Department offered their station precincts as shelter to more than 100,000 homeless people a year during the 1880s (Monkkonen, 1981). Almost a century later, in the 1980s, U.S. cities started noticing a significant increase of homeless people and blamed the recession as one of the major causes. According to the National

Law Center on Homelessness and Poverty (NLCHP), approximately 3.5 million people, including over 1 million school-aged children will experience homelessness each year (NLCHP, 2013).

Estimated Count of Homeless on a Single Night

Each year the U.S. Department of Housing and Urban Development (HUD) releases its "Point-In-Time" (PIT) estimate on data reported to them by more than 3,000 cities and counties for the scope of homelessness over the course of one night every January. The one night counts are conducted by Continuums of Care (CoC) and the following 2012 data shows the key findings of HUD's estimated number on a single night (HUD, 2012):

1. There were 633,782 homeless people. This shows a drop of 0.4 percent from January 2011 and a reduction of 5.7 percent since 2007.
2. Individuals represent 62 percent of the homeless population. This is a decline of 1.4 percent from 2011 and 6.8 percent since 2007.
3. People in family households represented 38 percent of the homeless. Families increased by 1.4 percent in 2011 and declined 3.7 percent since 2007.
4. Veterans represent about 13 percent of the homeless population. This dropped by 7.2 percent since January 2011 and by 17.2 percent since January 2009. HUD housing vouchers along with case management through the Department of Veterans Affairs have helped in this reduction.
5. People experiencing long-term or chronic homelessness was near 16 percent, but has declined 6.8 percent from 2011 and 19.3 percent since 2007.
6. Unsheltered homelessness (street homelessness) was 38 percent and unchanged from 2011, but declined 13.1 percent since 2007.
7. Sheltered homelessness (living in emergency shelter or transitional housing) was 62 percent.
8. Five states accounted for almost half of the nation's population in 2012: California, 20.7 percent; New York, 11 percent; Florida, 8.7 percent; Texas, 5.4 percent; and Georgia with 3.2 percent.

Criticism on the Estimated Counts of Homelessness

In 2011, there were 46.2 million people in poverty in the United States (U.S. Census Bureau, 2011).

Advocates for the homeless believe the HUD "Point-In-Time" (PIT) estimates are low and do not accurately track the homeless population numbers. As noted by the National Coalition for the Homeless (NCH), the PIT method only counts those who are homeless at a particular time. The number may stay stable, but the population can change greatly because some homeless may secure housing while others become newly homeless. An alternative to the PIT method would be "Period Prevalence Counts" (PPC) which would examine the number of people who are homeless over a period of time (NCH, 2009). The NCH points out other problems with studies of the homeless include only counting people who are in shelters or on the streets. Moreover, this approach may provide useful information about the number of people who use services such as shelters and soup kitchens; however, it can often result in under reporting the number of homeless who may be living in cars or alternative places (NCH, 2009).

Homelessness in U.S. Cities

In December 2012, the U.S. Conference of Mayors released its "Hunger and Homelessness Survey" on the extent of homelessness in 25 surveyed cities from September 1, 2011, to August 31, 2012. The following findings are of significance in its study (U.S. Conference of Mayors, 2012):

1. There was an average 7 percent increase in homelessness.
2. There was an average 8 percent increase of families experiencing homelessness.
3. There was an average 5 percent increase in the number of unaccompanied individuals experiencing homelessness.

4. An average of 17 percent of homeless persons needing shelter did not receive it because there were no beds available.
5. Emergency shelters in 64 percent of the surveyed cities turned away homeless families with children.
6. Emergency shelters in 60 percent of the surveyed cities turned away unaccompanied individuals.
7. Among those requesting emergency food assistance, 51 percent were persons in families, 37 percent were employed, 17 percent were elderly, and 8.5 percent were homeless.
8. Across the survey cities, 19 percent of the people needing emergency food assistance did not receive it.

Race, Ethnicity, Gender, and Age

In 2010, the U.S. Department of Housing and Urban Development (HUD) estimated the homeless population to be: 41.6 percent white, 37 percent African American, 16.4 percent Hispanic, 4.5 percent other single race, and 7.2 percent multiple races. With reference to gender, HUD estimated 62.3 percent were males and 37.7 percent were females. Further, the following age information was included in its 2010 Annual Homeless Assessment Report to Congress (HUD, 2010):

- Under the age of 18 was 21.8 percent
- 18 to 30 years of age was 23.5 percent
- 31 to 50 years of age was 37.0 percent
- 51 to 61 years of age was 14.9 percent
- 62 and older was 2.8 percent

LGBT Youth

According to the National Alliance to End Homelessness, LGBT youth represent approximately 20 percent of homeless youth. It estimated each year over 300,000 LGBT youth experience at least one night of homelessness (NAEH, 2013). The National Coalition for the Homeless reports the following information on homeless LGBT youth (NCH, 2012c):

- Are at higher risk for victimization, mental health problems, and unsafe sexual practices
- 58.7 percent of LGBT homeless youth have been sexually victimized compared to 33.4 percent of heterosexual homeless youth
- LGBT homeless youth commit suicide at higher rates (62%) than heterosexual homeless youth (29%)

Quality-of-Life Concerns

In America, the homeless are constantly in need of food, water, and shelter, so it is not uncommon for many homeless people to panhandle for food or money. Homeless people deal with poor health, inadequate health care, an unsatisfactory diet, poor personal hygiene, and sleep deprivation. Unfortunately, the average life expectancy for a homeless adult is between 42 and 52 years of age (O'Connell, 2005). The following 2012 data show more quality-of-life concerns for the homeless (U.S. Conference of Mayors, 2012):

1. Shelter: Emergency shelters in 64 percent of the surveyed cities had to turn away homeless families with children because there were no beds available. Emergency shelters in 60 percent of the cities turned away unaccompanied individuals.
2. Mental Health Issues: 30 percent of homeless adults were severely mentally ill.
3. Disabled: 18 percent were physically disabled.
4. Working Class: 17 percent were employed.

5. Domestic Violence: 16 percent were victims of domestic violence.
6. HIV Positive: 4 percent were HIV positive.

Federal Law Definitions of Homelessness

Following are two definitions for homelessness under federal law. One is a general definition of homelessness for adults and the second definition specifically applies to homeless children and youth. These definitions are delineated in the federal law known as the McKinney–Vento Act and are under U.S. Code, Title 42: The Public Health and Welfare, Chapter 119. The two definitions and their key elements are as follows:

Homeless adult person　(1) An individual or family who lacks a fixed, regular, and adequate nighttime residence; (2) an individual or family who resides in a public or private place not designed for or ordinarily use as a regular sleeping accommodation for human beings, including a car, park, abandoned building, bus or train station, airport or camping ground; (3) an individual or family living in a supervised publicly or privately operated shelter designed to provide temporary living arrangements (including hotels and motels paid for by Federal, State, or local government programs for low-income individuals or by charitable organizations, congregate shelters, and transitional housing); (4) an individual who resided in a shelter or place not meant for human habitation and who is exiting an institution where he or she temporarily resided (Subchapter 1: General Provisions Section 11302).

Homeless children and youths　Have similar residency and shelter/transitional housing as a homeless adult, but includes sharing the housing of other persons due to loss of housing; living in motels, hotels, trailer parks, or camping grounds; or abandoned in hospitals; or are awaiting foster care placement (Subchapter VI: Education and Training, Part B: Education for Homeless Children and Youth, Section 11434a).

Causes for Homelessness

There are many interrelated causes for people experiencing homelessness. History shows that a poor economy, coupled with high unemployment, contributes to increased poverty and housing shortages. Personal bankruptcy, chronic alcohol and drug abuse, domestic violence, family break-ups, lack of family or government support, and mental illness are contributing factors as well. Being an undocumented immigrant or a runaway can also be a cause for homelessness. Unfortunately for LGBT youth, family conflict related to their sexual orientation and gender identities are added factors contributing to homelessness (NAEH, 2013).

When asked to list the three main causes of homelessness among families with children in 2012, the U.S. Conference of Mayors identified lack of affordable housing, poverty, and unemployment. Eviction, domestic violence and low-paying jobs finished the list for causes (U.S. Conference of Mayor, 2012). Regarding individuals, the top reasons for homelessness were lack of affordable housing, unemployment and poverty, followed by mental illness and the lack of treatment, substance abuse and the lack of treatment, and low paying jobs (U.S. Conference of Mayors, 2012).

When There Are No Shelters

People who experience homelessness become creative and adaptive when they need temporary shelter. Safety is a concern for homeless people when they sleep, and shelter is important in extreme (cold, wet, or hot) weather. Exhibit 14.4 shows the locations where homeless people sleep and congregate.

1. Abandoned buildings	12. Parks
2. Alleys	13. Patios
3. Awnings	14. Picnic Tables
4. Benches	15. Rest Areas
5. Bus Stations	16. Sidewalks
6. Cardboard Boxes	17. Subway Stations
7. Cars	18. Tarps
8. Construction Sites	19. Tents
9. Covered Bus Stops	20. Train Stations
10. Homeless Camps	21. Vacant Buildings
11. Overpasses	22. Vacant Houses

EXHIBIT 14.4   When There Is No Shelter, 2013

Homeless people are continually forced to leave from most, if not all, of these temporary locations by the police, business owners, or other government representatives. When homeless people do not leave, they are subject to arrest by police officers for trespassing or disorderly conduct offenses. This is referred to as criminalizing homelessness. Police officers need to learn from firefighters and other first responders to be more respectful and compassionate to homeless individuals. Instead of telling a homeless person to leave a public or business area, police officers should make every effort to locate an emergency shelter. Advocates for the homeless from all across the United States are uniting with homeless people to resolve the issue through public awareness, in legislation, and in the courts.

Crime Victimization

The homeless are extremely vulnerable to person and property crimes. The NCH indicated that from 1999 to 2010 there were 1,184 acts of violence against homeless people resulting in 312 murders across 47 states and Puerto Rico, and Washington, D.C. (NCH, 2012a). The NCH also reported that on average, for the murder victims, almost 36 percent were between the ages of 40 and 50, 65 percent were between the ages of 40 and 60, and 93 percent of the victims were males. Nearly 85 percent of the perpetrators were under the age of 25 and the majority were males; one in four violent attacks on the homeless resulted in death (NCH, 2012a). Exhibit 14.5 shows the number of homicides classified as hate crimes against homeless people.

Individual crimes committed against homeless people are not coded and classified by most local, state, and federal law enforcement agencies because the FBI's Uniform Crime Report does not collect homelessness status in its crime victimization and suspect statistics. Further, homelessness status is not protected by federal hate/bias crime laws.

State Laws Protecting the Homeless from Hate Crimes

As of July 2013, six states and the District of Columbia have enacted hate crime statutes to protect the homeless; these states are Alaska, Florida, Maine, Maryland, Rhode Island and Washington (NCH, 2012b). Advocates for the homeless reference cases like the one in South Baltimore in 2001, where three teenage males, over a period of four months attacked and beat to death three homeless men and assaulted several other homeless persons. All three teenagers called their actions "bum stomping" and were sentenced to prison for the brutal murders and assaults (Klein, 2003). According to Michael Stoops (personal communication, July 2013), Director of Community Organizing of the NCH, the passage of these laws allow judges to increase penalties for people who attack the homeless. "We need to send a symbolic and practical message that attacks against the homeless will not be tolerated," Stoops said. In making recommendations, the NCH calls for an amendment to the federal Hate Crimes Statistics Act to include crimes against the homeless, and for supporting state legislative efforts to add homeless persons as a protected class to state hate crime statutes (NCH, 2012b).

Year	Homicides Classified as Hate Crimes (FBI Data)	Fatal Attacks on Homeless Individuals (NCH Data)
1999	17	49
	(9 racial, 2 religion, 3 sexual orientation, 3 ethnicity)	
2000	19	43
	(10 racial, 1 religion, 2 sexual orientation, 6 ethnicity)	
2001	10	18
	(4 racial, 1 sexual orientation, 5 ethnicity)	
2002	13	14
	(4 racial, 3 religion, 4 sexual orientation, 2 ethnicity)	
2003	14	8
	(5 racial, 6 sexual orientation, 2 ethnicity, 1 disability)	
2004	5	25
	(3 racial, 1 religion, 1 sexual orientation)	
2005	6	13
	(3 racial, 3 ethnicity)	
2006	3	20
	(3 racial)	
2007	9	28
	(5 sexual orientation, 2 racial, 2 ethnicity)	
2008	7	27
	(5 sexual orientation, 1 racial, 1 ethnicity)	
2009	8	43
	(6 racial, 1 sexual orientation, 1 ethnicity)	
2010	(FBI information unavailable at the time of this report)	24
12 Year Total	111	312

EXHIBIT 14.5   Comparison of FBI Defined Hate Crime Homicides versus Fatal Attacks on Homeless
Source: Hate Crimes Against the Homeless: Violence Hidden in Plain View, 2012a. Used by permission of National Coalition for the Homeless. (2012a).

PEACEKEEPING STRATEGIES TO MITIGATE THE HOMELESSNESS CRISIS

Public trust and confidence in government and law enforcement agencies are essential for effective responses to the homelessness crisis. Homeless people in communities must believe they will be protected and treated with respect by the police, before relationships can develop. They must sense that the police are attentive and responsive in their efforts to help them and there is no risk of being harassed or assaulted. Further, homeless people and their advocates must see positive behavior from the police that match their rhetoric to help. Chapter 12 discussed humane law enforcement strategies for responding to hate/bias crimes and the same strategies identified have value for people experiencing homelessness. The following are just a few examples of jurisdictions that have made the effort to be attentive and responsive to the needs of the homeless (NLCHP, 2011):

- Seattle, WA. In late 2010, as a result of the efforts of local and national homeless advocates, the City of Seattle reversed a police department policy allowing police officers to ban homeless persons from private property open to the public, such as store and coffee shops, for no reason. The new policy allows homeless individuals to remain on these properties during business hours as long as they are not violating city business codes.
- Puyallup, WA. In 2010, Puyallup passed a city ordinance allowing religious organizations to host temporary encampments for homeless persons. The new ordinance seeks to address homeless sweeps and enforcement of anti-camping laws despite a shortage of affordable housing and shelter space.
- Minneapolis and Hennepin County, MN. In January 2007, Hennepin County developed a 10-year plan to mitigate homelessness. The Street Outreach Program was created to join homeless persons with needed services and divert them from contact with the criminal justice system. The program has been successful in reducing public funds spent on each homeless person.

Federal Strategic Plan to Prevent and End Homelessness

In June 2010, the United States Interagency Council on Homelessness (USICH) and its 19 federal member agencies initiated *Opening Doors,* the first comprehensive federal strategic plan to prevent and end homelessness. Its mission is "to coordinate the federal response to homelessness and to create a national partnership at every level of government and with the private sector and end homelessness in the nation while maximizing the effectiveness of the Federal Government in contributing to the end of homelessness (USICH, 2012). The USICH's goals are to prevent and end homelessness for individuals, veterans, families, youth, and children. Moreover, it has 52 strategies under 10 objectives that address five themes. The five themes are (USICH, 2012):

1. Increase Leadership, Collaboration, and Civic Engagement
2. Increase Access to Stable and Affordable Housing
3. Increase Economic Security
4. Improve Health and Stability
5. Retool The Homeless Crisis System

Exhibit 14.6 identifies the organizational objectives under each theme. To illustrate USICH's ability to respond to feedback from national advocates and service providers, it amended several of its objectives in 2012 related to youth and education. Criminal justice professionals would benefit in reviewing each objective and amended objective for problem-solving strategies.

Education and Training

Awareness training on homelessness should be considered if a police department doesn't teach it at its academy or offer it at in-service training. At a minimum, the curriculum should include the causes and solutions to homelessness along with how to interact with homeless people in a humane and respectful manner. Some law enforcement and public safety training

Themes and Objectives

Theme 1: Increase Leadership, Collaboration, and Civic Engagement

Objective 1: Provide and promote collaborative leadership at all levels of government and across all sectors to inspire and energize Americans to commit to preventing and ending homelessness.

Objective 2: Strengthen the capacity of public and private organizations by increasing knowledge about collaboration, homelessness, and successful interventions to prevent and end homelessness.

Theme 2: Increase Access to Stable and Affordable Housing

Objective 3: Provide affordable housing to people experiencing or most at risk of homelessness.

Objective 4: Provide permanent supportive housing to prevent and end chronic homelessness.

Theme 3: Increase Economic Security

Objective 5: Improve access to education and increase meaningful and sustainable employment for people experiencing or most at risk of homelessness.

Objective 6: Improve access to mainstream programs and services to reduce people's financial vulnerability to homelessness.

Theme 4: Improve Health and Stability

Objective 7: Integrate primary and behavioral health care services with homeless assistance programs and housing to reduce people's vulnerability to and the impacts of homelessness.

Objective 8: Advance health and housing stability for youth aging out of systems such as foster care and juvenile justice.

Objective 9: Advance health and housing stability for people experiencing homelessness that have frequent contact with hospitals and criminal justice.

Theme 5: Retool The Homeless Crisis Response Team

Objective 10: Transform homeless services to crisis response systems that prevent homelessness and rapidly return people who experience homelessness to stable housing.

• Amendment objective—Refer to Amendment document for full report.

EXHIBIT 14.6   Overview of the Federal Strategic Plan to End Homelessness: Themes and Objectives
Source: USICH (2012).

programs already include this topic in their cultural diversity courses or community-policing courses. Criminal justice and emergency services college students, police officers, and other first responders greatly benefit from homelessness awareness instruction. Some practical tips that can be included in such instruction and in community meetings are listed in Exhibit 14.7.

Soup Kitchens and Emergency Shelters

Soup kitchens, located in many cities throughout the entire United States, provide meals to those who are hungry, poor, and homeless. Many churches, mosques, and synagogues help in providing emergency shelter during extreme weather periods. When law enforcement officers and criminal

1. Offer food (a meal or food pack), water, or meal vouchers.
2. It is not recommended that you give cash to homeless individuals unless there are mitigating circumstances.
3. If you choose, provide cash or other donations to a soup kitchen, shelter, rescue mission, or other nonprofit organization to help the homeless.
4. Assist homeless individuals in locating emergency shelter if needed.
5. Treat homeless individuals with respect.

EXHIBIT 14.7   Five Tips for Encounters with a Homeless Person on the Street

Mini Case Study: What Would You Do?

Consider the following case study picturing two scenarios: (1) the individuals involved are U.S.- born and speak English fluently; (2) the individuals involved are immigrants and speak limited English. Describe the challenges in each scenario, as you answer the questions following the case study.

You are a police officer on duty and you are having lunch with another police officer at a family style restaurant in your patrol district. A homeless adult male with a small child walks into the restaurant, and both approach you and the other officer at your table. The man tells you he is homeless and that he and his nine-year old daughter are looking for temporary

shelter and haven't had a meal in 24 hours. The man tells you he was laid off from his part-time job one month ago and was evicted from his apartment one week ago. He mentions he has no family and friends to turn to for assistance, and suddenly his nine-year old daughter looks at you and starts crying, pleading "please help me and my daddy."

• How do you feel about this situation?
• What are you going to say to the child and her father?
• How are you going to help these two individuals with your current knowledge, skills, and resources?

justice students volunteer their time at soup kitchens and emergency shelters that serve the disadvantaged, they have an opportunity to get to know the homeless in their community, and conversely, the homeless get to know them.

MENTAL ILLNESS CHALLENGES IN MULTICULTURAL COMMUNITIES

In 2010, the Substance Abuse and Mental Health Services Administration (SAMHSA) estimated 45.9 million (20.0%) of Americans 18 or older suffered from a diagnosable mental disorder or mental illness, and about 11.4 million (5%) from a serious mental illness. Eight percent or 1.9 million youth age 12–17 had a major depressive episode, while another 2.9 million (12.2%) of the population received treatment or counseling for problems with emotions or behavior (SAMHSA, 2012).

Mental illness A mental-health disorder characterized by alterations in thinking, mood, or behavior associated with distress and/or impaired functioning (U.S. Department of Health and Human Services, 1999).

According to the Alzheimer's Association in 2013, an estimated 5.0 million (11%) Americans, age 65 and over had Alzheimer's disease while approximately 200,000 persons (4%) under age 65 had the disease.

> Alzheimer's disease is the most common type of dementia. "Dementia" is an umbrella term describing a variety of diseases and conditions that develop when nerve cells in the brain (called neurons) die or no longer function normally. The death or malfunction of neurons causes changes in one's memory, behavior and ability to think clearly. In Alzheimer's disease, these brain changes eventually impair an individual's ability to carry out such basic bodily functions as walking and swallowing. Alzheimer's disease is ultimately fatal. (Alzheimer's Association, 2013)

For a police officer in America, these percentages are significant because an estimated 5 percent to 20 percent of police contacts across the nation involve the severely mentally ill (Bouchard, 2012). People with severe mental illness can include anyone—children, teenagers, adults, and senior citizens. Mental illness transcends race, ethnicity, gender, and sexual orientation. Serious mental illness includes major depression, schizophrenia, bipolar disorder, obsessive compulsive disorder (OCD), panic disorder, posttraumatic stress disorder (PTSD), and borderline personality disorder (National Alliance on Mental Illness, 2009). Most trained and experienced law enforcement officers are familiar with these disorders and the term "psychotic episode," as they have had encounters with people with mental illness. Police officers know that psychotic episode is a critical period of time for the person with a mental illness. Stabilization of the person without injury or loss of life should always be the primary objective in these encounters.

> **Psychotic episode** A period of time when a person with a serious mental illness is impaired and at risk of endangering himself or herself, or others.

All law enforcement officers and other first responders should acquire knowledge and skills in the area of mental health. The following information reflects the volume of contacts that two different police departments reported on mental-health incidents over the course of one year.

- In Portland, Maine, after taking steps to improve data collection, Police Chief Michael Sauschuck reported that mental health–related calls almost quadrupled from 856 calls in 2010 to 3,311 calls in 2011 (Bouchard, 2012).
- In Raleigh, North Carolina, the city police department responded to nearly 2,000 mental health commitment calls in 2009 (Sheehan, 2010).

Mental illness is a problem for police, medical services, and social services, and places a burden on the local community as well. Since there is a large potential for miscommunication and misunderstanding when dealing with those afflicted with a mental illness, many encounters can quickly turn negative. Police officers must be prepared when dealing with people who have mental illness, and studying the types of calls involving people with mental illness will prove invaluable for them.

Types of Calls

Regardless of the time of the day or the size of the agency, law enforcement officers encounter people with mental illness in a variety of situations. According to the U.S. Department of Justice, these types of calls involve criminal offenders, disorderly persons, missing persons, complainants, victims, and persons in need of care. Exhibit 14.8 shows examples for each role.

Individually and collectively, law enforcement officers are trained to handle different types of incidents in various types of scenarios. Likewise, police officers will benefit from studying and formulating response strategies to the five most frequent types of people-with-mental-illness scenarios, which are as follows (Peck, 2003):

1. A family member, friend, or other concerned person calls the police for help during a psychiatric emergency.
2. A person with mental illness feels suicidal and calls the police as a cry for help.
3. Police officers encounter a person with mental illness behaving inappropriately in public.
4. Citizens call the police because they feel threatened by the unusual behavior or the mere presence of a person with mental illness.
5. A person with mental illness calls the police for help on account of imagined threats.

Even though these are the five most frequent scenarios law enforcement officers may have with people with mental illness, no two contacts or encounters are ever the same. Further, it is worth mentioning that police officers will continually have such types of contacts at places such as parks, schools, colleges, businesses, care facilities, and any other locations where there are people. Law enforcement officers must always be attentive and sensitive to the behavior and needs of each mentally ill person.

Role	Examples
Offender	• A person with mental illness commits a person or property crime.
	• A person with mental illness commits a drug crime.
	• A person with mental illness threatens to commit suicide.
	• A person with mental illness threatens to injure someone else in the delusional belief that the other person poses a threat to him or her.
	• A person with mental illness threatens to injure police as a means of forcing police to kill him (commonly called "suicide by cop").
Disorderly person	• A family or community member reports annoying or disruptive behavior by a person with mental illness.
	• A hospital, group home, or mental health facility calls for police assistance in controlling a person with mental illness.
	• A police officer on patrol encounters a person with mental illness behaving in a disorderly manner.
Missing person	• A family member reports that a person with mental illness is missing.
	• A group home or mental health institution reports that a person with mental illness walked away and/or is missing.
Complainant	• A person with mental illness calls the police to report real or imagined conditions or phenomena.
	• A person with mental illness calls the police to complain about care received from family members or caretakers.
Victim	• A person with mental illness is the victim of a person or property crime.
	• A family member, caretaker, or service provider neglects or abuses a person with mental illness.
Person in need of care	• Police are asked to transport a person with mental illness to a hospital or mental health facility.
	• Police encounter a person with mental illness who is neglecting his or her own basic needs (food, clothing, shelter, medication, etc.).

EXHIBIT 14.8 Roles of People with Mental Illness in Law Enforcement Encounters

Source: "People with Mental Illness," U.S. Department of Justice, Office of Community Oriented Policing Services, May 2006.

POLICE PROTOCOL IN ENCOUNTERS WITH PEOPLE WHO HAVE MENTAL ILLNESS

Law enforcement officers exercise a great amount of discretion when they encounter a person who has a mental illness. Generally, there are three options: (1) arrest, (2) hospitalization, and (3) informal disposition. Arrest is based on a crime that has been committed.

Arrest

The police officer takes the mentally ill person into custody and transports him or her to jail where the arrested person is booked for the crime and later released, similar to any other person under the same circumstances. Some officers may believe that arresting a mentally ill person may result in treatment for that person in a correctional facility. In almost all cases this is not the reality in the criminal justice system. All arrests should be made on the probable cause that a crime has been committed and law enforcement officers should always follow the due process protection guarantees of the U.S. Constitution. The arrest of people with mental illness, for the sole reason of getting them treatment, is discouraged.

Hospitalization

Hospitalization of a person with mental illness is accomplished through voluntary and involuntary commitments. Often law enforcement officers will become involved with helping family members who need assistance in the voluntary commitment of another family member who consents to be taken to a hospital or clinic for mental health treatment. The police officer generally will stand by until the ambulance arrives to transport the person, or, depending on the law enforcement agency's protocol and the totality of the circumstances, make the transport themselves to the hospital or clinic. If the person with mental illness in this scenario refuses a voluntary commitment, the police officer must then decide if the individual is a danger to himself or herself, or to others. When it is determined that the mentally ill person is indeed a danger to himself or herself, or others, then the police officer can legally place a police officer hold on the person to make it an involuntary commitment. In this case, the police officer would take the person into custody and transport to a local hospital that treats and accommodates people with mental illness. Law enforcement officers should follow mental health professionals' guidelines, local laws, and their agency's procedures when making a voluntary or involuntary commitment on any person.

Informal Disposition

Informal disposition is the third alternative to arrests or hospitalizations in encounters between law enforcement officers and persons with mental illness. Usually there is no written report by the police officer as is required in an arrest or hospitalization. Commonly, the only documentation of the informal disposition is in the police officer's notebook and in the 911 Center's Computer Aided Dispatch (CAD). Informal dispositions can range from calming down a mentally ill person and having a responsible family member or friend watch over, to doing nothing at all.

Use of Force

Police interactions with people with mental illness have the potential of being dangerous, but usually are not. As of 2006, which was the last comprehensive study on the use of force between police officers and those with mental illness, the U.S. Department of Justice reported there were 982 police officers assaulted and 15 police officers feloniously killed between 1993 and 2002 by "mentally deranged" assailants. These assaults and murders are tragic, but these attacks by people with mental illness represent one out of every 59 assaults on officers and one out of every 42 officers killed. In providing its analysis on the data of police officers killed by mentally ill offenders from the years of 1980 to 2010, the Department of Justice reported that the number of police officers killed ranged from 2 to 11 each year (U.S. Department of Justice, 2012). For the person with severe mental illness, it is estimated that he or she is four times more likely to be killed by the police in encounters than are other citizens (U.S. Department of Justice, 2006a). Unfortunately for the person who has a severe mental illness, he or she is vulnerable to excessive force by police officers who may not possess the mental health training and skills to diffuse a potentially dangerous contact. Too often in every city, county, and state, there are reports of a mentally ill person either injured or killed by a police officer who did not use alternate methods in the encounter.

Certainly, police officers must always be alert to their own safety when there is any type of encounter with a person; however, there is a need for the police to approach a person with mental illness in a calm and nonthreatening manner. Furthermore, police officers, when they have exhausted all other means, should only use the minimum amount of force necessary to physically restrain any person. Unfortunately, the average number of classroom hours that recruits spend on

Recommendations for Police Officers Who Encounter Mentally Ill Persons

1. Communicate in a respectful manner.
2. Speak in a calm and nonthreatening voice.
3. Be direct in your inquiries and requests.
4. Rephrase your inquiries and requests, if needed.
5. Be patient and take the extra steps to communicate, and over communicate, if needed.
6. Do not argue with, talk down or belittle the person with mental illness.
7. Do not make threats toward the individual with mental illness.
8. Protect the person with mental illness, others, and yourself from any physical injuries.
9. If the person with mental illness is having a psychotic episode and requires physical restraint, use the appropriate techniques to minimize any physical injuries to him or her.
10. Only use the minimum amount of force that is necessary and justified, if the person with mental illness becomes violent with you or others.
11. Notify a supervisor and, at a minimum, document in your police report any use of physical force against a person with mental illness.
12. Follow your department policy as to how to handle the encounter, specifically in the areas of: (1) the arrest, (2) hospitalization, and (3) informal disposition.
13. Always seek medical treatment for a person with mental illness if they are physically injured.

EXHIBIT 14.9   Recommendations for Police Officers Who Encounter Mentally Ill Persons

mental illness issues in the police academies nationwide is a shockingly low 6.5 hours and sometimes, though not guaranteed, maybe one or two hours at in-service training (Hails & Borum, 2003). As of 2013, the training topic of mental illness issues is not listed in the curriculum for state and local law enforcement training academies. The Police Executive Research Forum recommends a minimum of 16 hours of training on mental illness issues at the police academy level. In the meantime, police departments across the United States need to examine what practices have worked well for police officers who have had encounters with persons with mental illness and highlight these effective methods in their training programs. Exhibit 14.9 lists recommendations for police officers, who have contact with mentally ill persons.

Mentally Ill Persons in the Corrections System

In a 2006 study, the U.S. Department of Justice reported that 56 percent of state prisoners, 45 percent of federal prisoners, and 64 percent of local jail inmates were identified to have a mental health condition.

Noted in the same study was the prevalence of violence associated with criminal activity. An estimated 61 percent of state prisoners and 44 percent of jail inmates who had a mental health problem had a prior violent offense. In addition, inmates with a mental health problem had high rates of substance dependence or abuse in the year before their admission. Those who were dependent on or abusing drugs/alcohol accounted for 74 percent of state prisoners and 76 percent of local jail inmates (U.S. Department of Justice, 2006b).

Inmates receiving mental health treatment since being incarcerated amounted to about one in three state prisoners, one in four federal prisoners, and one in six local jail inmates. Those receiving a prescribed medication were the most common type of treatment receivers, with 27 percent in state prisons, 19 percent in federal prisons, and 15 percent in local jails (U.S. Department of Justice, 2006b).

RESPONSE STRATEGIES BETWEEN POLICE AND PEOPLE WITH MENTAL ILLNESS

In June 1999, President Bill Clinton's administration convened the first Conference on Mental Health to address ways of reducing the stigma of mental illness and discrimination against people with mental disorders. The Attorney General chaired a session on mental health and the criminal justice system. The purpose was to address the recurring cycle of people with mental disorders being incarcerated for crimes (often minor offenses) and receiving minimal or no treatment for their underlying mental health problems. The session focused on legislative proposals to address these issues, including a mental health court proposal and other proposed legislation to improve services to the mentally ill within correctional settings. Following up on the Conference on Mental Health, the Office of Justice Programs, and the Department of Health and Human Services (DHHS), Center for Mental Health Services hosted a conference in July 1999 on the treatment of people with mental disorders within the justice system. Issues included the challenges of integrating criminal justice and mental health systems, diverting mentally ill offenders to appropriate treatment through mental health court programs, improving mental health services in the juvenile justice system, and creating community partnerships to respond to the needs of people with mental illness.

One of the many benefits that resulted from the 1999 Clinton administration conferences on mental illness and other similar conferences is the ongoing awareness that respect and civil rights protection of people with mental illness must always be a priority as it is essential with all multicultural groups. Government and specifically the criminal justice system must be responsive and adaptive, and make changes in how it deals with people who have mental illness. Law enforcement agencies should follow five strategies to deal with the challenges facing people with mental health issues:

1. Partnerships with multicultural community leaders, local faith-based organizations, and other community-based agencies (e.g., homeless shelters, food banks, social services, hospitals/mental health clinics) to provide a network of support for people with mental health problems.
2. Assistance to local multicultural business organizations that wish to work voluntarily with mental health issues within the community.
3. Creation and updating of specific police training programs and continuing education for encounters with people with mental health problems.
4. Development and updating of policies, procedures, and practices within the law enforcement agency for dealing with mental health problems (e.g., crisis intervention teams).
5. Collaboration with local fire departments, emergency medical services, 9-1-1, and surrounding law enforcement agencies to pool resources and strategies to mitigate the mental health challenges.

Treatment for Mental Illness

Mentally ill individuals, without adequate family or support systems, have limited to no capacity to care for themselves, often experiencing, from the time of the onset of their mental illness, repeated hospitalizations, and psychiatric trauma. They are usually not able to track their medication, frequently deny that they are sick, and refuse to be treated. This becomes law enforcement's challenge as these individuals pose threats to others. New York State has enacted legislation that occurred as a result of a woman's death (Kendra Webdale) in 1999 when she was pushed in front of a train by a mentally ill individual who was neither taking medication nor receiving treatment for his schizophrenia. "Kendra's Law" in short, mandates, via court order, that certain individuals must receive outpatient treatment for their illness (New York State, Office of Mental Health, 2006). The majority of United States have similar laws, but New York has put significant resources into developing this legislation; a study has shown that patients who must receive treatment (because of laws such as Kendra's Law) are not arrested or rehospitalized as frequently as those receiving no treatment (Belluck, 2013). This conclusion is intuitive, and officers would be well advised to become familiar with their state's form of Kendra's Law.

Mini Case Study: CIT (Crisis Intervention Team)

The strategies of the CIT model in Memphis, Tennessee, explained below are impressive. Read the following, and then identify and explain at least two barriers that could potentially prevent a police department from adopting the CIT model. After you identify the barriers, discuss ways of overcoming these obstacles so that the model becomes more feasible for a police department.

Memphis, Tennessee

In recent years, the most effective approach to improving police response to incidents involving people with mental illness, and especially crisis incidents, has been specialization. More departments have seen the value of having trained officers or even specialized units dispatched to handle these situations. The Memphis, Tennessee, Crisis Intervention Team has used a (CIT) model whereby a team of selected patrol officers are trained and then serve as generalists/specialists. The role of the specialists would be to perform the full range of regular patrol duties, but respond immediately whenever crisis situations involving people with mental illness occur. In those situations, these officers assume on-scene command as soon as they arrive. They are trained to handle crisis situations as well as facilitate the delivery of treatment and other services. The specialists quickly become knowledgeable about voluntary and involuntary commitments, and they develop good working relationships with professionals in the mental health community (U.S. Department of Justice, 2006a).

According to the University of Memphis, research indicates that the CIT model works efficiently for crisis response times and jail diversion for those with mental illness. Further, the CIT positively impacts and improves psychiatric symptomatology for those suffering from a serious mental illness as well as substance abuse. Moreover, CIT partnership with mental health care services is user friendly to individuals with mental illness, family members, and police officers. Last, research shows that police officer injury rates have been significantly reduced (University of Memphis, 2011). Numerous police departments throughout the United States have embraced the CIT model and have achieved similar results (National Alliance on Mental Illness, 2013).

Summary

- *Community policing* is a term frequently used by law enforcement officers, criminal justice educators, elected officials, and community leaders. It refers to a style of policing in which law enforcement agencies and communities form partnerships to help problem-solve crime and public safety issues. The presence or the lack thereof of community policing is pivotal to the success of every law enforcement agency's stated mission. Public safety and quality-of-life concerns are important to all of America's multicultural cities and communities. Both police and multicultural communities benefit when there is citizenship participation and relevant activities that build bridges for ongoing relationships.

- There are three major types of gangs: (1) street gangs, (2) prison gangs, and (3) outlaw motorcycle gangs. Typical gang-related crimes include alien smuggling, armed robbery, assault, automobile theft, drug trafficking, extortion, fraud, home invasions, identity theft, murder, weapons trafficking, and hate crimes. There are approximately 1.4 million criminal gang members in the United States. Street gangs have the largest membership and most members are 18 years and older, but the majority of youth who join a gang belong to a street gang. The next largest group of gangs is prison gangs, followed by outlaw motorcycle gangs.

- The terms *youth* and *street gang* are commonly used interchangeably, but the use of the term *street gang* for *youth gang* often results in confusing juvenile gangs with adult criminal organizations. Causation variables for youth gang membership include five risk factors which are: (1) prior delinquency in violence and alcohol/drug use; (2) poor family management and problematic parent–child relations; (3) low school attachment and academic achievement, and negative labeling by teachers; (4) association with peers who engage in delinquency; (5) and disorganized neighborhoods where large numbers of youth are in trouble and where drugs and firearms are readily available.

- By promoting coordination and information sharing between federal, state, and local law enforcement agencies, the FBI has been able to and continues to identify violent gang enterprises that pose a significant threat. The FBI has also been able to pursue these criminals with coordinated investigations that support successful prosecutions. State and local law enforcement agencies have been responding to the gang threat since their inception but have not always maintained a consistent level of responsiveness. Major multiagency gang operations involving federal, state, county, and city law enforcement officers illustrate the need for law enforcement officers, especially in certain regions of the country, to familiarize themselves with the cultural, racial, and ethnic dimensions of gangs. Organizations such as COPS (Community Oriented Policing Services), an office of the U.S. Department of Justice, continue to provide excellent resources to law enforcement to mitigate the gang threat.

- A homeless person is an individual who lacks a regular and adequate nighttime residence. Homelessness is a growing problem in the United States that impacts all multicultural groups. The main causes for homelessness include a lack of affordable housing or shelter, poverty, and unemployment. People who are homeless are targeted victims of hate crimes. As of July 2013, six states and the District of Columbia have enacted hate crime laws to protect the homeless.

- Before the police can be effective in responding to mitigate homelessness problems, homeless people must perceive that they will be protected and treated with respect by the police. Law enforcement officers need to demonstrate compassion to the homeless and be unbiased in their treatment to homeless people. Law enforcement officers need to be knowledgeable about organizations that help the homeless.

- Mental illness is characterized by alterations in thinking, mood, or behavior associated with distress and/or impaired functioning. There are many challenges faced by people with mental illness when they are in the roles of criminal offenders, disorderly persons, missing persons, complainants, victims, and persons in need of care. Unfortunately, due to their mental illness they are at an unfair disadvantage and are often treated with bias and disrespect.

- Most police officers have limited training on dealing effectively with mental health issues. Officers need to be aware that the use and level of force directed against a person with mental illness may be unnecessary unless there is a risk to the officer's safety. Other methods of dealing with the mentally ill are available to law enforcement, and more training is needed on the local, state, and national levels. Law enforcement must be responsive and adaptive, and make changes in how it deals with people who have mental illness. Strategies include (1) partnerships with the leadership of multicultural communities, local faith-based organizations, and other community-based services (i.e., hospitals/mental health clinics) to provide a network of support for people with mental health problems; (2) assistance to local multicultural business organizations that voluntarily wish to work with mental health issues within the community; (3) creation and updating of specific police training programs and continuing education for encounters with people with mental health problems; (4) development and updating of policies, procedures, and practices within the law enforcement agency for dealing with mental health problems; and (5) collaboration with local fire departments, emergency medical services, 9-1-1, and surrounding law enforcement agencies to pool resources and strategies to mitigate the mental health challenges.

Discussion Questions and Issues

1. *Community Policing.* Why is community policing in minority, ethnic, and immigrant communities especially crucial to the success of law enforcement in any given city or rural community? Discuss the two examples presented in this section of the chapter (i.e., the police department in Garden Grove, California, without community policing in place [at the time of the fall of Saigon] and the Chicago Police Department whose community policing efforts resulted in a dramatic decline of violent crimes and property crimes in the city). What lessons can you extract from these two examples that may be applicable to your jurisdiction?

2. *Types of Gangs.* Make a list of the specific street gangs and outlaw motorcycle gangs within the law enforcement jurisdiction that you work or live in. Research information regarding each gang's membership and reported criminal activity. After compiling this information, discuss three strategies a police department could use to curtail each gang's membership and criminal activity.

3. *Homelessness.* Compile a list of the homelessness conditions and causes in the law enforcement jurisdiction that you work or live in. Research the number of people who are homeless and indicate their race, ethnicity, age, and gender. Identify the number of temporary emergency shelters, rescue missions, and soup kitchens in the area. Also, refer to Exhibit 14.4: "When There Is No Shelter" and identify all of the 22 types of places homeless people stay in your area. Upon completing these tasks, identify strategies you could take individually and collectively with other people, to help people who are homeless in your multicultural community.

4. *Police Encounters with Mental Illness.* Select a city, county, or state law enforcement agency in your community and collect the following information:

a. How many hours of training do police recruits receive at the academy on mental health issues?

b. How many hours a year do police officers receive for mental health issues at in-service training?

c. Review the police department's written policy, procedures, and practices for encounters with people who have mental illness.

d. Does the police department track and keep record of all police officer contacts with people who have mental illness?

e. Does the police department follow the five response strategies law enforcement should use to deal with problems of people with mental health issues? You can review the five strategies on p. 408.

References

Alzheimer's Association. *2013 Alzheimer's Disease Facts and Figures,* 2013. Retrieved August 25, 2013, from www.alz.org/downloads/facts_figures_2013.pdf

Archibold, Randal C. (2009, March 22). "Mexican Drug Cartel Violence Spills Over, Alarming U.S." *The New York Times.* Retrieved July 19, 2013, from www.nytimes.com/2009/03/23/us/23border.html?_r=2&scp=1&sq=mexican%20drug%20cartel%20violence&st=cse

Belluck, Pam. (2013, July 30). "Program Compelling Outpatient Treatment for Mental Illness Is Working, Study Says." *The New York Times.* Retrieved August 25, 2013, from www.nytimes.com/2013/07/30/us/program-compelling-outpatient-treatment-for-mental-illness-is-working-study-says.html?pagewanted=all&_r=0

Berry, Ondra. (2013, July). Retired Deputy Police Chief, Reno, Nevada, Police Department, personal communication.

Bouchard, Kelly. (2012, December). "Limited data on police, mentally ill encounters." *Portland Press Herald.* Retrieved April 22, 2014, from www.pressherald.com/news/projects/Shoot-Limited-data-on-police-mentally-ill-encounters.html l

Boys & Girls Club of America (BGCA). (2013). "Gang Prevention through Targeted Outreach." Retrieved July 26, 2013, from www.nationalgangcenter.gov/SPT/Programs/67

Carcamo, Cindy. (2013, July 12). "Gun smuggling to Mexico dented, but hardly slowed, by border searches." *Los Angeles Times.* Retrieved August 23, 2013, from articles.latimes.com/2013/jul/12/nation/la-na-ff-gun-trafficking-20130713

Center for Disease Control and Prevention (CDC). (2012). "Gang Homicides—Five U.S. Cities, 2003-2008." *Morbidity and Mortality Week Report.* Retrieved July 25, 2013, from www.cdc.gov/mmwr/pdf/wk/mm6103.pdf

Chicago Police Department. (2011). "Chicago Police Department 2010 Annual Report," p. 33.

Community Oriented Policing Services (COPS). (2013a). Office of Community Oriented Policing Services Fact Sheet: "2013 Cops Hiring Program." Retrieved July 15, 2013, from cops.usdoj.gov/pdf/2013AwardDocs/CHP/2013_CHP-Preaward-FactSheet.pdf

Community Oriented Policing Services (COPS). (2013b). "Gangs Toolkit." Retrieved July 26, 2013, from www.cops.usdoj.gov/default.asp?Item=1309

Decker, Scott and G. David Curry. (2003). Suppression without prevention, prevention without suppression. In S. H. Ecker (Ed.), *Policing Gangs and Youth Violence* (pp. 191–213). Belmont, California: Wadsworth/Thompson Learning.

Esbensen, Finn-Aage. (2000). *Preventing Adolescent Gang Involvement.* Youth Gang Series. Washington, D.C.: U.S. Department of Justice, Office of Juvenile Justice and Delinquency Prevention.

Esbensen, Finn-Aage, L. Thomas Winfree, Jr.,, Ni He, and Terrance Taylor. (2001). "Youth Gangs and Definitional Issues: When is a Gang a Gang, and Why Does it Matter?" *Crime and Delinquency, 47,* 105–130.

Federal Bureau of Investigation (FBI). (2009b). "Massive Racketeering Case Targets Hawaiian Gardens Gang Involved in Murder of Sheriff's Deputy, Attacks on African-Americans and Widespread Drug Trafficking." Retrieved May 28, 2009, from losangeles.fbi.gov/dojpressrel/pressrel09/la052109.htm

Federal Bureau of Investigation (FBI). (2013). "Violent Gang Task Forces." Retrieved July 26, 2013, from www.fbi.gov/about-us/investigate/vc_majorthefts/gangs/violent-gangs-task-forces

Gang Resistance Education and Training (G.R.E.A.T.). (2013). "Welcome." Retrieved July 26, 2013, from www.great-online.org/

Glover, Scott and Richard Winton. (2009, May 22). "Dozens arrested in crackdown on Latino gang accused of targeting blacks." *L.A. Times.* Retrieved May 28, 2009, from www.latimes.com/news/local/la-me-gang-sweep22-2009may22,0,6857156.story

Gottfredson, G. D. and Gottfredson D. C. 2001. *Gang Problems and Gang Programs in a National Sample of Schools.* Ellicott City, Maryland: Gottfredson Associates, Inc. Retrieved April 22, 2014 from www.nationalgangcenter.gov/About/FAQ#RefGottfredson2001

Hails, Judy and Randy Borum. (2003). "Police Training and Specialized Approaches to Respond to People with Mental Illnesses." *Crime and Delinquency, 49*(1), 52–61.

Hill, Karl. G., Christina Lui, and J. David Hawkins. (2001). *Early Precursors of Gang Membership: A Study of Seattle Youth.* Bulletin. Youth Gang Series. Washington, D.C.: U.S. Department of Justice, Office of Juvenile Justice and Delinquency Prevention.

Howell, James C., and Arlen Egley, Jr. (2005). "Moving Risk Factors into Developmental Theories of Gang Membership." *Youth and Juvenile Justice, 3*(4), 334–354.

Klein, Allison. (2003, November 20). "Friend testifies defendant took part in bum stomping." Baltimore Sun. Retrieved April 23, 2014 from http://articles.baltimoresun.com/2003-11-20/news/0311200114_1_waterbury-daniel-ennis-holle

Klein, Malcom W. (1995). *The American Street Gang.* New York, NY: Oxford University Press.

Miller, Walter. (1982/1992). *Crime by Youth Gangs and Groups in the United States.* Washington, D.C.: Government Printing Office.

Monkkonen, Eric H. (1981). *Police in Urban America, 1860–1920.* Cambridge, England: Cambridge University Press.

National Alliance to End Homelessness. (2014). "LGBTQ Youth." Retrieved April 22, 2014, from www.endhomelessness.org/pages/lgbtq-youth

National Alliance on Mental Illness. (2009). "About Mental Illness." Retrieved April 6, 2009, from www.nami.org/template.cfm?section=About_Mental_Illness

National Alliance on Mental Illness. (2013). "The Facts about Crisis Intervention Teams." Retrieved August 25, 2013, from www.namidupage.org/news-events/nami-line/may-2012-nami-line/232-the-facts-about-crisis-intervention-teams

National Coalition for the Homeless. (2009, July). "How Many People Experience Homelessness?" Retrieved July 30, 2013, from www.nationalhomeless.org/factsheets/How_Many.pdf

National Coalition for the Homeless. (2012a, January). "Hate Crimes against the Homeless: Violence Hidden in Plain View." Washington D.C. Retrieved July 15, 2013, from www.national-homeless.org/publications/hatecrimes/hatecrimes2010.pdf

National Coalition for the Homeless. (2012b, January). "Hate Crimes against the Homeless: An Organizing Manual for Concerned Citizens." Washington D.C. Retrieved July 31, 2013, from www.nationalhomeless.org/publications/hatecrimes/hatecrimesmanual12.pdf

National Coalition for the Homeless. (2012c, February). "LGBT Homeless." Retrieved April 22, 2014, from www.national-homeless.org/factsheets/lgbtq.html

National Gang Intelligence Center (NGIC). (2009). *National Gang Threat Assessment.* Product No. 2009-M0335-001. Retrieved July 23, 2013, from www.fbi.gov/stats-services/publications/national-gang-threat-assessment-2009-pdf

National Gang Intelligence Center (NGIC). (2011). National Gang Threat Assessment—Emerging Trends. Retrieved July 19, 2013, from www.fbi.gov/stats-services/publications/2011-national-gang-threat-assessment/2011-national-gang-threat-assessment-emerging-trends

National Law Center on Homelessness and Poverty (NLCHP). (2013). "From Wrongs To Rights: The Case for Homeless Bill of Rights Legislation." Retrieved April 22, 2014, from http://nlchp.org/documents/Wrongs_to_Rights_HBOR

National Law Center on Homelessness and Poverty. (2011, November). "Criminalizing Crisis: The Criminalization of Homelessness in U.S. Cities." Washington D.C. Retrieved April 22, 2014, from www.nlchp.org/documents/Criminalizing_Crisis

National Gang Center (NGC). (2011). National Youth Gang Survey Analysis. Retrieved July 23, 2013, from www.national-gangcenter.gov/Survey-Analysis

New York State, Office Mental Health. (2006). An Explanation of Kendra's Law. Retrieved January 15, 2014, from www.omh.ny.gov/omhweb/Kendra_web/Ksummary.htm

O'Connell, James J. (2005, December). "Premature Mortality in Homeless Populations: A Review of the Literature." Nashville: National Health Care for the Homeless Council, Inc. Retrieved July 29, 2013, from santabarbarastreetmedicine.org/wordpress/wp-content/uploads/2011/04/PrematureMortalityFinal.pdf

Osborne, A. L. (2013, July). "Skipper." Former President of NAACP, Portland, Oregon, personal communication.

Peck, Leonard W. Jr. (2003). "Law Enforcement Interactions with Persons with Mental Illness." *TELEMASP Bulletin,* 10(1), 1–12.

Police Athletic League (PAL). (2013). "Welcome to the New National PAL Website" Retrieved July 26, 2013, from www.nationalpal

Police Executive Research Forum (PERF). (2004). "Community Policing: The Past, Present, and Future." Washington, D.C. Retrieved April 23, 2014 from www.policeforum.org/assets/docs/Free_Online_Documents/Community_Policing/community%20policing%20-%20the%20past%20present%20and%20future%202004.pdf

Substance Abuse and Mental Health Services Administration (SAMHSA). (2012, January). "Results from the 2010 National Survey on Drug Use and Health: Mental Health Findings." NSDUH Series H-42, HHS Publication No. (SMA) 11-5667. Rockville, MD. Retrieved July 31, 2013, from www.samhsa.gov/data/NSDUH/2k10MH_Findings/2k10MHResults.pdf

Sheehan, Ruth. (2010, January 15). "Shuttling patients burdens deputies." *News & Observer.* Retrieved August 1, 2013, from www.newsobserver.com/2010/01/15/285369/shuttling-patients-burdens-deputies.html

Spergel, Irving A. (1995). *The Youth Gang Problem.* New York, NY: Oxford University Press.

Stoops, Michael. (2013, July). Director of Community Organizing, National Coalition for the Homeless, Washington, D.C., personal communication.

Thornberry, Terrence. P. (1998). "Membership in Youth Gangs and Involvement in Serious and Violent Offending." In R. Loeber, and D. P. Farrington (Eds.), *Serious and Violent Juvenile Offenders: Risk Factors and Successful Interventions,* Thousand Oaks, Calif.: Sage Publications.

Thornberry, T. P., M. D. Krohn, A. J. Lizotte, C. A. Smith, and K. Tobin. (2003). *Gangs and Delinquency in Developmental Perspective.* New York, NY: Cambridge University Press.

University of Memphis. (2011). "About CIT." Retrieved August 24, 2013, from cit.memphis.edu/aboutus.html

U.S. Census Bureau. (2011). "Poverty Highlights." Retrieved July 29, 2012, from www.census.gov/hhes/www/poverty/about/overview

U.S. Conference of Mayors. (2012, December). *Hunger and Homelessness Survey: A Status Report on Hunger and Homelessness in America's Cities:* A-25 Survey. U.S. Conference of Mayors, Washington, D.C. Retrieved July 30, 2013, from usmayors.org/pressreleases/uploads/2012/1219-report-HH.pdf

U.S. Department of Health and Human Services. (1999). "Mental Health: A Report of the Surgeon General. "Retrieved April 22, 2014 from http://profiles.nlm.nih.gov/ps/access/NNBBHV.pdf

U.S. Department of Housing and Urban Development. (2010). "The 2010 Annual Homeless Assessment Report to Congress."

Retrieved August 24, 2013, from www.onecpd.info/resources/documents/2010HomelessAssessmentReport.pdf

U.S. Department of Housing and Urban Development. (2012). "The 2012 Point-in-Time Estimates of Homelessness." Volume 1 of the 2012 Annual Homeless Assessment Report. Retrieved July 29, 2013, from www.onecpd.info/resources/documents/2012AHAR_PITestimates.pdf

U.S. Department of Justice. (2006a). Office of Community Oriented Policing Services: "People with Mental Illness." Retrieved April 23, 2014, from http://cops.usdoj.gov/Publications/e04062003.pdf

U.S. Department of Justice. (2006b). Office of Justice Programs, Bureau of Justice Statistics: "Study Finds More than Half of All Prison and Jail Inmates Have Mental Health Problems." Retrieved April 23, 2014, from www.bjs.gov/content/pub/press/mhppjipr.cfm

U.S. Department of Justice. (2009a). Office of Justice Programs, Bureau of Justice Statistics: "State and Local Law Enforcement Training Academies, 2006" Special Report, February 2009, NCJ222987. Retrieved July 18, 2013, from www.bjs.gov/content/pub/pdf/slleta06.pdf

U.S. Department of Justice. (2012, January 26). "Officer Safety and Wellness (OSW) Group Meeting Summary: Officer Deaths and Injuries from Gunfire." Retrieved August 1, 2013, from www.cops.usdoj.gov/pdf/OSWG/Meeting_01-26-2012.pdf

U.S. Department of Justice. (2013a). "Prison Gangs." Retrieved July 24, 2013, from www.justice.gov/criminal/ocgs/gangs/prison.html

U.S. Department of Justice. (2013b). "Motorcycle Gangs." Retrieved July 23, 2013, from www.justice.gov/criminal/ocgs/gangs/motorcycle.html

U.S. Interagency Council on Homelessness. (2012). "Opening Doors: Federal Strategic Plan To Prevent And End Homelessness, Amendment 2012." Retrieved August 24, 2013, from www.usich.gov/resouces/uploads/asset_library/USICH_OD_Amendment)WEB_091112v2pdf

APPENDIX A

Multicultural Community and Workforce: Attitude Assessment Survey*

The first set of questions that follow ask for your opinions about how certain segments of the community view the police. Using the response sheets (Attitude Assessment Survey Response Sheet) on pages 415–419, put the number of the response that you think best describes each group's perception. Remember, give the response based on how you feel each group would answer the statements.

1. In your opinion, how would this group rate the job this police department does? (See response sheet.)
2. This group generally cooperates with the police.
3. Overall, this group thinks that police department acts to protect the rights of individuals.
4. Which of the following, this group feels, describes the current relationship between the police and the community?
5. Overall, this group feels this department responds to citizen complaints about officers in an objective and fair manner.
6. This group thinks most contacts with police are negative.

The next set of questions ask for your opinions about procedures and practices within the police department.

7. Overall, police supervisors in this department respond to citizens' complaints about employees in an objective and fair manner.
8a. Most police officers in this department are sensitive to cultural and community differences.
8b. Most civilian employees in this department are sensitive to cultural and community differences.
9a. This department adequately prepares officers to work with members of the community who are of a different race or ethnicity than the majority of the population.
9b. This department adequately prepares civilian employees to work with members of the community who are of a different race or ethnicity than the majority of the population.
10. The police administration is more concerned about police–community relations than it should be.
11a. Special training should be given to officers who work with community members who are of a different race or ethnicity than the majority population.
11b. Special training should be given to civilian employees who work with community members who are of a different race or ethnicity than the majority population.
12. Special training should be given to assist officers in working with each of the following segments of the community.
13. How often are racial slurs and negative comments about persons of a different race or ethnicity expressed by personnel in this department?
14a. Persons of a different race or ethnicity in this city are subject to unfair treatment by some officers in this department.

---

*Adapted with permission from the Alameda, California Police Department, 2013.

14b. Persons of a different race or ethnicity in this city are subject to unfair treatment by some civilian employees in this department.

15a. Prejudicial remarks and discriminatory behavior by officers are not tolerated by line supervisors in this department.

15b. Prejudicial remarks and discriminatory behavior by civilian employees are not tolerated by line supervisors in this department.

16. Transfer policies in this department have a negative effect on police–community affairs.

17. Citizen complaint procedures in this department operate in favor of the citizen, not the employee.

18. Internal discipline procedures for employee misconduct are generally appropriate.

19. The procedure for a citizen to file a complaint against a department employee should be which of the following?

20. With regard to discipline for misconduct, all employees in this department are treated the same in similar situations, regardless of race or ethnicity.

21. What kind of discipline do you think is appropriate for the first incident of the following types of misconduct? (Assume intentional.)

This section examines your views about police–community relations training and community participation. Please circle the response that best describes your opinion.

22. Do you think training in police–community relations was adequate to prepare you to work with all segments of the community?

23. How often do you have opportunities to participate in positive contacts with community groups?

24. Do you think this department has an adequate community relations program?

25. What subject areas related to community relations would be helpful on an in-service training basis?

26. What do you think is the most important thing that citizens need to understand about the police?

27. How can the police department best educate the public about police policies and practices?

28. Listed are steps that police departments can take to improve police services as they relate to community relations. How important you think each of them should be to this administration?

Attitude Assessment Survey Response Sheet

Place the number that corresponds to your response in each column.

	Business community	Minority residents	Community leaders	Most residents	Juveniles
Question 1:					
(1) Very good					
(2) Good					
(3) Fair					
(4) Poor					
(5) Very Poor					
Question 2:					
(1) Most of the time					
(2) Sometimes					
(3) Rarely					
(4) Never					

	Business community	Minority residents	Community leaders	Most residents	Juveniles
Question 3:					
(1) Strongly agree					
(2) Agree					
(3) Disagree					
(4) Strongly disagree					
Question 4:					
(1) Very good					
(2) Good					
(3) Fair					
(4) Poor					
(5) Very poor					
Question 5:					
(1) Strongly agree					
(2) Agree					
(3) Disagree					
(4) Strongly disagree					
Question 6:					
(1) Strongly agree					
(2) Agree					
(3) Disagree					
(4) Strongly disagree					

Place check in column corresponding to your response for each question.

	Strongly agree	Agree	Disagree	Strongly disagree	Don't know
Question 7:					
Question 8a:					
Question 8b:					
Question 9a:					
Question 9b:					
Question 10:					
Question 11a:					
Question 11b:					

Check one response for each group.

Question 12:

	Strongly agree	Agree	Disagree	Strongly disagree
African American/black (includes Caribbean, Haitian, and so forth)				
Asian				
Hispanic				
Homosexual				

	Strongly agree	Agree	Disagree	Strongly disagree

Circle your response.

Question 13:   (1) Often   (2) Sometimes   (3) Rarely   (4) Never

Place check in column corresponding to your response for each question.

	Strongly agree	Agree	Disagree	Strongly disagree	Don't know
Question 14a:					
Question 14b:					
Question 15a:					
Question 15b:					
Question 16:					
Question 17:					
Question 18:					

Circle one response.

Question 19:

(1) Citizen sends complaint in writing to department.

(2) Citizen telephones complaint to department.

(3) Citizen comes to department.

(4) Any of the above is an acceptable means.

(5) None of the above is an acceptable means.

Please explain._____

Circle your response.

Question 20: (1) Strongly agree (2) Agree (3) Disagree (4) Strongly disagree

Check one response for each.

Question 21:

Type of misconduct	Verbal warning	Training/ counseling	Oral reprimand	Formal reprimand	Suspension	Termination
Excessive force						
False arrest						
Discrimination						
Use of racial slurs						
Criminal conduct						
Poor service						

Type of misconduct	Verbal warning	Training/ counseling	Oral reprimand	Formal reprimand	Suspension	Termination
Discourtesy to citizen						
Improper procedure						

Please circle the response that best describes your opinion.

Question 22:   (1) Yes (2) No (3) Did not receive training

If no, please describe why the training was not satisfactory.

Please explain._____

_____

_____

Question 23:   (1) Frequently (2) Sometimes (3) Rarely (4) Never

Question 24:   (1) Yes (2) No (3) Don't know

Please explain._____

_____

_____

Question 25: _____

_____

_____

_____

Question 26: _____

_____

_____

_____

Question 27:

Circle one only.

(1) Through patrol officer contacts with citizens

(2) Through public meetings

(3) Through the media

(4) Selected combinations of the responses above

(5) Other (explain):_____

_____

_____

(6) Don't know

Check one response for each

Question 28:

	Somewhat important	Important	Not at all important
Hire more police			
Focus on more serious crimes			
Improve response time			
Increase salaries			
Provide more training			

	Somewhat important	Important	Not at all important
Raise qualifications for potential applicants			
Be more courteous to public			
Increase foot patrols			
Reduce discrimination			
Provide dedicated time for community involvement			

APPENDIX B

Cultural Diversity Survey: Needs Assessment*

There has been a great deal of discussion in recent years about whether the job of police officer has been changing. Some of the discussion revolves around issues related to contact with people from different cultural, racial, or ethnic groups. Please check or enter one answer for each question.

1. Comparing the job of an officer today with that of an officer a few years ago, I think that today the job is
   ( ) a lot more difficult
   ( ) somewhat more difficult
   ( ) about the same in difficulty
   ( ) somewhat easier
   ( ) a lot easier

2. When I stop a car with occupant(s) of a different racial or ethnic group than mine, I must admit that I am more concerned about my safety than I would be if I stopped a car with the same number of occupant(s) of the same racial or ethnic group as mine.
   ( ) strongly agree
   ( ) agree
   ( ) disagree
   ( ) strongly disagree

3. If an officer notices a group of young people gathering in a public place and the young people aren't known to the officer, they should be watched very closely for possible trouble.
   ( ) strongly agree
   ( ) agree
   ( ) disagree
   ( ) strongly disagree

4. If an officer notices a group of young people from another racial or ethnic group gathered in a public place, the officer should plan on watching them very closely for possible trouble.
   ( ) strongly agree
   ( ) agree
   ( ) disagree
   ( ) strongly disagree

5. How often do you think it is justifiable to use derogatory labels such as "scumbag" and "dirtbag" when dealing with possible suspects?
   ( ) frequently
   ( ) some of the time
   ( ) once in a while
   ( ) never

6. When I interact on duty with civilians who are of a different race, ethnicity, or culture, my view is that
   ( ) they should be responded to a little more firmly to make sure that they understand the powers of the police
   ( ) they should be responded to somewhat differently, taking into account their different backgrounds
   ( ) they should be responded to the same as anyone else

---

*Adapted with permission: police department wishes to remain anonymous.

7. When I encounter citizens of a different race, ethnicity, or culture who have committed a violation of the law, my view is that
( ) they should be responded to a little more firmly to make sure they understand the powers of the police
( ) they should be responded to somewhat differently, taking into account their different backgrounds
( ) they should be responded to the same as anyone else

8. When interacting on duty with civilians who have a complaint or a question and who are of a different race, ethnicity, or culture, I try to be very aware of the fact that my usual gestures may frighten or offend them.
( ) strongly agree
( ) agree
( ) disagree
( ) strongly disagree

9. When interacting on duty with offenders who are of a different race, ethnicity, or culture, I try to be very aware of the fact that my usual behavior may frighten or offend them.
( ) strongly agree
( ) agree
( ) disagree
( ) strongly disagree

10. How often have you run into a difficulty in understanding what a civilian was talking about because of language barriers or accents?
( ) frequently
( ) once in a while
( ) hardly ever
( ) never

11. How often have you run into difficulty in understanding what an offender was talking about because of language barriers or accents?
( ) frequently
( ) once in a while
( ) hardly ever
( ) never

12. How often have you run into some difficulty in making yourself clear while talking to a civilian because of language barriers or accents?
( ) frequently
( ) once in a while
( ) hardly ever
( ) never

13. How often have you run into some difficulty in making yourself clear while talking to an offender because of language barriers or accents?
( ) frequently
( ) once in a while
( ) hardly ever
( ) never

14. How important is it that the police department provides training to make its members aware of the differences in culture, religion, race, or ethnicity?
( ) extremely important
( ) very important
( ) fairly important
( ) not too important
( ) not important at all

15. Personally, I believe that the training I have received on group differences is
    ( ) far too much
    ( ) somewhat too much
    ( ) about the right amount
    ( ) too little
    ( ) virtually nothing

16. The training in the area of group differences has been
    ( ) extremely helpful
    ( ) very helpful
    ( ) somewhat helpful
    ( ) not too helpful
    ( ) not helpful at all

17. My own view is that our department's quality of service could be improved by
    ( ) placing greater emphasis on hiring on the basis of the highest score obtained on the entrance exam, making no attempt to diversify by race, ethnicity, or gender
    ( ) placing greater emphasis on diversity by race, ethnicity, or gender and somewhat less emphasis on the numerical rank obtained on the entrance examination
    ( ) giving equal weight to both the score obtained on the entrance examination and diversification by race, ethnicity, or gender

18. What percentage of civilian or internal complaints against employees is adjudicated equitably?
    ( ) over 80 percent
    ( ) between 60 and 80 percent
    ( ) between 40 and 60 percent
    ( ) between 20 and 40 percent
    ( ) less than 20 percent

19. Some civilian or internal complaints are adjudicated more favorably toward people from diverse groups rather than toward the majority population.
    ( ) strongly agree
    ( ) agree
    ( ) disagree
    ( ) strongly disagree

20. I think that employees of a different race or ethnicity receive preferential treatment on the job.
    ( ) strongly agree
    ( ) agree
    ( ) disagree
    ( ) strongly disagree

21. The racial diversity of my coworkers has made it easier for me to see issues and incidents from another perspective.
    ( ) strongly agree
    ( ) agree
    ( ) disagree
    ( ) strongly disagree

22. To think that employees of a different race or ethnicity than mine receive preferential treatment on this job
    ( ) bothers me because I do not think it is justified
    ( ) does not bother me because I think it is justified
    ( ) is fair only because it makes up for past discrimination
    ( ) I do not believe minorities get preferential treatment

23. In certain situations, having a partner of a different race or ethnicity than mine is more advantageous than having a partner of my same race or ethnicity.
    ( ) strongly agree

( ) agree
( ) disagree
( ) strongly disagree

24. I have received negative feedback from members of the community regarding the conduct of other officers.
( ) strongly agree
( ) agree
( ) disagree
( ) strongly disagree

25. I have received negative feedback from members of the community regarding the conduct of officers who are of a different race or ethnicity in particular.
( ) strongly agree
( ) agree
( ) disagree
( ) strongly disagree

26. I have received more negative feedback from members of the community regarding the conduct of officers from different races and ethnic backgrounds than about the conduct of white officers.
( ) strongly agree
( ) agree
( ) disagree
( ) strongly disagree

27. In terms of being supervised
( ) I would much rather be supervised by a man
( ) I would somewhat rather be supervised by a man
( ) I would much rather be supervised by a woman
( ) I would somewhat rather be supervised by a woman
( ) It does not make a difference whether a man or a woman supervises me

28. In terms of being supervised by a man
( ) I would much rather be supervised by a nonminority
( ) I would somewhat rather be supervised by a nonminority
( ) I would much rather be supervised by a minority
( ) I would somewhat rather be supervised by a minority
( ) It does not make a difference to which group my supervisor belongs

29. In terms of being supervised by a woman
( ) I would much rather be supervised by a nonminority
( ) I would somewhat rather be supervised by a nonminority
( ) I would much rather be supervised by a minority
( ) I would somewhat rather be supervised by a minority
( ) It does not make a difference to which group my supervisor belongs

If this questionnaire is being used for a training class, please check one answer in the following questions that best applies to you.

30. What is your sex?
( ) male
( ) female

31. What is your race?
( ) white
( ) African American or black
( ) Hispanic
( ) Native American

( ) Asian American
( ) other

32. How many years have you been employed by the police department?
( ) 0–5 years
( ) 6–10 years
( ) 11–20 years
( ) more than 20 years

33. What is your current rank?
( ) officer
( ) sergeant
( ) lieutenant
( ) captain or commander
( ) deputy chief
( ) chief

34. What is the highest academic degree you hold?
( ) high school
( ) associate's degree
( ) bachelor's degree
( ) master's degree

APPENDIX C

Cross-Cultural Communication Skills Assessment for Law Enforcement Professionals

Self-awareness is a key factor in the development of an effective professional communication style and the sharpening of your cross-cultural communication skills. As you answer the following questions, think about cross-cultural communication both with citizens/noncitizens you encounter as well as coworkers in your department. Consider having a coworker fill out the assessment for you to the extent possible, and then compare your responses with his or hers.

While the following assessment focuses on cross-cultural skills, some of the categories also pertain to communication with people from the same background as oneself. Many of these topics are discussed in Chapter 4 of this text.

Instructions: Answer using the following ratings:

Usually	Sometimes	Seldom

1. I exhibit patience when communicating with individuals for whom English is not their first language. _____

2. I make a point of simplifying my language and refraining from using slang and idioms with people for whom English is not their mother tongue. _____

3. (Except for in emergency situations) I refrain from filling in words for individuals trying to communicate with me. _____

4. When using an interpreter, I maintain eye contact with the individual I am questioning or with whom I am interacting (i.e., rather than focusing on the interpreter). _____

5. I spend extra time explaining police procedures to new immigrants where required. _____

6. I am aware of the "baggage" that some new immigrants carry with them related to fear or distrust of police, and make efforts to communicate in a supportive, nonthreatening manner. _____

7. I am familiar with culturally different beliefs around eye-contact related to respect and authority. _____

8. To check understanding, I restate, paraphrase, or summarize what an individual has said in order to allow him or her the opportunity to correct/confirm my understanding. _____

9. I am aware of my biases toward groups from different backgrounds, and I make an effort to communicate professionally with all people, in spite of these biases. _____

10. I make an effort to not let citizens/coworkers push my "hot buttons" so that my communication remains nondefensive and professional. _____

11. When speaking with individuals from groups that speak English differently from the way I do, I try not to imitate their manner of speech in order to be "one of them." _____

12. With nonnative speakers of English, I try not to speak in an excessively loud voice in an attempt to make myself clear. _____

13. I encourage people to let me know when they have not understood something I have communicated. _____

14. I make it a point to convey respect to all citizens while on duty, regardless of their race, color, gender, religion, or any other dimension of diversity. _____

15. With all channels of communication and vis-à-vis all groups (i.e., face-to-face with coworkers, agency online communication, media), I avoid any derogatory remarks that can result in the breaking of trust. _____

APPENDIX D

Listing of Gangs and Identifying Characteristics

The following information lists national and regional gangs and their specific characteristics for the three major types of gangs presented in Chapter 14:

Section I: Street Gangs

Section II: Prison Gangs

Section III: Outlaw Motorcycle Gangs

This material does not include all gangs in the United States. Individual state, county, and city law enforcement agencies should be contacted for information on local and regional gangs in their jurisdictions. This listing was adapted and reproduced with permission from the National Drug Intelligence Center of which the *National Gang Threat Assessment for the National Gang Intelligence Center* is a part. Both centers are part of the U.S. Department of Justice. This information was published in 2009, and was current as of the writing of this text's sixth edition.

SECTION I: STREET GANGS

18th Street (National)

Formed in Los Angeles, 18th Street is a group of loosely associated sets or cliques, each led by an influential member. Membership is estimated at 30,000 to 50,000. In California, approximately 80 percent of the gang's members are illegal aliens from Mexico and Central America. The gang is active in 44 cities across 20 states. Its main source of income is street-level distribution of cocaine and marijuana and, to a lesser extent, heroin and methamphetamine. Gang members also commit assault, auto theft, carjacking, drive-by shootings, extortion, homicide, identification fraud, and robbery.

Almighty Latin King and Queen Nation (National)

The Latin Kings street gang was formed in Chicago in the 1960s and consisted predominantly of Mexican and Puerto Rican males. Originally created with the philosophy of overcoming racial prejudice and creating an organization of "Kings," the Latin Kings evolved into a criminal enterprise operating throughout the United States under two umbrella factions: Motherland, also known as KMC (King Motherland Chicago), and Bloodline (New York). All members of the gang refer to themselves as Latin Kings and, currently, individuals of any nationality are allowed to become members. Latin Kings associating with the Motherland faction also identify themselves as "Almighty Latin King Nation (ALKN)," and make up more than 160 structured chapters operating in 158 cities across 31 states. The membership of Latin Kings following KMC is estimated to be 20,000 to 35,000. The Bloodline was founded by Luis Felipe in the New York State correctional system in 1986. Latin Kings associating with Bloodline also identify themselves as the "Almighty Latin King and Queen Nation (ALKQN)." Membership is estimated to be 2,200 to 7,500, divided among several dozen chapters operating in 15 cities across five states. Bloodline Latin Kings share a common culture and structure with KMC and respect them as the Motherland, but all chapters do not report to the Chicago leadership hierarchy. The gang's primary source of income is the street-level distribution of powder cocaine, crack cocaine, heroin, and marijuana. Latin Kings continue to portray themselves as a community organization while engaging in a wide variety of criminal activities, including assault, burglary, homicide, identity theft, and money laundering.

Asian Boyz (National)

Asian Boyz is one of the largest Asian street gangs operating in the United States. Formed in southern California in the early 1970s, the gang is estimated to have 1,300 to 2,000 members operating in at least 28 cities across 14 states. Members primarily are Vietnamese or Cambodian males. Members of Asian Boyz are involved in producing, transporting, and distributing methamphetamine as well as distributing MDMA (methylenedioxymethamphetamine) and marijuana. In addition, gang members are involved in other criminal activities, including assault, burglary, drive-by shootings, and homicide.

Black P. Stone Nation (National)

Black P. Stone Nation, one of the largest and most violent associations of street gangs in the United States, consists of seven highly structured street gangs with a single leader and a common culture. It has an estimated 6,000 to 8,000 members, most of whom are African American males from the Chicago metropolitan area. The gang's main source of income is the street-level distribution of cocaine, heroin, marijuana and, to a lesser extent, methamphetamine. Members are also involved in many other types of criminal activity, including assault, auto theft, burglary, carjacking, drive-by shootings, extortion, homicide, and robbery.

Bloods (National)

Bloods is an association of structured and unstructured gangs that have adopted a single-gang culture. The original Bloods were formed in the early 1970s to provide protection from the Crips street gang in Los Angeles, California. Large, national-level Bloods gangs include Bounty Hunter Bloods and Crenshaw Mafia Gangsters. Bloods membership is estimated to be 7,000 to 30,000 nationwide; most members are African American males. Bloods gangs are active in 123 cities across 33 states. The main source of income for Bloods gangs is street-level distribution of cocaine and marijuana. Bloods members are also involved in transporting and distributing methamphetamine, heroin, and PCP (phencyclidine), but to a much lesser extent. The gangs also conduct other criminal activity including assault, auto theft, burglary, carjacking, drive-by shootings, extortion, homicide, identity fraud, and robbery.

Crips (National)

Crips is a collection of structured and unstructured gangs that have adopted a common gang culture. Crips membership is estimated at 30,000 to 35,000; most members are African American males from the Los Angeles metropolitan area. Large, national-level Crips gangs include 107 Hoover Crips, Insane Gangster Crips, and Rolling 60s Crips. Crips gangs operate in 221 cities across 41 states. The main source of income for Crips gangs is the street-level distribution of powder cocaine, crack cocaine, marijuana, and PCP. The gangs are also involved in other criminal activity such as assault, auto theft, burglary, and homicide.

Florencia 13 (Regional)

Florencia 13 (F 13 or FX 13) originated in Los Angeles in the early 1960s; gang membership is estimated at more than 3,000. The gang operates primarily in California and increasingly in Arkansas, Missouri, New Mexico, and Utah. Florencia 13 is subordinate to the Mexican Mafia (La Eme) prison gang and claims Sureños (Sur 13) affiliation. A primary source of income for gang members is the trafficking of cocaine and methamphetamine. Gang members smuggle multikilogram quantities of powder cocaine and methamphetamine obtained from supply sources in Mexico into the United States for distribution. Also, gang members produce large quantities of methamphetamine in southern California for local distribution. Florencia members are involved in other criminal activities, including assault, drive-by shootings, and homicide.

Fresno Bulldogs (Regional)

Fresno Bulldogs is a street gang that originated in Fresno, California, in the late 1960s. Bulldogs are the largest Hispanic gang operating in central California, with membership estimated at 5,000 to 6,000. Bulldogs are one of the few Hispanic gangs in California that claim neither Sureños (Southern) nor Norteños (Northern) affiliation. However, gang members associate with Nuestra Familia (NF) members, particularly when trafficking drugs. The street-level distribution of methamphetamine, marijuana, and heroin is a primary source of income for gang members. In addition, members are involved in other criminal activity, including assault, burglary, homicide, and robbery.

Gangster Disciples (National)

The Gangster Disciples street gang was formed in Chicago, Illinois, in the mid-1960s. It is structured like a corporation and is led by a chairman of the board. Gang membership is estimated at 25,000 to 50,000; most members are African American males from the Chicago metropolitan area. The gang is active in 110 cities across 31 states. Its main source of income is the street-level distribution of cocaine, crack cocaine, marijuana, and heroin. The gang is also involved in other criminal activity, including assault, auto theft, firearms violations, fraud, homicide, operation of prostitution rings, and money laundering.

Latin Disciples (Regional)

Latin Disciples, also known as Maniac Latin Disciples and Young Latino Organization, originated in Chicago in the late 1960s. The gang is composed of at least 10 structured and unstructured factions with an estimated 1,500 to 2,000 members and associate members. Most members are Puerto Rican males. Maniac Latin Disciples are the largest Hispanic gang in the Folk Nation Alliance. The gang is most active in the Great Lakes and the southwestern regions of the United States. The street-level distribution of powder cocaine, heroin, marijuana, and PCP is a primary source of income for the gang. Members are also involved in other criminal activity, including assault, auto theft, carjacking, drive-by shootings, home invasion, homicide, money laundering, and weapons trafficking.

Mara Salvatrucha (National)

Mara Salvatrucha, also known as MS 13, is one of the largest Hispanic street gangs in the United States. Traditionally, the gang consisted of loosely affiliated groups known as cliques; however, law enforcement officials have reported increased coordination of criminal activity among Mara Salvatrucha cliques in the Atlanta, Dallas, Los Angeles, Washington, D.C., and New York metropolitan areas. The gang is estimated to have 30,000 to 50,000 members and associate members worldwide, 8,000 to 10,000 of whom reside in the United States. Members smuggle illicit drugs, primarily powder cocaine and marijuana, into the United States and transport and distribute the drugs throughout the country. Some members also are involved in alien smuggling, assault, drive-by shootings, homicide, identity theft, prostitution operations, robbery, and weapons trafficking.

Sureños and Norteños (National)

As individual Hispanic street gang members enter prison systems, they put aside former rivalries with other Hispanic street gangs and unite under the name Sureños or Norteños. The original Mexican Mafia members, most of whom were from southern California, considered Mexicans from the rural, agricultural areas of northern California weak and viewed them with contempt. To distinguish them from the agricultural workers or farmers from northern California, members of Mexican Mafia began to refer to the Hispanic gang member prisoners who worked for them as Sureños (Southerners). Inmates from northern California became known as Norteños

(Northerners) and are affiliated with Nuestra Familia. Because of its size and strength, Fresno Bulldogs are the only Hispanic gang in the California Department of Corrections (CDC) that does not fall under Sureños or Norteños but remains independent. Both the Sureños and the Norteños gang members' main sources of income are retail-level distribution of cocaine, heroin, marijuana, and methamphetamine within prison systems and in the community and extortion of drug distributors on the streets. Some Sureños members have direct links to Mexican drug trafficking organizations (DTOs) and broker deals for Mexican Mafia as well as for their own gang. Both Sureños and Norteños gangs are also involved in other criminal activities such as assault, carjacking, home invasion, homicide, and robbery.

Tango Blast (Regional)

Tango Blast is one of largest prison/street criminal gangs operating in Texas. Tango Blast's criminal activities include drug trafficking, extortion, kidnapping, sexual assault, and murder. In the late 1990s, Hispanic men incarcerated in federal, state, and local prisons founded Tango Blast for personal protection against violence from traditional prison gangs such as the Aryan Brotherhood, Texas Syndicate, and Texas Mexican Mafia. Tango Blast originally had four city-based chapters: Houstone, Houston, Texas; ATX or La Capricha, Austin, Texas; D-Town, Dallas, Texas; and Foros or Foritos, Fort Worth, Texas. These four founding chapters are collectively known as "Puro Tango Blast" or "The Four Horsemen." From the original four chapters, former Texas inmates established new chapters in El Paso, San Antonio, Corpus Christi, and the Rio Grande Valley. In June 2008, the Houston Police Department estimated that more than 14,000 Tango Blast members were incarcerated in Texas. Tango Blast is difficult to monitor. The gang does not conform to either traditional prison/street gang hierarchical organization or gang rules. Tango Blast is laterally organized, and leaders are elected sporadically to represent the gang in prisons and to lead street gang cells. The significance of Tango Blast is exemplified by corrections officials reporting that rival traditional prison gangs are now forming alliances to defend themselves against Tango Blast's growing power.

Tiny Rascal Gangsters (National)

Tiny Rascal Gangsters are one of the largest and most violent Asian street gang associations in the United States. It is composed of at least 60 structured and unstructured gangs, commonly referred to as sets, with an estimated 5,000 to 10,000 members and associates, who have adopted a common gang culture. Most members are Asian American males. The sets are most active in the southwestern, Pacific, and New England regions of the United States. The street-level distribution of powder cocaine, marijuana, MDMA, and methamphetamine is a primary source of income for the sets. Members are also involved in other criminal activity, including assault, drive-by shootings, extortion, home invasion, homicide, robbery, and theft.

United Blood Nation (Regional)

Bloods is a universal term that is used to identify both West Coast Bloods and United Blood Nation (UBN). While these groups are traditionally distinct entities, both identify themselves by "Blood," often making it hard for law enforcement to distinguish between them. The United Blood Nation group started in 1993 in Rikers Island GMDC (George Mochen Detention Center) to protect its members from the threat posed by Latin Kings and Ñetas, who dominated the prison. UBN is a loose confederation of street gangs, or sets, that once were predominantly African American. Membership is estimated to be between 7,000 and 15,000 along the U.S. eastern corridor. UBN derives its income from street-level distribution of cocaine, heroin, and marijuana; robbery; auto theft; and smuggling drugs to prison inmates. UBN members also engage in arson, carjacking, credit card fraud, extortion, homicide, identity theft, intimidation, prostitution operations, and weapons distribution.

Vice Lord Nation (National)

Vice Lord Nation, based in Chicago, is a collection of structured gangs located in 74 cities across 28 states, primarily in the Great Lakes region. Led by a national board, the various gangs have an estimated 30,000 to 35,000 members, most of whom are African American males. The main source of income is street-level distribution of cocaine, heroin, and marijuana. Members also engage in other criminal activity such as assault, burglary, homicide, identity theft, and money laundering.

SECTION II: PRISON GANGS

Aryan Brotherhood

Aryan Brotherhood, also known as AB, was originally ruled by consensus but is now highly structured with two factions—one in the CDC and the other in the Federal Bureau of Prisons (BOP). The majority of members are white males, and the gang is active primarily in the southwestern and Pacific regions of the United States. Its main source of income is the distribution of cocaine, heroin, marijuana, and methamphetamine within prison systems and on the streets. Some AB members have business relationships with Mexican DTOs that smuggle illegal drugs into California for AB distribution. AB is notoriously violent and is often involved in murder for hire. Although the gang has been historically linked to the California-based Hispanic prison gang Mexican Mafia (La Eme), tension between AB and La Eme is increasingly evident, as seen in recent fights between whites and Hispanics within CDC.

Barrio Azteca

Barrio Azteca is one of the most violent prison gangs in the United States. The gang is highly structured and has an estimated membership of 2,000. Most members are Mexican national or Mexican American males. Barrio Azteca is most active in the southwestern region, primarily in federal, state, and local corrections facilities in Texas, and outside prison in southwestern Texas and southeastern New Mexico. The gang's main source of income is smuggling heroin, powder cocaine, and marijuana from Mexico into the United States for distribution both inside and outside prisons. Gang members often transport illicit drugs across the U.S.–Mexico border for DTOs. Barrio Azteca members are also involved in alien smuggling, arson, assault, auto theft, burglary, extortion, intimidation, kidnapping, robbery, and weapons violations.

Black Guerrilla Family

Black Guerrilla Family (BGF), originally called Black Family or Black Vanguard, is a prison gang founded in the San Quentin State Prison, California, in 1966. The gang is highly organized along paramilitary lines, with a supreme leader and central committee. BGF has an established national charter, code of ethics, and oath of allegiance. BGF members operate primarily in California and Maryland. The gang has 100 to 300 members, most of whom are African American males. A primary source of income for gang members is cocaine and marijuana distribution. BGF members obtain such drugs primarily from Nuestra Familia/Norteños members or from local Mexican traffickers. BGF members are involved in other criminal activities, including auto theft, burglary, drive-by shootings, and homicide.

Hermanos de Pistoleros Latinos

Hermanos de Pistoleros Latinos (HPL) is a Hispanic prison gang formed in the Texas Department of Criminal Justice (TDCJ) in the late 1980s. It operates in most prisons and on the streets in many communities in Texas, particularly Laredo. HPL is also active in several cities in Mexico, and its largest contingent in that country is in Nuevo Laredo. The gang is structured and is estimated to have 1,000 members. Members maintain close ties to several Mexican DTOs and are involved in trafficking quantities of cocaine and marijuana from Mexico into the United States for distribution.

Mexikanemi

The Mexikanemi prison gang (also known as Texas Mexican Mafia or Emi) was formed in the early 1980s within the TDCJ. The gang is highly structured and is estimated to have 2,000 members, most of whom are Mexican nationals or Mexican American males living in Texas at the time of incarceration. Mexikanemi poses a significant drug trafficking threat to communities in the southwestern United States, particularly in Texas. Gang members reportedly traffic multikilogram quantities of powder cocaine, heroin, and methamphetamine; multiton quantities of marijuana; and thousand-tablet quantities of MDMA from Mexico into the United States for distribution inside and outside prison. Gang members obtain drugs from associates or members of the Jaime Herrera-Herrera, Osiel Cárdenas-Guillén, and/or Vicente Carrillo-Fuentes Mexican DTOs. In addition, Mexikanemi members maintain a relationship with Los Zetas, a Mexican paramilitary/criminal organization employed by the Cárdenas-Guillén DTO as its personal security force.

Mexican Mafia

The Mexican Mafia prison gang, also known as La Eme (Spanish for the letter M), was formed in the late 1950s within the CDC. It is loosely structured and has strict rules that must be followed by the 200 members. Most members are Mexican American males who previously belonged to a southern California street gang. Mexican Mafia is primarily active in the southwestern and Pacific regions of the United States, but its power base is in California. The gang's main source of income is extorting drug distributors outside prison and distributing methamphetamine, cocaine, heroin, and marijuana within prison systems and on the streets. Some members have direct links to Mexican DTOs and broker deals for themselves and their associates. Mexican Mafia is also involved in other criminal activities, including controlling gambling and homosexual prostitution in prison.

Ñeta

Ñeta is a prison gang that began in Puerto Rico and spread into the United States. Ñeta is one of the largest and most violent prison gangs, with about 7,000 members in Puerto Rico and 5,000 in the United States. Ñeta chapters in Puerto Rico exist exclusively inside prisons; once members are released from prison they are no longer considered part of the gang. In the United States, Ñeta chapters exist inside and outside prisons in 36 cities across nine states, primarily in the Northeast. The gang's main source of income is retail distribution of powder and crack cocaine, heroin, marijuana and, to a lesser extent, LSD, MDMA, methamphetamine, and PCP. Ñeta members commit assault, auto theft, burglary, drive-by shootings, extortion, home invasion, money laundering, robbery, weapons and explosives trafficking, and witness intimidation.

SECTION III: OUTLAW MOTORCYCLE GANGS

Bandidos

Bandidos Motorcycle Club, an outlaw motorcycle gang (OMG) with 2,000 to 2,500 members in the United States and 13 other countries, is a growing criminal threat to the nation. Law enforcement authorities estimate that Bandidos is one of the two largest OMGs in the United States, with approximately 900 members belonging to more than 88 chapters in 16 states. Bandidos is involved in transporting and distributing cocaine and marijuana and producing, transporting, and distributing methamphetamine. Bandidos is most active in the Pacific, southeastern, southwestern, and west central regions and is expanding in these regions by forming new chapters and allowing members of support clubs to form or join Bandidos chapters. The members of support clubs are known as "puppet" or "duck" club members. They do the dirty work for the mother club.

Hells Angels

Hells Angels Motorcycle Club (HAMC) is an OMG with 2,000 to 2,500 members belonging to more than 250 chapters in the United States and 26 foreign countries. HAMC poses a criminal threat on six continents. U.S. law enforcement authorities estimate that HAMC has more than 69 chapters in 22 states with 900 to 950 members. HAMC produces, transports, and distributes marijuana and methamphetamine and transports and distributes cocaine, hashish, heroin, LSD (lysergic acid diethylamide), MDMA, PCP, and diverted pharmaceuticals. HAMC is involved in other criminal activity, including assault, extortion, homicide, money laundering, and motorcycle theft.

Mongols

Mongols Motorcycle Club is an extremely violent OMG that poses a serious criminal threat to the Pacific and southwestern regions of the United States. Mongols members transport and distribute cocaine, marijuana, and methamphetamine and frequently commit violent crimes, including assault, intimidation, and murder, to defend Mongol's territory and uphold its reputation. Mongols have 70 chapters nationwide, with most of the club's 800 to 850 members residing in California. Many members are former street gang members with a long history of using violence to settle grievances. Agents with the ATF have called Mongols Motorcycle Club the most violent and dangerous OMG in the nation. In the 1980s, the Mongols OMG seized control of southern California from HAMC, and today Mongols club is allied with Bandidos, Outlaws, Sons of Silence, and Pagan's OMGs against HAMC. The Mongols club also maintains ties with Hispanic street gangs in Los Angeles.

Outlaws

Outlaws Motorcycle Club has more than 1,700 members belonging to 176 chapters in the United States and 12 foreign countries. U.S. law enforcement authorities estimate that the Outlaws have more than 94 chapters in 22 states with more than 700 members. The Outlaws are also known as the American Outlaws Association and Outlaws Nation. Outlaws are the dominant OMG in the Great Lakes region. Gang members produce, transport, and distribute methamphetamine, and transport and distribute cocaine, marijuana and, to a lesser extent, MDMA. Outlaws members engage in various criminal activities, including arson, assault, explosives operations, extortion, fraud, homicide, intimidation, kidnapping, money laundering, prostitution operations, robbery, theft, and weapons violations. It competes with HAMC for membership and territory.

Sons of Silence

Sons of Silence Motorcycle Club (SOSMC) is one of the largest OMGs in the United States, with 250 to 275 members among 30 chapters in 12 states. The club also has five chapters in Germany. SOSMC members have been implicated in numerous criminal activities, including murder, assault, drug trafficking, intimidation, extortion, prostitution operations, money laundering, weapons trafficking, and motorcycle and motorcycle parts theft.

APPENDIX E

Selected Examples of Foreign Terrorist Organizations

The following is a list of foreign terrorist organizations or FTOs (see Chapter 10) current as of September 28, 2012. The list is based upon a National Counterterrorism Center (NCTC) report. The FTOs are designated such by the Secretary of State in accordance with section 219 of the Immigration and Nationally Act (INA). The 50 FTOs identified are as follows:

- Abdallah Azzam Brigades (AAB)
- Abu Nidal Organization (ANO)
- Abu Sayyaf Group (ASG)
- Al-Shabaab
- Ansar al-Islam (AAI)
- Asbat al-Ansar
- Aum Shinrikyo (AUM)
- Basque Fatherland and Liberty (ETA)
- Communist Party of the Philippines/New People's Army (CPP/NPA)
- Continuity Irish Republican Army (CIRA)
- Gama'a al-Islamiyya (Islamic Group)
- HAMAS (Islamic Resistance Movement)
- Haqqani Network (HQN)
- Harakat ul-Jihad-i-Islami/Bangladesh (HUJI-B)
- Harakat ul-Mujahidin (HUM)
- Hizballah (Party of God)
- Islamic Jihad Group (IJU)
- Islamic Movement of Uzbekistan (IMU)
- Jaish-e-Mohammed (JEM) (Army of Mohammed)
- Jemaah Anshorut Tawhid (JAT)
- Jemaah Islamiya (JI)
- Kahane Chai (Kach)
- Kata'ib Hizballah (KH)
- Kongra-Gel (KGK, formerly Kurdistan Workers' Party, PKK, KADEK)
- Lashkar-e-Tayyiba (LT) (Army of the Righteous)
- Lashkar-e-Jhangvi (LJ)
- Liberation Tigers of Tamil Eelam (LTTE)
- Libyan Islamic Fighting Group (LIFG)
- Moroccan Islamic Combatant Group (GICM)
- National Liberation Army (ELN)
- Palestine Liberation Front (PLF)
- Palestinian Islamic Jihad (PIJ)
- Popular Front for the Liberation of Palestine (PFLP)
- PFLP-General Command (PFLP-GC)
- Al-Qa'ida in Iraq (AQI)
- Al-Qa'ida (AQ)
- Al-Qa'ida in the Arabian Peninsula (AQAP)
- Al-Qaida in the Islamic Maghreb (AQIM, formerly GSPC)
- Real IRA (RIRA)
- Revolutionary Armed Forces of Colombia (FARC)
- Revolutionary Organization 17 November (17N)

- Revolutionary People's Liberation Party/Front (DHKP/C)
- Revolutionary Struggle (RS)
- Shining Path (Sendero Luminoso, SL)
- United Self-Defense Forces of Colombia (AUC)
- Harakat ul-Jihad-i-Islami (HUJI)
- Tehrik-e Taliban Pakistan (TTP)
- Jundallah
- Army of Islam (AOI)
- Indian Mujahidin (IM)

National Counterterrorism Center (NCTC). (2012). "Foreign Terrorist Organizations." Retrieved August 6, 2013, from www.nctc.gov/site/other/fto.html

GLOSSARY*

Acculturation: The process of becoming familiar with and comfortable in another culture. The ability to function within that culture or environment, and retain one's own cultural identity.

Affirmative action: Legally mandated programs whose aim is to increase the employment or educational opportunities of groups that have been disadvantaged in the past.

African American Vernacular English: A recognized language and a dialect of English that meets all of the requirements of a language; it possesses a coherent system of signs; it has a grammar of elements and rules; and it is used for communication and social purposes. (*Source:* Patrick, 2006 [Ch. 6])

Alien: Any person who is not a citizen or national of the country in which he or she lives.

Al-Jihad: Struggle (literal translation in Arabic). The term has also been used by some to mean "holy war" against infidels or nonbelievers.

Al-Qaida: Also spelled al-Qaeda. An international terrorist network consisting of loosely affiliated cells of operatives around the globe; the organization provides money, logistical support and training to a variety of Islamist terrorist groups, and carries out attacks and bombings in order to disrupt the economies and influence of Western nations. (*Source:* Adapted from the American Heritage Dictionary)

Alzheimer's disease The most common type of dementia. "Dementia" is an umbrella term describing a variety of diseases and conditions that develop when nerve cells in the brain (called neurons) die or no longer function normally. The death or malfunction of neurons causes changes in one's memory, behavior and ability to think clearly. In Alzheimer's disease, these brain changes eventually impair an individual's ability to carry out such basic bodily functions as walking and swallowing. Alzheimer's disease is ultimately fatal. (*Source:* Alzheimer's Association, 2013)

Anti-Semitism: Latent or overt hostility toward Jews, often expressed through social, economic, institutional, religious, cultural, or political discrimination and through acts of individual or group violence.

Assimilation: The process by which ethnic groups that have emigrated to another society begin to lose their separate identity and culture, becoming absorbed into the larger community.

Asylee: A foreign-born individual in the United States or at a port of entry who is found to be unable or unwilling to return to his or her country of nationality, or to seek the protection of that country because of persecution or a well-founded fear of persecution. Persecution or the fear thereof must be based on the individual's race, religion, nationality, membership in a particular social group, or political opinion. (*Source:* Adapted from Department of Homeland Security, Definition of Terms, 2008)

At-risk communities: Communities having a high level of criminal activity or disorder and usually a higher number of incidents of civil rights violations—hate/bias crimes, discrimination, racism, and bigotry.

Awareness: Bringing to one's conscious mind that is only unconsciously perceived.

Bias: A preformed negative opinion or attitude toward a group of persons based on their race, religion, disability, sexual orientation, ethnicity, gender, or gender identity.

Bias-based policing: The act (intentional or unintentional) of applying or incorporating personal, societal, or organizational biases and/or stereotypes in decision making, police actions, or the administration of justice.

Bigot: A person who steadfastly holds to bias and prejudice, convinced of the truth of his or her own opinion and intolerant of the opinions of others.

B-NICE incident: An acronym for any terrorist incident involving Biological, Nuclear, Incendiary, Chemical, and/or Explosive weapons of mass destruction.

Bisexual: Of or relating to people who are physically, romantically, sexually, and/or emotionally attracted to both men and women.

Community policing: A partnership between the police and the local community that identifies strategies to reduce crime, increase traffic safety, and deal with all other public safety problems.

Community profiling: Demographic analysis of a community with regard to the ethnicity/national origin, race, religion, and sexual orientation of groups whose members work or reside there.

Consent decree: An out-of-court settlement whereby the accused party agrees to modify or change behavior rather than plead guilty or go through a hearing on charges brought to court. (*Source:* CSIS Project Glossary http://csisweb.aers.psu.edu/glossary/c.htm)

Cross-cultural: Involving or mediating between two cultures.

Culture: Beliefs, values, habits, attitudes, patterns of thinking, behavior, and everyday customs that have been passed on from generation to generation. Culture is learned rather than inherited and is manifested in largely unconscious and subtle behavior. Culture is passed on from generation to generation.

Cultural competence: A developmental process in which individuals gain awareness, knowledge, and skills that enable effective

---

*The glossary is adapted, in part, from *Transcultural Leadership: Empowering the Diverse Workforce.* Houston, TX: Gulf Publishing Company (1993), with permission from the authors: Simons, G., C. Vazquez, and P. Harris. Additional definitions are provided with notations to the chapter in which the source can be found. We also indicate when a definition comes from a known entity such as the "Alzheimer's Association" or the "Department of Homeland Security."

organizational work across cultures and equitable cross-cultural and cross-racial treatment of all citizens. A "culturally competent organization" is one that has developed and adheres to a set of principles, attitudes, and policies that enable all individuals in an organization to work effectively and equitably across all cultures and ethnicities.

Department of Homeland Security (DHS): The cabinet-level federal agency responsible for preserving the security of the United States against terrorist attacks. This department was created as a response to the 9/11 terrorist attacks.

Dirty bomb: "Is one type of a radiological dispersal device (RDD) that combines a conventional explosive, such as dynamite, with radioactive material. The terms dirty bomb and RDD are often used interchangeably in the media. Most RDDs would not release enough radiation to kill people or cause severe illness—the conventional explosive itself would be more harmful to individuals than the radioactive material. A dirty bomb is not a 'Weapon of Mass Destruction' but a 'Weapon of Mass Disruption,' where contamination and anxiety are the terrorists' major objectives." (*Source:* U.S. Nuclear Regulatory Commission, 2013)

Disability bias: A preformed negative opinion or attitude toward a group of persons based on their physical or mental impairments, whether such disability is temporary or permanent, congenital or acquired by heredity, accident, injury, advanced age, or illness.

Discrimination: The denial of equal treatment to individuals or groups because of their age, disability, employment, language, nationality, race, ethnicity, sex, gender and gender identity, sexual orientation, religion, or other form of cultural identity.

Diversity: The term used to describe a vast range of cultural differences that have become factors needing attention in living and working together. It is often applied to organizational and training interventions having to do with the interface of people who are different from each other. Diversity (and "diverse groups") includes race, ethnicity, gender, disability, sexual orientation, age, class, and educational background.

Domestic terrorism: "The unlawful use, or threatened use, of force or violence by a group or individual based and operating entirely within the United States or Puerto Rico without foreign direction committed against persons or property to intimidate or coerce a government, the civilian population, or any segment thereof in furtherance of political or social objectives." (*Source:* FBI, 2010)

Dominant culture: Refers to the value system that characterizes a particular group of people that dominates the value systems of other groups or cultures. See also **Macroculture/majority or dominant group.**

Ebonics: See African American Vernacular English.

Émigré: An individual forced, usually by political circumstances, to move from his or her native country and who deliberately resides as a foreigner in the host country.

Ethnic group: Group of people who conceive of themselves, and who are regarded by others, as alike because of their common ancestry, language, and physical characteristics.

Ethnicity: Refers to the background of a group with unique language, ancestral, often religious, and physical characteristics. Broadly characterizes a religious, racial, national, or cultural group.

Ethnicity bias: A preformed negative opinion or attitude toward a group of people whose members identify with each other, through a common heritage, often consisting of a common language, common culture (often including a shared religion) and/or ideology that stresses common ancestry. The concept of ethnicity differs from the closely related term *race* in that "race" refers to grouping based mostly upon biological criteria, while "ethnicity" also encompasses additional cultural factors.

Ethnocentrism: An attitude of seeing and judging other cultures from the perspective of one's own culture; using the culture of one's own group as a standard for the judgment of others, or thinking of it as superior to other cultures that are merely different; an ethnocentric person would say there is only one way of being "normal" and that is the way of his or her own culture.

Foreign-born: Refers to an individual who is not a U.S. citizen at birth or who is born outside the U.S., Puerto Rico, or other U.S. territories, and whose parents are not U.S. citizens. The terms "foreign born" and "immigrant" are used interchangeably. The term includes naturalized U.S. citizens, legal permanent residents, temporary migrants (e.g., foreign students), humanitarian migrants (refugees), and unauthorized migrants. (U.S. Census Bureau, State and Country Quick Facts: Foreign-Born Persons, 2010)

Formal profile: Typically a document containing explicit criteria or indicators issued to officers to guide them in their decision-making. It is often based on data collected and interpreted to signify a trend or suggest that given behavioral or situational commonalties, a person could believe that something may result. It can be an outline or short biographical description, an individual's character sketch, or a type of behavior associated with a group. Officers use behavioral or situational indicators to develop reasonable suspicion or probable cause to stop subjects. A profile is a summary of data that also relies upon expert advice about "average" or "typical" appearance that can *potentially* identify perpetrators of criminal activities.

Gang: The definition of a gang varies among most law enforcement agencies and jurisdictions at the federal, state, and local levels in the United States. The National Gang Center (NGC) promotes a functional definition for criminal justice professionals and educators. The following five criteria are widely accepted and recognized among researchers for classifying groups as gangs (*Source:* NGC, 2011):

1. The group has three or more members, generally aged 12–24.

2. Members share an identity, typically linked to a name, and often have shared symbols, typically including style of clothing, graffiti, tattoos, and hand signs.

3. Members view themselves as a gang, and are recognized by others as a gang.

4. The group has some permanence and a degree of organization.

5. The group is involved in an elevated level of criminal activity.

Gay: A male homosexual. Generally this word is used to refer to gay men, but may also be used to describe women; the term "gay" is preferred over the term "homosexual."

Gender: This term is used synonymously with *sex* to denote whether a newborn is male or female at birth, for example, "it's a boy" or "it's a girl."

Gender bias: A preformed negative opinion or attitude toward a person or group of persons based on their actual or perceived gender, for example, male or female.

Gender identity: A person's internal sense of being male, female, or a combination of both; that internal sense of a person's gender may be different from the person's gender as assigned at birth. Note: A transgender person may express their gender identity through gender characteristics, such as clothing, hair, voice, mannerisms, or behaviors that do not conform to the gender-based expectations of society.

Gender identity bias: A preformed negative opinion or attitude toward a person or group of persons based on their actual or perceived gender identity, e.g., bias against transgender or gender nonconforming individuals.

Gender nonconforming: Describes a person who does not conform to the gender-based expectations of society, for example, a woman dressed in traditionally male clothing or a man wearing makeup. Note: A gender nonconforming person may or may not be a lesbian, gay, bisexual, or transgender person but may be perceived as such.

Glass ceiling: An invisible and often perceived barrier that prevents some ethnic or racial groups and women from becoming promoted or hired.

Hate group: An organization whose primary purpose is to promote animosity, hostility, and malice toward persons of or with a race, religion, disability, sexual orientation, ethnicity, gender, or gender identity that differs from that of the members or the organization. Examples include the Ku Klux Klan and the American Nazi Party.

Heterogeneity: Dissimilarity; composed of unrelated or unlike elements. A heterogeneous society is one that is diverse, and frequently refers to racial and ethnic composition.

Heterogeneous: Dissimilar, or composed of unrelated or unlike elements.

Heterogeneous Society: Is one that is diverse, and frequently refers to racial and ethnic composition.

Heterosexual: Of or relating to people who are physically, romantically, and/or emotionally attracted to people of the opposite sex. Note: The term *straight* is a synonym.

Hierarchy: A deeply embedded system of societal structure whereby people are organized according to how much status and power they have. Hierarchical societies have specific and defined ways in which people must behave toward those lower and higher on the hierarchy. Communication is restricted in hierarchical societies, and people are always aware of where they stand in terms of status and power vis-à-vis other individuals.

High-context/low-context communications: Frameworks of communication, largely but not exclusively influenced by culture, related to how much speakers rely on messages other than from words to convey meaning; explicit and specific communications is valued in the low-context style, and conversely, an intuitive and relatively indirect style characterizes high-context communication.

Holistic: View that the integrated whole has a reality independent and greater than the sum of its parts. (*Source:* Webster's New World Dictionary)

Homeland security: Federal and local law enforcement programs for gathering, processing, and application of intelligence to provide the United States with a blanket of protection against terrorist attacks.

Homeless adult person: (1) An individual or family who lacks a fixed, regular, and adequate nighttime residence; (2) an individual or family who resides in a public or private place not designed for or ordinarily use as a regular sleeping accommodation for human beings, including a car, park, abandoned building, bus or train station, airport or camping ground; (3) an individual or family living in a supervised publicly or privately operated shelter designed to provide temporary living arrangements paid for by Federal, State, or local government programs for low-income individuals or by charitable organizations, congregate shelters, and transitional housing; (4) an individual who resided in a shelter or place not meant for human habitation and who is exiting an institution where he or she temporarily resided. (*Source:* Subchapter 1: General Provisions Section 11302, U.S. Code, 2010)

Homeless children and youth: Have similar residency and shelter/transitional housing as a homeless adult, but includes sharing the housing of other persons due to loss of housing; living in motels, hotels, trailer parks, or camping grounds; or abandoned in hospitals; or are awaiting foster care placement. (*Source:* Subchapter VI: Education and Training, Part B: Education for Homeless Children and Youth, Section 11434a, U.S. Code, 2010)

Homophile: Same as homosexual.

Homosexual: Of or relating to people who are physically, romantically, and/or emotionally attracted to people of the same gender. Note: This is an outdated term considered derogatory and offensive by many people.

Human trafficking: The transportation of persons for sexual exploitation, forced labor, or other illegal or criminal activities.

Hybrid gangs: Nontraditional gangs with multiple affiliations and ethnicities.

Immigrant: Any individual admitted to the United States as a lawful permanent resident; also referred to as "permanent resident alien." (*Source:* Department of Homeland Security, Definition of Terms, 2008)

Informal profile: Represents the "street sense," personal experiences, and strongly held beliefs that officers use to evaluate people or situations.

Indian Country: "All land within the limits of any Indian reservation under the jurisdiction of the United States Government; . . . , all dependent Indian communities within the borders of the United States whether within the original or subsequently acquired territory thereof, and whether within or without the limits of a state, and all Indian allotments, the Indian titles to which have not been extinguished . . ." (*Source:* U.S. Code, 2007)

Indian tribe: Any Indian or Alaska Native tribe, band, nation, pueblo, village, or community that the Secretary of the Interior acknowledges to exist as an Indian tribe. (*Source:* U.S. Code, 2012b)

Informal networks: A system of influential colleagues who can, because of their position or power within an organization, connect the employee with information, resources, or other contacts helpful to his or her promotion or special assignment prospects.

Institutional racism: The failure of an organization (public or private) to provide goods, services, and opportunities to people because of their color, culture, ethnic origin.

International terrorism: "Involves violent acts or acts dangerous to human life that are a violation of the criminal laws of the United States or any state, or that would be a criminal violation if committed within the jurisdiction of the United States or any state. These acts appear to be intended to intimidate or coerce a civilian population, influence the policy of a government by intimidation or coercion, or affect the conduct of a government by assassination or kidnapping." (*Source:* FBI, 2010)

Jihad: See **Al-Jihad.**

Juvenile Gangs: The terms *youth* and *street gang* are commonly used interchangeably however, the use of the term *street gang* for *youth gang* often results in confusing youth gangs with adult criminal organizations. (*Source:* NGC, 2013). To eliminate the confusion, it is important to remember that street gangs are composed of juveniles and young adults.

Leadership: Exercised when one takes initiative, guides, or influences others in a particular direction.

Legal immigrant: An individual granted legal permanent residence; granted asylum; admitted as a refugee; or admitted under a set of specific authorized temporary statuses for longer-term residence and work. This group includes "naturalized citizens," legal immigrants who have become U.S. citizens through naturalization; "legal permanent resident aliens," who have been granted permission to stay indefinitely in the U.S. as permanent residents, asylees, or refugees; and "legal temporary migrants," who are allowed to live and, in some cases, work in the U.S. for specific periods of time (usually longer than one year).

Lesbian: A homosexual woman. Some lesbian women prefer to be described as gay women; preferred over the term "homosexual."

LGBT: Common initialism for "lesbian, gay, bisexual, and transgender," used here to refer to community organizations or events that serve lesbian, gay, bisexual, transgender, and allied people.

Macroculture/majority or dominant group: The group within a society that is largest and/or most powerful. This power usually extends to setting cultural norms for the society as a whole. The term majority is falling into disuse because its connotations of group size are inaccurate in certain cities or regions of the country.

Mental illness: A mental health disorder characterized by alterations in thinking, mood, or behavior associated with distress and/ or impaired functioning. (*Source:* U.S. Surgeon General's Report, 1999)

Mentor: "A trusted counselor or guide." (*Source:* Webster's New World Dictionary). A mentor is usually a more experienced person who helps a less experienced one. The mentor provides information, advice, support, and encouragement to someone who is usually an apprentice, protégé, or a less experienced person. It involves leading, developing, and guiding by example in his or her area of success.

Minority: The terms *minority* or *minorities* are used within the text to describe groups of individuals who represent a numeric minority within a racial or ethnic population.

Minority group: A group which is the smaller in number of two groups that constitute a whole; part of the population that differs in certain ways from the majority population and is sometimes subjected to differential treatment.

Multiculturalism: The existence within one society of diverse groups that maintain their unique cultural identity while accepting and participating in the larger society's legal and political system.

Neighborhood office: A temporary office located in a neighborhood, usually an apartment business office complex where the police officer conducts routine business.

Order maintenance: The police handling of incidents that are not crimes, but public nuisance matters about which the police officer uses discretion to decide a course of action.

Outlaw Motorcycle Gangs: Highly structured and organized networks whose members commit such criminal acts as violent crimes, weapons trafficking, and drug trafficking. Outlaw Motorcycle Gang chapters in the United States range in size with hundreds of chapters and thousands of members worldwide.

Paradigm shift: What occurs when an entire cultural group begins to experience a change that involves the acceptance of new conceptual models or ways of thinking and results in major societal transitions (e.g., the shift from agricultural to industrial society).

Parity: The state or condition of being the same in power, value, rank, and so forth; equality.

Pluralistic: The existence within a nation or society of groups distinctive in ethnic origin, culture patterns, religion, or the like. A policy of favoring the preservation of such group with a given nation or society.

Prejudice: A judgment or opinion formed before facts are known, usually involving negative or unfavorable thoughts about groups of people.

Prison gangs: Prevalent throughout the federal and state prison system in the United States, these are highly structured and organized networks, having an influence in prison operations and in street gang crime.

Probable Cause: Probable cause is a higher level of reasonable belief, based on facts that can be articulated, that is required to arrest a person and prosecute him or her in criminal court. Also, before a person or a person's property can be searched, police must possess probable cause. All states have similar constitutional prohibitions against unreasonable searches and seizures.

Professionalism: Approach to one's occupation or career, with a sense of dedication and expertise.

Profile: A "profile" is typically a document that contains explicit criteria or indicators issued to officers to guide them in their decision making. It is usually based on data collected and interpreted to signify a trend or suggest that, given a particular set of characteristics (behavioral or situational commonalties), a person could believe that something may result based on that particular cluster of characteristics. A profile relies on using expert advice provided to law enforcement agencies to identify perpetrators of criminal activities. It can be an outline or short biographical description, an individual's character sketch, or a type of behavior associated with a group. It is a summary of data presenting the average or typical appearance of those persons situations under scrutiny. Officers use these indicators of physical, behavioral, or situational commonalties to develop reasonable suspicion or probable cause to stop subjects.

Profiling: Any police-initiated action that uses a compilation of the background, physical, behavioral, and/or motivational characteristics for a type of perpetrator that leads the police to a particular individual who has been identified as being, could be, or having been engaged in criminal activity.

Psychotic episode: The period of time when a person with a serious mental illness is impaired and at risk of endangering himself or herself, or others.

Race: A group of persons of (or regarded as of) common ancestry. Physical characteristics are often used to identify people of different races. These characteristics should not be used to identify ethnic groups, which can cross racial lines.

Racial bias: A preformed negative opinion or attitude toward a group of persons who possess common physical characteristics, such as color of skin, eyes, and/or hair, facial features, and so forth, genetically transmitted by descent and heredity, which distinguish them as a distinct division of humankind, for example, Asians, blacks or African Americans, whites.

Racially biased policing: Occurs when law enforcement inappropriately considers race or ethnicity in deciding with whom and how to intervene in an enforcement capacity.

Racial profiling: Any police-initiated action that relies on the race, ethnicity, or national origin rather than the behavior of an individual or information that leads the police to a particular individual who has been identified as being, or having been, engaged in criminal activity.

Racism: Total rejection of others by reason of race, color, or, sometimes more broadly, culture.

Racist: One with a closed mind toward accepting one or more groups different from one's own origin in race or color.

Refugee: Any person who is outside his or her country of nationality who is unable or unwilling to return to that country because of persecution or a well-founded fear of persecution. Persecution or the fear thereof must be based on . . . race, religion, nationality, membership in a particular social group, or political opinion. (*Source:* Department of Homeland Security, Definition of Terms, 2013). People with no nationality must generally be outside their country of last habitual residence to qualify as a refugee. An individual can also be an "economic refugee," fleeing conditions of poverty for better opportunities elsewhere.

Religious bias: A preformed negative opinion or attitude toward a group of persons who share the same religious beliefs regarding the origin and purpose of the universe and the existence or non-existence of a supreme being, for example, Catholics, Jews, Muslims, Protestants, and atheists.

Reasonable suspicion: A police officer may briefly detain a person for questioning or request identification only if the officer has what is called a "reasonable suspicion" that the person's behavior is related to criminal activity. Reasonable suspicion requires that the officer have specific facts that must be articulated to support his or her actions; a mere suspicion or "hunch" is not sufficient. Reasonable suspicion can be based on the observations of a police officer combined with his or her training and experience, and/or reliable information received from credible outside sources. A police officer possesses reasonable suspicion if he or she has enough knowledge to lead a reasonably cautious person to believe that criminal activity is occurring and that the individual played some part in it. Reasonable suspicion is a level of belief that is less clear-cut than probable cause.

Scapegoat: To blame one's failures and shortcomings on innocent people or those only partly responsible.

Sexual orientation: The term for a person's physical, romantic, and/or emotional attraction to members of the same and/or opposite sex, including lesbian, gay, bisexual, and heterosexual (straight) individuals. Note: Avoid the offensive terms "sexual preference" or "lifestyle."

Sexual-orientation bias: A preformed negative opinion or attitude toward a person or group of persons based on their actual or perceived sexual orientation.

Stereotype: To believe or feel that people are considered to typify or conform to a pattern or manner, lacking any individuality. Thus, a person may categorize behavior of a total group on the basis of limited experience with one or a few representatives of that group. Negative stereotyping classifies people in a group by slurs, innuendoes, names, or slang expressions that depreciate the group as a whole and the individuals in it.

Schoolfront office: A temporary office located in a school where the police officer conducts routine business. Schools that have a regular police school resource officer are not considered schoolfront offices.

Storefront office: A temporary office located in a business office or shopping center where the police officer conducts routine business.

Street gangs: National, regional, and local street gangs, represented in urban, rural and Indian Country, are the largest types of gangs and control the greatest geographic areas; while, the majority of gang members identified by law enforcement agencies are 18 year and older, juveniles also comprise a percentage of street gang membership, a actively participating in criminal behavior and violence. (*Source:* National Gang Center, 2011)

Subculture: A group with distinct, discernible, and consistent cultural traits existing within and participating in a larger cultural grouping.

Suspect-specific incident: An incident in which an officer lawfully attempts to detain, apprehend, or otherwise be on the lookout for one or more specific suspects identified or described, in part, by national or ethnic origin, gender, or race.

Synergy: The benefit produced by the collaboration of two or more systems in excess of their individual contributions. Cultural synergy occurs when cultural differences are taken into account and used by a multicultural group.

Terrorism: "Terrorism is defined in the *Code of Federal Regulations* as the unlawful use of force and violence against persons or property to intimidate or coerce a government, the civilian population, or any segment thereof, in furtherance of political or social objectives (28 C.F.R. Section 0.85)." (*Source:* FBI, 2010)

Terrorist Attack Pre-Incidence Indicators (TAPIs): A term used by the intelligence community to describe actions and behaviors taken by terrorists before they carry out an attack. (*Source:* Nance, M. W. (2003). *The Terrorist Recognition Handbook.* Guilford, CT: Lyons Press).

Terrorist incident: "A violent act or an act dangerous to human life, in violation of the criminal laws of the United States, or of any state, to intimidate or coerce a government, the civilian population, or any segment thereof, in furtherance of political or social objectives." (FBI, 2010).

Terrorism prevention: "A documented instance in which a violent act by a known or suspected terrorist group or individual with the means and a proven propensity for violence is successfully interdicted through investigative activity." (*Source:* FBI, 2010)

Transgender: Of or relating to a person who identifies as a different gender from their gender as assigned at birth. Covers a range of people, including heterosexual cross-dressers, homosexual drag queens, and transsexuals who believe they were born in the wrong body, and may take hormones or undergo a sex change operation to alter their gender.

Unauthorized/Undocumented immigrant: All foreign-born noncitizens residing in the country who are not "legal immigrants" and who entered the country without valid documents or arrived with valid visas but stayed past their visa expiration date or otherwise violated the terms of their admission. (*Source:* Passel and Cohn, 2011 [Ch. 1]). Although the term "unauthorized immigrant" is increasingly in use, it has not entirely replaced the term "undocumented immigrant."

U.S.-born: Describes those who are U.S. citizens at birth, including people born in the United States, Puerto Rico, or other U.S. territories, as well as those born elsewhere to parents who are U.S. citizens.

Weapons of Mass Destruction (WMD): "Any weapon or device that is intended, or has the capability, to cause death or serious bodily injury to a significant number of people through the release, dissemination, or impact of (a) toxic or poisonous chemicals or their precursors; (b) a disease organism; or (c) radiation or radioactivity." (Title 50, US Code, Chapter 40, Section 2302).

White supremacist group: Any ongoing organization, association, or group of three or more persons, whether formal or informal, having as one of its primary activities the promotion of white supremacy through the commission of criminal acts.

INDEX

Note: The 'b' and 'e' following the locators refer to boxes and exhibits cited in the text.